2/14

Y0-BYZ-428

South Florida

AN EXPLORER'S GUIDE

South Florida

Includes Sarasota, Naples, Miami & the Florida Keys

Sandra Friend, Trish Riley & Kathy Wolf

THE COUNTRYMAN PRESS · WOODSTOCK · VT

The Countryman Press ✳ Woodstock, Vermont

SECOND EDITION

We welcome your comments and suggestions. Please contact Explorer's Guide Editor, The Countryman Press, P.O. Box 748, Woodstock, VT 05091, or e-mail countrymanpress@wwnorton.com.

South Florida: An Explorer's Guide
ISBN: 978-0-88150-870-3

Maps by Mapping Specialists, Ltd., Madison, WI
Cover and interior design by Joanna Bodenweber
Text composition by PerfecType, Nashville, TN

Published by The Countryman Press, P.O. Box 748, Woodstock, Vermont 05091

Distributed by W. W. Norton & Company, 500 Fifth Avenue, New York, NY 10110

Printed in the United States of America

10 9 8 7 6 5 4 3 2

DEDICATION
To Niki and Clyde, for drawing me into the magic of South Florida.
—Sandra Friend

To my beautiful children, Rachel and Bud.
—Trish Riley

Also by Sandra Friend and Kathy J. Wolf
North Florida & the Florida Panhandle: An Explorer's Guide

Also by Sandra Friend
50 Hikes in North Florida
50 Hikes in Central Florida
50 Hikes in South Florida
Along the Florida Trail (with Bart Smith)
Exploring Florida's Botanical Wonders
Florida
Hiker's Guide to the Sunshine State
*The Hiking Trails of Florida's National Forests, Parks, and Preserves
    (with Johnny Molloy)*
Orlando, Central & North Florida: An Explorer's Guide
Sinkholes

Also by Trish Riley
The Complete Idiot's Guide to Greening Your Business (with Heather Gadonniex)
The Complete Idiot's Guide to Green Living
Great Destinations: Palm Beach, Miami, Fort Lauderdale & the Florida Keys
*The Unofficial Guide to the Best RV and Tent Campgrounds in Florida & the
Southeast* (with Grace Walton)

EXPLORE WITH US!

Welcome to this edition of *South Florida: An Explorer's Guide,* the most comprehensive travel guide you'll find covering this region. We've included attractions, accommodations, restaurants, and shopping on the basis of merit (primarily close personal inspection by your authors) rather than paid advertising. The following points will help you understand how we've organized the guide.

WHAT'S WHERE

The book starts out with a thumbnail sketch of the most important things to know about traveling in South Florida, from which beaches you should head to first to how to deal with hurricane season. We've included important contact information for state agencies and advice on what to do when you're on the road.

LODGING

All selections for accommodations in this guide are based on merit; most of them were inspected personally or by a reliable source known to us. No businesses were charged for inclusion in this guide. Many bed & breakfasts do not accept children under 12 or pets, so if there is not a specific mention in their entry, ask them about their policy before you book a room. Some places have a minimum-stay requirement, especially on weekends or during the high season (winter).

Rates: All rates quoted are for double occupancy, one night, before taxes. When a range of rates is given, it spans the gamut from the lowest of the low season (which varies around the state) to the highest of the high season. A single rate means the proprietor offers only one rate, unless noted "and up." Rates for hotels and motels are subject to further discount with programs like AAA and AARP and

DINING ON THE BEACH AT SHARKEYS

Sharkeys

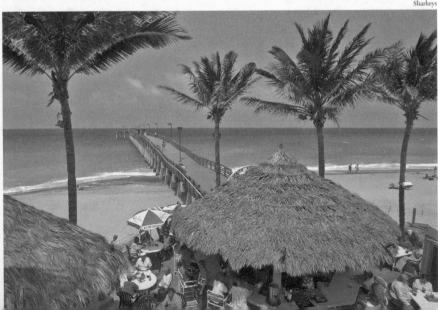

may be negotiable depending on occupancy. Many places offer reduced rates for Florida residents, and bargains can be had at the last minute and through online booking services. For South Florida, high season is typically January to April.

RESTAURANTS

Our distinction between *Eating Out* and *Dining Out* is based mainly on price, secondarily on atmosphere. Dining in Florida is more casual than anywhere else in the United States—you'll find folks in T-shirts and shorts walking into the most exclusive restaurants. If a restaurant has a dress code, we note it. Expect Dining Out choices in urban areas to require business casual dress.

   Smoking is no longer permitted within restaurants in Florida, if the bulk of the business's transactions are in food rather than drink. Many restaurants now provide an outdoor patio for smokers.

KEY TO SYMBOLS

☯ **Special value.** The special value symbol appears next to lodgings and restaurants that offer quality not usually enjoyed at the price charged.

& **Handicapped access.** The wheelchair symbol appears next to lodgings, restaurants, and attractions that provide handicapped access, at a minimum with assistance.

✑ **Child-friendly.** The crayon symbol appears next to places or activities that accept children or appeal to families.

▼ **Gay-friendly.** The inverted triangle symbol indicates establishments that make an extra effort to cater to a gay clientele.

🐾 **Pets.** The pet symbol appears next to places that accept pets, from bed & breakfasts to bookstores. All lodgings require that you let them know you're bringing your pet; many will charge an additional fee.

∞ **Weddings.** The wedding symbol appears next to venues that are experienced with hosting weddings.

("¡") **Wi-Fi.** Locations that offer wireless Internet

⊶ **Ecofriendly establishments.** In the case of lodgings, denotes certified participants in the Florida Green Lodging Program. In the case of other businesses, properties noted by the authors as taking special initiatives to reduce, reuse, and recycle.

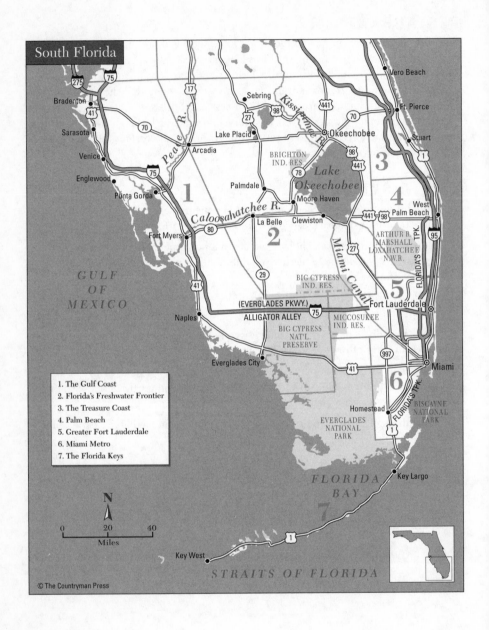

South Florida

Bradenton
Sarasota
Venice
Englewood
Punta Gorda
Fort Myers

Sebring
Lake Placid
Arcadia
Palmdale

Okeechobee
BRIGHTON
IND. RES.
*Lake
Okeechobee*
Moore Haven
Clewiston

Vero Beach
Ft. Pierce
Stuart

West
Palm Beach

ARTHUR R.
MARSHALL
LOXAHATCHEE
N.W.R.

Peace R.
Caloosahatchee R.
La Belle

1

2

3

4

5

6

Kissimmee R.

Miami Canal

GULF
OF
MEXICO

Naples

(EVERGLADES PKWY.)
ALLIGATOR ALLEY

BIG CYPRESS
IND. RES.

BIG CYPRESS
NAT'L.
PRESERVE

MICCOSUKEE
IND. RES.

Fort Lauderdale

Miami

Everglades City

EVERGLADES
NATIONAL
PARK

Homestead

BISCAYNE
NATIONAL
PARK

1. The Gulf Coast
2. Florida's Freshwater Frontier
3. The Treasure Coast
4. Palm Beach
5. Greater Fort Lauderdale
6. Miami Metro
7. The Florida Keys

N

0   20   40
Miles

*FLORIDA
BAY*

7

Key Largo

Key West

STRAITS OF FLORIDA

© The Countryman Press

CONTENTS

INTRODUCTION

I (Sandra) never thought I'd fall in love with a swamp. But that's what happened when I was researching the second edition of 50 Hikes in South Florida. I spent a month living in Fort Myers, getting my feet wet several times a week on hikes in and around the Big Cypress Swamp. When the time came for the book debut, Clyde and Niki Butcher invited me to sign books at their annual Labor Day Muck-A-Bout. I took my first "total immersion" swamp walk with their volunteer crew, where the water was so deep I had to swim a short ways, and I was hooked. Each year thereafter I have returned to introduce others to the amazing experience of walking through a shallow, sluggish river of crystal-clear raindrops beneath a tightly knit canopy of cypresses decorated with colorful bromeliads and fragrant orchids. For seven years, I've considered this wilderness a second home, a place to draw strength from the natural beauty of one of the country's most unique national parks and the many resident artists who call it home.

TAKING A SWAMP WALK IN BIG CYPRESS
NATIONAL PRESERVE

Sandra Friend

Such is the magic of South Florida. It has captured the imagination of explorers since the Spanish set foot on these shores in the 1500s in search of gold. The farther south you go in Florida, the clearer and bluer the oceans become. South Florida is on the tropical fringe, with its native flora originating in the Caribbean and growing as far north as West Palm Beach and Pine Island. It is a place where rare indigenous species roam, including the elusive Florida panther and the reclusive

10

American crocodile. The central portion of Florida's peninsula is graced with quiet rural towns, cattle ranches, and citrus groves until you reach the mighty swamps of South Florida, the Everglades, and Big Cypress.

South Florida is also an amalgam of cultures. The Seminoles, descendents of Creeks who migrated into Florida in the 1700s, moved south to escape persecution and deportation during the 1800s, as did their cousins, the Miccosukee. Japanese pineapple farmers formed the Yamato farming colony at Delay Beach in 1905. The Amish established a community near Sarasota, and Cuban refugees flooded Miami after Fidel Castro's coup of Cuba in 1953.

A flurry of land speculators flooded the region in the early 1900s, ditching and draining the Everglades in exchange for massive grants of land from the state. Land scam shenanigans ensued through the 1920s Florida boom and subsequent bust, building up coastal communities that today are sprawling cities. South and Central Americans seeking investment properties have flocked to cosmopolitan Miami and Miami Beach, as have celebrities from around the world. Many South Florida cities are the termini of highways starting in the Northeast and Midwest, and so it is here that many people end up when looking for a retirement home or a getaway from fierce winter weather, which is why "snowbirds" make the population swell tremendously during the winter months.

With its arts communities and historic sites, seaside resorts and forests to roam, rural retreats, urban chic, and some of the best fishing and diving in the United States, South Florida is a destination with plenty to explore.

I'm pleased to introduce Trish Riley as my new collaborator in this very large swath of the state. Trish has lived in Fort Lauderdale for 17 years, is an award-winning environmental journalist, and is the author of several books about the region, including *Great Destinations: Palm Beach, Miami, Fort Lauderdale & the Florida Keys,* an ecoguide to the region, as well as *The Complete Idiot's Guide to Green Living;* she is also the coauthor of *The Complete Idiot's Guide to Greening Your Business*.

Prices for lodgings and restaurants are subject to change, and shops come and go. Your feedback is essential for subsequent editions of this guide. Feel free to write us in care of The Countryman Press or Explorer's Guide, P.O. Box 424, Micanopy 32667, or e-mail eg@genuineflorida.com or GoldCoast@trishriley.com with your opinions and your own treasured finds. You'll find updates to this book posted at www.genuineflorida.com.

"Certainly, travel is more than the seeing of sights; it is a change that goes on, deep and permanent, in the ideas of living."
—Miriam Beard

ACKNOWLEDGMENTS

Covering South Florida is a big project, so we'd like to thank those who took their time to assist with our research:

Sandra Friend:
Sue Arnold, Arnold's Wildlife Rehabilitation Center; Toni Badovinac, Oak Park Inn; Arnold Boston, Bayfront Inn; Kat at Billie Swamp Safari; Becky Bovell and Jennifer Huber, Charlotte County Visitors Bureau; Becky Bragg, Canoe Outpost Peace River; Dina Craig, SunStream Hotels & Resorts; Cynthia Dobyns and the Harradens, The Ivey House; Roxie Smith and Ellis Etter, Pink Shell Beach Resort and Spa; Terry Felder, SeaRocket USA; Annette Figueroa, Sun Splash Family Water Park; Virginia Haley and Erin Duggan, Sarasota Visitors & Convention Bureau; Nancy Hamilton and Katie Meckley, Lee County Visitor & Convention Bureau; Maria Hayworth, Hayworth Creative Public Relations; Christa Hill, The Clewiston Inn; Amanda Kliegl, The Sundy House; Larry Levey, Avon Park Depot Museum; Cindy Malin, Seminole Tribe of Florida; JoNell Modys and Jack Wert, Naples Marco Island Everglades CVB; Kent Morse, Dolphin Explorer; Deborah Petty-Cole, Best Western Ambassador Suites; Michelle Phillips, Florida's Freshwater Frontier; Harriet and Bob Porter, Lake Placid Mural Society; Patty Register, Gatorama; Mary Rude, Six Mile Cypress Slough Preserve; Marianne Saltz, South Seas Island Resort; Krissy Simone, Esterra Spa; Howard Solomon and family, Solomon's Castle; and Liz Sparks, Florida Fish and Wildlife Conservation Commission.

Sandra would also like to thank her friends who aided and abetted these adventures, including Linda Benton, Lori Burris, Clyde and Niki Butcher, Paul Cummings, Phyllis Malinski, Jackie Butcher Obendorf, Mike Owen, Chuck and Betty Wilson, and my husband, Rob Smith Jr.

Trish Riley would like to thank Gentry Baumline with Hayworth Creative PR, Diane D'Amico at Jupiter Beach Resort, Dania Kahn and Jason Alexander at Courtyard Marriott Boynton Beach, Josie Gulliksen of Newman PR, and the folks at Coral Lagoon Resort in Marathon and at Ambrosia House in Key West. I'd also like to thank my assistant, Jennifer Jenkins, for her painstakingly hard work fact checking and updating the South Florida information, and friends and colleagues Teresa Mears, Barb Freda, and Patti Roth for their help in finding the best new treasures in the region. Last, I'd like to thank my sweethearts, Teddi (my Yorkie) and Stella (Rachel's cat), for keeping me company while I wrote up our interesting experiences as we researched this guide. Teddi even helped vet a good portion of South Florida, and—glamour queen that she is—she was especially welcomed throughout the Keys.

WHAT'S WHERE IN SOUTH FLORIDA

ADMISSION FEES If an admission fee is $7 or less, it's simply listed as "fee." Fees greater than $7 are spelled out. Although fees were accurate when this book went to press, keep in mind that *yearly increases are likely*, especially for the larger attractions and theme parks.

AIRBOAT RIDES Airboats are an exciting way to get out in the backcountry of Florida. These shallow boats can skim over only a few inches of water. Boat sizes range from small four-seaters to massive floating buses holding up to 30 people and dictate the type of experience you can expect. The smaller intimate boats will be more one-on-one, will get into tighter places, and may be more expensive. Most of the larger boats provide handicapped assistance. All airboats require hearing protection, which is provided by the operators.

AIR SERVICE Major international airports in the region covered by this book include Sarasota-Bradenton International Airport in Sarasota, Southwest Florida International Airport in Fort Myers, Palm Beach International Airport in West Palm Beach, Fort Lauderdale–Hollywood International Airport in Fort Lauderdale, and Miami International Airport. Smaller regional airports served by commuter flights are listed in their respective chapters.

ALLIGATORS AND CROCODILES No longer an endangered species, the American alligator is a ubiquitous resident of Florida's lakes, rivers, streams, and retention ponds. Most alligators will turn tail and hit the water with a splash when they hear you coming—unless they've been fed or otherwise sensitized to human presence. Do not approach a sunning alligator, and never, ever, feed an alligator (it's a felony and downright dangerous) in the wild—when people feed gators, they come to associate people with food and may attack people they encounter. Nuisance alligators *and* violations of feeding alligators should be reported to the **Florida Fish and Wildlife Conservation Commission** (1-888-404-FWCC; www.floridaconservation.org). South Florida is also home to the endangered American crocodile, a reclusive species that prefers the mangrove swamps and open shallows of Biscayne Bay and Florida Bay. Individual crocodiles have been spotted as far north as Pine Island Sound on the west coast and Fort Lauderdale on the east coast, and chances are you'll see at least one at the Flamingo Marina in Everglades National Park.

AMTRAK One daily **AMTRAK** (1-800-USA-RAIL; www.amtrak.com) train makes its way from New York to South Florida: the Silver Service/ Palmetto, ending in either Tampa or Miami. Stops are noted in *Getting There.*

ANTIQUES The antiques districts are particularly hot in Arcadia, Delray Beach, and Sarasota, each worth a full day for browsing. You'll find nice clusters of antiques shops in Fort Myers and Venice as well. Since 1985 the free magazine *Antiques & Art Around Florida* (352-475-1336; www.aarf.com) has kept up with the trends throughout the Sunshine State; pick up a copy at one of the antiques stores you visit, or browse their Web site to do a little pre-trip planning.

ARCHAEOLOGY Florida's archaeological treasures date back more than 10,000 years, including temple mound complexes on the Gulf Coast, such as those found at Emerson Point, Spanish Point, and Terra Ceia. Remnants of the Calusa culture have been unearthed all along Pine Island Sound; you can walk through the remains of a Calusa city in Pineland. In the middle of Estero Bay, Mound Key was once the capital of the Calusa culture. Even out in the sugarcane fields of Belle Glade and the hammocks of Ortona, mounds have been discovered: evidence of the Calusa's travels. On the Atlantic Coast, remnants of the Ais, Jeaga, and Tequesta remain, including the Miami Circle and burial mounds at the Deering Estate at Cutler. And the reefs of the Florida Keys provide a treasure trove of shipwrecks for divers.

For information about archaeological digs and shipwrecks, contact the Florida Division of Historical Resources, Bureau of Archaeological Research (www.flheritage.com/archaeology).

AREA CODES As Florida's population increases, its area codes continue to fragment. In general, in urban areas you must dial the area code with every local call. The need for the area code varies depending where you are in any particular county since the phone systems do not correspond to county lines.

ART GALLERIES Florida is blessed with many creative souls who draw their inspiration from our dramatic landscapes, working in media from copper sculpture and driftwood to fine black-and-white photography, giclee, and watercolor. Many artists gravitate into communities; look for clusters of art galleries in places like Bradenton, Coconut Grove, Delray Beach, Islamorada, Matlacha, Sanibel Island, Sarasota, and Key West. Naples offers the finest of the fine arts, with dozens of galleries downtown and two major art museums.

ARTS COUNCILS Many cities and counties have public art displays thanks to their local arts councils. The Florida Cultural Affairs Division (www.florida-arts.org) offers resources, grants, and programs to support the arts throughout Florida. Its Florida Artists Hall of Fame recognizes great achievements in the arts.

AVIATION While Florida may not be the birthplace of aviation, it is definitely its nursery school and postdoctorate program. Florida's aviation history includes many World War II training bases—especially in South Florida— and the birth of naval aviation in 1914;

the first scheduled commercial airline flight from St. Petersburg to Tampa was also in 1914, and the first nonstop flight across the nation came soon after. The rocket technology of NASA brings modern aviation into the space age.

BASEBALL Florida is home to Major League Baseball's annual spring training, so baseball fans flock down south every spring to catch the action when the Boston Red Sox and the Minnesota Twins play in Fort Myers; the Cincinnati Reds in Sarasota; and the Pittsburgh Pirates in Bradenton. Many of these teams have farm teams that continue to play the season out at their stadiums.

BEACHES Where to start? Florida's 2,000-mile coastline means beaches for every taste, from the busy social scene at South Beach to the remote serenity of Keewaydin Island. Public lands are your best places to enjoy pristine dunes and uncluttered beachfronts— our favorites include Bahia Honda State Park, Cayo Costa State Park, Caspersen Beach, and Bowman's Beach on Sanibel Island.

BED & BREAKFASTS Because of the sheer number of bed & breakfasts throughout Florida, we don't list every one in the region covered by this book, but we have given you selections from what we feel are the best we've encountered. There is a mix of historical bed & breakfasts, working ranches, rustic lodges, and easygoing family homes. Some of our choices, but not all, are members of associations such as **Superior Small Lodging** (www .superiorsmalllodging.com) or the **Florida Bed & Breakfast Inns** (281-499-1374 or 1-800-524-1880; www .florida-inns.com), both of which conduct independent inspections of prop-

erties. All the bed & breakfast owners we stayed with were eager to tell their stories; most have a great love for the history of their homes and their towns. We find bed & breakfast travel to be one of the best ways to connect with genuine Florida, and we strongly encourage you to seek out the experiences we've listed throughout the book. Some motels will offer breakfast so that they can list their establishment as a bed & breakfast, and we have tried to note this wherever possible as Internet sites can be misleading.

BICYCLING Check with **Bike Florida** (www.bikeflorida.org) for bicycling opportunities in Florida, where regional groups have done a great job of establishing and maintaining both on-road bike routes and off-road trails suitable for mountain biking. Information on these routes and trails is listed in the text. The Office of Greenways and Trails (see *Greenways*) can provide maps and specific information on rail-trail projects throughout the state.

BIG CYPRESS NATIONAL PRESERVE Established by Congress in 1974 as the first National Preserve in the United States, **Big Cypress National Preserve** (239-695-1201; www.nps.gov/bicy), between Naples and Miami along the Tamiami Trail, protects more than 900 square miles of cypress and sawgrass habitats dependent on seasonal rains. Stop in at the Oasis Visitor Center, Ochopee, for an orientation to the preserve.

BIG CYPRESS SWAMP The Big Cypress National Preserve is only one in a network of public lands protecting the Big Cypress Swamp, more than a million acres of gently sloping watery wilderness fed by summer rainfall that moves slowly south in a shallow river through cypress strands and sloughs.

Other public lands protecting this fragile environment are Collier-Seminole State Park, Corkscrew Swamp Sanctuary, Fakahatchee Strand Preserve State Park, Florida Panther National Wildlife Refuge, Picayune Strand State Forest, and the Ten Thousand Islands National Wildlife Refuge, where the fresh water mingles with the mangrove fringe of the Gulf of Mexico. Most of these preserves provide exploration of the habitat via boardwalks, paddling trails, or hiking trails—expect to wade them most of the year.

BIRDING As the home to millions of winter migratory birds, Florida is a prime destination for bird-watching; see the **Great Florida Birding Trail** (www.floridabirding trail.com). The Florida Game and Fresh Water Fish Commission (www.floridaconservation.org) has a bird-watching certificate program called Wings over Florida. My top pick for birding in South Florida: Ding Darling National Wildlife Refuge. If you can fit no other visit into your schedule, go there during the winter migratory months to see a vast variety of birds, including the bright pink roseate spoonbills feeding on the mud flats.

BLACK HERITAGE TRAIL In 1990, the Florida Legislature created the Study Commission on African-American History in Florida to document African-American contributions to Florida history and culture. To promote these sites for tourism, the Florida Department of State and VISIT FLORIDA created the **Florida Black Heritage Trail** program (www.fl heritage.com/services/trails/bht) and guidebook, which is available online or through the Department of State.

BOAT AND SAILING EXCURSIONS Exploring our watery state by water is part of the fun of visiting Florida, from the blasting speed of an airboat skipping across the marshes to the gentle toss of a schooner as it sails along the Intracoastal Waterway. Many ecotours rely on quiet electric-motor pontoon boats to guide you down Florida's rivers. With South Florida's multitude of islands and massive Lake Okeechobee, boat tours and charter boats can be found at almost every major marina.

BOOKS To understand Florida, you need to read its authors, and none is more important to read than Patrick Smith, whose *A Land Remembered* is a landmark piece of fiction tracing Florida's history from settlement to development. A good capsule history of Florida's nearly five hundred years of European settlement is *A Short History of Florida*, the abbreviated version of the original masterwork by Michael Gannon. To understand Florida's frenetic development over the past century, *Some Kind of Paradise: A Chronicle of Man and the Land in Florida* by Mark Derr will offer serious insights.

South Florida's settlers had a much harsher time of homesteading than their North Florida brethren, since mosquito-borne diseases, Seminole attacks, and ravaging hurricanes were common. To introduce yourself to the

The Crows Nest

hardships of these early days, seek out *Their Eyes Were Watching God* by novelist Zora Neale Hurston for a touching fictionalization of the 1928 hurricane that decimated the southern communities along Lake Okeechobee, and *Crackers in the Glade* by Rob Storter, a memoir and history of his family's settlement of the Ten Thousand Islands. Peter Matthiessen wrote a trilogy of novels using the true tales of early settlers in the Ten Thousand Islands. It kicks off with *Killing Mr. Watson,* a fictionalized account of the events that led up to one fateful day in Chokoloskee. The trilogy has been reworked and edited by the author and is now available as a single volume, *Shadow Country.* And although it's well out of print, *The Mangrove Coast* (1942) by Karl Bickel is one of the best books written on the settlement of southwest Florida.

No discussion of the Everglades is complete without *The Everglades: River of Grass* by Marjory Stoneman Douglas. By putting pen to paper to write "There are no other Everglades in the world," she spearheaded a conservation effort in the 1940s to preserve the unique Everglades habitat and establish Everglades National Park. Also of note are the classic history *Man in the Everglades* by Charl-

ton Tebeau and the recent *Liquid Land* by Ted Levin. David McCally gives an informative account of how the original Everglades ecosystem has been razed by agriculture in *The Everglades: An Environmental History,* and Alex Wilkinson explains the way of life for sugarcane workers in *Big Sugar.* The chronicler of Okeechobee lore is Lawrence Will, who wrote *Cracker History of Okeechobee* and *Okeechobee Hurricane* among others. Moving on to the wonders of the Big Cypress Swamp, explore this watery region through the words of Jeff Ripple and photos by Clyde Butcher in *Southwest Florida's Wetland Wilderness: Big Cypress Swamp and the Ten Thousand Islands.* Connie Bransilver and Larry Richardson collaborated on a beautiful coffee-table book, *Florida's Unsung Wilderness: The Swamps.* And to connect the dots between the swamp and the orchid growers of Redland, seek out *The Orchid Thief* by Susan Orlean. The natural history of the Florida Keys is thoroughly explained by Jeff Ripple in *The Florida Keys: Natural Wonders of an Island Paradise.* *Last Train to Paradise* by Les Standiford gives a thorough picture of Flagler's Folly, the Overseas Railroad, while *Charlotte's Story: A Florida Keys Diary* by Charlotte Niedhauk is a memoir of living as the caretaker on Lignumvitae Key in the 1930s.

Key West authors are known for their fine literature and plays, headed up by Ernest Hemingway and closely followed by Tennessee Williams, Truman Capote, John Hershey, and Alison Lurie among many others. But South Florida fairly bubbles over with mystery writers, and most of their settings take place within the cities covered in this book. Best beloved is John D. MacDonald, whose Travis McGee is a model for many modern sleuths. Carl

Sandra Friend

Hiaasen and Tim Dorsey are known for madcap mysteries, while Randy Wayne White, James W. Hall, Edna Buchanan, and Barbara Parker tend more toward the mainstream. These folks are only the tip of the iceberg; ask around at any South Florida independent bookseller to find many more.

BUS SERVICE Greyhound (1-800-229-9424; www.greyhound.com) covers an extensive list of Florida cities; see their Web site for details and the full schedule. Stops are noted in the text under *Getting There*.

CAMPGROUNDS Rates are quoted for single-night double-occupancy stays; all campgrounds offer discounts for club membership as well as weekly, monthly, and resident (6 months or more) stays and often charge more for extra adults. If pets are permitted, keep them leashed. Also see the *Green Space* section of each chapter for campgrounds at state and county parks. Florida State Parks uses Reserve America (1-800-326-3521; www.reserveamerica.com) for all campground reservations; a handful of sites are kept open for drop-ins. Ask at the gate.

CHILDREN, ESPECIALLY FOR The crayon symbol ✐ identifies activities and places of special interest to children and families.

CITRUS STANDS, FARMER'S MARKETS, AND U-PICKS Citrus stands associated with active groves are usually open seasonally November through April. We've listed permanent stands as well as places you're likely to see roadside fruit and vegetable sales (often out of the backs of trucks and vans) from local growers. All U-pick is seasonal, and Florida's growing seasons run year-round with citrus in winter

and spring, strawberries in early spring, blueberries in late spring, and cherries in early summer. If you attempt U-pick citrus, bring heavy gloves and wear jeans: Citrus trees have serious thorns. Also, don't pick citrus without permission: It's such a protected crop in Florida that to pluck an orange from a roadside tree is a felony. For a full listing of farmer's markets around the state, visit the Florida Department of Agriculture (www.florida-agriculture.com/consumers/farmers_markets.htm) Web site.

CIVIL WAR As the third state to secede from the Union, Florida has a great deal of Civil War history to explore. Although most battle sites are in North Florida and the Panhandle, skirmishes and raids occurred in places like Fort Myers and are commemorated annually. See Florida Civil War Reenactors Event Roster (www.floridareenactorsonline.com/EventRoster.htm) for a calendar of reenactments held throughout the state.

CORAL In the Florida Keys, avoid stepping on coral. You'll damage the living organisms, and they'll damage you with dangerous cuts that can quickly become infected. Washed up on beaches or embedded in sandy soil, dead coral can cut bare feet as easily as broken glass.

CORAL REEFS The coral reefs paralleling the Florida Keys are the only living coral reefs in the continental United States, and scientists say that all reefs have diminished by as much as 90 percent in recent years due to pollution and global warming. The most extensive reefs formed along Key Largo and from Big Pine Key west to Key West. The coral reefs of Florida are similar to those in the Caribbean,

Sandra Friend

sharing many species of fish and crustaceans. There are several types of reefs in the Keys, including bank reefs, which, heavily affected by wave action on one side and protected by the coral structure on the other, harbor a great diversity of species; patch reefs, which form on little fossil reef outcrops at 6- to 30-feet deep and are surrounded by seagrass; and spur-and-groove reef, where the reef grows around eroded limestone formations, as it does at Looe Key.

CRABBING From mid-October through May, it's perfectly legal for you to dive offshore to collect stone crab claws—if you can stand the thought of removing them from their owners. The good news is the crabs grow them back, so take only one from each critter. Limits set by the Florida Fish and Wildlife Conservation Commission (www.floridaconservation.org) are 1 gallon of claws per person (2 gallons per vessel), and all claws must be a minimum of 2¾ inches from elbow to tip. Divers must fly a diver-down flag.

CRABS Florida can lay claim to some of the freshest crabs in its seafood restaurants, thanks to fishermen who set crab traps in the shallows to catch stone crabs in season in such places as Chokoluskee, Cortez, Matlacha, and

the Keys. Eat your crab legs with melted butter for optimum effect.

DIVE RESORTS Dive resorts cater to both open-water and cave divers, with an on-site dive shop. They tend toward utilitarian but worn accommodations—wet gear can trash a room! Lodgings categorized as such will appeal to divers because of their location.

DIVING South Florida divers focus on the sea, for there are shipwrecks to be explored, stone reefs to follow, and the wondrous beauty of the living coral reefs of the Florida Keys to experience. A diver-down flag is a must when diving off a boat, even in relatively shallow water.

THE DIXIE HIGHWAY Conceptualized in the 1910s by Carl Graham Fisher and the Dixie Highway Association as a grand route for auto touring, the Dixie Highway had two legs that ran along the East Coast of the United States into Florida, both ending in Miami. Since it ran along both coasts of Florida, you'll find OLD DIXIE HIGHWAY signs on both US 1 and US 17 on the east coast and along US 19, 27, and 41 on the west coast, and even US 441 in the middle.

EMERGENCIES Hospitals with emergency rooms are noted at the beginning of each chapter. Dial 911 to connect to emergency service anywhere in the state. For highway accidents or emergencies, contact the Florida Highway Patrol at VFHP on your cell phone or dial 911.

THE EVERGLADES When rainfall lands on the prairies and lakes of Central Florida, it starts a southward journey down its creeks and rivers to the Kissimmee River and Fisheating

Creek, which empty into Lake Okee-chobee. Prior to the construction of the Herbert Hoover Dike, the waters of Okeechobee seeped south into creeks and the "river of grass" known as the Everglades. Decades of flood control and irrigation and drainage for agricultural development have disrupted this natural system, flushing phosphates and other chemicals into Everglades National Park. The congressionally approved Everglades Restoration Plan (www.everglades plan.org) seeks to undo the damage by returning water flow to its natural course and by forcing the agricultural industry to clean its water before releasing it into natural systems. The Everglades are a complex environment. Fifty miles wide, only a few inches to a few feet deep in places, the natural sheet flow of rainwater moves slowly southward to nourish sawgrass prairies punctuated by tree islands, with cypress sloughs forming where the water is deepest. As it flows into the Gulf of Mexico and Florida Bay, the water mingles with the saline mangrove estuaries, nourishing these important nurseries for marine life. Water polluted by agricultural run off causes an overgrowth of algae and marine plants, threatening the habitats of sea creatures. Serious declines in water quality and fish population point to the need to clean and restore the Everglades. The Comprehensive Everglades Restoration Project, initiated with great fanfare in 2000, has since stalled, giving way to rising costs and continuing development. Florida governor Charlie Crist has pledged to revive the program and introduced a proposal to buy a large tract of sugar cane farms with an eye toward ceasing farming eventually. During the dry season (December through April), the jagged limestone karst bedrock becomes evident across the Ever-

glades, and animals cluster around deep ponds dug by alligators. The remainder of the year, it's a shallow watery landscape as far as the eye can see.

EVERGLADES NATIONAL PARK

Now protecting 1.5 million acres of the Everglades ecosystem, Everglades National Park (www.nps.gov/ever) was dedicated on December 6, 1947, by President Harry Truman. It was the culmination of years of effort by devoted activists concerned about drainage projects in South Florida and how they were affecting the landscape. Among those who most visibly contributed to the cause of protecting the Everglades were Ernest Coe, a landscape architect who founded the Tropical Everglades Park Association in 1928 with the intent of establishing a national park in South Florida, and Marjory Stoneman Douglas, an outspoken conservationist who rallied the public with *The Everglades: River of Grass* in 1947 and continued to fight for the natural Everglades sheet flow to be restored until her death in 1988 at age 108. The park enjoys the highest visitation of any public land in Florida, with more than 1.1 million visitors a year. There are three major gateways to the park: the Everglades National Park Gulf Coast Visitor Center in Everglades City, Shark Valley along the Tamiami Trail in the Miccosukee Reservation, and the main public-access portion of the park in South Dade County along Main Park Road, starting at the Ernest Coe Visitor Center. Recreational pursuits in the park include paddling, fishing, camping, nature walks and hiking, and bicycling the park roads. Keep in mind that this is a wild natural environment and is home to numerous species of mosquitoes. To avoid tampering with the habitat, no mosquito-control spraying is done within the park. Mosquitoes are at their peak during the summer months but can be a problem almost any month of the year. January and February are when the mosquito population ebbs and are the best months for outdoor activities. In addition to your insect repellent, consider carrying a mosquito head net for those unexpected swarms at dusk and after a sudden rain—I'm happy I did.

EVERGLADES TRAIL With 20 stops along the route, this new driving tour introduces you to the flow of water through South Florida, starting at its northernmost headwaters in the Shingle Creek basin outside Orlando and moving down into Lake Okeechobee and the Everglades "river of grass" itself. Visit www.evergladestrail.com for a map and guide.

FACTORY OUTLETS You've seen the signs, but are they really a bargain? Several factory outlets offer brand and designer names for less, but you may also get a great deal at smaller shops and even the local mall. We've listed some factory outlets that we found particularly fun to shop at that also had a nice selection of eateries and close access to major highways.

FERRIES Florida has few remaining ferryboats; in the region covered by this book, you'll find a private car ferry crossing to Palm Island, and several passenger ferries.

FISH CAMPS An important Florida tradition, fish camps are quiet retreats for anglers to relax along a lake or river and put in some quality time fishing. Sometimes the family comes along, too! Accommodations listed under this category tend to be older cabins, mobile homes, or concrete block structures, sometimes a little rough around the edges. If the cabins or motel rooms

at a fish camp are of superior quality, we list them under those categories.

FISHING The Florida Fish and Wildlife Conservation Commission (www.myfwc.com) regulates all fishing in Florida, offering both freshwater and saltwater licenses. To obtain a license, visit any sporting goods store or call 1-888-FISH-FLO for an instant license; you can also apply online at www.floridaconservation.org. No fishing license is required if you are on a guided fishing trip, are fishing with a cane pole, are bank fishing along the ocean (varies by county), or are 65 years or older; choose from short-term, annual, 5-year, or lifetime options.

FLORIDA GREEN LODGING PROGRAM Established in 2004 by the Florida Department of Environmental Protection, this innovative program recognizes lodgings that go the extra mile to protect Florida's natural resources by lessening their environmental impact. The program is entirely voluntary and encompasses not just linen reuse but energy efficiency, waste reduction, clean air, and communications. There are several levels of achievement for which lodgings earn one, two, or three palm ratings. Designated Green Lodgings are marked with a ✽ symbol in this guide; to date, 66 lodgings statewide have earned this honor. To learn more about the program, visit www.dep.state.fl.us/green lodging.

FLORIDA TRAIL The Florida Trail is a 1,400-mile footpath running from the Big Cypress National Preserve north of Everglades National Park to Fort Pickens at Gulf Islands National Seashore in Pensacola. With its first blaze painted in 1966, it is now one of only eight congressionally designated National Scenic Trails in the United States and is still under development—but you can follow the orange blazes from one end of the state to the other. The Florida Trail and other trails in state parks and state forests, known as the Florida Trail System, are built and maintained by volunteer members of the nonprofit **Florida Trail Association** (352-378-8823 or 1-877-HIKE-FLA; www.floridatrail.org), 5415 SW 13th St., Gainesville 32608. The association is your primary source for maps and guidebooks for the trail.

FORESTS, STATE The Florida Division of Forestry (www.fl-dof.com) administers Florida State Forests, encompassing thousands of acres of public lands throughout Florida. There are fewer state forests in South Florida than the rest of the state, but you'll find solitude on the trails at Myakka State Forest and Picayune Strand State Forest. Most (but not all) developed state forest trailheads charge a per-person fee of $2–3 for recreational use. For $30 you can purchase an annual day-use pass good for the driver and up to eight passengers: a real bargain for families! If you're a hiker, get involved with the Trailwalker program, in which you tally up miles on hiking trails and receive patches and certificates. A similar program for equestrians is the Trailtrotter program. Information on both programs can be found at trailhead kiosks or on the Florida Division of Forestry website.

GAS STATIONS Gas prices fluctuate wildly around the state—and not in proportion to distance from major highways, as you might think. You'll find your best bargains for filling your tank near Fort Pierce, North Miami, Key Largo, and Okeechobee. The highest prices seem to be in Palm Beach County and Sarasota.

GENEALOGICAL RESEARCH In addition to the excellent resources found in some local genealogical libraries, check the State Library of Florida, Florida Collection (www.flgenweb.net) for the Florida GenWeb project, census data, vital records, pioneer families, and links to the state's many historical societies.

GENUINE FLORIDA After writing more than a dozen guidebooks to Florida, Sandra realized that what she cared about the most were the honest-to-goodness down-home experiences that often get lost in the shuffle when visitors are looking for what's hot and new in the Sunshine State. She and her husband started Genuine Florida (www.genuineflorida.com) with the intent of promoting these rural, natural, and cultural heritage gems, and keep an active blog (www.genuineflorida.com/blog) featuring Florida book reviews, roadside Floridiana, and funky finds as they travel within their home state.

GOLFING Golfing is a favorite pastime for many Florida retirees, and there are hundreds of courses across the state, impossible to list in any detail; a good resource for research is Play FLA (www.playfla.com), the state's official golf travel Web site. Courses that are particularly interesting or feature exceptional facilities are listed. Florida is home to both the PGA and LPGA headquarters.

GREAT FLORIDA BIRDING TRAIL The Great Florida Birding Trail (www.floridabirdingtrail.com), supported by the Florida Fish and Wildlife Conservation Commission, provides guidance to birders on the best overlooks, hiking trails, and waterfront parks to visit and which species you'll find at each location. Sites listed in the regional Great Florida Birding Trail brochures are designated with brown road signs displaying a stylized swallow tailed kite. Certain sites are designated "Gateways" to the Great Florida Birding Trail, and you can pick up detailed information and speak with a naturalist at those. In the region covered by this guidebook, these sites include Corkscrew Swamp Sanctuary, Myakka River State Park, many sites on the Gulf Coast and the Everglades, as well as the Florida Keys.

GREENWAYS Florida has one of the nation's most aggressive greenway programs, overseen by the **Office of Greenways and Trails** (850-245-2052 or 1-877-822-5208; www.dep.state .fl.us/gwt/), which administers the state land acquisition program under the Florida Forever Act and works in partnership with the Florida Trail Association, Florida State Parks, water management districts, and regional agencies in identifying crucial habitat corridors for preservation and developing public recreation facilities.

HANDICAPPED ACCESS The wheelchair symbol & identifies lodgings, restaurants, and activities that are, at a minimum, accessible with minor assistance. Many locations and attractions provide or will make modifications for people with disabilities, so call beforehand to see if they can make the necessary accommodations.

HERITAGE SITES If you're in search of history, watch for the brown signs with columns and palm trees that mark official Florida Heritage Sites— everything from historic churches and graveyards to entire historic districts. According to the Florida Division of Historical Resources (www.flheritage .com), to qualify as a Florida Heritage Site a building, structure, or site must

be at least 30 years old and have significance in the areas of architecture, archaeology, Florida history, or traditional culture, or be associated with a significant event that took place at least 30 years ago.

HIKING The best hiking experiences in each region are under the *Hiking* section, and you can find additional walks mentioned under *Green Space.* Your most comprehensive hiking guides for this portion of Florida include Sandra Friend's *50 Hikes in South Florida* (Backcountry Guides) and (with Johnny Molloy) *The Hiking Trails of Florida's National Forests, Parks, and Preserves* and *Hiker's Guide to the Sunshine State* (University Press of Florida), also by Sandra Friend.

HISTORIC SITES With nearly five centuries of European settlement in Florida, historic sites are myriad—so this book's coverage of Florida history is limited to sites of particular interest. For the full details on designated historic sites in Florida, visit the state-administered Florida's History through Its Places (www.flheritage.com/facts/ reports/places) Web site. Historic sites that belong to the Florida Trust for Historic Preservation (www.floridatrust .org), P.O. Box 11206, Tallahassee 32302, honor Florida's Historic Passport program, which offers membership (www.floridatrust.org/member ship) to member sites—some for free, others for discounted admissions.

HUNTING Hunting is regulated by the Florida Fish and Wildlife Conservation Commission (www.myfwc.com), with general gun season falling between October and February in various parts of the state. Check the Web site for specific hunt dates, the wildlife management areas (WMAs) open to hunting, and hunting license regulations.

HURRICANES Hurricanes can strike anywhere in Florida, and in 2004, our state suffered a historic four hurricanes in just six weeks. I live about as far from both coasts as you can get, and while my home, protected by ancient live oaks, was spared damage, all of my neighbors lost parts of their roofs. While traveling during hurricane season (June through October), be aware of hurricane evacuation routes from coastal areas and keep daily tabs on the weather forecasts. Check before you visit and change plans if a hurricane is in the forecast; call the Florida emergency hotline (1-800-342-3557). If a landfall is predicted, do not wait until the last minute to evacuate the area: Be proactive and get out fast. Better safe than sorry, even if it means a radical change to your vacation plans.

IGUANAS Currently there are hundreds of thousands of feral iguanas from the Florida Keys upward to Palm Beach County, with a sizable population in Broward and Miami-Dade Counties. An invasive species not native to Florida, they are often spotted on the side of the highway or on boat docks, basking in the sun. You'll even see cautionary road signs in Key Biscayne. Three members of the *Iguanidae* family, the green iguana, the Mexican spiny tailed, and the black spiny tailed, are causing quite a ruckus

Sandra Friend

with the locals as they breed like rabbits and munch vegetation faster than a locust. But for those who consider capturing one, take heed. A whip from a tail or a bite will certainly require medical attention. Iguanas, like all reptiles, carry salmonella and require special handling. The illegal release of exotic species in Florida is punishable by a $1,000 fine and up to one year in jail.

INFORMATION Numerous kiosks and roadside billboards will taunt you to come in for vacation deals. Most are tied to time-shares or are operating in their own interest. True visitors centers will offer information without trying to sell you something. At the beginning of each section under Guidance we have listed the visitors bureaus and chambers with no commercial affiliation.

INSECTS Florida's irritating insects are myriad, especially at dawn and dusk during summer months. We love our winters when they get chilly enough to kill the little buggers off. If you don't like poisonous DEET, you might want to try using lemon eucalyptus essential oil, which scientists say is just as effective. If you can't stand the odor of this oil or citronella, you'll spend 99 percent of your time indoors. Flying annoyances include the mosquito (which comes in hundreds of varieties), gnat, and no-see-um; troublesome crawling bugs are the chigger (also known as redbug), a microscopic critter that attaches itself to your ankles to feed; the tick, which you'll find in deeply wooded areas; and red ants, invaders that swarm over your feet leaving painful bites if you dare step on their nest. Bottom line—use insect repellent, and carry an antihistamine with you to counter any reactions you have to communing with these native residents.

JELLYFISH At almost any time of the year you will find jellyfish in the ocean and washed up on the shore. Take particular care with the blue man o'war jellyfish; the sting from this marine creature is excruciatingly painful. Do not touch the dead ones on the beach as their venom is still potent. Contrary to popular belief they won't chase you down, but in case you get stung, consider carrying a small bottle of white vinegar in your beach bag; this seems to help alleviate some of the pain. Then seek medical attention. Just as with bee stings, reactions vary.

LOBSTERING August 6 through March 31 marks the annual Florida lobster season, when you're welcome to scuba or snorkel for your own dinner. Limits are six per day or 24 per boat, and specific areas, such as the waters of John Pennekamp Coral Reef State Park and Everglades National Park, are excluded. For the full list of rules and regulations, contact the **Florida Marine Patrol** (1-800-342-5367 or 1-800-ASK-FISH) or the **National Marine Fisheries Service** (813-570-5305 or 305-743-2437).

MANGROVES The mangroves that grow along our barrier islands and coastline provide a natural anchor for the buildup of sand and sediment to expand the land. During a storm they serve as a buffer between the raging water and the coastal habitats. Three types of mangroves grow in Florida: black, white, and red. Red mangroves have a distinct network of prop roots, roots that look like arches holding up the tree, and tend to be the "island builders." Black mangroves are broader and are surrounded by a network of short breathing roots protruding from the soil under the plant that look like miniature cypress knees. White mangroves look the most treelike, with oval light green leaves (the other mangroves have dark green, elliptical leaves).

MARITIME HERITAGE In a state where many still pull their living from the sea, it's only appropriate that we have a Florida Maritime Heritage Trail (www.flheritage.com/archaeology/underwater/maritime) that ties together the elements of our maritime heritage: working fishing villages such as Placidia; coastal fortresses built to defend Florida from invasion; lighthouses; historic shipwrecks; and our endangered coastal communities such as the coastal pine flatwoods and coastal scrub. Visit the Web site for a virtual travel guide to Florida's maritime heritage.

MOTELS, HOTELS, AND RESORTS We've included resorts with motels and hotels for this guide since many properties refer to themselves as resorts but do not offer everything you need to stay put on the property, such as an on-site restaurant, shopping, and tours. In general, chain motels and hotels are not listed in this guide because of their ubiquitous nature; however, we've included a handful that are either the only lodging options in a particular area or happen to be outstanding places to stay.

MUSEUMS Explore our centuries of history: The **Florida Association of Museums** (850-222-6028; www.flamuseums.org) provides a portal to more than 340 museums throughout the state. Their Web site also provides a calendar of exhibits in museums around the state.

NATIONAL WILDLIFE REFUGES Founded by President Theodore Roosevelt on March 21, 1903, with the dedication of Pelican Island National

Wildlife Refuge in Florida's Indian River Lagoon, the National Wildlife Refuge system protects lands used by migratory birds and vanishing species. With nine refuges in South Florida, the U.S. Fish and Wildlife Commission manages a significant chunk of the South Florida landscape. Some National Wildlife Refuges (such as Crocodile Lakes National Wildlife Refuge in the Florida Keys) are entirely closed to public access. Others, like Ding Darling, Loxahatchee, and the National Key Deer Refuge, provide public access on a limited basis. When visiting a National Wildlife Refuge, keep in mind that all animals and plants are protected—visitors have been arrested and fined for removing tree snails, orchids, and bromeliads from preserves in South Florida.

ORCHIDS South Florida is an orchid-lovers' paradise. In addition to viewing them in the wild on many public lands, you can purchase your own to take home from growers ranging down the Atlantic Coast from Boynton Beach to Coral Gables and Redland into the Keys. There is a particularly high concentration of orchid growers along Krome Avenue in South Dade County. The international headquarters of the American Orchid Society (www.orchid web.com) is in Delray Beach.

PADDLING Canoeing and kayaking are extraordinarily popular activities in Florida, especially during the summer months, with sea kayaking a favorite along the barrier islands and the Keys. Most state parks have canoe livery concessions, and private outfitters are mentioned throughout the text. The newly opened Circumnavigational Salt-water Paddling Trail (www.florida dep.org/gwt/paddling/saltwater.htm) offers 1,600 miles of sea kayaking along the edges of our state. Portions

of the trail are already in place as Blueways, mentioned in the text.

PARKS, STATE The Florida State Parks system (www.floridastateparks .org) is one of the United States's best and most extensive state park systems, with more than 160 to explore. All Florida state parks are open 8 AM–sunset daily. If you want to watch the sunrise from a state park beach, you'll have to camp overnight. Camping reservations are centralized through Reserve America (www.reserve america.com) and can be booked through each individual state park Web site. Walk-in visitors are welcome on a first-come, first-served basis. An annual pass is a real deal if you plan to do much traveling in the state: Individual passes are $40 plus tax, and family passes are $80, plus tax, per year. The family pass is good for up to a maximum of eight people in one vehicle. Pick up a pass at any state park ranger station, or order through the Web site.

PARROTS A favorite pet of the early 1990s, Quaker parrots were thrown into the ecomix after Hurricane Andrew in 1992. The loud, lime green birds put on an impressive and often humorous display and are frequently seen in flocks of a dozen or more throughout Southeast Florida and in the Tampa Bay area. Former pet macaws have also been spotted, now breeding fifth and sixth generations of wild birds.

PETS The dog-paw symbol 🐾 identifies lodgings and activities that accept pets. Always inform the front desk that you are traveling with a pet, and expect to pay a surcharge.

POPULATION According to the 2007 federal census estimates, Florida's population is more than 18 million people.

What's scary to those of us who live here is that there continues to be a net gain of 800 people moving into Florida every day—which means an increasingly serious strain on our already fragile water resources.

PYTHONS Snake owners who decide their pets are too big to contain have unfortunately released many exotics into the Everglades, so many Burmese pythons have been seen in and around Everglades National Park—to the extent that they are actively breeding at a rapid rate, with estimates as high as 100,000 within the wild lands of South Florida. Feeding off rats, squirrels, and birds, the giant pythons, some as long as 15 feet and weighing as much as 250 pounds, have even been seen battling alligators. They have no natural predators in this environment. Because of this exponentially growing problem, and the 2009 death of a child by a "pet" Burmese python, the Florida Fish & Wildlife Conservation Commission is now issuing a limited number of permits for hunters to assist them in eradicating these troublesome snakes.

RAILROADIANA Florida's railroad history dates back to 1836 with the St. Joe & Lake Wimico Canal & Railroad Company, followed shortly thereafter in 1837 with the opening of the mule-driven Tallahassee & St. Marks Railroad, bringing supplies from the Gulf of Mexico to the state capital. Railroad commerce shaped many South Florida towns, with Henry Plant's Plant System (later the Seaboard Air Line) on the west coast and Henry Flagler's Florida East Coast Line on the Atlantic coast changing the course of history for South Florida and especially the Florida Keys. This category notes sites of interest to railroad-history buffs.

RATES The range of rates provided spans the lowest of low season to the highest of high season (which varies from place to place) and does not include taxes or discounts such as AARP, AAA, and camping club discounts.

RESERVATIONS The Seminole and Miccosukee tribes have reservations scattered throughout South Florida as sovereign lands granted to them by the U.S. government. The Seminoles hold more than 90,000 acres in South Florida and in recent times have served as hosts with grand casinos and hotels. For an understanding of tribal culture, visit the Big Cypress Seminole Reservation to walk through the Ah-Tah-Thi-Ki Museum, the world's largest museum devoted to Seminole culture and heritage.

RIVERS Unfortunately, most of South Florida's rivers vanished in the early 1900s as part of the "Everglades Reclamation" spearheaded by Governor Napoleon Bonaparte Broward and later carried forward by the Army Corps of Engineers under the banner of flood control and water management. Instead, you'll see hundreds of canals. But there are still a few rivers that run free, and as you can imagine, they are extraordinarily popular for kayaking, among them the wild and scenic Loxahatchee River in Palm Beach County, the St. Lucie River in St. Lucie County, and the Peace, Little Manatee, Myakka, Hillsborough, and Estero Rivers on the Gulf Coast. The Kissimmee River is undergoing a restoration effort to undo the damage done, but Fisheating Creek is the only wild waterway that still flows into Lake Okeechobee.

SCENIC HIGHWAYS The Florida Department of Transportation has designated nine scenic highways throughout the state. In South Florida, enjoy a drive on the Gulf Coast Heritage Trail, which leads you from Bradenton south along the barrier islands to Venice; the most scenic segment is the lushly canopied narrow road on Manasota Key. The Big Water Heritage Trail leads you on a loop around Lake Okeechobee to explore historic and scenic sites. But nothing else in the Southeast compares to driving the Overseas Highway, as US 1 jumps from island to island through the Keys, with expanses of ocean stretching off to both horizons. The Tamiami Trail through Big Cypress National Preserve leads you through the heart of South Florida's watery southern wilderness, where you'll see flocks of rare white pelicans on the salt flats and hundreds of wood storks roosting in the cypresses.

SEASONS South Florida's temperate winter weather makes it ideal for vacationers, but we do have a very strong tropical delineation of wet and dry seasons. Daily afternoon thundershowers are an absolute from June through September. Winter is generally dry and crisp, with nighttime temperatures falling as low as the 40s, with rare dips into the 20s.

SEMINOLE WARS Two years into the Second Seminole War, Col. Zachary Taylor led U.S. Army troops south from Fort Basinger on the Kissimmee River toward the coast, running into a large Seminole ambush along the shores of Lake Okeechobee on Christmas Day 1837, led by medicine man Abiaka, known as "Sam Jones." The Battle of Okeechobee raged nearly three hours, felling more than 100 men from both sides with injuries and leaving 26 dead. Although the Seminoles were outnumbered two to one, the heavy army casualties prevented the troops from following the Seminoles' retreat into the Everglades.

Several months after a trading post opened on the northern boundary of Seminole Territory near the Peace River in 1849, five Seminoles attacked the trading post and killed officers stationed there, precipitating unrest between the settlers and the Seminoles. The U.S. Army moved back in and continued to build new forts along the reservation boundary. On December 20, 1855, Billy Bowlegs (Holata Micco) led a band of Seminoles who attacked and killed federal soldiers surveying within the Seminole lands. Seminole raiding parties then attacked the Braden plantation and others near the Manatee River, and the U.S. Army sent soldiers into the Everglades to attack Seminole settlements. The Third Seminole War was under way. By 1858 Billy Bowlegs agreed to leave Florida with his family and be relocated to reservation lands in the west—the ultimate goal of the Seminole Wars, so the federal government could open up all of Florida to settlement. After the U.S. Army departed South Florida, Abiaka was the only remaining Seminole leader in the state, and fewer than three hundred Seminoles remained in Florida, all deeply hidden in the Everglades. The Seminoles never signed a peace treaty to end this war. It was not until 1957 that the U.S. Congress recognized the Seminole tribe and permitted them to apply for reservation lands in Florida. (For the Seminole Tribe's description of the wars and their aftermath, please visit www.seminoletribe .com/history/index.shtml.)

SHARKS Yes, they are in the water. At any given time there are a dozen or more just offshore, but for the most part they will leave you alone. To avoid being bitten, stay out of the water if there is a strong scent of fish oil in the air, which means that fish are already being eaten and you may be bitten by mistake. You will also want to avoid swimming near piers and jetties, which are active feeding zones.

SHRIMP South Florida is a shrimp-lover's dream, with fresh shrimp in virtually every seafood restaurant, especially on the Gulf Coast. Look for shrimp fried, broiled, sautéed, and blackened in creative recipes by Florida chefs. Pink shrimp in the Keys are especially delectable.

STINGRAYS In the Gulf of Mexico, wading calls for the "stingray shuffle." Set each foot down on the ocean floor with a resounding stomp on each step, which alerts the stingrays to stay clear. As you'll discover by visiting aquarium touch tanks in South Florida, stingrays are relatively docile and don't mind being touched—but they do react to being stepped on.

THE SUNSHINE STATE The moniker Sunshine State was an effective 1960s advertising slogan that was required on motor vehicle tags; it became the state's official nickname in 1970 by a legislative act.

Holiday Isle James Steele

TAXES Florida's base sales tax is 6 percent, with counties adding up to another 1.5 percent of discretionary sales tax. In addition, a tourist development tax of up to 10 percent may be levied on hotel accommodations in some cities and counties, including Miami-Dade and Monroe.

THEME PARKS South Florida doesn't cater to the same crowd that heads to the theme parks in the north. Down here, attractions tend more toward the classics—look to Sunken Gardens in St. Petersburg or Monkey Jungle in Homestead as examples, since the parks of South Florida focus on wildlife and flora.

TOADS The *Bufo Marinus* toad (or cane toad), growing as large as 9 inches in length and more than 2 pounds in weight, is usually spotted at night catching bugs under lights. In the 1960s it was originally released in sugarcane fields to control rats and mice, and now it can be seen in almost every residential neighborhood. When attacked or threatened, the nuisance species secretes a milky toxin from the back of its head. Contact with the poison will cause a nasty rash and is lethal enough to kill even large dogs within a few hours, so make sure to keep kids and Fluffy away from these critters.

TRAIL RIDING Bringing your own horses? Under state law, riders utilizing trails on state land must carry proof of a negative Coggins test for their horses. If you're interested in riding, hook up with one of the many stables listed in the text. Under state law, equine operators are not responsible for your injuries if you decide to go on a trail ride.

VISIT FLORIDA Visit Florida (www.visitflorida.com), the state's official tourism bureau, is a clearinghouse for every tourism question you might have. Their partners cover the full range of destinations, from quaint small towns like Okeechobee to the snazzy new hotels on Miami Beach. Utilize their Web site resources to pre-plan your trip, from the interactive map that lets you explore destination possibilities in regions to Sunny, the online vacation planner that assists you in compiling your itinerary.

WEATHER Florida's weather is per-haps our greatest attraction. Balmy winters are the norm, with daytime temperatures in the 80s and evenings in the 60s common for South Florida. And don't even think about snow—it's the rare freeze that reaches south of Lake Okeechobee (although we've seen it happen!). Summers are hot and wet, with temperatures soaring up to the 90s. In the Florida Keys the trade winds help keep summer temperate, but you won't avoid the rains. Florida thunderstorms come up fast and carry with them some of the world's most violent and dangerous lightning. It's best to get inside and out of or off the water should you see one coming. Contrary to popular belief, you are not safe in an automobile due to the rub-ber tires. Our car was hit by lightning while we were driving across Alligator Alley, a great vista for storm watching. Our car was totally disabled by the hit, requiring thousands of dollars in repair, though we felt no impact and were unharmed. And watch for approaching storms. Even if the sky looks clear, a lightning bolt may still strike if thunder is rumbling nearby.

WHERE TO EAT We've limited our choices to local favorites and outstand-ing creative fare, avoiding the chains seen everywhere across America. Sev-eral Florida-based chains deserve a mention, however; you'll enjoy their

cuisine when you find them. Flanigans, known for its excellent burgers and diverse menu, started in Pompano Beach in 1985, and now there are near-ly 20 locations along the Atlantic Coast. Hooters got its start in Clearwater, and Fred Fleming's Barbecue hails from St. Petersburg, as does Outback Steak-house. TooJay's, a New York–style deli, shines with big breakfasts, stellar sand-wiches, and its yummy Mounds cake. You'll also find the Stuart-based Ice Cream Churn, with 28 flavors of home-made ice cream, tucked away inside convenience stores throughout the state. Miami is an incubator for world-class chefs and boasts numerous out-standing restaurants, as do the Florida Keys, although some of the best restau-rants are the small, independently owned regional eateries, many of which we've included in this guide.

WINERIES Florida's wineries run the gamut from small family operations to large production facilities, and some partner together to provide a store-front in a high-traffic region while the growing, fermenting, and bottling is done in an area more favorable for agriculture. Native muscadine grapes are the cornerstones of the state's wines, and a few entrepreneurs have created interesting wines from the plethora of tropical fruits that thrive in south Florida. For an overview of Florida wineries, contact the **Florida Grape Growers Association** (941-678-0523; www.fgga.org), 343 W Cen-tral Ave., #1, Lake Wales 33853.

WI-FI The Wi-Fi symbol "₁" indicates places that provide wireless Internet access, which may or may not be free. The forward-thinking city of Sarasota offers free Wi-Fi throughout the entire downtown area—sit on a park bench and check your e-mail.

The Gulf Coast

FLORIDA'S GULF ISLANDS:
MANATEE COUNTY

SARASOTA AND HER ISLANDS

CHARLOTTE HARBOR AND
THE GULF ISLANDS

THE BEACHES OF FORT MYERS AND
SANIBEL ISLAND

THE PARADISE COAST: NAPLES,
MARCO ISLAND & EVERGLADES

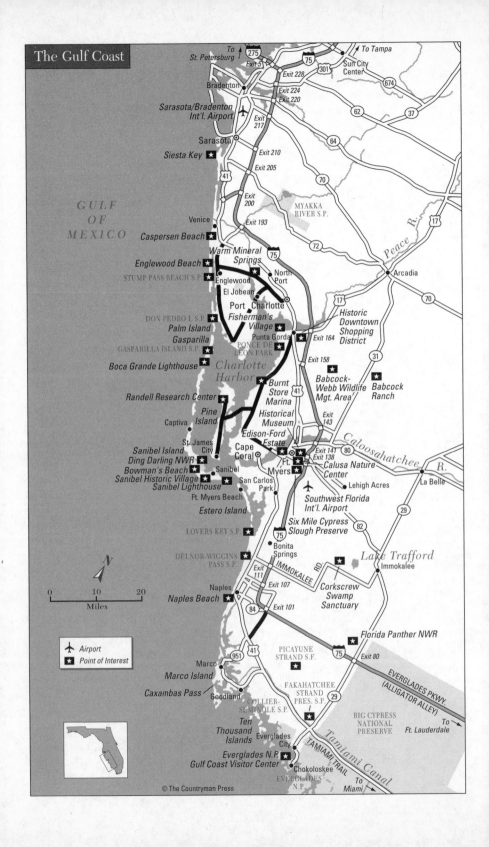

The Gulf Coast

GULF
OF
MEXICO

To
St. Petersburg

To Tampa

Exit 5

Sun City
Center

Exit 228

Bradenton

Exit 224
Exit 220

Sarasota/Bradenton
Int'l. Airport

Exit 217

Sarasota

Siesta Key ★

Exit 210

Exit 205

MYAKKA
RIVER S.P.

Exit 200

Venice

Exit 193

Caspersen Beach ★

Warm Mineral
Springs

Englewood Beach ★

STUMP PASS BEACH S.P. ★

Englewood

North
Port

El Jobean

Port
Charlotte

Fisherman's
Village ★

DON PEDRO I. S.P. ★

Palm Island

Gasparilla

GASPARILLA ISLAND S.P. ★

Punta Gorda

PONCE DE
LEON PARK

Boca Grande Lighthouse ★

Charlotte
Harbor

Exit 164

Exit 158

Burnt
Store
Marina

Babcock-
Webb Wildlife
Mgt. Area

Babcock
Ranch ★

Randell Research Center ★

Pine
Island

Captiva

Historical
Museum

Edison-Ford
Estate

Exit 143

St. James
City

Sanibel Island

Cape
Coral

Exit 141
Exit 138

Ding Darling NWR ★

Bowman's Beach ★

Sanibel Historic Village ★

Sanibel

Ft.
Myers

Calusa Nature
Center

Sanibel Lighthouse ★

San Carlos
Park

Lehigh Acres

La Belle

Ft. Myers Beach

Estero Island

Southwest Florida
Int'l. Airport

LOVERS KEY S.P ★

Six Mile Cypress
Slough Preserve

Bonita
Springs

Lake Trafford

DELNOR-WIGGINS
PASS S.P. ★

Immokalee

0   10   20
Miles

Corkscrew
Swamp
Sanctuary

Naples

Exit 107

Exit 111

Naples Beach ★

Exit 101

Florida Panther NWR ★

✈ Airport
★ Point of Interest

PICAYUNE
STRAND S.F. ★

Exit 80

EVERGLADES PKWY.
(ALLIGATOR ALLEY)

Marco

Marco Island

FAKAHATCHEE
STRAND
PRES. S.P. ★

BIG CYPRESS
NATIONAL
PRESERVE

To
Ft. Lauderdale

Caxambas Pass

Goodland

COLLIER-
SEMINOLE S.P.

Tamiami Canal

Ten
Thousand
Islands

Everglades
City

TAMIAMI TRAIL

Everglades N.P.
Gulf Coast Visitor Center ★

Chokoloskee

To
Miami

© The Countryman Press

EVERGLADES
N.P.

FLORIDA'S GULF ISLANDS: MANATEE COUNTY

Known for its beautiful beaches and vibrant cultural offerings, **Manatee County** is on the south shore of Tampa Bay and stretches deep inland, encompassing massive ranches and farmlands that are important contributors to Florida's economy. This region has deep roots in the past, with archaeological sites that date back thousands of years and historic sites from the earliest pioneer settlement of Florida. It is the landing site of Spanish explorer Hernando De Soto, who in 1539 arrived with his troops near the mouth of Tampa Bay in search of gold. Near the end of the Second Seminole War in 1841, Josiah Gates arrived by boat and homesteaded along the river in the area now known as Old Manatee. Major Robert Gamble established his 3,500-acre sugar plantation along the Manatee River in 1843. By 1855, enough people had settled around the river for Manatee County to be formed from southern Hillsborough County.

After the Civil War, settlers streamed into the interior to establish cattle ranches, citrus groves, and large farms in places such as Parrish and Miakka (now Myakka), leading to a local agricultural boom. The city of Bradenton grew up around the Civil War–era village of Manatee, with businesses lining downtown avenues and imposing Victorian homes built across the river in Palmetto. Rivers define Manatee County—Little Manatee at its northern end, the Manatee River between Ellenton and Bradenton, and the Braden River to the south.

The barrier islands of Manatee County have been a vacation destination for savvy Floridians for generations. Inhabited in ancient times by Timucua and, more recently, Calusa; explored by the Spanish in the early 1500s; and permanently settled after Florida gained statehood in the 1800s, Anna Maria Island has three charming villages—Anna Maria, Holmes Beach, and Bradenton Beach—with a mix of old-fashioned seaside residential communities, motels, and low-rise condo complexes (thanks to an ordinance prohibiting buildings from being more than three stories tall). Miles of public beaches offer easy access and free parking. Longboat Key is split across neighboring Sarasota County. It's primarily residential—including the site of the original historic village at the north end—and boasts superb beaches, resort and beach-home rentals, and some classic motels.

GUIDANCE **Florida's Gulf Islands** (www.floridasgulfislands.com) is the official tourism Web site for the **Bradenton Area Convention & Visitors Bureau** (941-729-9177 x231), P.O. Box 1000, Bradenton, FL 34206, and encompasses activities throughout the county. Walk-in information is available at the **Manatee County Tourist Information Center** (941-729-7040), 5461 Factory Shops Blvd., Ellenton, at Prime Outlet Center and the **Anna Maria Island Chamber of Commerce** (941-778-1541; www.amichamber.org), 5313 Gulf Dr. N, Holmes Beach.

GETTING THERE *By car:* I-75, US 19, US 301, and US 41 provide primary access to the region.

By air: **Sarasota Bradenton International Airport** (941-FLY-2-SRQ; www.srq-airport.com) has regular service by nine major carriers, including Air Canada, AirTran, Delta, and US Airways.

GETTING AROUND *By car:* **US 19** south from I-275 (Sunshine Skyway) leads you through Terra Ceia and Palmetto before ending in Bradenton. **US 41** south crosses I-275 to connect Palmetto, Bradenton, and Sarasota. **US 301** sweeps in from the northwest through Parrish, Ellenton, and Palmetto to Bradenton en route to Sarasota. Use **SR 64** (Manatee Ave.) to reach the northwest corner of the county and to get to Bradenton and Anna Maria Island. **CR 789** runs north-south down the islands, connecting Anna Maria Island with Bradenton Beach and Longboat Key. **SR 70** is the southernmost east-west route in the county, from South Bradenton to Myakka City. **CR 684** (Cortez Rd.) passes through the old fishing village of Cortez to reach Bradenton Beach, crossing one of the oldest manned drawbridges along the Intracoastal Waterway.

By bus: **Manatee County Area Transit** (941-747-8621; www.mymanatee.org) has 10 routes with hourly bus service between Bradenton, Ellenton, Palmetto, and the Gulf Islands communities 6 AM to 7 PM Monday through Saturday. Fare $1.25, transfers $.25, discounts for seniors and students. Routes connect with the free trolley on Anna Maria Island.

By trolley: A **free trolley service** is offered on Anna Maria Island between the City Pier and Coquina Beach, 6 AM to 10:30 PM daily. The **Longboat Key Trolley** runs from Coquina Beach at the south end of Anna Maria Island to downtown Sarasota. Daily service every 30 minutes from 6 AM to 11 PM. Fare $.75.

By taxi: Yellow Cab of Bradenton (941-748-4800), Diplomat Taxi (941-365-8294).

PUBLIC RESTROOMS Beachfront parks include public restrooms and changing areas.

PARKING Beachgoers rejoice! Parking is free at natural-surface lots on Anna Maria Island, Bradenton Beach, and Longboat Key. Downtown Bradenton has metered spaces.

MEDICAL EMERGENCIES **Manatee Memorial Hospital** (941-746-5111; www.manateememorial.com), 206 Second St., East Bradenton.

AQUARIUM ♿ 🐾 Yes, you can see manatees in Manatee County at the 60,000 gallon **Parker Manatee Aquarium**, part of the educational complex at the **South Florida Museum** (see *Museums*). Home to three adult manatees, including the museum's mascot "Snooty," it is an accredited second stage rehabilitation facility for injured manatees to be returned to the wild.

ARCHAEOLOGICAL SITES

Bradenton
At **Shaw's Point**, now inside **De Soto National Memorial** (see *Historic Sites*), archaeologist S. T. Walker discovered a shell mound in 1879 that had been created by an early culture along the shores of Tampa Bay, complete with fire pits. The mound was nearly 600 feet long and 20 feet high at its highest. Despite the discovery of pottery shards within the mound, there was no government protection for such important artifacts back then. By the 1930s, the mound had been pulled apart and trucked away for road fill. If you walk the trail to Shaw's Point, you'll see the bleached oyster shells that were once a part of this large mound. Together with adjacent **Riverview Pointe Preserve**, the area is known as the **Shaw's Point Archaeological District** and was inhabited between 356 B.C. and A.D. 110.

Snead Island
At **Emerson Point Preserve** (see *Parks*), stop at the Portavant Temple Mound to capture a bit of prehistory. This flat-topped mound along the Manatee River is 150 feet long and 80 feet wide, and it once commanded a spectacular view, now obscured by centuries-old oaks. More than 1,000 years ago, a village of the ancestors of the Timucua sat on this site. A smaller rounded subsidiary mound and several middens are scattered throughout the forest.

Terra Ceia
Purchased and preserved by Karl and Madira Bickel in 1948, the ancient ceremonial mound now encompassed by **Madira Bickel Mound Archaeological State Park** (941-723-4536; www.floridastateparks.org/madirabickelmound) was the first designated state archaeological site in Florida. A paved concrete path winds through the palm hammock to a set of stairs leading to the top of the 20-foot-tall temple mound along Terra Ceia Bay. Paleoindian, Weedon Island, and Safety Harbor culture artifacts have been unearthed on the site, which is located off US 19 east 1.3 miles along Bayshore Drive.

ART GALLERIES

Bradenton
An artist's colony just outside downtown, the **Village of the Arts** (941-747-8056; www.artistsguildofmanatee.org), between Ninth St. W and 14th St. W, south of Milk Ave., is a working artists' neighborhood of colorful historic bungalows, with a mix of studios, galleries, and housing. With an Artwalk on the first Friday and Saturday of each month and regular "open shopping" hours of 11 AM–4 PM Saturday, it's a great place to shop for unique and whimsical art direct from the artists.

Longboat Key
Grab some fun at **KK's ARTique** (941-383-0883), 5360 Gulf of Mexico Dr., where appealing scenes of Sarasota mingle with classy art glass, mirror mosaics, fiber craft, and pottery.

BASEBALL Every spring, the **Pittsburgh Pirates** head to historic **McKechnie Field** (941-747-3031; www.mlb.com/spring_training/ballpark.jsp?c_id=pit), 1611 Ninth St. W, Bradenton, which was originally built for them in 1923 and named for Pittsburgh native, Bradenton resident, and Hall of Fame manager Bill McKechnie. The ballpark can handle more than 6,000 fans, and it's a busy place when the Pirates are in town. **Pirate City** (941-747-3031), 1701 27th St. E, is the official training facility.

EQUESTRIAN EVENTS One of the best-kept secrets in this area are the shows presented by **Herrmann's Royal Lipizzan Stallions** (941-322-1501; www.hlipizzans.com), 32755 Singletary Rd., Myakka City. Colonel Herrman assisted General George Patton in smuggling the horses out of Austria during World War II, and his heirs continue the tradition of training the horses in leaps and plunges, and touring the stallions throughout the world. Their winter home encompasses 200 acres; brood mares live here full time. See these powerful and graceful stallions with their trainers. Shows are presented Thursday through Friday at 3 PM and Saturday at 10 AM. Private riding lessons are available October through mid-May by appointment.

HISTORIC SITES

Anna Maria Island
Built in 1910, the **Anna Maria City Pier** anchors the north end of the island and looks out over Tampa Bay. On a clear day, you can see Egmont Key, Fort De Soto, and the Sunshine Skyway Bridge in the distance. In addition to providing a place to fish, the pier has a restaurant where you can savor the view.

Bradenton
✐ Commemorating Spanish explorer Hernando De Soto's arrival at Tampa Bay in 1539, **De Soto National Memorial** (941-792-0458 x105; www.nps.gov/deso), end of 75th Ave., at Shaw's Point, was commissioned in 1940 as the probable landing site of the Spanish fleet. In addition to Uzita, a replica Spanish camp with living-history interpreters, and a visitors center with artifacts, exhibits, and a video on De Soto's expedition, the park has more than a mile of trails leading through the mangrove fringe to various points of historic interest. Cattle were shipped from the peninsula during the 1800s and U.S. Navy blockaders used the point as a lookout post during the Civil War. As you walk the path along the Manatee River, you'll encounter the Holy Eucharist Monument, commissioned by the Diocese of St. Augus-

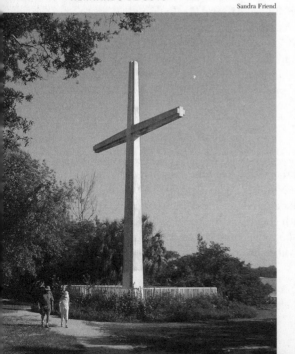

CROSS MARKING THE LANDING OF HERNANDO DE SOTO

Sandra Friend

tine in 1960 as a Catholic memorial in honor of De Soto. The nearby Memorial Cross remembers the 12 priests who accompanied De Soto on the expedition. Open 9 AM–5 PM daily. Free.

Florida Heritage District signs on SR 64 at 27th St. E direct you to **Braden Castle Park**, the site of the first **Tin Can Tourist Camp** in Florida and the former homestead of Dr. Joseph Braden. There isn't much left of his old tabby castle, but the view of the Manatee River is spectacular. The ruins are in the middle of a quaint village of tiny bungalows dating from 1924. It is still an active retirement community, so please be respectful when you visit, and don't block driveways or bother people.

✐ At **Manatee Village Historical Park** (941-741-4075; www.manateeclerk.com/ ClerkServices/HisVill/mchvillage.htm), 1404 Manatee Ave. E, explore historic landmarks brought here for preservation, such as the Bat Fogarty Boat Works, the Bunker Hill School, the Stephens House, and Wiggins Store. Open 9 AM–4:30 PM Mon.–Fri. and the second Sat. of each month. Free. Behind the park (on an adjacent tract outside the fence) is the city's oldest cemetery, the **1815 Manatee Burying Ground**, where most of the county's earliest settlers are buried. The nearby business district at Ninth St. E and SR 64 is the heart of Old Manatee, the first settlement in the county. Josiah Gates claimed his homestead here along the river in 1841.

Most of **downtown Bradenton** is a business district from the 1920s boom, but the city itself was founded as Braidenton in 1878. Watch for the Heritage District signs near 12th St. W directing you to the Italianate Post Office and the **Bradenton Carnegie Library** (941-741-4070), 1405 Fourth Ave. W, established in 1918 by Andrew Carnegie and an important repository of the early history of the region.

Bradenton Beach
Downtown Bradenton Beach is a quaint historic district with homes and businesses dating from the turn of the last century. At the end of Bridge Street, walk down the newly restored **Bridge Street Pier**, once part of the original plank bridge that was the only access to Anna Maria Island for nearly 40 years.

Cortez
With homes and boathouses dating back to the late 1800s, the **Cortez Fishing Village** (www.cortezvillage .org) is on the National Register of Historic Places; a walking tour map is available on their Web site.

BRADENTON BEACH PIER

Sandra Friend

ELLENTON

That imposing antebellum home along US 301 is indeed the southernmost remaining example of an architecture common along Florida's rivers in the early 1800s. Flanked by three-hundred-year-old oaks, the grand entrance to the **Gamble Plantation Historic State Park** (941-723-4536; www.florida stateparks.org/gambleplantation), 3708 Patten Ave., evokes Tara. Established in 1843 by Major Robert Gamble, the 3,500-acre sugar plantation along the Manatee River needed a grand estate home. Built of tabby (a mix of oyster shells and lime) with walls 2 feet thick, this Greek Revival mansion was designed to trap cool air like a cave and to utilize rainwater cisterns for fresh water. The plantation played a pivotal role at the end of the Civil War, when Confederate Secretary of State Judah P. Benjamin disguised himself as a French journalist, "M. Bonfal," and fled to Florida. Capt. Archibald McNeil, the plantation owner in 1865, hid his famous guest until arrangements could be made for a boat to Nassau. Both men had to flee to elude capture, but Benjamin succeeded in escaping the United States and went on to have a long career in law in London.

In 1925 the United Daughters of the Confederacy purchased the land and donated it to the state with the proviso that it be designated the Judah P. Benjamin Confederate Memorial. Now restored to its original glory, the home features period furnishings and artwork and is one of the few remaining examples of a Florida antebellum plantation. The UDC restored and maintains the Patten House (circa 1895) on the grounds of the state park, open by appointment and during special events. The state park has a nominal entrance fee, and there is an additional fee for a guided tour of the home.

Longboat Key
Blue historic markers along the sidewalks paralleling Broadway Street denote key homes and businesses in the original **Village of Longbeach** (www.longbeach village.com) founded in 1885. There are still many quaint cottages on the side streets, but most of the historic village has been replaced by modern upscale homes.

Palmetto
✏ At the **Palmetto Historical Park** (941-723-4991; www.manateeclerk.com/ ClerkServices/HisVill/palmetto_park.htm), 515 10th Ave. W, experience a 1920 kindergarten schoolroom, peek into the town's first freestanding post office from 1880, and visit the military museum in the Cypress House. The **1914 Carnegie Library** has an extensive amount of genealogical and historical information, as well as one of the few basements in the region—it was a requirement for the grant for the library to be built. Open 10 AM –4 PM Tues.–Fri. and on the first and third Sat. each month. Free.

Terra Ceia
While there's little left of the original village save an enclave of rural homesteads, Terra Ceia (north of Palmetto, off US 19) has two distinctive historic sites—the old **Palmetto Elementary School** and the **post office** (circa 1891) at the corner of Terra Ceia Drive and Center Road.

MUSEUMS

Anna Maria City
✒ At the **Anna Maria Island Historical Museum** (941-778-0492; www.amihs .org), 402 Pine Ave., you can pose inside the Old City Jail (no prisoners, no windows!) with a jailbird costume on, or go on a scavenger hunt with the kids for baby turtles, shark's teeth, and more. Open Tues.–Sat. 10 AM–1 PM (May–Sept.) and 10 AM–4 PM (Oct.–Apr.). Free.

Bradenton
On the campus of Manatee Community College, the **Family Heritage House Museum** (941-752-5319; www.familyheritagehouse.com), 5840 26th St. W, is a gallery and resource center for the study of African American achievements, as well as part of the National Underground Railroad "Network to Freedom" program, with extensive research materials. Open Tues.–Thurs. 11 AM–6 PM, Sat. by appointment.

✒ The **South Florida Museum** (941-746-4131; www.southfloridamuseum.org), 201 10th St. W, is one of Florida's more intriguing collections of archaeological and historic interest. While you'll hear a lot about Snooty, the museum's resident manatee (see *Aquarium*), the real treasure here is the amazing Tallant Collection of Paleoindian artifacts, including many excavated from mounds near Lake Okeechobee. In the Great Hall, a series of dioramas on Florida's long prehistory and history usher you back to the Tallant Gallery, where golden icons, pottery shards, and precious metal jewelry are on display. The 60,000-gallon Parker Manatee Aquarium is Snooty's home, where you'll learn about manatees and their part in Florida's ecosystems. In the Spanish Plaza, a replica home (to scale, where you'll learn how short early explorers were) shows off life as it was in Spain when Hernando De Soto came to these shores in the 1500s. The main floor also features the Bishop Planetarium and Discovery Place, a hands-on workshop for kids. Upper-floor exhibits focus on regional history. Stop by the museum store on your way out to purchase replicas from the Tallant Collection, books, and great games and toys for the kids. Open daily 10 AM–5 PM Mon.–Sat., 12 PM–5 PM Sun. during Jan.–Apr., July; closed Mon. in May–June and Aug.–Dec. Adults $15.95, seniors $13.75, ages 4–12 $11.75, under 4 free.

Palmetto
✒ The **Manatee County Agricultural Museum** (941-721-2034; www.manatee clerk.com/clerkservices/hisvill/ag_museum.htm), 1015 Sixth St. W, presents an excellent overview of the history of agriculture in this region, from citrus groves to commercial fishing. Did you know, for instance, that the region was famous for gladiolas in the 1920s? And this was the first place that pink grapefruit was bred? Five galleries present artifacts, photos, tools, and exhibits explaining how farming built this county. Junior Agriculture activities provide fun stuff for the kids to do, such as mazes and puzzles. It's located in the **Palmetto Historical Park** (see *Historic Sites*) and shares the same hours. Free.

RAILROADIANA ✍ At the **Florida Railroad Museum** (1-877-869-0800; www.frrm.org), 83rd St. E off US 301, Parrish, the museum is the train, run by volunteers, and it operates every weekend on a 6-mile stretch of original Seaboard Air Line Railroad track from Parrish north to the town of Willow near the Little Manatee River. Choose from air-conditioned coaches or open-air cars as the locomotive takes you on a smooth two-hour ride. Departures are at 11 AM and 2 PM. Adults $12, ages 3–11 $8, under 3 free. A small gift shop is tucked away in rolling stock on a siding.

WINERY In the rolling hills near Lake Manatee, **Rosa Fiorelli Winery** (941-322-0976; www.fiorelliwinery.com), 4250 CR 675, brings authentic Italian wine-making to Florida. Moving from Sicily, the family established vineyards in an area that "felt like home." They offer free wine tastings, or you can sign up for a tour (fee) or a tour with a delicious Italian luncheon or buffet ($17–23). Open 10 AM–5:30 PM Mon. and Wed.–Sat., 12 PM–5 PM Sun.

✳ To Do

BIRDING The secret sweet spot for birding on **Anna Maria Island** is well away from the crowd at the northern residential tip of the island, where the beach can be up to 300 feet wide, attracting flocks of colony birds such as terns, skimmers, and gulls. Park at **Bayfront Beach Park** and walk up Bay Street to the pathway leading to the beach. Scan the salt marsh at **Robinson Preserve** (941-748-4501 x4602), 1690 99th St. in Bradenton, from the top of the observation tower. I've also had great success at Terra Ceia, where flashes of pink on the mudflats of **Terra Ceia Preserve State Park** (941-721-2068, www.swfwmd.state.fl.us/recreation/areas/terraceia.html) mean roseate spoonbills are feeding. For sightings of Florida scrub jays, head west to **Rye Preserve** (941-776-0900), 905 Rye Wilderness Trail, for a trek through scrub habitats along the Little Manatee River.

BOATING For a spin on Sarasota Bay, rent your own runabout, deck boat, or open skiff at **Cannons Marina** (941-383-1311; www.cannons.com), 6040 Gulf of Mexico Dr., Longboat Key, with rates running from $160 for a half day to $440 for a full day. You are required to put down a $200 security deposit and are responsible for gas and oil.

FLORIDA RAILROAD MUSEUM

Sandra Friend

ECOTOURS With so many natural areas to explore, more and more nature tour operators are showcasing the best of the beach, the bays, and the interior forests. ✍ A freebie the kids will love is a walk with the **Anna Maria Island Turtle Watch** (941-778-5638; www.islandturtles.com) 2213 Ave. B Bradenton Beach, a volunteer group that monitors turtle nesting. Guided walks are offered each June through

August, call for reservations. **Around the Bend Ecotours** (941-794-8773; www.aroundthebend.com), 1815 Palma Sola Blvd., takes groups on a variety of adventures in local natural areas. One week, it may be a dig at Manatee Mineral Springs, another trip a journey into pioneer history out on the open prairie. Tours are led by certified Florida Master Naturalists. Shawn at **Native Rentals** (see *Watersports*) is now offering kayak tours, too. He's an Anna Maria Island native and knows the sweet spots, whether you're watching wildlife or casting for redfish.

FAMILY ACTIVITIES ⬦ Did you ever wonder where your milk comes from? Treat the family to a day on the farm at **Dakin Dairy Farms** (941-322-2802; www.dakindairyfarms.com), 30771 Betts Rd., Myakka City. Take a self-guided tour through the dairy on weekdays or a guided tour on Saturdays. Feed the goats, pet the farm animals, and just plain play outdoors—there's a fossil dig, hay tunnels, and cow train rides for fun, plus a farm market for Mom and Dad to browse for fresh local produce and dairy products. Don't forget the ice cream! Open Mon.–Sat. 10–5. While **Hunsader Farms** (941-331-1212; www.hunsaderfarms.com), 5500 CR 675, Bradenton is a popular U-Pick destination, they also have a petting zoo in their barnyard, a playground for the kids, and picnic space for families. Their Pumpkin Festival and Country Christmas draw big crowds. Open mid-Sept.–mid-June. At **Napier's Family Farm and Animal Rescue** (941-750-8185; www.napierfamilyfarm.com), 20010 E SR 64, the children can ride a pony or visit with rescued horses, some of which are up for adoption. Trail rides are offered for a $25 donation.

FISHING No angler should miss the historic **Cortez Fishing Village** (off Cortez Rd.), where **Annie's Bait & Tackle** (see *Eating Out*), 127th St. W, is the smart stop to ask around for a captain who knows these waters well. Departing from **Catchers Marina** (941-778-1977), 5501 Marina Dr., Holmes Beach, **Anna Maria Island Fishing Charters** (941-778-4498; www.fishtampawaters.com) offers in-shore and nearshore excursions with local expert Captain Tom Chaya. Both historic piers on the islands draw visitors who want to drop a line in the bay—the **Anna Maria City Pier** (941-779-1667), 100 S Bay Blvd., and the **Bridge Street Pier** at Bradenton Beach. In Palmetto, the **Green Bridge Fishing Pier** is a part of the old Green Bridge over the Manatee River. To enjoy a quiet day casting the shallows along the mangrove-lined shores, head out with **Paddle & Cast Kayak Fishing Tours** (941-228-0530), 7224 7th Ave. NW, Bradenton.

GOLF ⛳ One of America's top golf courses is the **Legacy Golf Club at Lakewood Ranch** (941-907-7067; www.legacygolfclub.com), 8255 Legacy Blvd., a par 72 Arnold Palmer signature course where nearly every hole is framed by sand and water. The fairways are 360 feet wide, providing expansive views. Fees range from $49–99 and include cart with cooler and ice, greens fee, tees, yardage card, and warm-up practice balls. The club offers a variety of instructional courses, including the "Uncomplicated Golf" School.

HIKING As regional conservation efforts have put more land into the public trust, the availability of hiking trails has expanded. Virtually all listings under *Green Space* and *Wild Places* provide day hiking. Some of my favorites include **Coquina Baywalk**, **Emerson Point Preserve**, and **Rye Wilderness Park**.

PADDLING Nearly 75 miles of Blueway trails are now a part of the Paddle Manatee program (www.co.manatee.fl.us/paddle.html), which includes the Terra Ceia Paddling Trail, Manatee River Paddling Trail, Braden River Paddling Trail, and Sarasota Bay Paddling Trail. Contact the county for a free comprehensive guide, which includes access points, points of interest, and maps. For a guided trip or a rental, launch with **Almost Heaven Kayak Adventures** (941-504-6296; www .kayakfl.com). Enjoy a trip down the twisting, winding scenic Little Manatee River with **Canoe Outpost** (813-634-2228; www.canoeoutpost.com), 18001 US 301 S, Wimauma. At **Ray's Canoe Hideway** (941- 747-3909, 1-888-57CANOE; www .rayscanoehideaway.com), 1247 Hagle Park Rd., head out on an adventure on the Upper Manatee River into Rye Wilderness Park. Rent their canoes or kayaks ($25–50) or launch your own.

SCENIC DRIVE Following coastal highways and byways from the Sunshine Skyway Bridge over Tampa Bay to the southern tip of Manasota Key, the **Gulf Coast Heritage Trail** leads you on some of the region's most scenic roads. More than one hundred points of interest are detailed on the brochure and map. Watch for the distinctive brown signs for key points of interest. For a copy of the map, contact a tourism center (see *Guidance*).

SEGWAY TOURS I didn't believe it until I tried it—a Segway really does balance your weight, no matter how you lean! **Manatee Segway Tours** (941-224-8079; www.manateesegwaytours.com) provides a training session before you head out on one of their three guided trips along Bradenton's Riverfront. The hour-long tours are offered daily, $35–65 and are by reservation only.

SWIMMING The Gulf of Mexico is shallow and warm, so the beaches along **Anna Maria Island, Bradenton Beach,** and **Longboat Key** attract splashers, waders, and swimmers along with sun worshippers. For family fun, **G. T. Bray Park** (941-742-5923), 502 33rd Ave. Dr. W, Bradenton, offers an Olympic-sized swimming pool and a splash park with lifeguards on duty.

TRAIL RIDING Across from Lake Manatee State Park (see *Parks*), **Lake Manatee Stables** (941-746-3697), SR 64, Rye, offers trail riding on the park's trail system. For something completely different, try a little "horse surfing" with **Great World Ecotours** (941-650-1820 or 1-800-807-7656; www.greatworldway.com), 8374 Market St., Lakewood Ranch. They'll not only outfit you for a small group trail ride at one of the many area preserves but they offer horseback riding on the beach, where you can swim with the horses and surf with them, too!

WALKING TOURS The **Manatee Riverwalk** is a designated walking tour that covers historic sites in Palmetto, Bradenton, and Village of the Arts. Contact the chamber of commerce (see *Guidance*) for a brochure and map.

WATER SPORTS On Anna Maria Island, visit **Native Rentals** (941-778-7757; www.mysitontopkayak.com), 5416 Marina Dr., where they have ocean kayaks, snorkeling and fishing gear, giant bicycles, and body boards for rent.

✳ Green Space

BEACHES For a taste of Old Florida, the beaches of Florida's Gulf Islands are as authentic as they come. They hearken back to the earliest days of beach tourism, when beach bungalows and cottages and tiny motels by the sea beckoned families to return year after year. You'll find no towering condos shading you as you explore the white sand shores. Paralleled by Gulf Drive with numerous access points, the beaches of **Anna Maria Island** stretch nearly eight miles and are typically lined with dunes topped with sea oats. Since **Manatee Beach** (941-742-5923), 4000 Gulf Dr., is closest to Bradenton, it tends to get busy. Head farther south to **Coquina Beach**, 2603 Gulf Dr., on Leffis Key. It's popular with families thanks to its picnic tables, playground, concessions, and restrooms. The northern end of Longboat Key is a peninsula known as **Beer Can Island,** a beauty spot overlooking emerald waves. Access it from North Shore Road off Gulf of Mexico Drive. Thanks to its unique shape, it's the best spot along the shore for shelling.

PARKS

Bradenton Beach
⚐ A unique gateway to the natural communities along the bay, **Leffis Key** (941-742-5923), 2603 Gulf Dr., protects 17 acres of waterfront. Access to the park is via gentle hiking trails and boardwalks through the mangrove forests and coastal berm, where you can peer out of overlooks across the bay and down into crystal-clear water to watch sea squirts and sponges on the rocks. Free.

Longboat Key
⚐ A 32-acre oasis on residential Longboat Key, **Joan M. Durante Community Park** (941-316-1988), 5550 Gulf of Mexico Dr., is a city park with extensive walkways through natural habitats and a man-made wetland, great views of Sarasota Bay, and picnic and playground facilities. Free.

Rye
With miles of equestrian trails and plenty of lakefront to keep anglers happy, **Lake Manatee State Park** (941-741-3028; www.floridastate parks.org/lakemanatee), 20007 SR 64, is a popular recreation area on the remote eastern side of the county. Swimming is permitted in the lake, and there's a full-facility campground near the lake. Fee.

SARASOTA BAY AT LEFFIS KEY
Sandra Friend

Snead Island
Encompassing 365 acres at the northern tip of Snead Island, **Emerson Point Preserve** (941-748-4501 x4602), Tarpon Rd., protects the ancient **Portavant Temple Mound** (see *Archaeological Sites*) as well as an interesting mix of habitats, including a

rare look at the Tampa Bay estuary from its southern shore. Both a limestone path and a paved biking trail run around the park, and anglers can gain access to Tampa Bay down at the point. Snaking around the island, several hiking-only trails can be strung together with the limestone path for an easy and interesting 2.7-mile walk. Free.

PUBLIC GARDEN Preservation of a 10-acre nursery formed what is now the **Palma Sola Botanical Park** (941-761-2866; www.palmasolabp.com) 9800 17th Ave. NW, in northwest Bradenton. Its location near Palma Sola Bay allows the growth of tropical plants not generally found elsewhere in the county. Open 8 AM– dusk, free.

SPRINGS Once known as Indian Spring, **Manatee Mineral Springs**, 2nd Ave. E and 14th St. E, is noted by a historic marker in this small neighborhood park in the Old Manatee district of Bradenton, not far from **Manatee Village Historic Park** (see *Historic Sites*). A giant black bead tree grows next to the spring.

WILD PLACES Set aside as wilderness for the residents of Manatee County, **Duette Preserve** (941-776-2295), 2649 Rawls Rd. off SR 64, Duette, encompasses 22,000 acres of sandhills, prairie, river hammocks, and scrub and is the site of an active Florida scrub jay restoration program. It is the prime destination for the region's deer hunters in the winter and attracts anglers who enjoy fishing in a relaxed wilderness setting. Ongoing restoration of the scrub habitat is bringing back a Florida scrub jay population. Most of the park roads (designated "trails") are accessible only by four-wheel-drive vehicles, but they can be bicycled or hiked. Tent camping, offered Friday through Saturday nights, costs $20/night for up to four people. Fee.

Offering a smorgasbord of short hikes along and around the Upper Manatee River near the Lake Manatee Dam, **Rye Wilderness Park** (941-776-0900), 905 Rye Wilderness Trail, Rye, also features a tent campground open on weekends for $20 a night. The preserve has upland scrub habitats as well as gorgeous oak hammocks along the river. Free.

✳ Lodging
BED & BREAKFAST

Holmes Beach 34217
A grand 1925 coquina and cypress beach house surrounded by dunes, the **Harrington House Beachfront Bed & Breakfast Inn** (941-778-5444 or 1-888-828-5566; www.harringtonhouse .com), 5626 Gulf Dr., comes with all the comforts of home—and more. Borrow a bike or a kayak, or just lie on the beach and read. If it rains, you can watch movies in the living room. And don't miss breakfast—the food is top-notch, too. There are 8 well-appointed rooms in the Main House, plus numerous rooms and suites in a variety of nearby historic beach houses owned by the family, including bungalows across the street. Seasonal rates range from $149–329 for single rooms, $229–529 for multiroom suites and a Gulf view villa. Children 12 and over welcome.

CAMPGROUND

Cortez 34215
⛺ Tucked under a canopy of trees, **Holiday Cove RV Resort** (941-792-

1111 or 1-800-346-9224; www.holiday coverv.com), 11900 Cortez Rd. W, is an appealing destination minutes from the beach and seconds from an exploration of the estuary. Take advantage of their boat launch to putter or paddle out to the bay, or relax around the heated pool. The park caters to motor homes, travel trailers, and fifth wheels only, with full hookups on new brick paver 30/50 amp sites; $35–65 daily, with discounted weekly and monthly rates.

COTTAGES

Longboat Key 34428

✦ 🐾 Established in 1948, **Rolling Waves Cottages** (941-383-1323; www.rollingwaves.com), 6351 Gulf of Mexico Dr., is the kind of old-fashioned family beach getaway that I truly treasure. These eight cottages (one- and two-bedroom) are absolutely authentic, a slice of local history tucked under the palms and pines and overlooking the dunes. Each cottage ($175–250) has an updated kitchen, several beds, and large televisions with cable television. Cribs and high chairs available on request; discounts for weekly stays.

HOTELS, MOTELS, AND RESORTS

Anna Maria 34216

The **Rod & Reel Resort** (941-778-2780; www.rodandreelmotel.com), 877 North Shore Dr., is your basic 1940s Florida motel, refurbished but with no real frills—and appealing as all get out because it's the kind of place that my family would stay at when I was a kid. Most of the kitchenettes ($114–208) have one double bed, some have two, and they're all on a nicely landscaped courtyard overlooking the bay. With the historic pier right here and an easy walk to the quiet north end beaches,

it's a great location if you just want to get away and fish or read.

Bradenton Beach 34217

& With an architectural style that enhances the old Bridge Street historic district, **Bridgewalk** (941-779-2545 or 1-866-779-2545; www.silverresorts .com/bridgewalk.asp), 100 Bridge St., offers luxurious modern studios, suites, and townhomes within an easy walk of beach and bay, $132–283. The three-building complex includes the Sun House Restaurant & Bar, a heated pool, and a day spa, and the quaint shops of historic Bradenton Beach are just footsteps away.

Families find a place in the sun at **Silver Surf Gulf Beach Resort** (941-778-6626 or 1-800-441-7873; www .silverresorts.com/silver_surf.asp), 1301 Gulf Dr. N, where the beach is just across the street and the rooms are spacious enough to accommodate the entire brood. Choose from standard, studio, or suite ($118–193). With bead board–style walls, wicker furnishings, and touches of greenery, it feels like you're in the islands—and you are! On-site pool, free beach chairs, and rentals of Vespas, sea kayaks, and sailboards. If you're eligible, ask for Florida resident pricing.

🐾 "❢" Settle into the **Tortuga Inn Beach Resort** (941-867-8842 or 1-877-867-8842; www.tortugainn.com), 1325 Gulf Dr. N, and take advantage of one of the 14 private docks on Sarasota Bay or the expansive beach across the street. The upscale rooms (hotel, studio, suite, or multibedroom luxury apartment, $125–355) center around a tropical courtyard and spacious heated pool.

🐾 "❢" Charming cottages tucked amid tropical vegetation await you at **Tradewinds Resort** (941-779-0010 or 1-888-686-6716; www.tradewinds resort.com), 1603 Gulf Dr. N.

Although they look like historic Old Florida seaside cottages, they are new and modern, with full amenities and daily housekeeping. Enjoy the beach across the street, or the pool just steps from your door. Choose from studios or one- or two-bedroom units, $125–320 daily or $645–1,095 weekly, with special discounts for Florida residents.

Holmes Beach 34217

🎖 🐾 "🎱" Add some retro zing! to your vacation with a stay at **Haley's Motel** (941-778-5405 or 1-800-367-7824; www.haleysmotel.com), 8102 Gulf Dr., where owners Tom Buehler and Sabine Musil-Buehler celebrated this classic resort's 50th anniversary in 2003. From the glass block corners and brightly painted doors to the tropical birds in their cages, this is a very eclectic and fun place. Tuck yourself into one of the updated-but-period 1950s rooms, or pick one of the neatly renovated rooms, studios, or apartments. Lounge at the pool, or read a book by the frog pond in the secret garden. Bikes and beach accoutrements free to guests. All pets welcome! The 14 units of varying configurations start at $119, with weekly rates available.

THE RETRO HALEYS MOTEL

Sandra Friend

An old-fashioned family seaside motel, the **White Sands Beach Resort** (941-778-2577; www.whitesandsbeach resort.com), 6504 Gulf Dr., has rooms to fit every size group, with full kitchens, tiled floors, big bathrooms, and barbecue grills outside ($119–275; weekly rates available). The heated swimming pool overlooks the Gulf of Mexico, and it's an easy walk down to the beach.

Longboat Key 34228

🐾 Enjoy seaside serenity at the **Sandpiper Inn** (941-383-2552; www.sand piperinn.com/FL), 5451 Gulf of Mexico Dr., an appealing little hideaway of apartments and studio rooms right on the Gulf. Sit out on your patio and listen to the waterfall in the tropical garden, or soak in the small heated pool after a dip in the sea. Large, tiled one- and two-bedroom suites with kitchens run $139–249, with weekly rates available.

✳ Where to Eat
DINING OUT

Longboat Key

Wine Spectator rates **Euphemia Haye** (941-383-3633; www.euphemia haye.com), 5540 Gulf of Mexico Dr., as worthy of its Award of Excellence for its wine cellar, and the folks at Florida Trend give them the Golden Spoon for creative cuisine, intimate dining, and a dessert room—the Hayeloft. Tucked away in a tropical forest, this local gem offers a getaway for you and your sweetheart to savor a truly international menu, with gourmet creations such as Grecian lamb shank, shrimp Taj Mahal, roast duckling, and calves' sweetbreads grenoblois. Expect to drop $100 for dinner for two, and save room for delights at the Hayeloft, where you can choose from a dazzling display of desserts.

Terra Ceia

From the outside **Lee's Crab Trap** (941-722-6255), US 19 at the Terra Ceia Bridge, has that casual seafood house look, but let me assure you—it's not. This is a classy place with a 30-year history of pleasing locals with certified Angus steaks and seafood dishes with a gourmet touch. Lunch includes oyster and shrimp po'boys and Florida gator burgers. Crab is served 13 different ways at dinner, including imperial, supreme, and Norfolk. Dress well (business casual or better); reservations suggested.

EATING OUT

Anna Maria

On the historic pier, **The City Pier Restaurant** (941-779-1667; www.pier jewelry.com/restaurant.php), 100 Bay Blvd., offers great views of Tampa Bay with your meal, which might include fish-and-chips, coconut shrimp, or a cherry snapper sandwich at lunch ($7–9), or a sirloin steak or big steamer pot full of veggies, king crab, and shrimp for dinner, entrées $13 and up.

Rotten Ralph's (941-778-3953; www .rottenralphs.com), 902 S Bay Blvd., is the classic Florida waterfront restaurant that everyone sent me to—it's got that Cracker fish camp feel but is right in the heart of the marina at the end of the road. Cruise in, drive, or walk, and settle down for the basics. All-you-can-eat British-style fish-and-chips ($10) are the specialty of the house.

Bradenton

With its loyal following tagging along, the original **Anna Maria Oyster Bar** (941-792-0077; www.oysterbar.net), 6696 Cortez Rd. W, moved landside, offering hot wings, frozen margaritas, their famous giant grouper sandwiches, and 25 cent oysters in a casual setting. Dig into steamer pots of veggies, potatoes, and shellfish, or sample tasty

seafood preparations like Cajun onion crusted salmon, nutty grouper, and tilapia almondine, entrées $11 and up. Two additional locations: 6906 US 41 and at 1525 51st Ave., Ellenton.

Grandma Yoders (941-739-2918), 5896 53rd Ave. E, is a little strip-mall treasure that one of my girlfriends took me to for dinner. Enjoy good Amish cooking—especially heaping slices of pie—in a family atmosphere, where Manhattans (open-faced sandwiches on homemade bread) come with real mashed potatoes smothered in gravy. Open 11 AM–8 PM Mon.–Sat.

French toast, pecan and banana pancakes, and Southern pancakes with grits—it's all part of the fare downtown at **Theresa's** (941-747-7066), 608 14th St. W, where breakfast ($4 and up) is served up friendly and fast. Open weekdays 7 AM–2 PM, weekends 8 AM–2 PM.

For a dainty spot of tea, go with the girlfriends to **Truffles & Treasures** (941-761-3335), 7445 Manatee Ave. W. This Victorian tearoom is lace and frills and downright popular, especially for Mums bringing daughters out on the town. Formal teas include the Queens Tea and Lady Tiffany's Tea, or you can opt for daily fare such as Truffles' signature spinach salad. Open 11 AM–3 PM Tues.–Sat. Reservations recommended.

Bradenton Beach

Breakfast at the **Gulf Drive Café** (941-778-1919), 900 Gulf Dr., is a delightful way to start your day, enjoying a platter of hotcakes while watching the seagulls wheel over the Gulf. Breakfast ($5 and up) is served anytime. Even at 8 AM there's a line for the seaside patio, where sea oats frame a panorama of blue, so arrive early! Their Belgium waffles are top-notch.

Cortez

Annie's Bait & Tackle (941-794-3580), 4334 127th St. W, is a good old-

I kept seeing snakes out of the corner of my eye. Sharp objects hung over our heads—crosscut saws and scythes—and weird ones, too, like a pair of snowshoes, a saddlebag, a ceramic jug, and a hornet's nest. Strapped to the wall behind me was a massive alligator, and in every direction, rattlesnakes dripped from the walls and ceiling. Behind the bar was a veritable zoo of Florida critters frozen in taxidermy, from otters to raccoons. This is dining at the **Linger Lodge** (941-755-2757; www.lingerlodgeresort.com), 7205 Linger Lodge Rd., off Tara Blvd. and SR 70, one of the weirdest restaurants I've ever set foot in. Set beneath ancient oaks and palms along the bluff above the Braden River, it's a one of a kind experience, thanks to Frank Gamsky, a taxidermist who built the current restaurant in 1968. It started as a fish camp in 1945 and is still a true Old Florida destination, surrounded by a pleasant full-service campground. The menu fits the setting, serving up genuine Southern cooking like frog legs, fried green tomatoes, BBQ pulled pork, and River Bottom Pie. Grab a great dinner for under $15 or linger on the screened porch and enjoy your lunch, $6 and up.

LINGER LODGE

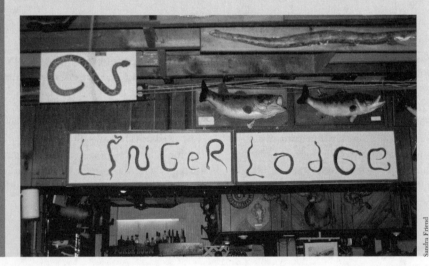

Sandra Friend

fashioned fish camp befitting this historic fishing village, where you can grab a bucket of shiners and a fresh grouper sandwich or burger. Breakfast served weekends 6:30 AM–11 PM, lunch and dinner daily. Bait shop open daily, with fishing licenses and charters on the spot.

Holmes Beach
🐚 There's heavy voodoo going down at **Mr. Jones BBQ** (941-778-6614), 3007 Gulf Dr., where New Orleans meets the Far East with burgers rubbed in secret spices, five kinds of ribs (your choice of spare or baby back), and awesome exotics such as chicken shish

kebob with rice biryani served up tikka masala style with a mass of my favorite sautéed veggies—peppers, onions, mushrooms, and tomatoes—and sides of raita, mango, and fresh coriander chutneys, as well as strips of French bread for dipping and a boatload of cold beer. Open for lunch and dinner daily.

Longboat Key
The busiest breakfast spot on the island is the **Blue Dolphin Café** (941-383-3787; www.bluedolphincafe.com), 5370 Gulf of Mexico Dr., where the specialties include a breakfast wrap with homemade veggie chili, cheddar cheese, and scrambled eggs, or Belgium waffles with fresh fruit. Serving breakfast and lunch, $6 and up.

Palmetto
Model planes and historic photos of aviation set the tone at **Hot Rodd's Hanger** (941-729-2950), 120 Seventh St. W, a busy restaurant with breakfast all day ($4 and up), lunch sandwiches and salads, and lots of dinner choices, with roast pork and baked ham, alligator and coconut shrimp among them. But what'll really get you in the door are the milk shakes—choose from blueberry or peanut butter, as well as the traditional flavors.

ICE CREAM

Anna Maria
What's a beach without an ice cream parlor? **Mama Lo's By The Sea** (941-779-1288), 101 S Bay Blvd., serves up more than 40 different flavors of ice cream, frozen yogurt, and sorbet in every combination you can think of, and some of the choices are just awesome—coffee crunch, coconut, peppermint stick, and gator tracks, to name a few. They serve lunch and fancy coffee drinks, too. Open 7 AM–9 PM daily.

Bradenton
🍴 Everyone in town stops at the **Shake Pit** (941-748-4016; www.shake pit.com), 3810 Manatee Ave. W, between errands, a local favorite since 1959. It's a family business with that 1950s flair and funky touches like local celebrities leaving autographs (and sometimes cartoons!) on the ceiling. They make great burgers, dogs, and short order sandwiches like grilled cheese, Philly cheesesteak, and BLTs, but the big draw is the ice cream—in cups and sundaes, sodas and floats, and even with a fried banana! Open for lunch and dinner except Wednesday.

Just up the road, **Sweetberries Frozen Custard** (941-750-6771; www .sweetberries.com), 4500 Manatee Ave. W, has frozen custard, sandwiches, and soups in a sit-down café where everything is made fresh.

✷ Entertainment

On the grounds of Seagate, a grand Mediterranean Revival–style mansion built by Powel Crosley Jr. in 1929, the **Powel Crosley Theatre** (941-722-3244; www.powelcrosleytheatre.com) offers a series of fine theatrical productions from December through April. $20 adults, $16 seniors, ages 5–12, $10.

✷ Selective Shopping

Anna Maria
You'd hardly believe that **Ginny's and Jane E's at the Old IGA** (941-778-3170; www.annamariacafe.com), 9807 Gulf Dr., was once a supermarket, with its chic indoor "garden of antiques" feel. Local art mingles with antiques, a juice bar (featuring smoothies and coffee), and organic fruit and vegetables to make a comfy kick-back-and-relax atmosphere. Closed Mon.

Across from the Old City Pier, Bayview Plaza, at the corner of Bay and Pine, offers some great little shops, including **White Egret Boutique** (home decor and gifts), the Paper Egret (sundries and gourmet food), and **Two Sides of Nature,** with whimsical colorful toys and kitchen items, as well as a prolific stock of bright island T-shirts. But my favorite, **The Museum Shoppe** (941-779-0273), 101 South Bay Blvd., is up on the second floor and takes a little effort to find, but it is well worth it if you love giving eclectic gifts. I found quill-and-ink sets for writers, sealing wax, heirloom toys, maps, and globes, and local metal art depicting sea life.

Bradenton

A giant rooster tops **Bungalow Antiques** (941-750-6611), 1910 Manatee Ave. E, making it easy to spot from the highway. This 1940s bungalow has rooms and rooms of great collectibles and decor items—lots of fun stuff!

At **Carriage House Antiques** (941-747-9234), 3307 Manatee Ave. W, I reveled in a room of Florida kitsch, picking up finds such as 1970s citrus trivets and 1940s playing cards. You'll also find fine furniture, vintage glassware, a book nook, and more from nearly 24 dealers within the maze of rooms in this cottage.

Break out those comfortable shoes! The **Red Barn Flea Market** (941-747-3794 or 1-800-274-FLEA; www.redbarnfleamarket.com), 1707 First St. E, is one of the region's largest, with more than four hundred vendors indoors and two hundred more booths outside. Open 8 AM–4 PM Wed. and Fri.–Sun.

Bradenton Beach

The funky little downtown surrounding the Bridge Street Circle in Bradenton Beach has quite a few shops and restaurants, including **Two Sides of Nature** (941-779-2432), 119-B Bridge St.; Island Creperie (941-778-1011),

127 Bridge St.; the **Banana Cabana** (941-779-1930; www.bananacabana seafood.com), 103 Gulf Dr. N; and the **One Stop Shell Shop** (941-778-9195), 101 Gulf Dr., where the sign on the door says, WE WELCOME ICE CREAM CONES, BEACH ATTIRE, AND BARE FEET . . . AFTER ALL, THIS IS FLORIDA!

Cortez

Ahoy, mates! Stroll the salvage garden at **The Sea Hagg** (941-795-5756; www.seahagg.com), 12304 Cortez Rd. W, for a jumble of nautical goodies— some antique, some new, some indoors, some out. Open Mon.–Sat.

Ellenton

The sprawling **Feed Store Antique Mall** (941-729-1379), 4407 US 301, is full of dealer booths inside an old-fashioned barn—a maze of bargains, just like an old-fashioned flea market. I found books, collectibles, a W. C. Fields lamp, and costume jewelry. Open daily.

Holmes Beach

At **Niki's Island Treasures & Antique Mall** (941-779-0729), 5351 N Gulf Dr. in Dolphin Plaza, shop for stained-glass windows, retro chairs and tables, and all sorts of funky stuff.

Longboat Key

Creativity is in high swing at **KK's Artique** (941-383-0883), 5360 Gulf of Mexico Dr., with floral-patterned art glass, mosaic-framed mirrors, fiber craft, clay sculpture, and paintings of appealing Sarasota scenes.

Palmetto

With dozens of dealers under one roof, **Emiline's Antiques and Collectibles Mall** (941-729-5282), 1250 10th St. E, offers plenty of possibilities, including everything from a 1916 cash register to Plasticville houses, pottery, salt shakers, fine china, and Fenton glass.

PRODUCE STANDS AND U-PICK

Bradenton

Since 1939, **Mixon Fruit Farms** (1-800-608-2525; www.mixon.com), 2712 26th Ave. E, has served the region with farm-fresh citrus from their groves east of the city, which are open for guided tours November through April. Their store is open 9 AM–5 PM Monday through Saturday and features orange swirl ice cream, homemade cream and butter fudge, and many Florida gifts.

Between mid-August and September, the **Rosa Fiorelli Winery** (see *Winery*) offers fresh u-pick bronze or black muscadine grapes.

Myakka City

Grab farm fresh dairy products at **Dakin Dairy Farms** (see *Family Activities*) and stop in at the u-pick at **Hunsader Farms** (see *Family Activities*).

Terra Ceia

At **Goodson Farms Produce** on US 41 just south of I-275, stop in for fresh fruit milk shakes and strawberry short-cakes during the growing season, November through May.

With 150 acres of groves in and around Palmetto, **The Citrus Ranch** (239-723-0504 or 1-888-723-2006; www.citrusranch.com) has a stand at 4805 Buckeye Rd., 1.5 miles east of US 41, where they sell packed citrus fruit gifts, loose fruit, and fresh-squeezed juices. Free samples! Open 9 AM–5 PM Mon.–Sat., Nov.–May.

✳ Special Events

January: Discover the region's agricultural bounty at the **Manatee County Fair** (941-722-1639; www.manateecountyfair.com), held at the fairgrounds in Palmetto.

February: The **Bradenton Beach Festival** (941-778-1005; www.cityof bradentonbeach.com/events_bridge .php) features boat rides and other watersports along historic Bridge Street at Bradenton Beach.

Eat more seafood at the **Cortez Fishing Festival** (941-794-1249; www .fishnews.org/festival), where you can nosh on nuggets direct from the sea, browse arts and crafts, and learn how to repair a net. Third weekend of the month.

February/March: The **Rubonia Mardi Gras** (941-46-7470; www.rubonia mardigras.org) has been "parading for a purpose" in fun costumes since 1980. The Mystic Crewe forged an alliance with nearby Terra Ceia and it became a funky party/parade/fund-raiser for both small communities, still going strong today. Check the Web site for the exact date.

April: CSO Festival, **Gamble Plantation Historic State Park** (see *Historic Sites*), first Sat. Entertainment, food, antique autos, arts and crafts, and the Patton House open for tours.

July: Visit the **South Florida Museum** (see *Museums*) for Snooty the Manatee's Birthday Bash, a fun party for the kids.

November: Celebrate the harvest at the **Tomato Festival** (941-722-1639), Sutton Park, Palmetto, with cook-offs, entertainment, and crafts.

December: The Civil War returns to Ellenton at the **Gamble Plantation Holiday Open House** (941-723-4536). See the encampments and a live cannon display, as well as Civil War field equipment in action.

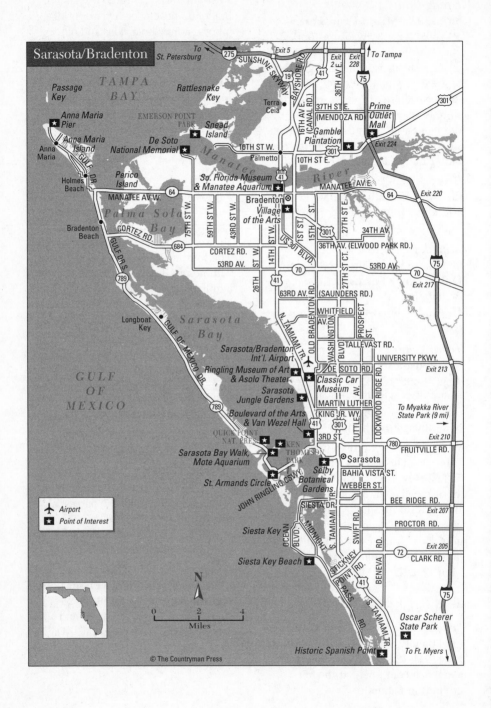

Sarasota/Bradenton

To St. Petersburg

To Tampa

Exit 5

275

SUNSHINE SKYWAY

Exit 2 228

To Tampa

75

TAMPA BAY

Passage Key

Rattlesnake Key

Terra Ceia

19

41

36TH AV. E.

6TH AV. E. (CANAL RD.)

BAYSHORE RD.

301

37TH ST. E. (MENDOZA RD.)

Prime Outlet Mall

Exit 224

Anna Maria Pier

Anna Maria Island

EMERSON POINT PARK

Snead Island

De Soto National Memorial

Gamble Plantation

Palmetto

10TH ST. W.

10TH ST. E.

Anna Maria

Holmes Beach

GULF DR.

So. Florida Museum & Manatee Aquarium

Manatee River

41

301

64

MANATEE AV. E.

Exit 220

MANATEE AV. W.

64

Perico Island

Bradenton Village of the Arts

1ST ST.

15TH ST.

27TH ST. E.

34TH AV.

Palma Sola Bay

Bradenton Beach

CORTEZ RD.

75TH ST. W.

59TH ST. W.

43RD ST. W.

US 301 BLVD.

301

36TH AV. (ELWOOD PARK RD.)

75

684

CORTEZ RD.

14TH ST. W.

53RD AV.

27TH ST CT.

53RD AV.

70

Exit 217

GULF DR. S.

70

26TH ST. W.

41

63RD AV. RD. (SAUNDERS RD.)

789

Longboat Key

Sarasota Bay

N. TAMIAMI TR.

OLD BRADENTON BLVD.

WHITFIELD AV.

WASHINGTON ST.

PROSPECT ST.

TALLEVAST RD.

UNIVERSITY PKWY.

Exit 213

GULF OF MEXICO DR.

GULF OF MEXICO

Sarasota/Bradenton Int'l. Airport

DE SOTO RD.

LOCKWOOD RIDGE RD.

Ringling Museum of Art & Asolo Theater

Classic Car Museum

Sarasota Jungle Gardens

TUTTLE AV.

MARTIN LUTHER KING JR. WY.

To Myakka River State Park (9 mi)

Exit 210

789

Boulevard of the Arts & Van Wezel Hall

41

301

3RD ST.

780

FRUITVILLE RD.

QUICK POINT NAT. PRES.

Sarasota Bay Walk, Mote Aquarium

KEN THOMPSON PARK

Sarasota

BAHIA VISTA ST.

St. Armands Circle

Selby Botanical Gardens

WEBBER ST.

BEE RIDGE RD.

Exit 207

JOHN RINGLING CSWY.

SIESTA DR.

S. TAMIAMI TR.

SWIFT RD.

PROCTOR RD.

✈ Airport

★ Point of Interest

Siesta Key

OCEAN BLVD.

MIDNIGHT PASS RD.

72

CLARK RD.

Exit 205

BENEVA RD.

75

Siesta Key Beach

STICKNEY POINT RD.

41

S. TAMIAMI TR.

N

0   2   4
Miles

Oscar Scherer State Park

Historic Spanish Point

To Ft. Myers

© The Countryman Press

SARASOTA AND HER ISLANDS

No one is quite sure where the name "Sarasota" came from, but it certainly is unique. It may have originated with the native peoples, who had a trading post marked "Saraxota" on early European maps. The name popped up on a Florida map in 1839 as "Sara Sota," and it's been there ever since. This region has a long and storied history, with human occupation dating back thousands of years along the coast, as evidenced by archaeological finds at sites like Little Salt Spring, Warm Mineral Springs, and Spanish Point. When the Florida frontier opened under the Armed Occupation Act, settlers began to work their way slowly down the coast. William Whitaker was the first to drive his cattle in and claim a stake, in 1847. He later built a log cabin at Yellow Bluffs along Sarasota Bay, the location now marked by Whitaker Gateway Park.

After the Civil War, more settlers—especially soldiers who'd been given land grants—moved in. John Webb opened a sugar cane processing plant and built guest cottages, the first tourism destination for the area—Webb's Winter Resort on Little Sarasota Bay. Small communities sprung up near the bay, like Nokomis and Osprey. But the first major influx of new residents to the area between Phillipi Creek and Hudson Bayou came from a real estate scheme. Set up in Edinburgh, Scotland, the Florida Mortgage Investment Company, led by Sir John Gillespie, purchased 50,000 acres near Sarasota Bay and sold tracts to potential colonists. When members of the "Ormiston Colony" arrived in 1885, they found a coastline with a forbidding wilderness, not the lush land of plenty they'd been sold. With the help of the Whitakers, a few stayed, but most dispersed. Gillespie's son took over the enterprise and headed to the newly platted "Sara Sota" in 1886. He had a dock built on the bay, the first hotel and golf course, and stores and houses. He made sure that a school, a church, and a cemetery also formed the core of the new community. And people came. The Spanish-American War helped the economy as cattle drives sent beef to the soldiers. Citrus growers flourished. When the Seaboard Coast Line arrived, Sarasota was buzzing with activity. John Hamilton Gillespie became Sarasota's first mayor when the town incorporated in 1902, still part of Manatee County. Sarasota Key became Siesta Key in 1907.

By 1913, Sarasota was a city, with its patterns of growth set by Mrs. Bertha Honore Palmer, wife of Chicago magnate Potter Palmer. She was a socialite with a winter home in Osprey and bought up a great deal of the county's land before the 1920s boom hit. Looking for a winter home for his circus, John Ringling came to town and threw his hat in the developer's ring by underwriting downtown skyscrapers and an artfully conceived causeway meant to open up development on his lands on the outer islands. High society flocked to this waterfront playground, with its brash new casinos and fine hotels, and established a tradition of fine arts that lives on to this day. In 1921 Sarasota became its own county, including the city of Venice, named after the city in Italy when the post office was established in 1888. Venice is one of Florida's first planned cities, designed by noted architect John Nolan in the 1920s as an Italian Renaissance village.

Just off the coast of Sarasota are the barrier islands, St. Armands Key is now a bustling shopping district. Adjacent Lido Key is topped with condos. Just south, Siesta Key is a magnet for family vacations, with dozens of excellent accommodations and their famous "baby-powder soft" beaches. Offshore from Venice—which boasts its own fabulous beaches—Casey Key and Manasota Key are primarily residential, their narrow roads hidden beneath a tunnel of tropical vegetation.

GUIDANCE You can't miss the **Sarasota Visitor Information Center** (941-955-0991; www.sarasotafl.org), 655 N Tamiami Trail, as it's in a large complex with the Center for the Arts and the Auditorium, right next to Boulevard of the Arts. Stop in for brochures and recommendations and to visit the new History Museum. The **Siesta Key Chamber of Commerce** (941-349-3800;www.siestakeychamber.com), 5118 Ocean Blvd., is in a shopping center in Siesta Village. You'll find their services very helpful when booking a room during the high season, as accommodations check in with them with availability reports. You'll find the large and helpful **Venice Chamber of Commerce** (941-488-2236; www.venicechamber.com), 597 Tamiami Trail S, right downtown. At Englewood, stop in the Englewood–Cape Haze Area Chamber of Commerce (941-474-5511; www.englewoodchamber.com), 601 S Indiana Ave., along US 41, for information.

GETTING THERE *By car:* **I-75**, **US 301**, and **US 41** provide primary access to the region.

By air: **Sarasota Bradenton International Airport** (941-FLY-2-SRQ; www .srq-airport.com) has regular service by nine major carriers, including Air Canada, AirTran, Delta, and US Airways.

By bus: The **Greyhound** (1-800-231-2222; www.greyhound.com) bus station is at 575 N Washington and Sixth, along US 301 and 2 blocks north of Fruitville Rd., Sarasota.

GETTING AROUND *By car:* Both **I-75** and **US 41** run north-south, connecting Sarasota and Venice with Bradenton and Charlotte Harbor. US 41 provides the best access to most things to see and do in the region. Use **Fruitville Road** (SR 780) east to **SR 789** to reach St. Armands and Longboat Key; **SR 72** (Clark Rd) in Sarasota to reach Siesta Key; and **SR 681** from I-75 for the most efficient route to the Laurel/Nokomis/Venice area. Albee Road and Black Point Road connect Casey Key with the mainland, and **SR 776** takes you south from Venice to Englewood.

By bus: **SCAT** (941-861-5000; www.scgov.net/SCAT), 5303 Pinkney Ave., run all over Sarasota County between 5 AM and 8 PM. Bus fare is 75 cents, and unlimited monthly passports are $40. Pick up timetables at the visitors center or public libraries, or download detailed schedules and route maps from their Web site.

By taxi: **Yellow Cab** (941-349-3341; www.yellowcabofsarasota.com), 2011 Cornell St.

By trolley: The **Longboat Key Trolley** runs from Coquina Beach at the south end of Anna Maria Island through Longboat Key and St. Armands to downtown Sarasota. Daily service every 30 minutes from 6 AM to 11 PM. Fare $.75.

PUBLIC RESTROOMS In **Venice**, you'll find them downtown in Centennial Park on Venice Ave. Stop in the **Sarasota Visitor Information Center** (see *Guidance*) for restrooms in downtown Sarasota. **Beachfront parks** include public restrooms and changing areas.

PARKING The availability of parking varies tremendously, but the good news is that most of it is free—including the natural-surface beach parking lots at **Siesta Key** and the beachfront county parks in **Venice**. Downtown **Sarasota** has metered spaces in high traffic areas, and time-limited spaces (up to 5 hours) in low-traffic areas. You can park along the bayfront in Sarasota for free (3-hour limit) and walk to the shopping district. **St. Armands** also has free three-hour street parking, and a large flat lot hidden behind the shops between Ringling Boulevard and Boulevard of the Presidents, with free five-hour parking. In **Venice** there is a large free lot right off Venice Avenue in the middle of downtown, and plenty of free street parking in the shopping district.

MEDICAL EMERGENCIES Hospitals with 24-hour emergency rooms include **Sarasota Memorial Hospital** (941-917-9000; www.smh.com), 1700 S Tamiami Trail and **Venice Regional Medical Center** (941-485-7711; www.venice regional.com), 540 The Rialto, off Business US 41.

WI-FI "Downtown Unplugged" is the new **downtown Sarasota**, where wireless Internet access is free and available to all—a great amenity in a place with so many sidewalk cafes. Connect to the network "unplugged" for your free surfing.

✳ To See

AQUARIUM ♿ The world's first marine research center devoted to shark studies, **Mote Marine Aquarium** (941-388-2451; www.mote.org), 1600 Ken Thompson Pkwy., City Island, Sarasota, features these creatures of the deep in the Shark Attack Theater, or use the Sharktracker to find out real-time information about tagged sharks in the Gulf of Mexico. Entering the main aquarium, you walk through a darkened room filled with tanks of saltwater creatures and engaging exhibits. Pause and enjoy the beauty of jellyfish with their trailing tentacles glowing. The outdoor tanks showcase mollusks and squid, with a giant squid (pickled, not live) for you to compare your size to. Then it's on to tanks of Gulf of Mexico sea life, including killifish and fiddler crabs, and Contact Cove, a large touch tank with clams, sea urchins, and horseshoe crabs. Kids cluster around Remarkable

MANATEES AT MOTE MARINE
Sandra Friend

Rays, a touch tank with stingrays. In the Goldstein Marine Mammal Visitor Center (follow the walk across the island), kids can climb through a turtle excluder device and marvel at the many manatees (the permanent residents could not be returned to the wild after rehabilitation). Don't miss Immersion Theater, which is a game and a movie that puts you in the food chain. Open daily 10 AM–5 PM, including holidays; adults $17, over 65 $16, children 4–12 $12, members free.

ARCHAEOLOGICAL SITES

Osprey

At **Historic Spanish Point** (see *Historic Sites*), there are several sites of significant archaeological interest, most notably the Archaic period midden near the Guptill House, ca. 3000 B.C., and the Shell Ridge midden, which juts out into Little Sarasota Bay and is wonderfully presented inside "Window to the Past," an exhibit hall of windows showing off 1,000 years of human history in the layers of the midden as explored by archaeologists as far back as 1871, when the Smithsonian helped landowner John Webb identify artifacts and bones.

North Port

The University of Miami overseas **Little Salt Spring,** an underwater archaeological preserve that has yielded some of the most ancient cultural remains found in the United States, thanks to the water itself, which has extremely low levels of oxygen. Preserved organic materials such as textiles, hair, skin, and a sharpened wooden stake have been carbon-dated up to 12,000 years old. The site is not open to the public. Nearby **Warm Mineral Springs** (see *Springs*) has also yielded a wealth of finds and shares the same lack of dissolved oxygen in the water below a certain depth. Remains of saber-toothed cats, mammoths, prehistoric camels, and an 11,000-year-old skull with intact brain matter have been found in the depths by archaeologists. You are not permitted to dive in this deep sinkhole, but you can swim and snorkel in the 87°F water.

ART GALLERIES

Englewood

Local artists such as Jeff Cornell, Colleen Henry, and Melissa Searle take center stage at the **Lemon Tree Gallery** (941-474-5700; www.lemontreegallery.com), 420 W Dearborn St., where delightful original paintings evoke the playfulness of life near the beach.

St. Armands

You'll find galleries scattered throughout the shopping district on the Circle. **Maui Art** (941-388-5305; www.mauiarts.com), 321 John Ringling Blvd., features giclee paintings of ocean scenes. Artist David Miller often works in the front window. Art is fun at **Garden Argosy** (941-388-6402), 361 John Ringling Blvd., which features colorful metal pop sculptures perfect indoors or out, mermaid art, and vivid mirrors framed with inspirational art. At the **Giving Tree Gallery** (941-388-1353; www.thegivingtreegallery.com), 5 N Blvd. of the Presidents, look for kinetic sculptures, carved wooden birds, and metal art.

Sarasota

Visit Palm Avenue for more than a dozen upscale fine-art galleries, including **A Step Above Gallery** (941-955-4477; www.astepabovegallery.com), 1288 N Palm

Ave., with its collection of art glass, including pieces from Dale Chihuly, and the **Medici Gallery** (941-906-949; www.medicigallery.com), 75 S Palm Ave., featuring five contemporary Italian artists working in a variety of media. The street is best experienced during a **First Friday Gallery Walk**, which starts at 6 PM. Looking for working artists? You'll find them at the **Towles Court Artist Colony** (941-363-0087; www.towlescourt.com), 1943 Morrill St., located between US 301, Osprey Ave., Morrill St., and Adams Ln., downtown. In this neighborhood of 1920s bungalows, look for the **Katharine Butler Gallery** (941-955-4546; www .kbutlergallery.com), 1943 Morrill St., with rotating exhibits monthly in various media; **The Gallery** (941-730-6265), 252 S Links Ave., showcasing artists from around the world; and **The Celery Barn** (941-952-9889), 266 Links Ave., with painting, sculpture, and portraiture from local artist Jini Mount. There are many other galleries as well, so park your car in one of the two large lots and wander through the community. Galleries and shops generally open 12 PM–4 PM Tuesday through Saturday, with **Third Friday Gallery Walks** at Towles Court 6 AM–10 PM all year with live music and refreshments.

Venice

Bold acrylics drew me into **Artemisa** (941-484-9432), 219 W Venice Ave. Inside, I found beautiful Florida wildlife art and landscapes, including evocative scenes of the Big Cypress Swamp and Boca Grande by local artist James Crafford.

Lose yourself in a wild Florida landscape at **Clyde Butcher's Venice Gallery and Studio** (941-486-0811; www.clydebutcher.com), 237 Warfield Ave., where fine art black and white photography in immense scale captures the essence of Florida's special places. An acclaimed photographer sometimes called "the Ansel Adams of the Everglades," Clyde seeks to inspire others to help preserve the essential natural spaces of Florida. His original gallery is in the **Big Cypress Swamp** (see *Paradise Coast*), but this is where he does his darkroom work. If you'd to see how these giant photos are printed, ask for a tour. Open Mon.–Fri. 10 AM–5 PM, Sat. 11 AM–3 PM.

CIRCUS HERITAGE Thanks to John and Charles Ringling, Sarasota and Venice have deep roots in the circus industry. Sarasota was the winter home for circus animals and performers alike until the circus moved to Venice in 1959. A new **Circus Heritage Trail** (www.sarasotacircushistory.com) brochure leads you through circus-related locations and to little-known sites like the memorial statue of Guther-Gabel Williams near the Venice Depot. Pick up a copy at the **Sarasota Visitor Information Center** (see *Guidance*).

HISTORIC SITES

Osprey

At **Historic Spanish Point** (941-966-5214; www.historicspanishpoint.org), 337 N Tamiami Trail, explore layers of history dating back thousands of years along the waterfront of Little Sarasota Bay, from Archaic period middens (see *Archaeological Sites*) to mansions built over the past two hundred years by various inhabitants of the land—among them Mrs. (Bertha Honore) Potter Palmer, wife of a Chicago magnate and a savvy player in Florida's 1920s land boom. At one point, she owned more than a quarter of what is now Sarasota County. A museum on the property tells her story. Historic buildings of particular interest include Mary's Free Chapel, built with funds from friends of a young lady in the early 1900s who died of tuber-culosis; the packing house, which shipped citrus fruit for many decades; the White Cottage, Jack Webb's home atop the Shell Ridge midden; and the Guptill Home, where in 1877, Frank Guptill built boats known as "sharpies," open flat-bottomed sailboats that could handle the shallow estuaries of Florida's coast. A replica of the boatwright's shop and of one of his boats, the *Lizzie G,* are on display. You are wel-come to stroll the deeply forested grounds at your own pace. Take the side trails to explore secret gardens and eerie swamp forests. Four formal tours are offered daily for no additional charge, and volunteers present living history throughout the property on Sunday. The admission is well worth it: adults $9, Florida residents and seniors $8, ages 6–12 $3.

Sarasota

At **Phillippi Estate Park** (941-861-5000), 5500 S Tamiami Trail, the historic Edson Keith Mansion is a beautifully restored two-story 1916 Italian Renaissance home designed by Otis and Clark that is used for civic functions. Walk the grounds, peek in the windows, and imagine what it was like to have this view all to yourself a century ago. It is occasionally open for viewing.

Venice

In 1910, Mrs. Bertha Honore Palmer, wife of Chicago magnate Potter Palmer, snapped up more than 140,000 acres in the area and formed the Sarasota-Venice Company. Pending expected development, the railroad was extended south from Sarasota and a canal built to connect **Venice** to the north by water and rail. Dr. and Mrs. Fred Albee purchased some of the Palmer's land and retained the servic-es of city planner John Nolen to design a new city. Approached by the Brother-hood of Locomotive Engineers (BLE) from Cleveland, who saw potential in Venice as a retirement community for their railroad brethren, Albee sold the land. The Union retained Nolen and followed his comprehensive plan. By the summer of 1926, Venice had its town center firmly established, with Venice Avenue leading visitors down a broad boulevard to the beach. Hotels, restaurants, shops, and resi-dences constructed under strict design codes—echoing the Northern Italian Ren-aissance—took form. This attention to detail can be seen today throughout the city. The neighborhoods of Venice are architectural gems with a great deal of Mediter-ranean and Spanish Mission architecture from the 1920s. Make a point of driving through them after exploring the downtown area in the Venezia Park district, where there are more than 25 Mediterranean Revival homes; a tour brochure is available from the chamber of commerce. The **Old Venice Depot** (see *Railroadi-ana*) is also home to the Venice Historical Society.

MUSEUMS

Sarasota

Known as Bellm's when I was a kid, the **Sarasota Classic Car Museum** (941-355-6228; www.sarasotacarmuseum.org), 5500 N Tamiami Trail, still showcases the stuff Dad loves best—vintage autos, antique cameras, and antique phonographs. Open since 1953, the museum has more than one hundred automobiles in its col-lection and frequently refreshes the stock by trades and acquisitions. Open daily 9 AM–6 PM. Adults $8.50, seniors $7.65, ages 13–17 $5.75, ages 6–12 $4.

The **Sarasota Historical Society Museum** is evolving inside space shared with the **Sarasota Visitor Information Center** (see *Guidance*). On my visit, exhibit panels

Recognized worldwide for its Baroque masterpieces, the **Ringling Museum of Art** (941-358-3180; www.ringling.org), 5401 Bay Shore Blvd., is much more than a fine-art collection—it's a complex of museums that will satisfy everyone in the family. To start, a visit to Ca' d'Zan celebrates the life and times of John and Mable Ringling, who lived on the 66-acre grounds in this Venetian-style mansion, built in 1924 as Mable Ringling's dream home. Enter through the 24-carat gold-leaf doors into the solarium and tour this classic structure, which still contains 95 percent of the original items installed by the Ringlings. In its time, it was the largest home within Sarasota city limits, and it had a soundproof ballroom, central heating, and an Otis elevator. Of the four levels, two are shown on your tour. Afterward, walk the grounds to the Circus Museum, which contains an interactive "Magic Ring"—ideal for kids to play out their circus fantasies—and showcases circus wagon art, props and costumes, and the history of the "Greatest Show on Earth." Finally, explore the grand salons of the Museum of Art, each with its own color backdrop and tone presenting such masterpieces as Simon Vouet's *Time Discovering the Love of Venus and Mars,* and Peter Paul Rubens's *Triumph of the Eucharist.* This is Florida's top art destination. Open daily, 10–5:30. Admission $19 adult; $16 senior; $6 for students, ages 6–17, Florida teachers, and active military. Included in your general admission is a tour of Ca' d'Zan but spaces are limited, so head there first—the first tour starts at 9:45 AM. Advance ticket purchase is recommended to guarantee a spot.

were up and the first artifact cases were in place. Stop and see what's new, including a time line of historic Sarasota and gallery space for exhibitions, as well as a gift shop.

PUBLIC ART Walk around St. Armands Circle for a dose of the Renaissance. In 1927, John Ringling purchased **classical Greek and Roman statues** to install as a major part of this shopping district. In recent times, as the originals were renovated, an additional 21 new statues were created, some replicas of ones in the Ringling Museum collection. A walking guide is available at a kiosk along the circle, with detailed information about each of the statues.

RAILROADIANA The Brotherhood of Locomotive Engineers (BLE) from Cleveland was instrumental in the growth of Venice. In 1925 the organization bought more than 50,000 acres and began developing around the waterways, with the city incorporated in 1927. Beneath the Venice Avenue Bridge, the **Old Venice Depot** stands from the Florida boomtown heyday, where the Seaboard Air Line provided passenger service until 1971, and the last circus train stopped here in 1992. ॐ A **Seaboard Air Line caboose** sits outside the station in a small park with picnic tables. The old rail line is now part of a bike path along the Intracoastal waterway, incorporating railroad history themes. The interior of the station has been restored and includes some exhibits and a gift shop. Open 10 AM–4 PM Mon., Wed., and Fri.—and sporadically, as it is staffed by volunteers. Fee.

ZOOLOGICAL PARK One of Florida's classic attractions, **Sarasota Jungle Gardens** (941-355-5305; www.sarasotajunglegardens.com), 3701 Bay Shore Rd., is going on 65 years old and is still as much fun as when I was a kid. Wander narrow, winding, natural footpaths through tropical plantings on 10 acres to explore themed areas such as the Tiki Gardens, the alligator and crocodile habitat, a fruit and nut garden, and Gardens of Christ. There are five animal-related shows throughout the day in various parts of the park. Of particular interest are the lakes where the flamingos hang out. The garden participates in an active American flamingo breeding program, so the flamingos nest on an island in Mirror Lake. Open 9 AM–5 PM daily. Adults $14, seniors $13, children 3–12 $10.

✴ To Do

BICYCLING ♿ On Siesta Key, rent bikes at **C.B.'s Saltwater Outfitters** (see *Boating*) to ride the island roads, or at **Siesta Sports Rentals** (941-346-1797; www.siestasportsrentals.com), 6551 Midnight Pass Rd., where they also have all-terrain wheelchairs perfect for beach access. Bike the **Venetian Waterway Park** (941-488-2236; www.vabi.org/vwp.htm) paralleling the Intracoastal Waterway on both sides for 5 miles from downtown past the airport to Caspersen Beach Park. When it's complete, there will be 10 miles of paved trail to enjoy. Rent a snazzy new bike from **Florida Bike & Beach** (941-412-1411; www.floridabikeandbeach .com) to cycle this bikeway or to head out through challenging sand trails in the backcountry of **Oscar Scherer State Park** (see *Parks*), $18 per day or $45 per week.

BIRDING At **Myakka River State Park** (see *Parks*), the **Birdwalk** (elevated walkway) out into the river provides excellent opportunities for spotting all varieties of wading birds. Little-known **Red Bug Slough Preserve**, 5200 Beneva Rd., is listed as a "hot spot" by the local Audubon chapter for viewing bald eagles and wading birds within a 72-acre urban refuge. In search of Florida scrub jays? This elusive threatened species can be seen along the trails at **Oscar Scherer State Park** (see *Parks*) and at **Shamrock Park & Nature Center** (see *Nature Centers*). An urban gem in south Venice is the **Venice Area Audubon Rookery** (941-493-9476; www.veniceaudubon.org), accessed via US 41 to Annex Road on the east side of the South Sarasota County Municipal Complex.

BOATING **C.B.'s Saltwater Outfitters** (941-349-4400; www.cbsoutfitters.com), 1249 Stickney Point Rd., Siesta Key, offers rentals ranging from a 17-foot runabout to a deck boat, with rates starting at $95 for a half day. Captains and tours are available for inexperienced boaters. At the **Turtle Beach Marina** (941-349-9449), 8865 Midnight Pass Rd., rent Wave Runners, kayaks, sport boats, and pontoon boats by the hour or day, or anchor for the weekend at the full-service marina.

ECOTOURS ✍ Departing from Mote Marine Aquarium (see *Aquarium*), **Sarasota Bay Explorers** (941-388-4200; www.sarasotabayexplorers.com), 1600 Ken Thompson Pkwy., offers a variety of tours, including Sea Life Encounter Tours, Kayak Tours, and Nature Safaris. Choose from dolphin watching, sight-seeing, nature exploration, and sunset cruises. Rates start at $26 adult, $22 children 4–12, and some tours can be arranged in tandem with aquarium tours.

🐊 At Myakka River State Park (see *Parks*), **Myakka Wildlife Tours** (941-365-0100; www.myakkariver.org/airboat.html), 3715 Jaffa Dr., offers cruises on the Myakka Maiden and the Gator Gal, the world's largest airboats that take you up into the shallow wetlands. Or opt for a Tram Safari on the park's back roads for wildlife viewing. Tours are $12 per person, $6 ages 6–12.

Further south on the Myakka River in North Port, Snook Haven (see *Eating Out*) offers a trip back in time on **Captain Terry's River Tour**, a nature cruise along a very wild section of the river. Call ahead (941-255-0400) for reservations.

FAMILY ACTIVITIES 🐊 **G.WIZ—The Hands-On Science Museum** (941-309-4949; www.gwiz.org), 1001 Boulevard of the Arts, Sarasota, was designed with families in mind. Kids and adults interact in the various "zones" of the museum, including the WaveZone, where you experiment with light and sound, and the EcoZone, with critters and a butterfly garden. The KidsZone is for little ones 6 and under. Open 10 AM–5 PM Tues.–Sat., 12 PM–5 PM Sun. Adults $9, seniors $8, ages 3–18 $6. Free parking.

🐊 **Smugglers Cove Adventure Golf** (941-351-6620; www.smugglersgolf.com), 3815 N Tamiami Trail, Sarasota, is known for its pirate ships and live gators on the course—which the kids are allowed to feed!

FISHING Head for the flats of Sarasota County's bays with a guide from **C.B.'s Saltwater Outfitters** (see *Boating*) for tarpon, snook, and redfish on light tackle. All guides endorsed by Orvis.

GAMING Bet on the greyhounds at the **Sarasota Kennel Club** (941-355-7444; www.sarasotakennelclub.com), 5400 Bradenton Rd., Sarasota, racing nightly at 7:30 except Sunday, with matinees at 12:30 PM on Monday, Wednesday, Friday, and Saturday.

GENEOLOGICAL RESEARCH Settlers started pouring into Venice in the 1860s, eager to homestead free land offered by the U.S. government under the Homestead Act. Settling near Osprey, the Webb family was the first to take up the offer. Trace your local ancestry and study regional history at the **Venice Archives and Area Historical Collection** (941-486-2487; www.venicegov.com/archives.htm), 351 S Nassau St., Venice, which is open 10 AM–4 PM Monday and Wednesday, plus Tuesday January through April.

GOLF Winding through lush woodlands and waterways, **Pelican Pointe Golf & Country Club** (941-496-GOLF; www.pelicanpointeclub.com) Center Rd. off Jacaranda Blvd., offers 27 holes of play, lessons from PGA professionals, a dining room, and full-service pro shop. Generous fairways await at the semiprivate **Bird Bay Executive Golf Course** (941- 485-9333), 602 Bird Bay Dr. W, where the signature hole is #14, a 168-yard par 3 over a ditch. Find more options at www.golfinvenice.com.

HIKING There are dozens of excellent places to hike in the region; virtually all listings under *Green Space* and *Wild Places* provide day hikes. **Myakka River State Park**—which includes a 40-mile backpacking loop detailed in *50 Hikes in*

South Florida—is one of the most popular hiking destinations in the area, but some of my other favorites include **Quick Point**, **Jelks Preserve**, and **Lemon Bay Preserve**.

PADDLING To explore Sarasota Bay on your own, rent your craft at **Economy Tackle/Dolphin Dive Watersports** (941-922-9671; www.floridakayak.com), 6018 S Tamiami Trail, Sarasota. If you're a newbie to sea kayaking, consider a guided tour or ACA-certified instruction in an "Introduction to Kayaking" course. If you're headed out on your own, rent a kayak at **C.B.'s Saltwater Outfitters** (see *Boating*) to paddle up to Palmer Point, the remote south tip of Siesta Key. For inland waters, **Snook Haven** (see *Eating Out*) offers 1.5-hour canoe rentals on the scenic Lower Myakka River for $15 (longer rentals available, too) with all safety equipment provided. Rentals are also available at the park concession at **Myakka River State Park** (see *Parks*).

SCENIC DRIVES Following coastal highways and byways, the **Gulf Coast Heritage Trail** leads you on some of the region's most scenic roads, including canopied Manasota Key Drive. Watch for the distinctive brown signs for key points of interest. For a copy of the map, contact a tourism center (see *Guidance*).

SEGWAY TOURS With the nation's first city Segway Tour, **Florida Ever-Glides** (941-363-9556; www.floridaever-glides.com), 200 S Washington Blvd., #11, Sarasota, offers guided trips around downtown Sarasota on their quiet little machines—after a training session so you feel comfortable maneuvering your craft. Tours run 2.5 hours, including a brief how-to orientation, and cost $61 per person.

SWIMMING Siesta Key and Longboat Key (see *Beaches*) are considered prime beachfront on the Gulf of Mexico, excellent for swimming. At **Warm Mineral Springs** (see *Springs*), you can "take the waters" in the old European style—with a lot of European visitors—in Florida's only truly "hot" spring at 87°F.

TRAIL RIDING To get a taste of what early settlers and Cracker cowmen experienced in the frontier days, bring your own horse to **Myakka State Forest** to ride the extensive trail system through the vast open scrub, or enjoy a shorter ride along the trails at **Myakkahatchee Creek Preserve** (see *Wild Places*).

WATER SPORTS Siesta Key has them! Stop by **C.B.'s Saltwater Outfitters** (see *Boating*) for Wave Runner rentals ($85 per hour) from **Siesta Key Jet Ski** (941-313-7547; www.siestakeyjetski.com).

✳ Green Space

BEACHES Since **Manasota Key** is primarily residential within Sarasota County, the beaches hidden along the canopied road are less crowded and more enjoyable. Stop at 14-acre **Manasota Beach,** 8570 Manasota Key Rd., or **Blind Pass Beach**, 6725 Manasota Key Rd., where you'll find a bayside nature trail.

Siesta Key is undisputedly tourist oriented, but with its unique soft sand—which rarely heats up underfoot—it's no wonder this beach is an international destination. The primary public beach access with the most parking is at **Siesta Beach,**

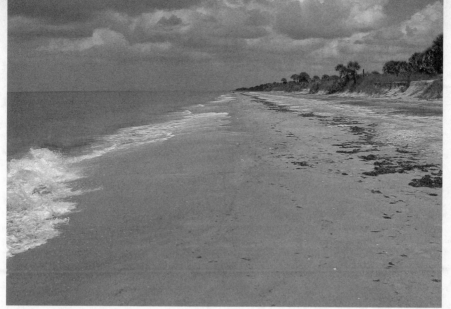

Sandra Friend

CASPERSEN BEACH

948 Beach Rd., where volunteers will help orient you to the beach ecosystems and the town. My favorite place is **Point O'Rocks Beach Access #13**, off Midnight Pass Rd. south of Stickney Pt. Rd. There isn't a lot of parking here, but unless you're staying waterfront at Crescent Beach, it's the best way to get to the Point O'Rocks, a rocky reef formation with tidal pools, excellent for snorkeling and examining sea creatures up close in their natural habitat.

Venice Beach, 326 S Nokomis Ave., is best known for its shark's teeth. Fossil collectors from around the world come here in search of the Holy Grail—enormous teeth from *Carcharodon megalodon,* a prehistoric shark 52 feet in length. More commonly, you'll find small black fossil teeth from more average-sized sharks. Along the Venice coastline, my favorite place is **Caspersen Beach**, 4100 Harbor Dr. S, which has several miles of unspoiled natural waterfront to roam. If you're bringing Fido, stop instead at 🐾 **Brohard Beach & Paw Park** (941-861-1602), 1600 Harbor Dr. S, where dogs are welcome to frolic in the surf.

BOTANICAL GARDEN ♿ 🐾 ⊙⊙ For a relaxing afternoon, visit **Marie Selby Botanical Gardens** (941-366-5731; www.selby.org), 811 S Palm Ave., an oasis of formal gardens and natural habitats along Sarasota's waterfront. Start your tour by walking through the airlock of the Tropical Display House, where you'll marvel at a tunnel of tropical blooms. Stand still and take in the fragrance of hundreds of orchids before you head into the fernery. Following the pathway toward the bay, enjoy gardens of ferns, cycads, and bamboo, and take a side trip on the canopy walk en route to the succulent garden with its towering giant agave. Shaded by sea grapes, the path continues along Hudson Bayou to "The Point," where a bo tree shades the view. A boardwalk winds through the bayfront mangroves. Beneath the banyan trees, Michael's in the Garden is a café with self-serve gourmet sandwiches, ice cream, coffee, and tea. The classy building was once the Selby family's residence, and the dark pool in front of the home is a memorial to the family. Tropical plantings accent the native habitat along the waterfront on the way to Paynes Mansion. Look up into the trees for a bromeliad garden! The 1934 mansion houses exhibits of botanical art and a gift shop. At the Tree Lab, kids can play in the tree house canopy and peek in the frog nursery, with its colorful poison dart frogs. Behind the buildings are herb, fruit, and container gardens. Open 10 AM–5 PM daily; closed Christmas. Adults $17, ages 6–11 $6.

GREENWAY The **Venetian Waterway Park** (see *Bicycling*) follows the Intracoastal Waterway from Nokomis to Venice, with trails on both side of the waterway. Bicyclists and walkers can enjoy the 5-mile paved section that is open to the public; another 5 miles are planned.

NATURE CENTERS

Englewood

⚘ Enjoy the cool Gulf breezes at **Lemon Bay Park & Environmental Center** (941-474-3065), 570 Bay Park Blvd., where eagles nest amid the pines, and trails wind across 195 waterfront acres surrounding a nature center. Free.

Sarasota

⚘ Encompassing 190 acres along the Myakka River, **Crowley Museum & Nature Center** (941-322-1000; www.CrowleyMuseumNatureCtr.org), 16405 Myakka Rd., offers a variety of activities. Walk the boardwalk through Maple Branch Swamp and nature trails through the pine woods, visit the old Crowley pioneer homestead from the 1880s, watch living-history demonstrations at the blacksmith shop and sugarcane mill, and explore the museum filled with artifacts from Old Miakka. Open 10 AM– 4 PM Tues.–Sun. (Jan. 1–Apr. 30) and Thurs.–Sun. (May 1–Dec. 31). Fee.

Venice

⚘ At **Shamrock Park & Nature Center** (941-486-2706), 4100 W Shamrock Dr., scrub jays range across the 82 acres along the Intracoastal Waterway, but the real reason to come here is for the kids: The nature center is excellent, and the playground is a lot of fun, especially if they love dinosaurs. Free.

PARKS

Sarasota

⚘ Established in 1934, **Myakka River State Park** (941-361-6511; www.florida stateparks.org), 13207 SR 72, provides endless opportunities for outdoor recreation on more than 28,000 acres. Day-trippers can experience the only **Canopy Walk** in the United States—a swinging bridge more than 40 feet up in the live oak canopy, giving you a bird's eye view of bromeliads. Stop at the Myakka Outpost to board a modified airboat for a one-hour tour along the river (see *Ecotours*), or rent bikes to ride dozens of miles of trails throughout the park. Birdwatchers will appreciate the **Bird Walk**, a long boardwalk out into the river with numerous opportunities for birding, while backpackers can enjoy the best multiday experience that southwest Florida has to offer—a 40-mile series of stacked loops passing through prairies, oak hammocks, and dozens of other habitats. Fee.

Whitaker Gateway Park (941-316-1172), 1455 N Tamiami Trail, marks the location of the original homestead of the Whitaker family, the first post-statehood settlers along Sarasota Bay. It offers fishing and picnicking along Yellow Bluff. Free.

Venice

Best known for its ever-expanding Florida scrub jay population, **Oscar Scherer State Park** (941-483-5956; www.floridastateparks.org/Oscar Scherer), 1843 S Tamiami Trail, is a great place for a weekend getaway. Covering more than 1,300 acres of land, the park preserves a crucial chunk of scrub and scrubby flatwoods in the midst of burgeoning Gulf Coast development. Here you can bike and hike for dozens of miles, rent a canoe or kayak and paddle down South Creek, fish from the boardwalks or along Osprey Lake, or camp beneath the sand under live oaks. Fee.

Sandra Friend

MYAKKA CANOPY WALK

SPRINGS ✔ Dubbed "the Original Fountain of Youth," **Warm Mineral Springs** (941-426-1692; www.warmmineralsprings.com), 12200 San Servando Ave. (along US 41), North Port, boasts Florida's only truly hot spring, with 87°F water year-round. Known for its significant archaeological artifacts (see *Archaeological Sites*), it opened as a tourist attraction in the 1940s, attracting bathers who wanted to "take the waters" for their health. These deep waters have the highest concentration of minerals found in any United States spring, and it's obvious when you step in—the water is both warm *and* soft, with a pH of 7.36. It's a popular destination for foreign tourists, especially those from Eastern Europe and Russia, and families. While the buildings show their age, they're nicely decorated in murals of natural Florida. Wellness services are offered as an adjunct to a dip in the spring, including acupuncture, chi balancing, and massage. Buy bottled water in the gift shop, asserted to enhance your good health. The springs were sold at auction the day after my visit—and it's my hope they'll become a public park—so check their website before your visit. General admission $20, 12 and under $8.

WILD PLACES

North Port

Myakkahatchee Creek Environmental Park (941-486-2547), 6968 Reisterstown Rd., protects 160 acres along Big Slough, with scenic trails along this picturesque natural waterway sometimes perched on sand bluffs above the creek. Picnic area and canoe launch. Equestrians, bicyclists, and hikers welcome. Free.

With more than 8,500 acres of pine flatwoods, **Myakka State Forest** (941-255-7653; www.fl-dof.com/state_forests/myakka.html), 4723 53rd Ave. E, has miles of forest roads for off-road bicycling, horseback riding, and hiking. Tent camping is permitted. Fee.

Venice

Along the wild southern reaches of the Myakka River, **Jelks Preserve** (941-486-2547), along N River Rd. (north of Center Rd.), has a network of trails (with a 3.3-mile perimeter trail) meandering through pine flatwoods, scrubby flatwoods, and oak hammocks on uplands above the Myakka River. Some trails lead to river views. Free.

West of I-75, the **T. Mabry Carlton, Jr. Memorial Reserve** (941-486-2547), 1800 Mabry Carlton Pkwy., encompasses 234 acres of pine flatwoods, scrubby flatwoods, oak hammocks, and open prairies. A 1.7-mile loop trail touches on some of the habitats, and a 7.9-mile linear trail works its way north to the entrance to Myakka River State Park. Free.

✳ Lodging

BED & BREAKFASTS

Sarasota 34236

Capture the spirit of Old Sarasota at **The Cypress** (941-955-4683; www .cypressbb.com), 621 Gulf Stream Ave. S. The inn is infused with a sense of artistry and style; jazz drifts through the corridors. Constructed by Jarvis Hardisty, a sailing instructor, this 1940 gem retains the elegant spirit of its past, especially as a lone holdout against a line of condos along the waterfront. There are 12 mango trees shading the property, and the owner, Robert Belott, a retired photographer and gourmet chef, makes excellent use of them in breakfast and snack preparations. Each room ($150–289) is decorated with his brilliant photographs and filled with his family antiques. Kathyrn's Garden Room looks out into the mango trees, while the romantic and extremely popular Martha Rose Suite has a private balcony overlooking the bay and a sitting area with a Victorian sofa. Sitting out on the porch, cocktail in hand, with an assistant, George, offering you crêpes and cheese, you feel a sense of calm in this oasis in the city, knowing that numerous dining options lie within easy walking distance. It is a venue worthy of Hardisty's storied legacy—sophisticated and stylish, yet down-home Florida.

Venice 34285

⊕ ⁍⁝⁍ One of the oldest homes in Venice, the **Banyan House Historic B&B** (941-484-1385; www.banyan house.com), 519 Harbor Dr., is shaded by an enormous banyan tree planted by Thomas Edison, a friend of the original owner, and boasts the first swimming pool built in Venice, carefully maintained with its original tile by the current owners. There are guest rooms ($139–179) in three buildings, including the main house, the carriage house, and the servant's quarters. The tropical courtyard is a great place to relax, and the breakfast room overlooks the Cherokee red patios. Three rooms have balconies and kitchenettes; a full breakfast is served to all guests. Closed December; apartments outside the main home are available during those periods on a monthly basis.

🐾 ⅍ ✿ ⁍⁝⁍ **The Horse & Chaise Inn** (941-488-2702 or 1-877-803-3515; www.horseandchaiseinn.com), 317 Ponce de Leon Ave. In the family for more than 30 years, this 1926 Mediterranean Revival house (expanded years ago into a rest home) was converted by Lois and Jon Steketee into a relaxing inn showcasing the region's long and storied history in each of its eight rooms ($115–169). Stay in the Ringling Room to relive old circus memories, or settle back in the red, white, and blue Patriot Room, commemorating the old Venice Army Air Force Base. Guys can't help but play in the BLE Room—a Lionel train runs on an elevated track around the room. With a bottomless cookie jar in the kitchen, snacks and drinks always available in the dining room, and cold bottled water in your room, the inn will make you feel right at home. It's easy to mingle with fellow guests in the open, comfortable common areas, including the garden courtyards, but I especially appreciated being able to check my e-mail on the personal computer, with high-speed Internet access, provided for guests. Closed July 5–Sept. 30.

COTTAGES

Siesta Key 34242

▼ ☀ "ℐ" Fifteen years ago, Gail and David Rubinfeld found a tumbledown fish camp at the south end of Siesta Key and had a dream of turning it into a couples' getaway. And indeed, I've found few accommodations as romantic as the **Turtle Beach Resort** (941-349-4554; www.turtlebeachresort.com), 9049 Midnight Pass Rd., where you can lie in bed and look out over your own private bay view, or bask in your own private hot tub. Grab a kayak or bicycle to explore the island. The complex consists of ten cottages ($270 and up), with weekly rates available. Reserve early, as there are many repeat customers.

& ▼ "ℐ" At the **Inn Behind the Beach** (941-349-4554; www.turtle beachresort.com), 9049 Midnight Pass Rd., enjoy the same relaxed comfort as the cottages across the street at Turtle Beach Resort, but with a larger variety of suites and studios (starting at $230 in the low season) to choose from, each with its own private hot tub. You'll feel pampered with soft robes and sherry, and feel ready to spring into action with access to bicycles, canoes, and kayaks included in your room rate. Nap in your own private hammock and grill a steak for dinner. All units include a full kitchen. No children or pets permitted.

Casey Key 34275

Built in 1947, the **Gulf Shore Beach Resort Motel** (941-488-6210; www.gulfshoresresortmotel.com), 317 Casey Key Rd., features bungalows (efficiencies, one bedroom, and two bedroom, $95–200 in season) with a classic Florida beachfront feel, each with terrazzo floors, wooden ceilings, and a tiled mural in the shower. The units include a bedroom and dining–full kitchen area, plus a front porch overlooking the common green with shuffleboard courts, and a walk over the rise to the dunes of the Gulf.

Siesta Key 34242

✐ ☀ "ℐ" Dangle a line (or your toes) off the deck on Heron Lagoon at the **Banana Bay Club Resort** (941-346-0113 or 1-888-622-6229; www.banana bayclub.com), 8254 Midnight Pass Rd., an appealing Superior Small Lodging surrounded by mangroves. This older motel has been completely converted to classy units in Caribbean tones, all very roomy, with full kitchens. Several waterfront rooms available, and all are nonsmoking and come with pillow-topped beds and one hundred minutes in free phone calls to anywhere. Rates run $99–269, depending on room size and season.

🐾 "ℐ" ↩ An intimate home away from home, the **Captiva Beach Resort** (941-349-4131 or 1-800-349-4131; www.captivabeachresort.com), 6772 Sara Sea Cir., is only moments from the beach. Since 1981 the Ispaso family has carefully updated and tended this 1940s motel nestled in a tropical forest. It boasts sparkling clean rooms and suites in a variety of eight different configurations ($115–250) with full kitchens, and bottled water flowing out of every kitchen's tap! Visit their Web site for a virtual tour of every room and a virtual walk to the beach.

⚓ Enjoy a touch of the circus at **The Ringling Beach House** (941-349-1236 or 1-888-897-9919; www.siesta keysuites.com), 523 Beach Rd., where suites in this 1920s Ringling home have playful names such as "Ringmaster" and "Seal," as well as roomy, fully updated interiors ($120–252, discounts for longer stays). The adjoining **Siesta Key Suites** offers even more options on this steps-from-the-beach property.

🦐 ♿ ⚓ 🐾 After my visit, I directed my own relatives to **Tropical Shores Beach Resort** (941-346-0025 or 1-800-235-3493; www.tropicalshores .com), 6717 Sara Sea Cir., a very family-friendly motel just a few minutes' walk from Point O' Rocks. There are 30 large, inviting units; tropical plantings throughout the property; and two heated pools. The staff is friendly and the rooms are spotless, with daily housekeeping (not a norm in these parts!). In business since 1955, the resort is family-owned and strives for 100 percent guest satisfaction. Their room rates start at $77 off-season for a mini efficiency. Their adjacent property, the **Tropical Sun Beach Resort** (www.tropicalsunresort.com) is a large 1950s motel just like I stayed in as a kid, with retro lime and black tiled showers, large rooms ($68 and up) with futons, efficiency kitchens, and a guest laundry.

Venice 34285

♿ ⁿⁱⁿ ↝ Right off I-75, the **Best Western Ambassador Suites** (941-480-9898; Ambassador.BestWestern .com), 400 Commercial Ct., is a newly certified Green Lodging that makes a great launch point for outdoor recreation along the corridor of lands surrounding the Myakka River; for after-workout recuperation, they have a heated pool, and Jacuzzis in some

rooms. Stretch out and relax in the spacious suites ($89 and up), where you can curl up on the sofa with your laptop or sit at a dedicated business desk. Each suite includes a kitchen nook with microwave, wet bar, coffeemaker, and mini-fridge, as well as a kitchen table. An expanded continental breakfast is included in your stay.

A landmark of the Venice boomtown years, the historic **El Patio Hotel** (941-488-7702 or 1-800-941-0993; www.elpatiohotel.com) dates back to 1926 and has been operated since 1949 by the Miles family. It's right in the heart of the downtown shopping district, above the shops—centrally located for forays on foot. An exterior walkway overlooks gardens, and an interior common space provides a comfortable place to read or have a cup of tea. Choose from standard rooms and one-bedroom suites ($120–160): basic, spacious, and clean; the baths are small, reflecting their era.

♿ ⚓ **Inn at the Beach Resort** (941-484-8471; www.innatthebeach.com), 725 W Venice Ave., is just steps from Venice Beach and the shopping district, offering large motel rooms with tiled floors and a mix of 13 different configurations among their 49 units. Rates start at $99 off-season.

LONG-TERM RENTALS

Siesta Key 34242

There are only seven units at **Siesta Sunset Beach House** (941-346-1215; www.siestasunset.com), 5322 Calle de la Siesta, which makes it an appealing home away from home with an easy walk to shops and restaurants in Siesta Village. I appreciated the oh-so-comfortable bed and bright, roomy interior, but each sparkling-clean unit also offers a fully equipped kitchen (dishes, linens, and all appliances), television and VCR (a 150-title library resides downstairs for your pleasure), and robes for the bath. Up to four bedrooms may be combined to accommodate large families. A crow's-nest sundeck on the top floor provides a perch to watch the sunset, and the courtyard contains a swimming pool and hot tub. You can borrow beach chairs as you head across the street to Siesta Beach Access #7, or grab a bike and head into the village. The weekly rental runs $550–1,300, with shorter stays possible during the off-season and package deals available.

✳ Where to Eat

Looking for local restaurants featuring, locally grown food? **The Originals** (www.freshoriginals.com) includes cafes, bistros, and mom-and-pop restaurants that preserve the culinary heritage of the region, drawing on the produce of local farmers and the bounty of the sea. There are nearly 50 participants, and I wish I had the time to sample them all! Best of all, they offer gift certificates good at any of their locations.

DINING OUT

Englewood
Relax and pass the tapas at trendy **Vino Loco Wine & Tapas** (941-473-3816; www.vinolocowine.com), 420 W Dearborn St., a bottle shop with live music and delectable organic delights like Shrimp Chueca, Pescada Blanco, oyster shooters, and cheese plates with seasonal fruits. Open Mon.–Sat. at 11 AM.

Sarasota
Almost completely hidden by a giant banyan tree, **5-One-6 Burns** (941-906-1884; www.fiveonesixburns.com), 516 Burns Ln., is a sophisticated bistro with appealing offerings such as vanilla bean–glazed sea scallops, hummus,

and grilled Brie. Lunch 11 AM–5 PM and dinner after 5; menus change daily, with entrées starting under $20.

They're not on the waterfront, but it doesn't matter—fine fresh seafood is what you'll get at **Barnacle Bill's** (941-365-6800; www.barnaclebills seafood.com), 1526 Main St., a local favorite where seafood specialties include seafood strudel, shrimp and lobster Newburg, sesame-crusted salmon, and crab Alfredo. My Crab Cakes Benedict was a delightful twist on an old favorite, perfect for lunch. Their extensive menu also includes seafood baskets and sandwiches, Kobe beef, aged steaks, veal, and old-fashioned pot roast; entrées $15–40. I especially appreciate the half portion options. There is a fresh fish market on the premises.

Overseen by Executive Chef Jean-Pierre Knaggs and his wife, Shay, since 1986, **The Bijou Café** (941-366-8111; www.bijoucafe.net), 1287 First St. at Pineapple Ave., is highly recommended as a superb downtown restaurant. Their wine list is extensive, and the classy entrées (starting around $20) include veal Louisville, grilled salmon Verde, and grilled lavender honey-glazed quail, the recipes influenced by Jean-Pierre's South African and French heritage.

Dine in the middle of downtown at **Mattison's City Grill** (941-330-0440; www.mattisons.com), One Lemon Ave., where you can listen to live jazz while savoring a fresh pizza as the sun sets. A slice is $4. While the aroma of the brick oven tempts, you may prefer other Italian-influenced fare such as veggie panini, ripe tomatoes and bocconcini mozzarella, or antipasta mista. They serve burgers and grouper sandwiches, too. Lunch $4–13, entrées $16–33.

At the **Selva Grill** (941-362-4427; www.selvagrill.com), 1345 Main St. #2, Chef Darwin Santa Maria brings his native Peruvian cuisine to Sarasota palates, with ceviches ($14 and up) being a specialty of the house. Selva's own Selva Ceviche is a wild mix of fresh corvinae, lime, onion, cilantro, Cusco corn, and roasted camote. *Platos fuertes* (main dishes) use Hawaiian swordfish, venison, roasted lamb, and steak in creative ways. Entrées from $25.

Siesta Key

Peruvian cuisine shines at **Javier's Restaurant and Wine Bar** (941-349-1792; www.javiersrestaurant.com), 6621 Midnight Pass Rd., where ethnic specialties such as *picante de camarones* (large shrimp in spicy pepper sauce) and *lomo saltado* (beef tenderloin tips sautéed with Spanish onions, fresh tomato, garlic, and cumin) complement fine American favorites such as pepper steak, pasta jambalaya, and barbecue baby back ribs. Small plates, $6–11; entrées $18–22, and a 4-course Tapas dinner for $23. Open Tues.–Sat., 5–9 PM.

🦐 For a romantic dinner on the bay, head to **Ophelia's on the Bay** (941-349-3328; www.opheliasonthebay.net), 9105 Midnight Pass Rd., where large picture windows showcase the bayfront as you dine by candlelight. Savor a glass of wine as you experience a parade of sensory delights—my organic-greens salad was topped with pecans dipped in maple sugar, a crunchy sweet counterpoint to the greens and Gorgonzola cheese; my scampi had a garlicky zing; and the butternut squash was nutty sweet. The menu changes frequently, but one constant is the pleasant and attentive waitstaff. Entrées start at $25. There is an extensive wine list and a martini menu.

St. Armands

At **Cork** (941-388-CORK; www.cork onthecircle.com), 29 N. Blvd. of the Presidents, wine is an essential ingredient to a relaxed meal and fusion is the name of the game, with old favorites, like fried green tomatoes served with sliced fresh mozzarella, lemon basil oil and aged balsamic, and old world standards, like foie gras, an integral part of the menu. Entrées ($23 and up) include creations like roast duckling, rubbed with Cointreau and roasted with Florida oranges, lemons, and limes; and porchetta osso bucco, a slow-cooked pork shank with garlic, basil, plum tomato, and citrus zest. The specialty of the house is dessert soufflés, so save room!

Venice

Seafood's the thing at **The Crow's Nest** (941-484-9551; www.crowsnest -venice.com), 1968 Tarpon Ctr. Dr., a favorite at the Tarpon Center Marina since 1976. Grab some raw Apalachicola oysters and fresh Gulf shrimp, or savor the seafood bisque and steamed mussels as you watch the ships sail in along the Venice jetties. Fresh catches and entrées ($15–43)

AHI TUNA APPETIZER AT THE CROW'S NEST
The Crow's Nest

include such delectables as walnut crusted filet of salmon and pesto baked striped bass, paired up with an award-winning wine list.

Sharky's on the Pier (941-488-1456; www.sharkysonthepier.com), 1600 Harbor Dr. S, has a beachy keen party atmosphere, but their culinary creativity is out of this world. Try the shrimp and blue crab au gratin made with Florida blue crab, Gulf shrimp, and cheddar, or feast on flounder San Juan, with artichoke hearts, spinach, and lobster sauce. In the intriguing Seafood Rainforest, shrimp and scallops mix it up with veggies, mango, pineapple, and cashews. Their not-to-be-denied pasta offerings include a lobster brie sauté, perfect for a romantic sunset dinner at the only beachfront eatery in Venice. Entrées from $15.

🐚 For a romantic evening in Venice, drift away from shore and inland to **Valentis** (941-484-1888), 1200 E Venice Ave., a gathering place with a true Venetian feel. The aroma of fresh-made plum tomato marinara infuses the restaurant, where muted light creates islands of intimate conversation as Italian crooners softly sing in the background and attentive, friendly servers look to your every need. Entrées ($13 and up) include oven baked favorites like manicotti and lasagna; specialty pizzas; a delightful pork pizziola sautéed in green bell peppers and onions; octopus and calamari; and specials like seafood ravioli stuffed with ricotta, lobster, scallops, water chestnuts, spinach, crabmeat, and shrimp—these were a delight.

EATING OUT

Nokomis
It doesn't come fresher than **Pop's Sunset Grill** (941-488-3177; www .popssunsetgrill.net), 112 Circuit Rd. (off W Albee Rd. at the bridge), where

I watched for dolphins while waiting on a sampler skewer of shrimps and scallops and fresh green bean salad. Steamer pots, however, have been their stock in trade for more than 20 years and include corn on the cob, red potatoes, onions, carrots, celery, and your choice of fresh oysters, shrimp, snow crab, and middle neck clams. Feed a hungry appetite (or two) with one of these! Sunset sandwiches and beach baskets of fried seafood run $8–14.

St. Armands Key
Hungry Fox Restaurant (941-388-2222), 419A St. Armands Cir., offers a nice break from your day of shopping, serving "Floribbean cuisine with a flair" in dishes such as Caribbean French toast, Sarasota club, shrimp Islamorada, and jambalaya. Open for breakfast, lunch, and dinner.

Sarasota
Savor tasty Greek cuisine at **El Greco Café** (941-365-2234; www.elgrecocafe .com), 1592 Main St., a clean, crisp modern-day taverna with large picture windows and faux Greek columns. Lively Greek pop music fills the air as you fill yourself with moussaka, Athenian chicken, or lamb chops, $10 and up. The last Thursday of every month is Greek Night, with live entertainment, wine specials, and Greek entrées not normally on the menu.

In the Gulf Gate neighborhood, en route to Siesta Key, park and walk around the block to select from an interesting mix of restaurants, including a taste of New York's Little Italy at the **Italian Village Deli** (941-927-2428), 6606 Superior Ave.; pasta and Philly sandwiches at **Walt's Tuscany Grill** (941-927-1113), 6584 Superior Ave., where everything is made from scratch; fusion food at **Going Bistro** (941-926-2994), 2164 Gulf Gate Dr.; and eclectic seafood entrées at **Greer's**

Grill (941-926-0606), 6566 Gateway Ave., a local favorite.

A waterfront restaurant with a classic Florida fish camp feel—picnic tables and all—the **Phillippi Creek Village Restaurant & Oyster Bar** (941-925-4444; www.creekseafood.com), 5353 South Tamiami Trail, is a local favorite for fresh seafood. The extensive menu includes steamer pots and combination platters ($12 and up). I savored my blue crab Norfolk, a buttery preparation with a side of spicy parsley potatoes.

🍴 Enjoy Pennsylvania Dutch treats at **Yoder's Restaurant** (941-955-7771; www.yodersrestaurant.com), 3434 Bahia Vista St., which opened in 1975 as the region's first Amish restaurant (a cuisine that continues to spread, thanks to a substantial Amish community in rural Sarasota County). Patrons come from afar to sample their 25 different varieties of homemade pies. At breakfast it was busy; don't let the lack of cars in the lot fool you. The stuffed French toast stuffed me but good, and the folks at the next table looked puzzled by the heaps of food that came with their breakfast. Take home an award-winning pie! Serving 6 AM–8 PM, with meals under $10; closed Sun. Cash only.

Siesta Key

🍴 The **Broken Egg Restaurant & Gallery** (941-346-2750; www.the brokenegg.com), 210 Avenida Madera, is where locals and visitors rub shoulders over a spectacular breakfast and lunch menu, including crab cakes Benedict, Jerry's pancake (one massive buttermilk pancake with blueberries, bananas, and wheat germ), and cheese blintzes. Dining at the adjoining table, NBA announcer Dick Vitale signed posters as my companions and I feasted on fresh fruit. Check out the art gallery on your way out—it's full of great little gifts!

Drop by for a daiquiri at the **Siesta Key Oyster Bar** (941-346-5443; www.skob.com), 5238 Ocean Blvd., where fresh seafood and hot wings are the hot stuff. Enjoy fresh oysters and clams on the half shell, plus award-winning wing sauce, or try one of their many seafood entrées, $12 and up.

🍴 Despite a popular bar as the centerpiece of the dining room, **Turtles Restaurant** (941-346-2207; www .turtlesrestaurant.com), 8875 Midnight Pass Rd., is the family place on Siesta Key to take kids to dinner, with a kids' menu (meals under $6) and plenty of activity out on the marina to keep them curious. Colorful giclee murals by David Utz decorate the walls. The crab bisque hints of tomato, while the fresh snapper amandine is just superb. Serving lunch and dinner, $7 and up.

Venice

🍴 Chili dogs and root beer floats—staple foods from my childhood. And since 1957, **The Frosted Mug** (941-497-1611), 1856 Tamiami Trail, has been serving these and other old-time fast-food favorites daily, $2–9. Dig into chili cheese fries, blue cheese bacon burgers, and 15 types of hot dogs, including New York, Polish, and Italian.

🍴 Fried yam patties and dynamite cake are a part of the Southern charm at **Gold Rush BBQ** (941-483-3137), 661 Tamiami Trail S. We caught this one when the sign for fried chicken special on Wednesday nights caught my husband's eye, and what a delightful find. Midweek, the restaurant was packed with happy customers chowing down on a variety of barbecue—pulled pork, baby back ribs, barbecued chicken—with perfect sides like redskin mashers with horseradish and garlic. Sweet cornbread comes with every meal. Barbecue starts at $7, but if you want a real taste treat, go with the "Mother

Lode Combo" with enough smoked meat to take a plate home afterward. With spectacularly quick service, good food fast, and a home-style atmosphere, it's a winner!

Escape to Old Florida at **Snook Haven** (941-485-7221; www.snook havenretreat.com), 5000 Venice Ave., a classic fish camp with live music every day and picnic tables on the porch. It's literally at the end of the road, as far east of Venice as you can go on Venice Ave. as it becomes a bumpy dirt road leading to the Myakka River. Snook Haven is more cultural experience than restaurant, with weekend jam sessions, canoe rentals, and tour boat rides on the Myakka River. Still, it's a place to grab lunch (under $10) in a gorgeous riverside setting. Dine on gator bites and grouper or go for one of their fresh-made shrimp salads served in a tomato; the fresh potato chips with buttermilk ranch dip are delectable.

BAKERY AND ICE CREAM

St. Armands

Family-owned **Big Olaf Creamery** (941-388-4108; www.bigolaficecream .com), 561 N Washington Dr., is a local favorite with great homemade ice cream, thick and creamy like it should be. They have 32 flavors of ice cream (I picked peppermint!) and frozen yogurt, including sugar-free varieties, tempting with tasty treats—sundaes, shakes, malts, and cones.

A Michigan transplant, **Kilwins** (941-388-2000), 312 Blvd. of the Presidents, is an old-fashioned candy and ice cream shop with excellent lemonade—an important resource on a hot day—as well as Mackinaw Island fudge, and ice cream flavors such as Traverse City cherry to choose from.

Step into the 1950s at **Scoop Daddy's** (941-388-1650; www.scoopdaddys

.com), 373 John Ringling Blvd., where magnets and movie posters take you back in time while you slurp down that chocolate shake.

Sarasota

Delightful pastries await at **Pastry Art** (941-955-7545; www.pastryartonmain .com), 1512 Main St., where I was tempted by both tiramisu and a raspberry parfait while savoring the aroma of fresh-brewed coffee. Open daily, serving lunch salads and sandwiches, as well as sweets.

Enjoy delicious homemade ice cream at **Sarasota Scoops** (941-921-1003), 5353 S Tamiami Trail, handmade by mother-daughter team Janie and Becca McClain. And what flavors! They include black raspberry with chocolate chips, Gator Tracks, Rasamataz (vanilla with chocolate chips and raspberry syrup), key lime sorbet, and much more. Enjoy a scoop or a sundae in this snazzy little ice cream shop, where soft jazz complements the mosaic tables and bistro-style art. Open late.

Venice

An old-fashioned ice cream parlor, **The Soda Fountain** (941-412-9860), 349 W Venice Ave., offers traditional favorites served up at their classic marble tables and fountain.

✳ Entertainment

Sarasota

Asolo Theatre Festival (941-351-8000 or 1-800-361-8388; www.asolo .org), FSU Center for the Performing Arts, 5555 N Tamiami Trail, offers professional actors in productions such as *The Imaginary Invalid* and *Inventing Van Gogh* at the Mertz Theatre, a restored five-hundred-seat 1903 opera house transported here from Dunfermline, Scotland. Student productions from the MFA program at the

Jane B. Cook Theatre offer a more intimate experience.

Performances are fun at the **Golden Apple Dinner Theatre** (941-366-5454 or 1-800-652-0920; www.the goldenapple.com), 25 N Pineapple Ave., a local landmark since 1971. Former Broadway thespians Roberta MacDonald and Robert Ennis Turoff, who established this venue as one of the nation's first dinner theaters, oversee a slate of Broadway musicals and theatrical productions accompanied by fine dining ($37–45). Closed Mon.; Sat. matinee offered at noon.

At the **Van Wezel Performing Arts Hall** (1-800-826-9303; www.vanwezel .org), 777 N Tamiami Trail, enjoy a smorgasbord of productions—top-quality dance, musicals, symphony orchestra, and comedy, including Broadway productions such as *Ain't Misbehavin'* and *Beatlemania,* the magic of David Copperfield, and the music of Englebert Humperdinck. From October through May there's such an array of shows, you'd think you were in New York.

✱ Selective Shopping

Englewood

Established as a fishing village in 1896, **Olde Englewood Village** (www.olde englewood.com) is now the heart of a quaint shopping district. Wander Dearborn Street and pop in on the various galleries, restaurants, and boutiques, including **Day Lilies Tropical** (941-474-1070), 452 W Dearborn, enticing you in with wooden flowers, artsy palms and yuccas, metal birds, and mobiles. **Ester's Antiques** (941-475-1846), 409 W Dearborn, is full of my great-grandmother's treasures, like cut glass egg plates, tea sets, quilts, and oriental cabinets. Integrate mind, body, and spirit at **Mystic See** (941-473-3816), 411 W Dearborn St., with cards,

incense, candles, and spiritualist readings. The **Amherst Depot** (941-475-2020), 349 W Dearborn, is my Dad's kind of store, a Lionel dealer with a Santa Fe symbol painted on the front door and plenty of miniatures and rolling stock inside.

On the site of the historic Woodmere sawmill, the **Dome Flea Market** (941-493-6773; www.thedomeflea market.com), 5115 SR 776, has offered up bargains since 1974. Browse the many dealer booths for one-of-a-kind art and Florida gifts. Open 9 AM–4 PM Fri.–Sun.

St. Armands

Walk around the entire circle, and you'll be rewarded with a dizzying array of shops, far too many to mention here. Don't miss the side alleys, too, where more shops await. Here are some of the places that caught my eye:

Artisans (941-388-0082), 301 John Ringling Blvd., has neon sculptures, glass art, and other fun and functional pieces. I found classic travel stickers for my antique steamer trunk and a great shawl here.

I loved it when I walked into **Circle Books** (941-388-2850; www.circle books.net), 478 John Ringling Blvd., and picked up one of my books—and the gal at the counter said it was selling briskly! This busy independent bookstore does a great job of promoting Florida authors, with frequent book signings by names big and small.

Add a splash of Provence to your life with **Décor de France** (941-388-1599; www.decordefrance.com), 24 N Blvd. of the Presidents, with table linens, pottery, and original paintings to add the spirit of the French countryside to your dining room.

Grab your Florida souvenirs at **Destination Florida** (941-388-2119), 465B John Ringling Blvd., where you can choose from local art, bold T-shirts, and "Life is Good" products.

A top spot for creative craft, the **Giving Tree Gallery** (941-388-1353; www.thegivingtreegallery.com), 5N Blvd. of the Presidents, isn't just about art, but artistic spirit expressed in everyday things, like lamps, clocks, and furniture. For instance, those big butterfly benches you see in parks? You'll find them here.

At **People's Pottery** (941-388-2727), 362B John Ringling Blvd., look through boldly colored handbags and pottery, art glass, and jewelry.

Sarasota—Downtown

A cluster of antiques shops and boutiques around Historic Burns Square makes **Pineapple Avenue** a great destination for browsers and buyers. Go for retro period home decor at **Jack Vinales** (941-957-0002; www.Jack VinalesAntiques.com), 539 S Pineapple Ave., including Mission and art deco. At **Pineapple Bay Trading Company** (941-951-1965; www.pineapple -bay.com), 500 S Pineapple Ave., dig through gemstones and creative jewelry, antiques, and gifts brought back from travels owners B. J. and Kari Graf make around the world.

Main Street is long and easy to walk, with street and lot parking nearby. Buskers are a spirited new addition—young men strumming indie rock tunes, a 60s flower child belting out protest songs, fellows in body paint playing drums. There's a Saturday farmer's market, too, to add to the atmosphere, and numerous sidewalk cafes. It's a mecca for bibliophiles, with several shops to choose from. Three stories tall, **Main Bookshop** (941-366-7653; www.mainbookshop.com), 1962 Main St., fills the bottom floor with current books, the middle with over-runs, and the top floor with used books. Open 9 AM–11 PM daily, 365

days a year. **A. Parker's Books** (941-366-2898; www.aparkers.com), 1488 Main St., has well-arranged, packed narrow aisles filled with classic books, a special first-edition section, and many autographed books. **Sarasota News & Books** (941-365-3662; www.sarasotanewsandbooks.com), 1341 Main St., anchors the bay end of the block with a great selection of magazines and current favorites. The coffee shop and outdoor tables provide a place for friends to meet.

Since 1978, **Pagliacci** (941-388-4070; www.pagliacci.com) 1429 Main St., has been the go-to place for collectibles—everything from fine figurines to Superman lunchboxes to clown paintings.

Visit **The Toy Lab** (941-363-0064), 1529 Main St., for educational games, replica critters, and fun science toys.

From Dean Martin CDs to that perfect straw hat, **2 For Me, 1 For You** (941-316-0343), 1515 Main St., has great goodies to choose from, including gourmet kitchen items and humorous handbags.

Siesta Key

Lotions & Potions (941-346-1546; www.lotionspotions.com), 5212½ Ocean Blvd., has fine stuff for your hands and face. Browse the stacks at **Used Book Heaven** (941-349-0067), 5216 Ocean Blvd. **C.B.'s Saltwater Outfitters** (see *Boating*) is, according to the owner, "a smelly old bait shop turned into a boutique," and not only do they sell bait, they have high-end Orvis gear and sportswear.

Venice—Downtown

Downtown Venice has enough shops to satisfy even the hard-core shopper, with a variety ranging from fine art to absolute kitsch. Paralleling the busy face of the city, Venice Avenue, quiet Miami Avenue is where you'll find the antiques shops. Explore the cross streets for even more bargains. Here's a sample.

If antique glass is your weakness, stop in **Buttercup Cottage** (941-484-2222; www.buttercupcottage.com), 227 W Miami Ave., for ornate perfume bottles as well as cobalt, Fenton, jade, Vaseline, and ruby glass.

Shop for fat quarters at **Deborah's Quilt Basket** (941-488-6866), 337 West Venice Ave., where you'll find fine fabrics and quilting supplies.

The Green Butterfly (941-485-6223), 209 W Miami Ave., is brimming with antiques for your dining room, including ruby glass, flatware, pottery, and fine china.

Pick up a special memento of your visit to Venice—a solid gold or silver shark's tooth pendant—at **Heitel Jewelers** (941-488-2720) 347 W Venice Ave. They originally opened in Sarasota in 1903 and showcase creative and unique Venice charms and jewelry.

With numerous dealer booths, the massive **Merchant of Venice** (941-488-3830), 223 W Miami Ave., offers a great selection of gifts and antiques from every genre. Look for vintage toys and games, comics, Mexican pottery, fishing lures, and more.

Step into the past at **Nifty Nic Nacs** (941-488-8666; www.niftynicnacs.com), 203 W Venice Ave., in the historic 1926 Johnson-Schoolcraft Building. It's my kind of antiques store. Dig through lots of cool kitsch from the 1950s, '60s, and '70s and check out all the harvest gold and avocado kitchenware, political buttons, and retro furniture.

The Paper Pad (941-488-8300; www.paperpadofvenice.com), 327 W Venice Ave., isn't just a card and stationary shop—they also have sushi sets, board games and puzzles, pottery, and gourmet gift items.

Much like the shell shops of my youth, **Sea Pleasures & Treasures** (941-488-3510), 255 W Venice Ave., is brimming with seashells from around the world, gifts made from seashells, and beach-related gifts and clothing. It's the place to pick up the specialized scoops for sifting for shark's teeth, and it has a museum display of fossilized shark's teeth found around the area.

Brighten a girlfriend's day with a snazzy handbag from **Venice Island Purses** (941-484-7877), 235 Miami Ave.

I found fun gifts for my nieces and nephews in the back corner of **Venice Stationers** (941-488-6113), 211 W Venice Ave., a shop that's much more than a stationery store. Look here for mementos, knickknacks, office supplies, and books about the area.

PRODUCE STAND

Sarasota
Founded in 1880 by a Civil War veteran, **Albritton Fruit Company** (941-923-2573; www.albrittonfruit.com), 5430 Proctor Rd., can stake a claim as Florida's oldest family-owned business. In addition to citrus, they sell fresh-squeezed, nonpasteurized juices and gift items. They have four additional retail outlets in the region, so don't be surprised to stumble across one in your travels.

✴ Special Events

January: **Sarasota County ArtsDay** (941-365-5118; www.sarasota-arts .org/artsday.cfm), held midmonth, is a community celebration of the arts in Sarasota on the streets of downtown.

March: **Sarasota Comedy Festival** (941-365-1277), held midmonth, is a week of fun and funny seminars, events, performances, and dinners benefiting the United Way of Sarasota County.

Sarasota Film Festival (941-364-6514; www.sarasotafilmfestival.com), held the last week of the month, features more than 25 films, celebrity participants, and fun events, including an outdoor film screening, a gala party, and more.

Sarasota Jazz Festival (941-366-1552; www.jazzclubsarasota.com/festival.php), held during the month, features headline acts and jazz in public places.

April: Top wine makers make this a weekend to remember. The **Florida Wine Festival** (941-952-1109 or 1-800-216-6199; www.floridawinefest.org) brings together vintners to talk trade, but gets the public in the act with seminars, tastings, and a grand auction.

Venice Sharks Tooth Festival (941-412-0402; www.sharkstoothfest.com), first weekend, is a weekend of food, fossils, and fun at the beach near the Venice Pier, with more than one hundred artists showing off their work.

Spring Festival of Sarasota Ballet (941-351-8000), end of the month. A celebration of outstanding artistry and technique, held at the FSU Center for Performing Arts.

June: **Sarasota Music Festival** (941-953-4252; www.sarasotaorchestra.org), most of the month. Started in 1964, this annual three week celebration features more than 40 world-renowned guest artists and a hundred exceptional music students.

October: **St. Armands Art Festival** (941-388-1554), second weekend. More than 175 artists and crafts-people display their original artwork, including pottery, oils, watercolors, ceramic jewelry, and sculpture.

November: **Art Fest—Downtown Venice** (941-484-6722), first weekend. Juried show with 150 booths, food, and entertainment on Venice Avenue West.

CHARLOTTE HARBOR AND
THE GULF ISLANDS

I t is a quaint town of brick streets and century-old bungalows hidden by screens of tropical vegetation, the bright red blooms of hibiscus standing out against lush green foliage. It is a waterfront town, along a vast rippling current in which dolphins play and cormorants dive. Established in 1887, **Punta Gorda** is one of Florida's most charming cities, where historic cottages come in island colors such as mango, avocado, and lavender. As the heart of Charlotte County, it has a vibrant downtown with arts and dining. Nightlife bustles on Marion Avenue. Art is everywhere, especially murals—striking images on downtown historic buildings and even a sea turtle swimming across the side of the Dairy Queen at a prominent intersection at FL 776 and US 41.

Punta Gorda is only one facet of this large county that surrounds Charlotte Harbor, where the Myakka and Peace Rivers meet. Imagine miles of mangrove-lined shoreline dense with the activity of egrets and herons, and vast sandy beaches where plovers and terns race along the sand. Or thousands of acres of pine flatwoods protected from development, where red-cockaded woodpeckers nest, eagles fly, and sandhill cranes gather in the open prairies. This is a birder's paradise, where every little park and preserve yields another find for your life list, from the vast Babcock-Webb Wildlife Management Area to the sandy tip of Stump Pass Beach State Park at Englewood. It's an angler's paradise, too, one of the world's top sport fishing destinations. You'll have a shot at tarpon, snook, redfish, barracuda, cobia, and grouper in the rich estuaries where the rivers meet the Gulf of Mexico. Cast off from the sleepy fishing village of **Placida**, or drop a line off the bridge at El Jobean.

In the early 1900s, developers with big dreams and land schemes moved into the wet prairies surrounding Charlotte Harbor, including Joel Bean, who made an anagram of his name to dub his new community **El Jobean**.

ONE OF THE MANY MURALS IN
DOWNTOWN PUNTA GORDA

Sandra Friend

He wasn't the first. It started with John Milton Murdock, who obtained thousands of acres to resell to farmers and settlers. The new owners quickly discovered the seasonal flooding that is a natural part of southwest Florida ecosystems, and Murdock had to create drainage canals to make the farmland usable, creating the community of **Charlotte Harbor**. Former Florida Governor Albert Gilchrist was a founder of Punta Gorda and lived there until his death; he, too, participated in development of the area, particularly at Boca Grande.

Once the fishing grounds of the Calusa, the barrier islands have stories to tell, including those of pirate treasure. Among the most persistent is the legend of Jose Gasper, born of noble Spanish blood but turned pirate in the early 1800s, cruising the coast of Florida for his prey of Spanish and British ships. Local lore places **Gasparilla Island** as his longtime hideout, and the islands surrounding Boca Grande as the place where he and his brother buried multiple casks and chests of Spanish gold coins. While most of Boca Grande lies in adjoining Lee County (see *The Beaches of Fort Myers Sanibel*), access by road—and a portion of the islands—lies in Charlotte County, along with a string of barrier islands that include **Don Pedro Island**, **Palm Island**, and **Manasota Key** off the coast of **Englewood**.

GUIDANCE Your official source for tourism information is **Charlotte Harbor & the Gulf Islands** (941-743-1900 or 1-800-652-6090; www.charlotteharbortravel.com), 18501 Murdock Cir., Ste. 502, Port Charlotte. For brochures, maps, and reservations, drop in at the **Southwest Florida Welcome Center** (941-639-0007; www.puntagordavisitor.info), 26610 S Jones Loop Rd., Punta Gorda, for information, or stop at their kiosk in Fishermen's Village (see *Selective Shopping*). In addition, the **Punta Gorda Chamber of Commerce** (941-639-3720; www.puntagorda-chamber.com), 252 W. Marion Ave., Ste. 121 has information for getting the most out of a day in Punta Gorda, including walking tour guides. Visiting Boca Grande? Stop at the **Boca Grande Area Chamber of Commerce** (941-964-0568; www.bocagrandechamber.com), 5800 Gasparilla Rd., Ste. A1, next to Boca Grande Resort.

GETTING THERE *By car:* **I-75** and **US 41** provide primary access to the region, with US 17 following the Peace River south from Arcadia to end in Punta Gorda.

By air: **DirectAir** (1-877-432-DIRECT; www.visitdirectair.com) launched commuter service to the **Charlotte County Airport** (941-639-1101 or 1-888-700-2232; www.flypgd.com), 28000 Airport Rd., Punta Gorda, in 2008. The nearest large airports include the **Sarasota International Airport** (see *Sarasota & Her Islands*) and **Southwest Florida International Airport** (see *The Beaches of Fort Myers Sanibel*).

By bus: **Greyhound** (1-800-231-2222; www.greyhound.com), 900 Kings Hwy., has a terminal in Port Charlotte.

By rail: **AMTRAK** (1-800-USA-RAIL), 909 Kings Hwy., connects from the nearest station to Port Charlotte via motor coach.

GETTING AROUND *By car:* **US 41** is the primary artery linking Punta Gorda, Charlotte Harbor, and Port Charlotte. **SR 771** connects Port Charlotte with Placida, where **SR 775** is the north-south route between Boca Grande, Cape Haze, and

Englewood. **SR 776** is the direct route from Port Charlotte to Englewood. There is a toll of at least $5 to cross the bridge to Boca Grande.

By taxi: **Voyager Taxi** (941-629-2810) provides 24-hour taxi service throughout the area, while **Charlotte Shuttles & Airport Transportation, Inc**. (941-255-9117 or 1-888-663-2430; www.charlotteshuttles.com), 2158 Gerard Ct, offers a 24 hour airport shuttle service.

By water taxi: **Pirates Water Taxi** (941-697-5777), 6301 Boca Grande Causeway, provides water transportation to Little Gasparilla Island, Don Pedro State Park, the outer islands, and restaurants from 8:30 AM–5:15 PM, and with advanced notice can operate anytime; $7.50 per person, $15 minimum for a trip.

MEDICAL EMERGENCIES There is a 24-hour emergency room at **Charlotte Regional Medical Center** (941-639-3131; www.charlotteregional.com), 809 E Marion Ave., Punta Gorda, and emergency care available at **Englewood Community Hospital** (941-475-6571; www.englewoodcommunityhospital.com), 700 Medical Blvd., Englewood. In Boca Grande, call the **Boca Grande Health Clinic** (941-964-0099), 280 Park Ave., or 911.

✳ To See

ARCHAEOLOGICAL SITE Peoples of the Safety Harbor and Weedon Island cultures (circa 499 A.D.) resided on islands and ridges near Placida, including **Big Mound Key** in Charlotte Harbor, where graves and a temple mound that rises nearly 23 feet high have been found

ART GALLERIES

Placida
Whimsical fish and turtles decorate walls, ceiling, and windows at **Margaret Albritton Gallery** (941-698-0603; margaretalbrittongallery.com), 13020 Fishery Rd., where it's tough to resist picking up at least one piece of her wildlife art, or a beach knickknack for the home.

CHOCOLATES AT THE SWISS CHOCOLATE EUROPEAN CAFE

Sandra Friend

Punta Gorda
The **Joe Matthis Gallery** (941-639-8488; www.swissconnections.usa), 403 Sullivan St., Ste. 113, honors the work of this distinguished Swiss artist, a graphic designer and muralist whose daughter manages the chocolatier next door. Special thematic exhibitions bring in the work of regional artists as well. Open Mon.–Sat. 10 AM–5 PM, third Thurs. until 8.

At the **Presseller Gallery & Delicatessen** (see *Eating Out*), you can dine among the creations of regional fine artists and digital media artists. The giclees of wildlife artist Robert Binks are among the many pieces of local art featured at the adjacent **Sunart Gallery & Framing** (941-639-3956), 307 Taylor St., where the art glass bowls evoke Chuiluly and wood parquet bowls fascinate with their natural whorls. Both galleries are owned by the Presseller family.

The **Sea Grape Art Gallery** (941-575-1718; www.seagrapegallery.com), 113 W Marion Ave., is a cooperative staffed by nearly 20 local artists. I particularly enjoyed Vicki Glynn's watercolors of the flora and fauna of Charlotte Harbor's coastlines.

At the **Visual Arts Center** (941-639-8810; www.visualartscenter.org), 210 Maud St., you can savor the art on display, browse through an extensive art library, take a workshop, or pick out an original gift from the gift shop. There are four main galleries with 12 shows per year, and more than 3,000 art books, tapes, and DVDs in the library. Classes are offered year-round, but the center does close on weekends during the summer months. In the courtyard you'll see a fountain preserved from Punta Gorda's first hotel. Free; donations appreciated.

The Punta Gorda Gallery Walk (941-743-1900) is held the third Thursday of every month from 5 to 8 PM. Walk (follow the flip-flops painted on the sidewalks) or ride the trolley to enjoy the galleries, shops, and restaurants celebrating the evening with live music and good food.

ATTRACTION Punta Gorda businessman Rick Treworgy has been crazy for classic cars since he got behind the wheel of a Pontiac GTO in 1965. He's brought his collection public at **Muscle Car City** (941-575-5959; www.musclecarcity.net), 3811 Tamiami Trail, taking over a former Wal-Mart to house more than 200 automobiles dating back to the 1920s. Talk about immense: it's a virtual warehouse with rows and rows of sleek driving machines, their well-detailed high-powered engines open for inspection. Each vehicle is immaculate and identified, enabling enthusiasts to gather around and swap memories about their favorite Corvette or GTO. Muscle Car City also includes a 50s-themed diner and a large gift shop with automobile memorabilia, including a few lovingly-restored cars for sale. Open Tues.–Sat. 9 AM–5 PM, $10 admission.

EL JOBEAN POST OFFICE

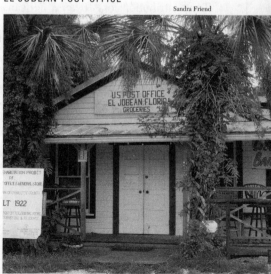

Sandra Friend

HISTORIC SITES

El Jobean
Undergoing restoration, the historic **1922 El Jobean Post Office & General Store** (941-627-3344), 4370 Garden Rd., when open, shows off artifacts from the early days of this planned community, which went bust in 1920. In 1931 the building served as a hotel and housed film crews from MGM. The original wooden railroad bridge over the Myakka River at the end of Garden Road is now the Myakka North Fishing Pier.

Placida

On the grounds of **Grande Tours** (see *Nature Tours*), Capt. Marian Schneider preserved two interesting historic artifacts from the area: the original bridge tender's cottage from the first wooden railroad bridge (now a fishing pier) to Gasparilla Island, and a homesteader's cistern that once sat on her parents' property to accumulate much needed fresh water from rainwater.

Punta Gorda

Stroll the downtown and waterfront streets to see classic Old Florida architecture reflected in homes, cottages, and bungalows, all privately owned. Built in 1903, the **A. C. Freeman House**, also known as the Gilchrist House, was once a mayor's residence. It's the last Queen Anne Victorian house in town and was moved for preservation from Hargreaves Avenue to Retta Esplanade, where it now houses the Punta Gorda Chamber of Commerce (see *Guidance*). The old **First National Bank of Punta Gorda**, built during the 1920s boom, is now the **Turtle Club** (see *Dining Out*) at 133 W Marion Ave. The **Punta Gorda Atlantic Coast Line Depot** (see *Railroadiana*) is one of only six Mediterranean-style railroad depots remaining in the United States.

At **Punta Gorda History Park** (941-639-1887), 501 Shreve St., historic buildings were moved here to avoid demolition. The collection includes the original city jail, a Cuban cigar worker's home, and **Trabue Cottage**, the first land sales and post office in the city.

MUSEUMS

Charlotte Harbor

Overlooking Charlotte Harbor, the **Charlotte County Historical Center** (941-629-7278; www.charlottecountyfl.com/historical), 22959 Bayshore Rd., presents exhibits ranging from prehistory to today on local history topics, as well as regular workshops. The Live Oak Emporium gift shop has educational toys, games, and books. Exhibits are open 10 AM–5 PM Tues.–Fri. and 10 AM–3 PM Sat. Fee.

Punta Gorda

The contributions of African Americans who helped to found Punta Gorda are memorialized in a museum established in 2004 to tell their stories over the past century. The **Blanchard House African American Heritage Museum** (941-575-7518; www.blanchardmuseum.org), 406 Martin Luther King Blvd., includes exhibits on pioneer families, the old Cochran Street Business district, Trabue Woods, and Baker Academy. Housed in a historic cottage, the museum also oversees the Colored Waiting Room exhibit at the **Punta Gorda ACL Depot** (see *Railroadiana*). A gift shop and history library complements the museum's holdings. Open 10 AM–2 PM on Mon., Wed., and Fri.; donation.

It's hard not to be moved by the exhibits at the **Military Heritage & Aviation Museum** (941-575-9002; www.mhaam.org), 1200 W Retta Esplanade B-4, inside Fisherman's Village. More than 20,000 military artifacts donated by veterans are used to interpret military history from the Civil War through Iraqi Freedom, with the bulk of the museum dedicated to World War II and the Vietnam War. There is a small gift shop with emblems and insignia items. Open 10 AM–6 PM Mon.–Sat., noon–5 PM Sun. Free admission, donations appreciated.

RAILROADIANA Built in 1928 to ship fish to northern markets, the **Punta Gorda Atlantic Coast Line Depot**, 1009 Taylor Rd., Punta Gorda, is the only remaining Spanish Mission style depot on the old ACL Railroad. The ticket office contains railroad memorabilia, historic items from the fishing industry, and ephemera from World War II troops who passed through the station. Both the "Colored" and "White" waiting rooms have been restored and contain period exhibits. Access to the station is through the **Punta Gorda History Park** (see *Museums*), which runs periodic tours. An excellent mural depicting the railroad era is across the street.

Although no structure remains from that era, you'll find a historic marker for the **Southernmost Railroad Terminal** in front of the Isles Yacht Club on West Marion Ave., past Fishermen's Village. In 1887, the U.S. Florida Southern Railway's narrow gauge railway ran out past this point on a 4,000-foot dock to connect with steamers of the Morgan Line.

✳ To Do

BICYCLING A paved path connecting communities in the eastern part of the county, the **Cape Haze Pioneer Trail** (941-627-1628), 1688 Placida Rd., starts at SR 771 near Rotunda and works its way for 4.5 miles through the massive circular-shaped planned community to the coast at Cape Haze along the route of the former Charlotte Harbor and Northern Railroad. Plans are to continue the route to Placida to connect to the Boca Grande Trail to Gasparilla Island.

BIRDING Of historic interest to bird lovers, Columbus G. McLeod was an Audubon warden watching over the **Placida rookery** in 1908. Like Guy Bradley, the famed Audubon warden who was shot and killed in the Everglades in 1905 while protecting the rookeries from plume hunters, McLeod vanished while on watch and was presumed murdered. His death further ignited the national furor over the wearing of feathers in hats, shifting public sentiment to protection of our now-common egrets and herons. The wilds of **Charlotte Harbor State Park** (see *Wild Places*), an aquatic preserve encompassing more than 80 miles of mangrove-tangled shoreline, is home to the elusive mangrove cuckoo, which can sometimes be seen at **Ponce de Leon Park** (see *Parks*). For red-cockaded woodpeckers and sandhill cranes, visit the wide open spaces of **Babcock-Webb Wildlife Management Area** (see *Wild Places*). Eagles return to nest every winter at **Cedar Point Environmental Park** (see *Parks*). Virtually all of the public lands bordering Charlotte Harbor will help you add more species to your life list.

BOATING

Boca Grande
Charter boats (with captain and crew) are available from **Boca Boats** (1-888-416-BOAT) at **Boca Grande Resort** (see *Lodgings*) to enjoy the barrier islands along Charlotte County's coastline. Half-day rentals start at $550.

Englewood
Explore Lemon Bay on a skiff from **Bay Breeze Boat Rental** (941-475-0733; www.baybreezeboats.com), 1450 Beach Rd., with rates starting at $140 for a 17-foot Key Largo, or **Beach Road Watersports** (941-475-9099; www.beachroad

watersports.net), 1350 Beach Rd., where skiffs are $90 for a half day and pontoon boats $245 for the whole day. They rent Wave Runners and kayaks as well.

Placida

Gasparilla Marina (941-697-2280 or 1-800-541-4441; www.gasparillamarina .com), 15001 Gasparilla Rd., is one of the largest marinas in the area, with 225 slips, overnight dockage with showers, and a ship's store, large boat storage, and fuel. They rent boats, too, 20–21 foot for $210 half day, $275 full day.

Punta Gorda

Providing easy access to Charlotte Harbor and Pine Island Sound, **Burnt Store Marina** (941-637-0083; www.burntstoremarina.com), Burnt Store Rd., is a favorite for boaters headed to the south end of this region. Dockage runs $1.75 per foot per day, 30 foot minimum.

Holidaze Boat Rental (941-505-8888; www.holidazeboatrental.com), 1200 W Retta Esplanade at Fisherman's Village, offers rentals of power boats, pontoon boats, fishing and sailing skiffs, and Jet Skis at this location near the mouth of the Myakka River. Rentals start at $55 an hour or $165 per half day for a 17.5-foot Cobia.

Board a sunset cruise or nature tour at **Fishermen's Village** (see *Selective Shopping*) with the **King Fisher Fleet** (941-639-0969; www.kingfisherfleet.com), 1200 W Retta Esplanade; advance reservations suggested. Six different trips are offered throughout the week (see *Nature Tours*). As you cruise out into the bay, dolphins frolic in the waves made by the boat's wake. If you're visiting at Christmastime, ask about their special Christmas Light Canal Tours that take you up into residential areas to see the lights from the water.

CRABBING From October 15 through May 15, it's perfectly legal for you to dive offshore in Charlotte County to collect **stone crab claws**—if you can stand the thought of removing them from their owners. The good news is the crabs grow them back, so only take one from each critter. Limits set by the Florida Fish and Wildlife Conservation Commission (www.myfwc.com) are 1 gallon of claws per person (2 gallons per vessel), and all claws must be a minimum of 2¾ inches from elbow to tip, plus you may not take females with eggs. Divers must fly a diver-down flag.

ECOTOURS Sloshing in the shallows of Charlotte Harbor off the shore of **Ponce de Leon Park** (see *Parks*), we had our nets ready and were at attention on our feet, as we walked deeper into the waves. Led by a naturalist from **Charlotte Harbor Environmental Center** (see *Nature Centers*), the wet walk was an experience in learning about the smaller inhabitants of the harbor, caught in our nets and set in a tray for quick examination. From shore, a yellow-crowned night heron kept watch on our activities. This particular interpretive expedition, called a **Shallow Water Wading Trip**, is offered through CHEC on a regular basis to budding marine biologists of all ages, along with many other estuarine and upland tours. Check their Web site for details and reserve in advance: www.checflorida.org; the tours are free.

Enjoy a narrated voyage with **Grande Tours** (941-697-8825; www.grandetours .com), 12575 Placida Rd., Placida, and pick your subject: shelling, dolphins, buried treasure—you name it! Take a cruise, rent a kayak, or book a guided fishing trip—

To see the Florida that Patrick Smith describes in *A Land Remembered,* take a trip back in time at the Babcock Ranch with **Babcock Wilderness Adventures** (1-800-500-5583; www.babcockwilderness.com), 8000 SR 31, Punta Gorda. On a 90-minute ride on a school bus converted into a swamp buggy, you'll tour a portion of the 91,000-acre Crescent B Ranch, a working operation where cowmen still ride the range for days after the herds of up to 7,000 head of cattle. Babies raised here are auctioned off to live on other ranches around the country. Along the route, you'll encounter herds of Cracker cattle, descendents of those brought to Florida by the Spanish in the 1500s, and historic Rouxville, a 1920s lumber town where nearly two hundred people once lived along the railroad in boxcars—the first "mobile home" park in Florida. Keep alert, as your driver will point out wildlife in the pine woods and through Telegraph Cypress Swamp, where herds of wild hogs roam and alligators sun on the banks of the creeks at the old railroad trestle. A stop in the swamp lets you experience the ancient cypresses along a boardwalk and meet resident Florida panthers in a large enclosure. When you return to the registration and gift shop area, walk through a cabin used in the movie *Just Cause* that now serves as a small museum recounting how R. V. Babcock came from Pittsburgh in 1914 and purchased hundreds of thousands of acres to expand his timber business.

these knowledgeable natives can do it all. Their guided paddling tours are especially popular, given how easy it is to get lost in the mangrove maze, and they offer a narrated boat tour/shuttle to Don Pedro Island State Park daily at 10 AM, returning at 3 PM, for $21. Reservations are recommended.

King Fisher Fleet (see *Boating*) offers six different tours during the course of the week, including Out Island Day Cruises to Cabbage Key and Cayo Costa State Park, where dolphin sightings are virtually guaranteed. Two of their tours are a custom fit if you're looking for a narrated nature cruise. Sailing on Friday at 10 AM, the **Half Day Harbor Cruise** explores the shoreline of Charlotte Harbor State Park, perfect for birding; $21.95 adults, half price ages 3–11. On Wednesday, the Half **Day Peace River Nature Cruise** heads upriver into a slice of Old Florida, where grand live oaks and cabbage palms crowd the shores and alligators rest in the shallows; $21.95 adults, half price

CHEC WADING TOUR IN CHARLOTTE HARBOR

Sandra Friend

KAYAKING THE PEACE RIVER

ages 3–11. A 1.5-hour dolphin-watching afternoon tour is only $13.95 adults, half price children. Reservations are recommended.

FAMILY ACTIVITIES ♂ Along Charlotte Harbor, **Fish Cove Miniature Golf** (941-627-5393; www.coral caygolf.com/fishcove), 4949 Tamiami Trail, isn't just about the putt. It provides the kids some fun and adults an opportunity to unwind, with a playground on- site and great views of the harbor. Tropical plantings accent the mini golf faux cliffs and water hazards. At Port Charlotte, take the kids to **Sun Flea Market & Kidstar** (941-255-3532), 18505 Paulson Dr., with its slate of old-fashioned carnival rides, including a Ferris wheel. Of course, there's the flea market to browse, too.

FISHING If tarpon's your fish, you've found the holy land. For more than a century, anglers have descended on Charlotte Harbor as one of the world's top sportfishing destinations. You'll have a shot at tarpon, snook, redfish, barracuda, cobia, and grouper in the rich waters where the rivers meet the Gulf. Numerous private guides are registered locally; your best bet is to check at one of the marinas (see *Boating*). Two captains I know personally and will recommend for your outing is **Captain Van Hubbard/Let's Go Fishin', Inc.** (941-740-4665; www.captvan .com) and **Captain Ralph Allen** of the King Fisher Fleet (see *Boating*). Many fishing charters depart from Fishermen's Village (see *Selective Shopping*) in Punta Gorda, while others center around Placida.

GOLF Endless meandering waterways mark the course at **Deep Creek Golf Club** (941-625-6911; www.deepcreekgolf.com), 1260 San Cristoball Ave., a par 70 course designed by Mark McCumber. **Kings Gate Golf Club** (941-625-7615; www.kingsgategolf.com), 24000 Rampart Blvd., is a tough par 60 executive golf course. And a top pick by *Golf Digest*, the **Riverwood Golf Club** (941-764-6661; www.riverwoodgc.com), 4100 Riverwood Dr., offers true challenges created by its setting in a lush natural landscape of pines and oaks.

HIKING Explore wilderness around Charlotte Harbor at **Charlotte Harbor State Park** (see *Wild Places*), where there are three trailheads providing access to day hikes. Between Rotunda and Placida, the **Catfish Creek Trailhead** offers access to pine flatwoods and marshes and is best hiked using a GPS. The 1.8-mile **Old Datsun Trail** off Burnt Store Road circles a large flatwoods pond and is easy to follow. Along Pine Island Road (in neighboring Lee County), the **Little Pine Island High Marsh Trail** is a 2-mile loop through marl mud flats (often mucky) and mangrove forests.

Charlotte Harbor Environmental Center manages both **Cedar Point Environmental Park** at Cape Haze and **Alligator Creek Preserve** at Punta Gorda (see *Nature Centers*), both of which have excellent networks of hiking trails that are easy to follow and family-friendly. A 1-mile nature trail on the land side at **Don Pedro Island State Park** (see *Beaches*) loops through pine flatwoods and along the sometimes-wet mangrove fringe before leading you down to the ferryboat dock. **Babcock-Webb Wildlife Management** Area (see *Wild Places*) has a 1-mile trail through prime red-cockaded woodpecker habitat, best visited at dawn. On **Babcock Ranch,** which is now in state stewardship, there are two new places to hike. From its trailhead on CR 74, there are two loops to the **Footprints Trail**, 2 miles or 4.7 miles. The trail leads you into pine flatwoods and around cypress domes, through hardwood hammocks and across open prairies. You can now also hike at **Babcock Wilderness Adventures** (see *Nature Tours*), part of the attraction at the ranch.

PADDLING Grande Tours (see *Nature Tours*) rents kayaks and leads guided kayaking trips, including overnight trips with camping on some of the region's unspoiled barrier islands and on the new **Charlotte County Blueway Trail** (see *Blueway*). Launch your own expedition from **Ponce de Leon Park** (see *Parks*) or **Sunrise Park** along Alligator Bay; access via Edgewater Drive in Port Charlotte.

RACING At the **Charlotte County Speedway** (941-575-7223; www.charlotte countyspeedway.net), 8655 Piper Rd., Punta Gorda, experience Saturday-night racing on the ⅜-mile figure-eight asphalt track. Open Labor Day through June, with numerous special events.

SAILING Learn to sail in the broad expanse of Charlotte Harbor with the **International Sailing School** (1-800-824-5040; www.intlsailsch.com) based at Fisherman's Village, 1200 W Retta Esplanade, Punta Gorda, or with & **B&D Sailing** (941-627-1727; www.bdsailing.com), 19246 Palmdale Ct., Port Charlotte.

SCUBA Hit the depths with professional assistance from **DepthFinders Dive Center** (941-766-7565; www.DepthFinders.com), 1225 Tamiami Trail, or **Fantasea Scuba** (941-627-3888; www.fantaseascuba.com), 3781 Tamiami Trail, both in Port Charlotte.

SHELLING Seashells along the sandy strands of the barrier islands can grow to impressive sizes—but you'll have to be the early bird after high tide recedes to claim your treasure. Look for the best shells where the tides sweep around curved land at the tip of **Stump Pass Beach State Park** (see *Beaches*).

TROLLEY TOURS On the second and fourth Tuesday of each month, the Punta Gorda Chamber of Commerce (see *Guidance*) runs tours to get you familiar with the businesses of Punta Gorda. The tours start at Fisherman's Village at 10 AM on the second Tuesday, 3 PM on the fourth Tuesday. Call ahead for reservations.

WILDLIFE REHAB ✿ Volunteers look after injured birds and small mammals at the **Peace River Wildlife Center** (941-637-3830; www.peaceriverwildlifecenter .com), 3400 W Marion Ave., Punta Gorda, permanent home to nearly one hundred raptors, herons, and songbirds. Animals brought here go through triage in a "birds only" emergency room, stabilization in cages out of public view, and then a flight cage or home care until they are able to be returned to the wild. Many of the permanent residents are pelicans injured by discarded monofilament fishing line, and they have their own big pool in the back, where you can watch them gobble down fish at feeding time. Guided tours are given on a regular basis, or you can walk through at your own pace. Donations greatly appreciated, as this has been a fully nonprofit labor of love for more than a decade, with local veterinarians donating their time and equipment to care for injured wildlife.

✳ Green Space
BEACHES

Cape Haze
Beachgoers seeking beachfront solitude in Charlotte County will find it at **Don Pedro Island State Park** (941-964-0375; www.floridastateparks.org/donpedro island), a state-owned island accessible only by private boat or water taxi (see *Getting Around*) to Knight Island. The land base along SR 776 has a nice nature trail loop through a tall stand of pines and is a launch point for kayaking to the island.

Englewood
Where North Beach Road meets Gulf Boulevard, **Chadwick Park** (941-473-1018), 2100 N Beach Rd., is an enormous county beachfront park with ample parking, beach crossovers, and restaurants across the street. However, the best beach on the island is at its south end, where the highway ends. **Stump Pass Beach State Park** (941-964-0375; www.floridastateparks.org/stumppass), 900 Gulf Blvd., is several miles of a sliver of sand topped with maritime forest. A kayak launch lets you paddle up the bay side and view numerous osprey nests on the smaller surrounding keys. Parking can be tough on weekends. Fee.

DON PEDRO ISLAND

www.CharlotteHarborTravel.com

Punta Gorda
At **Ponce de Leon Park** (see *Parks*), Rotary Beach is the closest stretch of sand to town. It's a gathering place for locals to watch the sunset. Bring your lawn chair!

BLUEWAY Trace the ancient trails of the Calusa along the **Charlotte County Blueway Trail** (www.charlotte countyfl.com/parks/blueway.asp), a key part of the Florida Saltwater Circum-navigational Trail.

NATURE CENTERS Charlotte Harbor Environmental Center (www .checflorida.org) manages two popular nature centers and preserves along the coast. Protecting 115 pristine acres along an undeveloped coastline on Lemon Bay, **Cedar Point Environmental Park** (941-475-0769), 2300 Placida Rd., Engle-wood, offers a quiet place to walk the trails and become familiar with natural habi-tats that have vanished due to development in the area. Start at the visitor's reception center for a cinematic overview and information to take with you out in the field. Roam the seven marked trails to explore coastal pine flatwoods, coastal scrub, mangrove forests, and more. Enjoy the picnic area and playground near the front entrance, and launch your kayak into Oyster Creek for exploration of the pre-serve by water. Open sunrise to sunset, except when posted to protect eagle nest-ing; visitors center open 8:30 AM–4:30 PM Mon.–Fri. Just south of Punta Gorda, **Alligator Creek Preserve** (941-575-5435), 10941 Burnt Store Rd., provides access to more than 3,000 acres of Charlotte Harbor Preserve State Park, on which CHEC maintains their administrative office and classroom facilities. Several miles of trails and boardwalks run through a variety of ecosystems, from pine flatwoods to open prairies, needlerush marshes, and mangrove-lined lakes. Visitors center open 9 AM–3 PM Mon.–Sat., 11 AM–3 PM Sun.

PARKS Explore Punta Gorda's waterfront with a walk along the Retta Esplanade, starting at **Gilchrist Park**. It's the beginning of a string of parks along Charlotte Harbor at Old Punta Gorda Point. Follow the walkway toward Fishermen's Village through Shreve Park and Pittman Park, each protecting a slender slice of water-front dense with sea grapes and mangroves.

Deep in a mangrove forest, **Ponce de Leon Park** (941-575-3324), 4000 W Mari-on Ave., commemorates the Spanish explorer's reach to these shores with a small memorial and statuettes. De Leon died after he was wounded by Calusa warriors at nearby Pine Island Sound. The park offers a small beach, boat ramp, a board-walk through the mangroves, and restrooms and is home to the **Peace River Wildlife Center** (see *Wildlife Rehab*). It's a popular spot to pull up a camp chair and watch the sunset. Open dawn–dark daily. Free.

GILCHRIST PARK

Sandra Friend

WILD PLACES Adjacent to **Babcock Ranch** (see *Nature Tours*), the **Babcock-Webb Wildlife Management Area** (941-575-5768; www.myfwc.com/recreation/babcock _webb), 29200 Tuckers Grade, covers more than 79,000 acres of pine flat-woods, prairie, wetlands, and oak ham-mocks to the east of Punta Gorda on Tuckers Grade. There are 37 miles of unimproved roads throughout the pre-serve, open to hiking, biking, and horseback riding, and a short hiking loop through a red-cockaded wood-pecker colony. Fall brings in hunters from all over the region as they seek deer and wild hogs. But perhaps the most popular activity on the preserve is fishing at 395-acre Webb Lake, which is stocked with largemouth bass, bluegill, freshwater snook, and many other species for catch-and-release. Fee.

Stretching across two counties to protect more than 80 miles of mangrove coast-line and islands, **Charlotte Harbor State Park** (941-575-5861; www.florida stateparks.org/charlotteharbor), 12301 Burnt Store Rd. (CR 765), rings the harbor, preserving key habitat for bird rookeries and fish nurseries. While most of the park is an extremely remote wilderness area accessible only by kayak, there are two pri-mary access points for exploration on foot: the Old Datsun Trail along Burnt Store Road, 1 mile south of CHEC Alligator Creek (see *Nature Centers*), and the Cat-fish Creek Trailhead on the east side of CR 771, 1.5 miles north of Placida. Trails are seasonally wet and muddy.

✻ Lodging

BED & BREAKFASTS

Port Charlotte 33948

&. At **Tropical Paradise Bed & Breakfast** (941-624-4533; www .tropicalparadisebb.com), 19227 Moore Haven Ct., Joanne and Clift McMahon will treat you like part of the family. Choose from the Hibiscus Room ($85–105), a cheery Caribbean-themed bedroom with adjoining pri-vate bath, or the sumptuous Island Suite ($95–125), with hand-carved Honduran furnishings, en suite bath with whirlpool tub, and a private exit to the pool area, which overlooks a sce-nic waterway. Kayak or fish or bring your own boat and dock it—with direct access to Charlotte Harbor and right along the **Charlotte County Blue-way** (see *Blueway*), the McMahons enjoy the live-aboard cruiser life, and they offer discounts to MTOA (Marine Trade Owners Association) members.

⁰↑⁰ For rooms with pizzazz, check into the **Upper Room Bed and Break-fast** (941-625-0695; www.upperroom bedandbreakfast.com), 21010 Midway Blvd., a quiet haven surrounded by a residential community and churches. Five spacious rooms ($70–149), each lushly decorated, including the Princess Suite with its own dining area, cater to business travelers and those looking to refresh the spirit.

Punta Gorda 33982

Talk about a special experience. **The Cypress Lodge at Babcock Ranch** (941-628-6658; www.babcockwilder ness.com/lodge.htm), 8000 SR 31, is a slice of Florida history you won't soon forget. Surrounded by 92,000 acres of ranchland and wilderness, in the mid-dle of the 10,000 acre Telegraph Swamp, the lodge was once a hunting retreat for Fred Babcock, founder of the ranch, and you'll see that legacy reflected in the decor. Perched over a creek where alligators cruise the depths and wood storks sit in the trees, it's an intimate immersion in nature. The lodge is rented as a package, com-plete with the services of Casey Bruni, resident chef and manager, who'll see to your needs—whether a girlfriends getaway or a corporate retreat. Rates are negotiated depending on the activi-ties, meals, and number of guests involved.

CAMPGROUNDS

Port Charlotte 33953

A massive campground en route to the beach, **Harbor Lakes RV Resort Encore SuperPark** (1-800-468-5022; www.rvonthego.com/Harbor-Lakes-RV -Resort.html), 3737 El Jobean Rd., offers a vast array of activities and guest services—enough that most of the folks each winter are here for the season. Overnight guests welcome ($32–40): 30 amp service on back-in sites, or tent sites with no hookups.

Punta Gorda 33955

🐾 ⚑ Tucked away in the woods off US 41 on the way to Fort Myers, **Sun-N-Shade Campground** (941-639-5388; www.sunnshade.com), 14880 Tamiami Trail, provides a serene getaway for you and your RV with amenities such as a clubhouse, heated pool, shuffleboard, horseshoes, and a nature trail. Electric hookup and dump station; $30–35 per night, $180–240 per week.

HOTELS, MOTELS, AND RESORTS

Cape Haze 33946

You're whisked into another world at **Palm Island Resort** (941-697-4800 or 1-800-824-5412; www.palmisland.com), 7092 Placida Rd.—namely, acres upon acres of an offshore island to explore. Bound to the mainland by a ferry service with prices high enough to discourage gawkers, Palm Island lies between Manasota Key and Little Gasparilla Island, and it was developed in the early 1980s while taking into careful account the natural habitats, especially the mangrove fringe and tidal flats. It's a great destination for families looking for a relaxing week on an unspoiled beach, with miles of tidal flats to walk. With the exception of the Harborside Villas, all units face the Gulf and sit behind the dune line. The fully equipped units range from one to three bedrooms (seasonal rates of $140–550 daily, $915–4,505 weekly) and include several free rides on the car ferry, depending on your length of stay. Once you park your car, transportation is limited to foot traffic and golf carts. The resort employs naturalist and native plant expert Al Squires

to lead interpretive walks, provide narration on nature cruises, run a weekly series of nature talks at the clubhouse, and to keep an eye on the unique species found here, such as the least terns nesting along the beach. Amenities include four heated swimming pools and hot tubs, tennis courts and a tennis pro on staff, a nature center at the clubhouse, playgrounds, a recreation center, and rental of bicycles, golf carts, and all types of water sports items, including canoes and kayaks. Leave the kids at the Island Kids club to have fun doing crafts with Redbeard while you soak in the sun. A full-service marina makes this a great stop for boaters, with 90 wet slips for dockage plus 30 slips with water and electric for craft under 30 feet. To dine, guests can walk to the casual Rum Bay Restaurant; have pizza, hot dogs, and ice cream at Coconuts; or take a free passenger ferry to Johnny Leverock's Seafood House on the other side of the channel, which has a sports bar.

Englewood 34223

🐚 **Englewood Beach & Yacht Club** (1-800-382-9757; www.vacationfla.com/ebyc.htm), 1815 Gulf Blvd., caught my eye as I drove down to the end of Manasota Key—lots of families frolicking around the pool, and a neatly kept common area. Units come in one, two, or three bedrooms and range from $660–950 per week.

🐚 It's how a Florida beach vacation used to be—**Weston's Resort** (941-474-3431; www.westonsresort.com), 985 Gulf Blvd., is a family-friendly property at the south end of Manasota Key, adjacent to miles of unspoiled sand at **Stump Pass Beach State Park** (see *Beaches*), with pools, dockage, fishing guides, and plenty of waterfront views. They feature efficiency rooms ($100–133) and suites up to three bedrooms ($130–230).

Port Charlotte 33980

ℹ Cozy 1940s rooms await you at the **Banana Bay Waterfront Motel** (941-743-4441; www.bananabaymotel.com), 23285 Bayshore Blvd., a perennial regional favorite. It's a Florida classic, with a little palm-lined sand beach on Charlotte Harbor, a pool overlooking the water, and tropical plantings throughout. Enjoy standard motel rooms and efficiencies, some with waterfront views ($49–119).

Punta Gorda 33950

♿ 🐾 ℹ Downtown has a new kid on the block—the **Wyvern Hotel** (941-639-7700; www.thewyvernhotel.com), 101 E Retta Esplanade. This upscale addition to the business district scores big points as one of the most luxurious yet intimate hotels I've reviewed in Florida. With a Spanish-influenced restaurant, **Lulu,** on the first floor and a busy bar adjoining the rooftop pool, they'll tempt you to stay and not walk a block to the downtown restaurant district. I appreciated the large and elegant bath with tub and shower, the free Wi-Fi, and free parking, but the crown jewel? The bed. My husband said he's never had a better night's sleep. Comfy and fluffy in all the right places, it was a bed that was just plain hard to get out of in the morning—it was that good. Rates $159–419.

✳ Where to Eat

DINING OUT

Punta Gorda

For a culinary adventure, The **Downtown Hookah Lounge** (941-639-0004), 307 E. Marion Ave., plunges you into the feel of a Middle-Eastern souk, with decor and music to set the tone. The restaurant is largely outdoors, since one of the prime draws (no pun intended) are the hookah pipes. Flavored tobacco is drawn through water and inhaled for effect: and we're talking flavors like sour apple and bubble gum. Not my cup of tea, but certainly popular. The kebabs are outstanding. That's the focus of the Lebanese menu found here: chunks of meat and vegetables seasoned, skewered, and roasted. The portions are massive and come with seasoned rice. Kebabs $9–20, mazzeh $3–9, open evenings.

With big picture windows all around, **Jack's** (941-637-8800; www.jackspunta gorda.com), 201 W Marion Ave., is the place to see and be seen downtown. The bar and widescreen televisions draw a sports crowd, but the feel is more bistro, especially with creative twists like coconut grouper fingers, turkey artichoke panini, and Bahamian chicken. If you're more a meat-and-potatoes eater, never fear: they serve up hearty burgers and pizza, too, and offer daily "signature select" lunch options. Sandwiches and salads, $8–10. Food as art: that's **The Perfect Caper** (941-505-9009; www.theperfectcaper .com), 121 E Marion Ave., where each appetizer, entrée, and dessert is its own perfect masterpiece. The kitchen is a stage, the restaurant a theater, the presentation creative. Borrowing heavily from Asian traditions, the fusion preparations are made with the freshest of ingredients, most flown in the same day. Waitstaff slips out of the shadows to exchange dishes and freshen water. Served atop mashed potatoes surrounded by a sea of butter sauce and asparagus, my horseradish-crusted flounder had a perfect texture and just the right zing. Desserts are made fresh daily and include indulgences such as chocolate sorbet and Grand Marnier mousse. Perfection has its price: You will drop a bundle here. Dinner for one (sans alcohol) ran $54 plus tip. Lunch prices fit a trimmer budget. Live jazz Thursday through Saturday in the lounge. Reservations recommended.

Englewood

For fresh seafood head to **Barnacle Bill's** (941-697-0711), 2901 Placida Rd., where they offer up broasted oysters (shuck 'em yourself!) in-season, grouper and shrimp prepared several different ways, and crab salad. Try their famous hamburgers, too. I'll avoid the liverwurst, but I can't say I've ever seen it on a menu before—my father will be pleased. Lunch and dinner, $5–14.

The name tempted me every time I passed, so I finally had to stop at **The Egg and I** (941-475-6252), 2555 Placida Rd., and you guessed it—worth the stop! Hearty breakfast offerings ($2–6) include eggs Benedict, creamed chipped beef, and *abelskiver,* Danish pancake dumplings. Of course you can get eggs and grits, omelets, and dozens of interesting sides. Open daily for breakfast and lunch.

Placida

With its own fish market and a fleet of fishing boats docked outside, **The Fishery Restaurant** (941-697-2451; www .sunstate.com/fishery), 13000 Fishery Rd., is a no-frills setting with just plain good seafood and a great view of Gasparilla Sound. Their specialties include Grouper Grande, pan sautéed and lightly crusted, and Gaspar Snapper Marsala, lightly sautéed with mushrooms and wine; entrées from $13, baskets from $9. Open daily 11:30 AM–9 PM.

Port Charlotte

Like a trattoria in Napoli, **Donato's Italian Restaurant** (941-764-1600), 1900 S Tamiami Trail, offers up the ambiance of the Old Country rather than the New York feel of most Italian places. Relax with the family and savor freshly made pasta, tasty soups, and soft, warm bread. I suggest the spicy pasta puttenesca, or delicious sausage parmigiana; entrées run $12 and up,

with nightly specials. It's classy enough to qualify as fine dining, but no pretensions here—the waitstaff will make you feel at home.

The parking lot is frequently full at **La Romana Café & Italian Grill** (941-629-0404), 3591 Tamiami Trail, recommended for their great pizza and a broad variety of Italian entrées, including shrimp scampi, chicken piccata, and eggplant rollatini.

Olympia Restaurant (941-255-3440), 3245 Tamiami Trail, serves traditional Greek favorites such as gyros, souvlaki, leg of lamb, and moussaka, as well as an eclectic variety of non-Greek food, from cheese omelets and beef liver to chicken à la king and crab cakes. Daily early-bird specials served 3 PM–5 PM.

Whiskey Creek Steakhouse (941-766-0045; www.whiskeycreek.com), 2746 Tamiami Trail, offers mouthwatering steak and burgers from prime beef raised in the Midwest, all seared over an aromatic open wood fire. Choose from entrées ($10 and up) such as bacon-wrapped filet mignon; loaded chicken with hickory-cured bacon, sautéed mushrooms, and melted cheese; or their signature pulled pork barbecue.

Punta Gorda

For authentic Irish food and grog, visit **The Celtic Ray** (941-505-9219; www .celticray.com), 145 E Marion Ave., a happening place every evening. It's in the oldest continually operating building in Punta Gorda, built in 1910. In addition to fine lagers, stouts, ales, and bitters on draught, they serve inexpensive classic pub fare such as bangers, chicken curry, shepherd's pie, and Cornish pasty, all with sides of Irish soda bread. Open daily, food served until 10 PM, live music Wed. night.

Fire it up at **Dean's Tex-Mex Cantina** (941-575-6100), 130 Tamiami Trail, with sizzling fajitas, enchiladas, and chile rellenos. A local favorite for nearly 30 years, they appeal to the milder palate, too, with ribs and crispy chicken, steaks and burgers served "North of the Border." Entrées from $9.

For a delectable breakfast, pop in at **Elena's South Restaurant** (941-575-1888), 615 Cross St. # 1111, where the full range of menu starts at one egg and hashbrowns and slides up to London broil and eggs. I'm a big believer in a hearty breakfast, and I didn't go away hungry here. It was tough to choose between stuffed or raisin French toast, crepes, or the long, long list of omelettes, but I finally settled on the most decadent French toast I've had yet, with sour cream and cottage cheese filling. Open 7 AM–8 PM.

🐚 For fresh, local wild-caught crab, **Peace River Seafood** (941-505-8440), 5337 Duncan Rd., a funky little shack along US 17 north of Punta Gorda, will have you wishing you could eat here every evening. It's an unpretentious place, an old Cracker house with a talkative parrot on the porch, dollar bills stapled on the walls, and a nautical theme like you'd expect in a seafood house. But the menu will wow you. It's all fresh local catch, direct from the crabbers—and they have a fish market so you can take some home. Every evening there's a special seafood soup or stew, and entrées range from $10–35. If you don't like seafood, go somewhere else and save the space for us! Open Tues.–Sat., closes 8 PM.

Choose from the masters at **Presseller Gallery & Delicatessen** (941-639-7776; www.pressellergallery.com), 213 W Olympia Ave., a unique and delightful meld of food and art. Dally with a Dalí (Prosciutto ham and manchego cheese on an appropriately crusty baguette) or savor a Renoir (Norwegian smoked salmon, goat cheese, onions, and tomatoes on a croissant); $5–9. Dine amid the creations of regional artists, or enjoy your meal outdoors. Open Mon.–Sat. 7 AM–3 PM, Thurs. 7 AM–8 PM with live entertainment.

Great for a hearty meal, the **River City Grill** (941-639-9080), 131 W Marion Ave., satisfies both meat and potato tastes and those desiring something more—and living in one of those mixed marriages, I know what a find this is. Let your meat lover salivate over the black angus burger or Sunday pot roast while you dabble in chile-rubbed ahi or roti chicken potpie. Entrées $15 and up; lunches $7–10.

COFFEE SHOPS AND ICE CREAM

Tucked away down a side alley, **Café Ruelle** (941-575-3553) 117 W Marion Ave., is a quiet coffee house and wine bar with tasty desserts.

In a 1910 building, **Cubby's Homemade Ice Cream & Deli** (941-637-9600), 264 W Marion Ave., puts a fresh spin on all their creations. Sure, you could pick up a BLT wrap or fresh spinach salad at lunchtime ($4–8), but with all those flavors of homemade ice cream in front of you, shouldn't you eat dessert first?

Indulge your senses at the **Swiss Chocolate European Café** (941-639-9484; www.swissconnection.usa), 403 Sullivan St., Ste. 112, where the fine designer truffles are presented on a small tray with a doily. I couldn't resist trying Florida orange and cinnamon roll; there are 28 flavors to choose from. Sugar-free cookies, candy, and biscotti complement the freshly ground coffee. Open Mon.–Sat. 10 AM–5 PM.

✳ Selective Shopping

Englewood

Boutiques, antiques, and eateries define the shopping district dubbed **Olde Englewood Village** (941-473-8782; www.oldeenglewood.com) on Dearborn St., the heart of the old city on Lemon Bay. The city spans two counties; see *Sarasota and Her Islands* for shopping details.

Placida

In addition to the **Margaret Albritton Gallery** (see *Art Galleries*), Placida is home to a cute village of gaily painted beach bungalows that house a variety of artsy shops, including **Hatch Limited Artistry & Collectibles** and the **Placida Cove Gift Shop**. Most shops open at noon.

Punta Gorda

In downtown Punta Gorda, the core shopping district includes Marion and Olympia Avenues west of US 41 and Sullivan Street, off Olympia. Wander the streets and you'll find some tempting shops! Here's a few.

At **Pomegranate & Fig** (941-205-2333), 117 W Marion Ave., shop for funky home décor, including pop art pieces and Christmas ornaments.

Sassy So Sausalito (941-575-6767), 308 Sullivan St., showcases snazzy women's wear. In the same complex, **Home Gallery Pottery & Gifts** has an eclectic mix of garden urns, resort wear, local art, and overstock kitchenware.

Take a peek at tropical resort wear at **Tiki's Clothing** (941-639-4310), 105 Marion Ave., where Brighton and Tommy Bahama beckon the ladies to get casual.

A massive complex of shops, restaurants, and housing, **Fishermen's Village** (1-800-639-0020; www.fishville.com), 1200 W Retta Esplanade, is a destination in itself. There are dozens of shops to explore, but some simply drew me right in. Buy your nautically themed Christmas ornaments at **Christmas by the Sea**, part of a larger gift shop, the **Sand Pebble**. I found great Christmas presents at **Laff Out Loud**, a nostalgia shop with games and toys appealing to my generation. **Hooked on Books** offers used and new books in an open bistro-style space, with a nice selection of mysteries and children's stories. **Pirates Ketch** has spiffy nautical home décor, including timepieces, wall art, and life-sized carved wading birds like herons and spoonbills. Don't forget a stop for ice cream at **Flamingo Yogurt**!

PRODUCE STANDS, FARMER'S MARKETS, SEAFOOD MARKETS, AND U-PICK Charlotte County Citrus (941-639-4584), 28900 Bermont Rd. (CR 74), is a working family citrus grove with a fruit stand, and they will ship your citrus home. And for more than 40 years, the folks at **Desoto Groves** (941-625-2737; www.desotogroves.com), 1750 Tamiami Trail, have been picking and packing citrus, and they won't let a little thing like hurricanes knock them down. Stop in and visit one of their local outlets for oranges, grapefruit, and more.

At **The Fishery** (see *Eating Out*), load up on fish fresh from the fleet that sails from Placida at adjacent **Miss Cindy's Placida Fish Market** (941-697-4930).

Every Saturday, the **Punta Gorda Farmers Market** is in full swing in front of the historic courthouse on Taylor Road, 8 AM–1 PM.

On Wednesdays, stop by Fishermen's Village for the **Worden Farm Greenmarket** (www.wordenfarm.com/farmersmarkets.html), in the center court. Pick up artisan breads and cheeses, fresh flowers and herbs, seafood from local waters, and organic fruits and vegetables.

✳ Entertainment

FINE ARTS With performances by traveling troupes and local groups, the **Charlotte Performing Arts Center** (941-637-0459), 701 Carmalita St., is the place where the play is just one of the things going on. Now more than 20 years running, the **Charlotte Chorale** (941-204-0033) presents concerts December through April. A community tradition since 1955, the **Charlotte Players Community Theater** (941-255-1022) present five plays during their season, October through May, and the **Charlotte Symphony Orchestra** (941-625-5996; www .charlottesymphony.com) performs November through April each season, with a holiday pops concert each Christmas. Check the Web site for schedules and tickets.

✳ Special Events

January: Held annually since 2000, the **Charlotte Harbor Nature Festival** (239-995-1777; www.chnep.org), at the Charlotte County Sports Park, Port Charlotte, runs the last Saturday of the month and includes environmental displays, live music, children's activities, wagon rides, and guided walks into the adjacent Tippecanoe Environmental Park.

February: **Charlotte County Fair** (941-629-4252), 2333 El Jobean Rd., Port Charlotte. Held the last week of the month, this old-fashioned county fair has food, crafts, enter-tainment, rides, and a petting zoo and features daily shows and major musical entertainers. Fee.

Florida Frontier Days (941-629-7278; www.charlottecountyfl.com/Historical/ FloridaFrontierDays), Bay Shore Live Oaks Park, 22967 Bayshore Rd., Charlotte Harbor, held the second weekend of the month, celebrates regional history with living-history demonstrations, artisans, old-fashioned games, storytelling, and classic Florida food.

Taking art to the streets, the **Plein Aire Art Festival** in downtown Punta Gorda encourages artists who paint in "open air" to capture city scenes and showcase their finished works at a gala cocktail reception.

March: Attracting seafood lovers from all over, the **Placida Rotary Seafood Festival** (941-697-2271) has fun events such as face painting, crab races, antique swap and sell, craftspeople—and, of course, lots of seafood!

For nearly 30 years, the **Florida International Air Show** (941-575-9007; www.floridaairshow.com), Charlotte County Airport, Punta Gorda, has been a destination for aficionados of vintage and military aircraft. Enjoy exhibits, precision-flying teams, stunt pilots, and evening pyrotechnics.

April: **Punta Gorda Block Party** (941-639-3200; www.puntagordablock party.com), held midmonth, brings in top music acts on four stages, vendors and craftspeople with booths lining downtown streets, and festivities all evening.

December: Unique to this region and its many waterways are the **Lighted Boat Parades** that occur just before Christmas in Englewood (941-475-6882) and on the Peace River (941-639-3720). If you haven't seen one, it's quite a delight. Top viewing spots are at Fisherman's Village, Edgewater Lake in Charlotte Harbor, and along the US 41 bridges. Download a map of the route from the Punta Gorda Chamber of Commerce (see *Guidance*) to make your plans.

THE BEACHES OF FORT MYERS AND SANIBEL ISLAND

LEE COUNTY

It's tropical. It's enticing. Royal palms line the boulevards, sandal-clad Jimmy Buffet fans share the bars with yachtsmen and golfers, and the sea glimmers green against soft white sands. Hundreds of small islands dot the bays and sounds, awaiting exploration by a sea kayak, a fishing boat, or a quiet skiff. Layers of history lie beneath the shimmering sands and mangrove thickets of these Gulf Coast islands.

In A.D. 100, the Calusa established a city on Mound Key in Estero Bay. Spanish explorer Ponce de Leon met his match in 1521, receiving a mortal wound from a Calusa warrior in Pine Island Sound. Swashbuckling José Gaspar took over **Captiva Island**, raiding passing galleons on his way to Tampa Bay. From **Bokeelia** to **Bonita Springs**, Florida's pioneers plied the waters, setting up fishing camps, vegetable farms, and banana and coconut plantations, with agriculture still a major force on **Pine Island**. During the Seminole Wars, the small fortress of Fort Myers provided safe harbor to pioneers settling Florida's frontier. With millions of acres of open range along the Caloosahatchee River, ranchers such as Jacob Summerlin made fortunes by driving their cattle down to Punta Rassa, where the captains of Spanish galleons would pay them in gold. In 1861 Summerlin enlisted in the Confederate army as a Commissary Sergeant and was appointed to oversee northbound cattle drives to ensure a steady supply of beef to soldiers in Georgia. When the Union army occupied Fort Myers in 1865, two hundred Confederate soldiers marched south from Tampa in an attempt to take the fort back and stop raids on their cattle drives. The resulting four-hour skirmish was the southernmost engagement of the Civil War. The fort itself vanished as settlers poured into the area, eager to establish land grant claims during Reconstruction. Torn down piece by piece, the boards of the fort ended up in new downtown homes and shops.

Incorporated in 1886, the city of **Fort Myers** became a winter destination for tourists hopping steamships down the Gulf Coast. After a short visit in 1889, Thomas Edison built a grand estate on the Caloosahatchee River, where he could assemble a new laboratory devoted to the study of tropical plants. Edison transformed the little town as his industrialist and scientist friends became frequent visitors. Henry Ford bought an adjoining estate. His sophisticated circle of friends established the cultural core of Fort Myers, with its graceful historic downtown.

By overseeing the planting of hundreds of royal palms lining McGregor Boulevard, the old cattle-driving route, Edison ensured Fort Myers a lasting legacy as the City of Palms. Some of the original settlers were flower growers from Europe who made Fort Myers famous many decades ago as the "Gladiolus Capital of the World."

When the Tamiami Trail opened in the 1920s, the land boom started. Among the developers who kick-started growth at the turn of the last century was former governor Albert Gilchrist, president of the Boca Grande Land Company, who played a large role in the development of **Gasparilla Island** and **Boca Grande**. The Charlotte Harbor and Northern Railroad was extended to the island to allow phosphate barges to offload their cargo to a shipping plant built in 1912, and phosphate was shipped out of the island until the 1970s. Simultaneously, wealthy Northeasterners discovered this island getaway, a hot spot in the 1920s when the Silver Star ran the rails from New York City direct to Boca Grande in 24 hours. Anglers came here for some of the best tarpon fishing in the world.

As the population grew, the county's economy shifted away from agriculture. After receiving gunnery training at Page Field and Buckingham, thousands of World War II airmen returned to Fort Myers to live after the war. Tourists discovered the unparalleled shelling on **Sanibel Island**, the captivating beauty of Captiva Island, and the thousands of migratory birds that wintered on rookery islands in Pine Island Sound. The economy of the Fort Myers region now revolves around tourism and land development, with nearly a half million residents spilling down the coastline.

GUIDANCE Contact the **Lee County Visitor & Convention Bureau** (239-338-3500 or 1-800-237-6444; www.FortMyersSanibel.com), 12800 University Dr., Ste. 550, Fort Myers 33907, or visit their Web site for extensive information. Pick up brochures at local businesses or at one of the **Estero Chamber of Commerce Visitor Centers** (239-948-7990; www.esterochamber.org/visitorInfoCenters.htm), located at the Miromar Outlets and Coconut Point (see *Selective Shopping*).

Visiting Boca Grande? Stop at the **Boca Grande Area Chamber of Commerce** (941-964-0568; www.bocagrandechamber.com), 5800 Gasparilla Rd., Ste. A1, next to Boca Grande Resort (see *Charlotte Harbor and the Gulf Islands*).

GETTING THERE *By car:* **I-75** provides direct access to Fort Myers, and **US 41**, the **Tamiami Trail**, shoots straight through its heart. Be especially cautious driving on I-75 between Fort Myers and Naples, as traffic is heavy and a lot of construction equipment clogs up the highway.

By air: **Southwest Florida International Airport (RSW)** (239-768-1000; www .flylcpa.com), 11000 Terminal Access Rd., Fort Myers, offers regular commuter service on more than 20 different airlines, including AirTran, American, Continental, Delta, Northwest, Southwest, United, and US Airways. International flights depart for Canada and Mexico daily.

By bus: **Greyhound** (239-334-1011; www.greyhound.com), 2250 Peck St., Fort Myers, provides transportation from the Jackson Street terminal, downtown.

GETTING AROUND

By bus: **LeeTran** (239-LEE-TRAN; www.rideleetran.com) provides bus service throughout the county with 18 fixed routes. Fare $1.25, all-day pass $2.50, 7-day pass $12.50; senior fare $0.60, 7-day pass $10, monthly pass $20. Children under 42-inches tall free. Buses operate 5 AM to 9:45 PM Monday through Saturday, with several routes operational on Sundays. Check the Web site for route maps and numbers.

By car: To reach Pine Island, use **Pine Island Road**. Cape Coral is best accessed by **Colonial Boulevard** and **Del Prado Boulevard**. During the winter "snow-bird" season, traffic south of downtown Fort Myers increases in intensity as you head toward Bonita Springs and Fort Myers Beach. **McGregor Boulevard** provides a great scenic alternative to **US 41**. From **I-75** use **Daniels Parkway** to access Fort Myers Beach and Sanibel-Captiva, and **Bonita Beach Boulevard** to reach Bonita Springs and Estero Island. To get to Boca Grande, you'll have to drive all the way around Charlotte Harbor, through Punta Gorda, Charlotte Harbor, and Placida (see *Charlotte Harbor and the Islands*) via **Burnt Store Road** or **US 41** to **SR 771** and **SR 775**. The turnoff is just past Placida. There is a toll of at least $5 to cross the bridge to Gasparilla Island.

By passenger ferry: The **Tropic Star** (239-283-0015; www.tropicstarcruises.com) is the official provider of ferry service to Cayo Costa State Park with scheduled trips at 9:30 AM and 2:00 PM daily, $35 adult, $25 ages 7 and under. They also offer private water taxi service ($150 per hour) from Bokeelia to most of the destinations surrounding Pine Island Sound, including Boca Grande, Cabbage Key, Cayo Costa, North Captiva, and Useppa.

The **Key West Express** (1-888-539-2628; www.seakeywestexpress.com), 2200 Main St., connects Fort Myers Beach to Marco Island and Key West using large modern catamarans with all the comforts for the 3–4 hour trip. Departures are from Salty Sam's Marina and 706 Fisherman's Wharf in Fort Myers Beach. One-way fare to either Key West or Marco Island is $86 adult, $57 child. Round-trip to Key West $139 adult, $129 senior, $75 ages 6–12; round-trip to Marco Island, $119 adult, $109 senior, $75 ages 6–12.

By taxi: **Checker Cab** (239-332-1712; www.bluebirdyellowtaxi.com); you'll find a taxi stand at the Southwest Florida International Airport.

By trolley: **LeeTran** (239-LEE-TRAN; www.rideleetran.com) provides a "Park and Ride" trolley service to and from Fort Myers Beach.

PARKING With rare exceptions, **beach parking** will cost you no matter where you go, and there are parking fees for most of the **parks** in Lee County, paid via a digital box for which you must have exact change or a credit card. Save those quarters! In **downtown Fort Myers**, there is two-hour metered street parking and a parking garage.

MEDICAL EMERGENCIES **Lee Memorial Hospital** (239-332-1111; www .leememorial.org), 2276 Cleveland Ave., serves Fort Myers and has several affiliates: **Cape Coral Hospital** (239-574-2323; www.leememorial.org/facilities/cape coralhospital.asp), 636 Del Prado Blvd.; **Gulf Coast Hospital** (239-768-5000; www.leememorial.org/facilities/gulfcoasthospital.asp), 13681 Doctor's Way, near the corner of Metro and Daniels; and **Southwest Florida Regional Medical Center** (239-939-1147; www.leememorial.org/swfrmc_gc), 2727 Winkler Ave., which is the closest hospital to Sanibel and Captiva Islands and Fort Myers Beach. In Boca Grande, call the **Boca Grande Health Clinic** (941-964-2276), 320 Parks Ave.

✳ To See

ARCHAEOLOGICAL SITES

Cabbage Key

It's the only place I know of where you can explore ancient Calusa culture *and* order yourself a mouthwatering "Cheeseburger in Paradise"—**Cabbage Key** is a giant pile of oyster shells cast here by the Calusa thousands of years ago. They built canals, too, and you can explore the island via a nature trail that starts and ends at the inn and restaurant that was once mystery writer Mary Roberts Rinehart's home in 1938. To get here, take a **water taxi** (see *Boating*) or hook up with the folks at **Tarpon Lodge** (see *Lodging*) in Pineland, who own the place.

Estero

Launch your kayak from **Koreshan Historic State Park** (see *Historic Sites*) for a paddle into Estero Bay to see **Mound Key**, a man-made island of oyster shells rising 32 feet high, once the capital city of the Calusa, where King Carlos received the Spanish explorers who came to his shores in the 1500s.

Pineland

At the **Calusa Heritage Trail at the Randell Research Center** (239-283-2062; www.flmnh.ufl.edu/rrc), 13810 Waterfront Dr., explore the interpreted remains of an ancient Calusa city overlooking Captiva Pass and encompassing nearly 60 acres. Engineered thousands of years ago, this was the original city called "Tampa" by the Calusa, who were a seagoing culture with tools based on shells. They subsisted by fishing the vast estuaries between Ten Thousand Island and Charlotte Harbor. Follow nearly a mile of interpretive trails to visit sites of interest, including several significant mounds on which temples and houses once perched, and a canal system that linked the village with the bay. An abrupt climatic change more than 1,500 years ago might have caused the inhabitants to abandon their waterfront property; the ridges show storm deposits from major hurricanes. Guided tours are offered weekly on Saturday at 10 AM (reservations a must), or you can walk the trails yourself. Stop at the visitors center for information. Open 10 AM–4 PM daily. Fee.

Useppa Island

Inhabited continuously for more than 10,000 years, **Useppa Island** was home to another major village of the Calusa, with shell middens today belying sites of significance. Findings from archaeological digs are presented in the **Useppa Island Museum** (see *Museums*).

ART GALLERIES

Boca Grande

Both the **Hughes Gallery** (941-964-4273; www.hughesgallery.net), 333 Park Ave., and **Paradise! Fine Art** (941-964-0774), 340 Park Ave., present fine art by nationally renowned artists, as well as traditional interpretations of Florida landscapes. Nearby, the **Serendipity Gallery** (941-964-2166), Olde Theatre Mall, 321 Park Ave., is a quirkier place, filled with colorful art that appeals to those of us with flamingos on the bathroom wall and fish platters in the kitchen.

Bokeelia

Under a bower of sea grapes, the **Crossed Palms Gallery** (239-283-2283; www.crossedpalmsgallery.com), 8315 Main St., showcases fine art and classy art glass, sculpture, and jewelry from local artists.

Cape Coral

A rotating slate of art shows fills the galleries at **Cape Coral Arts Studio** (239-574-0802; www.southwestfloridaarts.com/capestudio.cfm), 4533 Coronado Pkwy. If you're staying in the region for an extended period, check into their ongoing workshops and fine-art classes. Open Mon.–Fri. Free.

Captiva Island

At **Jungle Drums** (239-395-2266; www.jungledrumsgallery.com), 11532 Andy Rosse Ln., nearly three hundred Florida artists are represented in all media, and the result is a store with dozens of pieces of naturally themed art that you'll want to take home. I found the copper mangrove "Captiva candelabra" tables especially appealing, as are the clay studio sushi platters, "Happy Glass" balls, and beach treasure boxes decorated with shells, beach glass, and copper. Owner Jim Mazzotta is best known for his vibrant island creatures and scenes that celebrate the margarita-and-sailing lifestyle.

Matlacha

Art galleries are tucked amid the shops lining the waterfront, including **WildChild Gallery** (239-283-6006; www.wildchildartgallery.com), 4625 Pine Island Rd., with pottery, art glass, and vivid Florida landscape paintings; **Water's Edge Gallery** (239-283-7570), 4548 Pine Island Rd., with wildlife art; Matlacha Art Gallery (239-283-6453), 4643 Pine Island Rd; and **Lovegrove Gallery and Gardens** (239-283-1244; www.leomalovegrove.com), 4637 Pine Island Rd., filled with delightful and unique pieces, from whimsical wire people to fish mosaics, wooden critters, and infrared photography. Step outside to the garden for even more art. Leona Lovegrove is the primary artist, but more than 40 other local artists are also represented at this gallery. From February through June enjoy **Art Night on Pine Island** 4–9 PM on the second Friday of each month as galleries stay open late to showcase artists and gourmet goodies.

Sanibel Island

Dubbed the "Island of the Arts," **Sanibel** has more than a dozen art galleries hidden in its byways and little malls. Start your exploration at **BIG (Barrier Island Group) Arts** (239-395-0900; www.bigarts.org), 900 Dunlop Rd., the nonprofit cultural arts center downtown, where monthly displays are shown at the **Phillips Gallery**. Pick up a copy of the Sanibel Island art gallery guide here to discover the island's many other artists, among them Bryce McNamara's whimsical recycled art at the **Tin Can Alley Art Gallery** (239-472-2902), 2480 Library Way. Featuring oceanic art from local artists such as Nancy Wilson and Myra Robert, **Seaweed Gallery** (239-472-2585; www.seaweedgallery.com), 1989 Periwinkle Way, is a little niche of glass, ceramic, and paintings that evoke the magic of the sea.

BASEBALL Spring training is the hot topic in these parts, with the **Minnesota Twins** (http://minnesota.twins.mlb.com) as the fifth team in more than 65 years to train in Lee County. They play at the **William H. Hammond Stadium** (239-768-4210 or 1-800-33-TWINS), 4400 Six Mile Cypress Pkwy., Fort Myers, and their Class A farm team the **Miracle** play the remainder of the season. Downtown, the **Boston Red Sox** (http://boston.redsox.mlb.com) play at the City of Palms Park (239-334-4700 or 1-877-RED-SOXX), 2201 Edison Ave.; tickets $10–44.

Boca Grande

At Sandspur Park along Gulf Boulevard, the tall thin lighthouse you see is the **Rear Range Light**, an unmanned structure built in 1881 to be used in Delaware, and then moved to Boca Grande in 1927 for active duty. Built in 1890 to guide ships to Charlotte Harbor, the **Boca Grande Lighthouse** (see *Museums*) is one of the oldest structures in the region. It served as a working lighthouse for nearly 70 years and was fully restored in 1986 to serve as a museum. Nearby, the **Quarantine House** (to the left of the entrance to the state park where the lighthouse is located), circa 1895, housed sick crewmembers on ships visiting the city. It is privately owned.

Estero

Dr. Cyrus Teed founded a utopian settlement along the Imperial River in 1894. The well-preserved village is now part of **Koreshan Historic State Park** (239-992-0311; www.floridastateparks.org/koreshan), 8661 Corkscrew Rd. The Koreshans once numbered 250, and they believed in a hollow earth, the Golden Rule, communal property, and women's rights. Tours take you through the village, and you can enjoy the park's many other amenities—campground, picnic area, riverside nature trail, canoe launch, and fishing—on your own.

Fort Myers

& ∞ Few Florida historic sites see as many visitors as the **Edison and Ford Winter Estates** (239-334-3614; www.efwefla.org), 2350 McGregor Blvd., Fort Myers, managed by the City of Fort Myers. Encompassing 14 acres, this tropical paradise dates from 1886, when Thomas Edison established experimental gardens and a laboratory to determine the industrial uses of tropical plants. By the 1930s, he determined that 10 to 12 percent pure rubber could be extracted from a particular species of goldenrod. A tour through the estate is an immersion in a tropical forest, starting with what is claimed to be the third largest banyan tree in the

THE BOCA GRANDE LIGHTHOUSE MUSEUM

Sandra Friend

world, covering nearly an acre with its dense, glossy canopy supported by hundreds of tap roots as thick as tree trunks and providing a labyrinth of tree limbs to explore. The parade of botanical wonders continues along the tour route, beneath the dangling sala-mi-like fruits of the sausage tree, past poisonous apple trees, blooming orchids, and forests of bamboo. Knowledgeable guides lead each hour-long walking tour, which winds through the tropical plantings to stop at Edison's home office, swimming pool, and wharf before coming to Seminole Lodge, Edison's home.

As befitting the inventor of the electric light, in 1887 Seminole Lodge was the first building in Florida to be illumi-nated. The novelty drew Edison's friends from around the world. This traditional Florida home uses breeze-ways and screened rooms to keep the rooms cool with the constant breezes across the Caloosahatchee River. Orig-inal furnishings grace each room. At the adjoining Mangoes, purchased by Edison's protégé, Henry Ford, the tour continues past a garage housing an original 1914 Model T, 1917 Ford

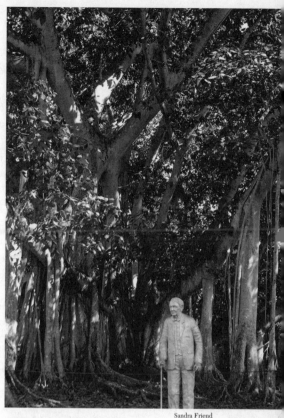

Sandra Friend

THE BANYAN TREE AT THE EDISON AND FORD ESTATES

Truck, and 1929 Model A before entering Ford's home for a look at life in the 1920s. Leaving the gardens, visitors explore Edison's original rubber laboratory—as intact as the day it shut down—and a museum containing Edison's many inven-tions, from the well-known lightbulb and phonograph to the lesser-known movie projector and stock ticker. Open daily, except Thanksgiving and Christmas, 9 AM–5:30 PM, last tour at 4 PM. Adults $20, children ages 6–12 $11. Botanical tours are offered Thursday and Saturday at 9 AM, and cost $24 adult, $10 child. Dis-counts offered for AAA and reciprocal museum members.

Sanibel Island

♿ Find the original Sanibel at the **Sanibel Historic Village & Museum** (239-472-4648; www.sanibelmuseum.org), 950 Dunlop Rd., where wooden walkways lead you through the village and gardens on the site of Bailey's landing, where the first general store stood. (Their family still has a store on Tarpon Bay Road.) His-toric structures were moved here from around the island, including the Burnap Cottage (1898), Miss Charlotte's Tea Room (1926), the original post office (1926), and others. The museum and houses are open limited seasonal hours, Nov. 7–Apr. 30 Wed.–Sat. 10 AM–4 PM, May 1–Aug. 11 Wed.–Sat. 10 AM–1 PM; fee.

Boca Grande

An excellent introduction to regional history, the **Boca Grande Lighthouse Museum** (941-964-0060; www.barrierislandparkssociety.org/lighthouse.html) at **Gasparilla Island State Park** (see *Beaches*) explains how these barrier islands, once occupied by the Calusa, became Spanish settlements where fishermen created "ranchos," offshore fish farms that they tended. When the railroad came to Boca Grande to serve the growing phosphate industry along the Peace River, it brought Northern visitors who sought recreation with sportfishing and changed the nature of the town from a working maritime port to the exclusive enclave it remains today. The lighthouse is open Wednesday through Sunday all year long, and Tuesdays February through April. Donation.

Inside the historic Teacherage House at the corner of Park Avenue and Banyan Street, the **Boca Grande Historical Society & Museum** (941-964-1600; www .bocagrandehistoricalsociety.com) offers a window into the past and an archive for the future, collecting and categorizing memorabilia to present online and in rotating exhibits in their small museum space. Browse their selection of books on the region in their gift store. Open Mon.–Fri., 10 AM–3 PM. Donation.

Located south of channel marker 7 on Boca Bayou, the **Gasparilla Island Maritime Museum** (941-964-4466) at historic Whidden's Marina (see *Boating*) revisits the grand era of commercial fishing in southwest Florida through artifacts and photographs displayed in the old Red Gill Fish House. Built in 1926, the marina is the oldest continuously operating business on the island and still serves its customers daily. Donation.

Cape Coral

The small **Cape Coral Historical Society Museum** (941-772-7037), 544 Cultural Park Blvd., offers exhibits on the local burrowing owl population, a rose garden,

BANYAN STREET IN BOCA GRANDE

Sandra Friend

a military museum, a Native American room, and a Florida Cracker homestead.
Open 1 PM–4 PM Wed., Thurs., and Sun., closed July and Aug. Fee.

Fort Myers

&. ♂ Housed in the city's original Atlantic Coast Line depot circa 1924, the **South-west Florida Museum of History** (239-321-7430; www.swflmuseumof
history.com), 2300 Peck St., offers a broad perspective on the people and events that
shaped this region. From the classy restored Pullman railcar Esperanza to vignettes
on the fishing villages of Pine Island Sound, the museum provides a diverse collection of artifacts to explore. Researchers will find the Archival Research Center an
invaluable resource for understanding the history of Southwest Florida, and the
museum store contains a good selection of Florida history books. The museum also
offers downtown walking tours from January through April. Admission for adults
$9.50, seniors $8.50, children 3–12 $5. Open 10 AM–5 PM Tues.–Sat.

&. ♂ Kids will have a blast at the **Imaginarium Hands-on Museum** (239-337-3332;
www.cityftmyers.com/imaginarium), 2000 Cranford St., where there's so much for
them to see and do inside a renovated water treatment plant, complete with a water
tower. The Animal Lab is full of critters, including turtles, frogs, and the ever-popu-
lar giant Madagascar hissing cockroach. There are coral reef and freshwater tanks,
and movies to watch at the Theater-in-the-Tank. New touch tanks are a centerpiece
of the museum, allowing you to get up close to sting rays, sea urchins, and crabs.
Kids ages 5 and under can play grown-up in Tiny Town. At Sporty Science, learn
physics by playing hockey and baseball. Mind Magic has plenty of hands-on exhibits,
including fun with magnets and pool balls, building noodle structures, and putting
on your own puppet show. In the Hands-On Hall, kids can play bee in a honeycomb
or get inside the Hurricane Experience (parents welcome!) where you're buffeted
with winds at hurricane force. Upstairs, play meteorologist on WIMG-TV, stand in a
thunderstorm, and touch a cloud. There's even a dinosaur dig! Behind the building is
a series of screened rooms with iguanas, doves, and finches, and the Fish-Eye
Lagoon, where turtles sun and swans glide. A giant sandbox is set in the shade, right
outside the snack bar. You'll keep the family busy for hours here. Open 10 AM–5 PM
Mon.–Sat., noon–5 PM Sun. Adults $8, seniors $7, ages 3–12 $5.

Pine Island Center

At the **Museum of the Islands** (239-283-1525; www.museumoftheislands.com),
5728 Sesame Dr., thousands of years of island culture are packed into the display
cases. Marvel at Calusa figurines, including icons of sea turtles, alligators, and
wolves, and look through photos and the family history of the earliest European
settlers on the island. There is a well-labeled shell and fossil collection, and artifacts from early settlers, such as an 1800s antique doll buggy. Browse the gift shop
for more books on regional history. Open 11 AM–3 PM Tues.–Sat. Nov. 1–Apr. 30
and Tues., Thurs., Sat. May 1–Oct. 31; fee.

Sanibel Island

&. ♂ You probably never knew that actor Raymond Burr of Perry Mason fame was
an avid shell collector, and neither did I until I visited the **Bailey-Matthews Shell
Museum** (941-395-2233; www.shellmuseum.org), 3075 Sanibel-Captiva Rd., a
mecca for anyone who enjoys the beauty of seashells. More than two decades ago,
Burr helped launch this museum, which prides itself on the most comprehensive
collection in the world. It's entirely fitting it's located on the one island in the

United States where shelling is world-class. A globe is the centerpiece of the Great Hall of Shells, showing where in the world you'll find specific species. Journey around the galleries to discover themed and regional exhibits, including shells as art: magnificent inlaid mother-of-pearl cabinetry and sailors' valentines. Natural bird and surf sounds add to the experience, and most of the exhibits put the shells in the context of where and how they live in offshore and inner bay habitats. The Children's Learning Lab has a touch tank and shell specimens, with hands-on games and puzzles. If you're planning to collect shells on this trip, don't miss the introductory movie, which gives important information on how to tell if your finds are alive or not before you remove them from their habitat. You're welcome to bring your own shells for identification. The gift shop has shell motif items, a great selection of guidebooks and serious scientific books on the subject, and children's toys and puzzles. Open daily 10 AM–5 PM, fee. Serious collectors will want to consider a membership to receive an information-packed newsletter.

RAILROADIANA

Boca Grande
Formerly the terminus of the Charlotte Harbor and Northern Railroad, which actively shipped phosphate brought to the wharf by barges until 1979, Boca Grande still has one of its original railroad depots downtown, built in 1911. It was one of three depots on the island and is now home to several shops and the **Loose Caboose Restaurant** (see *Eating Out*).

Fort Myers
Hop on board Florida's only dinner-train theater, the **Seminole Gulf Railway** (941-275-8487 or 1-800-SEM-GULF; www.semgulf.com), 4110 Centerpointe Dr. at Colonial Station, Colonial Blvd. and Metro Pkwy., Fort Myers, for a real treat as you figure out "whodunit" and feast on Black Angus steak, poached salmon, or chicken stuffed with walnut corn bread dressing. This diesel railway also offers scenic day trips of 20 and 30 miles up to and beyond the Caloosahatchee River trestle on Wednesday, Saturday, and Sunday, holidays excepted. Day excursions cost $19.95 adults, $11.95 ages 3–12, with discounts for families and special holiday outings.

WINERY Eden Winery (239-728-9463; www.edenwinery.com), 19709 Little Ln. off SR 80, Alva, is in the heart of the farming district and a popular stop for wine connoisseurs. Wine tastings run 30 to 40 minutes and include a discussion of the grapes and winemaking procedures. Fee.

ZOOLOGICAL PARK & WILDLIFE REHAB

Bonita Springs
& ✿ A classic Florida roadside attraction, **Everglades Wonder Gardens** (239-992-2591), 27180 Old US 41,

YOUNG ALLIGATORS AT EVERGLADES WONDER GARDENS

Sandra Friend

opened in 1936 as a wildlife rehab center by Lester and Bill Piper, and since my last visit was in the 1960s, I wasn't sure what to expect. Although habitats are slowly undergoing replacement, the winding paths under a canopy of tropical trees remain the same. A tour guide takes you on an interpretive walk through and past the enclosures, where you'll see Florida native species up close. Kids love the bouncing swinging bridge over the alligator pit, and you can let the kids feed fish and turtles along the route. The resident Florida panther, born in 1978, is the oldest in captivity; several have been bred here and released into the wild. There is a sad irony to the many plaques that read A PROTECTED SPECIES DUE TO LOSS OF HABITAT, as natural habitats surrounding the park have vanished at an incredible rate over the past few years. Check out the natural history museum in the gift shop, with pickled eggs, skulls, and photos from the founding of the park, once known as "Bonita Springs Reptile Gardens" and now in its third generation of family ownership. Before you head into the Everglades, see its native creatures up close. Open daily 9 AM–5 PM. Adults $15, ages 3–10 $8, 2 and under free.

Sanibel Island

C.R.O.W. (239-472-3644; www.crowclinic.org), 3883 Sanibel-Captiva Rd., aka the Clinic for the Rehabilitation of Wildlife, features a wildlife video and lecture to explain the efforts of this nonprofit organization to treat, stabilize, and rehabilitate injured birds. Check their Web site for entrance times, as they are renovating the animal hospital. Fee.

✷ To Do

BICYCLING

Boca Grande

To get around Boca Grande's narrow tropical-canopied streets, consider picking up a bike at **Island Bike 'n Beach Rentals** (941-964-0711), 333 Park Ave. A bike path parallels the main highway from downtown Boca Grande along the old railroad line all the way to the causeway.

Fort Myers

A system of **bike paths and bike trails** is evolving in and around Fort Myers, with new pieces in place every time I visit. It's now possible to bicycle to and from the city to Punta Rassa, gateway to the Sanibel Island causeway, via pathways that parallel Summerlin Road and Six Mile Cypress Parkway. New bike paths also stretch along Daniels Parkway, connecting to the southwest corner of Lehigh Acres. Cape Coral has a bike path paralleling Veteran's Parkway. For downloadable maps, visit the Lee County Metropolitan Planning Organization (www.mpo-swfl .org/bikeped.shtml) Web site.

Pine Island

Bike the entire length of 17-mile-long **Pine Island** along the bicycle path that parallels Stringfellow Road from Bokeelia to St. James City.

Sanibel Island

Everybody bikes on Sanibel Island—it beats sitting in long lines of traffic on Periwinkle Drive during tourist season, and it's good for you, too. A bike path parallels Periwinkle Drive and is heavily used. Side trails lead down to the Gulf, and the main trail continues the length of the island past Ding Darling National Wildlife

Refuge toward Captiva Island. Shade is limited. Rent bicycles at **Billy's Rentals** (239-472-5248; www.billysrentals.com), 1470 Periwinkle Way, or **Finnimore's Cycle Shop** (239-472-5577; www.finnimores.com), 2353 Periwinkle Way # 101.

BIRDING It's a fact: more migratory birds pass through this part of Florida each winter than any other. And it's the thousands of birds that draw thousands of visitors eager for their first glimpse of a roseate spoonbill picking its way across the mud flats, or a mangrove cuckoo patiently sitting on a tree limb. **J. N. "Ding" Darling National Wildlife Refuge** (see *Wild Places*) is one of the country's top destinations for birding, best done along its trails and along Wildlife Drive. I have never made a visit to the refuge without spotting at least one roseate spoonbill. At the refuge's nearby **Bailey Tract** on Tarpon Bay Road, watch for osprey and red-tailed hawks fishing in the freshwater impoundments. Birdwatchers also flock to the trails at the **Sanibel-Captiva Conservation Foundation** (see *Wild Places*), where benches along the Sanibel River and the island's freshwater marshes provide quiet spots for viewing. From December through June, you'll see swallow tailed kites nesting at **Six Mile Cypress Slough Preserve** (see *Preserves*) and all year long, families of Florida scrub jays flit through the scrub oaks at **Hickey's Creek Mitigation Park** (see *Wild Places*). On Pine Island, seek out the tough-to-find **St. Jude Nature Trail** of the Calusa Land Trust in St. James City, a narrow pathway that takes you out to a perfect birding spot in the midst of the mangroves.

BOATING

Boca Grande
At historic **Whidden's Marina** (941-964-2878; www.whiddensmarina.com), 190 First St. East, founded in 1926 and still owned by the same family, pick out your favorite craft from the large selection offered by **Capt. Russ' Boat Rentals** (941-964-0708).

Fort Myers Beach
Most of the region's marinas will rent or charter boats for you to explore the wondrous backwaters of Pine Island Sound and Estero Bay, including **Fish Tale Marina** (239-463-3600; www.fishtalemarinagroup.cc), 7225 Estero Blvd., where you can pick up a pontoon boat rental for less than $300 a day, and **Salty Sam's Marina** (239-463-7333 or 1-888-796-6427; www.saltysamsmarina.com), 2500 Main St.

At **Getaway Marina** (239-486-3600; www.getawaymarina.com), 18400 San Carlos Blvd., rent a 17- to 23-foot boat ($140–295) for 4 to 8 hours to putter around these mangrove-lined islands from **Bay Breeze Boat Rentals** (239-896-0284). Or take a spin on **Sea Rocket USA** (239-233-1578; www.searocketusa.com), a cigarette-style powerboat that zooms up to 70 MPH through the Gulf of Mexico. Head out on a 15-minute thrill ride ($35 adult, $25 ages 12 and under) past **Bowditch Point** (see *Beaches*), where the driver will do zigzags and 360° turns. You'll see dolphins racing to keep up! Or charter the boat for a private tour to Sanibel Island, Cayo Costa, and Cabbage Key, Naples and Marco Island ($500–1,000 for up to 14 people).

Pine Island
Out of Pineland Marina, **Island Charter Service** (239-283-3593), 13921 Waterfront Dr., offers charter service to the barrier islands of North Captiva, Cabbage Key, and Boca Grande. Call in advance for reservations and cost. **Tropic Star of**

Pine Island (239-283-0015; www.tropicstarcruises.com), sailing from Bokeelia, is the cruise I took for a day on Cayo Costa to hike the trails and look for seashells (see *Getting There*). They provide charters and water taxi service as well; arrange in advance.

CRABBING From mid-October through May, it's perfectly legal for you to dive offshore to collect **stone crab claws**—if you can stand the thought of removing them from their owners. At least the crabs can grow them back. Prime sites include along the Sanibel Causeway; off Big Carlos Pass Bridge; and near the Boca Grande phosphate docks. Limits set by the Florida Fish and Wildlife Conservation Commission (www.myfwc.com) are 1 gallon of claws per person (2 gallons per vessel), and all claws must be a minimum of 2¾ inches from elbow to tip. Divers must fly a diver-down flag.

ECOTOURS ∂ With miles of unsullied coastline and vast estuaries to explore, guided tours are the best way to get out and see dolphin, manatee, rare birds, and more.

Captiva Kayak Co. & Wildside Adventures (239-395-2925; www.captivakayaks .com), 11401 Andy Rosse Ln. at McCarthy's Marina, launches daily explorations to Buck Key, where you can paddle through a tunnel of mangroves and explore the estuaries of Pine Island Aquatic Preserve. More paddling tours are mentioned under *Paddling*. I've photographed dolphins frolicking in the wake of the *Lady Chadwick* on **Captiva Cruises** (239-472-5300; www.captivacruises.com), South Seas Island Resort Yacht Harbor, Captiva, which features shelling cruises and trips to the outer islands. The **Sanibel-Captiva Conservation Foundation** (see *Wild Places*) hosts a variety of guided outdoor adventures, from birding walks to paddling trips and interpretive cruises. Taking a unique spin on local history while introducing you to the wild side of the islands, **Calusa Ghost Tours** (239-938-5342; www.calusaghosttours.com), based out of Pine Island, include paddling trips along the ancient water trails of the Calusa in replica 14-passenger canoes and walks with a guide to burial mounds.

FAMILY ACTIVITIES ∂ When I was a kid, I remember counting down the miles waiting for the **Shell Factory** (see *Selective Shopping*) to appear on the horizon. These days, it's way more than the shell store where I loved to spend my allowance. Now, there's the **Shell Factory Nature Park and Botanical Garden** (www.shellfactory.com/about_nature_park.html), with prairie dogs and coatimundis, kinkajous, a gator slough, a petting zoo, and a 7,000-square foot rainforest aviary. The newest addition, guaranteed to thrill the kids, is the "Day of the Dinosaur" walk into prehistory, with life-sized dinosaurs. $10 adult, $8 seniors, $6 ages 4–12. Another part of the complex is the **Fun Park and Arcade**, where you can spin around in a bumper boat, slam around in a bumper car, or play miniature golf; fee.

Get in the swing of things! Take the kids out for some mini golf at **Golf Safari** (239-466-5855; www.golfsafariminigolf.com), 3775 Bonita Beach Rd., Bonita Beach, open 10 AM–10 PM daily; or **Smugglers Cove Adventure Golf** (941-466-5855; www.smugglersgolf.com), 17450 San Carlos Blvd., Fort Myers Beach, which is known for its pirate ships and live gators on the course, open 9 AM –11 PM daily.

Mini golf is also a part of **Mike Greenwell's Family Fun Park** (239-574-4386; www.greenwellsfamilyfunpark.com), 35 Pine Island Rd., Cape Coral, where you can try out batting cages, four go-cart tracks, and the video arcade. They're open 10 AM–10 PM Sun.–Thurs., 10 AM–11 PM Fri.–Sat.

FISHING Known as the "fishingest bridge in Florida," the **Matlacha Bridge** on Pine Island Rd., Matlacha, hosts an assortment of characters every day. But if sportfishing is your bag, you've come to the right place. Virtually any marina on the coast (see *Boating*) can hook you up with a professional guide to chase after tarpon or spend a day on the flats. If you've always wanted to cast but never tried, sign up for the **Backwater Fishing School** (1-800-755-1099; www.bwfishingschool.com), hosted at **Tarpon Lodge** (see *Lodging*), a three-day course with hands-on experience to make you the expert you've always dreamed of being.

Check in at **Getaway Marina** (see *Boating*) for their famous **night snapper fishing cruise**—you catch, they'll clean. The expedition departs on Tuesday and Friday nights at 6 PM and returns around 1 AM, and your fare includes rod, reel, license, bait, and tackle. During the day, they run the **Great Getaway** between 9 AM–3 PM, sailing up to 30 miles offshore for deep sea fishing with all the frills, including a full galley, separate accommodations for men and ladies, and crew that'll help teach you how to fish.

GAMING At **Naples–Fort Myers Greyhound Racing** (239-992-2411; www .naplesfortmyersdogs.com), 10601 Bonita Beach Rd., Bonita Springs, relax in the clubhouse or get involved in an unlimited-pot poker game during live races. Simulcasts are also offered.

HIKING Thanks to an aggressive public land–acquisition program, **Lee County** (www.leeparks.org) offers hikers dozens of spectacular choices for day hikes and a handful of places to take a backpacking trip. Many options are outlined in *50 Hikes in South Florida,* and most of the *Green Space* listings feature at least a nature trail for a short walk. If you only have time to sample a few short hikes, don't miss the haunting boardwalk loop through **Six Mile Cypress Slough Preserve** (see *Preserves*) in Fort Myers, a walk through the mangrove tunnels at **Four Mile Cove Ecological Preserve** (see *Preserves*) in Cape Coral, and an exploration of the trail system at the **Sanibel-Captiva Conservation Foundation** (see *Wild Places*).

PADDLING The **Great Calusa Blueway** (239-461-7400; www.GreatCalusa Blueway.com) is one of Florida's most comprehensive saltwater paddling trails, with more than 190 miles of coastline to explore. Rent a kayak or bring your own and explore the sheltered waters of Estero Bay, or follow the trail along the island coastlines of Pine Island Sound. Launch points for Estero Bay include the Imperial River at US 41, **Koreshan Historic State Park** (see *Historic Sites*), **Matanzas Pass Preserve** (see *Preserves*), and **Fish Tale Marina** (see *Boating*), among many others. Check the Web site or call for a comprehensive map of the paddling trail.

On the islands, rent kayaks at **Captiva Kayak Co.** (see *Ecotours*) or at **Gulf Coast Kayak** (239-283-1125; www.gulfcoastkayak.com), 4530 Pine Island Rd., Matlacha, where they also offer guided tours. Paddle the mangrove forests of Ding Darling National Wildlife Refuge by renting a kayak from **Tarpon Bay Explorers**

(239-472-8900; www.tarponbayexplorers.com), 900 Tarpon Bay Rd., on Sanibel Island; guided tours are also available by reservation. Tours of Mound Key are available from **Estero River Outfitters** (239-992-4050; www.esteroriveroutfitters .com), as well as rentals to take a canoe out on Estero Bay on your own.

SAILING For more than 40 years, Steve and Doris Colgate's **Offshore Sailing School** (1-800-221-4326; www.offshore-sailing.com) has trained students how to raise a sail, catch the wind, and then tack back to port with a series of in-depth hands-on courses that turn landlubbers into live-aboards. Offered year-round at the South Seas Island Resort marina on Captiva Island, *Learn to Sail* courses run from three to nine days. Check the Web site for seasonal pricing.

SCENIC DRIVES A slow drive—or, better yet, a bicycle ride—down **Banyan Street** in Boca Raton will leave you marveling at the wonder of these fast growing tropical trees, members of the ficus family that so quickly knit a dense canopy overhead while putting down roots from their branches. You'll feel like you're in a tropical tunnel! And if you see a giant lizard cross the road, well, it's not your imagination. Unfortunately for native wildlife, a colony of iguanas lives on the island, and there are Nile monitors as well.

SHELLING

Boca Grande

Seashells along the sandy strands of the barrier islands can grow to impressive sizes—but you'll have to be the early bird after high tide recedes to claim your treasure. Look for the best shells where the tides sweep around curved land at the tip of Boca Grande Pass within **Gasparilla Island State Park** (see *Beaches*).

Cayo Costa

It takes a **ferryboat ride** (see *Getting There*) or a boat to get to **Cayo Costa State Park** (see *Beaches*), but one of the best reasons to go is the shelling. On one visit there in the fall, I found pen shells scattered like leaves across the beach—a scene I hadn't seen in these parts since I was a kid. Tulip shells, apple murex, olive shells, and periwinkle were mine for the taking. From the campground, wander south along the beach for the best shelling.

Sanibel Island

The parking fees are a small price to pay for access to **Sanibel Island** on the morning after a raging storm, as this barrier island is renowned as having the best shell-collecting beaches in North America.

Beyond the typical jingle shells, quahogs, and cockles, you'll find such beauties as alphabet cone, sunray venus, thorny sea star, and apple murex. The secret? Sanibel is a barrier island with an east-west orientation, while Florida's barrier islands normally run north-south, protecting the coastline. Identify your finds with a visit to the **Bailey-Matthews Shell Museum** (see *Museums*). Peak season for

SEA SHELLS AT BOCA GRANDE

Sandra Friend

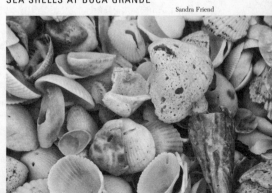

shelling is May through September, off-season from the usual crowds, and local charter captains offer expeditions to islands and sandbars.

SPAS

Fort Myers

A sanctuary set in a mangrove forest, the **Sanibel Harbour Spa** (239-466-2264 or 239-466-2156; www.sanibel-resort.com/spa) at the **Sanibel Harbour Resort** (see *Hotels, Motels, and Resorts*), offers tranquility through its broad range of treatments. Step inside a retreat of bamboo and stone, where the concierge will walk you through the possibilities: perhaps a Pedisage for those weary feet, or a Sea Shell Body Mask to nourish your body? For couples, the Caloosa Experience builds intimacy through relaxation. The spa also offers a BETAR (Bio Energetic Transduction Aided Resonance) bed, an immersive mind-body experience within a geodesic dome. Treatments start at $75; call ahead for your appointment.

Fort Myers Beach

A patrons-only elevator at the **Pink Shell Resort** (see *Hotels, Motels, and Resorts*) whisks you upstairs to the **Aquagene Spa** (239-463-8648; www.aquagenespa.com), where swirling, dimpled iridescent tiles evoke the calm of the sea. Whether it's a Romantic Rendezvous (complete with sugar scrub or salt glow, couples massage, champagne, and chocolate-dipped strawberries for two, $360) or a simple De-stress massage ($60 for 25 minutes), they're ready to assist, with a long list of services and spa packages to please. Open Mon.–Sat. 8:30 AM–6 PM, Sun. 8:30 AM–5 PM.

SWIMMING The beaches along Lee County's barrier islands are ideal for swimming—the Gulf waters are warm and clear. My favorite spot is **Bowman's Beach** on Sanibel Island, but you have dozens of places to choose from (see *Beaches*).

After hours spent walking on sand and stooping to pick up shells, I could think of no better pick-me-up than a massage to erase my burnout from the beach. And wrapped in flickering candlelight amid the muted earth tones at **Esterra Spa & Salon** (239-765-4SPA; www.esterraspa.com), 6231 Estero Blvd., it was more than a massage, it was a ritual of relaxation. My choice— hot stone massage, a new-to-me treatment that evolved into a sensory experience, not at all like the standard massages I typically request. I could not see the stones, but I could feel them, at once warm, smooth, round, and heavy, slipped into my palms, between my tired toes, and, in the hands of the masseuse, used to stretch my aching muscles. Afterward, I was ready for a nap. My experience was one of many available from an extensive menu that plays into the need for refreshing your body while at the beach, with treatments like milk and honey body wraps that help with sunburned skin, Salt Glow with Vichy shower to assist in exfoliation and hydration, and a Get the Red Out facial to help repair damaged cells. Open Mon.–Sat. 9 AM–6 PM, Sun. 10 AM–4 PM.

Sandra Friend

SUNSPLASH FAMILY WATERPARK IN CAPE CORAL

WATER PARK ✎ Built as a county recreation park in 1992, **Sunsplash Family Waterpark** (941-574-0557; www.sunsplashwaterpark.com) 400 Santa Barbara Blvd., Cape Coral has undergone an extreme makeover in 2008 to be one hopping water park. You'll keep the kids entertained all day with its variety of water play, including a frog pond with floating lily pads, a pool with drop slides just for teens, a lazy float down the "Main Stream River," racing slides for small children, the Tot Spot with water cannons and short slides in a shallow pool, another pool for the whole family, rollicking slides like the Electric Slide and Power Surge, and the drops for the daring—Thunder Bump, Terror Tube, and the X-celerator, all overlooking Lake Kennedy. A deli and café offer on-site eats, or you can get the family together at the picnic pavilion for a catered lunch. $17 for people over 48 inches tall (except seniors, $9), $15 for under 48 inches tall (except ages 2 and younger, $4), discount after 2 PM. Parking $3. Open Mar.–Sept. with varying hours.

✳ Green Space

BEACHES

Boca Grande

Gasparilla Island State Park (941-964-0375; www.floridastateparks.org/gasparillaisland) is a string of five beaches along Gulf Boulevard, with the best (in my opinion) to be found at the mouth of Charlotte Harbor, in front of the historic Boca Grande lighthouse. Sandspur Beach, closer to downtown, is popular with surfers trying to catch a wave when the weather's rough. Fee.

CATCHING A WAVE AT BOCA GRANDE

Sandra Friend

Bonita Springs

& Along a short stretch of secluded shoreline, **Little Hickory Island Beach Park** (239-949-4615), 26082 Hickory Blvd., offers a wheelchair-accessible strand of pure white sand, with restrooms, picnic tables, and showers. Fee.

Fort Myers

At the end of a lengthy mangrove-lined causeway is a hidden treasure—715 acres of protected waterfront known as **Bunche Beach** (239-765-6794), 18201 John Morris Rd., on San Carlos Bay. This natural area is a historic site, dedicated in 1949 to honor Dr. Ralph Johnson Bunche, the first person of color to win the Nobel Peace Prize. Prior to desegregation, this strip of sand was the designated beach for African-Americans who lived in the area. Free.

Fort Myers Beach

You won't go wrong with a visit to the beach, as the beaches around Fort Myers draw visitors from around the world. **Fort Myers Beach** provides easy access for visitors with small parking areas at the end of nearly every dead-end street along Estero Boulevard (FL 865), and a large parking area with facilities (showers and restrooms) and picnic tables at **Lynn Hall Park** on northern Estero Boulevard.

& Or continue down the dead-end road to the north end of Fort Myers Beach for a quiet piece of sand all your own at **Bowditch Point Regional Preserve** (239-463-1116; www.leeparks.org), 50 Estero Blvd., where you can meander bark-chip trails leading to great views of Matanzas Pass and Sanibel Island and find your own quiet slice of undeveloped beach tucked under the shade of mangroves. A wheelchair-accessible boardwalk leads from the central changing area and restrooms to the beach. Open 8 AM until a half hour after sunset. Fee.

For a unique beach experience, visit **Lovers Key State Park** (239-463-4588; www.floridastateparks.org/loverskey), 8700 Estero Blvd. (SR 865). A tram runs visitors through the mangrove swamps and out to the slim strip of beach, which is made up entirely of washed-up and eroded islands of seashells held together by cabbage palms, gumbo limbo, and mangroves. Shell collectors can have a blast just sifting through the bounty under their picnic table. Fee. The new bayside part of the park offers picnic tables, a playground, kayak launch, and restrooms. Free.
🐾 **Dog Beach** (941-463-2081), 160 Bahia Via, at Lovers Key just west of New Pass, is where you can let your canine friends romp in the surf. Free.

Pine Island

To feel like a castaway, take the ***Tropic Star*** (see *Getting Around*) from Pine Island to **Cayo Costa State Park** (941-964-1154; www.floridastateparks.org/cayocosta). No matter whether you spend a day or camp overnight at the primitive campground (cabins available by reservation), you'll enjoy the serenity of long walks along the beach of an unspoiled barrier island—great shelling guaranteed.

Sanibel-Captiva

Parking is more limited for the renowned beaches of **Sanibel and Captiva Islands**, and it'll cost you if you aren't staying on the island: In addition to the $6 toll for the Sanibel Causeway, you'll fork out an hourly charge at every beach parking lot on the islands. Some parking areas provide restrooms, a changing room with outdoor shower, and potable water. **Bowman's Beach** has a wilderness feel, while the **Sanibel Lighthouse Beach** is a popular sunning beach in the shadow of the historic lighthouse. **Gulfside Park** offers picnic tables and barbecue grills overlooking the ocean, as well as a nature trail. Anglers and sunset watchers head to **Turner Beach,** where Sanibel and Captiva Islands meet across the filled-in Blind Pass.

NATURE CENTERS Heaven and earth meet at the **Calusa Nature Center and Planetarium** (239-275-3183; www.calusanature.com), 3450 Ortiz Ave., Fort Myers, where a daily planetarium show (the only one in southwest Florida) complements the center's main mission of introducing you to the natural history of the Fort Myers area. Explore the reptile tanks to see the many species of turtles, snakes, lizards, and salamanders that inhabit the region, and learn the difference between the resident American alligator (pointed snout, dark body) and American crocodile (rounded snout, grayish body). A 0.6-mile wheelchair-accessible nature trail leads past an Audubon-maintained aviary of raptors and through a representative slough habitat, where volunteers battle to rid the swamp forest of invasive melaleuca. A rougher hiking trail starts at a replica Calusa village and loops around the center's 105 acres. Check the center's bulletin boards for information on ongoing environmental education programs open to the public. Open 9 AM–5 PM Mon.–Sat., 11 AM–5 PM Sun. Adults $9, ages 3–12 $6.

&. ✤ Lee County's first certified green building is the new Interpretive Center for **Six Mile Cypress Slough Preserve** (239-432-2004; www.leeparks.org/sixmile), 7751 Penzance Blvd. Stop here first for an understanding of the complexity of the habitats of southwest Florida, where rainfall seeps in sheet flows toward the sea. The network of boardwalks spanning this ecologically significant cypress slough enables you to enjoy lush bromeliads, primordial strap ferns, and flag ponds with resident alligators. Look closely in spring and summer for the delicate blooms of wild orchids in the cypress boughs. Join a guided interpretive walk to learn more about the swamp; walks are offered January through March daily 9:30 AM and 1:30 PM, May through October on Wednesday at 9:30 AM, and April/November/December daily at 9:30 AM. Fee.

PARKS

Alva
Several parks provide public access to the Caloosahatchee River, including the **W. P. Franklin Lock Recreation Area** off SR 80, with a picnic area and fishing. On the north side of the river, you can hike, camp, ride your bike, or bring a horse—the **Caloosahatchee Regional Park** (239-694-0398), 18500 N River Rd., has plenty of room for all sorts of activities. Walking trails lead out to riverside views, and wildlife encounters (especially with deer) are almost assured. Fee. **Manatee Park** (239-690-5030), 10901 Palm Beach Blvd., is a small park off the Caloosahatchee River providing seasonal access to view manatees near a power plant west of I-75. Free.

Fort Myers
Popular **Lakes Regional Park** (239-432-2000), 7330 Gladiolus Dr., provides 279 acres of outdoor recreation, from swimming and canoeing to bicycling and hiking. A 2.5-mile paved trail system winds through the park, bridging numerous islands within the lakes. Wander the Fragrance Garden to take in the complex aromas. On weekends, you can rent paddleboats, kayaks, and canoes to explore the waterways.

A water playground and a rock-climbing wall offer a place for kids to let off steam. Fee.

PRESERVES

Cape Coral

At **Four Mile Cove Ecological Preserve** (239-549-4606), SE 23rd Terrace, rent a canoe and explore secluded mangrove forests along the Caloosahatchee River, or take to the trail and enjoy a 1-mile stroll along a winding boardwalk. Walk softly, and you'll see yellow-crowned herons in the trees and little blue herons in the channels. Bring your fishing pole and relax along a pier with a broad view of the Fort Myers waterfront. This 365-acre saltwater marsh preserve provides a rare green space in the city of Cape Coral, next to the Midpoint Bridge. Free.

Fort Myers Beach

Walk down the mangrove-lined trails of **Matanzas Pass Preserve** (239-765-4222), 199 Bay Rd., to experience the unique estuarine mangrove forest environment. Clad in red and black speckled shells, mangrove crabs scurry down the gnarled roots of the red mangroves. The pathways lead you out to an unspoiled panorama of Matanzas Pass, where a canoe launch awaits your craft. Free.

WILD PLACES

Alva

With more than 1,100 acres protecting the realm of the Florida scrub jay and gopher tortoise, **Hickey's Creek Mitigation Park** (239-728-6240), 17980 FL 80, is a great getaway for long hikes, easy walks along the creek, and paddling on this winding cypress-lined blackwater creek. Fee.

Estero

Where the Estero River meets the bay, **Estero Bay Preserve State Park** (941-463-3240; www.floridastateparks.org/esterobay), end of Broadway west of US 41, has more than 5 miles of loop trails to walk and explore wet flatwoods and the tidal marsh on the edge of the estuary, where fiddler crabs scurry across the mud flats. Another access point is in Fort Myers—**Winkler Point** (239-992-0311), a watery wilderness along the edge of Estero Bay, at the end of Winkler Road. Roam wet flatwoods and estuarine fringe for up to 5 miles on trails where you are virtually guaranteed to get your feet wet. Free.

Sanibel Island

Encompassing more than half of Sanibel Island, **J. N. "Ding" Darling National Wildlife Refuge** (239-472-1100; www.fws.gov/dingdarling), One Wildlife Dr., hosts more than 100,000 visitors each year, the highest visitation in the entire National Wildlife Refuge system. Before taking to the trails or to Wildlife Drive, the popular one-way driving tour through the mangrove swamps, stop in at the visitors center for an excellent orientation on Sanibel's unique attraction to migratory birds. Closed Fri. Fee. Across the road, the **Sanibel-Captiva Conservation Foundation** (239-472-2329; www.sccf.org), 3333 Sanibel Captiva Rd., provides miles of hiking through tropical and coastal habitats, including a walk along the freshwater Sanibel River. The organization has actively been preserving every parcel of Sanibel they can buy; you'll see their signs in many places along the bike trails on the island.

✷ Lodging

BED & BREAKFASTS

Bokeelia 33922

∞ ✧ One of my most luxurious stays in Florida has been at the **Bokeelia Tarpon Inn** (239-283-8961 or 1-866-TARPON2; www.tarponinn.com), 8241 Main St., in the historic Poe-Johnson House, built 1914. There is no television in the great room, just a fine selection of music, board games, and books, and a pantry and fridge brimming with delights such as Dove ice cream bits, fresh tropical fruit, potpies, and cheese. Once a sea captain's home, this grand residence underwent $1 million in renovations to restore it to its natural beauty, with every heart pine and cypress board removed, refinished, and replaced. The simple, uncluttered furnishings of wood and white wicker make it easy to relax and enjoy the sea breezes off Boca Grande Pass. Each room ($159–325) has its own decorative flair, but you'll end up spending most of your time in the vast common areas, enjoying the views and the company. A gourmet breakfast is served for guests each morning. Guests have access to a boat ramp, dockage, and a 300-foot pier on the pass, perfect for idling away the day; the more active will appreciate the bicycles and golf carts for transportation, and kayaks for exploring Jug Creek.

Fort Myers 33901

& ⁏¹⁚ Dating from the days of Thomas Edison and built by timber magnate William H. Dowling in 1912 on the far shore of the Caloosahatchee River, the **Hibiscus House** (239-332-2651; www .hibiscushouse.com), 2135 McGregor Blvd., was sawed in two in the 1940s and sent across the river on a barge to be set up in its present location along the Avenue of Palms. With tongue-and-groove pine walls and ceilings, original glass windows, and classy furnishings, the five-bedroom bed & breakfast provides an excellent venue for visitors who want to explore downtown and the historic district on foot. Decked out in light tropical decor, each of the five rooms ($89–210) has a special ambiance themed after local flora. The Palm includes a writing desk and television. Common spaces include a poinciana-shaded sitting room in the rear of the house, a small front parlor where guests can watch television or chat, and a massive dining area where a full gourmet breakfast is served. Bring your swim suit—this is one of the few B&Bs that has its own pool, tucked in a tropical garden.

Matlacha 33993

⚓ ❀ With its four spacious guest rooms, **A Bayview Bed & Breakfast** (239-283-7510; www.webbwiz.com/bay viewbb), 12251 Shoreview Dr., is a great little getaway just off the main thoroughfare. Balconies overlook Matlacha Pass, and a resident osprey hangs out around the docks. Grab a canoe, and paddle the estuary behind the house. Each room ($109–199) has a television and phone and a small fridge. Well-behaved children and small pets welcome.

CAMPGROUNDS

Pine Island 33956

❀ If you're towing your rig and want to get away from it all, head for the quiet **KOA Pine Island** (239-283-2415; www.pineislandkoa.com), 5120 Stringfellow Rd., St. James City. In a secluded pine forest surrounded by mango groves, this campground offers a pool, spa, and exercise room, with tent sites, RV sites, and Kamping Kabins. Of the many amenities offered, one of the best is a free shuttle to the beach, attractions, and shopping, offered December through April. Rates $38 and up.

For a real deserted island getaway at an affordable price, pack your tent or reserve a cabin at **Cayo Costa State Park** (see *Beaches*), accessible only by boat. While marooned on this barrier island, explore more than 6 miles of hiking trails and walk miles of unspoiled beachfront, where shelling is some of the best in the United States. Primitive tent sites are $17; primitive cabins, $27. The park also manages the historic Jug Creek Cottages in Bokeelia, which start at $66 off-season and can be rented by the week.

North Fort Myers 33917

Along I-75 you'll see many camper manufacturers with large lots with RVs and trailers for sale off Luckett Road; many are factory outlets. Scout the region around them for campgrounds and RV parks east of the city, such as **Upriver Campground Resort** (239-543-3330 or 1-800-848-1652; www.upriver.com), 17021 Upriver Dr., and **Pioneer Village** (239-543-3303 or 1-877-897-2757; www.rvonthego.com), 7974 Samville Rd.

COTTAGES

Fort Myers 33916

Coral-rock cottages around a circular lake define **Rock Lake Resort** (239-332-4080 or 1-800-325-7596; www.bestlodgingswflorida.com/rocklake/index.html), 2937 Palm Beach Blvd., a 1940s classic with nine efficiencies offering a charming slice of Old Florida. Kick back on the porch and read a book, or paddle along scenic Billy Creek, a tributary of the Caloosahatchee. Cottages run $63–105 and adjoin a new city park.

Sanibel Island 33957

For an intimate getaway with your sweetheart, try **Seahorse Cottages** (239-472-4262; www.seahorsecottages.com), 1223 Buttonwood Ln., an "adults-only" property in Old Town

Sanibel. Lounge in the hammock, relax in the dip pool, take a bicycle and ride up to the shops, or grab beach umbrellas and towels and walk up the street to the Gulf. These housekeeping cottages include cable TV and VCR, CD and cassette players, and phones; guest laundry. Rates $90–255, depending on size and season.

HOTELS, MOTELS, AND RESORTS

Boca Grande 33921

Built in 1925, The **Anchor Inn** (941-964-5600; www.anchorinnbocagrande.com), 450 Fourth St., is the perfect getaway for aficionados of true Florida Cracker cottage style. Each room or suite ($170–321) comes with a full kitchen and your own courtesy golf cart for getting around the island. Multiday stays are expected, as there is an additional cleaning fee.

Touting "waterfront lodging on the bayou," The **Innlet** (941-964-2294; www.innletonthewaterfront.com), 11th St. and East Ave., has a very pretty location with waterfront rooms ($110–165) on a mangrove-lined canal, ample parking for boat trailers, a restaurant on the premises, and boat slips and a boat ramp for visitors.

Captiva Island 33924

Stay in quaint, colorful 1940s beach cottages with gingerbread trim at **Captiva Island Inn** (1-800-454-9898; www.captivaislandinn.com), 11509 Andy Rosse Ln., where the hand-sponged walls lend an artsy touch in this very artsy downtown. Each building has its own name and theme (and, in some cases, story), be it the Orchid Cottage, where Anne Morrow Lindbergh stayed while writing her classic *Gift from the Sea;* or the Jasmine Cottage, which overlooks a secret garden. The inn also has a large house with upscale rooms centered around a massive common area, perfect for family reunions. Rates start at $99 per night.

&. ✎ ⊙ "¶" Newly reopened and fully renovated, **South Seas Island Resort** (239-472-5111; www.southseas.com), 5400 Plantation Dr., has a new shine after five years of post-Hurricane Charley recovery, reorganization, and restoration. Captiva Island grows slender here, as it reaches its northern tip, and the access road through the resort sits right amid the mangroves and sea grapes. Along its length—which Uncle Bob's Trolley will take you up and down—are a variety of accommodations that make up the complex, starting with the Beach Villas and Gulf Beach Villas at Chadwick's Village, and the nearby Tennis Villas and Bayside Villas. I'd stayed here a decade ago, and a walk through several units convinced me that this is a whole new hotel. The furnishings have modern flair, the floors a natural feel, and small touches make all the difference, like glass block letting natural light illuminate a bathtub, and the televisions are flat-screen with a built-in DVD player. In all, there are more than 600 hotel rooms and a variety of privately owned beach homes available to choose from. At The Pointe, the very tip of the island, Harborside Village has more than a dozen different clusters of accommodations and is the hub of recreational activity. Here you'll find a zero-entry pool with an almost infinity view into Pine Island Sound, a 9-hole, par 3 seaside golf course, and the harbor itself, home to **Captiva Cruises** (see *Ecotours*), the **Offshore Sailing School** (see *Sailing*), Holiday Water Sports, and Best Boats. There's plenty for the younger set to do, including a large supervised arcade, the nature center, the Tiva Kids Club, and just splashing and snorkeling in the sea— the simple times I enjoyed greatly on my visits here. Make sure you stop for ice cream at the new Scoops, a homage-to-the-50s ice cream parlor. Prefer adult beverages? Try the Sunset Beach Bar, Starbucks, and Wine Flight Up, a trendy wine bar just outside the resort gates. Plan a weekend or a week of relaxation at this historic coconut plantation; they'll take care of everything for you. For rooms and suites, rates range from $109–350; small houses, $219–419; 5–6 bedroom houses, $899–2,500. Watch for their Florida resident specials.

&. ⊙ "¶" An enchanting mix of historic cottages and modern motel rooms, the **'Tween Waters Inn** (239-472-5161 or 1-800-223-5865; www.tween-waters .com), Captiva Rd., is an island getaway where authors, artists, and presidents have played since 1926. J. N. "Ding" Darling had his winter studio here, and you can now stay in it, or you can walk in the footsteps of Charles Lindbergh and Teddy Roosevelt by borrowing their getaways. The lovely Jasmine Cottage overlooks Pine Island Sound. The inn is a destination in itself—there are miles of uncrowded beaches, dockage, on-site fishing guides, guided kayaking tours, tennis courts, an Olympic-sized pool, children's pool, and several on-site restaurants and shops, plus a new day spa on the premises. Rates ($180–495) vary by season and size of unit, with special package rates, and all include continental breakfast.

Fort Myers 33916

&. ✎ "¶" ➷ At the tip of old Punta Rassa, **Sanibel Harbour Resort & Spa** (239-466-4000; www.sanibel -resort.com), 17260 Harbour Point Dr., is one of the premier resorts in the region, located where sport fishing truly began on this coast, when the Tarpon House was a draw for sportsmen in the late 1800s. With buildings tucked into the coastal forest and connecting boardwalks through the mangroves, the resort feels like it's been here forever. The grand lobby features broad windows overlooking San Carlos Bay and Sanibel Island. Guests can dine at six different restaurants in the complex, enjoying Charley's Cabana Bar for the ultimate sunset, or the Tarpon House for a more intimate meal. Guest rooms have relaxed Tommy Bahama décor, putting you in an island mood. Deluxe waterfront rooms include a private balcony and mini-bar; executive suites have spacious living rooms and king beds. There's an endless array of activities to enjoy on-site, from cruises on the *Sanibel Harbour Princess* to kayak rentals, lazing at the pool, or working out at the fitness center. Parents can drop the kids off at the Kids Club while they while away the hours at the Spa (see *Spas*). Rates start at $199, with many specials and packages available.

Step back into classic road-trip tourism at the **Sea Chest Motel** (239-332-1545), 2571 E First St., a good old-time Florida motel with 30 spacious rooms and kitchenettes ($40–85), all with updated furnishings. There is a private pier for guests, and the swimming pool overlooks the Caloosahatchee River.

Fort Myers Beach 33931
❝❞ Right on the beach, **The Beacon** (239-463-5264; www.thebeaconmotel .com), 1240 Estero Blvd., is the playful place to stay. The retro complex has 14 rooms ($69–209) and a cottage ($129–219) with private beach access, including several with a direct view of the Gulf. These are roomy accommodations with tile floors and updated furnishings. Some have full kitchens, all include a microwave, refrigerator, coffeemaker, and toaster. Breakfast is included with your stay.

The tropical ambiance of **Holiday Court Bayfront Villas and Suites** (239-463-2830), 925 Estero Blvd., drew me right in. It's an old-fashioned motel with villas decorated in bright Caribbean colors, with wicker chairs for relaxing, a shuffleboard court, and dockage right on the inlet, with no fee for guests who arrive by boat. Their swimming pool overlooks the harbor, or you can walk across the street to the beach. Most of the rooms are newly renovated, and those that aren't are available at a discount, $95–269.

 ❧ ▼ 🐾 ❝❞ Situated in the heart of downtown, the **Lighthouse Island Resort Inn and Suites** (239-463-9392 or 1-800-778-7748; www.lighthouse islandresort.com), 1051 Fifth Ave., provides a comfortable oasis of greenery where visitors can relax around the pools, make small talk at the tiki bar, and kick back on the balcony to watch the sunset. Easy access to the beach at Lynn Hall Park and the quaint shops and restaurants of downtown make this an ideal location for a multiday stay. This is a family-oriented facility, and pets are welcome for an additional charge. Most rooms contain either a kitchenette or full kitchen with full-sized appliances, great for the needs of a family on the go. Each suite provides multiple bedrooms, a kitchen, and living/dining area. Although many of the units date back nearly 50 years, extensive renovations ensure up-to-date facilities. The newest section of the inn, added in 2000, features the largest suites and elevator access to the upper floors. Rooms $79–255, depending on season, size, and features.

 ❧ Hidden under the bridge, the **Matanzas Inn** (239-463-9258 or 1-800-462-9258; www.matanzasinn.com), 414 Crescent St., offers pleasant and spacious waterfront apartments on the bay and motel rooms shaded by mango trees, with 26 units of various sizes ($69–284, weekly rates available) and a waterfront pool and spa; daily house-keeping, guest laundry, an award-winning restaurant, and dockage round out the amenities. You're within a few minutes walk of the bustling downtown and the beach.

  ♿ ✂ "Ⓘ" ↬ Evolving out of a lovely grouping of pink cottages along the tip of Fort Myers Beach, the new **Pink Shell Beach Resort & Spa** (1-800-237-5786; www.pinkshell.com), 275 Estero Blvd., embraces the fun of a family beach vacation. The original pink-shingled cottages (pink shingles were all the rage in the 1950s) were built by Roxie Smith's family, and several of the cottages still stand along the sound, available for guests who want to recapture the past. But the latest evolution of this resort reaches skyward, with five beachfront towers of varying heights offering guests stellar views of the Gulf of Mexico and Sanibel Island. The heart of the complex is the White Sand Villas, where you check in for your stay. This tower is home to the **Aquagene Spa** (see *Spas*), the poolside **Bongo's Bar & Grill, JoJo's at the Beach** (see *Eating Out*), and more. Dominated by a large faux tree draped in Spanish moss, the lobby and other common spaces have playful cat paintings in prominent places. Sparky, the resort mascot, is a cool cat who loves to surf, and you'll find him popping up around the undersea fantasy Octopool and at Sparky's Splash Pool, a zero-entry water playground with sprayers and coconut palms that dump water. Get the kids involved in activities at KiddsKamp, where they'll learn about native flora and fauna, go fishing, or compete in games at the pool. Next stop—the beach! Walk down the ramp into the soft, warm sand. Settle back in a beach chair, or take a slow walk down to Bowditch Point (see *Beaches*), scanning the shore for shells. One and two bedroom suites in the White Sand Villas are apartment-sized and immaculate, with spacious living and dining space, a full kitchen with an icemaker and water in the refrigerator door, and a bath that boasts both shower and garden tub. The Captiva Villas have kitchenettes, but the end units offer giant screened rooms overlooking the gulf and the sound. The Sanibel View Villas are farther from the action and closer to the wild shore at Bowditch Point, with a butterfly garden at their base. Guests enjoy free parking underneath their villas and in open lots. The cottages come with their own dock and gas grill, updated cabinetry, a large walk-in closet, and full kitchen, all overlooking Matanzas Pass. Room rates start at $149 off-season, with one bedroom suites $169–289 and two bedrooms $269 and up.

  🐾 Beneath the bridge you'll also find the **Sun Deck Resort** (239-463-1842; sundeckresort.com), 1051 3rd St., another classic motel from the 1960s, this one with seven unique units ($70–250) within a maze of pathways and levels under a canopy of tropical plantings. Some are kitchenettes, and one has a full kitchen. At the top of the stack is Hyannis, a 2-bedroom, 2-bath apartment with its own private decks and a spiral wooden staircase inside leading up to the sleeping quarters. It's a quirky, fun place just a short walk from Times Square and the beach.

Matlatcha

  🐾 "Ⓘ" ↬ You can't get more waterfront than the **Bridgewater Inn** (239-283-2423 or 1-800-378-7666; www.bridge waterinn.com), which sits on pilings right next to the "fishingest bridge" atop Matlatcha Pass. But who needs to walk to fish when you can drop a line off your deck? All nine rooms ($109–239) are accessed by the deck around the building, and many can interconnect, making this a great destination for big families. They come in a variety of configurations. Room #1 has a living room, full- and queen-sized beds, full kitchen, and dining room. Room #8 is a tropical nook with a fridge and three full-sized beds. And #2 is the deluxe model, a spacious corner suite with a primo view and a large flat-screen TV. Dockage is available for a small fee.

North Fort Myers 33903

&. "1" Spacious waterfront rooms make the **Best Western Fort Myers Waterfront** (239-997-5511 or 1-800-274-5511; www.bestwesternwaterfront.com), 13021 N Cleveland Ave., stand out from the typical chain hotel; every room has a balcony overlooking the Caloosahatchee River, facing downtown on the far shore. Each of the island-themed rooms ($81 and up) feature large closets, an oversized television, and a huge tiled bathroom, and you can walk right downstairs to Pincher's Crab Shack (see *Where to Eat*) for dinner.

Pineland 33945

∞ "1" Be pampered in historic surroundings at **Tarpon Lodge** (239-283-3999; www.tarponlodge.com), 13771 Waterfront Dr., where the Wells family continues to build on a long history of hospitality. This genteel getaway attracted anglers back in 1926 as the Pine-Aire Lodge and continues to do so today. Of the 21 inviting guest rooms ($115–245) overlooking Pine Island Sound, choose from a room in the Island House annex or in the historic original lodge. The Useppa and Cabbage Key Rooms have fabulous sunset views. The landscaped grounds include a beautiful waterfront swimming pool and a pier with a boathouse (now available as lodging, $235–310), where many visitors and locals amble out to watch the sun set over Useppa Island. The family also manages the rental cottages on offshore Cabbage Key, a quiet tropical getaway accessible only by private boat or local passenger ferry.

St. James City 33956

❀ A cute little complex with Old Florida flair, **Two Fish Inn** (239-283-4519; www.twofishinn.com), 2960 Oleander St., has five spiffy suites ($99 and up) named for fish you'll find in these waters, and the Island House, a spacious home away from home. The suites have just enough kitchen for you to prep your meals and enjoy them, too. Soak in the tropical pool, or borrow a bicycle, kayak, or canoe to explore the island. Captain Charlie runs charters for fishing ($350) or shelling ($200) right from their dock!

With free dockage right outside each front door, the **Water's Edge Motel and Apartments** (239-283-0515; www.thewatersedgemotel.com), 2938 Sanibel Blvd., is a gem of a family motel, now in the second generation of family ownership. Rooms range from standard motel through efficiency ($89 and up) and a one-bedroom apartment with hardwood built-ins. It's a popular family-reunion destination, so book ahead!

Sanibel Island 33957

When I was a kid, my family stayed at the **Anchor Inn & Cottages** (239-395-9688 or 1-866-469-9543; www.sanibelanchorinn.com), 1245 Periwinkle Way, and every time I've visited Sanibel since, passing by the distinctive A-frame cottages reminds me of those childhood days. So I was delighted when I stopped in and discovered everything still has that "stopped in time" feel, sparkling new and clean and 1960s—solid construction with concrete walls and wooden ceilings, old-fashioned terrazzo floors and tiled showers, and verandas outside each of the 12 rooms ($89–179 for standard efficiency to two-bedroom, and $150–270 for the spacious A-frame cottages).

Within walking distance of the beach, **The Palm View Inn** (239-472-1606 or 1-877-472-1606; www.palmviewsanibel .com), 706 Donax St., offers luxuriously themed suites amid a tropical garden, where quiet outdoor courtyard alcoves and a Jacuzzi and barbecue grill await guests. Each newly renovated unit offers a full kitchen, phone, and Internet access. Complimentary guest laundry and use of a kayak, bicycles, and beach toys are included with your stay. There are five units, including efficiencies and two-room suites ($85–185 depending on season and size).

The cozy, Caribbean-themed **Sandpiper Inn** (239-472-1529 or 1-877-227-4737; www.gosandpiper.com), 720 Donax St., has one-bedroom, one-bath suites with kitchen, sitting area, and a balcony or patio for you to catch the sea breeze. All housekeeping supplies are included, plus complimentary beach accessories, coolers, and bicycles. Adults only, $69–165.

Tucked away in a lush tropical garden, the intimate **Tarpon Tale Inn** (239-472-0939; www.tarpontale.com), 367 Periwinkle Way, has eight units along a private courtyard with hot tub and hammocks. Choose from partial or full kitchens. Each room has tiled floors and wicker furnishings, and guests can use the shelling table to clean their finds or borrow beach umbrellas and bicycles for an excursion; rates $90–220.

✳ Where to Eat
DINING OUT
Boca Grande
A local favorite since 1911, **The Pink Elephant** (941-964-0100; www.the -gasparilla-inn.com/din_pinkelephant

.php), 500 Palm Ave. (at the Gasparilla Inn), is best known for its fresh seafood, featuring locally caught grouper, pompano, and snapper served "Floribbean" style. An extensive wine list complements the menu, which also includes lamb, veal, and hand-cut Angus steaks.

In a historic downtown storefront, **The Temptation Restaurant** (941-964-2610), 350 Park Ave., has pleased its customers for more than 50 years with top-notch lunches and dinners featuring fresh local fish and seafood plus great steaks. Save room for dessert! Reservations recommended.

Captiva Island
🦐 It's fun, funky, and 1940s—a pink palace of movie memorabilia, Christmas ornaments, and tin toys. One of Captiva's most distinctive dining experiences, **The Bubble Room** (239-472-5558; www.bubbleroomrestaurant .com), 15001 Captiva Dr., offers sinfully delightful desserts and mouthwatering fresh breads with some of the island's best seafood. Although the prices say fine dining, the atmosphere is casual—T-shirts and sandals are acceptable. Decked out in a unique scouting uniform, your "Bubble Scout" attends to your every request. Served from 11:30 AM to 2:30 PM, lunch specialties ($9–13) include salads and sandwiches such as the Okra-Homa, with shrimp, okra, and corn cakes. For dinner ($20–33) try the Eddie Fisherman, a fillet of local grouper rolled in brown sugar and pecans and poached in a brown paper bag, or Some Like it Hot Hot Hot, tasty fresh Gulf shrimp in a garlic tequila butter sauce. Many patrons go for the Tiny Bubble, the least-expensive entrée option: a choice of appetizer, fresh breads, house salad, and a slab of one of the Bubble Room's tasty cakes. No matter how much room you leave for dessert, you'll be taking

some of the generous portion home. Don't miss the fluffy White Christmas Cake, stuffed with slivered almonds and coconut, topped with whipped-cream frosting. With nearly a dozen dessert choices, you'll find a perfect match.

In an elegant setting overlooking Pine Island Sound, **The Green Flash** (239-472-3337), 15183 Captiva Dr., offers tasty lunch ($7–10) and dinner ($14 and up) choices. I like the fruit de mer, with an assortment of sautéed seafood, and the grouper Café de Paris is the house specialty.

At 'Tween Waters Inn (see *Lodging*), the **Old Captiva House** serves up inspired variations on classic themes, including pecan crusted mahimahi with cherry buerre rouge, tropical rice and vegetable, and stuffed veal chop stuffed with rosemary and gouda, served with port wine glaze and saffron risotto; entrées $22 and up.

Fort Myers

Since 1982, **The Prawnbroker** (239-489-2226; www.prawnbroker.com), 13451 McGregor Blvd. #16, has served up fresh fish in its fish market; check the daily "Fresh Fish Report" as you walk in. Enjoy your favorites fried, broiled, grilled, or blackened, or have your seafood in a classic pasta dish, dinners $12–25. Your entrée comes with warm fresh bread, and the portions are nicely sized. I enjoyed a platter of light and tasty almond fried shrimp on my last visit. Open for dinner with "Early Catch" specials between 4 PM–5:30 PM, $11–14.

Fort Myers—Downtown

Rich, dark wood and tasteful furnishings underscore the classy feel of **The Veranda** (239-332-2065; www.veranda restaurant.com), 2122 Second St., a fine restaurant in one of Fort Myers's most historic venues. Built in 1902 by Manuel Gonzales, son of one of the original settlers, the complex joins together two homes at the corner of Second and Broadway, downtown. Diners look out over a secluded court-yard of tropical plants, accented with a waterfall flowing down into the fish-pond. First opened as a restaurant in the 1970s, The Veranda's lunch menu features tasty combinations such as Florida crab cakes with potato salad, or fried green tomato salad (my favorite!) with tidbits of Virginia ham and blue cheese sprinkled across a bed of mixed greens. Lunches are served 11 AM–2:30 PM and start at $8. The dinner menu ($28–39) shifts the emphasis to seafood and meat, with chateaubriand, veal Piccata, grilled fresh Florida grouper, and the Southern sampler of fresh fish, Gulf shrimp, and sea scallops in a lobster sherry cream sauce, delicious over a bed of fettuccine. Don't miss the tempting appetizers: oysters Rockefeller, escargot in puff pastry with Stilton blue cheese sauce, and Southern grit cakes with andouille sausage. Desserts include Bailey's Irish Cream Cheesecake and a delectable chocolate pâté with raspberry coulis, an artful presentation of a slab of cold fudgelike chocolate with a ribbon of maple walnut on a platter of raspberry sauce. Doors open for dinner at 5:30 PM, with meals served until 11 PM.

Pineland

A four-star culinary experience, the **Tarpon Lodge Restaurant** (239-283-2517; www.tarponlodge.com/dining), 13771 Waterfront Dr., at **Tarpon Lodge** (see *Lodging*), overlooks Pine Island Sound. The slate of top-notch entrées ($16–32) includes preparations such as rosemary roasted chicken breast, veal Piccata, and aged filet mignon, and the tasty marinated portobello mushroom salad is a wonderful variant on traditional spinach salad.

I appreciated the fresh-baked kalamata olive bread with olive oil for dipping; the rich and thick cream of mushroom soup was a delight. Meals are prepared using fresh herbs from the garden on-site. The friendly staff will gladly help you with recommendations to suit your palate. Reservations recommended.

Sanibel Island

As soon as it opened, eager fans showed up—**Doc Ford's Sanibel Rum Bar & Grille** (239-472-8311; www.docfordssanibel.com), 975 Rabbit Rd., is a big hit with the mystery lovers' crowd as it's owned by author Randy Wayne White and set just a few minutes from the now-closed marina where Randy and fictional Doc Ford lived and worked. The building is a part of this novelist's past—it's a former fish house that supplied fresh catches. The exterior is painted with Florida forest scenes, the warm wooden interior evokes the sea, and the menu reflects the rural tropics in which Randy spent many years on assignment for *Outside* magazine. Choose from an extensive array of creative appetizers, inspired entrées such as Campeche fish tacos or banana leaf snapper, and unique salads and sandwiches; meals from $7. It's a sports bar, too, so it gets noisy during the games, and there's no chance you'll miss the action with over a dozen flat-screen televisions around the place. The prominent and popular bar has a broad selection of premium rums, including Rum Jumbie and Myers Legend; some are aged a decade or two. Don't forget to browse the Doc Ford books and souvenirs, including Randy's own line of hot sauces inspired by his characters. Open daily 11 AM–close.

A top-notch seafood house, **Jacaranda** (239-472-1771; www.jacarandaon sanibel.com), 1223 Periwinkle Way, consistently wins "Taste of the Islands"

awards in all categories. Selections include Florida snapper en Papillote, sesame-encrusted yellowfin tuna, roast duckling, Sanibel cowboy steak, and more; entrées $20 and up. Enjoy fresh oysters at the raw bar on the patio.

EATING OUT

Boca Grande

Drop in for homemade ice cream at **Loose Caboose** (941-964-0440; www.loosecaboose.biz), 433 W Fourth St., in the old railroad depot, or take the time for mini-burgers or a soup and salad. Open for lunch daily ($5–13).

The only place to dine oceanfront in Boca Grande is the classic **South Beach Bar & Grille** (941-964-0765), 777 Gulf Blvd., a tropical-themed casual eatery with a screened room overlooking the placid waters of the Gulf framed by sea grapes. Lunch sandwiches and baskets include fried oysters, grouper Reuben, and grilled cheese. Entrées lean on the bounty of the sea, including Florida crab cakes and fresh peel 'n' eat shrimp.

Bokeelia

🌿 At the end of Stringfellow Road, the picture windows of **Capt'n Con's Seafood House** (239-283-4300) frame an idyllic Pine Island scene—fishing boats chug through the pass as brown pelicans dive in unison into schools of mullet shimmering beneath the waves. It's one of the oldest buildings in Bokeelia, the site of the original post office at the town's original steamer dock, circa 1904. Offering fresh fish, succulent steaks, and an ever-changing variety of down-home specials such as pot roast, meat loaf, and fried catfish, Capt'n Con's provides excellent value for your dollar (dinners under $20), with daily all-you-can-eat seafood specials. Top your dinner off with a slice of homemade pie, and don't miss Fran's shrimp bisque, offered on Thursday.

At Marker 8, the **Lazy Flamingo 3** (239-283-5959; www.lazyflamingo .com), 16501-B Stringfellow Rd., is a kick back and relax rustic Cracker shack with picnic tables and a bar— just the kind of place where you'll find the seafood you love. Grab shucked-to-order oysters, steamer pots, conch chowder, and grouper a few different ways, or go for the "Dead Parrot" wings and spicy french fries, with entrées under $20. It's a local favorite no matter the location (also found on Sanibel Island).

Captiva Island

The lilac and green **Keylime Bistro** (239-395-0882; www.captivaisland inn.com), 11506 Andy Rosse Ln., will certainly catch your eye, and it's a blast to settle down to the Sunday jazz brunch with a bunch of friends. Try the chicken voodoo, with sautéed artichokes, tomatoes, kalamata olives, capers, basil, and garlic; or paella Valencia, including shrimp, scallops, calamari, mussels, chicken, and sausage. Yum! Lunch runs $6–11, dinner $10–32. Across the street, **R.C. Otters Island Eats** (239-395-1142), owned by the same folks, is a fun and colorful restaurant with an extensive vegetarian menu and a kid's menu. They serve steamer pots, cold strawberry bisque, and lobster rolls, so the menu is not one to miss. Open daily for all meals.

I've strolled down the beach more than once to **The Mucky Duck** (239-472-3434; www.muckyduck.com), 11546 Andy Rosse Ln., for fish-and-chips, and that's why this British pub is a favorite around here: It has great views of the Gulf and reliable grub. Chow down on oyster po'boy or duck fingers, or try meat loaf à la Jaybird, a

specialty of the house. Lunch $5–15, dinner $18–38.

Fort Myers

From the outside, the building is clearly a renovated Long John Silver's. But the inside sparkles with bright walls, piñatas, and colorful pastel Mexican festival flags strung from the rafters. Boasting "Authentic Mexican Cuisine," **La Casita** (239-415-1050), 15185 McGregor Blvd., delivers with a menu that is anything but Tex-Mex. The owners hail from the Guanajato region of Mexico, where sautéed onions and peppers accompany roasted tomatoes and cilantro in freshly prepared enchiladas, chimichangas, tacos, and gorditas. Besides shredded beef or chicken, you can enjoy a mildly spicy potato filling. Platters come with soft, fresh Mexican rice and red beans. Enjoy house margaritas and a wide variety of Mexican and domestic beers. Platters $9 and up; thick homemade chips and a zesty cilantro salsa are provided as you peruse the menu.

Fort Myers—Downtown

Under the distinctive downtown Arcade marquee, **April's Eatery** (239-337-4004), 2269 First St., serves breakfast and lunch Monday through Friday to downtown workers and visitors. Choose from hot sandwiches, 8-inch subs, or cold sandwiches such as crab, dill, and shrimp salad. Morning choices include bagel sandwiches, toast, and muffins.

For lunch and dinner, **Delicious Things** (239-332-7797; www.delicious -things.com), 2262 First St., offers a taste of Italy with a twist. Entrée salads can come with ahi tuna, salmon, jumbo shrimp, and more and are made with fine mixed greens. While the lunch menu ($5–9) has many Italian favorites, such as panini, pastas, Pellegrino, and Lavazza coffee, it includes homemade wiener schnitzel with potato salad and a "DownTown Doener" comprised of homemade pita bread with red cabbage, mixed greens, onions, and a Turkish herb or garlic sauce. Dinners ($16–30) are elaborate presentations of fine cuisine, including fresh gnocchi stuffed with asiago cheese with fresh vegetables, manicotti, and filet mignon roasted with fresh thyme.

Fort Myers—East

I was very impressed by the ribs at the **Rib City Grill** (239-693-2223; www.ribcity.com), 13908 Palm Beach Blvd., which is a regional chain but darn good. Combo dinners "from the pit" cost under $15, and there are five types of salad on the menu, including crunchy grouper. I love the three-cheese fries, smothered in Monterey, cheddar, and pepper Jack with bacon. The coleslaw and baked beans are homemade, and desserts, such as the Chocolate Mousse Mania, just can't be passed up.

Fort Myers Beach

Haunted by the ghosts of Jim and Mary Galloway, whose Mermaid Club was burned by an arsonist in 1955, **The Beached Whale** (941-463-5505; www.thebeachedwhale.com), 1249 Estero Blvd., is a party-goers spot thanks to their rooftop bar, the Lookout Lounge, and a popular choice for its Whalewiches (no whales—think pulled pork, grouper, and other favorites), served with beans and rice, buttered parsley potatoes or fries, and their house coleslaw. Lunches $9–11, dinners $16–18.

After a day where I managed to squeeze in three hikes while visiting dozens of other locations—and no lunch—I was famished by the time I got to **Jojo's at the Beach** at the **Pink Shell Resort** (see *Hotels, Motels, and Resorts*). It was pouring rain, and the seating is open-air, but thank goodness

for the roof and roll-down windows. This casual restaurant overlooks the Gulf and specializes in Floribbean cuisine. Their crab fettuccine hit the spot, but other entrées ($16–29) tempted, too, including the center cut filet mignon. Feeling in a tropical mood, I savored a piña colada from Bongo's Bar & Grill for good measure. Jojo's serves lunch 11 AM–5 PM, dinner 5 PM–9 PM.

Dine beachfront at **Junkanoo on the Beach** (239-463-6139), 3040 Estero Blvd., where they fling open the sliding glass doors so you can enjoy the salty breeze while munching on a grilled portabello mushroom sandwich or the tasty shrimp and crab salad. Lunches $7–12, dinners $11 and up; it's a hangout for drinks and live music at night.

Enjoy homespun goodness at the **Split Rail Family Restaurant** (239-466-3400), 17943 San Carlos, where breakfast sides include fresh hot apples or grits (my favorites!) among many other choices. The atmosphere was pure country comfort, and although I was worried about getting to an appointment, I shouldn't have—the meal arrived in less than five minutes. I topped my pancakes off with real Wisconsin Gold sweet butter. Breakfast served 6 AM–2 PM, $4–8, including a variety of three-egg omelets and griddle favorites; they serve lunch and dinner, too.

Matlacha

Always busy at dinnertime, the **Matlacha Oyster House** (239-283-2544), 3930 Pine Island Rd., has a 1970s nautical look about it and keeps regulars coming back with fresh local shrimp and oysters, baked stuffed flounder, and other specialties, $10 and up.

Enjoy Italian specialties along the mangrove-lined estuary at **Moretti's Seafood Restaurant** (239-283-5825), 4200 Pine Island Rd., a family-owned restaurant with classic seafood pastas, pizza, grilled beef, veal, and chicken, entrées $10 and up.

🍤 A bustling breakfast stop, **Mulletville** (239-283-5151), 4597 Pine Island Rd., has good Southern classics on the menu, from grits to mullet, and features a mullet, shrimp, and Swiss omelet you just can't miss.

Offering a great view of the islands, the **Sandy Hook Fish & Rib House** (239-283-0113; www.sandyhookfish andribhouse.com), 4875 Pine Island Rd., serves up seafood classics in a comfortable family atmosphere. The "Sandy Hook Treasures" include more than a dozen seafood choices, from cracked conch to steamed crab legs and Florida lobster, $12 and up.

North Fort Myers
For casual waterfront dining, **Pincher's Crab Shack** (239-652-1313; www .pincherscrabshack.com), 13021 N Cleveland Ave. at the Best Western, is a fun and affordable choice with a great selection of seafood; the crab and corn chowder is spicy and downright addictive. If you order crab, you'll be pounding it with mallets on a brown paper–covered table; your fresh veggies and corn come served with real butter. Dinners start at $10; there are two additional locations in town.

Sanibel Island
Gaily painted roosters and chickens set the tone at **Amy's Over Easy Café** (239-472-2625), 630 Tarpon Bay Rd., where your view is of the tropical forest outside, and the extensive breakfast menu includes Gulf shrimp omelets, Reuben Benedict, and stuffed French toast; open for breakfast and lunch daily.

🍤 The fun place to eat on Sanibel is **The Island Cow** (239-472-0606; www .sanibelislandcow.com), 2163 Periwinkle Way, with a dining area that spills

out of a historic home and onto the front porch, where you can dine perched on pastel chairs while watching the world walk by. They serve amazing home-cooked breakfasts (Crab cakes and grits! Stuffed French toast!), grilled goodies, greens, quesadillas, wraps, barbecue, steaks . . . the list goes on and on and includes a kid's menu, too. Don't miss the treats, too—ice cream floats (such as Purple Cows and egg creams), pies, and cakes. Breakfast starts at $4, entrées at $11.

The Lighthouse Café (239-472-0303; www.lighthousecafe.com), 362 Periwinkle Way, claims bragging rights for the "world's best breakfast," and the way folks were lined up for it, I'd believe it. Inside the brightly painted café, try exquisite specialties such as seafood Benedict—a grilled croissant topped with sautéed shrimp, crabmeat, and scallops with broccoli, mushrooms, two poached eggs, and fresh Alfredo sauce. Breakfast all day ($3–11); lunch served 11 AM–3 PM.

St. James City
Breakfast is big at **Jackie's Family Restaurant** (239-283-4225), 3002 Stringfellow Rd., where their specials include a Fisherman's breakfast with fresh Pine Island mullet (when available), country fried steak, and a hearty helping of eggs, grits or potatoes, and toast, biscuit, or two small pancakes. They have biscuits and gravy, too. Here's where to fuel up (breakfast $3–9) before your outdoor adventure! Open Mon.–Fri. 8 AM–9 PM, Sat.–Sun. 8 AM–1 PM for breakfast only.

BAKERIES, COFFEE SHOP, AND SODA FOUNTAINS

Boca Grande
The **Boca Grande Baking Company** (941-964-5818; bocagrandebaking-co.com), 384 E Railroad Ave., features hearth-baked breads, fresh pastries,

muffins, and scones, and a full-service coffee bar with your favorite coffee drinks.

On a hot day, you'll want to have some cool ice cream treats ($4–6) at the **Pink Pony** next to historic Hudson's Grocery on Park Avenue, where if you catch them while the lunch counter's open, they'll make burgers and dogs, too. Located just across Park Avenue and the bike trail, the **Loose Caboose** (see *Eating Out*) dishes out ice cream, too.

Fort Myers

The place to grab baked goodies downtown is **Mason's Bakery** (239-334-4525; www.masonsbakery.com), 1615 Hendry Ave., where they make political cookies (yep, that's right!) and cakes and cookies with photos on them, along with muffins and pastries and other tasty treats; closed Sun.–Mon.

Fort Myers Beach

I stopped in for ice cream at **Strawberrie Corner** (941-463-1155), 7205 Estero Blvd., and discovered they offer a pretty complete array of sandwiches for lunch ($5 and up) in addition to sundaes, malts, cones, and, of course, strawberry shortcake.

✳ Selective Shopping

Boca Grande

Boca Grande Outfitters (941-964-2445; www.bocagrandeoutfitters.com), 375 Park Ave., carries "Life is Good" T-shirts and hats, a good selection of books on fishing, and sportswear. You can also pick up a pooper-scooper for your dog, a smart move if you're walking him to tiny Sam Murphy Park along the block, a tropical oasis in the shade of coconut palms.

Ruhama's Books in the Sand (941-964-5800), 333 Park Ave., is a great little independent bookstore with an emphasis on nautical books and local

authors. They also carry art supplies, including sketch pads and watercolor paints.

Bonita Springs

Packed with a good mix of collectibles and decor items, **The Motherload** (239-948-1177), 27796 Old US 41 Rd., has everything from Gilbert & Sullivan LPs and an original Battleship game to an Esther Williams swimming instruction book.

Captiva Island

Perk up your taste buds with a stop at the **Captiva Provision Company** (239-472-5111), 5400 Plantation Rd. It's a lovely gourmet grocery with fine artisan cheeses, a wine bar, fresh sandwiches, and deli items, and if you're staying at **South Seas Island Resort** (see *Hotels, Motels and Resorts*) they'll deliver right to your room.

Estero

 ♿ ✎ 🐾 "¶" Anchored by Dillards, Target, and Muvico Theaters, **Coconut Point** (239-992-4259; www.simon.com) is a massive outdoor mall along US 41 between Corkscrew Rd. and Coconut Pt., with most of the major chains represented, including some tough-to-find ones like the Apple Store and Trek Bicycles. There is a playground, fire pit, and a turtle pond, plus accommodations for your pet. Shuttles run throughout the property.

There's plenty to purchase at **Flamingo Island** (941-948-7799; www .flamingoisland.com), 200 yards west of I-75 on Bonita Springs Blvd., with more than six hundred dealer booths in a tropical setting. You can also pick up fresh fruits and veggies here. Fri.–Sun. 8 AM–4 PM.

Fort Myers

Get lost amid hundreds of booths at **Flea Masters Giant Flea Market** (941-334-7001; www.fleamall.com), on FL 82, 1 mile west of I-75, where

I stumbled across beautiful Balinese hand-carved cabinets for reasonable prices, fresh seafood and produce, and the usual booth after booth of cheap Asian goods.

A new mall complex off I-75 at Alico Road, **Gulf Coast Town Center** (239-267-0783; www.gulfcoasttown center.com), 10012 Gulf Center Dr., attracts an outdoorsy crowd with its massive **Bass Pro Shops** (239-461-7800; www.bassproshops.com), which pays homage to the Everglades.

Right near Punta Rassa and the Sanibel Causeway, the **Tanger Factory Outlet** (239-454-1974; www.tanger outlet.com), 20350 Summerlin Rd., contains factory outlet stores for popular top-name brands like Lane Bryant, Samsonite, and Rack Room Shoes, plus a few eateries.

Fort Myers—Downtown
In addition to the usual antiques store inventory, **Main Street Antiques & Collectibles** (239-689-6246), 2229 Main St., contains the contents of the old Flowers to 50s Vintage Department Store, which makes this a retro trip into your parent's 1970s basement—a delightful clutter of tree lamps, avocado easy chairs, and a paint-by-number-on-velvet Last Supper. Featuring goodies from the '50s, '60s, and '70s, the constantly changing inventory runs the gamut from psychedelic-patterned dresses and vintage Hawaiian shirts to Ronco appliances ("as seen on TV") still in the box since 1972. Poke through the shelves to find Viewmaster slides, 8 mm cartoon films, and other fun toys and books from your childhood. Note to album collectors—don't miss this selection!

Fort Myers—McGregor Boulevard
In the McGregor Boulevard Antique District, a handful of great shops are clustered near the College Parkway overpass. At the **McGregor Antique Mall** (239-433-0200), 12720 McGregor Blvd., browse collectibles such as political buttons and dolls, regional and national postcards, and salt cellars, as well as a fine collection of glassware and dishes. Poke through vintage purses **at Judy's Antiques** (239-481-9600), 12710 McGregor Blvd., where you'll find fine silver and glassware. **George Brown Antiques** (239-482-5101), 12730 McGregor Blvd, features tableware, fine furnishings, and estate jewelry.

Matlacha
Island Décor and More (239-283-8080; island-decorandmore.com), 4206 Pine Island Rd., is one of the largest gift shops in the area, and the prices are great. Pick up decor items with a nautical flair, select seashells, and browse through the books.

North Fort Myers
Sure, it's kitschy, with row upon row of alligator heads, shark jaws, and coconut monkeys. But nowhere else on earth other than **The Shell Factory** (1-888-474-3557), 2787 N Tamiami Trail, will you find a finer collection of seashells under one roof. From its humble beginnings in 1942 as a shell shop, the Shell Factory has ballooned to a sprawling megacomplex, with family entertainment (see *Family Activities*), adult entertainment (karaoke at Captain Fishbones bar), and a virtual department store of gifts beyond the thousands of seashells and corals for purchase. Browse for fossils, Christmas ornaments, touristy T-shirts, and fudge, too.

Sanibel Island
The Islander Trading Post (239-395-0888; www.islandertradingpost .biz) is an antiques shop with well-organized collections of collections,

from vintage drugstore items to ashtrays, Florida postcards and matchbooks, and even milk bottles.

The oldest bookstore on Sanibel Island is **MacIntosh Books and Paper** (239-472-1447; www.macintoshbooks.com), 2365 Periwinkle Way, a historic beach cottage with a nice selection of new fiction, a local-interest section, a goodly number of nature and children's books, and a back room filled with used books.

Jazz drifts through the **Sanibel Island Bookshop** (239-472-5223; www.sanibelbookshop.com), 1711 Periwinkle Way, where you can merge your right and left brain by browsing through both Sark's books and Ann Coulter. The store carries new books and has an extensive children's section, tasteful gifts and plush toys, and greeting cards.

PRODUCE STANDS AND FARMER'S MARKETS

Alva
Ritchey's Farm Fresh Produce (239-693-5092), 15500 Palm Beach Blvd., is a don't-miss family fruit stand along SR 80 with everything you can think of, from homemade jellies and jams to Hendry County citrus and Immokalee tomatoes; cash only.

Bonita Springs
Wednesday farmer's markets in **Bonita Springs** bring fresh produce in from the country. Stop by Riverside Park, 27300 Old 41 Rd., to sample the wares. Nov.–Apr., 7 AM–1 PM.

Fort Myers
There is nothing like the smell of Florida oranges being processed, and you'll pick up that scent as you step out of your car at **Sun Harvest Citrus** (239-768-2686; www.sunharvestcitrus.com), 14810 Metro Pkwy. Since 1940, this big green packinghouse has been the place to get the pick of the citrus crop for this region. Step inside and grab a supermarket cart to load up on fresh citrus, citrus-inspired sweets like key lime thimble cookies and candied orange slices, homemade fudge, and citrus dressings, jams, and jellies. Sip your own sample of juice while you peek through the big picture windows to watch the packing and juicing operation. They ship gift fruits, of course, but the one thing you shouldn't miss is the orange and vanilla swirl soft-serve ice cream at the deli counter! Open daily Mon.–Sat. 8 AM–9 PM, Sun. 10–6.

Fort Myers—Downtown
Farmers bring their produce into town for a true Green Market—only agricultural products that can be eaten or grown allowed—at the **Downtown Fort Myers Farmers Market** (239-332-6813), under the US 41 Caloosahatchee River Bridge in Centennial Park, at the corner of Heitman and First Streets. The market runs year-round from 7 AM–2 PM in Nov.–Apr. and 7 AM–1 PM May–Oct.

Fort Myers Beach
Every Friday 7 AM until noon November through April, peek under the Sky Bridge for the **Fort Myers Beach Farmer's Market** for booths and booths of fresh produce, seafood, cut flowers, houseplants, and baked goods. Parking is free during market hours.

Matlacha
The finest tropical produce from Pine Island's groves fills **Tropicaya Fruit & Gift** (239-283-0656; www.tropicaya.com), 3220 SW Pine Island Rd., where you can browse alligator brushes and hot sauces while waiting for your smoothie or juice. Nab a carambola (star fruit) or two to take home!

✷ Entertainment

FINE ARTS For an evening of fine music, check with the box office for the **Southwest Florida Symphony Orchestra** (239-418-1500; www.swflso .org), the only professional orchestra in the region. Playing both classical and popular music, they perform at both the **Barbara B. Mann Performing Arts Hall** (239-481-4849; www.bb mannpah.com), 8099 College Pkwy. SW, Fort Myers, and at **BIG Arts** (239-395-0900; www.bigarts.org), 900 Dunlop Rd., Sanibel Island.

In the 12,000-square-foot William R. Frizzel Cultural Center, the **Alliance for the Arts** (239-939-ARTS; www .artinlee.org), 11091 McGregor Blvd., Fort Myers, has public galleries with monthly exhibitions, theatrical productions, and art workshops.

THEATER ᕇ At **Broadway Palm Dinner Theatre** (239-278-4422; www.broadwaypalm.com), 1380 Colonial Blvd., Fort Myers, the buffet almost upstages the show at this regional theater—but not quite. Featuring professional performers, it hosts musicals and comedies year-round, with ticket prices starting at $25 for show only; reserve in advance.

✷ Special Events

February: For two days, downtown immerses in the arts during **Artfest Fort Myers** (239-768-3602; www .artfestfortmyers.com), bringing in more than 200 major artists from around the country and drawing on the talents of budding artists as well.

Brighten up at the **Edison Festival of Light** (239-334-2999; www.edison festival.org), midmonth, Fort Myers. Commemorating Thomas Edison's birthday, a lively lit-up parade kicks off this celebration of light and history, which includes a downtown block party, orchid show, huge arts and crafts fair, and the nation's largest after-dark parade.

✐ The **Lee County Fair** (239-543-8368; www.leeciviccenter.com) celebrates the agricultural bounty of the county, from fishing to veggies and ranching, with good old-fashioned family fun.

March: **Sanibel Shell Fair** (239-472-2155), 2173 Periwinkle Way, Sanibel Island. More than four hundred species of shells wash up on Sanibel's shores, and collectors enjoy showing off their prizes at this annual gathering that started back in 1937, hosted by the Sanibel-Captiva Shell Club. Donation.

April: Film buffs will love the **Fort Myers Beach Film Festival** (239-765-0202; www.fmbfilmfest.com), last week of the month, with screenings, filmmaker panel discussions, and workshops as well as an elegant celebrity gala and screenings at the Fort Myers Beach Theatre. Free.

July: Mangos are a serious cash crop on Pine Island, so the **Pine Island Mango Mania Tropical Fruit Fair** (239-283-0888; www.floridascreative coast.com/MM-home.html), mid-month, showcases these and other luscious tropical fruits during a weekend celebration at the German-American Social Club on Pine Island Rd. Fee.

October: Launched in 2005, the **Calusa Blueway Paddling Festival** (239-433-3855; www.calusablueway paddlingfestival.com), is a weeklong event that gets you out on the water, exploring both the freshwater rivers and the mangrove-lined coastline of Lee County, with activities held everywhere from Alva to Bonita Springs.

Be one with the birds during **Ding Darling Days** (239-472-1100; www .dingdarlingdays.com), a weeklong birding and ecoheritage festival at the **Ding Darling National Wildlife Refuge** (see *Wild Places*).

November: **American Sandsculpting Championship Festival** (239-454-7500; www.sandsculptingfestival.com), Fort Myers Beach. Try building the ultimate sand castle on the beach, where amateurs and pros compete for prize money while showing off their sand artistry. Free.

December: Celebrate the season in honor of the man without whom we'd be without Christmas lights at **Holiday House**, a special electrified tribute at the **Edison & Ford Winter Estates** (see *Historic Sites*). Local musicians play each evening.

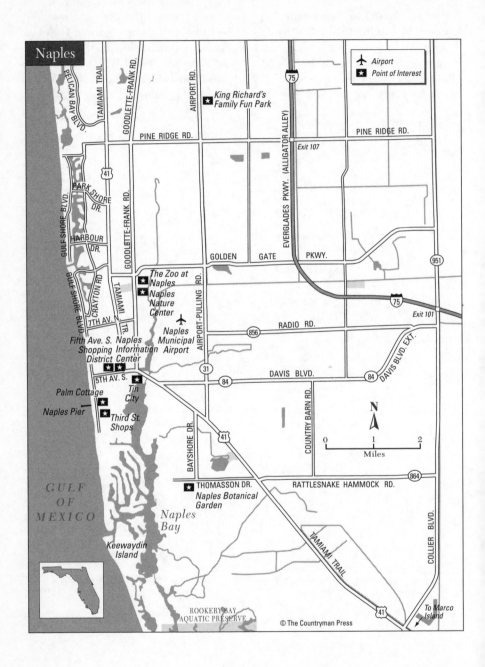

Naples

Legend
✈ Airport
★ Point of Interest

Map Labels

PELICAN BAY BLVD.

TAMIAMI TRAIL

GOODLETTE-FRANK RD.

AIRPORT RD.

75

★ King Richard's Family Fun Park

PINE RIDGE RD.

PINE RIDGE RD.

Exit 107

EVERGLADES PKWY. (ALLIGATOR ALLEY)

41

PARK SHORE DR.

GULF SHORE BLVD.

HARBOUR DR.

GOODLETTE-FRANK RD.

GOLDEN   GATE   PKWY.

951

75

Exit 101

CRAYTON RD.

GULF SHORE BLVD.

7TH AV. N.

TAMIAMI TR.

★ The Zoo at Naples
★ Naples Nature Center

AIRPORT-PULLING RD.

✈ Naples Municipal Airport

RADIO RD.

856

DAVIS BLVD. EXT.

Fifth Ave. S. Naples
Shopping Information
District Center
★ ★

RADIO RD.

84

DAVIS BLVD.

84

COUNTRY BARN RD.

5TH AV. S. ★

31

N

Palm Cottage ★
Tin City

Naples Pier ★
Third St. Shops

0   1   2
Miles

BAYSHORE DR.

41

864

GULF
OF
MEXICO

★ THOMASSON DR.
Naples Botanical Garden

RATTLESNAKE HAMMOCK RD.

COLLIER BLVD.

Naples
Bay

Keewaydin
Island

TAMIAMI TRAIL

ROOKERY BAY
AQUATIC PRESERVE

© The Countryman Press

41

To Marco
Island

THE PARADISE COAST: NAPLES, MARCO ISLAND & EVERGLADES

From ribbons of white sand to the mangrove-dense maze of the Ten Thousand Islands, the haunting fog-shrouded cypress strands of the Big Cypress Swamp, and the vast sawgrass prairies that define the world's only Everglades, the southwestern-most outpost of Florida's Gulf Coast is undeniably its most majestic.

After the Civil War, settlers Roger Gordon and Joe Wiggins came to the region with their families to homestead. A small settlement emerged along the bay, which promoters described as "surpassing the bay in Naples, Italy," and it was named **Naples**. In 1887, the owner of the Louisville Courier-Journal and his business partners formed the Naples Company and purchased nearly the entire town. They built a long pier into the Gulf of Mexico for shipping. Social life centered on the Naples Hotel, where celebrities such as Greta Garbo and Gary Cooper stayed.

At the age of 26, Barron Gift Collier was a millionaire flush with cash from streetcar advertising. Coming to Useppa Island in 1911 on vacation from New York City, he decided to invest in the rugged coastline, buying huge tracts of land until he owned a full third of Lee County. In 1923 he promised the state of Florida he'd underwrite the struggling federal construction of the Tamiami Trail across the Everglades if his land could be broken off into a separate county, and the state approved. To provide an engineering headquarters for the project and a county seat for the new Collier County, the Barron River was dredged to create **Everglades City**, Collier's first planned community and the county seat. It took 13 years of backbreaking labor to construct the highway, and Collier sunk his business profits into turning swampland into real estate by digging drainage canals and building roads, further advancing development around Naples Bay.

In 1513, Ponce de Leon discovered the Calusa settlements in the **Ten Thousand Islands**; he would continue north to receive a mortal blow from a Calusa warrior in Pine Island Sound. As along the coast to the north, Cuban ranchos—netted fish farms in the shallow estuary—were a mainstay of the local economy until the Seminole War of 1836. Hardy settlers cleared some of the mangrove keys and established plantations, growing corn and peas, pumpkins, tomatoes, citrus, and aromatic herbs. Settlers, traders, and Seminoles plied the waters to the **Smallwood Store** (see *Historic Sites*) on **Chokoloskee Island** to exchange goods, and the Storter family homesteaded most of the surrounding islands. Chokoloskee wasn't connected to the mainland until 1954, when a causeway was built.

The post-statehood settlement of **Marco Island** happened in 1870, when William T. Collier and his family homesteaded at Key Marco, where the Calusa once lived, and incorporated the area as Collier City. With fishing villages established at Key Marco and **Caxambas** (the southern point), the region stayed quiet until the 1960s, when it was carved up for residential development and some of the first high-rise condos on the Gulf Coast appeared along the shoreline. **Goodland**, founded by squatter Johnny Roberts in the late 1800s, grew up on a 40-acre Calusa shell mound and is one of the few places you can see what the islands looked like before modern development.

GUIDANCE Preplan your visit with the **Naples Marco Island Everglades Convention & Visitors Bureau** (1-800-688-3600; www.paradisecoast.com), 3050 N Horseshoe Dr., Ste. 210, Naples. Once in the area, stop in at the **Naples Area Visitor Information Center** (239-262-6141; www.napleschamber.org), 2390 Tamiami Trail N, a new interactive welcome center, to pick up brochures and maps and to make reservations. Open Mon.–Sat. 10 AM–5 PM.

GETTING THERE *By car:* **I-75** (also known as Alligator Alley as it passes through Big Cypress) and **US 41** (Tamiami Trail) provide primary access to the region.

By air: **Southwest Florida International Airport** (see *The Beaches of Fort Myers Sanibel*) offers regular commuter service daily. Naples Municipal Airport (239-643-0733; www.flynaples.com), 160 Aviation Dr. N, hosts **Gulf Coast Airways** (www.gulfcoastairways.com), a private high-end charter, flying in from locations around Florida, as well as an FBO for private pilots.

By bus: **Greyhound** (239-774-5660), 2669 Davis Blvd., Ste. 1, Naples.

GETTING AROUND *By car:* Unless you're staying in downtown Naples and plan to spend your time there, a car is essential for exploring this vast region. **US 41** intersects all major side roads to outlying towns—take **SR 846** to Vanderbilt Beach and Immokalee, **SR 951** to Marco Island, **CR 92** to Goodland, and **SR 29** to Everglades City.

By taxi: **Yellow Air Taxi** (239-261-2581; www.flyyellowairtaxi.com) and **Taxi Man Naples** (239-601-4444; www.taximannaples.com) are two of numerous providers in the area.

MEDICAL EMERGENCIES You'll find emergency services at **NCH Downtown Naples Hospital** (239-436-5000; www.nchmd.org) 350 7th St. N, and **NCH North Naples Hospital** (239-552-7000; www.nchmd.org) 11190 Health Park Blvd., as well as **Physicians Regional-Pine Ridge** (239-348-4000; www .physiciansregional.net), 6101 Pine Ridge Rd., and **Physicians Regional-Collier** (239-354-6000; www.physiciansregional.net), 8300 Collier Blvd., near Marco Island. There is a walk-in clinic at the **Marco Healthcare Center** (239-394-8234), 40 S Heathwood Dr., open daily 8 AM–7:30 PM. This is the closest medical care for Everglades City.

PARKING Downtown Naples provides free two-hour street parking, a large free parking garage just off Fifth Avenue, and a large, free, flat lot off Third Street. It does cost to park at most beachside parking areas, typically a flat fee of $4—which is a great bargain for all day, but not for a quick visit. Parking options are extremely limited on Marco Island, unless you are visiting a business or paying for beach parking. Nonresidents can purchase annual beach parking stickers for $50, good at all Collier County and City of Naples beach parks.

✱ To See

ARCHAEOLOGICAL SITES Noted as a center of Calusa culture—which can now be seen only in the **Marco Island Historical Museum** (see *Museums*)— Marco Island yielded spectacular treasures in 1896, when archaeologist Frank Cushing found an entire Calusa village preserved in muck at the site of what is now the **Olde Marco Island Inn & Suites** (see *Lodging*). Alas, Calusa shell mounds were long ago removed for roadfill or buried under construction sites; some remain hidden within the Ten Thousand Islands. The **Southwest** Florida Archaeological Society (www.explorationsinc.com/swfl-archaeology/index.html) hosts weekly open-to-the-public archaeology sessions at Craighead Laboratory (239-252-8517) on Tuesday and Thursday 9 AM–noon; call for details.

ART GALLERIES

Naples

It's claimed that Naples has more art galleries than any other city in Florida, and I have to concur—the sheer number of galleries is daunting even for a long weekend's worth of walk-about. I visited a handful, including the playful **Island House Gallery** (239-262-7455), 1100 Sixth Ave. along the dockside boardwalk; **Guess-Fisher Gallery** (239-659-2787), 824 Fifth Ave. S, featuring impressionist interpretations of Naples by artist Phil Fisher and batiks by his wife; the **Dennison-Moran Gallery** (239-263-0590), 696 Fifth Ave. S, a place of pure whimsy and ranked among the top 100 fine-art galleries in Florida; and **Native Visions Gallery** (239-643-3735; www.callofAfrica.com), 737 Fifth Ave. S, filled with wildlife and environmental art, featuring hot cast glass bowls and Judy Dy'Ans vivid renderings of Florida shorelines in oils. **Broad Avenue** is "Gallery Row" just east of Third Street, where you can park and visit gallery after gallery. The **Galerie du Soleil** (239-417-3450; www.galerie-du-soleil.com), 393 Broad Ave., is surrounded by beds of bright yellow blossoms. **Gallery One** (239-263-0835; www.gallery onenaples.com), 1301 Third St., appealed to my quirky sense of style with its playful raku pottery creatures, unusual statuettes, and colorful art glass.

Featuring the largest contemporary-art library in Naples, the **Von Liebig Art Center** (239-262-6517; www.naplesartcenter.org), 585 Park St., showcases more than a dozen rotating exhibits and permanent installations scattered throughout its two stories. Pieces are for sale in the Member's Gallery. Donation.

Ochopee

❧ Way down deep in the Big Cypress Swamp, motorists encounter an unexpected sight—**Clyde Butcher's Big Cypress Gallery** (239-695-2428; www.clydebutcher .com), 52338 Tamiami Trail N, a roadside oasis where alligators cruise the pond out front, and outstanding natural art awaits inside. Often referred to as "the Ansel Adams of the Everglades," Clyde makes massive black-and-white images that capture the many moods of Florida's wild places; much of his work focuses on the Everglades and Big Cypress ecosystems. You'll also find the color photography

BIG CYPRESS GALLERY

Sandra Friend

work of Oscar Thompson, Jeff Ripple, and Rick Cruz; creative cards and hand-painted photography by Clyde's wife, Niki; and books on wild Florida by their favorite authors. Every Labor Day weekend they host an open house on their property, a former orchid farm, featuring guided swamp walks (see *Swamp Walks*) to immerse you in the beauty and wonder of the swamp. Open daily 10 AM–5 PM.

HISTORIC SITES

Chokoloskee

✒ A private family-owned attraction, the **Historic Smallwood Store** (239-695-2989; www.florida-everglades .com/chokol/smallw.htm) is the oldest general store in Florida, notorious as the site of frontier justice in 1910 when the men of Chokoloskee dispatched Ed Watson, a suspected murderer, with a volley of gunfire. The store sits at the end of Mamie Street on the waterfront just as it did in 1897, when Ted Smallwood set up a trading post to swap goods with the Seminoles. Ted died in 1951, but it remained a working store in the family until 1982, and it reopened as a museum under the guidance of Ted's granddaughter. The bottles behind the counter (check out "Wintersmith's Chill Tonic") and the boxes on the tables are all original; the counter itself is beveled to allow ladies in hoop skirts to stand closer. Seminole artifacts fill some cases, as do many pieces of local history to sweep you back in time. A gift shop area has T-shirts, hats, and decor items. Open 10 AM–5 PM daily Dec. 1–May 1, 10 AM–4 PM Fri.–Tues. the rest of the year; fee.

Naples

In Naples, **Third Street South** is a designated historic district, although its anchor—the Old Naples Hotel—has been replaced with a parking lot and upscale shopping mall. Numerous business buildings date from the 1920s, and many to the original settlement of the area. Walk just a block or two in any direction to find streets where little Cracker cottages still hide under a canopy of mango and ficus.

One of the last tabby cottages in Collier County, **Palm Cottage** (239-261-8164; www.cchistoricalsociety.com), 137 12th Ave. S, built by Walter Haldemann in 1895, dominated the street when Naples was still a frontier outpost where Barron Collier's land office was a chickee with walls. The 3,500-square-foot cottage is made of insect-impervious Dade County pine and served many families over the years as well as for overflow accommodations for the Old Naples Hotel. Hedy Lamarr and other movie stars stayed inside these thick tabby walls, which help keep the rooms cool all year. Local spirit Alexandra Brown was the last owner prior to the cottage's purchase by the Naples Historical Society in 1978, and it's rumored she still keeps a kindly haunt over the place. A tour of the home showcases rooms with vintage details, including the 1906 kitchen with a GE icebox and antique stove. A gallery upstairs has fascinating scenes of Old Naples from the days when your address was "the house with green and white stripes" or "the house with diamonds." The Norris Garden is a new addition to the grounds.

Ochopee

The tiny **Ochopee Post Office** (239-261-8164), 3800 Tamiami Trail E, started its life as a toolshed but has housed the smallest post office in the United States since 1953 (it replaced the original 1932 post office, which burned down). Sitting all by itself along the roadside, it's an unmistakable landmark as you drive through the western Everglades.

MUSEUMS

Everglades City

Inside the 1927 Everglades Laundry building, the **Museum of the Everglades** (239-695-0008; www.florida-everglades.com/evercty/museum.htm), 105 Broadway Ave. W, opened in 1998 to educate visitors about the long and storied history of this once-frontier outpost, a city created in the midst of the Everglades. There are exhibits on Prohibition, the Seminoles, and early schools, and a special focus on what made Everglades City (founded as "Everglade," by the way)—the construction of the Tamiami Trail. The city became host to railroad and highway construction workers, and Barron Collier had a land office in town. Vintage laundry and dry-cleaning equipment are on display, as well as movie memorabilia. The front foyer houses a gift shop and art gallery featuring the work of local artists. Free; donations appreciated.

Immokalee

Learn about the earliest settlers to the wild frontier of Southwest Florida at the **Immokalee Pioneer Museum at Roberts Ranch** (239-658-2466; www.colliermuseums.com), 1215 Roberts Ave. Open Mon.–Fri. 9–5.

Marco Island

The **Marco Island Historical Society** (239-394-6917; www.theMIHS.org) is still searching for a permanent home for their important archaeological and historical collection. Presently, exhibits are at two different locations. The **Key Marco Museum**, 140 Waterview Dr., is in the lobby of the Marco Island Realtors Office. Open daily, 9–4. I visited the **Museum at Old Marco** (239-389-6447) 168 Royal Palm Dr., adjoining the Olde Marco Inn, in a former motel-turned-shops. The small

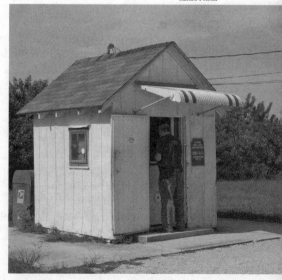

THE OCHOPEE POST OFFICE IS THE SMALLEST POST OFFICE IN THE UNITED STATES.

Sandra Friend

display focuses on Calusa culture (which is what Marco Island was famous for before the condos came along): The Key Marco Cat and Deer Head Mask were two spectacular finds in 1896, when archaeologist Frank Cushing found an entire Calusa village preserved in muck. Alas, the items removed from the muck mostly disintegrated, but there are models and photos to show them off. Prior to the 1960s real estate boom, Old Marco Village was home to numerous clam canneries, including Doxsee and Burnham, and residents made their living off the sea. Free.

In the Collier County Government Center, the **Collier County Museum** (239-774-8476; www.colliermuseums.com), 3301 Tamiami Trail E, depicts 10,000 years of local history, from prehistoric mastodons and the people who hunted them through the grand Calusa empire, the rise of the Seminoles, and the pioneers who settled this rough frontier. Set on 5 acres, it includes historic swamp buggies, a logging locomotive, and two early Naples cottages. Open 9 AM–5 PM Mon.–Fri., 9 AM–4 PM Sat. Free.

& "Art washes away from the soul the dust of everyday life" at the **Naples Museum of Art** (239-597-1111 or 1-800-597-1900; www.thephil.org/museum/museum .html), 5833 Pelican Bay Blvd., where a grand display of modern and classical art awaits. As you walk through the courtyard into the lobby, a massive Chihuly glass sculpture fills the space overhead, glinting in the sunlight. Rotating exhibits fill the first-floor Springborn Galleries—during my visit, modern Mexican masters. In the Von Liebig Galleries, I experienced innovative "correalism" with art suspended below eye level in a blue-curtained room, or popping out from curved paneled walls. Masters of Miniature in the Pistner Gallery showcased exquisite detail on miniature figurines and architectural models, including one of the Royal Opera, Versailles. A three-story glass sculpture is the centerpiece of the stairwell, and for an art glass aficionado like me, the Persian Ceiling corridor, another Chihuly creation, evokes a souk with glass as silk canopy, swirls of color and form punctuated by baubles and bowls. Exhibits spill into the adjacent Center for the Arts, where galleries showcased Winslow Homer's engravings and The Grand Tour in Miniature. Take a little piece of the museum home from the museum store, which offers colorful scarves, a great selection of art books, and objects d'art for the home. Open 10 AM–4 PM Tues.–Sat., noon–4 PM Sun., closed July–Oct. Admission starts at $8 adult, $4 student, and varies according to the season.

Originally a classroom exhibit by local students, the **Holocaust Museum of Southwest Florida** (239-263-9200; www.hmswfl.org), 4760 Tamiami Trail N, Suite 7, in Sandalwood Square, provides a chronological look at the events that shaped the Nazi empire and its reprehensible genocides. Open 1 PM–4 PM Tues.–Fri. and Sun. Free.

RAILROADIANA

Everglades City
An operational passenger and freight depot for more than 30 years, the **Atlantic Coast Depot**, at the end of Collier Ave., is now the **Everglades Seafood Depot** (see *Dining Out*), but its starring role was in *Winds Across the Everglades*, filmed in 1960. The depot marks the end of the Atlantic Coast Line (ACL) on the southwestern coast of Florida.

✐ Enjoy railroad history and model trains at the **Naples Depot Museum** (239-262-6525; www.colliermuseums.com), corner of US 41 and 10th St. S, where the historic Atlantic Coast Line depot houses a Lionel Train Museum with operational displays, exhibits on regional railroad history, an outdoor garden train to ride, and two significant pieces of rolling stock, the 1909 Soo Line Caboose and the 1947 Club Car. Take home railroad souvenirs and gifts from the Lionel Whistle Stop in the Southern RR baggage car. Open Mon.–Fri. 9 AM–5 PM, Sat. 9 AM–4 PM; now part of the **Collier County Museum.**

"Old Number 2," built by the Baldwin Locomotive Works, is one of the few remaining examples of logging locomotives left in the state. You'll see it at the **Collier County Museum** (see *Museums*).

SWAMP BUGGY RACES Invented in Naples in 1949 by Ed Frank to get through the rugged Big Cypress Swamp, the **swamp buggy** is a homegrown invention shown off on a regular basis at the **Florida Sports Park** (1-800-897-2701; www.swampbuggy.com), 8250 Collier Blvd., which features races between these enormous machines in January, March, and October.

ZOOLOGICAL PARK & WILDLIFE REHAB ♿ ✐ In a tropical setting established in 1919 as a botanical garden, the **Naples Zoo at Caribbean Gardens** (239-262-5409; www.napleszoo.com), 1590 Goodlette-Frank Rd., Naples, is an old family favorite of mine from the days of "Jungle Larry's Safari," a 1970s tourist attraction. An accredited zoo, it has large open-air enclosures with viewing platforms for most of its residents, from the big cats to alligators. The air echoes with the whoops of howler monkeys; these and other primates live on islands in a lagoon, where you can visit them on the Primate Expedition Cruise on a quiet electric boat, included free with your admission. There are several playgrounds scattered throughout the property, which still includes a bit of wild space and benches for quiet reflection amid the tropical landscaping, which dates back decades as a botanical garden. Renovations are still under way throughout the park. Regular "meet the keeper" and feeding events go on in the various enclosures all day; pick up a schedule as you enter the park. Before you leave, browse the gift shop, full of plush animals, nature-themed toys, and puzzles for the young ones. Ages 3–12 $12, 13–64 $20, 65 and up $19, military $12. Open 9 AM–5 PM daily.

✐ Injured wildlife find a new lease on life at the **Conservancy of Southwest Florida's Naples Nature Center** (see *Nature Centers*), where birds regain their flight capability in large enclosures tucked away in the pine forest. A large wading pool is home to dozens of pelicans and herons. Up to 70 percent of the injured mammals and birds received here can be reintroduced to the wild.

✳ To Do

AIRBOAT RIDES It's almost a cliché along the Tamiami Trail, but airboat rides through the Everglades are the only way to see the swamps up close and personal unless you go on a swamp walk (see *Swamp Walks*), and even those can't get you deep into the sawgrass. Ride with a reputable operator who doesn't feed the gators—not only is feeding wild alligators illegal, but it's a dangerous practice that makes them see humans as a food source. If you witness a violation, report it to Florida FWC (1-888-404-FWCC). And yes, you will see gators on these rides. Have your camera ready and hold on tight! At Lake Trafford, Ski Olesky will take you out on one of the most alligator-thick lakes in the state on **Airboats & Alligators, Inc.** (1-866-657-2214; www.laketrafford.com), 6001 Lake Trafford Rd., a ride you won't soon forget with a man who's a legend in these parts.

In Everglades City, ride with a knowledgeable native on **Captain Doug's Everglades Tours** (239-695-4400 or 1-800-282-9194; www.captaindougs.com), 200 Collier Ave., a narrated scenic tour with opportunities for photography.

BICYCLING Grab a bike to get around town at **Naples Cyclery** (239-566-0600; www.naplescyclery.com), 813 Vanderbilt Beach Rd. They rent road bikes, cruisers, or surreys by the hour, day, or week. Open Mon., Wed., Fri. 9 AM–8 PM, Sat. 9 AM–6 PM, Sun. 10 AM–4 PM. The historic district between Third Street and the beach is especially suited for a bicycle tour, but I've also biked around the north part of the county using bike lanes and sidewalks, and on the trail at **North Collier Regional Park** (see *Parks*). For a wilderness ride go to **Collier-Seminole State Park** (see *Parks*) for 3.5 miles of off-road biking through pine forests and tropical hardwood hammock.

BIRDING In Naples, driving along **Airport-Pulling Road** you'll see dozens of wood storks, herons, and other wading birds along the edges of the Airport Road Canal. At US 41 and Marco Island Road, **Eagle Lakes Community Park** (239-793-4414), 11565 Tamiami Trail E, is a top birding spot with more than 50 species spotted in an hour, including bald eagles and every variety of heron in the state. **Caxambas Park**, at the end of Marco Island, is a place to sit and watch thousands of birds fly in to their roosts on the islands of Caxambas Pass at sunset. Around Marco Island and Everglades City, the **Ten Thousand Islands** are home to large colonies of wading birds, best seen on a boat trip.

BOATING

Marco Island
Board the **Marco Island Princess** (239-642-5415; www.marcoislandprincess .com), 951 Bald Eagle Dr., for daily sight-seeing cruises in the Ten Thousand Islands. For a day trip to Key West during the winter months, check into **Key West Express** (1-888-539-2628; www.seakeywestexpress.com), departing from Marco River Marina daily between November and April; the massive catamaran leaves at 8:30 AM and arrives in Key West at 11:30, with return departure at 5 PM, $119 round trip, $75 for ages under 13. One of the best tours in the region is the **Dolphin Explorer** (see *Ecotours*), which also departs from this marina. Advance reservations required for all cruises.

To explore the Ten Thousand Islands at your own pace, rent your own craft at the **Cedar Bay Marina** (239-642-6717; www.cedarbayrentals.com), 705 E Elkham Cir., $220–315 for half/full day rentals.

Hang on for the ride of your life! A different way to see the Ten Thousand Islands by water is on a guided WaveRunner excursion by **Marco Island Ski & Watersports** (239-394-2511, ext. 2983), offered at the **Marco Island Marriott Beach Resort** (see *Lodging*). It's a fast-paced one-hour journey at high speed, where you're at the controls following the group. You start out over the open ocean to Caxambas Pass, then slide between the mangrove-lined islands on your way to Cape Romano. If you're a WaveRunner newbie, invest in an hour or two rental prior to your trip to get the hang of the machine before you follow your guide into the wilderness. Cost $150 per person; riders can be solo or doubled up depending on your preference, reservations are essential.

Naples

Day Star Charters (239-417-3474; www.naplescharterboats.com), 1221 5th Ave., runs trips of 2 to 8 hours for fishing, shelling, and sight-seeing. Each trip is chartered just for your party; call for details. **The Naples Princess** (239-649-2275; www.naplesprincesscruises.com), 550 Port-o-Call Way, offers daily sightseeing cruises as well as sunset dinner buffet cruises. Advance reservations required for all cruises.

ECOTOURS

Everglades City

Pick your own adventure! **Everglades Area Tours** (239-695-9107; www.ever gladesareatours.com) customizes explorations into the Everglades and Big Cypress based on your interests and needs, including camping, kayaking, airboating, and ventures on the mild side in their shuttle. They also provide guided half-day kayak tours.

Everglades Rentals & Eco Adventures (239-695-4666; www.evergladesadven tures.com), based at the **Ivey House** (see *Lodging*), offers a variety of guided trips into Big Cypress and the Everglades, including daily **Mangrove Tunnel Eco Adventures** ($124, lunch and equipment included) where you kayak beneath a bower of twisted mangrove branches and **Sunset Spectacular Eco Adventures** ($104), for a glide across the sawgrass at dusk. Both are led by naturalists with a

KENT KEEPS WATCH ON THE DOLPHIN EXPLORER

Sandra Friend

KEEWAYDIN ISLAND   Sandra Friend

MARCO ISLAND

Launching from the Marco River Marina, the **Sea Excursions Dolphin Explorer** (239-642-6899; www.dolphin-explorer.com), 951 Bald Eagle Dr., offers a catamaran nature tour of the Ten Thousand Islands. It's anything but ordinary. Started in 2006, the Sea Excursions Dolphin Project is a study tracking the behavior, movement, and distribution of Atlantic bottlenose dolphins between Bonita Beach and Everglades City. Information collected

deep knowledge of the area; discounts for Ivey House guests. Overnight guided trips into the Ten Thousand Islands and along the Wilderness Waterway start at $799 for 2 nights, 3 days.

Departing from the visitors center in Everglades City, **Everglades National Park Boat Tours** (941-695-2591) offer narrated voyages through the Ten Thousand Islands; buy your tickets (adults $21, ages 5–12 $11) inside the visitors center. The trip runs one and a half hours.

Naples

The **Conservancy of Southwest Florida** (see *Nature Centers*) offers free guided nature walks at many sites in the region, including Clam Pass and Tigertail Beach, as well as Good Fortune cruises ($25–35) on their pontoon boat for wildlife watching, sightseeing, and sunset birding. Check their Web site (www.conservancy.org/Page.aspx?pid=631) for details.

Sign up with **Pelican Tours** (239-267-0881; www.evergladesadventure.com) for a daylong whirlwind tour of the western Everglades and Big Cypress Swamp, with activities ranging from a historic walk through Everglades City to a jungle boat about the dolphins seen on each day's tour is shared with Mote Marine Laboratory in Sarasota to build a better database of dolphin behavior along Florida's southwest coast. On each trip, the naturalist collects photos of the dolphins, tracks locations by GPS, notes their associations—family groups, pairs, maternity groups—and activities. We're here to help by scanning the water to point out any dolphins we see. "There they are. Four o'clock! I see something floating!" Passing around a heavy photo album filled with photos of dolphin fins, master naturalist Kent Morse points out the obvious differences, such as bite marks and tears. Photographing fins helps him distinguish one dolphin from another. They all have names, of course. We spy Darwina (who was Darwin until she had a calf), Rangle, and dozens of others.

"In two years, I've only had one day we didn't see a dolphin," said Kent. "Where we're going today, about 100 dolphins have been sighted." He points to a riffle in the surface of the water. "Watch over there, near the sea wall." Sure enough, a dolphin surfaces. Then another. The chase is on. We keep a respectful distance, watching pods of mothers and babies, young males leaping, and one dolphin nosing around in the shallows near mangrove roots where brilliant pink roseate spoonbills are feeding. A landing on the lee side of Keewaydin Island offers us access to a broad sweep of beach with superb shelling. I pick up dozens of conchs and sand dollars and photograph sea urchins on the shore. We spent nearly an hour roaming the shore. Dolphins approach in the surf, to our delight.

At the end of the journey, Kent surprises us all with photos he took of us shelling and of the wildlife we saw—he had a printer tucked away in the back of the boat. Everyone leaves with a smile on their face. $54 for the 3-hour tour.

tour through the Ten Thousand Islands and a swamp walk in Big Cypress National Preserve. Reservations required; operators pick up participants in Fort Myers Beach, Bonita Springs, and Naples.

FAMILY ACTIVITIES ✐ **Coral Cay Adventure Golf** (239-793-4999; www .coralcaygolf.com), 2205 E Tamiami Trail, is the king of regional miniature golf, with two 18-hole courses set amid faux reefs, caves, and waterfalls. Open daily 10 AM–11 PM. At **King Richards Fun Park** (239-598-1666; www.kingrichardspark .net), 6780 N Airport Rd., the big castle beckons the family to an afternoon of fun activities—ride the only permanent roller coaster in the area, splash around the water park, or take on the go-carts. If the weather's troublesome, play laser tag or get wild with Dance Dance Revolution in the video arcade. Open Sun. 12 PM– 8 PM, Mon.–Thurs. 10 AM–8 PM, Fri.–Sat. 10 AM–10 PM.

For something completely different, head east on the Tamiami Trail into the wilds of Big Cypress for a stop at the **Skunk Ape Research Center** (239-695-2275; www.skunkape.info), 40904 Tamiami Trail E, Ochopee. Whether you believe it or not, Dave Shealy offers up evidence at the research center (free) in his Big

Cypress Trail Lakes Campground for Florida's version of Bigfoot, along with a reptile and bird exhibit (fee), and oversized statues of swamp critters for your family photos. Open 7 AM–7 PM.

FISHING

Everglades City
For saltwater fishing, take a guided trip through the meandering maze of the Ten Thousand Islands with any of the great outfitters around here, including **Chokoloskee Charters** (239-695-9107; www.chokoloskeecharters.com).

Immokalee
For the best freshwater fishing in the region, visit **Lake Trafford Marina** (239-487-3794 or 1-866-657-2214; www.laketrafford.com), 6001 Lake Trafford Rd., for an outing on 1,500-acre Lake Trafford.

Naples
Head down to the **Naples Municipal Beach & Fishing Pier** (239-213-3062; www.naplespier.com), 12th Ave. S and Eighth St., to drop a line and see what bites. For local guide services, both offshore and nearshore, consult with the folks at **Everglades Angler** (1-800-573-4749; www.evergladesangler.com), 810 12th Ave. S, or **Mangrove Outfitters** (1-888-319-9848; www.mangroveoutfitters.com), 4111 Tamiami Trail E.

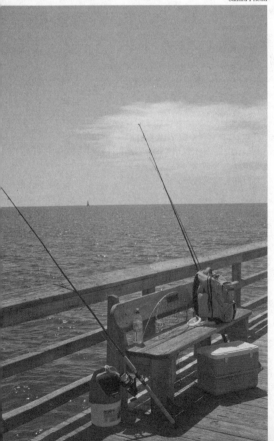

FISHING ON THE NAPLES PIER
Sandra Friend

GAMING Play the slots or go for high-stakes poker and blackjack at the **Seminole Casino Immokalee** (239-658-1313 or 1-800-218-0007; www.theseminolecasino.com), 506 S First St., Immokalee, open 24 hours.

GOLF There are more than 90 golf courses in the region, many affiliated with resort hotels or exclusive communities. A full list, which you can sort by number of holes, par, yardage, and type, can be found on the Naples Marco Island Everglades Web site (see *Guidance*). High handicappers will delight in **Arrowhead Golf Club** (239-596-1000; www.arrowheadgolf naples.com), 2205 Heritage Greens Dr., Naples, where the wide fairways and expansive greens make for a better-than-average day on the links. Designed to fit into its natural surroundings, The **Rookery at Marco** (239-793-6060; www.rookeryatmarco .com), 3433 Club Center Blvd., Marco Island, was recently redesigned by

Robert Cupp Jr., with generous fairways and oversized greens. Semiprivate, it's open to guests of the **Marco Island Marriott Beach Resort** (see *Lodging*) and is home to the Faldo Golf Institute.

HIKING This region is where I learned to get my feet really wet when hiking; the constant flow of clear, fresh rainwater in the Big Cypress Swamp and the Everglades means that if a trail isn't a boardwalk, you'll be slogging through a swamp. Not that it's a bad thing—it just takes getting used to walking where you can't see your feet. The southern terminus of the **Florida Trail** (1-877-HIKE-FLA; www .floridatrail.org) is at Loop Road in Big Cypress National Preserve. This National Scenic Trail continues north for nearly 45 miles before leaving Collier County. This particular section of the Florida Trail is the most rugged and remote in the state, best backpacked with a buddy. Stop by the **Kirby Storter Roadside** on the Tamiami Trail, Ochopee, for a pleasant 1-mile round-trip boardwalk through several Big Cypress habitats, courtesy of the Friends of the Big Cypress, or visit the **Florida Panther National Wildlife Refuge** for a wild walk through panther habitat. Virtually all the Green Space listings provide somewhere to hike; browse the Big Cypress chapter of *50 Hikes in South Florida* for details.

PADDLING If you love wilderness paddling, the **Big Cypress National Preserve** (see *Wild Places*) is a place to lose yourself in a maze of mangrove tunnels and cypress-lined channels. Pick up *Day Paddling Florida's 10,000 Islands and Big Cypress Swamp* by my buddy Jeff Ripple, who's the expert on paddling the Big Cypress, for options such as the Turner River and Halfway Creek. Rent canoes ($22–28) and kayaks ($28–52) from **Everglades Rentals & Eco Adventures** (see *Ecotours*) to explore both Big Cypress and the Gulf Coast of **Everglades National Park** (see *Wild Places*) by kayak. It takes two and a half hours to paddle to Sandfly Island, tides willing, where you'll find a 1-mile nature trail around this former stronghold of the Calusa. Nautical charts are recommended for all offshore paddling trips. For an extensive adventure, try out the new **Paradise Coast Blueway** (www.paradisecoastblueway.com), with a segment that currently stretches from Everglades City to Goodland through the Ten Thousand Islands, all mapped out with GPS waypoints. Eventually, the trail will include six days worth of paddling along the Collier County coastline and in Lake Trafford. In Naples, paddle out into Wiggins Pass with a rental from **Cocohatchee Nature Center** (see *Nature Centers*) for some saltwater kayak exploration of the mangrove shoreline.

SAILING Learn the ropes at **Sailboats Unlimited** (239-649-1740; www.sail boatsunlimited.com), Naples City Dock, on a bareboat charter, or take a sail on *Sweet Liberty* (239-793-3525; www.sweetliberty.com), 1484 Fifth Ave. S, with your choice of sight-seeing, dolphin watching, a shelling trip, or private charter.

SCENIC DRIVES For a tropical version of Beverly Hills, head south on **Gordon Drive** from the coconut palm–lined streets of Old Naples to gawk at the billionaires' seaside homes in Port Royal. Prefer a more natural setting? Head for the wilds east on the **Tamiami Trail** (850-410-5894), US 41 from Collier-Seminole State Park to the Big Cypress National Preserve, the first highway to slice through the Everglades. Grab a copy of the **Everglades Trail** (www.evergladestrail.com) brochure to make stops along the way at key places that affect the health and beauty of the Everglades habitats.

SHELLING 🐚 Imagine my delight to find the seashells piled high on my first visit to **Delnor-Wiggins Pass State Park** (see *Beaches*), right at the pass. Summertime is seashell time, thanks to the winds, waves, and storms that blow our way, churning up the bottom of the Gulf of Mexico. You'll find fabulous seashells on a long walk down to the end of **Tigertail Beach** (see *Beaches*) as well. A trip on the **Dolphin Explorer** (see *Ecotours*) includes time spent shelling for prime specimens on Keewaydin Island, an offshore gem that rarely gets picked over thanks to its lack of population.

SUNSET WATCHING Stay anywhere in Naples, and you'll find yourself drifting toward the Gulf of Mexico to watch the sunset with your neighbors each evening.

SWAMP WALKS It's an unsettling moment, when you first step into the water, knowing there are alligators about and although the forest is hot and humid, the water feels chilly to the touch as it soaks into your shoes and pants. After a few minutes, you're immersed in the wonderland of a cypress slough, in a shallow rain-fed river that slowly makes its way to the southwest through the Big Cypress Swamp. One of the few places on earth where a swamp is crystal-clear with a solid bottom, the **Big Cypress National Preserve** (see *Wild Places*) has grown in popularity in recent years with folks not afraid to venture out of their comfort zone and into the wet wilderness, where colorful orchids and bromeliads drip from the trees. While the **Florida Trail** (see *Hiking*) has been around for more than 40 years for swamp walkers to enjoy, it's only been in the past decade that the art of walking softly through water has been perfected at **Clyde Butcher's Big Cypress Gallery** (see *Art Galleries*). Reservations are necessary for these small group tours; book through their Web site. Naturalists at **Everglades Rentals & Eco Adventures** (see *Ecotours*) also lead six-hour guided **Swamp Stomps** into a freshwater slough within Big Cypress National Preserve, $104 (Ivey House guests, $83), ages 16 and over only.

Not long after breakfast, we were chasing a ghost. The whine of mosquitoes in the humid summer air made me glad I'd lathered up with bug spray. Splashing through the swamp, we were trying to stay close to Mike Owen, botanist for **Fakahatchee Strand Preserve State Park** (see *Wild Places*), as he zigzagged from pop ash to pond apple in search of signs of the most elusive of orchids, the **ghost orchid**. Barely 20 are known to bloom each year, and Mike has been studying them for decades. After two hours of slow progress, we found our treasure, suspended over our heads. A leaping frog in pale ivory, a sultry seductress of the swamp, the orchid bloom commanded our attention. Ranger-led swamp walks are offered occasionally. Visit their Web site for details.

Every numbered street ends at the Gulf, so you have plenty of palm-lined spots to choose from; the historic **Naples Pier**, however, tends to be a magnet for catching those final colorful rays. On Marco Island, enjoy a brilliant sunset at **Tigertail Beach** (fee), or watch the colors fade as the egrets flock home to roost at Caxambas Pass from **Caxambas Park** (free).

TOURS Naples Trolley Tours (www.naplestrolleytours.com) board at the Visitor Information Center (see *Guidance*) every hour from 8:48 AM to 3:48 PM. Tours run daily except Thanksgiving and Christmas and include all-day reboarding privileges, with tickets available when you board the trolley; $25 for a 2-hour tour (or buy online in advance). Check the schedule with your conductor before deboarding to be sure you do not miss the last pickup to get back to your starting point. For a different overview of Olde Naples, the guided **Naples Segway Tour** (239-262-1443; www.napleseventplanningandtours.com/tours.asp) involves 2 hours ($74) gliding down the sideways at speeds you won't approach on foot to visit far-flung points around downtown like Port Royal, the Pier, Tin City, Fifth Avenue, and Third Street South.

WALKING TOURS In Everglades City, pick up a brochure at the **Museum of the Everglades** (see *Museums*) for a **walking tour of historic Everglades City**, which was developed as a planned community by Barron Collier during the 1920s. For a walk through Naples, check at the kiosk of the Third Street South Association (813-649-6707) or at **Palm Cottage** (see *Historic Sites*) for the detailed **Historic Walking Tour of Old Naples**, a self-guided tour that includes gems such as Martha's Cottage (circa 1922) at 205 11th Ave. S and "Pineapple Plantation" at 1111 Gulfshore Dr., believed to have been designed in 1930 by Addison Mizner.

WATER PARK ✐ At **North Collier Regional Park** (see *Parks*), the **Sun-N-Fun Lagoon** (239-252-4021; www.colliergov.net/Index.aspx?page=358) is a colorful wet playground amid the watery wilderness of the Big Cypress. A lazy river circles the complex, which includes a dive/lap pool; a Tadpole Pool for the wee ones, with slides and swings; Turtle Cove, with water squirters and more for ages 5–12; and a large family pool. $5.50 for those under 48 inches, $12 for those taller; passes available. Closed Nov.–Jan., limited hours outside summer months.

✳ Green Space

BEACHES

Bonita Beach
A 342-acre barrier island accessible via a narrow drive through an exclusive residential community, **Barefoot Beach Preserve** (239-591-8596), end of Barefoot Beach Blvd. off Bonita Beach Rd., is one of those county parks that it's worth getting off the beaten path for. A mile-long nature trail leads to the north side of Wiggins Pass, and there is more than a mile of natural beachfront. Fee.

Marco Island
It's a beach that goes on forever—but you have to find it first. After parking at **Tigertail Beach** (239-353-0404; www.colliergov.net), Tigertail Ct., follow the boardwalk down to the sandy strip along the lagoon and turn left; once you've

rounded the lagoon, the full extent of the lengthy strand comes into view, arcing back toward Big Marco Pass. It's an excellent shelling destination and very much a place to get away from it all, if you just keep walking. Rangers lead free programs during the winter season, including sunset walks. A line of tall condos haunt **South Beach**, down at the end of the hotel strip on Collier Blvd. Fee.

Naples

Walking down to **Naples Beach** from the **Naples Pier** (see *Fishing*), I was reminded of a pristine shoreline I once visited on the Arabian Sea—lined with coconut palms, with residences hidden far enough back in the vegetation so as not to spoil the view. And that is why they call this the Paradise Coast. North of the city, **Lowdermilk Park**, Banyan Blvd. and Gulf Shore Blvd. N, is one of the more popular beachfront parks. Fee.

Vanderbilt Beach

Vanderbilt Beach Road ends at the water's edge at **Vanderbilt Beach**, a county park with beach access adjoining the Ritz-Carlton. The pristine portion of this strand is protected by **Delnor-Wiggins Pass State Park** (230-597-6196; www .floridastateparks.org/delnor-wiggins), 11100 N Gulfshore Dr., where the shelling is superb. Drive to the farthest most beach parking area to access the observation tower and nature trail leading out to the pass.

BOTANICAL GARDEN Still under development but coming along in stages, the **Naples Botanical Garden** (239-643-7275; www.naplesgarden.org), 4820 Bayshore Dr., is slated to reopen November 2009, with construction finally completed on the Vicky C. and David Byron Smith Children's Garden, Brazilian Garden, and Kathleen and Scott Kapnick Caribbean Garden. These will join the 90-acre Collier Enterprises South Wetlands Preserve and its birding tower. The Tropical Mosaic Garden near the entrance evokes the sea.

NATURE CENTERS

Marco Island

& ♪ Deep within in the mangrove forests of Rookery Bay near Marco Island, **Rookery Bay National Estuarine Research Reserve** (239-417-6310; www .rookerybay.org), 300 Tower Rd., has showcased the efforts of marine scientists to document and understand the complexity of life in this unique 110,000-acre marine preserve. Start your introduction with a movie that gives the feel of this mysterious puzzle of 10,000 mangrove islands, and then explore with the senses. Surrounding the cinema is a natural art galley with images by local artists. Move on to the Aquaria Showcase to watch creatures in underwater habitats such as oyster beds and seagrass, walk past the working labs, and head upstairs for more exhibits and an observation deck. A bridge and boardwalk are planned to expand the experience. Tours depart from the back dock, and you can follow signs to a short nature trail. Fee.

Naples

& ♪ Spread out over 14 acres, the **Conservancy of Southwest Florida** (239-262-0304; www.conservancy.org), 1450 Merrihue Dr., adjacent to Caribbean Gardens, provides an afternoon's worth of experiences for visitors. Begun in 1964 to save a key bird nesting area, Rookery Bay, from development, this nonprofit organization focuses on southwest Florida's natural areas through science, public policy, wildlife rehabilitation, and education. Their efforts have preserved more than 300,000 acres of habitat in southwest Florida. Enjoy guided walks on the Arboretum and Hammock Trails, or wander the trails on your own. In the museum, the "Florida: Coast to Coast" theme is reflected throughout the exhibits, from the nearshore touch tank to a walk through giant-sized mangrove roots and a massive interactive exhibit on seashells. Check out the relief map: as water flows into South Florida, who relies on it when it gets there? Rotating exhibits showcase habitats in other regions. Wander through the well-stocked gift shop with its natural science books and toys to board a quiet electric boat for an interpretive tour up the Golden Gate Canal to the Gordon River, cruising down a winding passage through a tunnel of mangroves past palm hammocks with giant leather ferns. Yellow-crowned night herons nest on an island at the confluence of waterways. Visit the wildlife rehabilitation center (see *Zoological Parks & Wildlife Rehab*) to meet some of the 2,500 creatures treated and released this year, and stop in the Wildlife Art Gallery near the parking area, where resident artist Chris Murray creates intricate wildlife sculptures in wood. More than seven hundred volunteers pull together to make this a very special place where you can touch nature while learning about it, too. Fee.

PARKS ✐ A city park with a broad range of on-site activities, **Cambier Park** (239-213-3058), 735 Eighth St. S, in the heart of downtown Naples, boasts an activity center, tennis courts, softball field, and massive "super playground" for the kids.

INSIDE THE CONSERVANCY NATURE CENTER

When Barron Collier died in March 1939, he was Florida's largest landowner. He wanted the federal government to create a national park that encompassed what was then the largest natural grove of royal palms in the United States, but the government wasn't interested. Instead, the state of Florida stepped in and created **Collier-Seminole State Park** (239-394-3397; www.floridastateparks.org/collier-seminole), 20200 E Tamiami Trail, Naples, which opened in 1947. In addition to the Bay City Walking Dredge, one of the original dredges used to build the Tamiami Trail, and a monument to Collier, the park offers several wilderness adventures. Launch your canoe or kayak for a paddling trip, experience miles of rugged bicycle trails, camp out in a pleasant tropical campground, walk the nature trail, or go for a hard-core

Sandra Friend

THE BAY CITY WALKING DREDGE AT COLLIER-SEMINOLE STATE PARK

6.5-mile hike-and-slog through the watery wilderness of Big Cypress on a Florida Trail loop, with optional primitive camping. Fee.

&. ✍ New **North Collier Regional Park** (239-252-4000; www.colliergov.net), 15000 Livingston Rd., offers a variety of activities for family fun beyond the usual ball fields. A 3-mile paved bike trail loops the park, and a boardwalk leads you into the heart of watery Big Cypress habitats. The park is home to the **Sun-N-Fun Lagoon** (see *Water Park*); the Can U Dig It playground, which has giant boulders and a covered "fossil" dig area; and a nature center with interactive exhibits and a gift shop selling nature books. Now that's a county park! Open daily 6 AM–10 PM.

PRESERVES &. ✍ With a world-class boardwalk through an old-growth cypress swamp, **Corkscrew Swamp Sanctuary** (239-348-9151; www.audubon.com/local/sanctuary/corkscrew), 375 Sanctuary Rd. W off CR 846, is a haunting place, a step into the past, into one of the last large virgin cypress stands in the United States within the wilds of the Big Cypress Swamp. Encompassing more than 11,000 acres, the sanctuary protects an important nesting colony of wood storks. It's a birder's delight, an official gateway for the Great Florida Birding Trail's southern region, which will tip you off to dozens of additional places to explore. Walk slowly along the 2.25 mile boardwalk to savor this watery wilderness. Adults $10, students $6, Audubon members $5, ages 6–18 $4. Open daily.

&. **Naples Preserve**, at the corner of Fleischmann and US 41, is a little patch of pine flatwoods in the middle of the city. It offers a visitors center and a boardwalk to explore the habitat.

WILD PLACES

Copeland

Best known for its population of rare ghost orchids, **Fakahatchee Strand Preserve State Park** (239-695-4593; www.floridastateparks.org/fakahatcheestrand), 137 Coastline Dr., comprises more than 85,000 acres, making it the biggest state preserve in Florida. It is truly a watery wilderness, where the Fakahatchee Strand runs 3 to 5 miles wide and 20 miles long, a swampy wilderness filled with natural wonders. Forty-four species of orchids have been found here, giving the park the nickname "Orchid Capital of the United States." Cruise **Janes Scenic Drive** in search of Florida panthers, or walk the old cypress logging tramways to explore the backcountry. The short **Big Cypress Bend Boardwalk** off US 41 provides a gentle introduction to this ancient swamp.

Protecting more than 26,000 acres of crucial habitat for Florida's most endangered species, the **Florida Panther National Wildlife Refuge** (239-353-8442; www .fws.gov/floridapanther), FL 29 north of I-75, has an interpretive trail through panther habitat. The same office manages the **Ten Thousand Islands National Wildlife Refuge** (www.fws.gov/southeast/tenthousandisland), which covers 35,000 acres where Fakahatchee and Picayune Strands spill their fresh water into the Gulf of Mexico. Visit by boat (powered or paddled) from Marco Island, Goodland, or Port of the Islands.

Estero
Spanning the county line, **CREW Marsh** (239-657-2253; www.crewtrust.org), 23998 Corkscrew Rd., protects more than 5,000 acres of Big Cypress Swamp habitat in a 60,000-acre watershed. It's a mosaic of wet flatwoods, cypress strands, and hardwood hammocks, with beautiful wildflower blooms each March. Walk the trail system to watch for wildlife, including sandhill cranes; guided hikes are offered throughout the year.

Everglades City
The westernmost extent of **Everglades National Park** (1-800-365-CAMP; www .nps.gov/ever), FL 29, comprises Collier County's southeastern corner and can be accessed only by boat. Stop at the **Everglades National Park Gulf Coast Visitor Center** (239-695-3311; www.nps.gov/ever), open 8–4:30 daily, which offers daily & wheelchair-accessible boat tours (fee), "bike hikes" of Everglades City historic sites, "Full Moon" canoe trips once a month, nightly programs under the stars, and daily talks under the chickee outside as well as guided canoe trips. The bulk of Everglades National Park, including the 99-mile Wilderness Waterway, is discussed in the *South Miami–Dade* chapter.

Naples
It stands as a monument to a Florida land scam: **Picayune Strand State Forest** (239-348-7557), accessed via Sabal Palm Rd., was once part of Golden Gate Estates, a 1960s planned community that just happened to seasonally flood when the salesmen weren't showing off the model homes. In the 1980s, the state started buying up the land for the state forest, but to do so, they had to track down and buy up acreage from more than 17,000 landowners—one of the most complex land acquisitions in Florida history. It's a watery wilderness enjoyed by swamp buggy enthusiasts, daring hikers on the Sabal Palm Trail, as well as hunters during deer season. It's now part of one of the large-scale Everglades Restoration Projects going on in South Florida to restore the sheet flow of water across the landscape.

Ochopee
Established by Congress in 1974 as the first National Preserve in the United States, **Big Cypress National Preserve** (239-695-1201; www.nps.gov/bicy), between Naples and Miami along the Tamiami Trail, protects more than 900 square miles of cypress and sawgrass habitats dependent on seasonal rains. Stop in

THE GULF COAST

at the **Oasis Visitor Center**, Ochopee, at an orientation to the preserve, and then immerse yourself into the environment via its trails, from the rugged **Florida Trail** (see *Hiking*) to the boardwalk at Kirby Storter Roadside and the Fire Prairie Trail off Turner River Road. The preserve is open to hunting and includes miles of off-road-vehicle trails primarily used by swamp buggies, as well as a number of campgrounds (see *Campgrounds*) with varying facilities. The visitor center is open 8:30 AM–4:30 PM daily year-round, except Christmas.

✳ Lodging
BED & BREAKFASTS
Everglades City 34139
🦐 ♿ "▮" ↝ There are two distinct faces to the **Ivey House** (239-695-3299; www.iveyhouse.com), 107 Camellia St., a popular launch point for adventures into the Everglades. The Ivey House Lodge, the historic part of the complex includes 11 rooms built in 1928 as quarters for workers building the Tamiami Trail. It has small rooms ($63–150) with a dorm feel, and the original bathrooms are down the hall. Guests mingle in a large living area with television. One of my favorite getaways in Florida is the Ivey House Inn, the newer part of the complex, which has 17 units ($90–250) centered on a tropical pool in a screened atrium, with shaded tables for guests to sit outside their spacious rooms. Each room has a tiled floor, large bathroom, and a workspace. A separate cottage houses up to four people ($126–287). All rooms come with continental breakfast, and you can arrange ecotours and kayak or canoe rentals at the front desk.

CABINS AND COTTAGES
Everglades City 34139
Glades Haven Everglades Cozy Cabins (239-695-2746 or 1-888-956-6251; www.gladeshaven.com), 901 S Copeland Ave., make up a modern fish camp with nice park-model cabins (bedroom, sleeping loft, living-dining-kitchen area with cable TV) either on or near the waterfront. Ask about dockage with your rental. Duplexes $89–99, full-sized $129–139.

CAMPGROUNDS
Big Cypress Preserve
🐾 **Big Cypress National Preserve Campgrounds** (see *Wild Places*), along the Tamiami Trail, are rugged wilderness outposts. Facilities vary with location, and many are not open during the summer. Primitive campgrounds (minimal to no fee; no restrooms) include the very remote **Bear Island** at the north end of Turner River Road; **Burns Lake**, along US 41; Pinecrest, off Loop Road; and **Mitchell's Landing**. I've camped at **Monument Lake** ($16, includes showers and flush toilets) and enjoyed it thoroughly; **Midway** ($16–19) recently reopened with new facilities.

Chokoloskee 34138
Along mangrove-lined waterways, **Outdoor Resorts of Chokoloskee Island** (239-695-3788; www.outdoor-resorts.com/ci), SR 29, provides waterfront RV camping with or without docks ($69–89); no tents. Boats, canoes, and kayaks can be rented on-site.

Marco Island 34145
🚣 🐾 "▮" Set in a lush tropical forest surrounded by Rookery Bay, the **Naples/Marco Island KOA** (239-774-5455 or 1-800-562-7734; www.koakampgrounds.com/where/fl/09109), 1700 Barefoot Williams Rd., is just moments

from nature centers and the beach for all sorts of outdoors fun; there's even an ecotour pickup at the park. Take your pick from RV and tent sites, Kamping Kabins, and a Kamping Lodge with kitchen and bath ($57 and up).

Naples 34102
❀ ⁀¹⁀ Shaded by tropical trees, the **Rock Creek RV Resort** (239-643-3100; www.rockcreekrv.com), 3100 North Rd., has 235 full hookup spaces ($47–60), a recreation room, shuffleboard, and a large heated pool. Slip your kayak in the creek and head down the Gordon River in a matter of minutes.

HOTELS, MOTELS, AND RESORTS

Everglades City 34139
There is no better place to settle into Collier County's past than the elegant **Everglades Rod & Gun Club** (239-695-2101; www.evergladesrodandgun.com), 200 Riverside Dr., a hunting and fishing lodge with humble beginnings in 1864 that grew to a large complex on the Barron River around settler Allen Storter's home. Dark pecky cypress walls and mounted trophies emphasize the outdoorsy atmosphere of this former private club, which has hosted a bevy of presidents and celebrities over the years. Arrival used to be by boat into the spacious lobby, so the walk from the parking lot is through the narrow back entrance lined with historic clippings, past an intimate bar with local murals and a jukebox. Guests stay in historic cottages with private baths ($95–140); cash only.

Goodland 34140
Since 1957, the little **Pink House Motel** (239-394-1313), 310 Pear Tree Ave., has had a fish-camp clientele and offers neat and clean paneled rooms overlooking the water. The one-

bedroom unit has twin beds, perfect for fishing buddies, and there is a four-person penthouse up top. Located at Marker 7, with plenty of tie-up space on the wharf.

Marco Island 34145
At the **Marco Island Lakeside Inn** (239-394-1161 or 1-800-729-0216; www.marcoislandlakeside.com), 155 First Ave., I settled blissfully into one of the most comfortable beds I've encountered in my travels. Massive renovations have made this family-owned, family-managed inn a perfect spot to unwind. Each one- or two-bedroom suite ($169–309) boasts a full kitchen and living room/dining area separate from the romantic bedroom, tastefully decorated with original art. Choose from lakefront or poolside, and enjoy the new on-site bistro, Sushi Blues & Steaks, a classy urban restaurant with sushi bar and live piano.

&. ✿ ⁀¹⁀ ↝ A beachfront destination, the **Marco Island Marriott Beach Resort & Spa** (239-394-2511 or 1-800-GET-HERE; www.marcoisland marriott.com), 400 S Collier Blvd., has something for everyone, from on-site shopping and an elegant full-service spa to sight-seeing cruises, Faldo golf school, guided tours of the botanical wonders around the hotel, parasailing, and the only WaveRunner ecotour in the United States (see *Ecotours*). While the folks are at a convention, kids can join the Tiki Tribe to have daytime scavenger hunts and outdoor and arts activities. In the low season, rooms without views start at $219.

Naples 34102
🦐 &. ⁀¹⁀ The Italianesque **Bayfront Inn** (239-649-5800 or 1-800-382-7941; www.bayfrontinnnaples.com), 1221 Fifth Ave. S, is Naples only waterfront boutique hotel, gleaming with marble and a white onyx wall, doors swept open to let in the breeze off the patio

on the bay. Each room ($99–155) and suite ($225–275) has that special touch, with sleek lines to the furnishings, a rattan-style headboard, 37-inch flat screen television, writing desk, and seafoam green glass sinks. Kitchenettes sport granite countertops. Downstairs, enjoy a drink at the Bamboo Grille, or wander out the door to browse the shops at **Bayfront Place** (see *Selective Shopping*).

&. ☙ In the heart of Old Naples, **Bellasera** (239-649-7333; 1-888-627-1595; www.bellaseranaples.com), 221 9th St. S shares a touch of Tuscany with guests, who have their pick of apartment-sized suites (studio through three bedrooms) throughout the complex. A one-bedroom suite ($149 and up) included a snazzy full kitchen with all the amenities, including a dishwasher. The complex includes the Verde Spa, an organic day spa, a large pool; Zizi, a classy bistro with an open kitchen; and free shuttle service to the beach and downtown shopping.

&. An all-suite hotel in Olde Naples, the **Edgewater Beach Hotel** (1-800-821-0196; www.edgewaternaples.com), 1901 Gulf Shore Blvd. N, offers 125 beachfront suites with private balconies or patios, living room, dining room, kitchen, and separate bedroom and bath. Daily maid service includes dishwashing; complimentary valet parking. Choose your view and pick a decor—West Indies or beach house— then plunk down $169 in the low season and up and c'mon down and relax. There are four on-site restaurants, a fitness center, water sports rentals, and children's activities.

&. ⁖ Enjoy old-world elegance at **The Inn on Fifth** (239-403-8777 or 1-888-403-8778; www.naplesinn.com/fifth), 699 Fifth Ave. S. The marble lobby and chandeliers echo an age when this was the First National Bank of Naples

in the heart of the commercial district. This two-story hotel surrounds a courtyard pool and hot tub. The large contemporary rooms (starting at $150 in the off-season) feature sliding French doors to let in the sea breeze, plenty of natural light, 12-foot ceilings, and comfy bathrobes. Inside the complex, relax at the Spa on Fifth, which offers a delightful array of body wraps, scrubs, facials, and massages.

◈ &. ⁖ One of a rapidly disappearing breed—the 1940s Florida motor court—the **Lemon Tree Inn** (239-262-1414 or 1-888-800-5366; www .lemontreeinn.com), 250 Ninth St. S, boasts luxuriously updated rooms around a courtyard with a Key West flair. Each room ($89–199, depending on season and size) speaks to an artist's sensibilities. I stayed in Casa Mara, #106, with the colorful fantasies of artist Mara Abboud adding vibrancy to a spacious room with a tiled kitchen area (bar sink, microwave, mini fridge, and coffeemaker); the furniture and linens evoked the tropics. On the patio, Adirondack chairs provide a place to read and relax. Continental breakfast is served poolside. It's an easy stroll to the shops on Fifth Avenue and about 8 blocks to the beach.

◈ I did a double-take when I realized the **Mariner Beach Motel** (239-261-7313; www.marineraptsmotel.com), 1295 Gulf Shore Blvd. S, was, indeed, a 1960s motel I'd missed on my prior visits. Built in 1966 and surrounded by tropical plantings, this little gem is just a block from the beach at the Naples Pier, closer than any other accommodations in downtown. Each of the spotless spacious rooms and suites ($80–200) make maximum use of space, including kitchenettes. With large windows that let the sun in, these are very appealing, especially for friends or families who need space to spread out.

&. ¶¹ With classic European styling, the **Trianon Hotel Old Naples** (239-435-9600 or 1-877-482-5228; www .trianon.com), 955 Seventh Ave. S, is the posh place to stay downtown, and it's within easy walking distance to all of Fifth Avenue. Spacious and comfortable, the rooms and suites include a writing desk and marble-tiled bathrooms; "superior" rooms add a sofabed and small fridge, and suites have a wet bar. Enjoy a very private courtyard and pool, and relax with complimentary cocktails in the evening. Continental breakfast is served each morning. Less than a decade old, this hotel is owned by a long-standing local family with ties to Ritz-Carlton, but the prices here make elegance affordable— starting at $95 low season, $170 high season.

Vanderbilt Beach 34108

&. ¶¹ ⊹ The coral pink **Inn at Pelican Bay** (239-597-8777 or 1-800-597-8770; www.innatpelicanbay.com), 800 Vanderbilt Beach Rd., towers over the surrounding pine forest. Inside, expect elegant surroundings; each spacious room (from $99 in the low season) has a balcony or terrace, large desk, safe, and two phones.

In a place where condos line the oceanfront, the **Lighthouse Inn** (239-597-3345), 9140 Gulfshore Dr., stands out as a preserved piece of Old Florida, with its jalousie windows and 1940s exterior surrounding a coconut palm–shaded pool. The rooms ($75–155) are pleasant and bright; efficiencies have a full kitchen and tiled shower. Buzz and Judy have run this place since 1978, and I wish them many more years of success.

🦐 At the **Vanderbilt Beach Resort** (239-597-3144 or 1-800-243-9076; www.vanderbiltbeachresort.com), 9225

Gulf Shore Dr. N, efficiencies ($124–155) look right out on the beach and are decorated with tropical flair. On the bayside, their one- to three-bedroom apartments and condos ($136–220) are bigger than most of the places I've lived in, ranging up to 1200 square feet, with fine furnishings that make you feel like you're living comfortably. Large screened porches overlook the Vanderbilt lagoon.

✳ Where to Eat
DINING OUT

Everglades City

A favorite of the celebrities who haunt this mangrove-lined frontier, the **Everglades Rod & Gun Club** (see *Lodging*) serves steaks and seafood with a focus on the native fish and shellfish that bring anglers here. Entrées include Swamp and Turf (frog's legs and a New York strip), honey crispy fried chicken, and steamed shrimp in beer, plus their specialty, stone crab claws (local, in season). Serves lunch and dinner; appropriate dress (business casual or better) please. Cash only.

Everglades Seafood Depot (239-695-3535), 102 Collier Ave. Inside a 1928 railroad depot at the end of the line, you'll find fresh shrimp, a large salad bar, and local signature entrées ($19 and up) such as the Sunshine Special, a steamed seafood platter with snow crab, shrimp, mussels, and half a Florida lobster tail.

The **Oyster House Restaurant** (239-695-2073; www.oysterhouserestaurant .com), 901 Copeland Ave., is where Chef Bobby shows off his expertise with the bounty of these local waters. Enjoy locally caught stone crab claws, fried gator, grouper "Oyster House style," and more ($9–23).

THE GULF COAST

Downtown, Fifth Avenue is the place to see and be seen at dozens of trendy bistros with outdoor seating, including **Yabba Island Grill** (239-262-1221; www.yabbaislandgrill.com), 720 Fifth Ave. S, where food is a work of art. "Island Style" means entrées like sweet chili glazed and wasabi pea crusted Chilean sea bass, served up with stir-fried island vegetables and snow peas, or grilled, marinated pork rib chop topped with spinach, mango, blue cheese and orange-tamarind demi. Entrées $18–29.

A genial and popular trattoria, **Campiello Ristorante** (239-435-1166; www.campiello.damico.com), 11777 Third St. S, features the best in Italian cuisine and seating that transports you to—well, Naples! True to its authentic roots, owners Richard and Larry D'Amico envisioned the restaurant as a lively center of neighborhood activity inspired by Florence and Sienna. Their extensive martini menu includes 28 choices (with The James Bond an option), and there is a page of fine wines to choose from. Lunch options ($13–19) include wood-fired oven pizzas, massive entrée salads, and muffuletta as one of many sandwiches. For dinner ($19–36), consider balsamic-glazed short ribs with smoked tomatoes and Sicilian onions.

Right along the downtown City Dock is **The Dock at Crayton Cove** (239-263-9940; www.dockcraytoncove.com), 845 12th Ave. S, a laid-back open air waterfront restaurant with upscale funky seafood offerings. Start off with some blue crab rolls or rock shrimp nachos, and move on to entrées ($23 and up) like Key lime grouper with purple mashed potatoes and Keewaydin lobster-clambake.

It's authentic—the interior of **McCabe's Irish Pub** (239-403-7170; www.mccabesirishpub.com), 699 Fifth Ave., came straight from Dublin, and you can start off your day with bangers and mash or have an Tatty Leek soup for lunch (one of my favorites!); serving traditional pub fare from $12. Open 7 AM–11 PM daily, and on weekends until last call.

At the **Ridgeway Bar & Grill** (239-262-5500), Third St. S & 13th Ave. S, lunch is meant to be savored in their green and white wicker chairs. With a colonial Caribbean feel, the restaurant brings the outdoors in, with large doors opening on to the wraparound porch. For lunch ($13–18) with a friend, I savored a delightful spinach salad with roasted pears, candied spiced walnuts, maytag blue cheese, shredded chicken, red onion, and orange zest.

Vanderbilt Beach

BHA! BHA! (239-594-5557; www.bhabhapersianbistro.com), 847 Vanderbilt Beach Rd., brings the tastes of the Middle East to southwest Florida with classic Persian delights, belly dancers, and fortune-tellers in a souk-like setting. Enjoy entrées ($19 and up) such as salmon *zahedan* (sautéed with tomatoes, herbs, and olives) or duck *fesenjune* (succulent braised duck with orange, pomegranate, and walnut sauce).

For the ultimate in beachfront dining, make it a special occasion at **The Turtle Club** (239-592-6557; www.theturtleclubrestaurant.com), 9225 Gulfshore Dr. N. With classic dishes ($26 and up) like pan seared low country shrimp and sausage, oak grilled rack of Colorado lamb, and their famous oysters "Turtlefeller," made with baby spinach, apple smoked bacon, and secret extras, this is a place to savor your dinner. An extensive wine list helps complement your entrée choices. As you might expect, chocolate turtle ice cream pie is my favorite on their dessert menu.

Everglades City

Hidden down a back street but worth the search, the **Camilla Street Grill** (239-695-2003), 202 Camilla St., catered the Muck-A-Bout (see *Swamp Walks*) last year, and I was blown away by their gator wraps (yup, you read that right), with ground-up gator meat seasoned so well it made me want to come back for more. Everything's made from scratch with fresh ingredients. Open daily.

It's a little bit historic site, a little bit art gallery, and a little bit museum. Unmistakable with the vintage cars and gas pumps out front, **Susie's Station Restaurant** (239-695-0704), 103 S Copeland Ave., has a pleasant country feel and serves up a variety of seafood baskets, fresh stone crab, and burgers ($6–15). Cash only, please.

Goodland

With a European feel, the **Little Bar Restaurant** (239-394-5663; www.little barrestaurant.com), 205 Harbor Pl., serves up fresh local avocados in their salads and a conch chowder worth stopping for. Open for lunch and dinner daily.

The quintessential Florida fish camp, **Stan's Idle Hour Seafood Restaurant** (239-394-3041; www.stansidle hour.net), 221 Goodland Dr. W, is a destination every Sunday noon for live concerts on the water. No frills, no fuss—just fresh seafood ($10 and up) at open-air picnic tables, and lots of appetizer choices.

Marco Island

After a walk on Tigertail Beach, I was famished when I stopped in at almost famous **Mel's SouthBeach Smokehouse BBQ** (239-394-7111), 657 S Collier Blvd. I settled on a Big House Burger, but my goodness, the Southern food they've got! Cornmeal-dusted fried green tomatoes, Cajun-spiced fried pickles, mixed greens, Mom's mac & cheese—what a lineup. They're known for their BBQ, which you can get as a pulled pork salad or as a big slab of ribs and red hot chicken on a Hogg Platter. Sandwiches start at $10, meals at $17.

Sit at picnic tables and eat your seafood off cafeteria trays at the it-can't-get-more-casual **Crazy Flamingo Raw Bar** (239-642-9600; www.the crazyflamingo.com), 1035 N Collier Blvd. at Town Center, where big steaming pots of oysters, mussels, and clams will tempt you with the aroma, and the smoked fish dip is fresh and good. The menu ($7 and up) is mostly fish, little bull, although they do have "The Required Burger." Open 11 AM–2 AM daily.

The "Best Darn Barbecue" at **Porky's Last Stand** (239-394-8727; www .porkyslaststand.com), 701 Bald Eagle Dr., comes recommended from friends who grew up with the owner, and it took one whiff of the smoke to convince me that this is an awesome place. Country family atmosphere, 1950s music, and great food—what more do you need? The meat is slow cooked over a wood fire, so enjoy spare ribs, smoked chicken, sliced pork or beef, and five different kinds of steak with choice of two sides, entrées $12 and up.

Right on the waterfront, the **Snook Inn** (239-394-3313; www.snookinn .com), 1215 Bald Eagle Dr., is a casual stop to drink margaritas and munch on shrimp; when I was asking around for the best place to eat, several folks suggested I have dinner here. The menu includes several preparations of grouper and shrimp, all the requisite shellfish, and a smattering of landlubber items, with entrées starting at $18. An extensive wine list complements your meal.

A shrine to the New York Yankees, **Susie's Diner** (239-642-6633), 1013 N Collier Blvd. at Town Center, is a bustling breakfast nook where I appreciated that the host did not sit me, a woman alone, at the counter stools but let me have my own little table despite the crowd. That morning's special was French toast topped with strawberries, blueberries, or banana, and you bet it was good! Expect lightning-fast breakfast service and crumbly fresh biscuits with your order, breakfast under $10. Cash only.

Naples

Since 1959, **Aurelio's** (239-403-8882; www.aureliosofnaples.com), 590 N Tamiami Trail, has been the king of regional pizzerias, offering both traditional and specialty toppings. Their secret trademarked dish, spinach Calabrese, is a spicy vegetarian alternative to stuffed pizza. Sandwiches come hot off the grill, and the antipasto is heaping. Open 4 PM–10 PM; closed Mon. Dine in or carry out.

Brunch at **Brambles** (239-262-7894), 340 Fifth Ave. S, an authentic English tearoom in a tropical garden, an oasis in the middle of the shopping district; lunches from $9.

Florida's oldest authentic British pub is **The English Pub** (239-774-2408; www.naplesenglishpub.com), 2408 Linwood Ave., where darts and pool are the order of the day, quiz night happens every Thursday evening, and traditional English breakfast (beans and toast, and even kippers!) is served every Sunday brunch, with roast beef and Yorkshire pudding Sunday evening, entrées $12–21.

🦐 Since 1952, **Kelly's Fish House** (239-774-0494; www.kellysfishhouse diningroom.com), 1302 Fifth Ave., has always been the place in Naples for fresh seafood, but you gotta love fish to come here—that's what the menu is all about. Perched along the Gordon River, it's a truly unique piece of old Naples, the pillars and crossbeams plastered with seashells and every table a miniature beach of sand and seashells beneath plate glass. Picture windows provide a great view of the waterfront. But let's not forget the food! I was offered (and accepted) anchovies for my Caesar salad, which came with subtle garlic dressing. The hushpuppies are homemade. My shrimp scampi was as fresh as could be. The Key lime pie has a smooth, silky texture and subtle bite. There are dozens of options on the menu, from Everglades frog's legs to genuine Gulf snapper, pompano, and shrimp Creole, with entrées $16 and up. If you arrive before nightfall, check out Kelly's Shell Shack in the parking lot—what an array of seashells to choose from!

With 50 varieties of gourmet burgers ($6 and up) to choose from, **Lindburgers** (239-262-1127), 330 Tamiami Trail S, is a must for the serious burger buff. If you love aviation history, you'll love it here, too—it's like stepping into an airport hangar filled with memorabilia.

Savor "Mediterranean soul food" at **Pelagos Café** (239-263-2996), 4951 N Tamiami Trail Ste. 105, a chic Greek restaurant tucked in a strip mall. Recognizable Greek pop music drifted through the background while I made my selections from gyros and *keftedes*, veggie falafel, a *mezede* platter with calamari and *saganaki*, and more. I settled on moussaka, which had a hint of cinnamon and was presented with a perfect Greek salad. Pleasant waitstaff, natural light, and the vivid paintings on the walls made for a great dining experience, with lunch under $15. Closed Sun.; reservations suggested.

Ochopee

🦀 Perch yourself on the edge of the Everglades and watch the gators swim past at **Joanie's Blue Crab Café**

(239-695-2682), 39395 Tamiami Trail, an unmistakable landmark on the Tamiami Trail famous for its fresh local seafood and "help yourself" service. Gator comes served with Indian fry bread, and you can try an Everglades Swamp Dinner, featuring gator nuggets and fritters and frog's legs. Their crab cakes are famous, and the grouper sandwich is delicious. Entrées $15 and up. Open 10 AM–5 PM daily.

ICE CREAM

Marco Island
In a strip mall at the corner of Bald Eagle and Collier, **Sweet Annie's Ice Cream Parlor** (239-642-7180; www .marcoislanddirectory.com/sweetannies .htm), 692 Bald Eagle Dr., has that old-fashioned feel, with classic soda fountain tables, black-and-white–tiled floor, and lots of "penny candy," although it costs more these days! Open 11 AM–11 AM daily.

Naples
The tempting aroma of hot fudge spills out of **Kilwins** (239-261-9898; www .kilwins.com), 743 Fifth Ave. S. They

dish up some tasty ice cream good for a hot day. Dean Martin and the Cat in the Hat overlook the scooping at **Regina's Ice Cream** (239-434-8181), 824 Fifth Ave. S, an old-fashioned ice cream parlor where it looks like a sock hop is about to start.

✳ Entertainment

FINE ARTS In addition to housing galleries associated with the adjacent Naples Museum of Art (see *Museums*), the **Naples Philharmonic Center for the Arts** (1-800-597-1900; www .thephil.org), 5833 Pelican Bay Blvd., hosts year-round performances from orchestras and chorale groups to headliner singers and more.

THEATER For top-notch community theater, visit **The Naples Players** (239-263-7990; www.naplesplayers .org), 701 Fifth Ave. S, at Sugden Community Theatre. Their season runs October through May and includes old standards such as *Annie Get Your Gun* as well as new critically acclaimed comedies like *The Sugar Bean Sisters*.

JOANIE'S BLUE CRAB IN OCHOPEE IS A POPULAR STOP ALONG THE TAMIAMI TRAIL FOR BEER AND SEAFOOD

Sandra Friend

✹ Selective Shopping

Marco Island

Customers can sip tea while browsing magazines at **Sunshine Booksellers** (239-393-0353), 677 S Collier Blvd., an independent bookstore with insightful new book selections and one of the most extensive children's book sections in the region.

Naples

In addition to being a mecca for art galleries, Naples offers more options for shopping in one compact area than any other Florida city I can think of—only St. Augustine and Key West come close. There are several distinct shopping districts in Naples, each with its own feel, including **Central**, **Fifth Avenue South**, and **Third Street South**.

Naples—Central

Across from Naples Community Hospital on US 41, there is a handful of narrow side streets with restaurants and shops—Central North, east to 10th—with a variety of options to explore. **Treasure Island Antique Mall** (239-434-7684), 950 Central Ave., is a rambling store with numerous dealer booths, including rare and antiquarian books from Wickham Books South, antiques and collectibles, classy armoires, 1970s retro decor items, antique clocks, and fine china.

Naples—Fifth Avenue South

Fifth Avenue South (239-435-3742; www.downtownnaplesassociation.com) feels like a 1940s movie set with a modern flair, the street lined with dozens of fascinating shops and restaurants, a mix of classic buildings surrounded by re-creations of the past.

Whimsical gifts await at the **Copper Cricket** (239-213-0500), 555 Fifth Ave. S.

Brighten your night at **La Luce** (239-263-LUCE), 837 Fifth Ave. S, where lamps are art—urban designs of fused glass create contemporary chic.

Glass baubles dangle at the **People's Pottery** (239-435-0018; www.peoples pottery.com), 769 Fifth Ave. S, a gallery filled with art glass, ceramics, and classy lapidary from artisans all over the United States.

"Fun things for fun people" is the motto at **Regattas** (239-262-3929), 760 5th Ave. S, and I certainly found plenty of gifts there I'd love to give, like silly pink flamingos, Lexees sandals, funny soaps, and local art cards.

A fanciful mural draws you to **The Wind in the Willows** (239-643-0663), 793 Fifth Ave. S, a clothing store where textiles have textures. We spent a lot of time in here browsing the charming children's clothing and toys and quirky handbags with bits of fluff and sparkly stuff. The resident parrot likes to make a fuss when new customers arrive.

Separate from the downtown shopping district a little farther south, you'll find the popular, touristy **Tin City** (239-262-6100; www.tin-city.com), 1200 Fifth Ave. S, with dozens of small shops featuring everything from home decor to fudge, T-shirts, and fine art. Across the street at the corner of Goodlette-Frank Rd. and US 41, **Bayfront** (239-649-8700) is a large boutique shopping mall on Naples Bay with complimentary valet parking; the shops and restaurants remind me of the upscale choices found in the resorts of Las Vegas. Behind Tin City you'll find **Dockside Boardwalk** (www.dockside-boardwalk.com), 1100 Sixth Ave. S, with a variety of shops.

Naples—Third Street South

Stop at the **Concierge Kiosk** (239-434-6533; www.thirdstreetsouth.com), Camargo Park, opposite Fleischmann Fountain, to get your bearings before hoofing it through this historic business district, where boutiques and art galleries nudge elbows with upscale restaurants. The Chumsky Building marks the original center of downtown Naples.

An old-school traditional hometown department store, **Gattle's** (239-262-4791; www.gattles.com), 1250 3rd St. S, is among the last of its kind. Dealing in fine linens since 1904, they've branched out to exquisite home décor, including Daum art glass, shell-studded lamps and mirrors, and pastel alligators for your walls. But linens are their forte, and you'll find plush Egyptian towels, traditional linen tablecloths, and Hamburg House custom embroidery for those monograms.

Check out the **Mole Hole** (239-262-5115), 1300 Third St. S, for unusual gifts; and **Au Cashmere** (239-261-8887), 1300 Third St. S, for luxurious clothing and accessories. **Tommy Bahama's** (239-643-7920), 1220 Third St. S, started right here and has both a sportswear store and a themed restaurant.

Naples—West

Wine, fresh fruit, and an indoor flea market with tiki bar—it's an unusual combination but makes up the core of **Big Cypress Market Place** (239-774-1690; www.bigcypressmarketplace.com), US 41 and Basik Rd., an innovative shopping complex between Naples and Marco Island, with farm fresh produce from local growers, the Big Cypress Winery, Trails End Tiki Bar, The Swamp Sport Den, an enormous "food arena," and gaming. After a drive into Naples on the Tamiami Trail, it's a must-stop!

Vanderbilt Beach

The Village on Venetian Bay (239-261-6100; www.venetianvillage.com), 4200 Gulf Shore Blvd. N, is an upscale shopping mall with art galleries, boutique shops, European clothing stores, and waterfront restaurants.

PRODUCE STAND, SEAFOOD MARKETS, AND U-PICK

Everglades City

Stop by **City Seafood** (239-695-4700), 702 Begonia St., for catch right off the dock as early as 9 AM. Stone crab claws come fresh off the boats during the season, October 15–May 15.

Goodland

You won't find it fresher than right off the boat at **Kirk's Seafood Market** (239-394-8616), 417 Papaya St., where in-season you can pick up stone crab claws at rock-bottom prices, and shrimp and fish all year long.

Immokalee

Harvest Blueberry Store and U-Pick (239-657-4888; www.about harvest.org), 1312 W New Market Rd. #1, is part of the "Harvest for Humanity" project, a 40-acre planned community for moderate- to low-income families. In the middle of the blueberry farm, the store offers fresh berries (in-season), or you may pick your own, as well as blueberry products such as syrup, preserves, T-shirts, and gifts.

✳ Special Events

January: **Swamp Buggy Races** (1-800-897-2701; www.swampbuggy.com), held the last weekend in Naples at Florida Sports Park. Time trials on Saturday, races on Sunday.

February: Celebrating the life and work of the woman who made a difference to the survival of the Everglades, the **Marjory Stoneman Douglas Festival** (239-695-0008) happens the last week of the month in Everglades City, with lectures, art, slide shows, music, and living history.

Held the first full weekend of the month, the **Everglades Seafood Festival** (239-695-4100; www.everglades seafoodfestival.com), is the biggest event to hit Everglades City all year, with three days of free concerts—always including a headliner like Chris Cagle—hundreds of vendors, and the freshest seafood straight from the boats.

March: **Swamp Buggy Races** (1-800-897-2701; www.swampbuggy.com), held the last weekend in Naples at Florida Sports Park. Time trials on Saturday, races on Sunday.

Florida's Freshwater Frontier.

June: Join in the mystical legends of the Big Cypress Swamp at the **Skunk Ape Festival** (239-695-2275; www.skunkape.info), held the second Saturday, Trail Lakes Campground, Ochopee, celebrating Florida's homegrown version of the yeti. Swamp buggy rides, live music. Fee.

Things get wild at **Spammy Jammy** (239-394-5663; www.LittleBar Restaurant.com), held the last Saturday, Goodland, at the Little Bar Restaurant. Join in the "Spam-a-Lot" spirit (this festival predates the Broadway play) by dressing in your "jimmies" and bringing your most artistic or tastiest Spam creation for judging.

SummerJazz on the Gulf (239-261-2222; www.naplesbeachhotel.com), held the second Saturday, June through September. Free beachside concerts at the Naples Beach Hotel & Golf Club, with food and beverages available.

October: **Swamp Buggy Races** (1-800-897-2701; www.swampbuggy.com), held the last weekend in Naples at Florida Sports Park. Time trials on Saturday, races on Sunday.

Florida's Freshwater Frontier

THE PEACE RIVER VALLEY: HARDEE
AND DESOTO COUNTIES

HIGHLANDS COUNTY

LAKE OKEECHOBEE

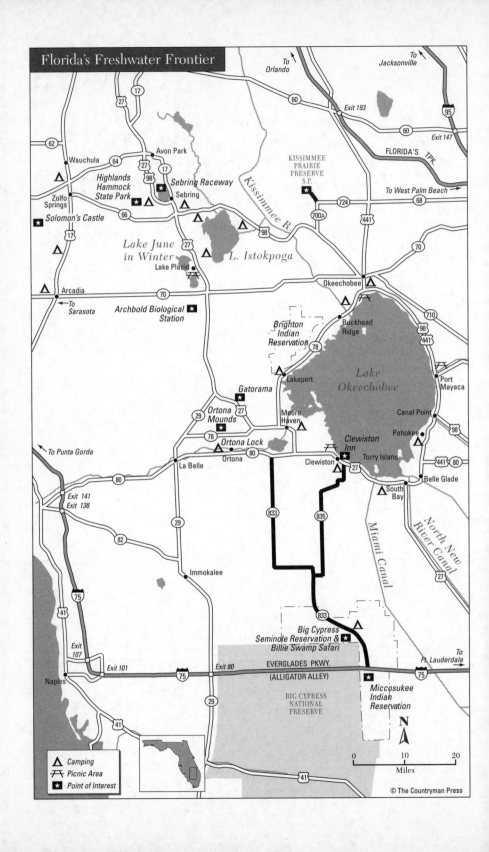

Florida's Freshwater Frontier

To Orlando
To Jacksonville

Exit 193
Exit 147
FLORIDA'S TPK.

KISSIMMEE PRAIRIE PRESERVE S.P.

To West Palm Beach →

Avon Park
Wauchula
Highlands Hammock State Park
Sebring Raceway
Sebring
Zolfo Springs
Solomon's Castle

Lake June in Winter
Lake Placid
L. Istokpoga

Okeechobee

Arcadia
← To Sarasota
Archbold Biological Station

Brighton Indian Reservation
Buckhead Ridge

Lakeport
Lake Okeechobee
Port Mayaca

Gatorama
Ortona Mounds
Moore Haven
Canal Point
Pahokee

Ortona Lock
Ortona
Clewiston Inn
Torry Island
La Belle
Clewiston
Belle Glade
South Bay

To Punta Gorda

Miami Canal
North New River Canal

Exit 141
Exit 138

Immokalee

Exit 107
Exit 101

Naples

Big Cypress Seminole Reservation & Billie Swamp Safari

EVERGLADES PKWY.
(ALLIGATOR ALLEY)
Exit 80

To Ft. Lauderdale

Miccosukee Indian Reservation

BIG CYPRESS NATIONAL PRESERVE

N

▲ Camping
⚷ Picnic Area
★ Point of Interest

0   10   20
Miles

© The Countryman Press

THE PEACE RIVER VALLEY:
HARDEE AND DESOTO COUNTIES

A crucial chapter of Florida's frontier history played out along the Peace River. As the northernmost border of the Seminole Territory, **Arcadia**, established in 1886, quickly earned a reputation as the rowdiest city in Florida, a frontier outpost where shootouts between cattle ranchers and cattle rustlers happened as a matter of course. The arrival of the Florida Southern Railroad through town created an economic boom that led to a thriving downtown through the 1920s. Lined with architectural marvels, the 58-block historic district has more than 370 buildings and homes on the National Register of Historic Places. Downtown is one of Florida's top destinations for antiques shoppers, where you can easily spend a day or two browsing the shops. While rustlers are no longer the problem they were, ranching and other agricultural interests remain the heart of DeSoto County's economy, with Ben Hill Griffin and more than a dozen other ranchers holding hundreds of thousands of acres in the region.

Farther north on the Peace River, **Wauchula**, Seminole for "cry of the sandhill crane," is the county seat of Hardee County, and **Zolfo Springs** was an important crossroads for cattle drovers moving herds from interior ranchlands to the coast. **Bowling Green** started as a trading post that marked the northern extent of Seminole lands.

GUIDANCE Florida's Freshwater Frontier (1-800-467-4540; www.florida freshwaterfrontier.com), P.O. Box 1196, Sebring, 33871-1196 brings together tourism information for all of the counties and small communities in this rural region. The **DeSoto County Chamber of Commerce** (863-494-4033; www .desotochamber.net), 16 S Volusia Ave., Arcadia, and downtown merchants association have a small visitors center adjacent to a public park near the railroad depot. **Hardee County Chamber of Commerce** (863-773-6967; www.hardeecc.com), 401 N 6th Ave. Ste. A, Wauchula, offers information on this rural county's attractions.

GETTING THERE *By car:* **US 17** links together the cities of this region, which sit 20 to 30 miles east of **I-75**. At least four exits along the interstate lead to Arcadia, so you won't miss it!

By air: **Sarasota Bradenton International Airport** (see *Sarasota and Her Islands*) is the nearest major airport.

GETTING AROUND A car is essential for getting around in this region.

MEDICAL EMERGENCIES For emergencies, visit **DeSoto Memorial Hospital** (863-494-8401; www.dmh.org), 888 N Robert Ave., Arcadia, or **Florida Hospital Wauchula** (863-773-3101; www.fhhd.org), 533 West Carlton St., Wauchula, at the corner of Florida Avenue.

PUBLIC RESTROOMS In Arcadia, you'll find them at the edge of the antiques district at the corner of DeSoto and Oak, behind the pavilion at Oak Park.

PUBLIC PARKING You'll find free street parking and surface lots in Arcadia, and some free and metered street parking in Wauchula near the restaurants.

✳ To See

ART GALLERIES

Arcadia
For evocative paintings of Florida landscapes and wildlife, stop in at **Debra Hollingsworth Galleries** (863-990-2800; www.debrahollingsworthgalleries.com), 4481 NE Cubitis Ave. (US 17). A fifth-generation Florida native, Debra reveals the soul of the land through her art.

Ona
At **Solomon's Castle** (see *Attractions*), playful art is everywhere—in the construction of the buildings, in the quirky galleries inside the castle, on the grounds, and in **The Alamo**, Howard Solomon's latest creation, where some of his work is for sale, such as "pet blocks" and bar cars. Just ask!

HISTORIC SITES

Arcadia
With a 58-block historic district, there are many architectural marvels to explore on foot in downtown Arcadia, including the original **1883 Post Office** and the **Old Opera House**. Stop in at **Wheeler's Cafe** (see *Eating Out*) to peruse photos and clippings that help interpret the town's long history.

Bowling Green
At **Paynes Creek Historic State Park** (see *Parks*), a significant chapter in Florida history unfolded in 1849 when the federal government built a trading post on the northern boundary of the Seminole Reservation on a creek that marked the land boundary. Several months after the trading post opened, on July 17, 1849, five Seminoles—one of whom was outlawed by his tribe—opened fire on the trading post. Captain George S. Payne, Dempsey Whiddon, and William McCullough were shot, and Payne and Whiddon died. Despite attempts by the tribes to appease the U.S. government, the incident sparked immediate conflict. With ground broken in October 1849, Fort Chokonikla was the first fort built, and the nearby creek was named for the captain killed at the trading post. Remains of the fort and a memorial to the fallen soldiers are an integral part of this park.

Wauchula

Wauchula's historic downtown district is primarily made up of commercial buildings and the **old City Hall** across from **The Quilter's Inn** (see *Lodging*).

MUSEUMS At **Pioneer Park** (see *Parks*), the **Cracker Trail Museum** (863-735-0119), 2822 Museum Dr., Zolfo Springs, showcases elements of the region's long history, from prehistoric bones found in the Peace River to an adze used to kill a Florida panther that attacked a pioneer's child back in the early 1800s. Artifacts in the museum and adjacent barn bring to life pioneer hardships during the post-statehood settlement of Florida—walk through an actual pioneer cabin and poke around the blacksmith shop. Open 9 AM–5:30 PM Tues.–Sat. Donations appreciated.

RAILROADIANA Historic railroad depots sit in both downtown Arcadia and Wauchula, and you'll find a **1914 Baldwin steam engine** (Engine #3) at the front corner of **Pioneer Park** (see *Parks*) in front of the **Cracker Trail Museum** (see *Museums*). It was used during the heyday of cypress logging along the Peace River Valley.

Sandra Friend

ARCADIA'S OLD OPERA HOUSE

RODEO The **All-Florida Championship Rodeo** (1-800-749-7633; www.arcadia rodeo.com), Arcadia, started in 1929 and is the state's oldest rodeo association in the middle of cattle country. Where better to watch the cowmen at play? Competitive events include bull riding, bareback riding, barrel racing, saddle bronc, steer wrestling, and tie-down roping. See a frontier shootout, and watch the quadrille—best described as "square dancing on horseback." Performances begin 2 PM each day of the event. Tickets are available in advance or at the box office after 11 AM. The rodeo, a nonprofit event that benefits the region, is presented in mid-March, with additional events held at the stadium throughout the year (see *Special Events*).

WILDLIFE REHAB A sanctuary for injured and orphaned wildlife, the **Hardee County Animal Refuge** (863 735-9531; www.hardeecounty.net), 650 Animal Way, can be found along the Peace River in the northwest corner of **Pioneer Park** (see *Parks*), Zolfo Springs. Visitors walk an elevated boardwalk to view the permanent refuge residents in a natural river hammock habitat. Open 10 AM–4 PM Tues. and Thurs.–Sun. Fee.

SOLOMON'S CASTLE

ATTRACTIONS
ONA

✐ You have to see it to believe it—**Solomon's Castle** (863-494-6077; www.solomonscastle.com), 4533 Solomon Rd., isn't just a rambling medieval pastiche complete with a replica of a 17th-century Spanish galleon, it's a collection of galleries and the home of sculptor Howard Solomon and his family. Set along the splendor of Horse Creek, a tributary of the Peace River, this unique little kingdom has a lot to explore. Walking in on the yellow brick road, you'll see sculptures that will have you cracking a smile. Solomon's creativity with "discarded stuff" dates back to the original ecoconscious era—he's been creating comic sculptures on this property since 1970—and he's entirely self-taught. It's the ultimate in recycled art. Oil drums, brake shoes, beer cans, turntables, pistons, cams, and universal joints become fantastical creatures and figurines, like the egg-eating gargoyle, the iron butter-

Animals of a different stripe roam the enclosures at **Peace River Refuge & Ranch** (863-735-0804; www.peaceriverrefuge.org), 2545 Stoner Ln., Zolfo Springs. Here, abandoned exotics are cared for, from African servals to tigers and lynx; you'll find black bears and other large native mammals as well. The sanctuary is not open to the public, but you can request a tour, either by phone or through their Web site. Donations appreciated.

✳ To Do

BIRDING Watch for red-cockaded woodpeckers in the longleaf pine forests of **Deep Creek Preserve** (see *Wild Places*), and for wading birds along the shoreline of the Peace River and Paynes Creek at **Paynes Creek Historic State Park**

fly, and "Evil Kornevil." The tour through the castle and around the grounds is a hoot, filled with puns and silliness, a walk through a series of galleries showcasing this detailed and unusual art plus a peek into the dungeon and a stroll through their home. Its incredible woodworking, including a massive three-sided door, speaks to Solomon's background as a cabinetmaker. More than 90 stained-glass windows decorate the castle. The tour continues through the **Boat in the Moat** (see *Eating Out*), yet another massive work of art, to the workshops where Howard Solomon does his welding and creates his whimsical world. Adjoining the restaurant is the Treetop Gift Shop, topped with a lighthouse and full of cute figurines, mini teapots, garden flags, urns— cute garden decor. If you call ahead, you can stay here, too, in the **Blue Moon Room** (see *Bed & Breakfasts*) inside the castle. The nature trail along Horse Creek leads beneath ancient oaks and returns to the grounds via a draw-bridge over the moat. Open 11–4 except Mon.; closed July–Sept. I highly rec-ommend the tour: adults $10, children under 12 $4, cash only; admission to the grounds and nature trail are free.

WHIMSICAL SCULPTURES SURROUND SOLOMON'S CASTLE

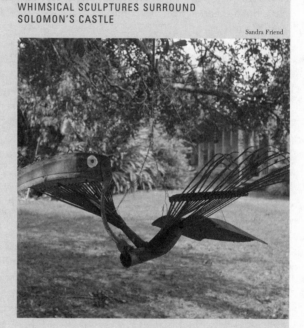

Sandra Friend

(see *Parks*). I saw several osprey nests while walking along the river at **Pioneer Park** (see *Parks*).

BOATING DeSoto Marina is part of the complex at the **Nav-A-Gator Grill** (see *Eating Out*) in Lake Suzy, offering dockage for cruisers coming up the Peace River; no live-aboards. Services include groceries, ice, bait, tackle, boat parts and supplies, the restaurant, cottages for rent, and kayak rentals. You can also charter a boat and captain; call for details.

DIVING DeSoto Divers (863-990-7425; www.desotodivers.cc), P.O. Box 1374, Arcadia 34265, offers courses from junior scuba through dive master as well as first aid and CPR.

ECOTOURS See the wild shorelines of the Peace River on **Nav-A-Gator River-boat Tours** (1-800-308-7506; www.nav-a-gator.com), 9700 SW Riverview Cir., Lake Suzy, where you're virtually guaranteed to spot osprey, alligators, and wood storks. **Pontoon boat trips** (lunch included) depart from the dock behind the Nav-A-Gator Grill; reservations required. Explore the river like early Florida pioneers in a **replica cargo canoe** with an interpretive guide; trips vary in length from an hour to a day.

FISHING A reclaimed phosphate mine is now home to **Hardee Lakes Park Fish Management Area** (http://myfwc.com/fishing/pdf/HardeeBrochure6.pdf), north of SR 62 on CR 663 and then west on Ollie Roberts Rd., Fort Green. Four lakes with irregular bottoms are stocked with bluegill, red-ear sunfish, black crappie, and largemouth bass. The **Peace River** is the major waterway through the region, and fishing is best from your canoe (see *Paddling*) or from any of the riverside parks when the water is low or near deep holes caused by snags. Largemouth bass, bream, and catfish are common, and snook have been caught as far north as Fort Meade.

FOSSIL HUNTING ✐ In the summer, the **Peace River** dries up, exposing countless fossils of prehistoric creatures buried in the creek beds. Bring a trowel or mattock to poke around for large shark's teeth, mammoth molars, and more. However, Florida archaeological laws prohibit the removal of prehistoric bones or Native American artifacts, so be selective!

GOLF With 27 holes (18 championship, 9 par 3), **Sunnybreeze Golf Course** (1-888-663-2420; www.sunnybreezegolf.com), 8135 SW Sunnybreeze Rd., off US 17 south of Fort Ogden, provides a challenge for golfers of all experience levels, with greens fees starting at $20. A fully covered driving range and pro shop round out the facility.

HIKING Don't miss the **Horse Creek Nature Trail** at **Solomon's Castle** (see *Attractions*) for an easy walk beneath ancient oaks and along a weaving, winding tributary of the Peace River. At **Brownsville Park** (see *Parks*) a short nature trail leads you through bottomlands along the Peace River. For a hike that combines history and scenery, head to **Paynes Creek Historic State Park** (see *Parks*) to walk a 2.9-mile circuit along Paynes Creek and the Peace River, with stops at the site of a frontier fort and trading post. For lengthier walks, see *Wild Spaces*.

PADDLING Starting at the Fort Meade Outdoor Recreation Area, north of Bowling Green, the 67-mile **Peace River Canoe Trail** provides a serene multiday journey down a slow-moving tannic river with sand bluffs, floodplain forests, and dense pine forests. Contact the Canoe Outpost for shuttles; the state **Office of Greenways and Trails** (850-245-2052 or 1-877-822-5208; www.dep.state.fl.us/gwt) can provide specific details and a map of the route. Check in with Becky or Trent at **Canoe Outpost–Peace River** (1-800-268-0083; www.canoeoutpost.com) to arrange a one- or two-day float down this majestic wilderness waterway, where towering cypresses and moss-draped live oaks line the shores. In addition to owning a large piece of riverfront property open to overnight camping, Canoe Outpost has two locations—upriver at Gardner, 855 River Rd., or downriver at Arcadia,

2816 NW CR 661. Now in their third generation of river rats running the show, these are Floridians you can trust to show off one of the state's most beautiful rivers. Guided trips available, or simply rent and arrange a drop-off or pickup.

THE PEACE RIVER VALLEY: HARDEE AND DESOTO COUNTIES

DeSoto Marina at the **Nav-A-Gator Grill** (see *Eating Out*) offers canoe and kayak rentals. Head out on the river and explore, but return to dock by 4:30 PM. Guided trips available.

SCENIC DRIVES Follow the Peace River along **US 17**, a scenic highway that leads you up the entire Peace River Valley from Punta Gorda (its southern terminus) north through Arcadia, Zolfo Springs, Wauchula, and Bowling Green. Between the towns, you'll enjoy the pastoral cattle-ranch scenery. Perhaps one of the most gorgeous drives in South Florida, **SR 66** east from Zolfo Springs to Lake Placid, part of the **Florida Cracker Trail Scenic Highway**, traverses wide open prairies with massive ranches and haunting stands of cypress.

✳ Green Space
PARKS
Arcadia
Brownville Park (863-491-5333), 1885 NE Brownville St., is a delightful Old Florida getaway north of town along the Peace River. Here, the forest is lush bottomland of hickory, sweet gum, and cypress, with a nature trail and canoe launch to let you take in the beauty of the river, and a campground (see *Campgrounds*) that makes a perfect base camp for fossil hunters. Free.

In an oxbow bend of the Peace River along SR 70 west of downtown, **Desoto Park** provides a quiet place to have a picnic or launch your canoe. Free.

Bowling Green
Protecting the confluence of the Peace River and Paynes Creek as well as an important historic site from the Second Seminole War, **Paynes Creek Historic State Park** (863-375-4717; www.floridastateparks.org/paynescreek), 888 Lake Branch Rd., has several miles of pleasant hiking trails, a large picnic area with playground, and canoe launch to reach the Peace River. A visitors center (open 9 AM–5 PM daily) interprets the significance of this site as it relates to the Seminole Wars. Fee.

Zolfo Springs
An expansive green space along the upper Peace River, **Pioneer Park** (863-735-0330), at the corner of US 17 and FL 64, has riverside picnic tables; a playground; a pleasant, shady campground (see *Campgrounds*); and a village of historic buildings surrounding the **Cracker Trail Museum** (see *Museums*). This is the regional venue for large outdoor events, and you can expect to find a flea market going on here most weekends. In March, crowds gather for **Pioneer Park Days** (see *Special Events*) to celebrate the region's past. Free.

WILD PLACES A place for a quiet hike, **Deep Creek Preserve** (941-475-0769; www.swfwmd.state.fl.us/recreation/areas/deepcreek.html), just off King's Highway in Lake Suzy on the way to the Nav-A-Gator Grill (see *Eating Out*), protects more than 2,000 acres along the Peace River and its tributaries. Nine miles of multiuse forest roads wind through the preserve to provide a network of trails.

Nearby, **R.V. Griffin Reserve** (1-800-423-1476; www.swfwmd.state.fl.us/recreation/areas/rvgriffin.html), CR 769 N, was saved from becoming a "planned community" in the early 1990s. This wilderness area encompasses 374 acres of pine flatwoods, prairies, and marshes, with 22 miles of multiuse trails. A 303-acre reservoir on the property exists to hold water for regional use during the months when the Peace River dries up.

✳ Lodging

BED & BREAKFASTS

Arcadia 34266

"⚑" Built in the late 1890s by Jasper Newton Parker, one of Florida's first cattle barons, the **Historic Parker House** (863-494-1060 or 1-800-969-2499; www.historicparkerhouse.com), 427 W Hickory St., is a true Florida treasure. Each of the Victorian rooms are immense, and owners Kay and Leonard Higley showcase the period with elegant furnishings and beautiful quilts. Enjoy a large screened veranda and the formal living room in addition to your own room or suite ($95); breakfast includes fresh fruits and freshly baked muffins and pastries as well as tasty breakfast entrées.

Ona 33865

Stare at the stars from your perch atop the ramparts at the **Blue Moon Room** (www.solomonscastle.com/bmr.htm), an efficiency apartment within **Solomon's Castle** (see *Attractions*); it's a work of art, with gorgeous stained-glass doors and hand-painted scenes on the closet doors, $99. Closed July—Sept. and on Mon.

Wauchula 33873

& "⚑" If you're an obsessive quilter like some of my friends, then your next destination should be **The Quilter's Inn** (863-767-8989 or 1-877-664-8989; www.thequiltersinn.com), 106 S Fourth Ave. Inside this 1925 bungalow, proprietor Pattie Detwiler, an avid quilter, displays her handiwork in all five guest rooms ($99–129). Each room features welcoming decor and is

uniquely appointed with period antiques. The comfortable rooms are a favorite for business travelers as well. Guests enjoy breakfasts in the in-house Patchwork Café, which is available for tea parties and other special functions.

CAMPGROUNDS

Arcadia 34266

🐟 At **Brownville Park** (see *Parks*), campers will appreciate the 24-space campground within this county park along the Peace River, as it is set on the high ground beneath ancient live oaks. There are spaces for tents ($20) and RVs ($25), electric and water included; primitive campsites are $15. Bathhouse and dump station on-site. Reservations suggested.

🐾 Bluegrass reigns supreme at **Craig's RV Park** (863-494-1820; www.craigs rv.com), 7895 NE US 17, a gathering place for campers who like a little pickin' and grinnin'. Home of the **Bluegrass Family Gathering** and the **Gold Wing Express Arcadia Bluegrass Festival** (see *Special Events*), it's also a pleasant, sunny, family-owned campground with daily rates of $35, monthly $600. The back section of the park is where the music happens.

A favorite with snowbirds, **Little Willies RV Resort** (863-494-2717 or 1-800-222-7675; www.littlewilliesrv resort.com), 5905 NE Cubitis Ave. (Old US 17), offers sunny grassy sites, full hookups, a clubhouse with scheduled activities, and a massive swimming pool. Open to RV and trailers only, $39, with discounts for members of motorcoach clubs.

✦ ☼ ⁙⚑⁙ Families flock to the **Peace River Campground** (863-494-9693 or 1-800-559-4011; www.peaceriver campground.com), 2998 NW SR 70, which was set under a shady canopy of live oaks until Hurricane Charley came along. It'll take a while for the trees to fully recover, but they're growing in— and the throngs who love this campground, especially tent campers, are increasing. It's no wonder, with all the activities they have available, including fossil hunts, a playground and game room, fishing and hiking, canoe rentals, and even Segway rentals. Primitive campers have 100 acres of wilderness to roam, where primitive sites are $15 for ages 12 and up. Full hookup sites are $52, tent sites with water and electric, $46.

Lake Suzy 34266

☼ ⁙⚑⁙ With frontage right on the Peace River, the **Riverside RV Resort & Campground** (863-993-2111 or 1-800-795-9733; www.riversidervresort .com), 9770 SW CR 769, is a very appealing destination for snowbirds and weekenders alike. Choose from shady or sunny sites, kick back at the pool and relax in the hot tub, or fish from the docks. There is boat trailer parking available and a boat ramp to slip your craft into the river. In-season daily rates for full hookup run $43–52; tent sites available Apr. 1–Sept. 30 for $41.

Zolfo Springs 33890

☼ Camp amid history at **Pioneer Park** (see *Parks*), where the cypresses and palms that shade your space watched as Seminoles camped here long ago. Most of the campsites overlook the wild beauty of the Peace

Sandra Friend

PIONEER PARK CAMPGROUND ALONG THE PEACE RIVER

River. Rates $7 without electric, $11 with electric; includes bathhouse with showers. Pets permitted, but they must be leashed.

HOTELS, MOTELS, AND RESORTS

Arcadia 34266

♿ ⁙⚑⁙ A renovation of the landmark D. T. Carlton Building has resulted in the snazziest accommodations to open in Arcadia, the **Oak Park Inn** (863-494-9500; www.oakparkinnarcadia.com). Downstairs, a single room with an outside entrance is wheelchair accessible. Upstairs, the rooms and suites open up into a large social space with a fireplace, and each has its own special round-the-world flair. Pick your mood. Room #7 looks over the historic train station and sports a Caribbean vibe; #1 is the bunkhouse, perfect for the kids, with bunk beds and cowboy art; #7 is distinctly Victorian; and #5 feels like a New York loft apartment, with a modern urban bath and stone floors. Guests have shared access to a washer and dryer, microwave, and complimentary drinks in the fridge. Rates range from $99 for the bunkhouse to $110 for a standard-sized room and $175 for the suites.

✳ Where to Eat

EATING OUT

Arcadia

Lovely Venetian murals accent **A Taste of Italy** (863-494-1700), 115 Oak St., inside the 1926 Koch Arcade. This popular Italian restaurant serves up culinary classics like eggplant parmesan, manicotti, lasagna, and spaghetti alongside brick oven pizza and subs, $7–15. Open Tues.–Sun. 4 PM–9 PM, Fri.–Sun. 11 AM–4 PM.

🍤 Since 1929, **Wheeler's Cafe** (863-993-1555), 13 S Monroe Ave., has been the place where the locals eat, and when my friend Becky took me there, we sat right down with some folks we'd never met before—a first for me in an American restaurant! Great conversation ensued, and the food was pure Southern. When the café opened as Goody's Restaurant, a meal cost 35 cents, and dinner specials are still a bargain at under $10, including roast beef, ham steak, fried catfish, and more, with home-style sides. A hearty breakfast costs only a few bucks and is served up in minutes. Leave room for their "world-famous" peanut butter pie! Open daily 6 AM–9 PM.

Lake Suzy

🍤 Now here's a place with real Florida character (and characters)—the **Nav-A-Gator Grill** (941-627-3474, www .nav-a-gator.com), 9700 SW Riverview Cir. It's a good old-fashioned fish camp that's a launch point for fishing, kayaking, ecotours, and more, but most folks come here for the food. Their grouper sandwiches are legendary, and local favorites such as sweet potato fries and swamp cabbage are not to be missed, with entrées $12 and up. Smokers (and those enjoying a beer) tend to gather 'round the fire ring out back, where you might catch someone strumming on a banjo or guitar. Walk back to the gift shop and the little museum—it's full of artifacts, from beads to pottery shards and bones, found on the bottom of the Peace River.

Ona

🍤 ✐ If you've never had lunch on a pirate ship, here's your chance! The **Boat in the Moat** is firmly aground in the moat around **Solomon's Castle** (see *Attractions*), and the gangplank leads to a different sort of dining adventure. The restaurant surrounding you is a handcrafted piece of art, from the uniquely themed stained-glass windows to each chair and table. It took Howard Solomon four years to build, and it sits on 105 pilings. His daughter Alane oversees the menu, which includes such lunch favorites as grilled chicken salad, homemade chicken pot pie, and corned beef on rye ($7–10). All of the food is homemade, including the desserts. Dinner is served Fri.–Sat. until 9 PM.

For bluegrass and barbecue, c'mon out to "the middle of nowhere" at **Herb's Limestone Country Club** (www .herbs.meanbikergirls.com), 5127 S CR 663. It's a biker bar, a bunker filled with beer and eclectic ephemera like a full-sized wicker motorcycle, plus Herb's detailed art. He handcrafted the bar, and the beautiful porch. Sit out there and enjoy a cold one, or show up for the fine barbecue Friday through Sunday and *especially* for the monthly "BBQ and Bands" bluegrass jams on the last Sunday of every month.

Wauchula

An appealing choice along US 17, **The Bread Board Restaurant** (863-773-2337), 902 US 17 S, offers good comfort food like country fried steak and catfish, and tasty Southern treats like fried green tomatoes and fried eggplant sticks. Lunch and dinner, $5 and up.

Zolfo Springs

Stop for Southern basics such as catfish, steak, and shrimp at the **Pioneer Restaurant** (863-735-0726), 2902 US 17, just across from Pioneer Park. Sandwiches and dinners $3 and up. Open daily for breakfast, lunch, and dinner; no credit cards.

A giant rooster tops **Rooster's** (863-735-2322), corner School House Rd. and FL 66, so you won't miss it from the road. Good, filling country breakfasts, an ice cream counter, and Southern selections for dinner.

SODA FOUNTAIN

Arcadia

Set in the pretty peppermint-pink Koch Arcade from 1926, the **Hot Fudge Shoppe** (863-494-6633), 117 W Oak St., has a '50s sock-hop atmosphere, accented by a popcorn machine with an aroma that entices you in. They offer cool treats and hot dogs, with hot fudge sundaes starting around $4 and plenty of fountain favorites. They make their own ice cream on the premises—sugar-free and fat-free versions included—and it is worth the trip.

✳ Selected Shopping

Arcadia

Downtown Arcadia is a serious destination for antique shoppers, with well over 300 different dealers tucked away in shops along Oak, Magnolia, and the side streets between them. Bring your wish lists and plan on a day on the town, as you'll have plenty to browse. Every fourth Saturday, there's an antiques fair along the streets. Here's a sampler of what you'll find on a stroll downtown.

A 1954 Coca-Cola sign dominates the wall at **Abigail's Antiques & Collectibles** (863-494-1434), 24 W Oak St., and it's for sale—along with a spectrum of vintage glassware, classic sheet music, costume jewelry, furniture, and much more.

I saw some very appealing cedar chests at **Antiques on Oak** (863-494-2038), 132 W Oak St., where unique furnishings are just a part of the setting—look for Tiffany lamps, stoneware jars, stained-glass windows, and fine glassware, too.

Check out the cheery Christmas corner in the back of **Cherry Hill Antiques** (863-993-2344; www.CherryHillAntiques.com), 120 W Oak St., and a collection of beer steins in the front of the store. Many of their items can be viewed (and purchased!) online.

Groaning under the weight of used paperbacks—more than 12,000 books stuffed into this little 1908 white and yellow cottage—**Crackerhouse Books** (863-993-1445), 236 N Brevard Ave., offers bibliophiles a treasure

ROOSTER'S DINER IN ZOLFO SPRINGS
Sandra Friend

trove to dig through, especially for paper ephemera. Call ahead, as their hours are offbeat.

Housed in the historic Dozier's Department Store, **Isabelle's Fine Antiques** (863-491-1004), 104 W Oak St., has a little bit of everything, from postcards to printer's trays, wooden rolling pins, a root beer barrel, and a back room full of books.

J&R Antiques (863-494-3398), 125 W Oak St, has classic lamps, tablecloths, and dishes among the home-decor related antiques in their collection.

The **Last Chapter Books & Cafe** (863-491-0250), 23 W Oak St., offers browsers books, books, and more books, including a fine little cache of antiquarian titles and classic comics, plus a nice little coffee shop.

Everything's folksy at **Maddy's Antiques** (863-494-2500; www.maddys antiques.com), 121 W Oak St., a fun place to browse for folk art, dried flowers, and antique wood.

Oak Leaf Antiques & Collectibles (863-491-5044), 101 W Oak St., offers dealer booths with upscale items such as intarsia trays, a sterling silver tea server, classy quilts, and unforgettable Florida scenes by the Highwayman artists.

The upper floor of the landmark Old Opera House, circa 1920, is home to **Pyewackets** (863-494-3006), 106 W Oak St., a real treat—the old-time cinema is chock-full of antiques. Most are for sale, but some aren't, as many constitute a museum dedicated to the heyday of this film house. A whole room is themed and maintained by the "phantom of the opera." The dealer booths and unique movie-history ephemera offer hours of browsing.

Fine furnishings and stained-glass lamps are among the treasures you'll uncover at **Timeless Treasures** (863-993-9393), 103 W Oak St.

Duck inside **Treasure Alley** (863-993-1838), 122 W Oak St., to browse their interesting mix of items, including military uniforms, mink stoles, and fishing rods.

A feminine display of Victoriana, **The Vintage Garden** (863-494-3555), 14 W Oak St., has classic cottage decor, plus vintage dresses and hats, purses, and costume jewelry.

PRODUCE STANDS AND U-PICK

Along US 17, watch for roadside stands with fresh seafood and local produce. **Nocatee Produce** is a roadside stand in Nocatee with local watermelons and tomatoes in season. At **Fort Ogden Gardens U-Pick,** near CR 761, grab organic vegetables, including tomatoes and onions, and fresh fruits in season.

In Wauchula, it's hard to miss **Sandy's Big Tree Produce** (863-767-0868), 906 S Sixth Ave., for some of the region's freshest veggies and fruit.

✳ Special Events

January: ✐ Experience the agricultural bounty of Arcadia at the **DeSoto County Fair** (863-494-5678; www .desotocountyfair.org), which began in 1953 to showcase livestock and produce. The fair has grown to be a fun family outing with a midway, beauty pageants, gospel music, and exhibit booths. Held late Jan.–early Feb.

The **Gold Wing Express Arcadia Bluegrass Festival** (www.craigsrv .com/bluegrass.html), a three-day weekend of bluegrass bands, kicked off a new tradition in January 2009, bringing more bluegrass to this musical region.

February–March: One week, 120 miles, all on horseback: **The Florida Cracker Trail Ride** (www.cracker trail.org) harkens back to the day when Florida's cattle drovers moved their herds down the Peace River Valley to Punta Rassa. To draw attention to Florida's cattle heritage, members of the Florida Cracker Trail Association ride 15 to 20 miles each day on "The Big Ride" from Bradenton to Fort Pierce. Catch the cowmen at **Pioneer Park** (see *Parks*) or at any of their stopping points on FL 64, US 98, or FL 68 along the route.

March: **All-Florida Championship Rodeo**, Arcadia (see *Rodeo*).

✍ The **Cracker Heritage Festival** (863-767-0330; www.mainstreet wauchula.com/cracker_heritage.htm), held on a mid-month Saturday by Main Street Wauchula, this festival focuses on regional heritage. Enjoy a pancake breakfast or barbecue lunch, Florida Cracker crafts, kids' activities, musical entertainment, and both silent and live auctions.

✍ Since 1968, **Pioneer Park Days** (863-773-2161; www.hardeecounty .net/Pioneer/index.cfm), at Pioneer Park, Zolfo Springs, has celebrated the region's rich history with pioneer craft demonstrations, country entertainment, good church food, and the fourth largest gathering of antique engines in the United States. Held the first weekend of the month.

May: ✍ **Watermelon Festival**, Arcadia. Includes plenty of watermelon eating, seed spitting contests, and the crowning of the Watermelon Queen, as well as a Sugar Babies contest.

HIGHLANDS COUNTY

I n the heart of Florida, Highlands County is a special place. Here, art, culture, and history come together with down-home hospitality and some of the most beautiful natural areas in Florida. A drive through the rolling hills offers glimpses of lakes surrounded by orange groves, colorful fields of caladiums, cattle ranches fringed by haunting cypress strands, and the bright splash of white sand that is the Lake Wales Ridge. Rising more than 200 feet above sea level, this portion of the ridge includes some of the highest land in the Florida peninsula, and some of North America's oldest lakes.

Highlands County separated from DeSoto County in 1921, adopting its name from the dominating topography. But its major communities took root prior to that. Settled in 1884 by Oliver Martin Crosby, incorporated as a town in 1886, and incorporated as a city in 1926, **Avon Park** reminded English settlers of Stratford-on-Avon, England. Known as the "City of Charm," the town is home to Lake Tulane, the oldest living lake in North America. From the 1940s through the 1980s, the board game checkers was a major-league sport, and you'll surely see some of the locals still playing today at the first "checker shelter," built during the 1940s and 1950s. Located in Veterans Square on the Mall on Main Street, the shelter honors veterans from World War I, World War II, and Vietnam. Avon Park is also home to South Florida Community College.

At the other end of the county, you'll find **Lake Placid**, the "Caladium Capital of the World." From July through October, the town is surrounded by thousands of acres of red and pink caladium fields in full bloom. Lake Placid is also home to the largest collection of murals in Florida, with more than 40 murals depicting local history, flora, and fauna, earning Lake Placid another moniker, "The Town of Murals." Named after a favorite get-

ORANGE GROVES ALONG SCENIC 17
Sandra Friend

away in New York by Dr. Melvil Dewey, creator of the Dewey Decimal System, in 1927, the town's former name was Lake Sterns. More clowns per capita live in Lake Placid than anywhere else in Florida, thanks to Toby's Clown College.

In 1911, Ohio pottery magnate George E. Sebring went on a fishing trip and was captivated by the area around Lake Jackson (then known as Lake Hare). He soon bought 9,000 acres of palmetto-covered prairie as the location for his dream city. Naming the town **Sebring** after his hometown in Ohio, he developed it to resemble a wheel, with the town center branching off in six spoke streets from a small central park. A devout Christian, Mr. Sebring offered free land to any church that would establish itself, and by 1912 the town was officially founded. In keeping with his vision of a green city, developers were instructed to plant a citrus tree in each residential lot. As the county seat, Sebring is said by some to be modeled after the ancient Syrian city of Heliopolis.

Sebring was also home to Hendricks Field, a military training base that housed B-17s gearing up for World War II. When sports-car enthusiast Alec Ulman flew into the airport in 1950, he thought it would make a great racetrack, and in 1952 the first sports car endurance race, the 12 Hours of Sebring, was held. Today the Sebring International Raceway is home to the American Le Mans endurance race and is one of the world's better known destinations for auto racing.

GUIDANCE For local tourism information, contact the **Highlands County Visitor & Convention Bureau** (863-386-1316 or 1-800-255-1711; www.visithighlands county.com), 1121 US 27 S, where you can stop in for brochures; the **Greater Lake Placid Chamber of Commerce, Inc.** (863-465-4331 or 1-800-557-5224; www.lpfla.com), 18 N Oak St., Lake Placid; or the **Avon Park Chamber of Commerce** (863-453-3350; www.apfla.com), 28 E Main St. You'll also learn more about the region from **Florida's Freshwater Frontier** (1-800-467-4540; www.florida freshwaterfrontier.com), P.O. Box 1196, Sebring, 33871-1196.

GETTING THERE *By car:* **US 27** and **US 98** run through the heart of the county. Both are met by **SR 64** in Avon Park, which comes in from the west from I-75 at Bradenton, as well as **SR 66**, which follows a similar route but ends up near Lake Placid. US 27 is also intersected by **SR 70** south of Lake Placid on its route between Bradenton to the west and Okeechobee and Fort Pierce to the east.

By air: **Sebring Regional Airport** (863-655-6444; www.sebring-airport.com), 128 Authority Ln., is available for private pilots. For commercial service, your nearest airports are the **Charlotte County Airport** (see *Charlotte Harbor and the Gulf Islands*) 2 hours southwest; Southwest Florida International Airport (see *The Beaches of Fort Myers Sanibel*) 2 hours southwest; and **Orlando International Airport** (www.orlandoairports.net), 2 hours north.

By rail: **AMTRAK** (1-800-872-7245; www.amtrak.com) provides regularly scheduled service to Sebring.

GETTING AROUND US 27 is the major north-south route connecting Avon Park, Sebring, and Lake Placid. **US 98** joins this route for the Avon Park—Sebring stretch, then branches off southeast along the north side of Lake Istokpoga to pass through Lorida en route to Okeechobee. **Scenic SR 17** is the pretty way to drive north from US 98 through historic downtown Sebring and Avon Park. Use **SR 66** or **SR 64** to reach the western side of the county.

MEDICAL EMERGENCIES For emergencies, head to the **Florida Hospital Heartland Medical Center** (863-314-4466; www.fhhd.org), 4200 Sun 'n Lake Blvd., Sebring; **Highlands Regional Medical Center** (1-800-533-4762; www .hrmc.org), 3600 S Highlands Ave., Sebring; or **Florida Hospital Heartland Medical Center** (863-465-3777), 1200 US 27 N, Lake Placid.

PUBLIC PARKING Free street parking can be found throughout the county.

✳ To See

ART GALLERIES

Avon Park

Inside the Hotel Jacaranda (see *Lodging*), **The Artists' Group at South Florida Community College** has a large gallery of student's work, some of which is for sale. They offer 6-week classes in basic instruction of painting with acrylics, oils, and watercolors.

Lake Placid

At the **Art Studio Gallery** (863-465-1710), 212 N Main St., drop in to see beautiful works of art by Jeni Novak, who runs a working studio where she teaches classes in a variety of techniques, including clay puzzling and watercolor. Or sign up for open "art time," where you (and the kids) can use the expansive studio space and its tools for less than $10 a day. Open Mon. and Thurs.–Sat. 10 AM–5 PM.

Founded in 1993, the **Caladium Arts & Crafts Cooperative** (863-699-5940; www.caladiumarts.org), 132 Interlake Blvd., features the work of more than 100 local artists, each with their own booths. You'll find fine art here that reflects local themes, including paintings and fine art photography of the Kissimmee River wilds, mist at morning in Highlands Hammock, and fishing on the coast. There are many folk artists and crafters, too, so expect a fair helping of homemade soaps and candles, Christmas crafts, hand-painted china, and quilts. Unique to Lake Placid, caladiums appear on treasure boxes and earrings. The co-op also sells postcards of the murals around town.

Sebring

I love pottery, so it was a delight to find **Gene Brenner Pottery & Craft Gallery** (863-471-2228; www.brennerpottery.com), 104 Circle Park Dr., where the in-store studio allows you to watch Gene at work on his wheel-thrown hand-turned bowls. There are full settings perfect for your dining room, plus a variety of whimsical sea creatures and fantasy fish for home decor. Gene's been an artist in Sebring for more than 30 years, and he's gotten to know a lot of fellow artists, whose work is exhibited here, such as Steve Vaughn's giclee on canvas Florida scenes, plus hand-blown art glass, batik, and more.

At **Art G—The Painting Studio** (863-314-0042), 215 N Ridgewood Dr., artist Janet King works on impressionist pieces like a row of four stadium chairs painted in folk art style. It's a gallery and art space where you can select from a variety of original artwork and historical Sebring prints and note cards.

Each second Friday 6–9 PM, merchants in downtown Sebring participate in a **Gallery Walk** (www.gallerywalksebring.com) to encourage residents and visitors to browse the shops.

CALADIUMS More than 98 percent of the world's **caladium bulbs** are grown in the Lake Placid area, and the annual **Caladium Festival** (see *Special Events*) in August draws more than 100,000 visitors each year. Throughout Lake Placid you will notice caladiums planted everywhere. Best viewed between July and October, fields of these large leafy plants can be seen on CR 621, as landscaping in residents' yards, on murals (see *Murals*), and even on trash cans! Bulbs can be purchased at the festival or through **Happiness Farms** (863-465-0044 or 1-866-892-0396; www .happinessfarms.com), 704 CR 621 E.

Sandra Friend

WORKS OF ART AT GENE BRENNER POTTERY

HISTORIC SITES

Avon Park

The Union Congregational Church, N Forest Ave., was built in 1892 on land donated by Avon Park founders Mr. and Mrs. O. M. Crosby. Previously founded as the Evangelical Church, the name was changed to Congregational in 1926.

The second oldest church in Avon Park is the **Episcopal Church of the Redeemer,** E Pleasant St., circa 1894. It was built with the assistance of the Diocese of Florida for communicants of the Church of England.

The **Bandstand** and a **Time Capsule** are located on Main St. between Lake Ave. and Forest Ave. The Bandstand was built in 1897 and previously stood in front of the Hotel Verona. The marble column Time Capsule was sealed in 1912 and is scheduled for opening in 2085.

The **Jacaranda Hotel** (see *Hotels, Motels, and Resorts*) opened during the roaring '20s in 1926. A place for high-class entertainment and good food, the hotel still serves up Southern hospitality (see *Dining Out*). The Revivalist-style hotel is named after the Jacaranda tree that used to sit in its footprint.

Veterans Square on the Mall on Main Street honors veterans of World War I, World War II, and Vietnam. This is also where you will find the first "checker shelter."

The former **Seaboard Air Line Depot** is now home to the **Avon Park Depot Museum** (see *Museums*). The depot, built in 1926, was in service until 1978.

Lake Placid

On US 27 you'll find the **Lake Placid Tower**. When this local landmark was built in 1961, it was the world's tallest concrete block tower. Also known as the Tower of Peace and Happiness Tower, the tower reaches a height of 270 feet and can be seen from all over the county.

Sebring

The Sebring City on the Circle 1920s town center houses many original buildings from the era. Currently being renovated for office and meeting space, the **E. L.**

Hainz Bloc Building, circa 1923, housed the first county courtroom. The **Edward L. Hainz House**, 155 W Center Ave., is a fine example of an "airplane" or "camel back" bungalow.

The Mediterranean Revival **Tobin Building** (circa 1926), 101 S Circle Dr., was built as a commercial building during the great Florida land boom. One of the oldest surviving commercial buildings can be seen at 113 S Circle. Built in 1913, it has been radically altered from the original, but it's still a significant historic structure. Take particular note of the concave facades on the **J. B. Brown Building**, 201–207 S Circle Dr. Built in 1922, the structure housed a hardware store owned by one Jesse B. Brown. The 1915 **Thomas Whitehouse Building**, 313 S Circle Dr., was built as a dry goods store, grocery, and hotel.

Just off the circle at 590 S Commerce Ave., you'll find the **Highlands County Courthouse**. The Classic Revival (circa 1927) building, designed by Fred Bishop, is Florida's oldest courthouse still in use today.

The **Nan-Ces-O-Wee Hotel** (circa 1923), 133 N Ridgewood Dr., the largest surviving commercial building in downtown Sebring, is said to be named after a Native American Princess. Sebring's first Jewish immigrants, Mike and Sadie Kahn, emigrated from Lithuania in 1921 and opened **Kahn's Department Store** on the ground floor of the hotel. In the 1960s the Kahn's created a Jewish cemetery by purchasing one hundred contiguous gravesites from the municipal cemetery. A time capsule in neighboring **Sadie Kahn Park** was sealed in 1923. Several Kahn descendants still reside in Sebring.

Not far from town center, on the corner of S Commerce and Eucalyptus, the 1930s **Stepping Stones Girl Scout Log Cabin** was a blast from the past for Kathy, who went to Girl Scouts in Maine in a similar lodge.

MURALS

Avon Park

Babe Ruth is honored with a mural on the side of a commercial establishment

BABE RUTH MURAL IN AVON PARK

Sandra Friend

Lake Placid

Lake Placid, The Town of Murals, has more than 42 murals within its city limits. It all started in 1992, when Bob and Harriet Porter brought together local artists to create the mural program, now a model for others around the country. Start your tour at the **Chamber of Commerce Welcome Center** (863-465-4331), 18 N Oak Ave., where a **mural gallery** (of paintings submitted by artists as proposals for their larger-scale work) is also home to a video overview of the project, which explains how the history of Lake Placid is being told by its art. Murals are painted with UV-resistant paint and clear-coated every other year for protection. Pick up your walking tour guide ($3) here and start wandering. Right on the outside of this building, **The Scrub Jay's World** appealed to me with its birders and celebration of Florida's only endemic bird. Kids will enjoy the grunting of bears and buzzing of bees at **The Lost Bear Cub** mural on Interlake Blvd. Perhaps the most well-known of the murals, since you can see it while driving north on US 27, is the 175-foot-wide **Cracker Trail Cattle Drive** on the side of Winn Dixie, which showcases the cattle drives of the area, both visually and with "ranch roundup" sound. Each mural has secrets to discover. **On the Rare Resident–Florida Panther** mural on W Park Avenue you'll want to look for the hidden kitten, owl, drag-onfly, lizard, and tree frog. Down the street, next to the Lake Placid Histori-cal Museum, find the word hello on the **Train Depot** mural. My favorite spot is Lake Placid Noon Rotary Park, an alley filled with flora and decorated with murals in every direction. Trash cans (see *Public Art*) have been dis-guised in artful ways as companion pieces to the murals. For more informa-tion about the murals, contact the **Greater Lake Placid Mural Society** (863-531-0211).

SCRUB JAY MURAL IN LAKE PLACID

Sandra Friend

along US 27 adjacent to the **Pizza Hut** (see *Eating Out*). Babe was one of the regulars in town when the St. Louis Cardinals had their spring training here in the 1920s–1940s.

Sebring

You'll find a variety of murals in several locations downtown, including around the circle and in the park behind Ridgewood Street.

MUSEUMS

Avon Park

Located in the cultural core of downtown, the **Avon Park Depot Museum** (863-453-3525; www.hsaponline.org), 3 N Museum Ave., presents the history of Avon Park inside a Seaboard Coast Line passenger station from 1926. The rooms of the depot are filled with local ephemera arranged in thematic groupings. One display honors the St. Louis Cardinals, who started spring training in Avon Park in 1926, after they won the World Series. Babe Ruth, Dizzy Dean, Lou Gehrig, and other Hall of Famers became regulars in town, and a commemorative bat given to Babe Ruth is displayed. Archives of the Avon Park Times date back to 1929. A representative kitchen shows off early life in Avon Park—did you know that Brown 'n' Serve rolls were invented here? See a switchboard used up until 1985 to connect people in this rural community. Prominently displayed is the novel *The Girl Who Loved Tom Gordon* by Steven King, loosely based on the New York Yankees' Tom (Flash) Gordon, a graduate of Avon Park High School. For more historic background, pick up a copy of *Yesterday, A Family Album of Highlands County* by Elaine and Larry Levey; you'll often find Elaine at the museum. Behind the depot, a gleaming chrome 1948 California Zephyr dining car, the Silver Palm, is permanently on a siding. It serves as a banquet hall and can be reserved for special functions. Open 10 AM–3 PM Tues.–Fri.; donation.

Museum of Florida Arts & Culture (863-453-6661; www.mofac.org), 600 W College Dr., on the SFCC campus. In the 1950s a small number of African American men painted Florida landscapes and sold them by the side of the road. The gorgeous renderings of the "Highwaymen" soon became highly collectible and now appear in many private collections and museums, including this one. In the concourse, you'll also find several striking murals and three-dimensional pieces by other talented Florida artists, and there is also an impressive display of Florida archaeological artifacts. Call for hours; free.

SWITCHBOARD DISPLAY AT THE AVON PARK DEPOT

Sandra Friend

Lake Placid

The **Lake Placid Historical Society Depot Museum** (863-465-1771), 12 Park St., is housed in the former ACL railroad depot, which is on the National Register of Historical Places. Here you'll see historic "sad" irons, Florida Native American artifacts, a linotype machine, a dress worn by Jacqueline Kennedy, and a unique collection of antique buttons artfully displayed. The history of the area is shown in photos and memorabilia. The museum is operated by the Historical Society of Lake Placid, which has been honoring their two eldest residents with the annual Pioneer Man and Pioneer Woman Award since 1982. Don't miss the museum's display of photographs of past recipients. Open Sept.–May Mon.–Fri. 1 PM–3:30 PM; free.

Toby the Clown College, Museum & Gift Shop (863-465-2920; www.toby theclownfoundationinc.org), 112 W Interlake Blvd. "Toby" has been clowning around at local hospitals, day care centers, and birthday parties since 1980, and as a member of the World Clown Association, he will teach you all you need to know to become a clown through education and entertainment. You'll soon be worthy of performing at charitable functions and other events, or just for the fun of it. The gift shop has many clown-related items for sale. Call for hours; donation.

Sebring

The **Florida CCC Museum** (863-386-6094; www.floridastateparks.org/highland shammock/CCCDisplay.cfm), paying homage to Florida men who worked in the Civilian Conservation Corps, is a prominent feature of **Highlands Hammock State Park** (see *Parks*). In the early 1930s the Depression, a land boom bust, and two major hurricanes left Florida's economy deeply depressed. With one in four workers out of work, the CCC was created as part of President Roosevelt's New Deal during the Great Depression. Young men between 17 and 25 entering into a military lifestyle were provided an income of $30 a month, and of that $25 was sent home to their families. Days were spent planting trees, fighting fires, constructing public parks, and restoring historic structures. The "CCC Boys" also received vocational and academic instruction along with a variety of sports and recreational activities. Some of these young men later went on to become leaders in the community. The Sebring camp was the first of 86 camps established. In 1935 eight of these parks became the first Florida State Parks. All the camps were closed in 1942 due to World War II, with many enrollees joining the armed services. This building, built in the late 1930s, is now a museum housing an impressive collection of historical CCC artifacts and memorabilia. Donation; open during park hours.

✆ **Children's Museum of the Highlands** (863-385-5437; www.childrensmuseum highlands.com), 219 N Ridgewood. This nonprofit hands-on facility is one of the best children's museums I have come across. The attentive staff will help you expand your kid's creativity and exploration through the Amazing Maze, Waterworks, Mini Grocery Store, Bubble Image, Doctor Scrubby's Office, WKID TV Station, Pedal Power, Note Nook, and Sebring Fire Tower. Open 10 AM–5 PM Tues.–Sat. (until 8 on Thurs.). Fee.

At the **Highlands Art League & Museum** (863-385-5312; www.highlandsart league.com), 351 W Center Ave., local residents Elsa and Marvin Kahn worked hard to make this "the village where art lives." This brightly colored artist colony is comprised of three historic homes overlooking Lake Jackson. Donation; call for hours.

You'll be greeted at the door by Howard Fleetwood, president of the **Military Sea Services Museum** (863-471-2386; www.milseasvcmuseum.com), 1402 Roseland Ave., where the Navy, Marine, and Coast Guard of the past and present are highlighted at this extensive military museum. Near the entrance there is an emotional exhibit that pays homage to MIAs and POWs. An empty place setting symbolizes the missing and captive who aren't home for dinner, while a wine glass is placed upside down to say, "I'm not here to toast with you." Then step through the watertight door, commonly found on naval vessels, and wander through 3,000 square feet of artifacts and memorabilia with a heavy emphasis on World War II. Mr. Fleetwood will be happy to show you items from the USS *Highlands* and discuss other historic ships and events. Named for Highlands County, this attack transport saw duty at both Iwo Jima and Okinawa. Other memorabilia include a "hook" from a Douglas A-4D used to catch the cable when landing on an air carrier, three types of shipboard bunks, and actual spikes made by Paul Revere in his foundry used to construct the USS *New Hampshire* (formerly the USS *Alabama*). Take note of a series of photographs of the USS *Ward DD-139*, the first U.S. ship to fire a shot just before Pearl Harbor. While guarding the entrance to the harbor on December 7, 1941, the Ward crewmen spotted a mini-submarine. The gun crew fired and sunk the sub just hours before the Japanese planes began their bombing campaign. The flag room houses a fine collection of military uniforms and flags from the three services and every state, including the rare 49-state American flag. Open 12 PM–4 PM Wed.–Sat. Fee.

Don't let the size of the small **Sebring Ridge Museum** (863-402-1611), 121 N Ridgewood, fool you. There is a wealth of Sebring memorabilia displayed in the ground floor of this 1920s historic building, including a scale model of the town and numerous unique history books, including *The Way Things Were: Short Stories of Past Experiences* by Reverend Robert J. Walker, which tells about growing up black, and *Ranch Boy* by H. Steven Robertson, a coming-of-age story told in great detail about ranch life in and around Sebring. Call for hours; donation.

PUBLIC ART In **Lake Placid**, it's not just about the murals. As you walk around, you can't help but notice the **unique trash containers** around town. Local artists again pooled their talents and created these receptacles as companion pieces to the murals. When you pull the handle on the Clown container, a clown pops up. Look for others, such as Barn, Fishing Shack, Comic School Bus, 1927 Chrysler, and the beautifully detailed Caladium container. Artists in Lake Placid are always coming up with new creative projects. Notice the **clowns** around town? These brightly colored clowns sit on benches or lean against fences at the RMCA Daycare Center on E Interlake Boulevard and throughout Lake Placid. Full-sized placards, they represent some of the clown graduates from **Toby the Clown College** (see *Museums*), all local residents whose faces grace the art. Another art trail, **Birds around Lake Placid** is a series of works of art, this time detailed images of native birds painted on more than four dozen discs scattered around downtown. Can you find them all?

RAILROADIANA Railroad history runs deep along this corridor where the Atlantic Coast Line and Seaboard Coast Line once flourished. Avon Park, Sebring, and Lake Placid all retain their original **passenger railway stations**, with the stations at Avon Park and Lake Placid now housing the local history museums (see *Museums*).

WINERY ♪ Planted in 1999 on 20 acres, the vineyards at **Henscratch Farms** (863-699-2060; www.henscratchfarms.com), 980 Henscratch Rd., Lake Placid, are now extremely productive and joined by extensive hydroponics including Verti-Gro towers filled with strawberries, zucchini, and other vegetables and fruits. Add over 300 chickens pecking their way across the property, and this makes for a fun family destination that's not just a certified Florida Farm Winery with southern-style wines from muscadine and scuppernong grapes, but an interpretive agricultural tour and, in season, a U-pick as well. The tour starts in a silo where a video presentation narrated by the founder walks you through how their wine is hand-processed, aged, filled, and corked, all manually. Follow the flapping yellow flags on a self-guided tour of the farm as you're followed by a flock of chickens fussing for Cheerios. The gift shop offers tastings and sells wine and gourmet foods, and if you're there early enough, you can also pick up a fresh dozen of free-range eggs laid daily by their resident hens. There's also a gift basket house for you to pick out wines and have your own custom label applied before shipping

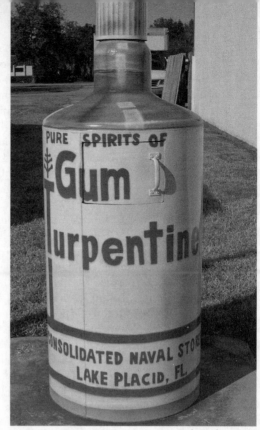

Sandra Friend

THE CREATIVE TRASH CANS OF LAKE PLACID

off to friends and family. Don't miss the annual **Blueberry Festival** (see *Special Events*) and Grape Stomp, where you can stomp your own wine! Open Dec.–May Tues.–Sat. 10 AM–5 PM, Sun. 12 PM–4 PM; Aug.–Nov. Tues.–Sat. 10 AM–4 PM, Sun. 12 PM–4 PM; closed June and July. Free.

✳ To Do

AIRBOAT RIDES Explore wild Lake Istokpoga on the *American Maid* on a private 1-hour tour departing from Mossy Cove Fish Camp & RV Resort (see *Fish Camps*) on Ray's **Air Boat Rides** (863-655-0119 or 1-800-833-2683), call in advance to arrange; $75 for two people, $25 for each additional adult. At Neibert's Fishing Resort (see *Fish Camps*), **Airboat Wildlife Adventures** (863-655-4737; www.airboatwildlifeadventures.com) handles six passengers at a time on a 1.5 hour tour following Arbuckle Creek out into Lake Istokpoga; call for rates and reservations.

BICYCLING The sidewalk around **Lake Jackson** in Sebring circles the lake for 11 miles, and there's plenty of room for bicyclists, hikers, and casual walkers. Another scenic ride is the new trail connecting US 27 paralleling SR 634 (Hammock Rd.) to Highlands Hammock State Park. Off-road cyclists will enjoy the loop at the **Preserve of Sun 'n' Lakes** (863-402-6812) off Sun 'n' Lakes Blvd. Great for beginner and experienced riders, the trails cover 1,600 acres of natural Florida wilderness. The multipurpose park is also a favorite of birders. The **Highlands County Pedalers Bicycling Club** (863-382-6464) does two 20-mile rides and two 40–100-mile rides each week. Membership is not required to ride along. Sebring is a favorite of bicycle clubs who hold century rides here, with rallies at the **Kenilworth Lodge** (see *Lodging*), including the **Annual Tour of Sebring** held every Labor Day Weekend since 1982. The **Ridge Trails Association** (863-382-3940; www.ridgetrails.org), 134 N Ridgewood Dr., Ste. 1, Sebring is actively working with land management agencies to establish an interconnect network of bikeways, walking trails, and paddling trails throughout the county.

BIRDING One of Florida's prime regions for birding, Highlands County has natural areas with birds that are on your life list. The **Archbold Biological Station** (see *Wild Places*) has been a center for research on the endemic **Florida scrub jay** since its founding. You'll find scrub jay families there as well as at **Lake June-in-Winter State Park** (see *Wild Places*) and **Avon Park Air Force Range & Wildlife Management Area** (see *Wild Places*), which is also home to the endangered **red-cockaded woodpecker**. I'm one of the fortunate few to document **crested caracara** mating in snags along the Kissimmee River at Bluff Hammock WMA; in adjacent Hickory Hammock WMA, I saw pileated woodpeckers and red-shouldered hawks. For the largest known population of **nesting osprey**, take a tour on **Lake Istokpoga**. These sites, as well as **Highlands Hammock State Park** (see *Parks*) are part of the Great Florida Birding Trail, which points out notable birding stops around the county.

DRUMMING Try some primal therapy by joining a drum circle at **Highlands Hammock State Park** (see *Parks*), coordinated by Primal Connection (863-402-8238; www.primalconnection.org) every third Sunday, October through June, from 3–5 PM. Free; bring your own drum or just a chair or dancing shoes to get in the spirit.

ECOTOURS Explore the vast prairies, pastures, and wetlands of the MacArthur Agro-ecology Research Center, part of **Archbold Biological Station** (see *Wild Places*) in the heart of Indian Prairie at Buck Island Ranch on a swamp buggy tour with **Indian Prairie Tours** (863-465-2571; www.maerc.org), where you'll see abundant wildlife. The three hour tours are offered year-round by reservation only, minimum 10 participants.

FISHING With 95 lakes in and around the county, there are numerous opportunities to fish. Check the fish camp listings (see *Fish Camps*) for best places to stay and launch your own boat or go out with a guide. **Captain Dave Miller** (941-915-9073 or 1-866-239-8101; www.thebasstamer.com) has more than 30 years experience guiding for bass fishing in the region's lakes.

GOLF Most of the region's hotels offer package deals with local courses, since Highlands County is a year-round destination for golfers. Designed in 1926 by Donald Ross, **Pinecrest Golf Club** (863-453-7555), 2250 S Little Lake Bonnet Rd., off Scenic 17, Avon Park, isn't just a golf course, it's a slice of local history. It was the site of the first television broadcast of a PGA tournament back in 1959.

The 18 holes are along fairways fringed with sweet-smelling orange groves, rambling beneath the tall pines above Little Lake Bonnet.

Guests golf free at the **Sebring Lakeside Golf Resort**, 603 Lake Sebring Dr. (see *Lodging*). The 9-hole, par 3 course is beautifully landscaped with ponds, streams, and waterfalls. **Sebring Municipal** (863-314-5919) and **Harder Hall** (863-382-0500), both 18-hole, par 72 courses, are within a half mile of the **Inn on the Lakes** (see *Lodging*).

The 18-hole, par 72, championship course at the semiprivate **Golf Hammock Country Club** (863-382-2151; www.golfsoftware.net/181), 2222 Golf Hammock Dr., circles the clubhouse, allowing for frequent rest and snack stops on hot Florida days. At **Crystal Creek Country Club** (863-465-5303), 135 Sun 'n' Lake Blvd., they welcome the general public on their 18-hole, par 64 course.

There are two challenging 18-hole courses at the **Springlake Golf Resort** (863-655-1276; www.springlakegolf.com), 100 Clubhouse Ln., bordering Lake Istokpoga. Recent upgrades to their "old Osprey ninth hole" (noted in the *Guinness Book of World Records* as the world's largest green) have converted it to the "World's Largest 18-Hole Putting Course," which includes sand and water hazards. It's a good course for beginners, but there is also enough to challenge seasoned players.

HIKING Head out into the wilderness along the **Florida Trail** following the Kissimmee River north from Hickory Hammock WMA through **Avon Park Air Force Range** (see *Wild Places*). Backpackers enjoy more than five days of backcountry along the Kissimmee River, with designated primitive campsites along the way. Day hikers shouldn't miss the network of hiking trails through ancient forests at **Highlands Hammock State Park** (see *Parks*). For an interpretive introduction to the Lake Wales Ridge scrub habitat, walk the short loop at **Archbold Biological Station** (see *Wild Places*) and then venture out on your own on longer trails through this desertlike landscape at **Lake June-in-Winter Preserve State Park** (see *Wild Places*).

PADDLING Popular paddling trips in the region include **Arbuckle Creek**, which starts north of **Avon Park Air Force Range** (see *Wild Places*) in Lake Wales Ridge State Forest; **Carter Creek**, which feeds into Arbuckle Creek; and **Josephine Creek** in Lake Placid. Rent a kayak ($19–59) from or launch on an expedition ($29–49) with **Sebring Kayak Tours** (863-202-0815; www.sebring kayaktours.com); they offer guided trips on Arbuckle Creek as well as playful "Paddle and Swim" outings on area lakes.

RACING For those who pay a bit more attention to their riding mowers than most, Avon Park is home to the **Florida Lawn Mower Racing Association** (www.floridalawnracing.net) with races are held at the Avon Park Mowerplex, Florida's only venue for this up-and-coming sport, which is sanctioned by the USLMRA (www.letsmow.com) to turn "a weekend chore into a competitive sport." Riding mower races are scheduled throughout the year, with the big event, the annual **NASGRASS Lawn Mower Race** (www.nasgrass.com), in March (see *Special Events*).

Since 1952, the **Sebring International Raceway** (1-800-626-7223; www.sebring raceway.com), 113 Midway Dr., Sebring, has provided fast action every March with their **12 Hours of Sebring** endurance race (see *Special Events*). The converted Hendricks Field, a World War II military training base, was also the site of the first Formula One race in North America in 1959. Since then, professional race car drivers, including Hollywood stars, have raced Cobras, Chapparels, Ferraris, Porches, and Ford GT40s on the 3.7-mile circuit. In 1970 Steve McQueen finished a close second to Mario Andretti. A multimillion-dollar renovation completed in 1999 added a new pit tower and media center. The **Four Points by Sheraton** (see *Lodging*) is just off the hairpin turn.

SCENIC DRIVES SR 17 is called **Scenic Highway** for a good reason. As it follows the rolling topography of the Lake Wales Ridge, it curves around lakes and takes you to the heart of fragrant orange groves. Heading west on **SR 66** out of Lake Placid, you'll drive through the heart of cattle country with prairie views that go on forever. July and August are the time to drive **CR 621**, when the colorful caladium fields are in bloom. A short scenic drive that shouldn't be missed is the loop in the end of **Hammock Road inside Highlands Hammock State Park** (see *Parks*). It's a one-way loop through one of the lushest forests in Florida, much like driving through a jungle.

SCUBA One of the clearest lakes in Florida, **Lake Denton** is a popular destination for scuba diver training sessions and divers looking for an interesting inland experience. Paid access is via a county park (if open) or through the friendly **Lake Denton Camp** (863-453-3627; www.lakedentoncamp.org), 790 Lake Denton Rd., Avon Park.

SPAS Back in Touch (863-402-0711; www.backintouchdayspa.com), a new day spa on the premises of the Inn on the Lakes (see *Lodgings*), offers tired golfers (and golf widows) a new retreat for facials, massages, and body scrubs, starting at $50 for treatments.

Founded by the former manager of the Château Élan Spa, the **Spa at Hammock Falls** (863-382-9646; www.thespaathammockfalls.com), #8 Hammock Falls Cir., provides a luxurious array of treatments, including body wraps, salt glows, and massage, within a classy, relaxed setting. Getaway packages start at $120 and treatments at $15 for hands/feet and $40 for massage.

SWIMMING Lake Verona is the place to swim in Avon Park, with sandy **Lake Verona Beach** along the shoreline, a short walk from downtown.

TRAIL RIDING ⚘ Guided **trail rides and riding lessons** are offered by **Orchid Hill Stables** (863-655-1582; www.orchidhillstables.com), 419 Ranchero Dr., Sebring; half-hour pony rides ($25), hourly rates $30–40 depending on group size. At **Lakeside Stables** (863-655-2252; www.horserentals.com/lakesidestables .html), 5000 US 98, take a trail ride ($20–50) along beautiful Arbuckle Creek; they offer on-site camping, too.

WALKING TOURS

Avon Park
The **Mile Long Mall** on Main Street extends from Lake Verona to US 27. The

Mall is lined with many antiques shops shaded under a canopy of centuries-old trees. Once a single-lane road designed for the horse and buggy, the street was divided in 1920 into two parallel roads, with a park created in the middle.

Lake Placid

Self-guided walking-tour booklets of the area's **colorful murals** (see *Murals*) and **artistic trash cans** (see *Public Art*) are available throughout town. The booklet also provides clues to hidden objects included in the murals.

Sebring

Stroll around **Sebring Circle** and see historic buildings from the early 1900s. Center, Ridgewood, and Commerce Streets branch out from **Circle Park** and offer many shops to explore (see *Selective Shopping*).

✳ Green Space

NATURE CENTERS Learn more about the Lake Wales Ridge at **Archbold Biological Station** (863-465-2571; www.archbold-station.org), Old FL 8, Lake Placid, a working research center with a public outreach facility on-site. Stop in at the Main Building (open 8 AM–5 PM Mon.–Fri.) to view a video and pick up interpretive information on the 0.5-mile nature trail that loops around the facility. Keep alert for Florida scrub jays, as they are often seen here. Free.

PARKS

Avon Park

Walk outside along Florida's only **Mile Long Mall** in Avon Park. Like the National Mall, this is a green strip through the city shaded by centuries-old trees, a fine place from which to enjoy the 1920s architecture found throughout downtown and a landmark kapok tree. Normally grown in tropical climates, the 60-foot tree produces an impressive canopy in January and February. The pods on the lower part of the tree contain silklike material that was used in World War II to stuff life preservers. **Veterans Square** honors veterans of World War I, World War II, Korea, and Vietnam, and the names of 427 Avon Park–area men are inscribed on the monument. A star next to each name indicates those killed while in service to our country. The "checker shelter" houses a Veterans Honor Roll with nine Avon Park military veterans from World War I, World War II, and Vietnam.

Lorida

At **Istokpoga Park** (863-402-6812), US 98 west of Lorida, stroll the Bee Island boardwalk and cast for bass. This small park has a boat launch into Lake Istokpoga and picnic tables with grills. Free.

Sebring

Medal of Honor Park, south of Sebring off US 27 on George Blvd., showcases 18 heritage oaks and bronze plaques honoring the 18 recipients of the Congressional Medal of Honor.

✍ Explore under a canopy of green at **Highlands Hammock State Park** (863-386-6094; www.floridastateparks.org/highlandshammock), 5931 Hammock Rd., one of Florida's oldest state parks. Five short interpretive trails lead you through ancient hardwood hammocks with centuries-old oak trees, along boardwalks following cypress-lined creeks and around marshy ponds, and through pine flatwoods.

Once home to the ivory-billed woodpecker, now more than half a dozen other woodpecker species can be seen throughout the park; a lengthy checklist for birders is available on the park Web site. Preserved by Margaret Roebling, the wife of Brooklyn Bridge builder John Roebling, this hammock of ancient oaks opened to the public in 1931. In 1935, it became one of four parks that started the Florida State Parks system. Much of the infrastructure dates back to efforts of the Civilian Conservation Corps. Florida's only **CCC Museum** (see *Museums*) is here on the grounds and relates the story of the Civilian Conservation Corps, which helped build the backbone of what is now the Florida State Park system. Tent and RV campers are welcome at the large campground. The park is a special destination for those with a sweet tooth for citrus, as its on-site café (see *Eating Out)*, serves sour orange pie and other goodies made from wild fruits gathered in the forest, as well as a popular Friday evening fish fry.

WILD PLACES

Avon Park

Founded in 1941, **Avon Park Air Force Range** (863-452-4254; www.avonpark fr.com), 29 South Blvd., encompasses more than 106,000 acres along the Kissimmee River floodplain and the Lake Wales Ridge. Of this 82,000 acres are open for public recreation. Their Wildlife Management Area is one of the largest in the state, open frequently for hunting and fishing, with 3 stocked ponds on-site as well as creek and river access. For backpackers, there is a 16-mile loop along Lake Arbuckle, and 12 linear miles of the **Florida Trail** (see *Hiking*) passing through the range. Day hikers will appreciate access to the 6-mile Sandy Point Wildlife Refuge Trail, as it passes through prime Florida scrub jay habitat. The range is an important destination for birders thanks to species like bald eagles, crested caracara, red-cockaded woodpeckers, and grasshopper sparrows. Primitive camping is permitted at several campgrounds within the range, such as Morgan Hole and Fort Kissimmee. Recreation passes cost $7 individual/$10 family for a day

THE BIG OAK OF HIGHLAND HAMMOCK

Sandra Friend

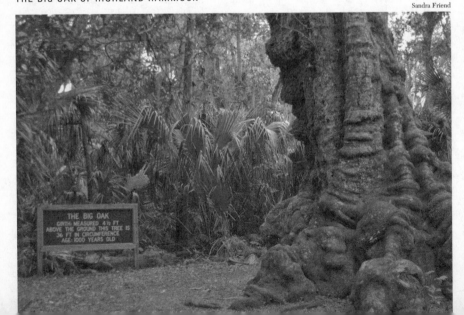

pass. Hunting is by permit only, first-come, first-served: $275 individual/$300 family. Recreation is only permitted when there are not military activities underway. Call 863-452-4119 x5 for a recorded message or check their Web site for an update before heading out to the range.

Just south of Avon Park is **Lake Tulane**, estimated to be the oldest living lake in North America—40,000 years old, with the deepest layer of sediment around 70,000 years old. Created by a sinkhole, the 70-foot-deep, crystal-clear lake covers 89 acres and has a clear, sandy bottom. Beneath that are layers of sediment reaching 60 more feet. Scientists are currently studying the lake, ideal for research, for information on what steers Earth's weather. The boat ramp for Lake Tulane is located on the west side of the lake. To get to the lake, take Anoka Avenue south from Main Street to Edgewood Street, and then turn left on Lakeview Boulevard and follow the road to the lake.

Lorida

Encompassing more than 4,000 acres along the Kissimmee River, **Hickory Hammock Wildlife Management Area** (1-800-250-4200; www.myfwc.com/recreation/cooperative/hickory_hammock.asp), along US 98, 9 miles southeast of Lorida, is open to fishing, hunting, and hiking. An extremely scenic 9.2-mile segment of the Florida Trail passes through Hickory Hammock, with trailheads on US 98 and at the end of Bluff Hammock Road. At the southern end, enjoy dark hydric hammocks and a pleasant primitive campsite 3.5 miles north of the trailhead. At the northern end, about a mile south of the Bluff Hammock trailhead, a lengthy boardwalk along the Kissimmee River is well worth a visit for birding and photography.

Lake Placid

Preserving a large swath of the imperiled Lake Wales Ridge, **Lake June-in-Winter Preserve State Park** (863-386-6094; http://www.floridastateparks.org/lake juneinwinter), end of Daffodil St., lets you explore the unusual scrub habitat of the ridge on several miles of hiking trails and a short nature trail. Rare plants such as scrub plum, scrub hickory, spike moss, and scrub beargrass can be seen along the trails. Open for day use only; fee.

Sebring

The 28,000-acre **Lake Istokpoga** has Florida's largest concentration of osprey nests and is world-renowned for its bass fishing. *Istokpoga* is a Native American word that means "waters of death." In the early 1900s Seminoles tried to cross the lake and were swallowed up by whirlpools, but today it is one of the best fishing lakes, with birds of many species and a large concentration of alligators. With a shallow depth of only of 4 to 6 feet, Florida's fifth largest lake is located to the east of US 27 between Sebring and Lake Placid. Boat ramps are located just off US 98 at RV Park on Arbuckle Creek (small fee) and Istokpoga Park near Lorida.

Lake Wales Ridge National Wildlife Refuge (www.fws.gov/merrittisland/subrefuges/LWR.html), with scattered parcels through the region, is notable in that it is the only NWR to be established primarily for the protection of rare plant species, 23 of which are on the endangered species list, including Florida ziziphus and scrub lupine. Because of the sensitive nature of these areas, they have not been opened to public access.

✷ Lodging

BED & BREAKFAST

🐾 ⁽ᴵ⁾ Built in 1925, the charming **Lake Verona Lodge** (863-452-9940; http://members.tripod.com/verona lodge), 310 E Main St., offers four spacious rooms in a historic home that took owners Steve and Gloria Vanderzee two years to renovate and modernize. They've done an outstanding job. The Kennedy includes an en suite bath with a large shower. Polished hardwood floors complement the original beadboard walls and ceiling, and the room includes one of my favorite amenities, a writing desk in the corner. Sunlight streams into the Washington through 13 windows and dapples across the Wedgewood blue walls. The bowed ceiling is made of Dade County pine. The Roosevelt and Lincoln rooms have two beds and share a bath with a claw-foot tub. Fresh fruit, cereals, homemade breads, and Welsh rarebit are often part of the extended continental breakfast served in the large sun-drenched dining room. Rates start at $89.

CAMPGROUNDS

Avon Park 33825

🐾 ⁽ᴵ⁾ **Adelaide Shores** (863-453-2226; www.adelaideshores.com), 2881 US 27

LAKE VERONA LODGE

Sandra Friend

Sandra Friend

BONNET LAKE RV RESORT

N, is perched along the shores of Lake Adelaide and has two golf pros on staff who offer free lessons, and a golf course across the street. $32 for RV sites, long-term stays discounted.

🐾 ⁽ᴵ⁾ At **Bonnet Lake RV Resort** (863-385-3700; www.bonnetlakecamp ground.com), 2825 SR 17 S, set up your tent or pull your rig beneath the tall pines and savor the orange blossom scented air. A large heated pool, horseshoes, bocce, and shuffleboard will keep you active; in the evenings, enjoy camaraderie in the recreation hall. Sites $25–40.

🐾 Make friends at **Lake Letta RV Park** (863-453-7700; www.lakeletta rv.com), 2455 S Lake Letta Dr., a pretty 55 and over campground set in the pine woods catering to RVers and long-term stays; campsites $20 daily, $135 weekly.

Lake Placid 33852

🐾 ⁽ᴵ⁾ Relax with your inner circle at **Camp Florida Resort** (863-699-1991 www.campfla.com), 100 Shoreline Dr.,

SUNSET OVER LAKE GRASSY

off US 27 S, where the campsites ($37.50) are broken up into rounded clusters with green space in-between, and the campground spills down the hill toward pretty Lake Grassy. Park models run $100–125. Small pets only.

Set along the shores of Lake Istokpoga, **Cypress Isle RV Park & Marina** (863-465-5241), 2 Cypress Isle Ln., offers tent sites ($15–25), and pop-ups and RV sites ($30). Each site has its own boat dock. Discounts are taken if you don't have a boat and for month-long and full-season stays. Three fully equipped one-bedroom cabins are also available ($70). No pets.

🌴 "🛈" **Sunshine RV Resort** (863-465-4815 or 1-800-760-7270; www.sunshine rvresorts.com), 303 SR 70 E, offers a variety of RV sites ($27–30) and park models ($58–68) in a quiet well-manicured setting along Ridge Lake. Enjoy their large pool and recreation area.

FISH CAMPS

Lorida 33857
Since 1972, **Mossy Cove Fish Camp & RV Resort** (863-655-0119 or 1-800-

833-2683; www.mossy-cove.us), 3 Mossy Cove Dr., off US 98, has catered to anglers looking for a quiet base camp for fishing for bass, crappie, and catfish on Lake Istokpoga. Bring your RV (30 amp service) or bunk down in one of their fully equipped cabins that sleep up to 8 people.

"🛈" Rent furnished waterfront cabins complete with cable TV, heat and air-conditioning, full bath with linens, and well-equipped kitchen at **Trails End Fishing Resort** (863-655-0134; www .trailsendfishingresort.com), 4232 Trails End. The "wife-friendly" resort on Lake Istokpoga also offers sites for RVs and doublewides. Laundry room, public showers, bait and tackle store, fish cleaning room, and dockside gas are also on-site.

Sebring 33876
There are no playgrounds or swimming pools at the rugged **Henderson's Istokpoga Fishing Resort** (863-465-2101), 35 Henderson Rd. (off US 27 and CR 621), but serious anglers can pull in their RVs or bunk in one of the cabins.

The casual **Neibert's Fishing Resort** (863-655-1416), 4971 US 98 on Lake Istokpoga, has sites for tents and RVs (both $20 per night), with discounts for long-term residents. Also on-site are laundry facilities and a cocktail bar.

HOTELS, MOTELS, AND RESORTS

Avon Park 33825

⁰ĭ⁹ Al Capone, Clark Gable, Babe Ruth, George Burns, and Gracie Allen are among those who walked through the doors of the **Hotel Jacaranda** (863-453-2211; www.hoteljac.com), 19 E Main St., to spend the night. Opened in 1926, this grand Classical Revival–style hotel has played many roles over the years, serving as a bunkhouse for World War II servicemen and most recently, student dormitories for its new owner, the South Florida Community College, which occupy half of the building. The carefully restored interior has a 1920s "titans of industry" feel, with rough plastered walls, window air conditioners, and heavy rolling doors that can separate the building into three sec-

HOTEL JACARANDA IN AVON PARK
Sandra Friend

tions for fire or hurricane protection. The antique elevator is one of only two I know of remaining in Florida that must be staff-operated. Many of the cozy standard rooms ($70) have original bathtubs and sinks as well as antique dressers. Suites ($75–83) and 2 or 3 bedroom Grand Suites ($135–205) are much more spacious. Rooms include a small fridge, microwave, and coffeemaker. Breakfast is included in your room rate from October 1 through June 1. Victor Borge once played piano here in the elegant formal dining room, the **Palm Room** (see *Dining Out*), and from November through May, pianist Jeff Klein entertains with tunes from yesteryear as students in culinary training attend to your needs.

🦞 🐾 ⊚ ⁰ĭ⁹ ↬ An old-fashioned motor court that has that retro zing, **Reed's Motel** (863-453-3194; www.reeds motel.com), 102 US 27 S, catches your eye with the neon diver that's been making a splash since 1957. With impeccable landscaping and 17 clean, spacious tropical-themed rooms, a heated pool with a chickee tiki hut, and a motel cat called Redland, this is one inviting place. Hidden behind the motel is another treasure—the Oasis Banquet Hall, with a dance hall, meeting space, kitchen, and a shaded outdoor space under a big thatched chickee roof. Taken by owner Tammy Lott, a nature photographer, images of wildlife in Highlands County grace the walls. There are also several large suites tucked away in corners of the complex, and I do mean large; these are full apartments with kitchen, living room, and dining room. Rates $69–200; golf packages available.

Lake Placid 33852

⁰ĭ⁹ A quiet night on the water was exactly what I needed when I checked into the **Valencia Suites** (863-465-

9200; www.valenciasuites.net), 1865 US 27 S. It's an intimate 13-room complex on the shores of Lake Grassy with spacious tiled rooms. I headed straight for the oversized tub in the elegantly tiled bathroom and relaxed watching movies on the big screen television. One entire wall of the room is a sleek kitchen with stainless steel refrigerator and dishwasher, microwave, toaster, and stovetop, plus all the dishes and supplies you'd need for an extended stay. Eat inside at the tall bar-style table, or outside on a picnic bench on your patio overlooking the lake. Rented weekly during the winter season, $308 and up, with daily rates available.

Sebring 33870

& ¶ In the lobby sits a full size Panoz GTS, a 385-horsepower high-end race car. This should give you an indication of the high-energy atmosphere at the **Four Points by Sheraton Sebring** (863-655-6252; www.chateauelan sebring.com), 150 Midway Dr., one of the few places in America you can stay right along a raceway. As the hotel is situated just off the legendary hairpin "Turn 7," you'll want to ask for a trackside room to experience all the sights and sounds of Le Mans racing without having to head over to the track. Room rates start around $110 but escalate dramatically during racing events.

& ❀ ☺ ¶ Straddling Lake Jackson and Little Lake Jackson, the **Inn on the Lakes** (863-471-9400 or 1-800-531-5253; www.innonthelakessebring .com), 3100 Golfview Rd., is within walking distance to two golf courses (see *Golf*). Guest rooms ($94–139) offer double- or king-sized accommodations, most with panoramic views. The elegant suites ($144–219) have room to really stretch out, with a huge walk-in closet that would make even the fussiest diva excited. Our room was just the tonic we needed for a day of

rest—spacious, spotless, and classy, with a panoramic view of the pool and lake. French doors open to a private balcony overlooking both lakes. When you are hungry, **Chicanes** (see *Dining Out*) serves up a fine selection of culinary delights.

☺ ¶ Listed on the National Register of Historic Places, **Kenilworth Lodge** (863-385-0111 or 1-800-423-5939; www.kenlodge.com), 836 SE Lakeview Dr., is a grand inn on a hill overlooking Lake Jackson. George Sebring, founder of this town, opened the lodge as a destination in 1916, and it's still a fascinating place to stay. The massive lobby has a grand staircase and 1950s television; one corner is taken up with a library from which you are free to borrow. The renovated-to-period guest rooms in the main lodge ($70 and up) are a little small by today's standards, but they all have a premium TV and a mini fridge; the bathrooms are surprisingly large. There are also more spacious suites (including a posh Presidential Suite) and apartments available, ranging from $95 to 160, with some of them overlooking the 80-foot heated pool. A deluxe continental breakfast is included in your stay.

¶ A stop at the **Safari Inn** (863-382-1148), 1406 US 27 N, revealed a basic but clean budget motel set in rounded buildings, like giant huts. Larger suites include a fridge and microwave, smaller rooms a shower instead of bath. Rates start at $59 in the low season.

✿ ☺ ¶ For a touch of Old Florida, take a personal retreat to **Sebring Lakeside Golf Resort** (863-385-7113 or 1-888-2SEBRING; www.2sebring .com), 500 Lake Sebring Dr., a lovely Spanish Mission–style inn built during the 1920s boom and opened in 1926 as the Lake Sebring Casino, a gathering place for swimming and dancing for the surrounding residential community.

Set on the shores of Lake Sebring, it's a place you can stroll out to the beach and soak in the sun, or out on the long, colorful dock, a piece of history in itself, and revel in the peace and quiet with only birdsong to interrupt your relaxation. Owners Mark and Maria Baker spent a lot of loving care on renovations; it took seven years alone to restore the original ballroom, which is now home to their popular **Sebring Lakeside Casino Tea Room** (see *Dining Out*). The Grand Suite ($235–255) overlooks the lake on three sides and has a fireplace open to both the bedroom and living room areas. The king-sized bed is dressed with sumptuous bedding, and the romantic bathroom has tiled arches to the private shower, scented candles in niches, and a large Jacuzzi overlooking a private garden. A full-sized kitchen ensures you will never need to leave the room. The complex includes 18 rooms ($101–175), some of which are duplexes, and efficiencies from the 1960s that gave me a trip in the way-back machine with their nifty retro furnishings and honeycombed bath tile floors. Family reunions are popular

here, what with the lakeside swimming pool, a complimentary round of golf (see *Golf*), complimentary bicycles, and paddleboats for exploring the lake. Three of the rooms have Jacuzzis, and most of them have lakefront views with screened porches. Reduced rates offered for extended stays.

✳ Where to Eat

DINING OUT

Avon Park

🍴 The all-you-can-eat buffet at the **Palm Room of Hotel Jacaranda** (see *Lodgings*), 19 E Main St., has all the elegance of yesteryear, including a resident pianist for most of the season. Southern fried chicken is always on the menu along with another Southern entrée, plus homemade mashed potatoes, veggies, salad and soup, and dessert, which could be their famed strawberry shortcake. Lunch buffets are served Aug.–May Mon.–Fri. 11 AM–2 PM, $9. Dinner buffets are Dec.–May 4:30 PM–7:30 PM, $9 on Mon.–Thurs., $11 for the Friday seafood buffet and the Sunday grand buffet.

Sebring

The cozy **Chicanes Restaurant & Bar** (863-314-0348) is located inside the Inn on the Lakes (see *Lodging*). For an appetizer, try the Tire Treads, deep-fried onions with Cajun dipping romelade. For smaller appetites there is the cedar planked salmon with a hint of brown sugar and Dijon mustard, or pork schnitzel, pan fried German style. Substantial entrées include chicken fusilli, bourbon chicken, and baby back ribs; dinner, $14–30. Save room for a dessert like the Pile Up, a chocolate concoction topped with vanilla ice cream, caramel, and hot fudge. The name "Chicanes" comes from the quick left-right zigzag bends found on racetracks, which require a quick suc-

THE DOCK AT SEBRING LAKESIDE RESORT
Sandra Friend

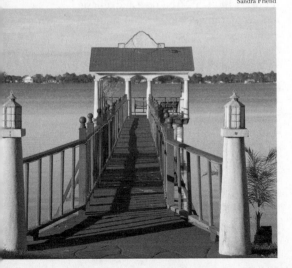

cession of braking, downshifting, and acceleration.

With a lakeside view, the **Sebring Lakeside Casino Tea Room** at **Sebring Lakeside Golf Resort** (see *Lodging*) provides an elegant escape for a formal lunch. The $14 fixed-price lunch includes a choice of ambrosia, pasta salad, or soup; a beverage; a selection from the dessert tray; and an entrée served with fresh fruit and veggies, such as chicken salad tossed with almonds, grapes, and apples; asparagus supreme, rolled in Virginia ham and aged Swiss cheese; medallions of pork tenderloin stuffed with ham and rosemary dressing; or finger sandwiches, among the other chef's specialties. Reservations suggested. 🍴 Occasionally, specially themed Children's Afternoon Tea Series are offered, providing a two-hour event with etiquette lesson, game or story, craft to take home, and a delicious lunch; reservations required.

Plan a night out at **Yianni's Prime Choice** (863-385-9222), 3750 US 27 N # 2A, where steak and seafood are the stars of the menu. Nine cuts of beef, including New York strip, filet mignon, and a 32-ounce porterhouse will tempt your inner carnivore, especially when you smell it sizzling on the open grill over their custom-built pit, fired with citrus, hickory, and oak logs. Can't handle that much meat? Try the shrimp scampi, Alaskan king crab, or rock lobster, or the Alexander's Great Salad loaded with vegetables, toasted nuts, and cheese and topped with your choice of grilled steak, salmon, or chicken. Save room for the Greek dessert tray, with temptations like baklava, carrot cake, rice pudding, and chocolate cake brought straight to your table. Rich, dark woods, white linen tablecloths, and the strumming of Spanish guitar set a mood for a relaxed dining experience.

Avon Park

A mural commemorating railroading sets the tone for **The Depot Restaurant** (863-453-5600), 21 W Main St., a popular lunch stop downtown. Open Mon.–Fri. 6 AM–2 PM, Sat. 6 AM–3 PM.

Classic car enthusiasts will love the theme at **Dutcher's Diner** (863-45-DUTCH; www.dutchersdiner.com), 1012 W Main St., which was hopping on a Saturday morning. Cars decorate the wallpaper and the walls, with posters and models of '50s–'70s classics. And then you open the menu. Try a '65 Chevy Malibu Deuce Coupe (translation: 2 eggs and an 8 oz. rib eye) for a hearty breakfast, or go for the more toned-down '70 Plymouth Roadrunner, with 2 eggs, 2 French toast, 2 bacon, and 2 sausage. Open 6 AM–3 PM daily, breakfast ($3–12) served all day.

Grab a great meal at the **Olympic Restaurant** (863-452-2700), 504 US 27 N, where the aroma of a fresh Greek salad begged me to stay when I walked in the door. You can get a gyro here, but the entrées ($8–13) are more mainstream—think country fried chicken, liver and onions, jumbo shrimp, and pork tenderloin. Open for lunch and dinner.

🐾 As you drive out toward the Avon Park Air Force Range, watch for **Smokin' Bear Bar-B-Que**, a roadside barbecue stand that shows up at the junction of CR 17A and SR 64, in an orange grove. The chicken and ribs smell *really* good, and a full meal costs less than $10. Opens at 11 AM Thurs.–Sun.

Lake Placid

Andy's Hot Dog World (863-699-5577), 340 E Interlake Blvd., has dogs your way with a variety of toppings, from NYC Coney Sauce to Chicago-style or with sauerkraut, $3–6. Stop here for ice cream cones, too! Open Tues.–Sat. 11 AM–3 PM.

You'll find hometown home-style cooking at **The Heron's Garden** (863-699-6550; www.heronsgarden.com), 501 US 27 N, a busy local restaurant where entrées run the gamut from frog's legs to ham steak, veal cutlet, and ravioli. A Greek influence and many vegetarian options on the menu make this a big favorite for the locals; I've enjoyed several meals here in my travels. It's no problem to find an entrée (served with salad or soup, potato, rice or vegetable) for under $10.

❝❦❞ Overlooking Lake Henry, **Jaxson's** (863-465-4674; www.hookiemelt.com), 443 Lake June Rd., is a place to meet up with friends for a great afternoon or evening meal. Lunch favorites ($4–11) include jumbo crab cake, Reubens, tuna melt, a prime rib wrap, and their extensive array of "Hamburger Heaven" half-pound burgers like the J-Bomb (chili and jack/cheddar), the Cowboy (onion rings and barbecue sauce), or the Jaxsonian (double beef, no toppings), all served up with salty spicy fries. The interior has a sports-bar feel; the covered back patio gives you a quiet spot to look out over the lake and savor your meal.

A mural drew me into **The Pastry Shoppe** (863-465-3814), 341 E Interlake Blvd., and the place was packed! True to their name, they make their own biscuits, muffins, and sticky buns and offer plenty of eggs and options for that morning meal, $5–7.

In a railroad themed restaurant near the historic depot, **Schooni's Italian American** (863-465-5060), 209 N Main Ave., is where folks go for Italian favorites downtown. Besides pizzas and calzones, they serve a variety of pasta dinners, hot subs, and burgers—including a pizza burger! Dinners and pizzas, $7–12.

Sebring

Dive into the **Blue Lagoon Saloon** (863-471-6001), 4120 US 27 N, a sports bar where the ceiling is a very amusing read and the tabletops are airbrushed with colorful sea scenes. Grab a bear and one of their 22 different appetizers ($3–9), or try the Zingers—chicken strips in wing sauce with blue cheese, cheddar, and jalapeño bites. More substantial platters, like yellowfin tuna, shrimp skewers, fried oysters, and fish and chips, run $6–14. Open late.

I love it when my syrup is prewarmed so my pancakes don't get cold, and that's what they do at **Dot's Restaurant** (863-382-2333), 950 Sebring Sq. along US 27, where their Grand Breakfast includes 2 pancakes, 2 eggs, 2 sausage, 2 bacon strips, and your choice of hashbrowns, homefries, or grits. Now that's a hearty hiker breakfast ($3–6)! It's a busy place at lunch, too, with specials ($6) like stuffed cabbage or ham and beans served with sides of corn, green beans, coleslaw, and mashed potatoes. Your short order is up in minutes. Open Mon.–Sat. 6:30 AM–2 PM, Sun. 7 AM–2 PM; cash only.

In a building dating back to the 1930s, the **Hammock Inn** (863-385-7025), Three Picnic Area Rd., located at Highlands Hammock State Park across from the **CCC Museum** (see *Parks*), serves up chili dogs, chicken salad, burgers, and grilled cheese sandwiches for lunch every day; grab a full meal for less than $10. But what draws the folks in for a special visit are their desserts. Don't leave without trying their wild orange pie (made from oranges picked right here in the park), banana split cake, or one of their many cobblers. Friday is fish fry night, and they make a popular Thanksgiving dinner. Food is also served during folk music events at the park.

🍴 Along Scenic 17, the **Sandwich Castle** (863-385-3809), 3416 SR 17 N, sits right in the middle of the orange groves. It's a good quick lunch stop, serving up favorites like BLT, ham and cheese, meatball parmesan subs, pizza, and buffalo chicken wings in an open kitchen where you can watch your meal ($5 on average) being prepped. There are also daily entrée specials on the board like roasted Cuban pork with black beans and rice, or meatloaf with mashed potatoes and green beans, $6 and up. Open Tues.–Sun. 11 AM–6 PM.

At **Sandy's Circle Café** (863-382-1942   ), 213 Circle Park Dr., breakfast ($3 and up) gets served up nice and fast, and it's good Southern home-style cooking, 7 days a week.

COFFEE SHOPS ⁰☕⁰ At **Rezultz Fitness** (863-699-1960; www.rezultz fitness247.com), 224 Interlake Dr., a corner of this 24/7 workout center in the historic Lake Placid Drugstore is a coffee and smoothie bar, great for a quick refresher when you're walking through town. You'll also find a coffee shop inside the **Golden Pineapple** (see *Selective Shopping*) on the downtown circle in Sebring.

✳ Selective Shopping

Avon Park

It's not just a dress shop. **Annabelle's of Avon** (863-452-2005; www.consign annabelles.com), 13 South Lake Ave., has a little bit of everything, from Limoges figurines to festival glass, classy hatboxes, purses, and shoes. Another whole storefront is devoted to furniture and home decor, with both antique and new items—tapestries, shadowboxes, pillows, and books.

Lake Placid

The core shopping districts of Lake Placid are along Interlake Boulevard and Main Street, but be sure to peep down the side streets as well. Walking the mural tour route, you'll find many fine shops, including these:

Columbia shirts and shorts, Tilley hats, sunglasses—I knew I'd found the right place. **Authentic Supply Company** (863-465-0113; www.shirtsnshorts.net), 295 E Interlake Blvd., carries outerwear for outdoors enthusiasts, including casual Hawaiibera shirts for the guys (that's "Hawaiian guayabera" to you); they have a men's big and tall room, too.

They have antiques, shabby chic, and other neat stuff at **Old Friends** (863-465-4196), 213 N Main St., including glycerin soaps and soy candles.

Find accent furniture and garden gifts at **The Blueberry Patch** (863-465-5111), 214 N Main St., where their kids' room is full of fun toys that I couldn't resist, like an Imagination Mat (laminated artwork with a space to draw on the back), message ribbons, and Happy Camper buttons.

At the **Garden of Alvyn** (863-531-0100), 206 E Interlake Blvd., "every day's totally different!" said the owner when I inquired as to their usual stock in trade. It's an antiques shop that spans eras and tastes. The day I stopped in, you could walk away with a giant oriental fan, a fire hydrant, or an ashtray fit into a tire. Shelves of pewter ware, Fiestaware, and blue glass looked to be a more permanent display, but I was eyeing that giant Ken-L-Ration advertising sign, big enough to shade a doghouse.

For holiday gifts and ornaments any time of year, visit **Holiday Treasures & Trinkets** (863-465-3884), 217 N Main St. They hand-make more than 90 percent of their wreaths and have goodies like mugs and cookie jars, an angel room, and snazzy home decor.

Looking for fine antique glass? **Jackie's Nik Naks** (863-699-0215), 244 E

Interlake Blvd., might have what you're searching for. In this open, airy, and bright store, bureaus and china closets hold an array of glassware, china, and figurines.

At **Lake Placid Embroidery** (863-465-7199), 211 N Main St., it isn't about the custom embroidered goods they do, it's the glam—glitzy handbags and matching costume jewelry. Although they do sell T-shirts and caps with slogans like "He Fishes, I Shop."

Find beachy keen home decor at **Tropical Island Wear** (863-465-5556), 213 N Main St., including wraps and covers with tropical scenes, and Florida orange crate art cards.

Search for a distinctive gift at **Goodness Gracious** (863-699-1711), 459 US 27 N, in the Tower Plaza, and say hi to owner Lorelei Dehne.

Sebring
With more than 50 dealer booths, **Alligator Antiques and Collectibles** (863 471-6255; www.alligatorantiques.net), 2651 US 27 S, is one snappy place. Find Roseville pottery and paintings from the Highwaymen, colorful carnival glass and books and records to browse. Open Mon.–Sat. 10 AM–6 PM, Sun. 10 AM–4 PM.

It's a Caribbean novelty shop, a travel agent, and a coffee nook rolled into one! The **Golden Pineapple** (863-414-0215) 209 Circle Park S, has dolls and salsa, rum cake, soaps and lotions, colorful Caribbean clothing, and some tempting java on the menu, including a Milky Way latte and Jamaican Blue coffee.

There are hundreds of T-shirts to choose from at **The Great Atlantic & Pacific T-Shirt Company** (863-385-0456), 239 N Ridgewood Dr., a fixture downtown for decades. They can even custom-letter a shirt with your pithy slogan while you wait. Take that, Cafepress!

✎ Find great gifts for the kids at **The Happy Owl** (863-385-4544), 227 N. Ridgewood Dr.; it's filled with educational supplies and party goods, diorama kits and games, railroad sets, and Melissa and Doug puzzles and toys.

Linda's Books (863-382-2649), 203 N Ridgewood Dr., is a treasure trove for bibliophiles like me, with aisles and aisles of shelves packed with hard- and soft-cover books, primarily used fiction.

In the 1923 George Sebring Building, **Wild Artist Jewelry** (863-385-7433), 125 N Ridgewood Dr., brings the fine art of beading to your creative hands. Make your own exquisite design with their instruction, or consider one of their spirit catchers or Asian curios as a great gift.

PRODUCE STANDS AND U-PICK

Depending on the season, you can pick your own strawberries (Dec.–Mar.), blueberries and blackberries (Apr.–June), or grapes (Aug.–Sept.) at **Henscratch Farms** (see *Winery*), where they also sell a great bottle of wine. Best of all, vegetables and fruits are grown vertically in hydroponic containers—no stooping required!

✎ It's quintessential Florida, a wooden building tucked away in the heart of an orange grove, selling fresh fruit right from the packing house floor. That's **Maxwell Groves** (863-453-3938; www.maxwellgrove.com), 607 E Circle St., which started in the 1920s as a 10-acre grove with a small log cabin. The current packing house and country store complex dates back to the 1960s. You can walk right in and see how oranges are processed after picked in the groves. Starting at the dump tank, they go through a sanitizer and a grader that separates them by size to pack commercially. I'll let you take the tour to learn the rest. There's nothing better than a sample of ice cold fresh-squeezed orange juice on a sunny morning! Take a taste of the good stuff, then shop around for some goodies, like the retro "Citra fruit spoons," a variety of honeys, candies, and dressings, and even citrus-scented lotions and soaps. Certified organic, the grove is open during the citrus season, Oct.–May.

✳ Entertainment

DINNER SHOWS Maintained and performed entirely by volunteers, the nonprofit **Highlands Little Theatre** (863-471-2522; www.highlandslittle theatre.org), 321 W Center Ave., is inside the Allen C. Atvater Cultural Center. Thanks to the dedication of patrons and residents, this little theater has been producing outstanding productions for more than 30 years. The 200-seat theater has a professional backstage area with brightly lit dressing rooms and two full stories above the stage, allowing for a quick change of sets. Tues. and Wed. evening performance $10 (no meal); Sun. matinee $15 (dessert only); Fri. or Sat. evening $30 (full dinner). A cash bar is also available during dinner shows.

FOLK MUSIC Bring a lawn chair or blanket and listen to champion bluegrass music and traditional Florida Cracker folk songs at the Hammock Inn (see *Eating Out*). Events are scheduled around the country-style restaurant throughout the year, which also serves up traditional food. Depending on the time of day, the park admission fee of around $4 per carload may apply. Don't forget your bug spray!

✳ Special Events

January: Started in 1937, the **Highlands County Fair** (863-385-FAIR;

www.hcfair.net) is a tradition during the last week of January, bringing the agricultural bounty of the county to light. With food, music, and ribbons for "The Best," this county fair is a down-home tradition to be enjoyed by young and old. The orchid contest is one of the highlights.

U.S. Sport Aviation Expo (www .sport-aviation-expo.com), Sebring Regional Airport, Sebring. Exhibits highlight ultralight aircraft, fixed wings, trikes, powered parachutes, and gyroplanes.

February: More than 200 crafters gather at the **Lake Placid Country Fair** (863-465-4331; www.lpfla.com/ events/fair.htm), held the first full weekend at DeVane Park

March: **12 Hours of Sebring** (1-800-262-7223). Racing enthusiasts gather for this historic endurance race (see *Racing*) near the end of the month.

Sod rebels from around the country compete on bladeless lawn mowers in the annual **NASGRASS Lawn Mower Race** (see *Racing*). Races run 12 minutes to mimic the 12 Hours of Sebring and are held at the Avon Park Mower-

INSIDE THE PACKING HOUSE AT MAXWELL CITRUS

Sandra Friend

plex on SR 64 west of Avon Park Airport, the nation's first dedicated lawn mower–racing facility.

May: **Annual Blueberry Festival** at **Henscratch Farms** (see *Winery*), with a blueberry pie baking and eating contests, arts and crafts, and bluegrass music.

August: **Lake Placid Caladium Festival** (863-465-4331; www.lpfla.com/events/caladium.htm), Stuart Park, Interlake Blvd. and Stuart St. After taking a bus ride to view the caladium fields and homes with caladium landscaping, you can purchase potted caladiums and pieces of art detailing these bright red and pink plants. Caladium history and growers' exhibits along with demonstrations on how to care for

the plant are featured. The festival is held the last full weekend of the month.

November: The **Wings & Wheels Festival**, Avon Park, first weekend, brings in aviators from all over the country to reminisce over vintage aircraft dating back to World War II. Two training fields were located here during the war.

December: **Sebring Historic Fall Classic** (863-655-1442 or 1-800-626-7223; www.sebringraceway.com). Legendary cars return for the Four Hours of Sebring endurance race with vintage, historic, GT, and prototype classes, the Rolex Endurance Challenge, and the American Muscle Car Challenge, first weekend Dec.

LAKE OKEECHOBEE

GLADES, HENDRY, OKEECHOBEE, WESTERN MARTIN & PALM BEACH COUNTIES

Covering 730 square miles, **Lake Okeechobee** is an inland sea. It's the second largest lake entirely within the United States, and it has a significant girdle around it called the Herbert Hoover Dike, built for flood control after two devastating hurricanes in the 1920s killed thousands of residents by pushing the water right out of this shallow bowl and into the surrounding prairies. Only 15 feet deep in most places, the lake was once an integral part of water movement through the Kissimmee Valley and into the Everglades; now, the River of Grass relies on locks and canals to feed its need for fresh water. Thanks to the dike, the entire shoreline is managed by the Army Corps of Engineers. There are no waterfront condos, no sprawling lakeside cities, and very few views—unless you climb atop the dike and take a walk.

Water has always been the lifeblood of the region. The Calusa found their way up from the southeastern coast and established villages along the lake they called "Mayami," the Big Water. In the 1800s settlers pushed their way up the Caloosahatchee River and founded **LaBelle**, named for Laura and Belle, the daughters of Civil War hero Capt. Francis Asbury Hendry. Farming and ranching became the backbone of the economy around the lake as the city of **Moore Haven**, founded in 1915 by James A. Moore, was settled on the western shore. **Okeechobee** is the largest settlement on the eastern shore of the lake and the heart of South Florida's cattle country. Dating from the late 1800s, this frontier town saw its first explosive growth around 1915 as a port city for the fishing industry along the lake. The 1920s Florida land boom brought cattlemen to the area, and the town's livestock market—still going strong—opened in 1939. Planned by famed city planner John Nolan and established as a company town by the U.S. Sugar Company, **Clewiston**, the "Sweetest Town in America," also sprung to life during the land boom as the Atlantic Coast Line railroad pushed south into lands drained and "reclaimed" for farmland around the southern edge of the lake, leading to an influx of farm workers into **South Bay**, **Belle Glade**, and **Pahokee** by the 1920s. Sugarcane fields stretch to the horizon in what was once part of the Everglades "river of grass," but they may vanish within the decade—an ambitious state project to turn agricultural lands back into the Everglades is underway, and the fruits of these efforts won't be known for at least another five years.

Refreshingly rural, this remains an agricultural region where cattle, sugar, oranges, and rice are the major crops. But that doesn't mean there's a lack of tourists. If you've ever wondered where all those RVs are headed down the inter-states every winter, chances are they're staking out camp at one of the many, many campgrounds around Lake Okeechobee. Anglers arrive here from around the globe for legendary fishing. With fishing, hiking, birding, boating, and historic sites to visit, you'll find plenty to see and do. I know; I've returned at least a week out of every year since 2002 to enjoy the outdoors here.

GUIDANCE Florida's Freshwater Frontier (1-800-467-4540; www.florida freshwaterfrontier.com), P.O. Box 1196, Sebring, 33871-1196 brings together tourism information for all of the counties and small communities around Lake Okeechobee. For Hendry County, visit the **Hendry County Tourist Develop-ment Council** (863-612-4783; www.visithendrycounty.com) at the Greater LaBelle Chamber of Commerce, 125 E. Hickpochee Ave. Along US 27, stop in at the **Clewiston Chamber of Commerce** (863-983-7979), 109 Central Ave. in the Clewiston Museum (see *Museums*) for brochures. In downtown Moore Haven, pick up information from the **Glades County Tourist Development Council** (863-946-0300; www.visitglades.com), on US 27 across from Beck's Gas Station, Moore Haven. In downtown Okeechobee at the visitors center adjoining the police station, the **Okeechobee Chamber of Commerce** (863-763-6464; www .okeechobeechamberofcommerce.com), 55 S Parrott Ave., can load you up with maps and brochures. **Okeechobee County Tourist Development Council** (863-763-3959 or 1-800-871-4403; www.okeechobee-tdc.com), 499 NW Fifth Ave., presents details about the area on their Web site. Contact the **Palm Beach Coun-ty Convention and Visitors Bureau** (561-233-3000 or 1-800-833-5733; www.palmbeachfl.com), 1555 Palm Beach Lakes Blvd., Ste. 800, West Palm Beach, in advance for a brochure on things to do and see in Pahokee, Belle Glade, and South Bay. For information about the lake, its water control structures (locks and dams), and campgrounds at those structures, contact the **U.S. Army Corps of Engineers South Florida Operations Office** (863-983-8101; www.saj.usace.army.mil), 525 Ridgelawn Rd., Clewiston.

GETTING THERE *By car:* **US 27** and **US 441** provide primary north-south access, with **SR 80** running east-west through LaBelle, Clewiston, and Belle Glade. **SR 78** links Okeechobee to Moore Haven via Lakeport.

By air: The nearest major airport to the eastern side of the region is **Palm Beach International Airport** (PBIA) in West Palm Beach (see *North Palm Beach Coun-ty*); to the west, it's **Southwest Florida International Airport** (see *The Beaches of Fort Myers Sanibel*).

By boat: The **Okeechobee Waterway** runs 152 miles from Port St. Lucie to Fort Myers utilizing the St. Lucie Canal, Lake Okeechobee, and the Caloosahatchee River. You can access Lake Okeechobee from either coast using your private boat.

GETTING AROUND *By car:* Unless you're boating, a car is necessary for explor-ing this region. To circle Lake Okeechobee clockwise starting at the city of Okee-chobee, follow **US 441** south to Canal Point, **CR 715** south to Belle Glade, **SR 80** west to Clewiston, **US 27** north to Moore Haven, and **SR 78** east back to Okeechobe. Mind the speed limits, especially around Clewiston, South Bay, and Belle Glade. **SR 29** connects US 27 in Palmdale with LaBelle, and SR 80 connects LaBelle back to US 27 to Clewiston. An unfortunately high number of speeders on SR 80 led to strict enforcement of speed limits for safety's sake.

By boat: Open-water crossing of Lake Okeechobee is generally rough and requires careful attention to depth readings. A navigable route follows the shoreline of the lake, utilizing the deep-water Rim Canal in places and channel markers in dredged areas of the lake in other places. Consult navigational charts for details.

MEDICAL EMERGENCIES For major emergencies go to **Hendry Regional Medical Center** (863-983-9121; www.hendryregional.org), 500 W Sugarland Hwy., Clewiston, or **Raulerson Hospital** (863-763-2151; www.raulersonhospital .com), 1796 US 441 N, Okeechobee.

✳ To See

ARCHAEOLOGICAL SITES Hidden in the sugarcane fields along the Herbert Hoover Dike near Belle Glade lie the **Chosen Mounds,** a multilayered burial complex unearthed by Smithsonian researchers led by George Tallant in the 1930s. In addition to bones of the Calusa, a coastal people from **Pine Island Sound** (see *The Beaches of Fort Myers Sanibel*), archaeologists discovered pottery shards, conchs used as hoes, and porpoise teeth used for engraving. Some of the artifacts removed from this site and from a burial complex near **Nicodemus Slough** (SR 78 near Moore Haven) can be viewed at the **South Florida Museum in Bradenton** (see *Florida's Gulf Islands*). At **Fort Center**, now accessible via a new interpretive trail at **Fisheating Creek WMA** (see *Wild Places*), archaeologists discovered a charnel platform decorated with wooden animal carvings; it was perfectly preserved by the muck at the bottom of a pond and is thought to be from the Belle Glade people, circa 500 A.D., who built earthen mounds and actively cultivated maize.

At the **Ortona Indian Mound Park** (863-946-0440), SR 78 west of US 27 and east of SR 29, walk through part of a village complex from 3,000 years ago and along canoe canals built by the Calusa not far from the Caloosahatchee River along Turkey Creek. A kiosk with interpretive information helps to orient you to the cultures that lived here and to follow trails around the site, which is heavily buried under vegetation. At 22 feet, the primary temple mound is the highest point in Glades County. Dispersed across 5 square miles, the overall complex is one of the largest prehistoric sites in Florida.

ATTRACTIONS

Okeechobee
For more than a decade, Sue Arnold has been rehabilitating and caring for native and exotic wildlife at **Arnold's Wildlife** (www.arnoldswildlife.org), 14895 NW 30th Terrace, off NW 144th Rd. With a group of dedicated volunteers, she handles more than 700 animals a year through the complex, and some have become permanent residents, including Florida panthers rescued from overpopulated zoos; hurricane victims like Dolly and Casper, a pair of cockatoos; lemurs without a home; and dozens of other raptors, marsupials, and felines. Guinea hens squawk as

BIG CYPRESS SEMINOLE RESERVATION

When the swamp buggy headed straight for the canal, it startled everyone in the high, bouncing vehicle, including me. Airboats zip down these canals and I didn't think our driver, Kat, could power that swamp monster through the muck and keep us afloat, but she did. At **Billie Swamp Safari** (863-983-6101 or 1-800-949-6101; www.seminoletribe.com/safari), Lemon Grove Rd., it's an immersion into the Big Cypress Swamp, ancestral home of the Seminole Tribe since the 1800s, but with a twist. Winding along trails through the dense forest and floodplain swamps along the swamp buggy tour, you'll see Asian water buffalo and ostriches, and other exotic animals as well as feral hogs, raccoons, alligators, and hundreds of wading birds. Along the way, your tour guide will fill you in on the flora and fauna of Big Cypress, the history of the Seminole, and interesting tidbits tied to the land, such as the best places for Florida panthers to take a perch. The rambling ride with its bumps and bounces is a counterpoint to the popular airboat tours, where you glide at high speed through the swamp with stops at key points, especially where it's possible to get up close to an alligator. The grounds include numerous animal displays, focused on native wildlife, including a Herpetarium with Florida snakes and some of the biggest alligators you'll see, and the Swamp Critters Show showcases more cuddly critters like armadillo, baby alligators, and snapping turtles. A nature trail winds along a boardwalk through a pop ash swamp. What's especially fun, however, is that you can stay overnight (see *Campgrounds*) in an authentic chickee, the Seminole version of a grass hut, and sit around a campfire listening to storytellers. It's a very different and authentic experience, one that will leave you with an appreciation of the Seminole and the habitats of the Big Cypress Swamp. Prices are à la carte with packages available. Swamp buggy $25 adult, $23 senior, $15 child; airboat $15; educational programs $8 adult, $4 child. Children must be 4 or older to ride in an airboat.

a panther paces a few feet away, and native deer roam through the garden. More than 720,000 children visit the center each year. But it's more than a wildlife rehab center with the addition of **Arnold's Butterfly Haven** (www.arnoldsbutterfly haven.com), an integral part of the outdoor experience on this family ranch. Step through the arbor and into a world where hundreds of butterflies flit about, entirely free-roaming, attracted by the colorful and aromatic plantings along garden paths arranged in the shape of our state butterfly, the zebra longwing. More than 57 species have been documented living, breeding, and feeding in this skillfully created garden. Climb to the top of the observation deck for a bird's-eye view. A 1.5-mile nature trail circles around the property. Open 9 AM–6 PM daylight savings time and 10 AM–5 PM the rest of the year; $10 donation.

Palmdale

A Florida classic since 1957, **Gatorama** (863-675-0623; www.gatorama .com), 6180 US 27, showcases an endangered Florida reptile that you won't see much of anywhere else—the American crocodile. Endemic to South Florida, these massive saltwater creatures breed from December through January; the colony here dates from the 1960s and now numbers more than 50. When you see owner Allen Register or one of his staff dangling food into the pond for the alligators to munch, you'll understand what a half century of growth means in gator terms: these creatures are huge! One large pond is divided in two by the walkway and fencing to keep the more aggressive alligators away from the American crocodile colony. Although the exhibits are old-style tiled pools, they showcase interesting creatures such as the mugger crocodile of India and the Nile crocodile. In 1987 the Register family began farming alligators for meat, and the demand still outstrips their supply. Covered walkways lead you past the exhibits, but you'll spend most of your time marveling at the size of the reptiles cruising the big pond. Open daily; $15 adults, children (under 60 inches) $7, little ones free.

CATTLE AUCTION Watch a live auction every week at the **Okeechobee Livestock Market** (863-763-3127; www.floridacattleauction.com), 1055 US 98 N, Okeechobee, where ranchers around the region round up their cattle for sale. It's free and fun. This is cattle country, where a 10,000-acre spread is not out of the ordinary. Florida has a long history of cattle ranching, dating from the Spanish explorers of the 1500s, and remains the third largest ranching state east of the Mississippi, with 1.1 million head of beef cattle and more than 150,000 head of dairy cattle. Calves are sold here between July and January through February.

HISTORIC SITES

Belle Glade

The **Torry Island Swing Bridge** on Torry Island Road at Point Chosen is a unique hand-cranked swinging drawbridge connecting the largest island in Lake Okeechobee with the mainland, and it is the oldest remaining manually operated bridge in Florida.

Clewiston

You'll find dozens of historic sites clustered around downtown, starting with the **Bond Street Historic Business District** at Bond and Sugarland Hwy. Stop in at the chamber of commerce or **The Clewiston Inn** (see *Lodging*) for a walking-tour brochure (see *Walking Tours*) to explore the area, by foot or by car. Significant historic homes include the **B. G. Dahlberg Executive House**, 125 W Del Monte Ave.; the **Captain Deane Duff House**, 151 W Del Monte Ave.; and the **Percy**

GATORAMA

Sandra Friend

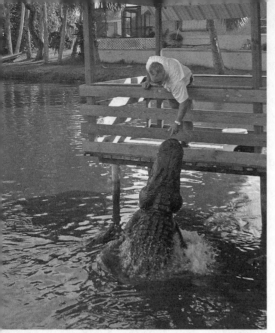

ALLIGATORS GROW HUGE AT GATORAMA

Bishop House, 325 E Del Monte Ave., all built on the original lakeside bluff. **St. Margaret Catholic Church**, 208 N Deane Ave., is the oldest church in town, built in 1931. The quaint wooden **Army Corps of Engineers Settlement Homes** between Ponce de Leon and Royal Palm Ave., crossing the streets of Balboa, Arcade and Crescent, were built for the men working on the Herbert Hoover Dike in the 1930s after the hurricanes. The dedication marker for the dike is the **Hoover Dike Memorial,** which is above the boat ramp near the Clewiston lock. The dike took six years to build.

LaBelle

On the National Register of Historic Places, the **Hendry County Courthouse**, SR 80 and SR 29, was built in 1926 in an Italian Renaissance Revival style. It features a four-story clock tower.

Moore Haven

Grecian columns flank the doorways to the **Glades County Courthouse** (863-946-6001), US 27 between Fifth and Sixth Sts., where you can walk inside and see the thick vault doors leading to the inner chambers, and huge historic maps on the wall. Designed by E. C. Hosford, the courthouse dates back to 1928.

By virtue of its age and location, the **Lone Cypress Tree** (also known as the Sentinel Cypress), Ave. J and the Caloosahatchee River, qualifies as a piece of history—it served as a navigational marker for sailors on the Lake Okeechobee for more than a century, as they used it to find the entrance to the newly dug Caloosahatchee Canal. Years later, the construction of a lock made the tree less useful for navigation, but it's a beautiful landmark around which the city grew.

Okeechobee

A significant **downtown historic district** lies between SE 4th Ave. and NW 8th Ave., which includes the **Okeechobee County Courthouse** and the **Old Jail**. The railroad station (see *Railroadiana*) dates back to the early 1910s. Stop and take a look at the massive **Okeechobee Freshman Campus Historical Mural** depicting the settlement of the area, painted on the side of the high school gymnasium at 610 SW 2nd Ave. and 6th St.

The **Battle of Okeechobee** (www.okeechobeebattlefield.com) is commemorated with a **Historic Marker** in front of what's left of the Old Habits Tavern, US 441 SE. For years, it's been all that that physically remains to point out the location of one of the most significant battles of the Second Seminole War. An annual reenactment (see *Special Events*) brings this turning point in Florida's history to life. In 2008, the state of Florida purchased 145 acres of land in this area that includes a portion of the battle site, with plans to eventually turn it into a state historic site.

Ortona

Cracker tales come alive, so to speak, at the **Ortona Cemetery**, SR 78 west of US 27 and east of US 29, in the middle of cattle country. Here, Seminole chief Billy Bowlegs III (who was 104 when he died) was interred in 1965, and saddles and cowboy boots decorate the resting places of the departed. A homemade headstone tells the story of a mother and children who died during the 1928 hurricane. This is the only interment site in Glades County.

MUSEUMS

Belle Glade

Commemorating the region's top folk historian, the **Lawrence Will Museum** (561-996-3453), 530 South Main St., in the Belle Glade branch library, offers a look into the research of the man who thoroughly studied the Okeechobee hurricanes, with artifacts and historical records. Free.

Big Cypress Seminole Reservation

A walk through the **Ah-Tah-Thi-Ki Museum** (863-902-1113; www.ahtahthiki .com), corner of CR 833 and Government Rd., is a walk through time, experiencing Florida through the eyes of the Seminole people. According to tribal history, ancestors of the Seminoles first crossed paths with European culture in 1510, when a Spanish slave ship landed in South Florida. A brief movie introduces you to Seminole culture and life, both ancient and modern, setting the stage for browsing the 5,000-square-foot exhibit hall. Interpretive information is provided by tribal members, recounting the use of certain arrows, how women ran the camp, how *sofkee* was made, and hundreds of other details that paint a picture of the evolution of their culture. The displays themselves are world-class, with extreme attention to detail, such as the waterway scene with its ripples and details of what's under the water. An exhibit on the Green Corn Dance illuminates the religious beliefs and practices of the Seminole Tribe. Each exhibit contains objects of historic importance; a temporary exhibit on Osceola, for instance, included his deerskin coat from 1835 worn by the warrior during the signing of the Lake Monroe Treaty. The outdoors is an extension of the museum, with a 1.5-mile boardwalk loop leading through 60 acres of typical Big Cypress Swamp habitats. Don't miss this part of the exhibit, as interpretive information is provided on the traditional medicinal uses of plants and trees. Along the trail, there's a meeting area used for ceremonial functions, and a group of chickees where Seminole artisans perfect and sell their crafts. Inside the museum, a gift shop sells art, books, and traditional items. Open 9 AM–5 PM daily. Adults $9; seniors, students, and military $6; children 4 and under, free.

DETAIL OF THE OKEECHOBEE PIONEER MURAL

Sandra Friend

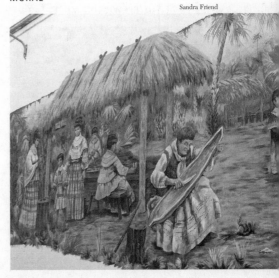

Clewiston

When I first visited the **Clewiston Museum** (863-983-2870; www.clewiston museum.org), 109 Central Ave., I was pleasantly surprised that it was packed with bits of local history that I knew nothing about before my visit, such as the No. 5 British Flying Training School housed in Clewiston during the 1940s, where British airmen came for fighter-pilot training, and the history behind why the Herbert Hoover Dike was built, with dramatic photos of the destruction from the hurricanes of 1926 and 1928. Now in its new spacious digs—the original home of the *Clewiston News*—the museum is bigger and better than ever, with a fossil room featuring a diorama and cases of fossils found within Hendry County, like a mastodon's lower jaw and tusk; a theater with presentations on natural and cultural history of the area; and extensive exhibits on early settlement, day-to-day life, and agriculture, especially the sugar industry. A gift shop with many history books and the official chamber of commerce brochure racks round out the complex. Open 9 AM–4 PM Mon.–Fri. Fee.

LaBelle

Housed in the historic home of the H. A. Rider family, the **LaBelle Heritage Museum** (863-674-0034), 150 S Lee St., features exhibits on local and regional history. Open 2 PM–5 PM Thurs.–Sat. Donation.

Okeechobee

Learn about life on Florida's frontier at the **Okeechobee Historical Society Museum & Schoolhouse** (863-763-4344); 1850 FL 70 N, the region's first one-room schoolhouse, built in 1907. Call to arrange a tour.

RAILROADIANA The **South Central Florida Express** (SCFE) Depot at W Aztec and W. C. Owen in Clewiston is home to the short line's rolling stock; stop here to take photos of the brightly painted locomotives. SCFE services the sugarcane fields to assist in the harvest. Okeechobee had a growth spurt when the Florida East Coast Railroad built a spur line into town, completed in 1915. The historic **Florida East Coast Railroad station** at 801 N Parrott Ave.—which in recent years was a stop on Amtrak until service cutbacks—is slated for renovation.

FOSSILS AT THE CLEWISTON MUSEUM
Sandra Friend

SCENIC VIEWS The **Harney Pond Canal Overlook** near Lakeport, SR 78 at CR 721, extends nearly a half mile out into the lake, with an observation platform great for birding. At **John Stretch Park** (see *Parks*), US 27 between Clewiston and South Bay, climb up the dike for a view of the Rim Canal and the marshes beyond. Stop **at Moore Haven Recreation Area** or the **Parrott Avenue Wayside** (aka Lock 7/Jaycee Park) along US 441 for views of the broad expanse of blue along the eastern shore of the lake. And for days and days of panoramic

Sandra Friend

THE RIM CANAL AT SOUTH BAY

views, walk the **Florida Trail** (see *Hiking*) around Lake Okeechobee, which has
my favorite scenic view—Indian Prairie.

✳ To Do

AIRBOATS *∂* Capt. Terry Garrels took me on one heck of a spin on **Big "O" Airboat Tours** (863-983-2037; www.bigofishing.com/airboat.html), 920 E Del Monte
Ave., departing from Roland Martin's Marina in Clewiston. Once through the lock
and out into the lake, we followed the Rim Canal until the captain found a good
break into the "grassy waters," the shallow marshes not far off the shoreline, and
whizzed us through narrow passageways where alligators lounged, moorhens floated,
and manatees surfaced. Unexpectedly, we came out into open water, which had
enough bounce to it to make me feel like we were on the ocean. On our 10-mile
route, Captain Terry made numerous stops to explain the habitats and wildlife we
were seeing, including pointing out a lone pond apple tree growing in the shallows—
according to historic accounts, a forest of these wizened trees once marched southwest from this lake's shores. Call for
rates, reservations required.

At **Billie Swamp Safari** (see *Attractions*), the airboat ride takes you
whizzing past a line of chickees in
front of a cypress dome before banking
into a series of canals through natural
habitats, including through a swamp
forest where colorful bromeliads dangle from the cypresses.

**Captain Don's Florida Airboat &
Pontoon Tours** (863-634-2109; www
.floridacrappiefishing.com) offers airboat tours on Eagle Bay near Okeechobee for $25 adult, $15 child for a

AN AIRBOAT ZIPS BY AT BILLIE SWAMP
SAFARI

Sandra Friend

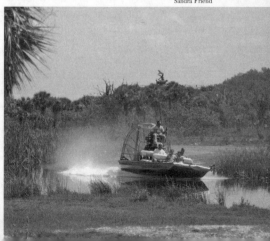

AGRICULTURAL TOURS Sugarland Tours (863-983-7979 or 1- 877-693-4372; www.clewiston.org), 544 W Sugarland Hwy., offers a glimpse into both the history of Clewiston and how sugar is processed, from the cane in the fields to the refined grains pouring into a bag. In this town, history and sugar are forever linked thanks to Charles Stewart Mott, who bought the bankrupt Southern Sugar Company in 1931 and reopened it as the U.S. Sugar Corporation, convincing investors that the Everglades muck was "black gold" for sugar growers. Most of the historic homes in town are a part of that era of rebirth and expansion, and as we rode through the shaded residential streets, our tour guide explained who built which grand old home and why.

Once out in the fields, we drove through the Southern Gardens Citrus Processing Plant and received a thorough explanation of how oranges become juice and concentrate, even though on that particular day, the plant wasn't in operation for us to get out and visit. We did disembark, however, along a string of railroad cars in a sugarcane field that was being harvested and watched the dinosaur-like harvester machines at work. Our guide pulled out a machete and chopped fresh cane for us to taste.

At the Clewiston Sugar Refinery, we watched from the safety of our bus as train cars offloaded their sugarcane into hoppers that carry the plant materials into the factory for processing. Donning shower caps and little plastic booties, we were allowed to watch processed sugar being bagged and stacked for shipment on the factory floor, with robotic arms spinning plastic webs around stacks of sacks and LP gas–driven loaders scurrying everywhere.

one-hour tour. He also offers pontoon tours on the Kissimmee River for $50 per hour, up to six people.

Eagle Bay Airboat Rides (863-824-0500; www.okeechobeeairboat.com), 900 SR 78 W, Okeechobee, takes you on an hour-long tour of Eagle Bay Marsh and Limpkin Creek, once a part of Lake Okeechobee's shores. Watch for alligators, spot eagles, and osprey, and bring your binoculars to spy the birds Captain Don points out. Ninety-minute tours out on Lake Okeechobee are also offered. Call for rates and reservations.

BICYCLING Atop the Herbert Hoover Dike, the **Lake Okeechobee Scenic Trail** (see *Greenways*) is now paved from Clewiston to the Pahokee Marina and Moore Haven to the Okee-tantie Recreation Area, providing nearly 50 miles for street bikes to traverse.

BIRDING Birding is fabulous all around the lake—I haven't been disappointed yet. White pelicans soar over the open water, sandhill cranes gather in groups on the prairies near **Okeechobee**, bald eagles nest on **Torry Island**, and osprey creel

The tour continues on to provide you a view of Lake Okeechobee, with history of settlement along the lake and the building of the Herbert Hoover Dike, and then wraps up with a buffet lunch at the Clewiston Inn. The comfortable 24-passenger bus totes you from stop to stop. Tours are offered weekdays at 10 AM; reserve your spot in advance by contacting the Clewiston Chamber of Commerce. Call for rates and reservations.

SUGAR CANE FIELDS NEAR BELLE GLADE

Sandra Friend

from snags all along the Rim Canal. For excellent birding, hit the **Florida Trail** (see *Hiking*) around the lake and to the south through Hendry County, where you'll spot caracara along the edges of the sugarcane fields. **Vance Whidden Park**, a low-lying area just up the road toward Lakeport, has great birding along the marshes. **Chandler Slough**, along US 98 in Basinger, is a prime place to stop and watch the birds in the cypress trees. For a place where you can spend days in search of caracara, sandhill cranes, red-shouldered hawks, and more, head out to the wide open spaces of **Kissimmee Prairie Preserve State Park** (see *Wild Places*), where the expanses of prairie and palmetto are brimming with birds, including the Florida grasshopper sparrow. Several **Wildlife Management Areas** (see *Wild Places*) in the region also offer excellent birding. At **Rotenberger WMA**, I saw groups of roseate spoonbills winging their way across the marshes, and crested caracara in the surrounding fields. The annual **Big O Birding Festival** (see *Festivals*) offers field trips into these productive areas and workshops on birding.

BOATING Public boat ramps are available at all major recreation areas around the lake, including **Clewiston Park**, **South Bay**, **Port Mayaca**, and **Alvin Ward**

Park in Moore Haven; there are numerous private ramps as well. Before heading out on the lake, boaters should pick up a navigational map at one of the marinas as this is one of the shallowest large lakes in the world. Among the many marinas servicing the lake are the **Belle Glade Marina** (561-996-6322), off SR 715 to SR 717, Belle Glade; **Buckhead Marina** (863-763-4716), 250 Buckhead Ridge Rd., west of Okeechobee off SR 78; **Okee-tantie Marina** at the Okee-tantie Recreation Area (see *Campgrounds*), and the **Pahokee Marina** (see *Campgrounds*). In Clewiston you can put in or dock at **Roland Martin's Lakeside Resort** (see *Lodging*), a full-service marina. West of Moore Haven off SR 80, **The Glades Resort** (see *Campgrounds*) has a deep-water marina along the Caloosahatchee River and can accommodate boats up to 60 feet.

ECOTOURS At **Kissimmee Prairie Preserve State Park** (see *Wild Places*), sign up for their **buggy tours**, the best way to see Florida's largest remaining prairie from on high and with interpretation. Each trip takes 2.5 hours and runs twice a day on weekends (8 AM and 1:30 PM) and on holidays. Call in advance to reserve a seat.

The Seminole Tribe of Florida offers tours through the wilds of their Big Cypress Reservation at **Seminole Tours** (1-800-949-6101 or 1-863-983-6101; www .seminoletours.com). In addition to package deals for **Billie Swamp Safari** (see *Attractions*) and the **Ah-Tah-Thi-Ki Museum** (see *Museums*), they offer overnight tours and personalized swamp buggy tours.

FAMILY ACTIVITIES ✔ Enjoy a real old-fashioned movie theater experience at **Mann's Clewiston Theatre** (see *Entertainment*) in Clewiston, a restored beauty from 1941, or take the kids down to **Woodworks Park** on Osceola Ave. in Clewiston, a gigantic wooden "super playground" from 1992, adjacent to the public library and pool complex. In Okeechobee, take the family bowling at "**I**" **Stardust Lanes** (863-467-1800), 1465 US 441 SE.

FISHING If you like to fish, you've come to the right place! **Lake Okeechobee** is a mecca for anglers and has long been known for its great bass fishing—although water management of inflow and outflow via locks and dams has caused serious problems to the quality of the fishery in recent years. But the tiny village of **Sand Cut** (population eight) along US 441 lays claim to being the speckled perch capital of the world, and I've seen some serious catfish in anglers' boats as they waited in the locks. If you're a first-timer here, it's best to check in with one of the marinas (see *Boating*) or fish camps (see *Fish Camps*), or contact the **Lake Okeechobee Guide Association** (1-800-284-2446; www.fishokeechobee.com). One recommendation from my Ontario friend who comes down to fish every year: stop in a bait-and-tackle shop such as **Garrard's Tackle Shop** (863-763-3416; www .okeechobeebassguides.com), 4259 US 441 S, Okeechobee, ask around, and you'll come up with a local who knows the waters like the back of his hand.

GAMING Who needs Vegas for slots? Here they are in the middle of cattle country at the **Seminole Casino Brighton** (1-866-2-CASINO; www .seminolecasinobrighton.com), on the Brighton Seminole Reservation west of Okeechobee between SR 78 and SR 70. In addition to more than 300 gaming machines, they run high-stakes poker and big-ticket bingo. They're open 24 hours,

7 days a week, with an on-site restaurant, the Josiah Lounge, open late.

GOLF With its greens within sight of the Herbert Hoover Dike, the **Belle Glade Golf and Country Club** (561-996-6605), 110 SW E Martin Luther King Ave., Belle Glade, is one busy place on weekends. This par 72 public course features 18 holes under tropical palms. At **The Glades Resort** (see *Campgrounds*) off SR 80, the 3,178-yard, par 36 course makes use of natural landscaping along its nine holes. This public course is inexpensive, too, with greens fees starting at $22 to walk, $20 with cart for 9 holes, $30 for 18 holes. Call 863-983-8464 for tee times.

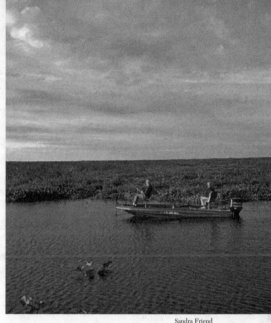

Sandra Friend

FISHING THE SHALLOWS OF LAKE OKEECHOBEE

GHOST TOUR Slip around the corridors of the **Clewiston Inn** (see *Lodging*) late at night on a guided walk to catch one of several apparitions that employees have been "seeing" for years—a former cook who rattles the kitchen pots, and two female guests who, it seems, checked out . . . without checking out. Ask at the front desk for details.

HIKING The granddaddy of hiking trails in this region is the **Florida Trail** (1-877-HIKE-FLA; www.floridatrail.org), which comes in from the south from Big Cypress Swamp and follows the water management canals through sugarcane fields and ranches for nearly 40 miles before reaching Lake Okeechobee, where it splits into two routes and encircles the lake for more than 110 miles. With numerous designated campsites (each with covered picnic bench and fire ring) on the lakeshore, this is a popular destination for backpackers, but it takes a special breed—you spend your time in the sun, and, recently, nearly half of the trail has been paved by the state to accommodate other users. The rewards are the amazing views and astounding amount of wildlife you see from the Herbert Hoover Dike. Those wanting to walk around the entire lake on day hikes join up with the annual **Big O Hike** (see *Special Events*) each year, as I've done. The linear Florida Trail continues north from Okee-tantie

ENTRANCE TO THE
BRIGHTON RESERVATION

Sandra Friend

Sandra Friend

AN EARLY ROUND AT THE BELLE GLADE GOLF COURSE

to follow the Kissimmee River upstream, with beauty spots accessible via trail-heads at **Yates Marsh**, **Chandler Slough** and **Micco Landing**. The 5-mile **Raphael Sanchez Trail** at Okeechobee Ridge Park, accessed from the Port May-aca Recreation Area, leads hikers on a shaded walk along the historic lakeshore. A backpacking route to the Atlantic Ocean, the 72-mile **Ocean to Lake Trail** is now accessible from a new trailhead along US 441 between Canal Point and Port May-aca and heads east to pass through **DuPuis Management Area** (see *Wild Places*), part of the Northeast Everglades Natural Area (NENA).

North of Palmdale, **Platt Branch Mitigation Park** (863-648-3203; www.myfwc .com/RECREATION/platt_branch), Detjens Dairy Rd., Venus, marks the south-ernmost extent of the Lake Wales Ridge, protecting more than 1,700 acres of scrub and scrubby flatwoods and the associated flora and fauna found in these rare habitats. Marked trails following forest roads create loop hikes of up to 5 miles; plans are for the trail system to be extended to allow backpacking along Fisheating Creek.

PADDLING Think of Lake Okeechobee like an inland ocean—it's big enough to get whitecaps and storm surges, and yet shallow enough to support a hefty alligator population. That said, not too many folks kayak out there, although following the shoreline looks like it would be nice. Instead, head to the **Fisheating Creek Canoe Trail** (863-675-5999; www.fisheatingcreekresort.com), 7555 US 27 N, managed by the folks at **Fisheating Creek Resort** (see *Campgrounds*). Open year-round, the trail roughly parallels the route of US 27 and offers one- or two-day trips starting at either Venus or Burnt Bridge. On your float trip, you are wel-come to camp in any dry, pleasant spot along this meandering cypress-lined creek, one of the most beautiful canoe runs in Florida. The livery provides shuttles ($20–25) and canoe rentals ($30 per day); reservations required. If you can do only one paddling trip in South Florida, do this one.

ROCKHOUNDING Dig for fossils in Florida? Better yet, serious collectors can uncover fossilized sea shells filled with honey-colored calcite crystals at the **Fort Drum Crystal Mine** (863-634-4579), a favorite destination for mineral collecting clubs. Known for years as Rucks Pit to collectors, it's the source of fossil shells like *Oliva roasa* and *Prunum bellum*, and rarer finds like *Iphocypraea rucksorum* and *Ventrilia rucksorum*, named for the owner. Prepare to get very wet and muddy, and bring your own prospecting tools, including shovel, bucket, and screen. Call for directions and cost.

SCENIC DRIVES Follow signs for the **Big Water Heritage Trail** (www.swfrpc .org/bigwatertrail.shtml) all around Lake Okeechobee to discover points of scenic and historic interest. You can pick up a map and brochure at any of the visitors centers around the lake (see *Guidance*) or download from the Web site.

Established in 2004 at the urging of Senator Bob Graham, the **Everglades Trail** (www.evergladestrail.com) is a driving tour that connects the dots of places linked to the natural heritage of the original Everglades. The entire region around Lake Okeechobee is a historic part of the Everglades drainage. Commemorating Florida's cattle ranching heritage, the **Florida Cracker Trail** passes through this region using US 98. Drive that route in the early morning, and you'll experience morning fog wrapping ranches in a dense mist and cows appearing like ghosts against silhouettes of cabbage palms.

SKYDIVING For a unique bird's-eye view of Lake Okeechobee, jump out of a perfectly good plane over sugarcane fields at **Air Adventures of Clewiston** (863-983-6151 or 1-800-533-6151; www.skydivefl.com), Air Glades Airport off US 27.

WALKING TOURS Pick up a **Clewiston Walking Tour** brochure at **The Clewiston Inn** (see *Lodging*) or **chamber of commerce** (see *Guidance*) and take a walk back into the 1920s by following the route down neighborhood streets to visit historic sites such as the original Clewiston School (circa 1927), St. Margaret's Catholic Church (circa 1931), and 15 homes from the 1920s, including several on the National Register of Historic Places. Four different routes range from 1 to 2.9 miles, all starting at The Clewiston Inn.

✳ Green Space

GREENWAYS Managed by the Office of Greenways and Trails, the **Lake Okeechobee Scenic Trail** follows the Herbert Hoover Dike around the lake and is paved for street bikes and roller blading between Port Mayaca and Okee-tantie and Clewiston and Pahokee. Mileages are painted on the asphalt, shaded benches provide resting spots, and kiosks at major access points provide maps of the route.

PARKS Enjoy riverfront picnicking at shady **Barron Park** in LaBelle along the Caloosahatchee River at SR 29, or explore the new **LaBelle Nature Park** (www .labellenaturepark.net), along the river at the end of Hardee St., off SR 80, along an old oxbow bend in the river.

Fishing, boating (with on-site launch), and picnicking are popular activities at **Clewiston Park** along the Herbert Hoover Dike, end of Francisco St.; it's also an access point to the paved Lake Okeechobee Scenic Trail and the Florida Trail.

John Stretch Park, 47225 US Hwy 27, between Clewiston and South Bay, is a favorite picnic spot for motorists, who scramble up the dike to see the Rim Canal and lakeshore marshes.

Between Belle Glade and Pahokee, **Rardin Park**, 4600 Bacom Point Rd., is set under the shade of massive ficus trees and has picnic tables and a playground; it's a steep but worthwhile walk up to the dike to see Torry Island and the sweep of the lake.

RECREATION AREAS/LAKE ACCESS POINTS Maintained by the Army Corps of Engineers, **recreation areas around Lake Okeechobee** provide a place for you to park and walk along the Herbert Hoover Dike; most of the recreation areas have boat ramps and picnic tables, and some have facilities. Key access points include **Port Mayaca**, at US 441 and SR 76; **Henry Creek** and **Nubbin Slough**, along US 441; and **Indian Prairie**, **Harney Pond Canal**, **Dyess Ditch**, and **Fisheating Creek**, along SR 78.

WILD PLACES
Devils Garden
Tough to get to, but worth the effort if you're an avid birder, there are several Wildlife Management Areas in southern Hendry County that are notable birding spots. **Dinner Island WMA** (www.myfwc.com/recreation/dinner_island), south of SR 80 along CR 833, protects 34 square miles of former pastures and prairies, flatwoods and oak hammocks. **Holey Land WMA** (www.myfwc.com/recreation/holey_land) is more than 35,000 acres and considered the northernmost original remaining portion of the Everglades River of Grass. Access is off US 27 south of South Bay. Nearby **Rotenberger WMA** (www.myfwc.com/recreation/rotenberger) protects thousands of acres of the original Everglades habitat of sawgrass marshes and hosts colonial nesting birds such as yellow-crowned night herons and cattle egrets.

Lakeport
Along SR 78 between Nicodemus Slough and Fisheating Creek, **Vance Whidden Park** is an undeveloped park with a dirt road leading out to the prairies along this single stretch of natural lakeshore on the northwest side of the lake, where there is a gap in the Herbert Hoover Dike for 3 miles to permit the Fisheating Creek floodplain to flow naturally into Lake Okeechobee. In the same general vicinity, on the southwestern side of Fisheating Creek, **Fisheating Creek WMA** (www.myfwc.com/recreation/fisheating_creek), Banana Grove Rd. off SR 78, features a brand-new 1.2-mile interpretive trail (accessed by a 2-mile round trip on a berm, bring a bicycle or walk 3.2 miles) with information about ecosystems and culture along this important waterway.

Okeechobee
Protecting 75 square miles of open prairies dotted with palm and oak hammocks, **Kissimmee Prairie Preserve State Park** (863-462-5360; www.floridastateparks.org/kissimmeeprairie), 33104 NW 192nd Ave., is Florida's second largest state preserve and a place that will humble you by its size. As I drove in the front gate and headed down the main road to the campground, I couldn't help but notice the similarities to driving along Main Park Road in Everglades National Park. The vis-

tas go on forever. Here, it's not sawgrass, but a combination of prairie grasses and saw palmetto stretching to the horizon. More than 100 miles of old roads crisscross the preserve. Some have been blocked off and set aside as hiking trails, others remain multi-use. This is a good place to bring your bicycle. The campground is a beauty spot, set under the shade of oaks yet open to the prairie, so you can enjoy the panorama from your tent or RV.

Port Mayaca

Open to equestrians, hikers, bicyclists, and hunters, the **DuPuis Management Area** (561-924-5314; www.sfwmd.gov/org/clm/lsd/dupindex.html), 23500 SW Kanner Hwy. (FL 76), encompasses more than 21,000 acres of forests, prairies, and wetlands. Stop at the nature center at Gate 5 for an orientation to this magnificent preserve.

✳ Lodging
CAMPGROUNDS

Big Cypress Seminole Reservation 33440

🐾 Get away from it all at the comfortable **Big Cypress RV Resort** (1-800-437-4102; www.bigcypressrvresort .com), CR 833, in the middle of the Big Cypress Seminole Reservation, just steps away from the **Ah-Tah-Thi-Ki Museum** (see *Museums*) and near the **Billie Swamp Safari** (see *Attractions*). RVs and tent campers welcome ($21–26), and well-appointed cabins are available ($65–75). The park has a clubhouse, aerobic trail, playground, miniature golf, heated swimming pool, and hot tub. Advance reservations suggested during the winter season.

Spend the night surrounded by the Big Cypress Swamp in an authentic Seminole chickee at **Billie Swamp Safari** (see *Attractions*). The small palm-thatched buildings sleep two for $35, or you can rent a chickee sleeping 8–12 people for $65. Linens, blankets, and bath towels included; all visitors share the bathhouse and have the opportunity to enjoy storytelling around the campfire or join a night swamp buggy tour (extra fee).

Clewiston 33440

ⁱⁱ The **Clewiston/Lake Okeechobee KOA** (863-983-7078 or 1-877-983-7078; www.clokoa.com), 194 CR 720, is in a nicely shaded grove north of town. RV spaces start at $36 daily and tent space (with hookups) for $28. There is one central bathhouse and a swimming pool. They also have rental cabins, including a honeymoon cabin with its own hot tub—ask about it.

ⁱⁱ **Okeechobee Landings** (863-983-4144; www.okeechobeelandingsrv .com), 420 Holiday Blvd., caters to the RV crowd with sun-drenched spaces on concrete pads with 50 amp service and full hookups ($35). Enjoy the heated swimming pool or hot tub, or arrange for a fishing guide.

LaBelle 33935

For a different type of outdoor experience, camp in the middle of an orange grove at **Grandma's Grove RV Park** (863-675-2567), 2250 W SR 80. You'll love it during the fragrant orange blossom season! $25 for full hookup; no tents.

🐾 The Army Corps of Engineers manages the **Ortona Lock Campground** (1-877-444-6777; www.reserveamerica .com), where groomed, grassy RV and tent sites ($24; water and electric) have a view of the Caloosahatchee River and access for fishing, off SR 80.

🐾 ⁱⁱ **Whisper Creek RV Resort** (863-675-6888; www.whispercreek

SLEEP IN A CHICKEE AT
BILLIE SWAMP SAFARI

.com), 3745 N SR 29 SW, offers a quiet getaway in the country, yet isn't far from the amenities of LaBelle, with many planned activities for campers to enjoy. While the resort mainly caters to long-term residents 55 and over, they have overnight rates of $35 for RV camping.

Lakeport 33471

🦀 **The Aruba RV Resort** (863-946-1324; www.okeedirect.com), 1825 Old Lakeport Rd., is as appealing inside the park as it is from the road. Many sites are shaded with tropical vegetation, waterway access is a cinch, and the heated pool, café, and tiki bar out front are available to all guests. Full-hookup sites include slabs with picnic tables ($31 in the trees, $37 waterfront). Weekly, monthly, and quarterly rates, too.

Moore Haven 33471

At The Glades Resort (863-983-8464; www.TheGladesResort.com), 4382 Indian Hills Dr. off SR 80, relax in a cabin along the golf course (see *Golf*) or bring your RV and settle into a shaded lot not far from the Caloosahatchee River at the marina (see *Boating*). There are full hookups at your choice of three different campgrounds within this 480-acre complex ($30–35; weekly, monthly, and annual rates

available). The comfy cabins have both a bed and futon and run $85 a day.

ⁿ Snuggled between the Herbert Hoover Dike and the Rim Canal, the **Marina RV Resort** (863-946-2255), 900 CR 720 NW, offers RV and tent camping right along the Florida Trail (see *Hiking*), with boating access to both the lake and the Caloosahatchee River. Shady sites are at a premium, but there is a nice central area with a pool, horseshoes, and shuffleboard, and the bathhouse is neat and clean. Full hookups $25, tents $18.

Okeechobee 34974

With a private boat ramp right on the Rim Canal, **Big Lake Lodge** (863-763-4638 or 1-866-256-5566), 8680 US 441 SE, is your destination for fishing. They offer a variety of accommodations for campers, including tent sites ($15), RV sites ($30–45), park models ($60–80), and furnished efficiency apartments ($45–65).

🦀 ⁿ It's not just a campground—it's a vacation destination. At the **Okeechobee KOA Resort & Golf Course** (863-763-0231 or 1-800-562-7748; www.okeechobeekoa.com), 4276 US 441 S, you can play nine holes of golf, relax in the hot tub, grab a bike for a spin, or sip a cold one in the tiki bar. Their massive list of amenities makes this one of the country's top KOA destinations, and in winter you'll find most of their seven hundred spaces filled with Canadian snowbirds. Choose from paved 50 amp sites with full hookup ($47–67), cottages or cabins ($65–155), or your basic tent site ($39–50).

With a great location on the Kissimmee River at Lake Okeechobee, the **Okee-tantie Recreation Area** (863-763-2622), 10430 SR 78, is a county-run facility with 270 sunny RV spaces ($31) and tent sites ($27, no utilities)—limit 2 people and one vehicle—plus a marina with boat rentals, bait and tackle, and ice and groceries.

Zachary Taylor RV Resort (863-763-3377 or 1-888-282-6523; www.camp floridarv.com), 2995 US 441 SE, is a pretty waterfront RV park on Taylor Creek that caters to the 55-and-over crowd with 240 full-hookup sites, screened-in heated swimming pool, and a recreation hall with many planned activities; sites available nightly, weekly, monthly, or for the season, with rates starting at $43 a night.

Pahokee 33476

Everglades Adventures RV & Sailing Resort (1-800-335-6560; www .evergladesadventuresresort.com), 190 N Lake Ave. at the Pahokee Marina, is the only waterfront campground on Lake Okeechobee, where the waves lap right up to your campsite ($27–39) and outside your cabin ($80–140) porch. Drop a line right into the lake!

Palmdale 33944

🐾 If you're looking for a getaway where the live oaks droop low and the Spanish moss waves in the breeze along a cypress-lined waterway, then head to **Fisheating Creek Resort** (863-675-5999; www.fisheatingcreek resort.com), 7555 US 27 N. This has been a favorite of my friends for years, but it's had a bad rap due to rowdy campers on the weekends. I'm assured the issue is under control, but weekdays are certainly the quiet days along this lazy creek. RV sites are clustered around a bathhouse/laundry area, with full hookups $20 a night. Primitive tent sites run $15 a night, and the best ones are along the creek, downstream from the camp store. Cabins cost $40 (no bathroom, next to bathhouse) to $65 per night. The livery service runs shuttles and offers canoe rentals (see *Paddling*).

South Bay 33493

Park your RV or pitch a tent at **South Bay RV Campground** (561-992-9045 or 1-877-992-9915), 100 Levee Rd.,off US 27, to relax in a pleasant, open campground surrounded by a series of ponds where you'll always see wading birds. You're right at the base of the Herbert Hoover Dike, with quick access for walking, bicycling, or fishing. Rates start at $14.

FISH CAMPS

Moore Haven 33471

A classic destination in these parts, **Uncle Joe's Fish Camp** (863-983-9421; www.unclejoesfishcamp.com), 2005 Griffin Rd. SE, opened in the 1940s and continues to serve serious anglers and their families with old-time cabins, tent space, and access straight into the lake via a boat ramp—no locks! Nothing fancy here, just serious fishing. Cabins have TV, air-conditioning, and heat and come fully equipped with dishes and linens. Cabins run $59 and up depending on size, tent space $15 a night, and reserved dock space $8 for guests. Laundry and shower room on premises. There is a $5 ramp fee for using their private ramp.

Okeechobee 34974

A quiet getaway for the fishing family, the **Angler's Villa Family Fishing Resort** (863-763-5060), 3203 SE 29th Ln., is just off the maze of waterways along Taylor Creek. Family owned and operated, this getaway offers a delightful setting under shady oaks. Rentals include fully equipped kitchens and cable TV (three-night minimum, $60 a night, $360 weekly). Heated, screened pool; gas and charcoal grills; and a fish-cleaning bench are on the premises, as well as a boat ramp and boat slips.

🐾 Evenings are always hopping at **J&S Fish Camp & Tavern** (772-597-4455;

www.jsfishcamp.com), 9500 SW US 441 S, where the music spills out over the water and onto the highway. This is a fun, funky little Florida fish camp with island style, offering RV sites and tent sites ($18), boat slips, cottages ($70–105, depending on size), and one of the cutest bathhouses I've seen. Friendly pets welcome.

HOTELS, MOTELS, AND RESORTS

Clewiston 33440

♣ ∞ "¡" Gracious Southern hospitality awaits in the historic elegance of **The Clewiston Inn** (863-983-8151 or 1-800-749-4466; www.clewistoninn.com), 108 Royal Palm Ave., an outstanding landmark in this rural community. Built in 1938 by the U.S. Sugar Corporation to provide accommodations for business travelers, it's been at the heart of community functions ever since. Step through the pillars to the elegant Southern lobby into a more genteel era, where it seems utterly appropriate to sip a mint julep in the Everglades Lounge while admiring J. Clinton Shepard's 1940s oil canvas mural of Everglades wildlife; birders will also appreciate the Audubon prints along the hotel's hallways. In 2007, the hotel was bought by two private investors who've made massive strides in upgrades and renovations to the 57-room complex, bringing modern flair and updated furnishings such as sleigh beds that accent the 1930s feel. Accommodations include standard rooms, suites, and spacious one- and two-bedroom apartments with their own kitchen nooks. Rates start at $99, with discounts for Florida residents. The **Colonial Dining Room** (see *Dining Out*) offers Southern-style fine-dining experience with a twist—the new owners have also revived the well-loved menu (and brought back the cook) from an old Clewiston favorite,

the Old South Bar-B-Que. The hotel also offers package tours, including ghost tours of the inn, and birding tours of the region.

Pro bass fisherman Roland Martin parlays his fame at **Roland Martin's Lakeside Resort** (863-983-3151 or 1-800-473-6766; www.rolandmartin marina.com), 920 E Del Monte Ave., where spacious rooms provide a good night's sleep before you hit the lake. Tie up your boat at one of the 130 covered boat slips ($8 per night) or along the lengthy dock; visit the marina store for bait, tackle, or to arrange a fishing guide. RV sites run $35 per night for full hookup. Call for room rates and reservations.

Lakeport 33471

The tiny **Aruba Motel** is part of the larger **Aruba RV Resort** (see *Campgrounds*), with four paneled motel rooms and three suites ($62 and up), each with a small fridge, microwave, and TV. Sit out front and watch the fish jump, or wander a few steps down to the tiki bar. Cash preferred; surcharge for credit card use.

The **Lakeport Lodge** (863-946-2020), SR 78 and CR 721, caters to anglers and is very busy on weekends. The 24 units include traditional motel rooms ($60) or suites ($70) offering a full kitchen, a living room/lounge area, and linoleum floors to minimize the impact of active outdoor enthusiasts. Smoking is permitted, but not in the bedrooms. The newly reopened Lakeport Restaurant, featuring burgers and steaks, is just steps away.

Okeechobee 34974

At Buckhead Ridge, **Angler's Waterfront Motel** (863-763-4031; www .guideservice.com), One Sixth St., just off SR 78, has basic, clean efficiencies and waterfront apartments ($70–80) with parquet floors, showers, and a fridge—just what the busy angler is looking for. Discount for 2 nights or more; guide service on-site.

🌸 "I" Under new ownership, the **Lakeview Inn & Suites** (863-763-1020 or 1-800-754-0428), 3225 US 441 SE, is an economical choice ($39–85) for your Okeechobee stay, featuring 20 rooms—some with kitchenette or full kitchen—and a nook under an arbor along the creek for relaxing, or barbecuing your catch.

♿ "I" **Pier II Motel** (863-763-8003 or 1-800-874-3744), 2200 US 441 SE, is a former chain motel renovated and now under local management. With enormous rooms, it's a comfortable place to stay ($70–80).

✳ Where to Eat
DINING OUT

Clewiston

🌸 The casual but elegant **Colonial Dining Room** at **The Clewiston Inn** (see *Hotels, Motels, and Resorts*) has brought back the charm of their original menu with its fine southern cooking, including entrées ($8–20) like buttermilk fried chicken breast, southern style chicken and dumplings, and country style pot roast. They've now accentuated it with a second menu, this one resurrecting a long-time favorite, the Old South Bar-B-Que. Having found one of the original cooks from that famed destination restaurant, they're serving up recipes ($6–25) that are mouthwateringly delicious, including their signature St. Louis ribs, 12-cheese macaroni and cheese (oooh, is that good!), and cornbread that's as soft as a slice of cake. Brunch served Sun. 11:30 AM–3 PM, all-inclusive luncheon buffet Mon.–Fri. for $9.

LaBelle

Don's Steak House (863-675-2074), 93 Hall St., is the place for steak in the region, what with all the cattle ranches to the north. Enjoy New York strip, Delmonico, top sirloin, porterhouse, prime rib, even filet mignon ($10 and up), or grab a taste of seafood favorites such as grouper, fried catfish, or fresh Florida frog's legs. Open for lunch and dinner; children's menu available.

Okeechobee

🌸 If it swims, crawls, or hops, they probably serve it at **Lightsey's Seafood Restaurant** (863-763-4276), at **Okee-tantie Recreation Area** (see *Campgrounds*), where Florida's marine bounty takes center stage on the menu and you can stare right back at it on the walls and in the aquariums. Enjoy entrées ($12 and up) like Florida lobster stuffed with crabmeat, fresh fried catfish and cooter, or a hefty plate of oysters, and leave room for some delicious pumpkin fry bread.

EATING OUT

Belle Glade

Even though it's attached to a gas station, **Mrs. Georgia's Catfish House** (561-996-6464), 1400 S Main St., is still worth a stop for dinner if you like your catfish and cole slaw in great big heaps. Dinner can be had for less than $10.

Big Cypress Seminole Reservation

When I hiked into the **Swamp Water Café** at **Billie Swamp Safari** (see *Attractions*) one fine winter day, I was glad that the portions were huge, because they fit my appetite—the massive Indian Taco is made up on Indian fry bread (delightful and calorie-heavy) and loaded with beef, lettuce, tomato, and salsa. I've been back several times since and have always been pleased. Open for lunch and dinner, meals $12 and up.

Clewiston

Authentic Mexican shines at the **Sunrise Restaurant** (941-983-9080), 842 E Sugarland Hwy., where "special plates" of your favorite Mexican dishes run $7 and up, and tacos, tamales, burritos, and more can be bought à la carte. I love their enchiladas, but you may opt for a seafood specialty, including shrimp tacos, frog's legs, or fried oysters. Open for lunch and dinner daily.

Fort Drum

North of Okeechobee, the **Pat's Country Kitchen** (863-763-8900), 32601 US 441, is an unassuming block building where you can sit and enjoy classic Clyde Butcher Florida landscape photography while the friendly staff serves up classic Cracker cooking (under $20) such as fried catfish, pork chops, and great homemade pies.

LaBelle

❦ Since 1933, **Flora and Ella's Restaurant** (863-675-2891), 550 SR 80 W, has been a fixture in LaBelle. Regulars come all the way from Fort Myers and Naples to enjoy their excellent country cooking and famous to-die-for pies. Their fine Southern cooking ($7 and up) includes such favorites as chicken and dumplings, Country Boy pot roast, catfish, and Hoppin' John. Yes, you can get okra, grits, and fried green tomatoes here! My dessert was a slide of coconut cream pie and as heavenly fresh and fluffy as it gets; we both gave a nod to one of the best pieces of pecan pie we've tasted yet.

Okeechobee

New in town but embracing the long-standing rancher culture, **Cowboy's Steak & BBQ** (863-467-0321), 102 SW 14th St., holds the Okeechobee image proudly for the world to see. The decor leans heavily on photos and paintings of local ranches and ranch families. Each table is named for a ranching family and decorated with their brand. Now that's touting Okee-choBEEF! I had a baked potato topped with shredded beef for a light lunch but will sample a hearty steak on my next trip. Lunch and dinner, $6 and up.

The aroma of fresh-baked pizza will draw you right in to **Gizmo's** (863-357-2188), 3235 US 441 SE, where their thin-crust pizza is the specialty of the house but their baked, not fried, chicken wings with secret rub are tasty, too. Subs, salads, sandwiches, and dinner specials, $6 and up.

You won't go wrong with breakfast at **Mom's Kitchen** (863-763-7553), 909 S Parrott Ave.—they serve it all day, they serve it up fast, and they serve it with grits if you like, all starting around $4. Choose from more than a dozen types of omelets, or have homemade biscuits and gravy. Open for lunch and dinner, too.

Named for the first sheriff of this frontier region, **Pogey's Restaurant** (863-763-7222), 1759 S Parrott Ave., is a good family restaurant with breakfast worth stopping for; most choices are less than $10. I like the French toast, but their specialty is biscuits with sausage gravy.

❦ A surprising find in the strip mall near Publix, **Pueblo Viejo VI** (863-357-9641), 3415 US 441 S, does a fine job of authentic Mexican dishes. The entrée ($9–16) portions are enormous, whether you order a simple combination dinner with enchiladas, tacos, or chile relleno, or go for one of their chef's specials like steak Tampiqueña (skirt steak and chicken enchilada) or Mojarra Frita (whole fried tilapia with pico de gallo and avocados). Savor it with a good margarita from their full bar.

Pahokee

Mister Jelly Roll's Coffee Shop
(561-924-0000), 129 Lake Ave., isn't
just for java—it's the local hangout for
scrumptious Mexican meals and general gossip and is named after a popular
local character. Open for breakfast,
lunch, and dinner.

Upthegrove Beach

❦ If you want a great steak, don't look
for a steakhouse—**Happy Hour** (863-
467-6420), a tavern along US 441 at
Upthegrove Beach, has the best steaks
in the region. Honest. We took a tip
from a local and discovered the best
value for your money in an honest-to-
goodness great steak. No frills, just
basic sides and perfect beef for $8 and
up. Open for dinner Mon.–Sat.

**COFFEE SHOPS AND SODA
FOUNTAINS** Kick back and relax at
Common Grounds (863-902-9889),
104 Bond St., Clewiston, a downtown
street-corner café serving breakfast
treats, soup and salad, and fresh tea
and coffee.

Don't miss **Gimme the Scoop** (863-
946-2663), 699 NW US 27, in Moore
Haven, for a sweet treat as you drive
through ranching country.

PRODUCE STANDS In Okeechobee,
The Market Place (863-467-6639),
3600 US 441, offers farm fresh produce and a weekend flea market.

✳ Entertainment

Restored by the Mann family, **Mann's
Clewiston Theatre** (863-983-6494),
100 E Sugarland Hwy., Clewiston, dates
from 1941 and still shows first-run films
in a great historic setting with a classic
old refreshment stand in the lobby.
Open Thurs.–Sun.; call for times.

✳ Selective Shopping

Clewiston

Bond Street downtown is the shopping
district, with boutiques, a coffeehouse,
and more. I've found plenty of goodies
at **Second Chance Boutique and
Gifts** (863-983-8865), 113 Bond St.,
where they have great prices on antique
glassware and newer decor items.

At Roland Martin's Lakeside Resort
(see *Hotels, Motels, and Resorts*), the
Marina Store is one of the best places
in town to shop. Sure, you can buy
bait, but why not a tie-dyed T-shirt for
the kids? They carry sportswear from
Columbia and Fresh Produce, Guy
Harvey T-shirts, Hawaiian shirts, and
even hula dancer and tiki salt and pepper shakers.

LaBelle

You'll find a bevy of unique items at
Country Peddler Antiques (863-
675-3822), 265 N Bridge St.—when I
poked around, I came up with a traveling pulpit for circuit preachers, Nori-
take china, and an elaborately gilded
clock amid primitives and glassware.

I know of no other honey outlet in
Florida, so make a beeline to **Harold
P. Curtis Honey Co.** (863-675-2187
or 1-888-531-9097; http://curtishoney
.hypermart.net), Bridge St., in the historic downtown district. It's a storefront for a family business that dates
from 1921. You've heard of orange
blossom honey, but how about palmetto and mangrove? In addition to
honey and honey products, they have
beautiful beeswax candles for sale, too.

Okeechobee

Park Avenue is the historic downtown
district just steps away from the chamber of commerce, where you'll find a
handful of antiques shops and boutiques. Among them are **The Outpost**
(863-763-7255), 330 Park Ave., a

sportswear shop with Columbia, Quicksilver, and Roxy, as well as surf-related hats and sandals.

The oldest flea market in the region, **Cypress Hut Flea Market**, 4701 US 441 N, is a giant garage sale with everything including the kitchen sink—even fine antiques, sterling jewelry, and fine leather.

Along US 441, the massive **Trading Post Flea Market** (863-763-4114) is a popular draw on weekends (8 AM–3 PM), with both new cheapie items and vintage treasures on display.

✴ Special Events

January: **Battle of Okeechobee Reenactment** (www.okeechobee battlefield.com) Okeechobee, last weekend, near Kings Bay along US 441 SE. On Christmas Day 1837, the Seminoles, led by their medicine man Abiaka, ambushed a unit of U.S. Army soldiers led by Col. Zachary Taylor. The fighting raged for three hours, and more than a hundred men fell. This battle was a turning point that dubbed Taylor "Old Rough and Ready" and drove the Seminoles deep into the Everglades for nearly a century. The reenactment captures both sides of the story.

SANDHILL CRANES IN OKEECHOBEE
Sandra Friend

Pucker up at the **Sour Orange Festival**, Lakeport Community Center.

February: **Cane Grinding Festival** (863-946-0440), Ortona, first weekend. An old-fashioned sugarcane grind and boil held at **Ortona Indian Mound Park** (see *Archaeological Sites*), with music and food, too.

Since 1959, the **Speckled Perch Festival** (863-763-6464; www.okeechobee chamberofcommerce.com/speckled perch.htm) has been a celebration of fishing for one of Lake Okeechobee's most notable species. Held early Feb.

Swamp Cabbage Festival (863-675-0125), LaBelle, last weekend. Celebrate "hearts of palm" at riverfront Barron Park with food, music, and crafts.

Top of the Lake Art Fest (www .mainstreetokeechobee.com/arts _culture.htm), a new festival sponsored by Okeechobee Main Street, brings the arts to the lake with a juried fine art show and artist booths in the city parks along SR 70.

March: **Chalo Nitka Festival** (863-946-0440), Moore Haven, first weekend. "Day of the Bass" in Seminole, this long-time heritage festival celebrates the convergence of Seminole and ranching cultures along Lake Okeechobee, and is held at Chalo Nitka Park on 10th St., with Seminole crafts and food and a parade as well as local entertainers.

April: **Black Gold Jubilee** (561-996-2745), Belle Glade, third weekend, brings in artists, musicians, and a crafts fair to celebrate the end of the harvest from the rich, dark earth that gives sugarcane and vegetables grown here their sweet flavor.

Spanning sites in Glades and Hendry counties, the **Big O Birding Festival** (www.bigobirdingfestival.com) includes four days of exploration and workshops in a region well-known for its excellent birding for rare birds best seen in this region, such as the Everglades snail kite and the crested caracara. Fee.

Clewiston Sugar Festival (863-983-7979), Clewiston, third Saturday, is a celebration of the end of the sugarcane harvest with entertainment, food, and crafts.

September: **Okeechobee Cattlemen's Rodeo** (863-763-6464), at the Cattlemen's Rodeo Arena, US 441 N. Held annually on Labor Day weekend, the rodeo brings in the cowmen from the ranches surrounding Okeechobee to showcase their riding and roping skills.

November: **Big O Hike** (1-877-HIKE-FLA; www.floridatrail.org), Thanksgiving week. Since 1992, a group of hikers

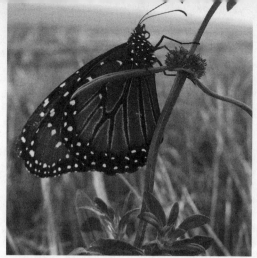

Sandra Friend

MONARCH BUTTERFLY ATOP THE HERBERT HOOVER DIKE

from the Florida Trail Association have walked around the lake on a 109-mile series of nine-day hikes each year, with designated group camping and social activities along the way.

The Treasure Coast

3

INDIAN RIVER COUNTY

ST. LUCIE COUNTY

MARTIN COUNTY

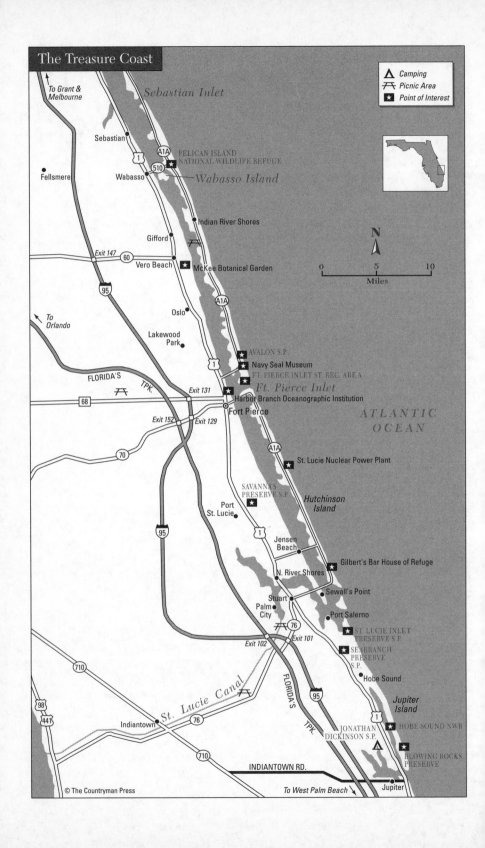

The Treasure Coast

Camping
Picnic Area
Point of Interest

0   5   10
Miles

N

To Grant & Melbourne

Sebastian Inlet

Sebastian

Fellsmere

1

A1A

510

Wabasso

PELICAN ISLAND NATIONAL WILDLIFE REFUGE

Wabasso Island

Indian River Shores

Gifford

Exit 147

60

Vero Beach

McKee Botanical Garden

95

To Orlando

Oslo

A1A

Lakewood Park

1

AVALON S.P.

Navy Seal Museum

FT. PIERCE INLET ST. REC. AREA

FLORIDA'S TPK.

Exit 131

68

Ft. Pierce Inlet

Harbor Branch Oceanographic Institution

Exit 152   Exit 129

Fort Pierce

ATLANTIC OCEAN

70

A1A

St. Lucie Nuclear Power Plant

SAVANNAS PRESERVE S.P.

Hutchinson Island

95

Port St. Lucie

1

Jensen Beach

Gilbert's Bar House of Refuge

N. River Shores

Sewall's Point

Stuart

Palm City

Port Salerno

76

ST. LUCIE INLET PRESERVE S.P.

Exit 102   Exit 101

SEABRANCH PRESERVE S.P.

710

FLORIDA'S TPK.

Hobe Sound

98

441

St. Lucie Canal

Jupiter Island

Indiantown

76

1

95

HOBE SOUND NWR

JONATHAN DICKINSON S.P.

710

BLOWING ROCKS PRESERVE

INDIANTOWN RD.

Jupiter

© The Countryman Press

To West Palm Beach

INDIAN RIVER COUNTY

When you hear the name Indian River, it's synonymous with citrus—and indeed, thousands of acres in the western half of the county are devoted to immaculate rows of grapefruit, orange, and other tangy fruits. But the earliest pioneers to this region found it to be a jungle, hard to pull a wagon through, and mostly underwater. In 1887 Henry T. Gifford and his family came to the bluffs of the Indian River Narrows to build their homestead. Within a few years, enough settlers joined them to petition for a post office, and Henry's wife, Sara, submitted the name "Vero," the Latin word for "truth." By November 1891, not only was there a post office, but Indian River County was carved out of neighboring Brevard and St. Lucie Counties. Mr. Gifford was behind the effort to build a road between Sebastian and Fort Pierce, which was dubbed the Dixie Highway. The Florida East Coast Railroad, Henry Flagler's rail line, began service through the county in 1893, providing citrus growers and fishermen fast shipping to northern markets.

When Waldo Sexton came to Vero in the early 1920s, he—like many other speculators in Florida's land boom—saw opportunity. An agricultural specialist from Purdue University in Indiana, he created the first dairy in the county and shipped out products in his refrigerator trucks, involved himself in citrus growing and packing, and established a real estate firm to draw northern investors south. He built the Driftwood Inn, a rambling two-story hotel in Vero Beach. Sexton took advantage of the tumbling fortunes of his neighbors in Palm Beach, buying up artworks and property for a song during the depression. He joined with Arthur McKee, to open the McKee Jungle Gardens, a revitalized tourist draw even today. Marshlands were drained for agriculture and housing residents poured in, and the population increased from 793 to 2,226 in 1930.

Today, this lightly populated, conservative county continues to hum along on a base of agriculture and light industry, its visitors mostly interested in the outdoors. They are attracted to the coast for the gentle beaches and great fishing and birding along the Indian River Lagoon, and to the marshy beginnings of the St. Johns River by the beauty of dense forests, cypress strands, and wide-open marshes. As you drive down US 1 toward Sebastian, notice the banana trees growing wild along the Indian River Lagoon—a reminder of an agricultural past that continues to be a strong anchor for this community today.

GUIDANCE For more information on the area, get in touch with the **Indian River Chamber of Commerce** (772-567-3491; www.indianriverchamber.com), 1216 21st St., Vero Beach 32960.

GETTING THERE *By car:* Use I-95 or US 1 to reach Fellsmere, Sebastian, Vero Beach, and Oslo. SR 60 connects Florida's Turnpike with Vero Beach.

By air: **Melbourne International Airport** (321-723-6227; www.mlbair.com), One Air Terminal Parkway, is the closest airport to the region, offering commuter flights daily on Delta. The region is also within range of Palm Beach International Airport (see *North Palm Beach County*).

GETTING AROUND *By car:* A car is necessary for visiting the county unless your destination is Vero Beach, where there is a lot to see and do within walking distance of hotels. Most services are along US 1 and SR A1A, and along SR 60 in Vero Beach.

MEDICAL EMERGENCIES For emergencies head to **Indian River Memorial Hospital** (561-567-4311), 1000 36th St., Vero Beach.

✳ To See

HISTORIC SITES

Fellsmere

Fellsmere was the vision of E. Nelson Fell, who in 1910 bought 118,000 acres from the railroad land company to create several cities. Fellsmere is the only one that has survived and thrived, in part due to having its own railroad that ensured shipment of citrus from surrounding farms to the Florida East Coast Railroad in Sebastian. Downtown Fellsmere is small and walkable, and its many historic sites include the **1913 City Hall, 1916 Fellsmere School,** several churches, the **1915 Fellsmere Inn,** and the **1920s land office,** now home of the **Marsh Landing restaurant** (see *Eating Out*).

Grant

Stop in at the **1916 Grant Historical House & Fisherman's Park** (321-723-8543), 5795 US 1, to see a restored pioneer Cracker home that is the centerpiece of this wayside park along the Indian River Lagoon. The home is open for tours 10–4 Tues.–Fri.; the park is open daily sunrise–sunset and has a walking trail, riverfront boardwalk, and fishing dock.

Sebastian Inlet

A hurricane in July 1715 sunk an entire flotilla of Spanish galleons loaded with gold and silver just off the coast of Sebastian Inlet. Nearly 1,500 men made it to shore and made camp at the inlet until they were rescued. Years later, the Spanish returned to the camp to attempt to raise some of their treasure and return it to Spain. The **Spanish Fleet Survivors and Salvors Camp** is on the National Register of Historic Places and is located inside **Sebastian Inlet State Park** (see *Beaches*).

MUSEUMS

Sebastian

Renowned for the treasures he recovered from the 1622 wreck of the *Atocha* off Key West, Mel Fisher is considered a giant in the field of treasure hunting. Stop in at **Mel Fisher's Treasure Museum** (772-589-9875), 1322 US 1, to see artifacts from the *Atocha* and from the 1715 Spanish fleet that sank off the coast between Sebastian Inlet and Fort Pierce. Open 10 AM–5 PM Mon.–Sat., noon–5 PM Sun. General admission is $6.50, children 6–12 $2, adults 55 and older $5, free for children age 5 and younger.

Sebastian Inlet

At **Sebastian Inlet State Park** (see *Beaches*), the **McLarty Treasure Museum** (772-589-2147), 13180 SR A1A, focuses on artifacts recovered from the ship-wrecked Spanish fleet of 1715, found along the Treasure Coast. The movie *Treasure: What Dreams Are Made Of* explains modern-day salvage efforts. Open 10–4:30 daily; small fee. ✑ Also inside the park, the **Sebastian Fishing Museum** (772-388-2750), on the south side of the Sebastian Inlet Bridge, covers the long history of the region's fishing industry, with replicas of a fish house and dock, and a 24-minute video on the Indian River Lagoon. Open 10 AM–4 PM; free with park admission.

Vero Beach

Inside the historic 1935 Vero Beach Community Building, dedicated in 1935, the **Indian River Citrus Museum** (772-770-2263), 2140 14th Ave., explores the history of citrus growing in the region, from the Spanish explorers who first brought orange trees to Florida to today's high-tech processing and packing. Archives, artifacts, and guided citrus tours are all part of the experience. Open 10 AM–4 PM Tues.–Fri. Donations appreciated.

Considered the largest facility of its kind on the Treasure Coast, the **Vero Beach Museum of Art** (772-231-0707; www.verobeachmuseum.org), 3001 Riverside Park Dr., offers four art galleries, a sculpture park, an art library, museum store, and numerous spaces for seminars and classes, including an outdoor foundry. Objects from the museum's permanent collection are rotated through several of the galleries; the Schumann Florida Gallery showcases Florida art. Classes are offered to the public on a regular basis. Open 10 AM–4:30 PM Mon.–Sat., 1 PM–4:30 PM Sun. Closed on Mondays June through August. Some exhibitions are free, others require a fee.

Indian River County Historical Society Office, Museum and Exhibit Center (www.irchistorical.org) includes the following three attractions, all of which are listed on the National Historic Register.

✑ Built in 1903, the former Florida East Coast Railroad Station is now the

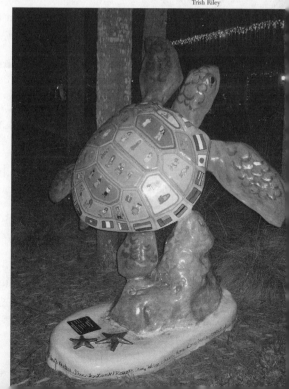

TURTLE WELCOMES YOU TO VERO BEACH

Trish Riley

Vero Beach Railroad Station Exhibit Center (772-778-3435), 2336 14th Ave. Stop in and see their permanent model-railroad display showcasing a journey through Indian River County. The railroad runs through a scale replica of Indian River County from the previous century. Open 10 AM–4 PM Wed.–Fri. Donations suggested.

The **Hallstrom Farmstead,** 1723 SW Old Dixie Hwy. (772-778-3435), a museum showcasing the farming lifestyle in this area from the early 1900s. Open 9 AM–1 PM Tues. and by scheduled tour. $5 donation.

Historical **Marian Fell Library,** 63 N. Cypress St., Fellsmere (772-571-0068), is a one-room library built in 1915. Mon.–Fri., 1 PM–5 PM, donations appreciated.

✳ To Do

BIRDING Don't-miss birding sites in the county include **Pelican Island National-al Wildlife Refuge** (see *Preserves*), with its nesting colony of brown pelicans; **Fort Drum Marsh Conservation Area** (see *Wild Places*), where sandhill cranes and crested caracara are commonly sighted; and **Blue Cypress Conservation Area** (see *Wild Places*), with foraging and nesting habitat for the snail kite. Many of the islands of the Indian River Lagoon are rookeries or roosts for colonial nesting birds such as herons, pelicans, and ibis, so a cruise along the waterway at dusk or dawn will yield spectacular sightings.

BOATING Cruising the Indian River Lagoon is a favorite pastime of locals. If you've brought your own, you can anchor in deep-water slips at the **Sebastian River Marina & Boatyard** (772-664-3029), 8525 N US 1, Sebastian, a full-service marina, or pull in at the **City Marina at Marker 139** (772-978-4960), 3611 Rio Vista Blvd. in Vero Beach; make reservations 48 hours in advance.

FISHING Saltwater or freshwater—your choice! **Sebastian Inlet** is a popular location where king mackerel, snapper, and grouper hang out around the jetties. If you hook up with a local captain for a deep-sea trip, expect to find wahoo, tuna, and marlin well offshore. Check in at **Captain Hiram's** (see *Eating Out*) to book an excursion with **Surfrider Charters** (321-917-4384). Inland, **Blue Cypress Lake** (see *Wild Places*) is known for its largemouth bass and black crappie, and **Stick Marsh,** a reservoir in the northwest corner of the county, has been named one of the Top 10 black bass lakes by the Florida Fish & Wildlife Conservation Commission.

HIKING While many of the county's trails are multiuse, there are several gems that are "hiking only" and well worth a morning's walk. Start with **Oslo Riverfront Conservation Area** (see *Preserves*) for a meander through the "jungle" that the early pioneers encountered. For more adventure head out to **Fort Drum Marsh Conservation Area** (see *Wild Places*), which has a beautiful boardwalk through a cypress dome and an often-challenging walk around Hog Island, a somewhat dry spot otherwise surrounded by the marshes from which the St. Johns River rises. And even if you're traveling without children, don't miss the **Environmental Learning Center** (see *Nature Centers*) at Wabasso Island, with its many boardwalks and short trails.

PADDLING Ply saltwater or freshwater with **Tropical Kayak Tours** (772-778-3044; www.tropicalkayaktours.com), where avid kayaker Ronda Good leads you on an adventure into the tropical heart of Indian River County. Her broad slate of tours includes numerous local destinations such as Blue Cypress Lake and the Sebastian River; tours of the Indian River start at $45. Call or e-mail (info@ tropicalkayaktours.com) to arrange reservations; lunch is provided on some of the trips.

✸ Green Space
BEACHES
Sebastian Inlet
Spanning two counties across one of the Indian River Lagoon's major inlets, **Sebastian Inlet State Park** (321-984-4852; www.floridastateparks.org/Sebastian Inlet/), 9700 S SR A1A, is a popular destination for surfers and anglers. A1A runs right through the park, which includes the beach and fishing pier, a full-service campground, a nature trail, and the **McLarty Treasure Museum** (see *Museums*). Park admission is $3 per person or $5 for 2 to 8 people in a vehicle. Separate $1 fee for McLarty Museum. Fee for boat ramp area is $3.

Vero Beach region
There are several oceanfront public parks along this strand, stretching from **Golden Sands Beach Park** (772- 581-4995), 1.4 miles north of CR 510, to **Round Island Beach Park** (772- 492-2412), south of Beachland Blvd. Most provide restrooms and showers, picnic tables and grills, a playground and lifeguards. Free.

Treasure Shores Beach Park, further north on A1A (772-581-4997), also has a lifeguard.

BOTANICAL GARDEN When I was a kid, it was a natural attraction called McKee Jungle Gardens that had been around since 1929. A victim of the Disney era, it closed its doors in 1976, and most of the land was sold to developers. But 18 acres of the original garden remained, and local enthusiasts rallied to save it. Reopened in 2001 as the **McKee Botanical Garden** (772-794-0601; www.mckee garden.org), 350 US 1, Vero Beach, this beautiful subtropical hammock bursts with brilliant natural color in every season. A botanical reference library is on-site. Open 10 AM–5 PM Tues.–Sat., noon–5 PM Sun. Fee for non-members.

NATURE CENTER ♿ ✐ Kids will love all there is to see and do at the 64-acre **Environmental Learning Center** (772-589-5050; http://discoverelc.org), 255 Live Oak Dr., Wabasso Island, with its hands-on interpretive stations along nature trails snaking through a variety of near-shore habitats, from coastal hammock to mangrove fringe. The Welcome Center has exhibits and a gift shop; pick up a map here to begin your exploration of the campus, which hides such goodies as the waterside pavilion for picnics, a tiki hut, a dry lab, a butterfly garden, a greenhouse, a native plant garden, and much more. Three-hour canoe trips on the Indian River Lagoon are offered every other Saturday morning (call for reservations). To reach the nature center, exit from CR 510 from the causeway onto Wabasso Island and drive north. Open 10 AM–4 PM Tues.–Fri., 9 AM–noon Sat. (until 4 in winter), 1 PM–4 PM Sun. Free; donations appreciated. Fee for canoe trips.

Sandra Friend

ALONG THE BEACH AT ORCHID ISLAND

PRESERVES

Orchid Island

In bits and pieces over 20 miles of coastline along SR A1A from Melbourne Beach to Wabasso Beach, **Archie Carr National Wildlife Refuge** (772- 562-3909 x275; www.fws.gov/archiecarr) protects the most significant sea turtle nesting ground in the United States. More than 25 percent of all loggerhead sea turtles and 35 percent of all green sea turtles return to this shoreline to nest. Named for University of Florida zoologist and conservationist Archie Carr, the refuge seeks to protect a total of 900 acres of coastal scrub and untrammeled beachfront for sea turtle nesting. Visitors are welcome to enter at adjacent beachfront park access points and walk the shoreline; turtle nests are marked—don't disturb them and don't disturb any nesting turtles you might encounter.

At **Sebastian Inlet State Park**, 9700 South A1A, Melbourne Beach, free guided sea turtle walks are offered in June and July, 9–midnight; advance reservations required (recommended up to a month in advance; phone 321-984-4852). Bring water, comfortable shoes and clothes, and bug repellent.

& ♪ In 1903 President Theodore Roosevelt dedicated **Pelican Island National Wildlife Refuge** (772-562-3909 x275; www.fws.gov/pelicanisland), SR A1A, 3.5 miles north of CR 510, as a preserve for a breeding colony of endangered brown pelicans, creating the nation's first National Wildlife Refuge. The preserve now encompasses 500 acres of impoundments along the Indian River Lagoon as well as 2.2-acre Pelican Island, which can be seen from an observation tower at the end of the Centennial Trail. The trail was the first of new visitor improvements added for the preserve's centennial. (Previously, birders had to visit by boat.) Two multiuse trails loop 2.5 miles each around the impoundments, perfect for a bike ride or a long walk, where, on my very first visit, I saw roseate spoonbills in the trees. The Centennial Trail is wheelchair accessible and another great birding spot. Open 7:30 AM–sunset daily. Free.

Protecting 336 acres along the Indian River Lagoon, **Oslo Riverfront Conservation Area** (561-778-7200), Oslo Rd., just east of US 1, is a haven for botanical diversity, with some of the tallest wild coffee you'll ever see and more than 20 rare species of plants, including Simpson's stopper, coral-root orchid, and whisk fern. Bromeliads grow densely on every tree in the hammock. Three miles worth of nature trails wind through the preserve, leading you to surprises such as an overlook on a mangrove-lined lagoon and to a historic coquina quarry. Open sunrise–sunset daily; free. Informative guided walks are offered Wednesday and Sunday at 9 AM; meet at the park entrance.

WILD PLACES

Fellsmere

With nearly 22,000 acres straddling the C-54 canal and waterfront along the St. Sebastian River, **St. Sebastian River Preserve State Park** (321-953-5004; www.floridastateparks.org/stsebastian/default.cfm), 1000 Buffer Preserve Dr., spills across Brevard and Indian River Counties and offers outdoor activities that include nearly 60 miles of equestrian trails with primitive campsites, overlooks on the canal for manatee watching,, and nature trails. A visitors center (open 10 AM–4:30 PM Fri.–Sun., 8 AM–5 PM Mon.–Fri.) is located off CR 507 north of Fellsmere.

South Indian River County

Protecting 54,000 acres along the chain of lakes that is the lower St. Johns River, **Blue Cypress Conservation Area** (321-676-6614) has access points off Blue Cypress Lake Rd. and CR 507 north of SR 60. Most folks come here for the fishing, but you can launch a canoe or kayak and experience what Florida looked like centuries ago along these cypress-lined waterways. Access to miles of levees for birding is best from Blue Cypress Recreation Area off CR 507, where there are also several primitive campsites.

An excellent place for birding, **Fort Drum Marsh Conservation Area** (321-676-6614 or 386-329-4404), 9.2 miles east of Florida's Turnpike Yeehaw Junction exit along SR 60, is a 21,000-acre wilderness that encompasses the headwaters of the St. Johns River. Birders might see crested caracara, sandhill cranes, wood storks, bald eagles, or wild turkey. White-tailed deer and feral hogs are also common here. The preserve offers a day's worth of walking along the levees, as well as two developed hiking trails

SEA TURTLE NEST

Sandra Friend

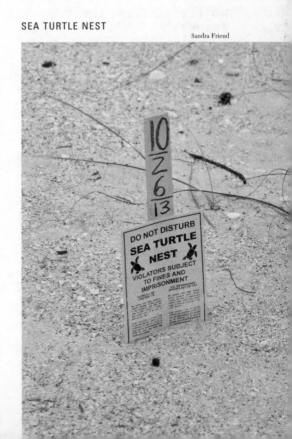

with primitive campsites; the Hog Island Trail has a gorgeous boardwalk bridging the "mainland" with Hog Island through a mysterious cypress swamp. The preserve also offers fishing, canoeing, bicycling, and seasonal hunting. Free. Located between State Road (SR) 60 and the Florida Turnpike, approximately 20 miles west of Vero Beach. Access from I-95, exit at SR 60, go west on SR 60 to the "20-Mile Bend." Access is located 10.9 miles west of County Road 512 and 10 miles east of Yeehaw Junction.

✳ Lodging

CAMPGROUNDS If you have a boat or canoe, bring a tent and sufficient fresh water and claim one of the hundreds of **uninhabited islands in the Indian River Lagoon** as your own for the night; leave-no-trace rules apply. For details contact **Sebastian Inlet State Park** (772-589-9659), 9700 S SR A1A, Melbourne Beach. Fees for parking and boat launching.

Landlubbers can head to one of the sites at **Sebastian Inlet State Park** (see *Beaches*) Book sites through 1-800-326-3521.

HOTELS, MOTELS, AND RESORTS

Sebastian 32958
Settle into the island mood at **Captain Hiram's Resort** (772-388-8588; www.hirams.com), 1580 US 1, part of a tropical resort complex along the Indian River Lagoon at Marker 66. Adding

to the relaxed atmosphere, there's a room to please everyone—from motel rooms to Jacuzzi suites to mini suites with wet bars, $120 and up.

A quiet, old-fashioned place, the **Sandrift Motel** (772-589-4546), 14415 US 1, has basic motel rooms and efficiencies, at reasonable rates ($55–75). You'll appreciate the sparkling pool and the Marker I restaurant just a few steps away.

Vero Beach 32963
Adding a little Miami chic to quiet, conservative Vero Beach, Gloria Estefan, a part-time resident of the area, opened the new $50 million hotel, **Costa d'Este Beach Resort** (772-562-9919; www.costadeste.com), 3244 Ocean Dr. Modern and stylish, the resort offers 90 guest rooms and four suites ($189–479), and **Oriente** (772-410-0100), a Cuban restaurant and bar.

The Driftwood Inn (772-231-0550; www.thedriftwood.com), 3150 Ocean Dr., is the same beachfront hotel built by Waldo Sexton in 1935 and includes an oceanfront restaurant, the Ocean Grill. Now a time-share resort, hotel rooms are still available ($90–120).

The Caribbean Court Hotel (772-231-7211; www.thecaribbeancourt.com), 1605 Ocean Dr., is a tropical-themed, pet friendly hotel across Ocean Drive from the beach. Rooms decorated with antiques ($139–239) complement the French cuisine at the hotel restaurant, Maison Martinique.

With a tropical setting and wrought-

COSTA D'ESTE HOTEL, VERO BEACH

Trish Riley

iron balcony railings, the **Sea Turtle Inn** (772-234-0788 or 1-877-998-8785; www.seaturtleinn.net), 835 Azalea Ln., offers a comfortable home away from home, just steps from the Ocean Drive shopping district and the beach. Accommodations include efficiencies and poolside apartments ($99–215).

✳ Where to Eat

DINING OUT

Vero Beach

Excellent food and an oceanfront view—what more can you ask for? The **Ocean Grill** (772-231-5409; www.ocean-grill.com), 1050 Sexton Plaza, is relaxing and satisfying. Dating from 1949, the restaurant sports unique decor with pioneer Waldo Sexton's imprint. Sexton, earning a good living as a citrus agriculturalist, took advantage of the depression to gather up priceless antiques at Palm Beach auctions, offering rolls of silver dollars for leftovers at auction's end. Not a bad strategy for anyone left with money during the current era! Each evening, several fresh catches are offered, broiled, Cajun, grilled, or fried. Roast duckling is a house favorite; other specialties include the coquilles St. Jacques, creamy and brimming with mushrooms and crab. Dinner with a glass of wine from their extensive list will set you back $30–50 a person, but the experience is well worth it. In between lunch and dinner, bar patrons can enjoy a tasty bleu cheese dip with crackers and beer.

Oriente (772-410-0100), at the Costa d'Este Beach Resort, 3244 Ocean Dr., brings owner Gloria Estefan's native Cuban cuisine to Vero Beach along with live music a few nights each week. Sample ropa veija, braised skirt steak with tomatoes and *sofrito* (a spicy blend of peppers), or ceviche vegetariano, grilled hearts of palm, baby bella

mushroom, with asparagus, avocado, pico de gallo (fresh salsa), with oregano citrus dressing. Sip Cuban coffee or mojitos at the daily happy hour (4:30–6:30 PM). Reservations recommended.

EATING OUT

Fellsmere

Worth driving out of your way for, **Marsh Landing** (772-571-8622), 44 N Broadway St., is a classic Florida Cracker restaurant serving up swamp cabbage, fried green tomatoes, and "swamp critters" such as gator, frog's legs, and catfish. You can't miss this historic building in downtown—it was the land office during the 1920s boom. Open for breakfast, lunch, and dinner daily; entrées $10 and up.

Sebastian

When on the sea, eat more seafood! **Captain Hiram's Restaurant** (772-589-4345; www.captainhirams.com), 1606 N Indian River Dr., offers a delectable selection of the finest around, from fresh oysters to half-pound broiled lobster tail to "angry" Dungeness crab and crab-stuffed baked shrimp. You won't go away hungry! Landlubbers can enjoy char-grilled rib eye and jerked chicken breast; there's a kid's menu, too. Serving lunch and dinner; entrées $13–25.

Vero Beach

From its humble beginning as an ice cream parlor in 1945, the **Patio Restaurant** (772-563-2844), 1103 21st St., has become one of the best-loved landmarks in Vero Beach. The stunning wrought iron and tile throughout the restaurant is centuries old and was imported from Europe by Addison Mizner, the architect renowned for his work throughout Palm Beach. And what's the connection? Credit Waldo Sexton, the restaurant's founder and 1920s boom developer, for piling up "old discards" such as tiles and chandeliers from various ritzy buildings in "the patio." These pieces were incorporated into the restaurant's decor in 1959. The restaurant was closed and renovated in 2008. Light and color play through the stained-glass panels above the French doors. It is a place to savor dinner, to enjoy the experience. The menu focuses on fresh local seafood and prime cuts of steak ($8 and up), but there are also pizzas, pastas, and Sunday brunch with mimosas for $20.

Dockside Grille (772-569-6865), 41 Palm Pointe, offers a lunch and dinner of seafood, burgers, and steaks from $8 and up.

✱ Selective Shopping

Vero Beach

An array of eclectic gifts, perhaps mirroring the art collection on display from the town's founder, is available in the gift shop of the Ocean Grill restaurant, 1050 Sexton Plaza.

A stroll away, you'll find fine men's wear at **G.T. Rhodes** (772-231-6424, www.gtrhodes.com), 1008 Beachland Blvd., and around the corner a lady's "chic boutique," at Blondies on the Ocean (772-231-4444), 3300 Ocean Dr.

If you're looking for that perfect kayak, look no further than **Indian River Kayak & Canoe** (772-569-5757; www .paddleflorida.com), 3435 Aviation Blvd., one of the largest paddle-sports outfitters on the Atlantic Coast, with "demo days" the first Sunday of each month.

With an extensive selection of children's books housed in a separate building with a teen reading loft (772-569-6650), the **Vero Beach Book Center** (772-569-2050; www.vero beachbookcenter.com), 2145 Indian River Blvd., is one of the larger independent bookstores in the state and stocks an excellent array of new books for grown-ups, too. Author events are frequent and feature top Florida authors. If you're a bibliophile, you won't want to miss this store!

ST. LUCIE COUNTY

In the late 1800s, more than 20 small settlements existed along the Treasure Coast, and it's along those same barrier islands and the Indian River Lagoon that you'll find the beauty of St. Lucie County. Named by Spanish explorers in the 1560s, the region was once populated by the Ais and Jeaga, indigenous hunters and gatherers whose people eventually died off after exposure to European illnesses. During the Second Seminole War in the 1830s, the First Artillery chose a high bluff about 4 miles south of the inlet to build a blockhouse they called Fort Pierce, in honor of their commander. The city of **Fort Pierce** is one of the oldest on Florida's South Atlantic coast, incorporated in 1901. Once known for its fisheries and pineapple farms, Fort Pierce evolved into one of Florida's 1920s boomtowns, which its architecture showcases today after successful downtown redevelopment efforts.

Once an outpost of unspoiled beaches and quiet villages, St. Lucie County has exploded in population growth over the past decade, changing the face that visitors see—especially along Florida's Turnpike and I-95 around **Port St. Lucie.** Where citrus groves and pine forests once stretched to the horizon, now there are residential communities. The western part of the county is still citrus and ranching country. Called the "Grapefruit Capital of the World," the county still leads all others in Florida in citrus production.

ARCHITECTURAL DETAIL AT FORT PIERCE
Trish Riley

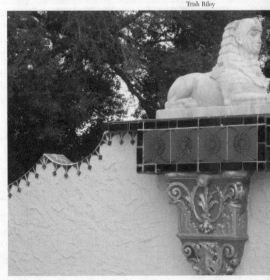

GUIDANCE St. Lucie County Tourism (1-800-344-TGIF; www .visitstluciefla.com), 2300 Virginia Ave., Fort Pierce 34982, and the **St. Lucie County Chamber of Commerce** (772-468-9152; www.StLucieChamber .org), 482 N. Indian River Dr., Fort Pierce 34950, and 1850 Fountainview Blvd., Port St. Lucie 34986 (772-340-1333), can provide more information about the area.

GETTING THERE *By car:* Use **I-95** or **US 1** to reach Fort Pierce, St. Lucie, Port St. Lucie, and Jensen Beach. **SR 70** connects Florida's Turnpike with Fort Pierce.

By air: **Palm Beach International Airport** (see *North Palm Beach County*) is the closest major airport.

GETTING AROUND *By car:* A car is necessary for visiting the county. Most services are along US 1 and SR A1A, and along SR 70 in Fort Pierce.

MEDICAL EMERGENCIES In Fort Pierce head for **Lawnwood Regional Medical Center** (772-220-6866; www.lawnwoodmed.com), 1700 S 23rd St. In Port St. Lucie your nearest emergency room is at **St. Lucie Medical Center** (772-335-1405; www.stluciemed.com), 1800 SE Tiffany Ave.

✳ To See

ARCHAEOLOGICAL SITES At **Spruce Bluff Preserve** (772-462-2526; www .stlucieco.gov/erd/spruce-bluff/ais.htm), Peru St. and Dar Ln., Port St. Lucie, follow the **Ais Mound Trail** to discover a midden from the ancient Ais culture of southeast Florida. The mound is 20 feet high and nearly 180 feet in diameter and is now topped with large trees.

ART GALLERIES Founded in 1961, **The A. E. "Bean" Backus Gallery** (772-465-0630; www.backusgallery.com), 500 N Indian River Dr., Fort Pierce, focuses on the work of Backus, whose lush impressionist Florida landscapes (1940s–1960s) captured the wild nature of the state's rugged beauty. Backus had many students over the years, and Alfred Hair, a talented African American protégé, brought Backus's inspiration to a group of fellow landscape painters now honored as the Highwaymen, who sold their impressionist landscapes out of the backs of their cars. Perched on the banks of the Indian River Lagoon, the 4,000-square-foot gallery showcases a portion of their permanent collection of Backus's work, plus several galleries displaying the works of other Florida artists. The gallery is open 10 AM–4 PM Tues.–Sat., noon–4 PM Sun., except during the summer months, when visits are by appointment. Free.

BASEBALL Spring training heats up in late February when the **New York Mets** arrive at Tradition Field Stadium (772-871-2115; www.traditionfield.com), 525 NW Peacock Blvd., Port St. Lucie, their 100-acre facility with a 7,300-seat stadium. The minor league St. Lucie Mets take the field in early April. Call ahead for tickets or buy them online.

HISTORIC SITES Downtown Fort Pierce boasts a broad range of classic Florida architecture, from Cracker homes to late-19th-century revival businesses and Spanish Mission buildings from the 1920s. Stop at the visitors center located in the **1910 Seven Gable House,** 482 Indian River Dr., to pick up walking-tour information. In 1875 the **P. P. Cobb Building,** 408 N Indian River Dr., served as one of the first trading posts along the Cracker Trail. This cypress-sided building is still used for retail businesses today. Built in 1925, the **historic City Hall,** 315 Ave. A, was in use until 1972; preservationists saved it from the wrecking ball, and it is now used for banquet rentals and office space. Visited by stars of the silver screen such as Sally Rand and Tom Mix, the **1923 Sunrise Theatre** (772-461-4775; www.sunrisetheatre.com), 210 S Depot Dr., was once the largest vaudeville theater on Florida's east coast. After extensive renovations, it recently reopened as the Theatre for the Performing Arts with regularly scheduled shows. The city itself was named after Fort Pierce, built by the U.S. Army during the Second Seminole War on the high bluff overlooking the Indian River Lagoon; a historic plaque at the site is all that remains to commemorate the spot. While passing through the historic center of town, a mix today of crumbling residences and sparkling Mediterranean architecture, I spotted a flock of peacocks strutting across the road as if they owned the town.

MUSEUMS

Fort Pierce
Explore the region's maritime past at the **St. Lucie County Historical Museum** (772-462-1795; www.stlucieco.gov), 414 Seaway Dr., where the wreck of the 1715 Spanish fleet comes alive in the Galleon Room, brimming with replicas of gold and silver coins, pottery and household items. In addition to the important Harry Hill photographic collection, which documents St. Lucie County between the 1880s and 1920s, the museum has a fire house with antique engines, a Seminole encampment, artifacts from the original Fort Pierce, and a 1907 settler's home. Open 10 AM–4 PM Tues.–Sat. Fee.

North Hutchinson Island
In the birthplace of the navy demolition teams, where better a museum to honor them? The National Navy **UDT-SEAL Museum** (772-595-5845; www.navyseal museum.com), 3300 N SR A1A, recounts the courage and history of navy frogmen, SEALS, and underwater demolition teams through well-interpreted artifacts and timeline based exhibits. Open 10 AM–4 PM Tues.–Sat., noon–4 PM Sun.; also Mon. 10 AM–4 PM Jan.–Apr. Fee $6 adults, $3 children ages 6–12. Free for members, group rates available.

✳ To Do

BOATING Located downtown, the **Fort Pierce City Marina** (772-464-1245 or 1-800-619-1780; www.fort piercecitymarina.com), One Ave. A, offers about 150 slips on the Indian River Lagoon, with fishing and sailing charters available dockside.

DIVING Dixie Divers Southeast Diving Institute (561-461-4488), 1717 S US 1, Fort Pierce, offers a full range of dive classes, including dive master. Certified scuba divers will want to head for **Fort Pierce Inlet State Park** (see *Beaches*), 905 Shorewinds Dr., Fort Pierce (772-468-3985), to check out a reef just 100

PEACOCKS STRUTTING THROUGH FORT PIERCE

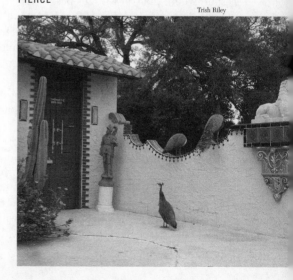

Trish Riley

yards from the beach; diver-down flag required. **Dive Odyssea** (772-460-1771), 621 N Second St., Fort Pierce, for fresh air and instructions on where best to charter a boat and head to the offshore reefs and wrecks.

DRIVING TOURS Celebrating the life of one of Florida's most important folklorists, the new Zora Neale Hurston "Dust Tracks" Heritage Trail starts at the Zora Neale Hurston Branch Library, 3008 Ave. D, Fort Pierce, and leads you on a journey through the novelist's many connections to Fort Pierce. There are eight stops along the way, with detailed interpretive information. Trail information can be found online at www.st-lucie.lib.fl.us/zora. For more information, call 772-462-1618.

ECOTOURS

Fort Pierce
Departing from the Fisherman's Wharf Marina, **Florida DolphinWatch** (772-466-4660; www.floridadolphinwatch.com) takes you on a narrated journey through the Indian River Lagoon, where dolphin sightings are frequent and the birding is superb. You'll tour both the fringe of Fort Pierce Inlet State Park and Jack Island Preserve. Reservations required; call for cruise schedule and current pricing. Also offers boat rentals and charters.

Port St. Lucie
River Lilly River Cruises (772-489-8344; www.riverlillycruises.com) offer two nature cruises from November through mid-June. The Eco Tour explores the North Fork of the St. Lucie River Aquatic Preserve, a beautiful backwater lined with palms and dense natural foliage. Watch for alligators, turtles, and birds, with occasional sightings of manatees and river otters. These tours launch from River Park Marina, 500 SE Prima Vista Blvd., in Port St. Lucie. A Nature Cruise to Bird Island launches from Veterans Memorial Park at Rivergate, 2200 SE Veterans Memorial Pkwy., in Port St. Lucie. Cruises are about $20 per person; call for schedule and current pricing; reservations required.

GAMING If you've not experienced the high speed game of jai-alai, a Basque sport where the ball whizzes past at speeds of up to 175 miles per hour, stop in at **Fort Pierce Jai-Alai** (1-800-JAI-ALAI or 1-800-524-2524), Kings Hwy., near Florida's Turnpike and I-95, Fort Pierce, to watch the mesmerizing action and, if you're so inclined, to bet on it. The complex includes elegant dining and intertrack wagering as well. Call for schedules; seasonal, running Nov.–Apr.

GOLF Since 1938, the **Indian Hills Golf Course** (772-465-8110), 1600 S Third St., Fort Pierce, has been an important part of the community, challenging golfers with a par 72 course.

HIKING For solitude amid the pines and ponds, head to the **Indrio Savannas** (see *Wild Places*) to stretch your legs; on **Jack Island** (see *Preserves*) work your way through a mangrove puzzle for 5 or more miles. With several miles of trails to choose from, the **Oxbow Eco-Center** in Port St. Lucie (see *Nature Centers*) is a sure bet for an enjoyable morning hike with or without the kids. There are many other public lands in St. Lucie County with shorter nature trails; see *Green Space* for more ideas.

HORSEBACK RIDING Enjoy the exhilaration of riding a horse down the beach along **South Hutchinson Island.** St. Lucie Parks & Recreation (772-489-4386) sponsors this unique experience, and reservations are essential for the 90-minute rides. Rides are typically arranged each Sunday, departing from **Frederick Douglass Memorial Park** (see *Beaches*), and riders must be at least 10 years old.

PADDLING By kayak, the **Indian River Lagoon** is a marvel of wildlife—there is no better way to see manatees and sea turtles up close. Check in at **Dolphin Watch** (see *Ecotours*) for rentals. If you've brought your own, consider a lazy paddle up the **North Fork of the St. Lucie River,** launching from either the Halpatiokee unit of the **St. Lucie Inlet Preserve State Park** (see *Wild Places* in *Martin County*) off US 1 in Port St. Lucie (where a handcart is a must to get down the 0.5-mile, often soggy nature trail to the dock) or from the more easily accessible **White City Park** (561-462-1521), 1801 W Midway Rd., Fort Pierce, where a paddle south lets you admire the moss-draped live oaks along the shoreline and explore the cul-de-sacs and oxbows where manatees hide in the wintertime.

SURFING For surfers in the know, **Fort Pierce Inlet State Park** (see *Beaches*) is a primo destination on the Treasure Coast. On the north side of the inlet, the North Jetty receives swells from the south and east, and no matter the time of year, the waves appear—best caught at high tide. The downside? The crowds. Hit the surf early on weekdays for the prime peaks.

WILDLIFE & MARINELIFE VIEWING

Fort Pierce
The world-renowned **Harbor Branch Oceanographic Institution** (772-465-2400; www.fau.edu/hboi/), 5600 N US 1, is the home port of Johnson-Sea-Link submersibles and offers lectures, trips, and tours, many open to the public. Scientists here explore the seas, discovering applications for medicine and studying environmental impacts on reefs and sea life. Exhibits are throughout the campus; call ahead for lecture and tour information.

✔ At the **Manatee Observation & Education Center** (772-466-1600; www .manateecenter.com), 480 N Indian River Dr., see manatees up close along Moore's Creek, a favored gathering spot. An observation tower provides a view from above, and the exhibition hall, complete with movies, will further your knowledge of these gentle giants. Open 10 AM–5 PM Tues.–Sat., noon–4 PM Sun. (Oct.–June); 10 AM–5 PM Thurs.–Sat. (July–Sept.). Fee.

✔ Adjacent to the **St. Lucie County Historical Museum** (see *Museums*), the **Smithsonian Marine Ecosystems Exhibit at the St. Lucie County Marine Center** (772-462-FISH; www.sms.si.edu/SMEE/smeehome.htm), 420 Seaway Dr., shows off a 3,300-gallon living coral reef and other living exhibits of Florida's coastal habitats, including mangrove forests and seagrass communities. These are not your typical aquarium exhibits—they are working models of the habitats, with interaction between all organisms living in each community. Open 10 AM–4 PM Tues.–Sat., noon–4 PM Sun. Fee. Free on Tues.

✳ Green Space

BEACHES

North Hutchinson Island

Surf's up at **Fort Pierce Inlet State Park** (772-468-3985), 905 Shorewinds Dr., one of the best places to hang 10 along this stretch of coastline. The 0.5-mile beach is popular for swimming, snorkeling, and sunbathing, and Dynamite Point was a training site for navy frogmen during World War II. Add picnic tables and nature trails, and it's a great family destination. Open 8 AM–sunset daily; fee. Nearby **Pepper Park,** north on SR A1A, provides a launch point north of the inlet for snorkelers and scuba divers to explore Spanish galleons wrecked in the 1700s, just yards offshore; free.

South Hutchinson Island

Driving south from Fort Pierce down SR A1A, you'll find many beach access points provided by **St. Lucie Parks & Recreation** (561-462-1521). Just 4 miles south is **Frederick Douglass Memorial Park,** 3500 S SR A1A, with picnic pavilions, bathrooms and showers, lifeguards, and a wheelchair-accessible beach crossover. Enjoy more of a wilderness feel at **Blind Creek Beach,** 5500 S SR A1A, just north of the nuclear power plant. South of the plant is **Walton Rocks Beach,** 6501 S SR A1A, with restrooms and picnic tables and a rocky reef exposed at low tide. **Herman's Bay,** 7800 S SR A1A, has paved parking and dune crossovers. Finally, **Waveland Beach,** 10350 S SR A1A, offers another large oceanfront park with lifeguards, restrooms and showers, a concession stand, and a boardwalk. One thing to be aware of is that a nuclear power plant sits on the waterfront here. Some families may prefer to explore beaches farther north or south along the coast.

BOTANICAL GARDENS Wander the garden rooms at **Heathcote Botanical Gardens** (772-464-4672; www.heathcotebotanicalgardens.org), 210 Savannah Rd., Fort Pierce, a collection of formal specialty gardens including an herb garden, a reflection garden, a palm and cycad walk, and more. Their gift shop offers local art, Florida gardening and plant books, and children's toys and trinkets. The gardens and shop are open 9 AM–5 PM Tues.–Sat. year-round and 1 PM–5 PM Sun. Nov.–Apr. Admission $6 for adults, $5 for seniors, and $2 for children. Guided tours available.

NATURE CENTER ♿ ✿ The **Oxbow Eco-Center** (772-785-5833; www.stlucie co.gov/erd/oxbow), 5400 NE St. James Dr., Port St. Lucie, is a 225-acre preserve along the North Fork of the St. Lucie River with trails radiating out from the nature center. Some of the trails are wheelchair-accessible boardwalks, but most take you out into the wilds of pine flatwoods, scrub, hardwood hammocks, and tall bluffs and swamps along the river. Wildlife is abundant; bring your camera! Guided walks available. Open dawn–dusk daily. Free.

PARKS

Fort Pierce

Offering a large campground with a view of the massive freshwater savannas along St. Lucie's coast, **Savannas Recreation Area** (772-464-1765 or 1-800-789-5776; www.stlucieco.gov/parks), 1400 Midway Rd., has freshwater fishing, nature trails, canoe rentals, and boat ramps. Fee.

Port St. Lucie

⚓ In a forest along the C-24 Canal, **Oak Hammock Park,** 1982 SW Villanova Rd., has two pleasant nature trails, with the Oak Trail meandering through a grove of ancient live oaks. There is a fishing boardwalk, picnic tables, and a playground as well. Free.

PRESERVES

North Hutchinson Island

Just 1.5 miles north on SR A1A from Fort Pierce Inlet, **Fort Pierce Inlet State Park** (772-468-3985; www.floridastateparks.org/fortpierceinlet) offers a place for solitude and the opportunity to watch ospreys in graceful flight above the Indian River Lagoon. A narrow bridge connects the parking area with 5 miles of trails for hiking and bicycling through mangrove-lined impoundments; an observation tower provides a bird's-eye view of surrounding islands. Open 8–sunset daily. Free.

South Hutchinson Island

⚓ An interpretive trail introduces you to the coastal dune habitat at **Ocean Bay Natural Area**, SR A1A, 4.5 miles north of Jensen Beach Blvd., where you'll tunnel through dense sea grapes, gumbo limbo, and strangler fig on a 15-minute walk. Free.

WILD PLACES

Indrio

Some of the area's best bird-watching can be found at **Indrio Savannas Natural Area** (772-462-2526), Tozour Rd. and US 1, where marsh impoundments attract a variety of wading birds in this 423-acre preserve, and Florida scrub jays are commonly seen in the scrub forest. More than 5 miles of hiking trails meander through pine flatwoods, open prairies, and along the impoundments. Open sunrise–sunset daily. Free.

Port St. Lucie

⚓ Stretching more than 10 miles from Fort Pierce to Jensen Beach, **Savannas Preserve State Park** (772-398-2779; www.floridastateparks.org/savannas), 9551 Gumbo Limbo Ln., protects the longest remaining freshwater savanna on Florida's east coast. Teeming with wildlife, these marshes are less than 3 miles from the sea.

✳ Lodging

CAMPGROUNDS

Fort Pierce 34982

Hang out on the wild side at **Savannas Recreation Area** (772-464-7855), 1400 Midway Rd., a county park on the western shore of Savannas Preserve State Park, where tent camping is available on unimproved sites, and there are improved sites for RVs and campers. Launch a kayak into the savannas, or walk along their edge on a nature trail to an observation tower.

Port St. Lucie 34952

The **Port St. Lucie RV Resort** (772-337-3340 or 1-877-405-2333; www.portstluciervresort.com), 3703 SE Jennings Rd., offers RV and camping spaces for $37 nightly. Most visitors are in for the season. Enjoy an air-conditioned clubhouse with big-screen TV, fax, and pool table, or lounge around the heated pool.

HOTELS, MOTELS, AND RESORTS

Fort Pierce 34946

& 🐾 "❙" Kick back and relax in a pleasant island-themed room at the **Fountain Hotel & Resort** (772-466-7041; www.fountainresort.net), 4889 N US 1, an intimate hotel with a heated pool and spa as the centerpiece of the grounds. Each room, suite, or efficiency ($79–109 May 1–Dec. 15 and $119–159 Dec. 16–Apr. 30) offers wireless Internet, satellite TV, and DVD players. Guests also enjoy a complimentary continental breakfast.

South Hutchinson Island 34950

Just 2 blocks from the beach at Fort Pierce Inlet, the **Dockside Harbor Light Inn** (772-468-3555 or 1-800-286-1745; www.docksideinn.com), 1160 Seaway Dr., offers a variety of well-kept rooms in a lush tropical setting. Guests have access to two heated pools and a whirlpool as well as fishing piers and dockage. Rates range from $70 off-season, $79 in-season for a standard room to $255 for the Presidential Waterfront Suite.

✳ Where to Eat

DINING OUT

Fort Pierce

Kick back along the Indian River at the original **Tiki Bar & Restaurant** (772-461-0880; www.originaltikibar.com), 2 Ave. A, an open-air chickee overlooking the Indian River where the music draws a crowd, and despite the Jimmy Buffet casual atmosphere, the food is top-notch, from Florida lobster tail to Black Angus steaks. Dinner entrées $15 and up.

Port St. Lucie

For a taste of the Caribbean, try **The Calypso Pot** (772-878-5044), 354 S Port St. Lucie Blvd., an authentic island restaurant serving curries and roti, with Trinidad specialties such as calypso rice, soursop, peanut punch, and homemade ginger beer. Entrées $3–12. Open for breakfast, lunch, and dinner.

The parking lot was packed at **Norris' Famous Place for Ribs** (772-464-7000; www.norrisribs.com), 6598 S US 1, and from the aroma inside, it was no surprise, since they serve award-winning baby back ribs, prime rib, and more to satisfy every meat lover, with entrées starting at $8. Open daily for lunch and dinner.

✳ Special Events

First Friday: Held the first Friday of every month. **Friday Fest** (772-466-3880; www.MainStreetFortPierce.org), held in downtown Fort Pierce from 5:30 to 8:30 PM, is the biggest street festival along the Treasure Coast, attracting more than 5,000 people each month for live music, food and drinks, and the arts. Free.

MARTIN COUNTY

Stretching from the Atlantic Ocean to Lake Okeechobee, the southernmost county of the Treasure Coast encompasses a mix of millionaires' mansions and orange groves, historic towns and burgeoning subdivisions, pine forests and beautiful beaches.

The region's communities have a long and storied history. Long before the first Europeans reached Florida's shores, the Ais, Jeaga, and Tequesta people lived along the region's waterways. Around 1565, Spanish explorers sailed down the Indian River looking for shipwreck survivors and setting up missions to convert the natives. They built a fort at the mouth of a large river and called it St. Lucie.

In 1696 the British ship *Reformation* sank along **Jupiter Island,** and its Quaker survivors, including Jonathan Dickinson and his wife, were found by the natives and spent six weeks working their way up the coast to St. Augustine. His diary serves as the only English-language record of interactions with these people. Today, Jupiter Island is most notable for its famous residents and their grand homes along the Indian River Lagoon—hometown boy Burt Reynolds among them. It's an enclave where the super rich enjoy the fruits of their labor.

James Hutchinson received a land grant from the Spanish governor of Florida in 1811. After losing crops and cattle to Seminole raiders, he petitioned for and received the barrier island that now bears his name, **Hutchinson Island,** and moved there, where pirates eventually attacked his plantation. In the 1860s Union gunboats and Confederate blockade runners played a game of cat and mouse around the islands and lagoons along the coast as the Confederates attempted to bring in supplies from the Bahamas.

By 1815 the government of Spain handed out land grants in the **Hobe Sound** area, where homesteaders started farms in the piney woods. A century later, the Olympia Improvement Corporation moved in and planned to turn the settlement into a Greek-themed village where movies could be made. Like most of the 1920s boom projects, this one collapsed after the 1928 hurricane. In the 1940s the army opened Camp Murphy as a training station for soldiers to learn a new technology—radar. The pine hills where Camp Murphy sat along US 1 were turned over to the state after the base was decommissioned and became Jonathan Dickinson State Park.

A Danish immigrant, John Laurence Jensen, arrived along the Indian River in 1881 and established a pineapple plantation around which the town of **Jensen Beach** grew. With the arrival of Henry Flagler's Florida East Coast Railroad in

1894, the ready markets for pineapples and citrus drove the economy. By 1895 Jensen was the "Pineapple Capital of the World," shipping more than a million boxes of pineapples each June and July. Fish houses opened along the Indian River for packing the sea's bounty.

The settlement that sprung up around the railroad in the 1880s was first dubbed Potsdam by a Dutch settler and was later renamed **Stuart** after Homer Hine Stuart Jr., a pineapple grower. In the early 1900s the Ashley Gang, a family of outlaws who lived in the south part of the county, terrorized Stuart with frequent robberies until a sheriff gunned them down in Sebastian in 1925. During the 1920s, the boom brought many new residents to the city and a great deal of new construction, shown in the architecture of the fine historic downtown.

With the railroad came tourists, and competition for them. In the early 1920s S. Davies Warfield, a Baltimore banker, bought up large tracts of land in the mostly uninhabited western reaches of the region and planned **Indiantown,** with its centerpiece his fine hotel, the Seminole Inn. His niece Wallis Warfield Simpson attended the grand opening; later in life, she became the Duchess of Windsor.

By 1925 residents became fed up with high taxes and lobbied Governor John Martin to allow them to secede from Palm Beach County. The governor showed as the guest of honor for the May 29, 1925, celebration that named the county in his honor. Stuart became the county seat. Today's Stuart is a mecca for sport fishing, and this gem of the Treasure Coast remains an undiscovered jewel that you'll enjoy exploring.

GUIDANCE The **Martin County Tourism Development Council** (772-288-5901; www.martin.fl.us), 435 SE Flagler Ave., Stuart, SR 34994, can provide you with more information about the area.

GETTING THERE *By car:* Use **Florida's Turnpike** to reach Stuart, and **I-95** for Jensen Beach, Palm City, Stuart, and Hobe Sound.

By air: **Palm Beach International Airport** (see *North Palm Beach County*) is the closest major airport.

GETTING AROUND *By car:* A car is necessary for visiting the county. Most services are along **US 1** and **SR A1A.** US 1 passes through all of the county's coastal towns. Cove Rd. and Bridge Rd. connect I-95 with US 1, Bridge Rd. leads from Hobe Sound to SR A1A on Jupiter Island, and **SR 76** heads west from Stuart to Indiantown.

MEDICAL EMERGENCIES Emergency-room care is available at **Martin Memorial Medical Center** (772-287-5200), 200 SE Hospital Ave., Stuart.

✳ To See

ARCHAEOLOGICAL SITES At **Indian Riverside Park** (561-221-1418), Palmer Ave. and Indian River Dr., Jensen Beach, most visitors are there for the pier, the riverside walkway, and the beautiful pavilion where you can sit and watch the sunrise. But this park also contains a large midden known as Mount Elizabeth and was the site of a village during the Late Archaic and early St. Johns periods, circa 1000 B.C. to A.D. 1. Open sunrise–sunset daily. Free.

Hobe Sound

Make an appointment to visit the **Midtown Payson Galleries** (772-546-6600), 11870 SE Dixie Hwy., to view the varied work of artists such as Cynthia Knott, Richard Mayhew, and William Thon.

Stuart

Open to a wide range of artists, the **Courthouse Cultural Center** (772-288-2542; www.martinarts.org), 80 SE Ocean Blvd., features installations overseen by the Martin Arts Council. Many of these are juried shows of local art, and exhibits change every six weeks or so.

At the **Geoffrey Smith Gallery** (772-221-8031; www.geoffreysmith.com), 47 W Osceola St., marvel at the bronze-cast sculptures of one of Florida's top sculptors, Geoffrey C. Smith. His work captures the beauty of South Florida's wildlife.

For more than 30 years, they've been throwing clay at the **Rare Earth Gallery** (772-287-7744; www.rareearthgallery.com), 41 SW Flagler Ave. In addition to pottery, the displays feature the work of more than 50 local artists. In winter, 10:30 AM–5:30 PM Mon.–Wed., 10:30 AM–8:30 PM Thurs.–Sat., noon–4 PM Sun. In summer, 10:30 AM–5:30 PM Mon.–Fri.

With more than a thousand original oils on display, the **Stuart Gallery** (772-283-9978), 55 SW Flagler Ave., is bound to have something that fits your home decor. 11 AM–5 PM Mon.–Wed., 11 AM–8 PM Thurs., 11 AM–9 PM Fri., 11 AM–10 PM Sat., noon–5 PM Sun.

HISTORIC SITES

South Hutchinson Island

At the St. Lucie Rocks, shipwrecked sailors swam to shore and safety at a place known to all on the sea—a House of Refuge. A system of these seaside houses ran up and down the Florida coast in the late 1800s, stocked with fresh water and provisions and manned by a lightkeeper. **Gilbert's Bar House of Refuge,** 301 SE MacArthur Blvd. (772-225-1875), is the last remaining of this maritime safety net. Built in 1875, it is the oldest standing structure in the county and contains a museum devoted to the maritime heritage of the region. Open 10 AM–4 PM Mon.–Sat., 1 PM–4 PM Sun. Fee.

Stuart

What is now the **Courthouse Cultural Center** (see *Art Galleries*) has a long and storied history. Built in 1908 as the first schoolhouse in Stuart, the building became the Martin County Courthouse. The staff outgrew the building by 1936, but rather than move, the county applied to the WPA for an addition. Designed by famed architect L. Phillip Clarke, the approved addition incorporates post-Depression art deco elements, including idealistic symbols and inscriptions, cast friezes, and cornices. Nearly demolished in 1989, the building was saved by a group of concerned citizens. Inside the building, the judges' vault, marble staircase, and terrazzo floors were restored, and some of the court's artifacts remain.

MUSEUMS

South Hutchinson Island

Opened by Harmon P. Elliot to honor his father, Sterling, an inventor, the **Elliot**

Museum (772-225-1961), 825 NE Ocean Blvd., celebrates American ingenuity and creativity and boasts a collection of local and Florida history. Open 10 AM–4 PM Mon.–Sat., 1 PM–4 PM Sun. Fee. **Gilbert's Bar House of Refuge** (see *Historic Sites*) sits adjacent.

Stuart

Love boating? Then don't miss the **Maritime & Yachting Museum** (772-692-1234; www.mymflorida.com), 3250 S Kanner Hwy., where volunteers bestow loving care on the restoration of a growing fleet of classic wooden boats, including the *Vintage Rose,* a 1934 Chris-Craft triple-cockpit motorboat; *Caretaker,* a 1950 Century Seamaid with its original engine; and *Annie,* a Bahamas dinghy from the 1950s. Their extensive collection covers not just antique boats but also ship models, maritime artifacts, traditional boatbuilding tools, marine engines, maritime art, and a maritime library. Open 11 AM–4 PM Mon.–Fri. Free

History buffs will enjoy the **Stuart Heritage Museum** (772-220-4600), 161 SW Flagler Ave., for a look back into the county's past, with artifacts, exhibits, and architecture dating from the 1890s. Open 10 AM–3 PM Mon.–Sat. Donation.

WILDLIFE & MARINELIFE VIEWING Explore 40 acres of coastal habitats at the **Florida Oceanographic Coastal Center** (772-225-0505; www.florida oceanographic.org), 890 NE Ocean Blvd., South Hutchinson Island, where mangrove-lined nature trails lead to the Indian River Lagoon. An ideal place to introduce children to marine science, the complex includes a children's activity center and stingray pavilion; plans are under way to add a coastal exhibit hall, and the Treasure Coast Fishing Center, focusing on game fish. Open 10–5 Mon.–Sat., noon–4 PM Sun. Adults $8, children 3–12 $4, younger children are free.

✳ To Do

BOAT TOURS Set sail on **Island Princess Cruises** (772-225-2100; www.island princesscruises.com), The Finest Kind Marina, 3585 SE St. Lucie Blvd., Stuart, to explore the county by water on any of their regularly scheduled cruises, including holiday dinner cruises; the Jupiter Island Luncheon Cruise, which showcases celebrity homes on the Indian River Lagoon; an afternoon cruise on the St. Lucie River; or the Nature Cruise through **St. Lucie Inlet Preserve State Park** (see *Wild Places*), accessible only by boat. Call for fees ($15 and up), reservations, and current schedule, since some cruises are seasonal.

HIKING With more than 20 miles of trails, **Jonathan Dickinson State Park** (see *Parks*) is one of Southeast Florida's top destinations for hikers. But the rest of the county offers some nice trails, too. The delicate coastal scrub at **Seabranch Preserve State Park** (see *Parks*) can only be explored via its hiking trails. **Hawks Bluff** at Jensen Beach in the south end of Savannas Preserve State Park (see *St. Lucie County*) showcases six habitats in less than a mile. For more possibilities see *Green Space.*

PADDLING Jonathan Dickinson State Park (see sidebar opposite *Parks*) is especially popular with paddlers for its access to the wild and scenic Loxahatchee River. For sea kayakers launching from the beaches, call the Florida Oceanographic Society at 772-225-2300 for daily weather information. At Port Salerno, **St. Lucie Inlet Preserve State Park** (see *Wild Places*) can be reached only by boat.

SNORKELING If you've brought your snorkel and fins, don't miss **Bathtub Reef** at Bathtub Reef Park (see *Beaches*), a perfect "starter" snorkel for the young ones because of its shallow, clear, waveless water. The reef is made up of tubes created by millions of tiny worms called *Sabellariid*.

✳ Green Space

BEACHES

Hobe Sound

At the end of Bridge Road, **Hobe Sound Beach** is the easiest-to-access beach in the region, popular for snorkeling and sailboarding. It has lifeguards, a concession stand, a picnic area, and restrooms. At the north end of Jupiter Island is a more remote beach popular with anglers, part of **Hobe Sound National Wildlife Refuge** (see *Wild Places*).

Jupiter Island

For a taste of the unexpected, visit **Blowing Rocks Preserve** (772-744-6668; www.nature.org), 574 S Beach Rd., where you'll find Florida's only sea caves. The barrier island is part of a rocky outcropping of Anastasia limestone that defines portions of the shoreline from Jupiter Island north to Fort Pierce, and here the rocky shelf is tall enough to have wave-sculpted caves inside. At times of high tide and high waves, water spurts out almost 50 feet from natural chimneys in the tops of the caves, hence the name. The caves can be explored only at low tide. A nature center on the Intracoastal side is the focal point of a natural habitat restoration area with trails. Swimming not permitted. Open 9 AM–4:30 PM daily. Beach access passes are $2 per person.

South Hutchinson Island

Cross SR 732 (Jensen Beach Blvd.) to Hutchinson Island to explore Martin County's northerly beaches. At the junction of SR 732 and SR A1A, **Jensen Beach Park** (772-334-3444) is a popular destination with picnic tables and volleyball courts. Head south to encounter a string of varied public beaches. You'll encounter **Chastain Beach** (772-221-1418), guarded only during the season, and the beaches at the tip of the island: **Stuart Beach,** with amenities including a playground and a 250-foot boardwalk, and **Gilbert's Bar House of Refuge** (see *Historic Sites*). Beach access is free at all parks.

NATURE CENTER ✄ The former Jensen Beach Elementary School, built by the WPA in the 1930s, is now the regional **Environmental Studies Center** (772-219-1887; www.esc.sbmc.org), 2900 NE Indian River Dr., Jensen Beach. Used for on-site education for more than 30 years, the facility has a marine life museum and saltwater aquariums. Ideal for family visits, the center is open to the public 9 AM–3 PM Mon.–Fri. during the school year. Free.

PARKS Along the North Fork of the St. Lucie River, **Halpatiokee Regional Park** (772-221-1418), 7645 SE Lost River Rd., Stuart, offers more than just the ball fields you see from the entrance. A paved bike path circles the park, and nature trails meander off into the woods to lead you through thickets of saw palmetto to the river. A canoe launch associated with the park is close to SR 76. Free.

Explore coastal scrub habitat at **Seabranch Preserve State Park** (772-219-1880; www.floridastateparks.org/seabranch), SR A1A, 1 mile south of Cove Rd., Stuart, where on my first visit I encountered both Florida scrub jays and a gopher tortoise while walking the 4.5 miles of hiking trails. Free.

In the middle of downtown Stuart, **Shepards Park**, at the intersection of West Ocean Blvd. and US 1, is the place to watch the sunset over the St. Lucie River along the river walk, or to have a picnic on the river's edge.

WILD PLACES

Hobe Sound

Nearly 1,000 acres of coastal habitats, including dunes and sand pine scrub, comprise **Hobe Sound National Wildlife Refuge** (772-546-6141; www.fws.gov/ hobesound), with the visitors center located 2 miles south of Bridge Road on US 1. A short nature trail loops through the scrub habitat at the visitors center; a separate unit of the refuge protects sea turtle nesting habitat at the north end of Jupiter Island. Summer sea turtle walks are offered June–July; call ahead for reservations. Free.

Jensen Beach

Stretching more than 10 miles from Fort Pierce to Jensen Beach, **Savannas Preserve State Park** (772-398-2779; www.floridastateparks.org/savannas), 9551 Gumbo Limbo Ln., protects the longest remaining freshwater savanna on Florida's east coast. Teeming with wildlife, these marshes are less than 3 miles from the sea. On the south end, access the park off Jensen Beach Road, where entrance is through a picnic and wildlife-watching area. For a short hike encompassing most of the region's ecosystems, stop at the Hawks Bluff entrance off Savannah Road; the 1.1-mile loop trail drops off the dunelike bluffs to follow the water's edge. Free.

Port Salerno

Accessible only by boat, **St. Lucie Inlet Preserve State Park** (772-219-1880; www.floridastateparks.org/stlucieinlet) encompasses a remote barrier island with mangrove forests, tropical hammocks, and a pristine beach favored by sea turtles for nesting in the summer months. Fee.

✳ Lodging

BED & BREAKFASTS

Indiantown 34956

Dating from 1927, the **Seminole Country Inn** (772-597-3777; www .seminoleinn.com), 15885 SW Warfield Blvd., is an important historic landmark from the 1920s land boom that still welcomes guests with the grace befitting Southern tradition. The inn boasts the original pecky cypress ceilings, polished hardwood floors, and brass fixtures enjoyed by those who attended the gala grand opening, including the owner's niece, Wallis Warfield Simpson, the future Dutchess of Windsor. The romantic rooms ($80–125) let you step back in time; snuggle under a quilt beneath a drape of mosquito netting. An in-house café offers lunch for guests and dinners in the grand Windsor Dining Room certain days of the week (see *Eating Out*).

Stuart 34994

Romantic old Key West–style rooms

await at **Inn Shepards Park Bed & Breakfast** (772-781-4244; www.inn shepard.com), 601 SW Ocean Blvd., complete with the swirl of mosquito netting billowing around your comfortable bed. Each of the four well-appointed rooms ($85–195) come with cable TV, DVD players, and soft-as-silk linens and robes. Located right in the downtown historic district, it's a relaxing home away from home with kayaks, bicycles, beach gear, and coolers available for guests.

CAMPGROUNDS

Hobe Sound 33455

Providing the full range of camping amenities, **Jonathan Dickinson State Park** (see sidebar opposite *Parks*) has everything, from 12 riverside cabin rentals to primitive backpacker campsites. The popular River Camp is near the Loxahatchee River and provides shady sites, while Pine Grove Campground, closest to US 1, provides easy access to the front gate if you're using the park as your home base during a vacation week. Pine Grove (undergoing an extreme makeover and slated to reopen Spring 2010) accepts leashed pets, but River Camp does not.

HOTELS, MOTELS, AND RESORTS

Jensen Beach 34957

Colorful and whimsical, the intimate **Four Fish Inn** and Marina (772-334-0936; www.aamarina.com), 2100 NE Indian River Dr., offers your choice of motel rooms, sparkling efficiencies, or single-bedroom apartments with modern kitchens and beautiful waterway views ($75 and up).

& ❦ Amid an 8-acre tropical paradise in the historic district, **River Palm Cottages & Fish Camp** (772-334-0401 or 1-800-305-0511; www.river palmcottages.com), 2325 NE Indian

River Dr., provides an Old Florida–style getaway that's become hard to find along the Atlantic Coast. The old-style bungalows have sparkling modern interiors with bold island decor, tiled floors, and full kitchens. Rates vary according to cottage size and season, starting as low as $120 for a bungalow that sleeps two. The grounds include a pool, putting green, hammocks between the palms, and a private beach on the Indian River Lagoon. Pets are welcome!

❊ Where to Eat

DINING OUT

Stuart

The Ashley Gang, notorious Florida outlaws, knocked off the Bank of Stuart numerous times between 1915 and their demise at the hands of the law nearly a decade later. In a unique nod to this period of Florida history, the **Ashley Restaurant & Bar** (772-221-9476), 61 SW Osceola St., in the historic Bank of Stuart building, offers an elegant place to dine. Tempting appetizers ($8–11) such as crunchy corn oysters and crispy Brie sticks are the warm-up for entrées ($13–25) that include pan-seared salmon, tuna, and chicken breast, and a delightful steamed and grilled vegetable platter for vegetarians. Open for lunch and dinner; entertainment offered most nights until last call.

Renowned for its extensive wine list (more than one hundred selections) and its uniquely Florida cuisine, **The Flagler Grill** (772-221-9517; www .flaglergrill.com), 47 SW Flagler Ave., is a "casual upscale" dining experience, thanks to restaurateurs Paul and Linda Daly, whose background with private clubs and fine wine bring the best to their guests. Savor escargot baked in blue cheese crème fraîche for starters ($11), and move on to a signature entrée such as herb-crusted red snapper ($28) or pan-seared, macadamia-crusted mahimahi with a coconut rum beurre blanc sauce ($27). Open for dinner only, daily during the winter season; reservations suggested.

Start your day early at the **Osceola Street Café** (772-283-6116; www .osceolastreet.com), 26 SW Osceola St., which opens at 6 AM for breakfast with fresh baked bagels, egg sandwiches, and a hot cup of joe. Lunch is served 11 AM–3 PM, including sandwiches and salads ($5–10). Dinner, Wednesday through Saturday, tempts with tapas and entrées ($16–30) prepared with the finest of fresh vegetables and meats, with an ever-changing menu.

EATING OUT
Hobe Sound
Harry & The Natives (772-546-3061; www.harryandthenatives.com), 11910 US 1, has old-fashioned cabins decorated with nautical bits and bobs, a plane crashing through one building, and signs, signs, signs—read 'em all. Opened as the Cypress Cabins and Restaurant on December 7, 1941, it's *the* local hangout, with great seafood and burgers for lunch and dinner, big drinks, and live music most nights. Serving breakfast ($4 and up) 7 AM–11 AM Tuesday through Sunday, with funky fun stuff such as bananas Foster French toast, coconut pancakes, and gator hash. The menus are a hoot, and as for payment, they'll accept "cash, dishwashing, honeydipping, oceanfront homes, table dancing, our gift certificates, Visa, and MasterCard."

Indiantown
The **Seminole Country Inn** (see *Bed & Breakfasts*) asks you to step back in time into the **Windsor Dining Room** (5–8:30 PM Tues.–Sat.), as elegant in its cypress walls and palladium windows as it was 80 years ago, for fine meals prepared "farm fresh," including

Grandma Mimi's fried chicken (that good buttermilk style), country roast pork loin, and fresh catfish ($7–14). A traditional southern country brunch is served every Sunday 9:30 AM–2 PM.

Stuart
I heard it in a hurricane—**Wahoo's on the Waterfront** (772-692-2333; www .wahoosstuart.com), 915 NW Flagler Ave., is a don't-miss stop for fabulous local seafood, with a stunning view of the Intracoastal. The fresh catch comes in daily, including swordfish, cobia, dolphin, and the namesake wahoo, and you can have it fixed up char-grilled, Cajun blackened, sautéed, poached, or Wahoo style with roasted peppers, onions, and garlic. Or choose off the menu with entrées starting at $14. Open for lunch and dinner, with a special Sunday brunch; live music nightly.

BAKERY AND COFFEE SHOP
Stuart
Stop in at **Aunt D's General Store** (772-781-9959), 5 SW Flagler Ave., for a taste of old New England—authentic Italian ice, coffee and cookies, and penny candy.

✱ Entertainment
Stuart
Built as a silent-movie theater in 1926, the **Lyric Theatre** (772-286-7827; www.lyrictheatre.com), 59 SW Flagler Ave., has been beautifully restored to its former glory and is *the* local venue for top-notch concerts, shows, and cultural events.

✱ Selective Shopping
Jensen Beach
She sells seashells at **Nettles Nest Shells and Gifts From the Sea** (772-229-8953), 11035 S Ocean Dr., where you'll find spectacular corals and fine specimens from around the globe.

Jonathan Dickinson State Park (772-546-2771;
www.floridastateparks.org/jonathandickinson), 16450 SE Federal Hwy., Hobe
Sound, has something for everyone. Hikers enjoy nearly 20 miles of trails,
including two backpacking loops (with a lengthier trail currently under construction); bicyclists have the Camp Murphy Off-Road Bicycle Trail to
explore; and paddlers can launch into the Loxahatchee River for a pleasant
trip up one of Florida's designated Wild and Scenic Rivers. When the tide is
up, a concessionaire runs a nature cruise up the river to the homestead of
Trapper Nelson, a legendary figure in Loxahatchee history. Nelson established an encampment with cottages, picnic shelters, and a zoo, a popular
getaway in the 1930s and 1940s. If the tides are right, the boat tour will drop
you off at Trapper Nelson's, where a ranger leads an interesting interpretive
walk around the encampment. If you do nothing else on your visit, don't miss
the climb up to the top of Hobe Mountain Tower, from which you can see
most of Jupiter Island and the Atlantic Ocean. This 11,000-acre park was
formerly a military installation, and you'll see remnants of old buildings
along many of the trails. There are two large campgrounds and cabins for
rent (see *Campgrounds*), canoe rentals, picnic areas, short nature trails,
a playground, and so much to do you'll visit again and again. Open 8 AM–
sunset daily. Fee.

LOXAHATCHEE RIVER

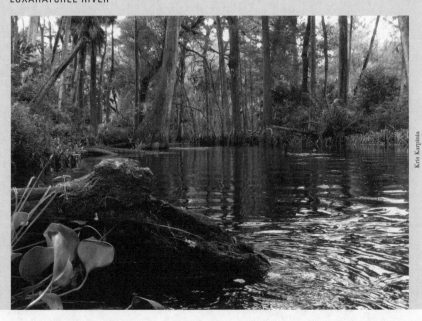

Kris Kurpinia

For classy collectibles stop in **Always & Forever** (772-287-8883; www .always-forever.com), 37 W Osceola St., where you'll find top names such as Waterford, Swarovski, Lladro, and Moorcraft.

At **Bella Jewelry and Gifts** (772-219-8648; www.bellajewelryandgifts.com), 39 SW Osceola St., the selection isn't just jewelry but includes home decor and New Age items—crystals, fossils, feng shui supplies, and aromatherapy.

Like a little museum, **Glass N Treasures** (772-220-1018), 53 SW Flagler Ave., is packed with collectibles, including Civil War items and travel brochures.

Victoriana awaits at the quaint **Humble Heart** (772-223-5505), 313 Colorado Ave., including a year-round Christmas room, garden accessories, and home furnishings.

Gardeners will love **The Love Garden** (772-287-5276; www.LoveGarden .us), 19 SW Flagler Ave., with its garden-themed decor for the home, splendid fountains, silk plants, and exotic pottery.

❦ Pups are welcome at **Puppuccino** (772-781-4202; www.puppuccino.com), Three SW Flagler Ave., a unique boutique for your favorite pet. Purchase accessories, canine fashions, and doggie treats!

The Gold Coast: Palm Beach to Miami

4

WEALTHY RETREAT:
PALM BEACH COUNTY

SUNNY HOMETOWN:
GREATER FORT LAUDERDALE

MAGIC CITY: MIAMI-DADE COUNTY

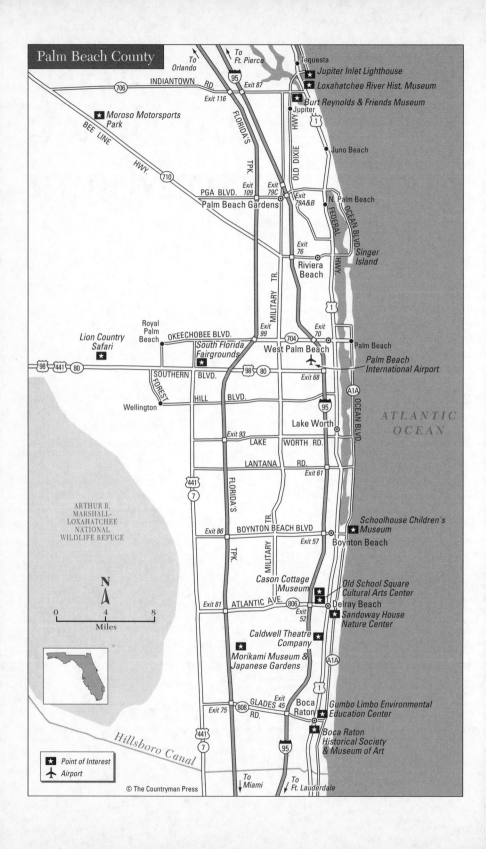

Palm Beach County

To Orlando
To Ft. Pierce

706   INDIANTOWN   RD.
95   Exit 87
Exit 116

FLORIDA'S TPK.

BEE LINE HWY.

★ Moroso Motorsports Park

710

Tequesta
★ Jupiter Inlet Lighthouse
★ Loxahatchee River Hist. Museum
★ Burt Reynolds & Friends Museum
Jupiter
HWY. 1
OLD DIXIE HWY.

Juno Beach

PGA BLVD.   Exit 109   Exit 79C
Palm Beach Gardens   Exit 79A&B
N. Palm Beach

OCEAN BLVD.

Exit 76

Singer Island

Riviera Beach

FEDERAL HWY.

MILITARY TR.

1

Lion Country Safari ★

Royal Palm Beach
OKEECHOBEE BLVD.
★ South Florida Fairgrounds
Exit 99   704   West Palm Beach   Exit 70
Palm Beach
Palm Beach International Airport ✈

98 441 80
SOUTHERN   BLVD.   98 80
FOREST   Exit 68
HILL   BLVD.
Wellington

A1A   OCEAN BLVD.

ATLANTIC OCEAN

95

Lake Worth

Exit 93
LAKE   WORTH   RD.
LANTANA   RD.
Exit 61

441
7

FLORIDA'S TPK.

ARTHUR R. MARSHALL-LOXAHATCHEE NATIONAL WILDLIFE REFUGE

N

0   4   8
Miles

Exit 86   BOYNTON BEACH BLVD.
Exit 57
★ Schoolhouse Children's Museum
Boynton Beach

MILITARY TR.

Cason Cottage Museum
★ Old School Square Cultural Arts Center
★★ Delray Beach   Exit 52
★ Sandoway House Nature Center

Exit 81   ATLANTIC AVE.   806

★ Caldwell Theatre Company

★ Morikami Museum & Japanese Gardens

A1A

Exit 75   808   GLADES   Exit 45
RD.   Boca Raton
1
★ Gumbo Limbo Environmental Education Center
★ Boca Raton Historical Society & Museum of Art

441
7

95

Hillsboro Canal

★ Point of Interest
✈ Airport

To Miami
To Ft. Lauderdale

© The Countryman Press

WEALTHY RETREAT:
PALM BEACH COUNTY

GUIDANCE For information about Jupiter, Tequesta, and Juno Beach, contact the **JTJB Chamber of Commerce** (561-746-7111; www.jupiterfl.org), 800 N US 1, Jupiter 33477. Also **Palm Beach County Convention and Visitors Bureau** (561-233-3000), 1555 Palm Beach Lakes, Ste. 800, West Palm Beach 33401.

GETTING THERE *By car:* From **I-95** take exit 79 for Palm Beach Gardens, PGA Blvd., and exit 87 for Jupiter, Indiantown Rd. From **I-95,** exits 66 to 76 take you Palm Beach and West Palm Beach. Exit 70, Okeechobee Blvd. (SR 704), and head east toward the downtown area, then cross over the bridge and you're there. Pay particular attention when you cross over the bridge, as Henry Flagler's home **Whitehall** (see *Historic Sites*) is to the right overlooking the water.

To get to Lake Worth from I-95, exit at either Sixth or 10th Ave. and head east about 1 mile to US 1/SR 805/Dixie Hwy. Lake Ave./SR 802 E is between Sixth and 10th. Go north on US 1 from Sixth Ave. and south on US 1 from 10th Ave. There are several one-way streets in the Lake Worth downtown area: Lake Ave. runs west to east from US 1 to the beach; Lucerne Ave. runs east to west from the downtown area to US 1. From I-95 take exits 56 to 59 for Boynton Beach, exits 51 and 52 for Delray Beach, and exits 44 to 50 for Boca Raton.

Exit I-95 at Atlantic Ave. for Delray Beach (not Atlantic Blvd., which takes you into Pompano Beach further south).

From Florida's Turnpike use exit 85 for Boynton Beach, Boynton Beach Blvd., exit 81 for Delray, Atlantic Ave., and exit 75 for Boca Raton, Glades Rd.

From Florida's Turnpike take exit 109 for Palm Beach Gardens and exit 116 for Jupiter; use exits 97, 98, or 99 for Palm Beach or West Palm Beach and exit 93 for Lake Worth.

By air: **Palm Beach International Airport (PBIA)** (561-471-7420), 1000 Turnage Blvd., West Palm Beach, is situated adjacent to I-95.

By rail: **AMTRAK** (561-832-6169 or 1-800-USA-RAIL; www.amtrak.com). Take the Silver Service/Palmetto route to 345 Congress Ave., Delray Beach. The nearest station to West Palm Beach is at 201 Tamarind Ave., West Palm Beach.

Tri-Rail (1-800-TRI-RAIL; www.tri-rail.com) service connects Palm Beach, Broward, and Miami-Dade Counties, and it also connects to several stations in central and south Palm Beach County. Catch the train at the **Gardens of Palm Beaches Mall,** 3101 PGA Blvd., Palm Beaches (561-775-7750), where it connects with Palm Tran routes at Mangonia Park Station, 1415 45th St.; West Palm Beach Station, 203 S Tamarind Ave.; and Lake Worth Station, 1703 Lake Worth Rd. Use Palm Tran Route 40 or 44 for West Palm Beach. It connects to Palm Tran routes at Boynton Beach Station, 2800 High Ridge Rd.; Delray Beach Station, 345 Congress Ave.; and Boca Raton Station, 601 NW 53rd St. Tri-Rail connects to several Palm Tran routes at Boynton Beach, Delray Beach, and Boca Raton stations.

By bus: **Greyhound** (561-833-8534 or 1-800-231-2222; www.greyhound.com), 205 S Tamarind Ave., West Palm Beach and service to 402 SE Sixth Ave., Delray Beach. The **Palm Tran** (561-841-4287; www.co.palm-beach.fl.us/palmtran) service area covers malls and tourist spots throughout Palm Beach County and south Palm Beach Gardens.

By trolley: **Lolly the Trolley** (561-586-1720), Lake Worth's community transit, covers all of Lake Worth every day 9 AM–5 PM. Fee. Tri-Rail connects with the **Boynton Beach Trolley** (561-572-0550; www.boyntonbeachtrolley.com). The Congress Ave. route runs 7:15 AM–6:15 PM Mon.–Fri.; the Ocean Ave. route runs 11 AM–10 PM Thurs.–Sun. Free for both residents and visitors.

By water taxi: **Water Taxi of the Palm Beaches** (561-775-2628; www.water-taxi .com), 11511 Ellison Wilson Rd. (at Panama Hattie's). **Palm Beach Water Taxi** (561-683-TAXI or 1-800-446-4577; www.palmbeachwatertaxi.com), Sailfish Marina, 98 Lake Dr., Palm Beach Shores (Singer Island). Pick up the water taxi at Sailfish Marina, or at Phil Foster Park, 900 E Blue Heron Blvd.; downtown West Palm Beach's Clematis Street District; Palm Harbor Marina, 400 N Flager Dr.; Riviera Beach Marina, 200 E 13th St. You can also catch a water taxi to Peanut Island from Panama Hattie's or the West Palm Beach Marina.

PARKING Public parking is readily available at no cost in the cities in the northern, western, and southern parts of the county. In the West Palm Beach, city garages and parking lots offer the first hour for free. **Garages** are located at Banyan Blvd. and Olive Ave., Evernia St. and Dixie Hwy., and the Police Garage at 600 Clematis St. Fees are $1 per hour 24 hours a day Mon.–Sat.; free Sun. All lots and garages charge a flat fee of $7 for overnight parking 10 PM–6 AM.

Parking lots in West Palm Beach are located at the corner of Datura St. and Dixie Hwy., the 500 block of Clematis St., and the City Hall lot at Banyan Blvd. and N Narcissus. Fees are $1 per hour, and lots are open 6 AM–10 PM.

Several meters are also located throughout West Palm Beach, Palm Beach, and the beach areas. Those also run about a $1 per hour.

MEDICAL EMERGENCIES Area hospitals include **Bethesda Hospital** (561-737-7733), S Seacrest Blvd., Boynton Beach; **Columbia Hospital** (561-842-6141), 2201 45th St., West Palm Beach; and **Palm Beach Gardens Hospital** (561-622-1411), 3360 Burns Rd., Palm Beach Gardens. Several fine hospitals are located near Lake Worth, the closest being the **JFK Medical Center** (561-965-7300), 5301 S Congress Ave., Atlantis. Also **Wellington Regional Medical Center** (561-798-8500), 10101 Forest Hill Blvd., Wellington.

PUBLIC RESTROOMS The beach areas and most city parks all have restrooms available to the public at no cost.

VALET Most restaurants and luxury hotels in the beach area, and especially on the "Island," offer valet services. Some restaurants and hotels have only mandatory valet parking. Inquire when making reservations.

NORTH PALM BEACH COUNTY

New World explorers and today's adventurers consider **Jupiter** an important navigational point when planning trips around Florida's coastline and points as far south as Latin America. Jupiter, the easternmost point in Florida, was named **Jupiter Inlet** in its early records. The legend goes that local Jeaga natives called themselves Jobe. When English settlers heard the name, it sounded to them like "Jove," which was also the name for the god Jupiter, so they began calling the region Jupiter, and it remains so to this day. The area became widely known after Jonathan Dickinson and his party were captured and held hostage by local Native Americans on the site where the DuBois pioneer home now sits. The most identifiable landmark in the area is the Jupiter Inlet Lighthouse. Erected in 1860, it remains an important navigational beacon. **Juno Beach** was once Dade County's link to northern Florida by way of the Celestial Railroad. The name Celestial Railroad came from the stops that were made: Juno, Venus, Mars, and Jupiter. In 1890 the village of Juno was named the county seat, covering the region of the railroad from just north of Jupiter and south to Biscayne Bay in Miami-Dade County. The Celestial Railroad was sold in 1896, and the county seat reverted to Miami four years later. To the north of Jupiter is the small village of **Tequesta,** named after the ancient Tequesta people.

Today, Jupiter provides the most rural coastal atmosphere on the Gold Coast, thanks to much as-yet-undeveloped property along the shoreline and inland. The beach is a quiet expanse shielded from the road by protected dunes with scenic wild grasses, which make for a pastoral view as well as protect both the endangered sea oats and the beach from erosion. Low-rise apartment and condominium complexes wind along the other side of the beach highway (SR A1A), but they're a far cry from the dense condo canyons created by high-rises in other coastal communities. Just a half hour north of West Palm Beach, Jupiter is close to nightlife and cultural activity as well, so visitors can enjoy the best of both sides of Florida here. There is a very well-heeled segment of the local population that has figured that out and settled in exclusive neighborhoods in Jupiter, however, property values and prices are generally much better here than farther south.

✳ **To See**

ART GALLERIES

Jupiter
The **Edna Hibel Museum and Gallery** (561-622-5560; www.hibelmuseum.org), 5353 Parkside Dr., at Florida Atlantic University, exhibits the fine art of South Florida artist Edna Hibel. She is the recipient of numerous prestigious awards, and her works have been exhibited in museums and galleries in more than 20 countries on four continents. Selections of her original paintings, lithographs, porcelains, drawings, and sculpture are also on display in Jupiter and Palm Beach.

Stuart

Beautiful marine and aquatic paintings can be admired and purchased at **Profile International Art Gallery** (561-220-3370; www.apbico.com/websites/others/progallery), 3746–48 E Ocean Blvd., Harbour Bay Plaza. You can almost feel yourself swimming underwater surrounded by tropical fish and manatees! The gallery is also an official frame maker to the President of the United States. There is another location at 50 S US 1, Jupiter (561-747-7094).

Tequesta

The **Lighthouse Center for the Arts** (561-746-3101; www.lighthousearts.org), 373 Tequesta Dr., was founded by Christopher Norton, son of the founders of the **Norton Museum of Art** (see *Central Palm Beach County*) in 1963. The center features a variety of exhibits and educational programs and is dedicated to bringing art to all ages. The nonprofit museum also has an excellent gallery store. Open 10 AM–4:30 PM Mon.–Sat. Free.

HISTORIC SITES A landmark for the region, the **Jupiter Inlet Lighthouse and Museum** (561-747-8380), 500 Captain Armour's Way, Jupiter, built in 1860, survived the Civil War (when its Fresnel lens was hidden by local Confederates in Lake Worth) and continues to be a navigational beacon today. It's quite a view from the top, and worth the dizzying spiral climb to get there. Tours start at the visitors center. Open 10 AM–5 PM Tues.–Sun. Fee.

MUSEUMS Burt Reynolds has made Jupiter his home for most of his movie and television career, so it is no wonder that he has assembled a fine collection of artifacts and memorabilia not only on his life, but also from his wide circle of friends. At the **Burt Reynolds & Friends Museum** (561-743-9955; www.burtreynoldsmuseum.org), 100 N US 1, Jupiter, sports fans and film buffs will enjoy seeing such items as Muhammad Ali's boxing gloves; Gene Autry's and Roy Rogers's boots; Trigger's original sales receipt; letters from Cary Grant, Carol Burnett, and Jack Lemmon; and movie props such as the canoe from *Deliverance* and the *Smokey and the Bandit* car. Open 10 AM–4 PM Fri.–Sun. Fee.

Call for an appointment to view archaeological artifacts being processed right before your eyes from **The Last Galleon** (561-747-7700), 603 Commerce Way, Jupiter, the oldest Spanish galleon found in Florida waters. This is the only facility in the United States that allows the public to watch while history is being uncovered.

✐ Learn about the ancient Tequesta, the shipwreck of Jonathan Dickinson, and the hardy pioneers who settled this region at the **Loxahatchee River Historical Museum** (561-747-6639; www.lrhs.org), 805 N US 1, adjacent to the Jupiter Inlet Lighthouse (see *Historic Sites*) in Jupiter. In addition to the artifacts and exhibits inside the museum, you can explore a replica Seminole village and the Tindall House, recently moved on-site. Open 10 AM–5 PM Tues.–Fri., noon–5 PM Sat. and Sun. Fee.

BASEBALL Catch a home run at **Roger Dean Stadium** (561-775-1818, www.rogerdeanstadium.com), 4751 Main St., Jupiter, where the Jupiter Hammerheads, Palm Beach Cardinals, Florida Marlins, and St. Louis Cardinals are up to bat. Tickets $7–22.

Juno Beach

⚓ Located inside **Loggerhead Park** (see *Parks*), the **Marinelife Center of Juno Beach** (561-627-8280; www.marinelife.org), 14200 US 1, specializes in the rescue and rehabilitation of sea turtles. The facility includes an interpretive center with aquariums showcasing native sea life, a library, and the large turtle tanks outside. Open 10 AM–5 PM Mon.–Sat., noon–3 PM Sun. Free; donations appreciated.

Jupiter

⚓ More than 3,000 wild animals receive care at the **Busch Wildlife Sanctuary** (561-575-3399), 2500 Jupiter Park Dr. The nonprofit facility provides an educational environment where you can learn about some of Florida's flora and fauna up close and personal. Open to visitors 10 AM–4 PM Tues.–Sat. Free; donations appreciated.

✳ To Do

BIRDING Most of the region's natural areas offer excellent bird-watching, particularly for wading birds and shorebirds. **Florida scrub jays** may be seen at **Jupiter Ridge Natural Area** (see *Preserves*), and herons and egrets along Lake Worth Creek at **Frenchman's Forest Natural Area** (see *Preserves*).

BOAT TOUR Tour the Intracoastal Waterway or Loxahatchee River on the *Manatee Queen* **Pontoon Boat** (561-744-2191; www.manateequeen.com), at the Crab House, 1065 SR A1A, Jupiter. The Jupiter Island tour showcases multimillion-dollar homes; the Loxahatchee River tour features wild and natural areas. Adults $24, children $15.

NATURE TOUR At **John D. MacArthur Beach State Park** (561-624-6952; www.macarthurbeach.org/), North Palm Beach, you can take guided nature tours (free) Wednesday through Sunday and kayak tours ($20 single kayak, $35 double kayak) daily at high tide or rent a kayak to explore on your own, $10–40. Local guides will take you snorkeling (bring your own gear) through the reefs June through August. Fee per carload for park admission.

PADDLING Canoe down Florida rivers with **Canoe Outfitters of Florida** (561-746-7053 or 1-888-272-1257; www.canoes-kayaks-florida.com), in Riverbend Park, 900 W Indiantown Rd., Jupiter, about 1.25 miles west of I-95. Located at the headwaters of the Loxahatchee River, Canoe Outfitters takes you on a six-hour journey from Jupiter all the way to Jonathan Dickinson State Park. Discover a peaceful, quiet environment as you pass through a forested area where eagles and osprey perch while alligators sun themselves on the banks. $40 per person in two-person canoe; includes guide.

The **Jupiter Outdoor Center** (561-747-9666; www.jupiteroutdoorcenter.com), 1000 FL A1A, Jupiter, offers stargazing adventures throughout the year. Guides take you around Pelican and Adventure Islands, and afterward you can toast marshmallows by the campfire. $30 and up.

WALKING TOUR The town of Jupiter's **Riverwalk** (561-746-5134) follows a 2.5-mile course along the Intracoastal Waterway from Jupiter Inlet past shops, restaurants, and natural areas, all the way to Jupiter Ridge.

WATER PARKS At **Rapids Water Park** (561-842-8756; www.rapidswaterpark .com), 6566 N Military Trail, West Palm Beach, the main event is the Big Thunder, a giant funnel 60 feet in diameter and 55 feet long. Float down the 9-foot tunnel through dark twists and curves as your speed increases, then drop 45 degrees through the funnel, slide around and around, and exit into the landing pool. Other high-speed thrills are also available, but for those who want to relax, there's the Lazy River. $31.95 for all, with children under two free.

🐾 **PlayMobil Fun Park,** 8031 North Military Trail, Palm Beach Gardens (772-691-9880), is a playground filled with PlayMobil toys, where children's imagination can be inspired. 10–6 Mon.–Sun.

✳ Green Space

BEACHES

Juno Beach

🐾 **Juno Beach** is a fine family beach for snorkeling and swimming in the emerald green waters. A very natural setting free of condos and hotels looming overhead, dogs are free to run in the surf here. Several parks provide access, including popular **Loggerhead Park** (see *Parks*). **Juno Beach Park** (561-626-5166), 14775 SR A1A, is one of the area's more popular beaches, with lifeguards on duty; a pedestrian pier (561-799-0185) offers access for fishing. Free.

Jupiter

Carlin Park, 400 S SR A1A, has nature trails, lifeguards on duty, and picnic facilities, and it's a good snorkeling beach. Free.

Jupiter Beach Park (561-624-0065), 1375 Jupiter Beach Rd., and Ocean Cay Park, 2188 Marcinski Rd., are two of the more popular lifeguard-attended beaches in Jupiter.

Riverbend Park (561-966-6617; www.pbcgov.com/parks/locations/riverbend.htm), 9060 Indiantown Rd., Jupiter, is a great spot for kayaking, biking, and horse riding (bring your own—no parking for horse trailers).

Tequesta

Off the beaten path a little, north of Jupiter along SR A1A, **Coral Cove** (561-966-6600; www.pbcgov.com/parks), 19450 Beach Rd., offers an unusual look at the Atlantic Ocean, thanks to the picturesque rocky shoreline and its many tidal pools and unusual formations. When the water is calm and clear, this is a great snorkeling spot, especially as there are 2 acres of natural rock reef for tropical fish to play in. Free.

PARKS

Juno Beach

Sandwiched between US 1 and SR A1A, **Loggerhead Park** (561-626-5166; www.pbcgov.com/parks), 1111 Ocean Dr., has a great children's playground, an observation tower overlooking the Atlantic from a tall dune, and access beneath SR A1A to the beach. It's also the gateway to two other natural attractions: the **Marinelife Center of Juno Beach** (see *Wildlife Rehab*) and **Juno Dunes Natural Area** (see *Preserves*). Open 8 AM–11 PM daily. Free.

Jupiter Farms

& With 800 acres in cabbage palm hammocks and restored marshes along the Loxahatchee River, **Riverbend County Park** (561-966-6660; www.pbcgov.com/parks), Indiantown Rd., just west of the river, offers river access for paddlers (with an on-site livery) and several miles of hard-packed hiking trails, suitable for wheelchairs with assistance. Free.

PRESERVES

Juno Beach

& ✍ Protecting a ribbon of saw palmetto–topped dunes along US 1, **Juno Dunes Natural Area** (561-233-2400) is accessed from **Loggerhead Park** (see *Parks*), with the nature trail starting across from the children's playground area. A paved wheelchair-accessible trail crosses ancient dunes to a high point with an

Sandra Friend

RUGGED ROCK FORMATIONS AT CORAL COVE

observation shelter overlooking the Atlantic Ocean. A natural-surface trail loops downhill and through the dense coastal scrub vegetation. Open sunrise–sunset daily. Free.

Jupiter

& ✍ To explore a scrub habitat where the dunes gleam like snow, visit **Jupiter Ridge Natural Area** (561-233-2400), 1 mile south of Indiantown Rd. on US 1. This beautiful 267-acre preserve along the Intracoastal Waterway almost ended up as a Wal-Mart two decades ago; now, as you walk the trails, notice the delicate scrub plants and colony of Florida scrub jays. A small portion of the trail is paved, with an overlook on the waterway. Open sunrise–sunset daily. Free.

A TOUCH OF WILD AT JUNO DUNES PRESERVE

Sandra Friend

Jupiter Island

For a taste of the unexpected, visit **Blowing Rocks Preserve** (561-744-6668), 574 S Beach Rd., where you'll find Florida's only sea caves. A rocky outcropping of Anastasia limestone defines portions of the shoreline from Jupiter Island north to Fort Pierce, and here the rocky shelf is tall enough to have wave-sculpted caves inside. At times of high tide and high waves, water spurts out natural chimneys in the tops of the caves, hence the name. The caves can only be explored at low tide. A nature center on the Intracoastal side is the focal point of a natural habitat restoration area with trails. No swimming permitted. Open 9 AM–4:30 PM daily. Fee.

Palm Beach Gardens

&. ✍ Explore natural habitats at **Frenchman's Forest Natural Area** (561-233-2400), Prosperity Farms Rd., where three trails wind through the forest along Lake Worth Creek; the red-blazed Cypress Trail leads you across a boardwalk through a cypress swamp. Open sunrise–sunset daily. Free.

✳ Lodging
CAMPGROUNDS

Riviera Beach 33404
Peanut Island Campground (561-845-4445), 6500 Peanut Island Rd., is run by the Palm Beach Parks and Recreation Department (www.pbcgov.com/parks) and is only accessible by boat. The island park has 20 tropical campsites, each with tent pad, grill, and picnic table. Restrooms on-site with showers. A park supervisor is always on-site for your assistance. Reservations are recommended.

RESORTS

Jupiter 33477
"♈" The only oceanfront hotel in Jupiter is the **Jupiter Beach Resort** (561-746-2511), Five N SR A1A, where the extensively remodeled rooms ($187 and up) have appealing tropical decor, marble floors, and shower stalls in each bathroom, furnished balconies, and high-speed Internet access. Guests have direct access to the beach or can enjoy the hotel pool; poolside café, spa, and fine dining on-site. Valet parking available.

Tequesta 33469
A family favorite for relaxing getaways, the **Jupiter Waterfront Inn** (1-888-747-9085, 561-747-9085), 18903 SE Federal Hwy., sits right along the Intracoastal with all 38 suites overlooking Jupiter Island. Guests enjoy a large heated outdoor pool and spa on a sun-deck along the water and can drop a line off the 240-foot pier. Room options include suites, studios, or Jacuzzi suites; rates $99 to 249.

✳ Where to Eat
DINING OUT

Jupiter
For fine dining, **BarryMore's Prime Steaks & Chops** (561-625-3757), 4050 S US 1, should be high on your local list. Their steaks are aged a month before serving, and their lamb chops are range-fed from Colorado; South African lobster tail is flown in daily. All entrées ($25–50, with a nightly chef's selections each evening) are satisfying, and the relaxed atmosphere encourages you to enjoy a cognac at the hand-tooled mahogany bar after dinner. Reservations recommended.

Dinner comes with a most excellent view at **Jetty's** (561-743-8166), 1075 N SR A1A, where the Jupiter Lighthouse is the centerpiece of the panorama. The menu is upscale seafood and steak and includes interesting combinations such as coconut shrimp with filet mignon tenderloin tips, and filet mignon with lump crabmeat in béarnaise sauce. Entrées $17 and up.

The Crab House (561-744-1300: www.crabhouseseafood.com), 1065 N SR A1A. Enjoy reliably delicious

Sandra Friend

THE JUPITER LIGHTHOUSE

seafood at this well-known and much-loved chain restaurant. Sample calamari, coconut shrimp, and a crab, avocado, and mango stack sauced with remoulade . . . mmmm. $14 and up.

Palm Beach Gardens

Palm Beach Gardens has a real four-leaf clover, and as I recently visited Ireland, I can't resist stopping at **Paddy Mac's** (561-691-4366; www .paddymacspub.com), 10971 N Military Trail, for traditional Gaelic fare. European Master Chef Kenneth Wade, Irish born and raised, previously worked at Ashford Castle, and his head chefs are also from the Emerald Isle. Chef Wade's culinary delights far surpass the usual pub fare, with reasonably priced entrées $15.95 and up. Lunch and dinner; traditional Irish music and dancing.

Jupiter

A hometown family burger joint, **Blondie's Bar & Grill** (561-743-3300), 10162 W Indiantown Rd., has deli sandwiches and salads, wings and dogs, and their special "Phyl-u-Up" Maryland crab soup. Serving lunch and dinner ($6–18).

A birch beer float and a junkyard dog—that's lunch for me at **The Dune Dog Drive In** (561-744-6667), 775 Alt SR A1A, a great stop after a long hike at nearby Jonathan Dickinson State Park. The place is a funky beach shack set in a parking lot along Old Dixie Highway, with Jimmy Buffet blasting and food ($4 and up) served at picnic tables. The family atmosphere at lunchtime makes way for barroom trolling after dark (margaritas are a specialty here).

🦪 Good food at bargain prices—that's the **Lighthouse Restaurant** (561-746-4811), 1510 N US 1, a local fixture where patrons Burt Reynolds and Tom Poston smile down from autographed photos on the walls. Breakfast is hearty and even the dinners pack a lot of food. I highly recommend the grilled crab cakes, a house specialty. They're open for breakfast, lunch, and dinner, but busiest at breakfast. Entrées $9–15.

When you have enough money, you can move anything—and such is the case with **Rooney's Public House Abacoa** (561-694-6610), 1153 Town Center Dr., where the entire pub was imported from Ireland. Good Irish cuisine, a properly stocked bar, succulent steak and seafood, and live music every weekend. What more can a redheaded lad or lass ask for?

Cathy's Beach Connection Restaurant (561-626-2262) offers reasonably priced breakfast, lunch, and dinner in a comfortable café. 12850 US 1, Juno Beach. Try a grouper reuben with cranberry juice/champagne mimosa. 8 AM–9 PM Mon.–Sat., 8 AM–4 PM Sun.

Tequesta

Pour me something tall and strong at the **Square Grouper** at Castaways Marina (561-575-0252), 1111 Love St., on the Intracoastal near Alan Jackson's house; the video for the Jackson-Buffet duet "5 O'Clock Somewhere" was partially filmed here. The menu is limited to your basic bar fare, but this is a great place to sit and sip a tall one while watching sailboats drift past. Live music Tues.–Sun.

✳ Entertainment
PERFORMING ARTS

Jupiter

The 225-seat **Atlantic Theater** (561-575-3271; www.theatlantictheater .com), 6743 W Indiantown Rd. #34, brings fresh, new drama and comedy to the area with insightful productions. Live music featuring local talent is also performed.

The historic **Maltz Jupiter Theatre** (561-743-2666; www.jupitertheatre .org), 1001 E Indiantown Rd., once the Burt Reynolds dinner theater, was renovated in 2004. Open since the 1980s,

the theater has been transformed into a 600-seat playhouse featuring professional productions of musicals, dramas, comedies, and classics, often with world-renowned celebrities.

Contemporary and classical productions are professionally presented at the **Shakespeare Festival** (561-575-7336; www.pbshakespeare.org), Carlin Park Amphitheater, 400 S SR A1A (just south of Indiantown Rd.).

✳ Selective Shopping
ANTIQUES AND COLLECTIBLES

Jupiter

There's a nice selection of antiques and collectible treasures at **Treasure Hunt Antiques** (561-748-0608), 1532 N US 1; **Sims Creek Antique Mall** (561-747-6785), 1695 W Indiantown Rd.

BOUTIQUE

Jupiter

Harbor Clothing Boutique (561-747-5330), 2127 US 1, offers an extensive line of Brighton purses and jewelry.

SPORTING CENTER

North Palm Beach

Once you've experienced the area's rivers and inlets, you'll want your own kayak, so head over to **Adventure Times Kayaks** (561-881-7218; www .kayakkayak.com), 521 Northlake Blvd.

MALLS AND OUTLETS

Palm Beach Gardens

Serious shoppers head to **The Gardens Mall** (561-622-2115), 3101 PGA Blvd., where you can find all the trendy fashions to make your style sizzle. Downtown at the Gardens, an outdoor mall just west of The Gardens Mall, features many fine shopping opportunities, including Macy's, Sur la

CATHY'S BEACH CONNECTION, JUPITER
Trish Riley

Table, Whole Foods, and Shoe Spa, where you can nurture your inner Carrie Bradshaw with owner Beth Weingarten's incredible bargains on $500 shoes. Just do it.

⊸ **Publix GreenWise Market** (561-514-5175), 11231 Legacy Ave. This market, across from the Gardens Mall on PGA Boulevard, is the first of the Publix chain's new green stores, designed to compete with the national champion, Whole Foods. The store is gigantic, with copious amounts of the finest in fresh organic produce, house plants, fresh meats and seafoods, and environmentally friendly cleaners and cosmetics and books to help educate shoppers about the trend toward ecofriendly lifestyles and choices. There is a full-service buffet with hot dishes and cold salads, fresh bakery, pizzeria, wine, and cheese sections. A great place to find an exceptional and healthy meal. I was also especially excited to discover that they carry my book *The Complete Idiot's Guide to Green Living* (Alpha Books, 2007)!

✳ Special Events

February: The annual **ArtiGras Fine Arts Festival** (561-694-2300; www

Trish Riley

PUBLIX GREENWISE, PALM BEACH GARDENS

.artigras.org), 800 US 1, Jupiter, just north of Donald Ross Road. Music, entertainment, ArtiKids, food, wine tasting, and lots of art. Fee.

March: Artists from all over the United States and Canada present their original paintings, crafts, photography, copper and wood sculptures, and jewelry at **Artfest by the Sea** (561-746-7111; www.jupiterfl.org), Juno Beach (SR A1A). Musicians playing everything from flutes to guitars walk around and serenade.

CENTRAL PALM BEACH COUNTY

The focal point of Central Palm Beach County is, of course, **Palm Beach.** The Intracoastal Waterway is all that separates the 16-mile-long barrier island from the mainland cities of Lake Worth and West Palm Beach. Land of the social elite, the "Island" is the winter home to many celebrities, including Rush Limbaugh, Jimmy Buffett, and the now infamous Bernie Madoff, who made off with the fortunes of many of his neighbors. Seasonal residents from social hot spots in New England, such as the Hamptons and Martha's Vineyard spend a great deal of time fund-raising for both humanitarian and artistic causes—the Kravis Center was built totally on donations. Created by Henry Morrison Flagler in 1894, after his opening of the Royal Poinciana Hotel, the island with small-town character displays spectacular Mediterranean architecture throughout. Flagler's **"Whitehall"** (see *Historic Sites*), built in 1901 for his wife, Mary Lily Kenan, can be seen to the north as you cross over the bridge on Okeechobee Boulevard (SR 704). Back on the mainland, West

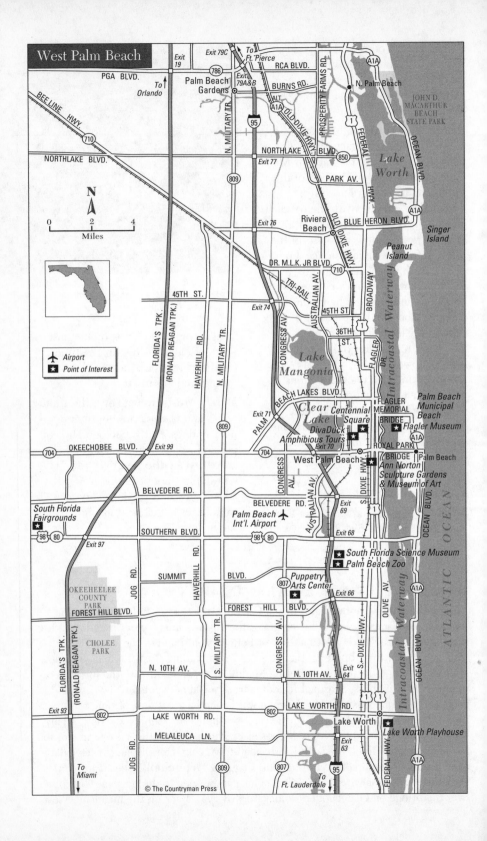

West Palm Beach

Palm Beach provided homes to those who built the grand homes on the "Island" and worked for its upper-class residents, or for many nouveau riche who couldn't quite afford the exclusivity of the "Island." However, the **City of West Palm Beach** has its own piece of paradise, with its scenic waterfront views of the Intra-coastal Waterway, sunny palm-lined streets, quaint shopping districts, and active downtown district. Be aware that this is a town where you'll want to stay within the city entertainment area—wander a bit north of town and you might find yourself in the crossfire of angry youths.

At the southwest side of Palm Beach on the mainland sits Lake Worth. A pol-ished gem, Lake Worth's original landowners, Samuel and Fannie James, actually first named the town Jewel. In 1911 the James' sold the town to Palm Beach Farms Company, and plans were formulated for a city along the water. In 1912 the town name was changed to the Townsite of Lucerne, but its name was changed yet again when it opened its first post office, as there was already a town in Florida named Lucerne. The city was incorporated in 1913 as the City of Lake Worth after Gen. William Jenkins Worth, who was instrumental in ending hostilities with indigenous people in 1842. Finnish immigrants are an integral part of the town's population and culture, and they constitute nearly half of the town's residents. They began migrating to the area as early as 1906 and bring one of the biggest events out for all to enjoy in the annual Finnish-American heritage celebration, Finlandia Festival (see Special Events).

Originally established as a colony for the workers employed by Flagler to build his railroad and empire for the rich in Palm Beach, West Palm Beach evolved into its own city. Many affluent businessmen wintering in South Florida soon began acquiring land to the west of Palm Beach for spacious estates and future invest-ment opportunities. New York businessman C. Oliver Wellington was one of them, purchasing a large plot of land and calling it the Flying C.O.W. Ranch after his ini-tials. The parcel spanned thousands of acres and remained private property until his death in 1959. As estate taxes grew, his heirs began developing some of the property as exclusive upscale plots, and the community of Wellington was born. By the 1970s, the first phase of the well-planned community was well under way. In the mid-1980s the Wellington Club was built as a central point for social gather-ings. In 1993, Glenn Straub, a mining and asphalt tycoon, bought the club, and it became the Palm Beach Club. Home to the Winter Equestrian Festival, the PBPC features past and future Olympians in jumping and dressage events, along with several "Sport of Kings" polo matches. The Village of Wellington wasn't incorporat-ed until 1995 and is now known as the winter equestrian capital of the world. As it's a true equestrian community, you'll find tack shops, show centers, miles of trail riding, and riding lessons for both novices and professionals.

Nearby Royal Palm Beach is the only landlocked Palm Beach County munici-pality with beach in its name. Purchased in 1959 by Philadelphia supermarket magnates Sam and Hattie Friedland, the former 65,000-acre Seminole Tribe hunt-ing ground was later sold to Miami developer Arthur Desser, and it has grown into a thriving suburban community.

Trying hard to stave off the onslaught of development, Loxahatchee Groves, founded in 1917, is the oldest of the western communities. An estimated 4,000 resi-dents live on just under 8,000 acres. It was founded in 1917 by Southern States Land sales manager George Bensil, who remained a resident until his death in 1961.

✱ **To See**

ART GALLERIES Bruce Webber Gallery (561-582-1045; webbergallery.com), 705 Lucerne Ave., Lake Worth. Nineteenth-century to contemporary original works of art in oil, acrylic, and watercolor along with fine-art photography. Next door, at 709 Lucerne Ave., **MaryAnne Webber's Gallery** showcases fine crafts, gifts, and jewelry from South Florida artists and around the United States. A trompe l'oeil mural along the side of the gallery complements the two structures.

HISTORIC SITES For information on many historical places throughout Palm Beach County, visit the **Historical Society of Palm Beach County** (561-832-4164; www.historicalsocietypbc.org), 1398 N Country Rd., Ste. 25, in the Paramount Building.

Lake Worth
During the 1920s Florida land boom, Pittsburgh socialite John Phipps developed the pineapple fields around the intersection of Pershing and Flagler Drives in Lake Worth into the **El Cid Neighborhood,** comprised of expensive Mediterranean Revival and Mission-style homes. The neighborhood was named after medieval Spanish hero Rodrigo Diaz de Vivar—*Cid* is a translation from Arabic, meaning "lord."

Lake Worth Pier (561-533-7367) has long been known as the site of some of the world's best pier ocean fishing. The 960-foot-long pier is as close to the Gulf Stream as you can get without a boat. You can fish for bluefish, snapper, and sand perch 24 hours a day or simply watch the sunrise over the crystal-clear ocean. Bait and rental poles are available.

Explore nearby **Peanut Island** (561-845-4445; www.pbcgov.com/parks), located in the Lake Worth Lagoon. This 79-acre island of lush mangroves and Australian pines is home to the **Palm Beach Maritime Museum** (see *Museums*), the historic former Coast Guard Station, and the nuclear fallout shelter built to protect President Kennedy in case of war during the Cuban Missile Crisis. Access is by boat or ferry from Phil Foster Park and Riviera Beach Marina (call **Seafare Water Taxi** at 561-339-2504 for transportation). Dock spaces are open to the public, and there are 20 tent sites for camping.

Palm Beach
Bethesda-by-the-Sea Episcopal Church (561-655-4554; www.bbts.org), Barton Ave. and N County Rd., is one of the more beautiful churches in all of Florida and the first Protestant church built in southeast Florida (in 1889). The church now serves all races, nations, and creeds, and many well-to-do socialites and celebrities have been married at the church, including Donald Trump, who exchanged vows here with Melania Knauss in January 2005. (You must be a member of the church, however, should you want to hold your own wedding here.)

Mar-A-Lago, meaning "from lake to sea," was purchased by Donald Trump in 1985 from the Post Foundation as a winter home. The grand estate, originally built in 1927 by legendary cereal heiress Marjorie Merriweather Post (then Mrs. Edward F. Hutton), required extensive restoration, and Mr. Trump spent the better part of 18 years ensuring careful and accurate historic restoration of the "Jewel of Palm Beach." The 110,000-square-foot Mediterranean Revival mansion has 118 rooms, including 58 bedrooms, 33 bathrooms, and 3 bomb shelters. The lush 20-

acre estate is now home to the members-only Mar-A-Lago Club. It can be seen from the water or Ocean Drive.

The second church erected in southeast Florida (after Bethesda-by-the-Sea Episcopal Church, above), **Old Bethesda-by-the-Sea Episcopal Church,** located in the Clematis Street Commercial Historic District west of Dixie Hwy., is now a private residence.

Henry Flagler constructed the **Royal Poinciana Chapel,** (561-655-4212; www .royalpoincianachapel.org) 60 Cocoanut Row, in 1898 to serve winter guests. The earliest organized church in Palm Beach, the chapel originally sat on Whitehall Way and was moved to its present location in 1973.

Palm Beach's oldest house and the first winter residence of Henry Flagler, the circa 1886 **Sea Gull Cottage,** 58 Cocoanut Row, is now the parish house of Royal Poinciana Chapel (see above). It was moved in 1984 from its original site next to the Royal Poinciana Hotel and restored in 1984. Please view from the exterior only.

Henry Morrison Flagler built his grand estate, **Whitehall** (561-655-2833; www .flaglermuseum.us), One Whitehall Way, in 1902 as a wedding present for his wife, Mary Lily Kenan Flagler. The 55-room, 60,000-square-foot Gilded Age mansion was grander than any other mansion at the time. The marble entrance hall, double staircase, colossal marble columns, and red barrel tile roof are just some of the exquisite details. Now a museum, the mansion's period rooms are decorated in such styles as Louis XIV, Louis XV, Louis XVI, Italian Renaissance, and Francis I. My favorite section is the china, of which there is a plate for every occasion. Located across from the Okeechobee Boulevard (SR 704) bridge, the home can partially be seen when you cross the bridge. Henry Flagler's private railcar #91 is part of the museum's collection (see *Museums*).

West Palm Beach

In 1893 the town of West Palm Beach was laid out in a grid pattern, leaving a triangular space, known as **Flagler Park,** on the east end of Clematis to be used as a public area. In 1923 the Memorial Library was built on the site, rebuilt in 1962, and remodeled in 1994. The plaza is still the center of downtown activities. Note the small, triangular, in-ground fountain resembling the original plot. A marker is at the corner of Clematis Street and Flagler Drive.

Built in the 1920s and '30s on the highest coast ridge between downtown West Palm Beach and Miami, the **Flamingo Park** subdivision was home to some of the area's most prominent residents. Homes were built in several architectural styles, such as Mission, Mediterranean Revival, Frame Vernacular, Masonry Vernacular, Art Moderne, American Foursquare, Colonial Revival, and Craftsman/Bungalow. One notable home, the Alfred Comeau House (circa 1924), is located at 701 Flamingo Dr. The neighborhood's historical marker is located at Park Place and Dixie Highway.

A unique example of early-20th-century railroad architecture in the Mediterranean Revival style, the **Seaboard Air Line Station,** 203 S Tamarind Ave., opened in 1925 and was the flagship station of the Seaboard line. AMTRAK and the Tri-Rail are both serviced from this station. See the historical marker in the station courtyard.

Lake Worth

The 2,600-year-old "Sport of Kings" is heralded at the **Museum of Polo & Hall of Fame** (561-969-3210; www.polomuseum.com), 9011 Lake Worth Rd. The permanent exhibit displays more than 2,000 years of polo history throughout the world and American polo history from 1904. Special exhibits change annually. Look for "A Day in the Life of a Polo Pony" in 2006. Open 10 AM–4 PM Mon.–Fri. and 10 AM–2 PM Sat. (during the season). Free.

The history and culture of Lake Worth's Polish, Finnish, and Lithuanian immigrants come alive at the **Museum of the City of Lake Worth** (561-586-1700; www.lakeworth.org), 414 Lake Ave., City Hall Annex. Seven rooms full of artifacts, books, photos, memorabilia, and antiques display "days gone by." Open 9:30 AM–4:30 PM Mon.–Fri.

Palm Beach

Henry Morrison Flagler Museum (561-655-2833; www.flagler.org), One Whitehall Way, is home to one of "America's Castles." Whitehall, built in 1901 by Henry M. Flagler, was a wedding present to his third wife, Mary Lily Kenan Flagler (see *Historic Sites*). The grand mansion is decorated in many European styles reminiscent of the Gilded Age. Flagler, cofounder of Standard Oil Co., was instrumental in bringing the railroad to the southeast region of Florida and down through the Keys. His private railroad car is on display in the new Beaux-Arts-style building next to the main house. The 8,000-square-foot building, built specifically to hold the car, is the first building of its kind constructed in the United States in the past 60 years. Whitehall is listed on the National Register of Historic Places and can be viewed 10 AM–5 PM Tues.–Sat. and noon–5 PM Sun. Adults $15, children 6–12 $3.

Opened in 1999, the **Palm Beach Maritime Museum** (561-540-5147; www.pbmm.org), in Currie Park, 2400 N Flagler Dr., has four facilities: the former U.S. Coast Guard Station, boathouse, and President John F. Kennedy command post and bomb shelter on Peanut Island (see *Historic Sites*); the marine science field office and dock on the Intracoastal Waterway; an educational center, preview building, and ferry dock at Currie Park in West Palm Beach; and the Palm Beach Maritime Academy K–8 Charter School. Access is by boat or ferry from Phil Foster Park and Riviera Beach Marina. Currie Park education center open 10:30 AM–3:30 PM Wed.–Sat.; Peanut Island Tours from 11 AM–5 PM Fri.–Sun. Cost for tour: Adults $10, children 5 and under free. The ferryboat is an extra charge. Call for more information.

West Palm Beach

Sitting on just under 2 acres, the **Ann Norton Sculpture Gardens** (561-832-5328; www.ansg.org), 253 Barcelona Rd., features monolithic sculptures set amongst three hundred species of tropical palms. The historic home, listed on the National Register of Historic Places, displays more than one hundred various sized sculptures created by Ann Weaver Norton. Open 11 AM–4 PM Wed.–Sun., closed August. $5 per person.

If you haven't been to the **Norton Museum of Art** (561-832-5196; www.norton.org), 1451 S Olive Ave., then this is a must-see. Florida's largest and most impressive art museum was recently expanded. Permanent collections feature many of the grand masters, such as Chagall, Gauguin, Klee, Matisse, Miró, Monet, Picasso, and an impressive collection of Jackson Pollock, along with other great American and international artists. The glass ceiling by Dale Chihuly, known for his expertise in glassblowing, feels like an undersea odyssey. Industrialist Ralph Hubbard Norton, who headed the Acme Steel Company in Chicago, and his wife, Elizabeth Calhoun Norton, founded the museum in 1941. Permanent collection: Adults $8, ages 13–21 $5, under age 13 free. Free admission to West Palm Beach residents on Saturday. Palm Beach County residents can view the museum at no charge on the first Saturday of the month. There is an extra charge for all on special exhibitions. Call for more information.

Open since 1980, the **Ragtops Motorcars Museum** (561-655-2836 or 1-877-RAGTOPS; www.ragtopsmotorcars.com), 2119 S Dixie Hwy., is housed in three buildings covering two entire city blocks. You'll experience yesteryear with vintage automobiles, memorabilia, a soda bar, and a 1954 vintage silver dining car. "The Station" features vintage station wagons and a unique gift boutique. Open 10 AM–5 PM Mon.–Sat. Admission $8 adults, $7 seniors, $4 children under 12. Classic cars from the collection are available for purchase.

The **South Florida Science Museum** (561-832-1988; www.sfsm.org), 4801 Dreher Trail N, is not your typical science museum. This facility houses Florida's only science-themed mini golf, along with a natural history display of Florida ice age fossils. There are also lots of hands-on and interactive experiments. You'll also find dozens of fresh- and saltwater tanks up to 900 gallons at the **McGinty Aquarium.** Their pair of white spotted bamboo sharks actually mated during Hurricane Wilma and produced one viable semitransparent egg. Over at the **Aldrin Planetarium** you'll embark on a galactic odyssey seeking out nebulas and constellations while sitting in comfy inclined chairs. Open 10 AM–5 PM Mon.–Fri., 10 AM–6 PM Sat., and noon–6 PM Sun. Museum admission: adults $9, seniors 62 and up $8, children 3–12 $6, under 3 free. Planetarium $4 additional.

Go way back in time to experience one hundred years of Florida's rich history from the 1850s to the 1950s. Sitting on 10 acres, **Yesteryear Village** (561-790-5232; www.southfloridafair.com/yesteryearvillage.html), South Florida Fairgrounds, 9067 Southern Blvd., displays a large collection of original and replicated buildings, fully furnished with period items from a simpler time. You'll walk through edifices such as an old school, a blacksmith shop, and a general store. **The Bink Glisson Historical Museum** is located inside a replica of an 1858 Haile plantation house. Bink Glisson, a self-taught wildlife and landscape artist, settled in Florida in the early 1920s and was instrumental in the development of Wellington. Many of his paintings are on display in the home. The original classic Cracker house still stands in Alachua County, Florida. The village is also home to the **Sally Bennett Big Band Hall of Fame Museum,** which displays memorabilia by such musicians as Tommy Dorsey, Buddy Rich, Glenn Miller, and Duke Ellington. Open noon–5 PM Tues.–Fri. Hours may change according to special events, so please call ahead. $5 fee for guided tours.

SPORTS

Wellington

Tournament play is at its best January through April at the **Palm Beach Polo & Country Club** (561-798-7000; www.palmbeachpolo.com), 11199 Polo Club. High-goal polo games are played on 11 world-class polo fields. The PBPC also presents the **National Horse Show and Winter Equestrian Festival** (see *Special Events*).

West Palm Beach

Learn how to play croquet the English way at the **National Croquet Center** (561-478-2300; www.croquetnational.com), 700 Florida Mango Rd. The 19,000-square-foot clubhouse presents tournaments and schedules classes throughout the year. Every Saturday morning the center offers free two-hour golf croquet starting promptly at 10. You must be at least 12 years old, and all instruction and equipment is provided. Reservations are recommended if there are more than four in your group. Flat-sole shoes are a must. For those who want to learn more, half-day clinics are held 8:30 AM–12:30 PM by Archie Peck, the center's director of croquet and four-time national champion. There is a fee for the clinic, and reservations are required. Hours vary depending on events; call for more information.

ZOOLOGICAL PARK Situated on more than 23 lush, tropical acres, the **Palm Beach Zoo at Dreher Park** (561-547-9453; www.palmbeachzoo.com), 1301 Summit Blvd., West Palm Beach, is home to more than nine hundred animals from Florida, Central and South America, Asia, and Australia. The new "Tropic of the Americas" features Mayan pyramids where you find bush dogs and jaguars, including a cub named Maya, who was born at the zoo on October 28, 2008. The zoo's paddocks house a variety of free-roaming animals, from the majestic Bengal tiger to the rabbit-sized Malayan mouse deer. Bring your bathing suit on hot days to cool off in the Interactive Fountain (changing cabanas available). Open daily 9 AM–5 PM. Adults $13, seniors 60+ $10, children 3–12 $9, under 3 free.

✴ To Do

CRUISES Take a trip over to Freeport, Bahamas, on the majestic *Palm Beach Princess* The 420-foot, 1,300-passenger Palm Beach Princess cruise ship (1-800-841-7447; www.palmbeachprincess.com) sails twice daily from the Port of Palm Beach for five-hour lunch or dinner cruises that include casino gambling, live entertainment, a pool, skeet shooting, and lavish buffets.

FAMILY ACTIVITIES Adventure Mini Golf (561-968-1111 or 1-877-580-3117), 6585 S Military Trail, Lake Worth. Two 18-hole courses feature cascading waterfalls, rapids, and hours of delight in the game room with snack bar.

The world's largest croquet complex, **National Croquet Center** (561-478-2300; www.croquetnational.com), 700 Florida Mango Rd., Lake Worth (see *Sports*), features its own "golf croquet" and is open year-round for sport and entertainment.

GOLF Lake Worth Municipal Golf Course (561-533-7365), One Seventh Ave. N, Lake Worth. Of the 145 golf courses in Palm Beach County, Lake Worth just happens to have one of the finest and most affordable. Designed by William Langford and Theodore J. Moreau, the municipally owned 18-hole, par 70 course has been open since 1924. Overlooking the scenic Intracoastal Waterway, the public golf course is one of the few on a waterfront venue. The **Lake Worth Country Club** is also open to the public and features leisurely lunches, elegant dinners, and a classic Sunday brunch.

HIKING One of the best places to go hiking is in the **Corbett Wildlife Management Area** (561-625-5122), off Seminole-Pratt-Whitney Blvd., with more than 60,000 acres of wild and watery wilderness. A 17-mile section of the **Ocean-to-Lake Trail** passes through the preserve. (See *Wild Places.*) Dozens of small county and city natural areas also offer short gentle walks, often paved or boardwalk, through patches of public land.

RACE CAR DRIVING More than seven hundred sports cars and motorcycle events are held each year at **Palm Beach International Raceway** (561-622-1400; www.racepbir.com), 17047 Beeline Hwy., Palm Beach Gardens. Driver-development programs and open test days for both sports cars and motorcycles are held on the 2.25-mile road course and 0.25-mile drag strip. Kids older than eight will want their turn at the wheel on the competition-grade 0.9-mile Kart Track.

SCUBA & SNORKELING **Lake Worth Lagoon** is recognized as one of the most important warm-water manatee refuges on the east coast of Florida. These "sea cows" are often observed resting or feeding near submerged seagrass beds during winter months. An artificial reef, completed in 1995, plunges to depths of 440 feet. It was created using tons of rock, barges, freighters, and even a Rolls Royce (!), this living reef system is home to many fish and other marine life.

SPA THERAPY Select one of the flavor-of-the-month body scrubs at **The Breakers** (561-655-6611 or 1-888-273-2537; www.thebreakers.com), One S Country Rd., Palm Beach, such as decadent chocolate, coffee, tropical mango, and Key lime, and seasonal offerings such as pumpkin spice.

TOURS It's a quacking good time! Part boat, part bus, the amphibious **DivaDuck** (561-844-4188; www.divaduck.com), 501 Clematis St., West Palm Beach, will take you over land and sea on a 75-minute, fully narrated musical tour of downtown CityPlace, historic Palm Beach neighborhoods, Lake Worth Lagoon, Peanut Island, and down the Intracoastal Waterway past magnificent mansions. All tours depart from Hibiscus Street in CityPlace, just west of the railroad tracks. Adult and children over 10 $25, children 4–10 $15, children under 4 $5.

WATER PARKS

Royal Palm Beach
Calypso Bay Waterpark (561-790-6160; www.pbcgov.com), 151 Lamstein Ln., is located in Seminole Palms Park, one of Palm Beach County's parks. It features an 880-foot river ride, two four-story-high water slides, and a lily pad walk, along with full-service concessions. Adults and children over 12 $10, children 3–11 $7, children 1–2 $3, infants under 1 free.

West Palm Beach
You'll find 22 acres of action-packed thrills at **Rapids Water Park** (561-842-8756; www.rapidswaterpark.com), 6566 N Military Trail. At Big Thunder, one of the largest water rides in Florida, you ride on a four-person tube through a 9-foot dark tunnel and then round and round through a funnel at speeds of up to 20 miles an hour before dropping to a landing pool below. You won't need tubes or rafts on Body Blasters as you slide your way through 1,000 feet of darkness, and at Pirate's

Plunge you zip down two speed slides before dropping seven stories. Tubin' Torna-does will have you twisting and turning, you'll spin and swirl through mist on one of two Superbowls, or you can ride a whitewater adventure over three waterfalls at Riptide Raftin. Over at Big Surf, you can catch a 6-foot wave in the 25,000-square-foot wave pool. Milder rides such as the Lazy River, Splish Splash Lagoon, and the toddler Tadpool ensure a fun day for everyone in your family. Open daily mid-Mar. to late Aug., and weekends Sept. to mid-Oct. Admission $32; children under two free.

✳ Green Space

BEACHES

Lake Worth

& At **Lake Worth Beach** (561-533-7367), SR A1A, there are 1,300 feet of guard-ed beach perfect for sunning, surfing, and volleyball, and you can rent cabanas, boogie boards, rafts, chairs, and umbrellas. The 962-foot fishing pier is sure to please anglers, and there are rental poles and bait available. Other amenities include restaurants and stores, showers, and picnic facilities. Lifeguards on beach 9 AM–5 PM; handicapped assistance if requested. Open daily. Free.

Singer Island

& ✎ Popular for sunning and snorkeling, **John D. MacArthur Beach State Park** (561-624-6950; www.macarthurbeach.org), 10900 Jack Nicklaus Dr., is a beautiful natural area between the Lake Worth Lagoon and the Atlantic Ocean. The park maintains an excellent nature center with interpretive information on the creatures of the lagoon and rocky reef. The main portion of the park connects with the beach via a broad boardwalk over the flats, a great spot for birding. There are two nature trails in the park, one through the tropical forest behind the dunes and the other, the Satinleaf Trail, a short interpretive trail that starts at the parking area and makes a loop through the native tropical hammock. At the beach, MacArthur's rocky reefs and tidal pools are ideal for snorkeling. Park rangers run guided kayak-ing tours of the lagoon; call for details and times. Open 8 AM–sunset daily. $4 per vehicle.

BOTANICAL GARDENS An oasis of beauty near the West Palm Beach Interna-tional Airport, **Mounts Botanical Garden** (561-233-1749; www.mounts.org), 531 N Military Trail, West Palm Beach, packs plants from around the globe into a 14-acre park. Themed sections break up your stroll through the gardens, from Florida natives to tropical fruits to Australian eucalyptus and African baobab trees. The Garden Shop stocks an excellent selection of books, including hard-to-find tomes on gardening and natural habitats in Florida. Open 8 AM–4 PM Mon.–Sat. and 12 PM–4 PM Sun. Donation.

Pan's Garden (561-832-0731; www.palmbeachpreservation.org), 386 Hibiscus Ave., is a tiny oasis in the heart of downtown Palm Beach, offering a quiet place to sit and reflect beneath the deep shade of native trees, with more than 300 species of Florida plants represented. Massive pond apple trees anchor one end of a cypress-lined pond, and a rare Geiger tree sports bright reddish-orange blooms in summer near the main entrance. Free.

NATURE CENTERS ♿ ✎ Perched on the edge of the Loxahatchee Slough, the water supply for West Palm Beach, **Grassy Waters Preserve** (561-804-4985; www.cityofwpb.com/park), 8264 Northlake Blvd., West Palm Beach, surrounds you with the Everglades as they always were, before cities along Florida's east coast drained them. The preserve features a nature center for orientation, the Rain-catcher Boardwalk for an immersion into the cypress slough habitat, and a set of rugged hiking trails just up the road behind the Fish & Wildlife Commission head-quarters building. Regular guided tours are offered, including off-trail swamp tromps and paddling trips. Fee.

♿ ✎ Hidden at the back of vast **Okeeheelee Park** (see *Parks*), **Okeeheelee Nature Center** (561-966-6660; www.pbcgov.com/parks), 7715 Forest Hill Blvd., West Palm Beach, provides interpretation of the habitats and their inhabitants found along a network of hard-packed lime rock trails that fan out behind the cen-ter for a couple of miles of walking. One path leads to a permanent deer exhibit. Free.

✎ **Pine Jog Environmental Education Center** (561-686-6600; www.pinejog .org), 6301 Summit Blvd., West Palm Beach, preserves a patch of pine flatwoods amid suburban sprawl. Park near the exhibit center and stop in for an interpretive brochure and overview of local habitats, then walk the 0.5-mile Wetland Hammock Trail around a flatwoods pond teeming with birds. Open 9 AM–5 PM Mon.–Sat. and 2 PM–5 PM Sun. Free.

PARKS

Lake Worth
Bryant Park (561-533-7359), corner of Golfview and Lake Ave., right on the Intracoastal Waterway. Regular concerts are held at the Bandshell, with seating for 500, or bring your own chairs and blankets. There are restrooms and a boat ramp on-site. Across the bridge, also on the water is **Barton Park,** by the Lake Worth Beach lower parking lot. It has picnic tables and pavilion, restrooms, and a play-ground.

John Prince Park (561-966-6660; www.pbcgoc.com/parks), 2700 Sixth Ave. S, stretches from Lake Worth Road to Lantana Road along Congress Boulevard, fac-ing Lake Worth. Tucked in the back of the park off Prince Drive, there's a delight-ful campground (265 sites for RV or tent camping—some on waterfront) and adjoining nature trail system. Other activities include a 3-mile paved bike/walking trail, fishing, canoeing, golfing, and birding. Pets welcome on a 6-foot leash.

West Palm Beach
One of the county's largest recreational parks, **Okeeheelee Park** (561-966-6660), 7715 Forest Hill Blvd., has a wide range of activities to choose from—dozens of picnic pavilions, ball fields, tennis courts, rental paddleboats, a water-ski course, paved bike trails, municipal golf course, and natural area with nature center and several miles of hiking trails winding through the pine flatwoods.

PUBLIC GARDENS Sitting on just less than 2 acres, the **Ann Norton Sculp-ture Gardens** (561-832-5328; www.ansg.org), 253 Barcelona Rd., West Palm Beach, features monolithic sculptures set among 300 species of tropical palms. The historic home, listed on the National Register of Historic Places, displays more than 100 various size sculptures created by Ann Weaver Norton. Open 11 AM–4 PM Wed.–Sun. Oct.–May and Fri.–Sat. June–Aug. Closed Aug. Fee.

¶ Marrying sculpture and formal gardens, the **Society of the Four Arts Gardens** (561-655-7226; www.fourarts.org), 2 Four Arts Plaza, is part of a larger cultural complex and features a breathtakingly beautiful Oriental garden among its many niche gardens. Most of the green space encompasses the Philip Hulitar Sculpture Garden, with its collection of statues set in garden nooks. Open 10 AM– 5 PM daily, free.

WILD PLACES At the western edge of "civilization" along Northlake Blvd., **Corbett Wildlife Management Area** (561-625-5122), off Seminole-Pratt-Whitney Blvd., West Palm Beach, encompasses more than 60,000 acres of wild and watery wilderness, brimming with blossoms in summer. A 17-mile section of the Ocean-to-Lake Trail passes through the preserve, accessed at Everglades Youth Camp along with the 1-mile interpretive Hungryland Boardwalk through a cypress slough. This is a popular winter destination for the county's deer hunters, who use large-tired swamp buggies to prowl off-road. Primitive camping is available to hunters and backpackers; day-use fee applies.

✴ Lodging

Lake Worth 33460

The first thing you notice when you drive up to the **Mango Inn** (561-533-6900; www.mangoinn.com), 128 N Lakeside Dr., is the immaculately groomed gardens surrounding the two-story building bathed in sunshine. Yes, you can't miss the eye-stopping yellow-painted inn nestled next to a delightful cottage. Tucked away on a quiet side street 2 blocks from the Intracoastal, the Mango Inn is within easy walking distance to the beach and the funky downtown area. Built in 1915, this local treasure was rescued and restored by Erin and Bo Allen, originally from Michigan. As you step through the front door you are greeted with the clean aroma of fresh cut flowers grown in the care-fully tended garden. Cozy up to the coral fireplace or stretch out and grab some rays next to the heated swimming pool and circular waterfall. When you are ready to rest your head, retire to your own immaculate room or suite, complete with private bath. Fall into the lush down pillows and curl up under the monogrammed designer bed

linens. For longer stays, request the cozy 1925 Pineapple Cottage, with fireplace and full kitchen; or the 1925 Mango Little House, complete with kitchen facilities. Mornings bring a new sensation with fresh baked blueberry gingerbread pancakes, cashew-mango muffins, and cinnamon-raisin scones with clotted cream and blackberry butter. Dine with other guests in the welcoming dining room or on the intimate veranda overlooking the pool. Before you head to the beach, have Erin pack you a picnic basket of light snacks and beverages. $165 and up.

The Bradley Park Hotel (561-832-7050 or 1-800-822-4116; www.bradley parkhotel.com), 280 Sunset Ave. Founded by Florida pioneer and Flagler contemporary E. R. Bradley, this hotel is a remnant from the days when Bradley ran the Beach House, an entertainment venue and casino adjunct to Flagler's hotel. Bradley won the reputation of "Mr. Lucky," the greatest gambler that ever lived. Today's hotel has 31 suites, from stu-

Trish Riley

CHESTERFIELD HOTEL, PALM BEACH

dios to penthouse, each with kitchen facilities. $359 and up.

The glamorous, European-style **Chesterfield Hotel** (561-659-5800; www.chesterfieldpb.com), 363 Cocoanut Row, is listed on the National Register of Historic Places. Built in 1926 as The Lido-Venice bed & breakfast, the hotel was renamed in 1928 as The Vineta. The three-story Mediterranean Revival–style structure is a good representation of resort hotels built during the Florida land boom of the 1920s. The name changed again in 1985 to The Chesterfield, and the boutique hotel is now a member of the Red Carnation Hotel Collection and Small Luxury Hotels of the World. It's plush and cozy, just a block from the beach. $359 and up.

✧ **The Breakers** (561-655-6611 or 1-888-BREAKERS; www.thebreakers .com), 1 S County Rd. A AAA five-diamond resort, the Breakers is simply incomparable to any other Gold Coast property. The Breakers earned its designation as a Florida Certified Green Hotel in 2006, the first Palm Beach hotel to make such an investment in the environment. Originally built in 1896 and twice reconstructed because

of fires, the hotel was created for the wealthiest Americans of the Gilded Age. While most remaining properties created during that time of opulence and luxury have become museums, the Breakers remains in full use, still serving the crème de la crème and giving the rest of us a glimpse at the good life, too, should we choose to accept it. Speaking from experience, my advice is this: treat yourself right. Everyone deserves to find out what it's like to live at the height of luxury. You may just be surprised to discover that this magnificent place is filled with people like you. From the 220-foot-long lobby to the carved and painted ceilings, this hotel is filled with luscious beauty. Patterns and colors combine everywhere—striped upholstery and diamond-patterned carpet and floral curtains and polka-dotted linens. Perhaps it's the pastel colors that make it all work so well, but it is simply richly

VIEW FROM THE BREAKERS, PALM BEACH

Trish Riley

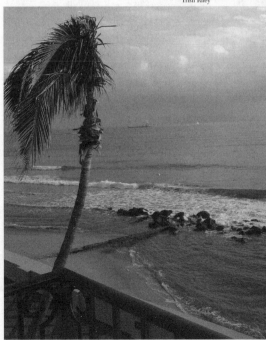

gorgeous. Then there are the marble baths, glass-walled shower, and the balcony overlooking the sea. There is a world-class spa, pools, and golf, and beach activities include guided trips to the offshore reef. A children's labyrinth garden and the chef's herb garden contribute to the award-winning grounds, all combining to give the feel of a grand estate—more like a stately home than a hotel. $380 and up.

The Colony (561-655-5430 or 1-800-521-5525; www.thecolonypalmbeach .com), 155 Hammon Ave. A few steps from Worth Avenue, the Colony offers simple, unpretentious finery. This luxurious Euro-style boutique hotel has rooms and villas (available by the month during the season). $375 and up.

↝ **Four Seasons Resort** (561-582-2800; www.fourseasons.com/palm beach), 2800 S. Ocean Blvd. This oceanfront resort brings a new sense of luxury to Palm Beach, with carefully appointed full-service rooms and suites, a spa, water sports, and golf. This is a good place for the ultimate luxury vacation, with fine dining and relaxation the only concerns on the agenda. Make it a romantic getaway, or bring the whole family and take a four-bedroom suite, with work spaces, sitting areas, and oceanfront balconies. $499 and up.

One of the few bed & breakfasts on the "Island," the **Palm Beach Historic Inn** (561-832-4009 or 1-800-918-9773; www.palmbeachhistoricinn.com), 365 S County Rd., is only a few steps from Worth Avenue and the beach. Complimentary continental breakfast is served in your room. Eight guest rooms and four suites, with king or queen beds, are all located on the second floor. Rates $145 and up.

West Palm Beach 33401
In the heart of the downtown shopping district near CityPlace is **Grandview**

Gardens Bed & Breakfast (561-833-9023; www.grandview-gardens.net), 1608 Lake Ave. The intimate 1923 Mediterranean Revival villa has only five guest suites. Decorated in Spanish Mediterranean style, each suite has its own private entrance and is set around the 30-foot swimming pool and tropical gardens. Innkeepers speak a variety of languages: English, German, Spanish, and French. Rates $199 and up and include a breakfast buffet.

West Palm Beach 33407
Innkeepers Elaine and Frank Calendrillo are your hosts in the Tuscany-style villa (circa 1926) **Casa de Rosa Bed & Breakfast** (561-833-1920 or 1-888-665-8666; www.casaderosa.com), 520 27th St., in Historic Old Northwood. Beautifully landscaped gardens surround the heated pool. With just four rooms, this is the perfect romantic getaway or an alternative from hotels for the executive business-person. The Italian architecture, painted in marigold yellow, features upper- and lower-story verandas with 22 arches. The luxurious 20-by-30-foot White Rose Room has a king-sized bed and a bathroom with two vanities—unique in bed & breakfasts, the room opens to the veranda through three French doors. The Beach Rose Cottage has a fun beachy theme complete with kitchen, the charming Tuscany Rose Room Suite features a queen-sized poster bed and French doors, and the comfortable Tropicana Rose Room ensures you a peaceful night's sleep. Rates $135 and up.

Built during the Florida land boom in 1922 by Mayor David Dunkle, the **Hibiscus House Bed & Breakfast** (561-863-5633 or 1-800-203-4927; www.hibiscushouse.com), 501 30th St., is on the National Register of Historic Places. Rooms have romantic queen-sized beds, such as the four-poster rice bed in the Green Room, and the Peach Room has a wood ceiling canopy. The two-room Burgundy Suite has a sitting room, fireplace, and a queen-sized cherry four-poster bed. A full breakfast is served on china, silver, and Waterford crystal in the formal dining room or in the tropical gardens surrounding the pool. Rates $189 and up.

✧ **Hilton Palm Beach Airport** (561-684-9400; www.hilton.com), 150 Australian Ave. With easy access to the airport, this is a good selection for a business trip, but there are better choices for vacation. The rooms and suites are well kept. $180 and up.

✧ **Hotel Biba** (561-832-0094; www .hotelbiba.com), 320 Belvedere Rd. This 43-room historic motor lodge that was reinvented as a sleek, hip hotel is on the fringes of the downtown scene of West Palm Beach. Coolest of cool decor and amenities include glass tiles—mosaics and terrazzo—Egyptian cotton linens, Aveda bath products, bamboo bead doors, and burlap headboards. The candle-lit wine bar, decorated with colorful silk, is the subject of wide acclaim, and I think the Biba has the coolest package on the Gold Coast: surf lessons with your room (call for prices). $125 and up.

CAMPGROUND

Lake Worth 33461
John Prince Park Campground (561-582-7992 or 1-877-992-9925), 4759 S Congress Ave., offers 265 rustic campsites with water and electric hookups for tents or RVs. Sites, especially the coveted waterfront sites, fill up fast, so reservations are recommended. The campground is operated by the Palm Beach Park and Recreation Department (www.pbcgov.com), and a manager resides on-site for your convenience.

DINING OUT

Lake Worth
At **Bizarre Avenue Cafe** (561-588-4488), 921 Lake Ave., Granny's attic meets Bizarro World in a creatively decorated, offbeat café. Settle into the overstuffed chairs and sofas, and if you like one, you can take it home! All of the furnishings and bric-a-brac are for sale. The carefully selected, ever-changing decor is arranged in intimate groupings and surrounded by rich red brick walls. The eclectic menu echoes the atmosphere with such scrumptious delights as chicken–artichoke heart crêpes and an assortment of tapas, sandwiches, pasta, and salads. Desserts are made fresh locally and complement the season—we had the Pumpkin Crunch when we visited in the fall. The wraparound bar serves wine and beer. Plan to stay late, as this place is open until 11 PM weekdays and midnight Fri. and Sat.

Dave's Last Resort and Raw Bar (561-588-5208), 632 Lake Ave. Looking for a place to relax with friends? The open, airy dining room/bar boasts a plethora of TVs, with a variety of broadcast sports. The booths and table-tops are laden with copper and outlined with etched maple leaves. Light knotty pine, lots of it, completes the rustic feel. This is the place to go when you have a "manly" appetite. Start with the raw bar sampler, which includes oysters, clams, snow crab, white and rock shrimp, and even crawdads. Still hungry? Then order up the house favorite—a 20-ounce porterhouse with garlic mashed potatoes. Open daily for lunch, dinner, and—as all good last resorts—late into the night.

Yama (561-582-5800), 809 Lake Ave., is getting rave reviews for sizzling Korean barbeque and all the amazing flavors and side dishes that go along with this cultural delight. $12.95 and up.

Palm Beach

Muer Seafood restaurants (www.muer .com) began as a family of restaurants in 1964, and while Landry now owns the chain, the culinary control is still in the hands of the Muer chefs. Along the water, **Charley's Crab** (561-659-1500), 456 S Ocean Blvd., offers the best in seafood dishes, from classics such as bouillabaisse ($19) to imaginative dishes such as the Szechuan-style Dungeness crab clusters ($23). At 207 Royal Poinciana Way, **Chuck & Harold's** (561-659-1440) caters to the well-heeled locals. Favorites are Chuck & Harold's Fishwich ($9) and the Muer classic Maryland crab cakes ($22). A great place to sip Bloody Marys is outside in the garden café. Both locations are celebrated for their Sunday brunch. Lunch and dinner served Mon.–Sat. (See also *Oceanside: Eastern Broward County* for **Pal's Charley's Crab,** on the Intracoastal Waterway in Deerfield Beach.)

A Palm Beach classic, the **Leopard Lounge and Restaurant** (561-659-

LEOPARD LOUNGE AND RESTAURANT AT THE CHESTERFIELD, PALM BEACH

Courtesy The Chesterfield, Palm Beach

8500 or 1-800-243-7871; www.red carnationhotels.com), 363 Cocoanut Row, serves breakfast, brunch, lunch, afternoon tea, and dinner. The jungle-themed lounge, British Colonial furnishings, and black and red lacquer trim evoke a private-club atmosphere, and it offers a variety of live music, entertainment, and dancing.

EATING OUT

Lake Worth

Every town has one or two culinary treasures, and **John G's** (561-585-9860; www.johngs.com), 10 S Ocean Blvd., is *the* local favorite. Start your day in this nautical setting, watching the sunrise while feasting on Canadian peameal bacon flanked with scrambled eggs, or try the cinnamon nut French toast or blueberry pancakes. This place is always rated at the top of the "Best" lists, so get there early, as it's known for its long lines. On Sunday, the owner, Mr. John G himself, serves chocolate-dipped strawberries to those patiently waiting. It's conveniently located across from the beach, so you'll want to come back and grab lunch as well. Try the some of the deep-sea favorites, such as fried clams and crab cakes or fresh fish fillets. And don't forget to save room for dessert! Open daily 7 AM–3 PM.

Key West Crossing (561-588-9900), 617 Lake Ave. Stop into this funky ice cream parlor for a piece of Key lime pie and coconut ice cream. Play checkers on one of the colorful tables, or shop for eclectic gifts and treats such as Key lime syrup. Open daily 11 AM–11 PM.

The hub of the Finnish community since 1955, the fabulous **Scandia Bakery and Coffee Shop** (561-582-1600), 16 S Dixie Hwy., is also the headquarters for the annual **Finlandia Festival** (see *Special Events*). Read the bulletin board, some of which is in English, while having your cardamom cake and coffee. Make sure to take home a fresh hot loaf of Finnish or Russian rye bread. Open for breakfast and light lunches 8 AM–4 PM Mon.–Sat. and 8 AM–2 PM Sun.

West Palm Beach

Montezuma Restaurant (561-586-7974), 5607 S. Dixie Hwy., W. Palm Beach.What's the best sign that a Mexican restaurant is authentic? The salsa, but more important, the clientele. Montezuma is just such a place. Even the babies are spoon-fed spicy beans and rice at this unassuming café, which caters to the strong local population of Mexican farm workers. The small gift shop and grocery of Mexican imports is interesting and has friendly service. $8 and up.

Bellagio (561-659-6160; www.il bellagiocityplace.com), 600 Rosemary Ave. at City Place. The aroma of delicious northern Italian comfort food greets you as you enter this fountain-side eatery at City Place. Try sautéed artichokes and mushrooms, or save your appetite for a main dish of chicken dressed with spinach and mozzarella in a cognac cream sauce. $16.95 and up.

Brewzzi (561-366-9753; www.brewzzi .com), 700 S. Rosemary at City Place. Take a break from shopping at this City Place brewery, where you can sit upstairs or on the open-air patio and look down upon the less-savvy shoppers. Try the award-winning brew, as well as the Gorgonzola chips, a huge Brewzzi salad, meat loaf, Farfalle à la Vodka, crusted snapper, Angus steaks, or pizza—there's something here for everyone. $12 and up.

E. R. Bradley's Saloon (561-833-3520; www.erbradleys.com), 104 Clematis St. This saloon was named for a Florida dandy who struck a deal with Henry Flagler to build and run a beach club alongside Flagler's hotel. Bradley became known as the world's luckiest gambler when his adopted homeland became the subject of Flagler's railway and glitterati of the Gilded Age. The saloon is the perfect way to keep his memory alive, and it does so with hallways lined with newspaper and magazine accounts from Bradley's day. The restored waterfront home is a lovely place to sit outside for views of the Intra-coastal, or inside after dark the barroom turns into a dance hall. Delicious soups and seafood are served, with fresh homemade pretzels served with lunch instead of bread. Open until the wee hours for dancing. Entrées $17 and up.

Leila (561-659-7373; www.leilawpb .com), 120 S. Dixie Hwy. At this tiny spot south of City Place, you'll find a casual atmosphere and fragrant, sensuous, and tasty fare. I love the curries and falafel, Mediterranean salads, and heady Lebanese specialties. The moderately sized portions make it fun to try several dishes at once. Choose a few or a sampler. Entrées $17 and up.

✳ Entertainment

PERFORMING ARTS

Lake Worth

Since 1987, the nationally renowned **Demetrius Klein Dance Company** (561-586-1889), 811 Lake Ave., has swept away critics across the country with their unique choreography and physical modern dance form. The company's active schedule produces a dozen full performances a year.

The fully restored **Lake Worth Playhouse** (561-586-6410), 713 Lake Ave., is comprised of two theaters. The 300-seat main theater presents Broadway-style plays and musicals to appreciative audiences. Built in 1924, the interior is a spectacular example of period design. The 70-seat **Stonzek Studio Theater,** at 709 Lake Ave., showcases experimental works and is reminiscent of New York's intimate off-Broadway scene.

Manalapan

Dedicated to introducing new and developing work, the 258-seat **Florida Stage Professional Theatre** (561-585-3433 or 1-800-514-3837; www .floridastage.org), 262 S Ocean Blvd., produces contemporary works by both established and emerging playwrights. Located in the Plaza del Mar between the Atlantic Ocean and the Intracoastal Waterway. Summer and season tickets $35–45; opening night $75.

West Palm Beach

Classical and contemporary dance is presented at **Ballet Florida** (561-659-1212 or 1-800-540-0172; www.ballet florida.com), 500 Fern St., at locations around the tri-county area. Under the direction of founder Marie Hale, celebrated choreographers from around the world direct 22 professional dancers in such works as Twyla Tharp's *Baker's Dozen;* Ben Stevenson's *Five Poems,* with costume and scenery designed by actress Jane Seymour; and, of course, the holiday favorite *The Nutcracker.*

The 400-seat **Cuillo Centre for the Arts** (561-835-9226; www.cuillocentre .com), 201 Clematis St., features live theater such as pre-Broadway shows, concerts, and play readings.

Conveniently located just east of I-95, **The Kravis Center for the Performing Arts** (561-832-7469 or 1-800-KRAVIS-1; www.kravis.org), 701 Okeechobee Blvd., was built totally on donations from local residents. The

Trish Riley

CUILLO CENTRE FOR THE ARTS, WEST PALM BEACH

center is named for its main benefactor, Raymond F. Kravis, a geologist from Oklahoma and winter resident of Palm Beach for more than 35 years. As such it has had the funding to produce some of the region's best ballet, theater, and musical performances. Three venues, the 2,200-seat Dreyfoos Hall, the 1,400-seat Gosman Amphitheater, and the 300-seat Rinker Playhouse, offer performances from intimate lecture series to large-scale Broadway productions.

Palm Beach Opera (561-833-7888 or 1-888-88-OPERA; www.pbopera.org), 415 S Olive Ave., holds performances at the Kravis Center. The opera company has a half dozen operas and symphonic concerts during the season and an outreach program to assist both children and aspiring opera singers. One of their educational programs, The Family Opera Series, is hosted by canine tenor The Great Poochini, a costumed character in tails.

✳ Selective Shopping

Lake Worth

Even if you don't own a dog, you'll want to stop at the delightful **Paws on the Avenue** (561-588-6533), 409 Lake Ave. Top dog Caroline Clore has created a doggone oasis for your furry friend. You'll want to adorn your canine or feline with an attractive bandanna or choose from the vast collection of clothing specifically created "fur" style and function. Your hungry canines will drool with delight at the gourmet pet treats at Café le Paws. And don't forget to pamper your little dah-ling at the Day Spa with an herbal bath, paw soak, and therapeutic massage.

SHOPPING AREAS

Lake Worth

The Lake Worth downtown area of Lake Avenue and Lucerne Avenue, is a virtual hub of the antiques community, so you'll be sure to find what you're looking for, whether it is collectibles, fine art, estate jewelry, Oriental carpets, or classic heirlooms. Fine linens are found at **RoundAbout Antiques** (561-845-1985), 824 Lake Ave.; and the **Lake Avenue Antiques Mall** (561-586-1131), 704 Lake Ave., has something for everyone.

Palm Beach

Worth Avenue (561-659-6909; www.worth-avenue.com) is the pinnacle of luxury shopping. All the big names are here, along with some new ones. You'll find old favorites such as **Cartier** (561-655-5913), 214 Worth Ave.; **Chanel** (561-655-1550), 301 Worth Ave.; and **Hermès** (561-655-6655), 255 Worth Ave.; along with some of the finest antiques shops in the world.

West Palm Beach

If Worth Avenue gives you sticker shock, there is still excellent shopping to be had on the mainland at **City-Place** (561-366-1000; www.cityplace.com), 701 S Rosemary Ave., where you find regulars such as **Banana Republic** (561-833-9841) and **Williams-Sonoma** (561-833-0659). To get to S Rosemary Ave., take I-95 exit 70 to Okeechobee Blvd., and go east less than a mile. Shops are open 10 AM–9 PM Mon.–Thurs., 10 AM–10 PM Fri. and Sat., and noon–6 PM Sun. Valet parking available at some locations.

FARMER'S MARKET West Palm Beach Greenmarket (561-822-1515; www.wpb.org/greenmarket), Second St. between Olive Ave. and Flagler Dr. and Narcissus St. between Clematis St. and Flagler Dr. Live music. Dog friendly and free parking. Every Sat. from 8 AM–1 PM Oct. 18–Apr. 25.

TIFFANY'S, PALM BEACH

Trish Riley

✳ Special Events

Weekly/Monthly: **Evening on the Avenues** (561-582-4401), Cultural Plaza near M St., Lake Worth. Held 6 AM–10 PM the first and third Fri. of every month. Enjoy live music, arts and crafts, food, and lots of shopping at specialty stores along Lake Avenue and Lucerne Avenue, as well as an array of classic cars lining J St.

Bonfire on the Beach, Lake Worth Beach. Held 7 AM–9 PM first and third Fri. in Nov. and Dec. and the second and fourth Fri. of Jan. and Feb. Stroll along the white-sand beach and let the balmy breezes blow through your hair. Then, cozy up with a loved one until the last embers wane. You'll want to toast marshmallows. 7 AM–9 PM. **Note:** no alcoholic beverages or pets.

Motown favorites come alive every Friday night at **The Colony Hotel** (see *Lodging*), Palm Beach, with music from the 1960s to the '80s, such as the Temptations, the Supremes, and Marvin Gaye, 9:30 AM–closing.

A few miles west of Palm Beach you'll find a treasure at **Lion Country Safari** (561-793-1084; www.lioncountrysafari.com), 2003 Lion Country Safari Rd., Loxahatchee. If you can't go to Africa, then we'll bring Africa to you. That was the thought in 1967 when a group of South African and British entrepreneurs opened the first "cageless" park in America. Drive through the 350-acre preserve where a thousand animals roam freely. The park is divided into seven sections: Las Pampas, grasslands where llamas, rhea, fallow deer, and Brazilian tapirs graze; Ruaha National Park, where you'll see greater kudu, impala, and aoudad; the dry Kalahari Bushveldt, where Gemsbok and Lechwe antelope leap past you; the Gir Forest, where you can look closely to see the impressive Asiatic water buffalo; The Gorongosa, where African lions dominate; the famed Serengeti Plains, home to the African elephant, eland, ostrich, wildebeast, and more; and the Hwange National Park, where you'll see herds of zebras running along with white rhinos while chimpanzees play and giraffes tower above you. You will be driving at a snail's pace through the park so as not to injure any animals, so allow about one to two hours for the 5-mile safari. And please, no matter how tempting, keep your windows rolled up just like they tell you, and never, ever get out of your car. These animals are wild and can be very inquisitive: The ostrich and giraffes especially love to surprise you. My favorite sections were the Hwange National Park, where a herd of zebras took off ahead of me, racing along the plain, and The Gorongosa, where the "King of Beasts" rules. The parks, which work as part of the Species Survival Plan (SSP) and are members of the American Zoo and Aquarium Association (AZA), have been instrumental in the continued survival of the white rhinoceros. And as a licensed rehabilitation facility, the park often takes in Florida rescues, such as the brown pelican. With the new Safari World expansion, the park adds

A one-hour Historic Walking Tour of Worth Avenue (561-659-6909; www .worth-avenue.com) starts at 11 AM at the Gucci Courtyard, 256 Worth Ave., West Palm Beach, the second Wed. of the month Oct.–May and the first Sat. of the month June–Aug. Call for reservations. Free.

On the first weekend of every month, hundreds of antiques and collectibles dealers feature items from knickknacks and fine collectibles to books and furniture at the **West Palm Beach**

Antique & Collectibles Show (1-800-640-FAIR; www.wpbantiques .com), 9067 Southern Blvd., South Florida Fairgrounds, West Palm Beach.

Clematis by Night (561-822-1515; www.clematisbynight.net), in Centennial Square at the top of Clematis St., West Palm Beach, features a fountain-side concert from 6:00 to 9:30 every Thursday night. Listen to rock, rhythm and blues, swing, blues, reggae, and soul while browsing through the inter-

an additional 53 acres to include a children's Safari Splash Interactive Spray Ground, a 55-foot Ferris wheel and other cool kiddie park rides, an Aldabra tortoise exhibit, a giraffe feeding exhibit, and a Safari Hedge Maze. A picnic area is also available, so plan to make a day of it. The park also has a KOA campground. To traverse the park, you may use your own approved vehicle (convertibles are not allowed, and open-bed trucks must be empty), or park your car ($5) and rent a car ($10) or van ($18). Rental cars and vans are first come, first served. No pets are allowed in the park, but they do offer free kennels while you visit. Open 10 AM–4:30 PM (with the park closing promptly at 5:30 PM) daily. Admission: Ages 10–64 $24, seniors 65+ $22, children 3–9 $18, ages 2 and under free. Check the Web site and local grocery stores and flyers for discount admission coupons.

ZEBRAS BLOCK THE ROAD AT LION COUNTRY SAFARI

Sandra Friend

national crafts bazaar. The free event is hosted by the City of West Palm Beach.

Pack up the family and bring a picnic basket to the **Meyer Amphitheater** (561-659-8007), West Palm Beach, to listen to local bands at sunset on the water every Sunday. Free.

January: The South Florida Fairgrounds, West Palm Beach, is home to the **South Florida Fair** (561-793-0333; www.southfloridafair.com).

Winter Equestrian Festival (561-793-5867; www.stadiumjumping.com) is held late Jan. to mid-Mar. at the Palm Beach Polo & Country Club at 11199 Polo Club and Stadium Jumping at 14440 Pierson Rd., Wellington. The largest equestrian event in the world is where the best of the best hunters and jumpers compete, along with dressage and equitation events on more than 4,000 horses.

February: **Finlandia Festival** (561-582-1600), Lake Worth. Since 1985, Bryant Park has been transformed into the *Tori,* a Finnish-style marketplace. Celebrate with this cultural community—the second-largest Finnish community in the world outside of Finland—and enjoy vibrant music, dancing, Finnish foods, and handicrafts.

The **Street Painting Festival** (561-582-4401; www.streetpaintingfestival.org) is held each year in downtown Lake Worth. The tradition of street painting originated in Italy in the 16th century, but it has been the main event in Lake Worth only in the past decade. Watch the streets come alive as more than 400 artists use chalk to transform the pavement into works of fine art. Strolling minstrels, jazz, classical music, dance, theater, improvisation, and an array of streetside cafés complete the old-world atmosphere. Children of all ages will love the Children's Meadow, where they can create their own street paintings.

Spring is in the air at the **Palm Beach Tropical Flower & Garden Show** (561-655-5522) in downtown Palm Beach.

March: The **Worth Avenue Association Pet Parade and Contest,** Palm Beach, puts even Westminster on notice. The "Island" society's best groomed dogs, cats, birds, and even bunnies strut their stuff at this annual event.

The **Annual Palm Beach Boat Show** (1-800-940-7642), along the West Palm Beach waterfront, displays more than a thousand boats and yachts.

April: The annual waterfront **Sunfest** (561-659-5980 or 1-800-SUNFEST; www.sunfest.com), downtown West Palm Beach, offers name-brand entertainment and the best of food and art for several days. Sometimes it is held earlier in the year, so call ahead or check the Web site.

May: The Puppetry Arts Center and Gold Coast Storyteller performs at the **Annual Storytelling Festival** (561-967-3231), West Palm Beach.

June: The **West Palm Beach Carnival** (561-255-7990; www.westpalmbeachcarnival.com), South Florida Fairgrounds, is a lively tropical celebration of island life and culture featuring live reggae music, arts and crafts, and a variety of Caribbean foods and activities.

December: A holiday favorite, the annual **Holiday Boat Parade of the Palm Beaches** (561-832-8444; www.pbboatparade.com) floats boats and yachts along the Intracoastal Waterway, north from Peanut Island to Jupiter.

In 1894, settlers began to push into southeast Florida. Nathan S. Boynton, a former Civil War major from Michigan, settled in **Boynton Beach,** naming it after himself. Major Boynton built the Boynton Beach Hotel as his family's winter residence, and around the turn of the century the hotel became a social destination for northerners escaping the cold winter months. Another group of Michiganders, led by William Linton and David Swinton, settled in **Delray Beach,** so named after the Spanish word for "the king." The town is a leader in the preservation of local history, with many buildings around town restored to their original glory. The area, rich for planting fruits and vegetables, brought a number of Japanese farmers around the turn of the 20th century. These farmers formed the Yamato Colony, growing pineapples on the land now just east of I-95 in **Boca Raton.** The Morikami Museum and Japanese Gardens is all that is left of the colony. The Spanish name Boca Raton is often translated into the "Mouth of the Rat" or "Rat's Mouth," but "Raton" was a term that was once used to mean a cowardly thief. So the true translation of the town's name is thought to mean "Thieves Inlet." In the 1960s South Florida experienced a huge land boom, and many technical companies, such as IBM, moved to the region. In 1981 the first IBM personal computer was developed here.

✳ To See

HISTORIC SITES Throughout the region, many markers have been erected to further detail certain historical moments and places.

Boca Raton

The marker located along the west side of SR A1A in Spanish River Park in Boca Raton memorializes the **Barefoot Mailman**. Between the 1880s and early 1890s, U.S. mailmen walked along this beach, delivering mail from Palm Beach to Miami. The round-trip was made in six days.

The **Boca Raton Town Hall,** 71 North Federal Hwy., houses the Boca Raton Historical Society. Architect Addison C. Mizner is mainly responsible for the Mediterranean Revival style found here and throughout the town of Boca Raton. Completed in 1927, the Town Hall also housed both the fire station and police department. The gilded dome on the bell tower is its shining jewel. Listed on the National Register of Historic Places in 1980, the building is now used by the Boca Raton Historical Society as a local history museum (see *Museums*).

A marker for the **Florida East Coast Railway Depot** is at 747 S Dixie Hwy. In 1895 Henry Flagler's railroad reached Boca Raton, and in 1930 a railway depot for passengers was built. The station operated until 1968. The station was restored in 1989 by the Boca Raton Historical Society and is

DELRAY BEACH

Trish Riley

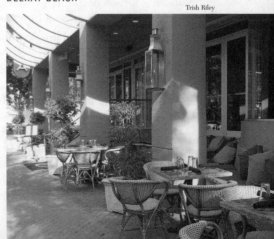

listed on the National Register of Historic Places. The beautifully designed building is in the Mediterranean Revival style. Take particular note of the arched loggia,
pitched gable roof, and delicate spiral columns.

Boynton Beach

If you follow Ocean Ave. to SR A1A, you'll come to a private residence sitting on
the land where the **Boynton Beach Hotel** once stood. The winter home of the
town's founder, Maj. Nathan S. Boynton, became victim to the 1926 hurricane and
was never rebuilt. The only remaining structures are two small cottages. Surviving
historical records are located at the Boynton Beach Library.

The circa 1925 **Boynton Beach Women's Club,** 1010 S Federal Hwy., was
designed by Addison Mizner in the Mediterranean Revival style. The two-story
structure has a loggia on three sides. It was the town's social hub until the 1930s
and is now privately owned.

One of Palm Beach County's sweetest landmarks is the **Little Red Schoolhouse**
(561-433-8550; www.palmbeachpreservation.org), 4485 Haverhill Rd. The 1886
schoolhouse was the first built in what was then Dade County. Educational tours
are given on weekday mornings. Free.

Delray Beach

The 1915 **Cason Cottage** (561-243-2577; www.db-hs.org) is built in the Old Florida Vernacular style with Dade County pine. Restored in 1988, it was the former
retirement home of the Rev. and Mrs. John R. Cason Sr., community leaders.
Many relatives of the Methodist minister still reside in the area. The Delray Beach
Historical Society office is located in a historic bungalow on the property. Open for
tours Tues.–Fri.

The oldest hotel in Delray and a member of Historic Hotels of America is the
Colony Hotel and Cabana Club, 525 E Atlantic Ave. (see *Lodging*). The 1926
Old Florida–style hotel is lovingly restored and sits in the heart of the downtown
cultural area amid fine restaurants and art galleries.

On the city's municipal beach along SR A1A, you'll find a marker commemorating
the **Delray Wreck.** About 150 yards offshore, at the bottom of the ocean in 25
feet of water, rests the SS *Inchulva,* grounded during a hurricane in 1903. The
ship, also known as the "Delray Wreck," is a popular diving spot.

At 200 NE First St. you'll find a marker for the **Florida East Coast Railway.**
Only a 40-foot freight section remains of the old 1896 railroad station. In 1994 the
only surviving section of the station was bought by the Delray Beach Historical
Society and moved to its present location.

One of the greatest historical preservation projects is the **Old School Square**
(561-243-7922; www.oldschool.org), 51 North Swinton Ave., at the corner of
Atlantic Ave. and Swinton Ave. Comprised of three buildings—the Delray Beach
elementary school (circa 1913), high school (circa 1925), and gymnasium (circa
1926)—it is now home to the **Cornell Museum of Art & History** (see *Museums*),
the **Crest Theatre** (see *Performing Arts*), the restored gym, and several vintage
classrooms.

A marker for **Orange Grove House of Refuge No. 3, 1876–1927** is found
along SR A1A, north of Atlantic. One of several homes built by the Treasury
Department for shipwrecked refugees, this site is named for the nearby wild sour
orange grove.

Stop into the **Sundy House,** 106 S Swinton Ave., for lunch or dinner, or stay overnight in the quaint bed & breakfast (see *Lodging*). The circa 1902 Victorian house is the oldest home in Delray Beach and home to the town's first mayor. The wide-open verandas are perfect for sipping an afternoon tea.

HISTORIC TOURS

Boca Raton
The **Boca Raton Historical Society** (561-395-6766; www.bocahistory.org), 71 N Federal Hwy., provides guided tours of the Boca Express Train Museum, the Boca Raton Resort & Club, and other places of historical significance throughout the City of Boca Raton.

Delray Beach
On the fourth Saturday of the month you can take a narrated trolley tour of historic Delray Beach offered by the **Museum of Lifestyle & Fashion History of Delray Beach** (561-243-2662; www.mlfhmuseum.org). The one hour and 45-minute tour explains the history of Delray Beach and the diversity of its multicultural settlers, along with stops at some of the town's historic churches, hotels, and homes. The trolley picks you up at 11 AM at downtown Delray Beach Public Library at 100 W Atlantic Ave. The $10 fee also covers admission to the museum (see *Museums*).

MUSEUMS

Boca Raton
Many historical exhibits are on display at the **Boca Raton Historical Society** (561-395-6766; www.bocahistory.org), 71 N Federal Hwy., where you will also see the Boca Express Train Museum (see *Railroadiana*). Historical tours available.

The 44,000-square-foot **Boca Raton Museum of Art** (561-392-2500; www.boca museum.org), 501 Plaza Rd., Mizner Park, features a fine collection of American and European art, along with an outdoor sculpture garden of contemporary pieces of monumental size. Open 10–5 Tues., Thurs., and Fri., 10 AM–9 PM Wed., and noon–5 PM Sat. and Sun. Adults $14, seniors $12, students $6. Prices reduce to about half during the off-season when special exhibitions are not shown.

⚓ At the **Children's Museum** (561-368-6875; www.cmboca.org), 498 Crawford Blvd., kids can use large magnetic pieces to create their own "Picasso," step back in time and shop for groceries in a replica of Boca Raton's first grocery store, make handmade postcards at Oscar's Post Office, and learn how to care for pets at the Audubon & Friends naturalist exhibition. Open noon–4 PM Tues.–Sat. $3 per person.

Boynton Beach
⚓ Walk into the **Children's Museum** (561-742-6780; www.schoolhousemuseum .org), 129 E Ocean Ave., and you'll be greeted by a replica of the **Jupiter Inlet Lighthouse** (see *North Palm Beach County*), then step back in time to the 1800s and dress up like a Florida pioneer and experience how life used to be. Different historic themes are presented throughout the year. Open 10 AM–5 PM Tues.–Sat. and 1 PM–4 PM Sun. Adults $5, children $3.

Delray Beach
Housed in the historic Delray Elementary School (circa 1913), the **Cornell Museum of Art & History** at Old School Square (561-243-7922; www.oldschool.org),

51 N Swinton Ave., features four galleries, a two-story atrium, a tearoom, and a gift shop. The town's historical archives, which contain photographs, books, and maps, are located on the second floor (see *Historic Sites*).

Japanese immigrant and pineapple farmer George Morikami donated 200 acres to use for a museum showcasing Japanese culture. The **Morikami Museum** (561-495-0233; www.morikami.org), 4000 Morikami Park Rd. (off Jog Rd. between Linton Blvd. and Clint Moore Rd.), is the only museum of Japanese culture in the United States. Surround yourself with serenity as you walk past a cascading waterfall and through pine tree–lined nature trails that wind around the lake while experiencing different types of gardens. The 9th- to 12th-century Shinden Garden is modeled after those found on estates of Japanese nobility. The Zen-inspired 14th- and 15th-century rock gardens display a contrasting stark simplicity. There's even a bonsai garden. Inside, discover more than 5,000 pieces of art and objects in the museum, and take off your shoes and walk through a traditional Japanese home. A library, gift shop, and teahouse are also on-site, and each Saturday you can take part in a traditional *sado* tea ceremony. The Morikami also offers classes, along with several educational events and cultural festivals throughout the year (see *Special Events*). Open 10 AM–5 PM Tues.–Sun. Adults $10, seniors $9, children $6.

RAILROADIANA The **Boca Express Train Museum** (561-395-6766; www.bocahistory.org), 747 S Dixie Hwy., offers guided tours of not one, but two 1947 streamliner railcars (both on the National Register of Historic Places), a 1940s Seaboard caboose, and a Baldwin steam engine, all housed in a 1930 FEC train depot that contains additional memorabilia relating to train travel in the 1940s. Open 1 PM–4 PM Fri. during the season (Nov.–Apr.). Adults $4, children $2.

MORIKAMI MUSEUM AND JAPANESE GARDENS, DELRAY BEACH
Courtesy Morikami Museum and Japanese Gardens

ART GALLERIES

Delray Beach

More than 100 different artists are represented in the **Avalon Gallery** (561-272-9155; www.avalononatlantic.com), 425 E Atlantic Ave., displaying organic forms in art glass and ceramics. It's rated one of the top 25 galleries in the United States.

✳ To Do

BOAT TOURS **Loxahatchee Everglades Tours, Inc.** (561-482-6107 or 1-800-683-5873; www.evergladesairboattours.com), 15490 Loxahatchee Rd., Boca Raton. Glide over the river of grass while seated on elevated airboats, from which you can see alligators, great blue herons, red shoulder hawks, turtles, and the occasional cottonmouth moccasin. Pass through sloughs and hammocks on airboats just right for your party, from the 8-person *Eagle* to the 20-person *Gator* and *Osprey*. Knowledgeable guides introduce you to the vast Everglades ecosystem and explain the history, biology, and geology of what you'll see on the tour. Open daily 9:30 AM–4 PM. Three types of tours: 30-, 60-, and 90-minute. Reservations recommended.

DAY SPAS

Delray Beach

Treat yourself to a massage inside the crisp treatment rooms or outdoors in your own private cabana overlooking the sunning pool at **Spa Eleven** (561-

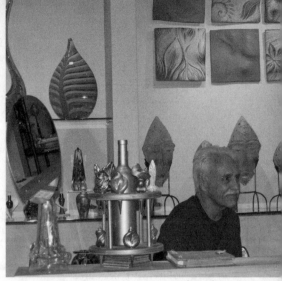

Sandra Friend

CLASSY ART GLASS AT THE AVALON GALLERY

278-1100; www.spaeleven.com), 14140 N Federal Hwy. Massages run $145 for 80 minutes and $220 for 110 minutes. Open 10 AM–6 PM Mon., 10 AM–8 PM Tues.–Thurs., 9 AM–7 PM Fri. and Sat., and 11 PM–6 PM Sun. Reservations are suggested, but they'll take walk-ins if there's an opening.

FAMILY FUN Drive go-carts and bumper cars at **Boomers! Boca Raton** (561-347-1888; www.boomersparks.com), 3100 Airport Rd., Boca Raton. Bumper boats, go-carts, mini golf, rock wall, arcade games, and laser tag. Open noon–10 PM Mon.–Thurs., noon–midnight Fri., 10 AM–midnight Sat., and 10 AM–10 PM Sun.

HIKING You can get lost for miles on the dikes of **Loxahatchee National Wildlife Refuge** (see *Wild Places*), but most of the hiking opportunities in this part of the county run more toward the mild side. Enjoy birding along boardwalks at Green Cay Wetlands and Wakodahatchee Wetlands; wander the nature trails at Sugar Sand Park and Delray Oaks. See *Green Space* for more ideas.

PADDLING Loxahatchee Canoeing Inc. (561-733-0192; www.canoetheever glades.com), 12440 SR 7, Boynton Beach. Paddle a canoe or kayak on a 5.5-mile trail through the **Loxahatchee National Wildlife Refuge** (see *Wild Places*). You can easily guide yourself, as interpretive signs are posted along the trail; or a knowledgeable guide is available to point out indigenous wildlife, such as rare birds, butterflies, and, of course, alligators. Rates are $32 for a half day, plus a $5 park fee. Reduced rates in the summer months.

TENNIS Home of the International Tennis Championship, the **Delray Beach Tennis Center** (561-243-7360; www.delraytennis.com), 201 W Atlantic Ave., Delray Beach, is where you'll see pro tennis tournaments with celebrities such as Venus and Serena Williams and Boca native Corina Morariu. Both kids and adults can play or take lessons on 14 clay courts and 7 hard courts.

WATER PARK You'll have a splashing good time at **Coconut Cove Waterpark & Recreation Center** (561-274-1140; www.pbcgov.com/parks), 1200 Park Access Rd., South County Regional Park, Boca Raton. The park's features include a 986-foot river ride, two 220-foot water slides, and a children's water playground. Open late spring to early fall. Adults 12 and up $10, children 3–11 $8, children 1–2 $3, infants are free. Reduced rates after 3 PM.

✳ Green Space

BEACHES

Boca Raton

Hitting the beach in Boca Raton is a pricey proposition—up to $18 per day for a parking pass (nonresident) to take advantage of **South Beach Park, Red Reef Park,** and **Spanish River Park** along Ocean Blvd. A cheaper alternative is the county-managed **South Inlet Park** (561-966-6600), 1298 S Ocean Blvd., an 11-acre facility with lifeguards, picnic area and pavilions, and a saltwater fishing pier.

Delray Beach

Delray Municipal Beach (561-966-6664) dates from 1922 and has public access through several parks along Ocean Blvd. Heading north from downtown, they are **Sarah Gleason Park, Sandoway Park, Anchor Park,** and **Atlantic Dunes Park.** Of these, Atlantic Dunes has the most natural feel and has surf chairs available for guests with limited mobility. Each of the beach-access parks has metered parking.

BOTANICAL GARDENS ⅙ Walk among some of the world's most colorful orchids at the headquarters to the **American Orchid Society (AOS) Visitors Center and Botanical Garden** (561-404-2000 or 1-877-ORCHIDS; www.aos.org), 16700 AOS Ln., Delray Beach, located next to the **Morikami Museum** (see *Museums*). View thousands of tropical flora as you wind through 3.5 acres of themed gardens, water features, and cypress-pond boardwalk, then relax and take in a peaceful moment inside the 4,000-square-foot atrium greenhouses. The large collection of orchids throughout the property is clearly labeled, and there are also other exotic species such as phais, palms, cycads, and a rare African baobab tree. The Orchid Emporium gift shop is full of books, gardening items, a selection of orchids (even the one that smells like chocolate!), and several fine orchid-related souvenirs and collectibles. Open 10 AM–4:30 PM Tues.–Sun. Adults $10, children under 12 free. Throughout the year classes are offered for only $35 for beginning and advanced orchidteers, which includes a free copy of *Orchid* magazine and an orchid plant for you to take home and nurture.

NATURE CENTERS

Boca Raton

⅙ ✑ In South County Regional Park, the **Daggerwing Nature Center** (561-488-9953), 11200 Park Access Rd., offers interpretive habitat displays and a 0.6-mile boardwalk into a lush, tangled jungle of strangler fig and pond apple trees. The nature center is open 1 PM–4:30 PM Tues.–Fri. and 9 AM–4:30 PM Sat.; boardwalk open during daylight hours. Free.

Sandra Friend

GREEN CAY NATURE CENTER

& ⌀ With touch tanks, hands-on activities, boardwalks, and an observation tower to explore, the **Gumbo Limbo Environmental Education Center** (561-629-8760), 1801 N Ocean Blvd., is a great family destination along the mangrove-lined shores of the Spanish River. Trails lead through bowers of mangroves and out to the edge of the clear waterway, where manatees and mangrove pufferfish may be seen. The center is open 1 PM–4:30 PM Tues.–Fri., 8:15 AM–4:30 PM Sat., and 1 PM–4:30 PM Sun.

Boynton Beach

& ⌀ Just a few years ago, **Green Cay Wetlands and Nature Center** (561-966-7000), 12800 Hagen Ranch Rd., was a pepper farm managed by my friends Ted and Trudy Winsberg. Rather than sell their land to developers as many farmers around them did, they wanted a lasting legacy for the community and worked with the county to create a wetlands water-reclamation park. And it worked—the marshes are now crowded with birds, from little blue herons and great white herons to colorful purple gallinules. A 1.5-mile boardwalk circles the park for optimal birding. The park is open sunrise to sunset daily; the beautiful new nature center, with indoor turtle and alligator ponds, a wetland diorama, movies and exhibits, and a gift shop, is open 1 PM–4:30 PM Tues.–Fri. and Sun., 8:15 AM–4:30 PM Sat. Free; donations appreciated.

Delray Beach

Located in a 1936 beachfront home is the **Sandoway House Nature Center** (561-274-7263; www.sandoway house.com), 142 S Ocean Blvd. Restored to its original condition, it provides a living history to the area with educational exhibits and events about natural ecosystems. Learn about ocean reef fish, the Florida spiny lobster, and nurse sharks during their Coral Reef Pool Shark Feedings held at scheduled times throughout the week; take in the night sky on the monthly astronomy nights; or discover the diversity of Florida's native plants and animals during the **Nature Walk,** held the last Saturday of the month (see *Special Events*). Open 10 AM–4 PM Tues.–Sat. Admission $4.

PARKS

Boca Raton

Red Reef Park (561-393-7810), 1400 SR A1A (North Ocean Blvd.). Snorkel

A LOUISIANA HERON AT GREEN CAY WETLANDS

Sandra Friend

the unique rock and reef outcroppings or take a nature walk through the 67-acre park. The oceanfront park is also home to the 20-acre **Gumbo Limbo Environmental Education Center** (see *Nature Centers*).

& $\mathscr{S}$ Kids will love the Children's Science Explorium at **Sugar Sand Park** (561-347-3913), 300 S Military Trail, featuring hands-on science experiments and oversize artifacts for play. Set in a sand pine scrub, the 132-acre park includes paved and natural surface nature trails, ball fields, and a large playground. Open 8 AM–sunset daily. Free.

Delray Beach

Head to **Lake Ida Park** (561-966-6600), 1455 Lake Ida Rd., for waterskiing and boating fun. The 209-acre park also has a fishing pier, observation platform, picnic areas, and a 2.5-acre dog park complete with Fido Fountain and separate sections for small and large dogs.

PRESERVES

Boca Raton

& $\mathscr{S}$ Accessed through George Snow Park, **Serenoa Glade Preserve** (561-393-7700), 1101 NW 15th St., protects a sliver of the original Atlantic Coastal Ridge in Boca Raton, topped with a pine forest. A 0.5-mile trail leads through the forest; the entrance is hidden back by the tennis courts. Open 8 AM–sunset daily. Free.

Boynton Beach

& $\mathscr{S}$ **Seacrest Scrub Natural Area** (561-233-2400), south of Boynton Beach Blvd. on Seacrest Blvd., protects a 58-acre patch of sand pine scrub habitat that is home to gopher tortoises. Several nature trails, including a paved trail, wind through the forest. Make sure you close the gate behind you to keep the tortoises in! Open sunrise–sunset daily. Free.

& $\mathscr{S}$ For fabulous birding, visit **Wakodahatchee Wetlands** (561-641-3429), 13026 Jog Rd., early in the morning, when wading birds and migratory visitors are most active. Built as a natural water reclamation facility, the preserve features an 0.8-mile boardwalk where I've seen purple gallinules roosting on every visit. Open sunrise–sunset daily. Free.

Delray Beach

& $\mathscr{S}$ A short walk takes you back to nature at the **Delray Oaks Natural Area** (561-233-2400), Congress Ave. at 29th St., where a 1-mile loop trail leads through 25 acres of picturesque oak hammock along what was once the Yamato Marsh. Open sunrise–sunset daily. Free.

WILD PLACES Covering 221 square miles of sawgrass, cypress, and tree islands, **Arthur R. Marshall Loxahatchee National Wildlife Refuge** (561-732-3684; http://loxahatchee.fws.gov), 10216 Lee Rd., off US 441 south of Boynton Beach Blvd., Boynton Beach, defines the eastern edge of the Everglades. Stop at the visitors center for interpretive information, exhibits, and a movie; walk the Cypress Boardwalk to immerse yourself in a forest primeval. Endless miles of dike-top walking or bicycling are available; most visitors complete the Marsh Trail, with an observation tower providing a bird's-eye view of the impoundments, or take to the canals via canoe. Birding here is superb, with sightings of Everglades snail kites possible. Day use only. Open dawn–dusk daily. Fee.

✳ Lodging

HOTELS, MOTELS, AND RESORTS

Delray Beach 33483

♿ 🐾 ⊘ ᵗ¹ᵗ ↬ Owned by the same family since 1938, **The Colony Hotel and Cabana Club** (561-276-4123 or 1-800-552-5363; www.thecolonyhotel .com), 525 E Atlantic Ave., beckons back to the era of destination hotels where the wealthy spent "the season." The lobby captures that spirit, with its wood-burning fireplaces and white wicker furniture. The rooms have an old Florida flair, where antiques mingle with fine furnishings and Florida art, such as Clyde Butcher fine art photographs. A member of the Historic Hotels of America, the Colony is a founding member of Green Hotels (www.greenhotels.com). Sensitive to environmental concerns, the hotel is active in recycling and water conservation and provides guests with educational information on environmental awareness. Its central location in the heart of busy downtown Delray Beach makes it an ideal destination for exploring the city on foot. Rates start at $99 in the off-season, with top-quality rooms ranging from $140–300.

🐾 ᵗ¹ᵗ Tropical paradise surrounds the secluded **Crane's Beach House** (561-278-1700 or 1-866-372-7263; www .cranesbeachhouse.com), 82 Gleason St., yet it is only a short walk from Delray Beach's trendy downtown area. Rooms and suites, decorated in beachy Key West style, range from $136 to 485, depending on season and room. Pet-friendly rooms are also available. Gated security entrance, two pools, sandy beach, Internet.

↬ **Delray Beach Marriott** (561-274-3200; www.delraybeachmarriott.com), 10 N. Ocean Blvd. Located at the beach end of trendy Atlantic Avenue, the Delray Beach Marriott is a popular choice for travelers seeking waterfront sports and sunny relaxation plus sophisticated shopping, dining, and nightlife. It's a great family location. Complimentary breakfast for two, free in-room movie. $289 and up.

↬ **Ritz-Carlton Palm Beach** (561-533-6000; www.ritz-carlton.com), 100 S. Ocean Blvd., Manalapan. This primo destination took a few potshots from the 2004 hurricanes that ripped into the land at the Palm Beach shoreline, but after several weeks the hotel reopened, ready to welcome customers. The Ocean Cafe & Bar serves light lunch items (I love the gazpacho), and the Lobby Lounge features high tea during the day and light bites and a live pianist later in the day. $399 and up.

♿ 🐾 ⊘ ᵗ¹ᵗ ↬ It's not just a historic site. The elegant **Sundy House Inn** (561-272-5678 or 1-866-663-0024; www.sundyhouse.com), 106 S Swinton Ave., is the cornerstone of an intimate retreat wrapped in a cloak of tropical forest, an artful presentation of nature and history called the Taru Gardens. More than 75,000 botanical species thrive on this acre in the city, carefully tended by an expert botanist. Amid the forest is South Florida's only naturalized swimming pond, a cenote with a

THE COLONY HOTEL IN DOWNTOWN DELRAY BEACH

Sandra Friend

gravel bottom where native fish swim in the depths and a double-osmosis filter keeps the crystalline water chemical free. The royal poinciana tree that anchors the garden is the oldest in Delray, standing there when John Sundy, the first and most popular mayor of Delray Beach, had this Early Revival–style Victorian home constructed in 1902. The grand house now serves as a restaurant (see *Dining Out*), while the 11 guest rooms, part of the Kessler Collection, are set in several restored structures, including a historic cottage ($499–669) and a renovated stable. Each room and suite ($249–599) boasts its own distinctive, classy decor, with local artwork and hand-painted walls and tiles, plasma televisions and, in some rooms, fireplaces. The bathrooms are luxurious. An equestrian theme carries through the rooms in the stable, each with tiled floors, large bath, and patios front and back. Coral rock walkways wind through stands of bamboo to connect the rooms. Tours of the gardens are offered Tues.–Sun. 10 AM–1 PM. Breakfast is included with your stay, and package deals are available.

THE BOCA RATON RESORT
AND YACHT CLUB

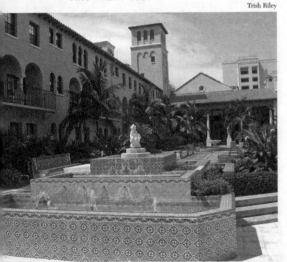

Trish Riley

⁰**ℐ**⁰ Spacious suites with fully equipped kitchens right on the beach make **Wright by the Sea** (561-278-3355 or 1-877-234-3355; www.wbtsea.com), 1901 S Ocean Blvd., a favorite for family reunions and business travelers. There's plenty of space to spread out, whether you want to lie by the pool, barbecue at the chickee hut, or walk along the private beach. Complimentary beach cabanas and wireless high-speed Internet. Studio and one- and two-bedroom suites $109–339.

Boca Raton 33432

⁰**ℐ**⁰ **The Boca Raton Bridge Hotel** (561-368-9500 or 1-866-909-2622; www.bocaratonbridgehotel.com), 999 E Camino Real. This boutique-style hotel is a little-known secret, even to locals. Located directly on the Intracoastal Waterway and a short stroll to the beach, it offers in-room Internet access, with Wi-Fi in the lobby and Internet Cafe. Check out their Sunday champagne brunch at Carmen's At The Top of the Bridge. Low- to high-season rates $159–269; junior suites $199–309; VIP suites $279–409.

↭ Built in 1926, the **Boca Raton Resort & Club** (561-447-3000 or 1-800-327-0101; www.bocaresort.com), 501 E Camino Real, is the pinnacle of luxury resorts on the Gold Coast. Elegant rooms, suites, and bungalows with inspiring views make this a sought-after destination for both tourists and locals. Accommodations feature Spanish-Mediterranean, Moorish, and Gothic antiques and architecture and cosmopolitan or nautical themes. Throughout the 356-acre resort you'll find six pools, a 0.5-mile private beach, par 71 golf course, golf practice range, and putting green, 18 Har-Tru clay tennis courts, oceanfront and lakefront restaurants, on-site shops and boutiques, a new children's playground with water park and tricycle track, Spa

Palazzo, and an enhanced fitness center. Rates $230–775, depending on style and season.

Boynton Beach 33424
⇔ **Courtyard by Marriott Boynton Beach** (561-737-4600), 1601 Congress Ave. This new hotel offers all the amenities desired by overnight, business, and family travelers, from sleek single rooms to townhouses for vacationers or business people seeking extended stays. With convenient access to highways, shopping, and the airport, this is a great location for those who don't desire beachfront property. $159 and up.

✳ Where to Eat
DINING OUT

Boca Raton
Undoubtedly one of the more beautiful restaurants in South Florida, **The Addison** (561-395-9335; www.the addison.com), Two E Camino Real, is a great place for that romantic dinner. American, steak, and continental entrées $22–35. Dinner nightly.

Always on the Top 10 lists, **Kathy's Gazebo Café** (561-395-6033; www .kathysgazebo.com), 4199 N Federal Hwy., is an elegant night out. The decadently rich food, extensive wine list, and top-of-the-line service are what you'd expect from a fine restaurant. The house favorites are the fresh Dover sole (flown from Holland) amandine or meunière ($37) and classic bouillabaisse with lobster, shrimp, clams, and mussels in a hearty broth flavored with garlic, saffron, and tomatoes ($38). Reservations strongly recommended. Gentlemen will need a jacket. Lunch Mon.–Fri.; dinner Mon.–Sat.

Delray Beach
Elegance meets bistro casual in the warm confines of **City Oyster** (561-

272-0220; www.bigtimerestaurants .com), 213 E Atlantic Ave., where the name of the game is shellfish, prepared in an infinite variety of ways. Fancy a Maine lobster roll? Oysters on the half-shell? Fish tacos? How about mahimahi grilled, fried, or blackened and served with watermelon-lime crème. Firm and fresh, my rock shrimp lunch was prepared in a piquant, light sauce. Open for lunch ($8 and up) and dinner, with an impressive bar.

At the **Sundy House Restaurant** (see *Lodging*) I experienced the classiest presentation of brunch I've encountered in Florida, with an ever-vigilant waitstaff that unobtrusively removed plates and refilled glasses. Before you dig into this elaborate Sunday feast, take the grand tour to scout your favorites with a ramble through the rooms of this historic 1902 home. A carving station and omelet station are supplemented with a seafood bar, Mediterranean bar, salad bar, fine breakfast breads and pastries, and desserts. It was tough making decisions, but I started with the eggs benedict Florentine and seared salmon with sweet onion marmalade. Pace yourself and savor the surroundings. Seating is broken into intimate groupings, scattered throughout several rooms and porches. My perch looked out over a view of the tropical gardens, the room decorated with paintings of native birds. Sunlight dappled the underside of a poinciana tree. Complimentary bloody Marys or mimosas compliment your meal. "It's like being on a cruise ship without the rocking," said the lady at the next table, and I smiled as I excused myself for one last trip, this time to pick from homemade delights on the pastry table, including chocolate-dipped strawberries, cannoli, banana bread, and a key lime tart. Brunch is served 10:30 AM–2 PM on

Sundays, $53, half price for ages 6–12, under 6 free; reservations essential. Dinners are served Tues.–Sun., 6 AM–9 PM.

Lemongrass (561-544-8181; www.lemongrassasianbistro.com), 101 Plaza Real South E. Enjoy authentic Asian flavors from Thailand, Japan, and Vietnam, presented in their most colorful beauty for your dining delight. Try the curried dumplings, lemongrass soup, tuna tataki, and Deep Blue Sea—seafood in a spicy Thai red curry sauce. $12 and up. Open for lunch and dinner.

Old Calypso (561-279-2300; www.oldcalypso.com), 900 E. Atlantic Ave. Creole and Caribbean flavors are combined with fresh Florida seafood and steaks at this friendly spot. Enjoy waterfront dining on the Intracoastal Waterway. $12 and up.

🐚 **The Old Key Lime House Restaurant** (561-582-1889; www.oldkeylimehouse.com), 300 E. Ocean Ave., Lantana. A renovation project surprised the owner when peeling back the layers of paneling and flooring applied over time revealed this to be the second-oldest house in Lantana. Today the rambling structure provides a fitting Cracker atmosphere for delicious Key lime pie heralded as the best in Florida by *Bon Appetit* magazine in January 2007 and fresh seafood dishes. With waterfront seating in Florida's largest tiki hut hand-built by Seminole natives, and a boat dock, this is as unpretentious as it is inexpensive and delicious. Lunch and dinner daily, Sunday brunch, raw bar open 'til midnight weeknights and 2 AM Friday and Saturday. $15 and up.

EATING OUT

Boca Raton
Anyone who works in or around Boca Raton is familiar with **Byblos Restaurant** (561-338-0300), 158 NW 20th St. Tucked at the end of a strip mall, the tiny eight-seat restaurant is more famous for its take-out than eat-in. But many business locals make it a quick stop for lunch, with lines out the door, so stop by early or later in the day. The authentic Middle Eastern foods are reasonably priced at around $6. The sampler platter includes your choice of Kebbe nuggets; spanakopita (spinach and feta pie); stuffed grape leaves (with or without lamb); *fatouch* or tabbouleh salad; cucumber, hummus, or baba ghanoush dips; and pita bread. If you still have room, they also have baklava. Open 11 AM–3 PM Mon.–Sat.

Carmen's at the Top of the Bridge (561-750-8354; 999 E Camino Real; www.bocaratonbridgehotel.com), famous for its view as well as its cuisine, Carmen's, at the Boca Raton Bridge Hotel, has live music Thursday through Saturday. Try the chef's favorite, escargot and caviar served with tomatoes, garlic, and basil on pasta, or try the Florida snapper or rack of lamb. Dinner and music Thurs.–Sat.; Sun. brunch. Closed Mon.–Wed. $36 and up.

Cote France Bakery and Sandwichery (561-392-2907), 110 Ne 2nd St. This little bakery, tucked into a strip mall at the end of Mizner Plaza, serves real French pastries, baguettes, quiche, and hot sandwiches. You'll be able to test the authenticity by practicing your French speaking skills with the staff. There are a few tables to dine in at, but with a big crowd always lining up, take away is nice and a continent better than any fast food joint. $7 and up. Open 7 AM–5 PM Mon.–Sat.

Open since 1979, **Tom's Place** (561-997-0920), 7251 N Federal Hwy., is a must-visit. The legendary rib shack used to be an army barracks, and now the bustling eatery offers pulled pork, ribs, and chicken on family-style platters, served with corn bread and greens. Hands down the best barbecue sauce, with many trying to figure out the recipe. Menu items are $8–15, with an early-bird special for $8.

Truluck's (561-391-0755; www .trulucks.com), 351 Plaza Real. Truluck's is a small chain of seafood restaurants that started in Texas and recently opened in Boca. While seafood is the specialty, crab is the focus, and no matter the season, crab from somewhere around the world will find its way onto the menu, which gives diners a chance to taste some lesser-known varieties. That said, Truluck's makes one of the most satisfying bowls of crab and corn chowder around. The atmosphere is elegant but welcoming with a lively piano bar area and extensive wine list. $21.95 and up. Open for dinner daily.

Delray Beach
The **Blue Anchor British Pub & Restaurant** (561-272 7272; www.the blueanchor.com), 804 East Atlantic Ave., was built in the late 1800s in London, England. It stood for nearly 150 years on Chancery Lane, greeting regulars like Jack the Ripper and Winston Churchill. The exterior was dissembled and shipped to Florida, and it boasts the claim of "Florida's most haunted pub." Stop in for a Guinness, a plate of fish and chips, or Shepherd's pie. Serving traditional British fare for lunch and dinner, $9–23, in an authentic pub setting.

Peel some shrimp, then grab a burger and a beer at **Boston's on the Beach** (561-278-3364; www.bostonsonthe beach.com), 40 S Ocean Blvd. The Key West Basket with fried shrimp, grouper fingers, catfish fingers, conch fritters, and french fries is a favorite of both tourists and locals. Breakfast,

lunch, and dinner $5–25. Open daily 7 AM–2 AM, with nightly entertainment. **The Upper Deck** is a little less casual, with lunch $7–20 and dinner $15–30. Sit out on the open-air patio for the best view of the beach.

ICE CREAM AND CHOCOLATES
Doc's All American (561-278-3627), 10 N Swinton Ave., Delray Beach, is an authentic 1950s drive-in where ice cream is the star of the show—in everything from malts to sundaes. You can get burgers and dogs here, too, but make my meal creamy and chocolate, please.

Chocoholics unite and meet at **Kilwin's** (561-278-0808; www.kilwins .com), 402 E Atlantic Ave., Delray Beach, where you'll find everything from barks, bonbons, and brittles to truffles, turtles, and taffy.

✳ Entertainment
PERFORMING ARTS
Boca Raton
Student and professional performances are presented at **Boca Ballet Theatre** (561-995-0709; www.bocaballet.org) at Florida Atlantic University's University Theater at 777 Glades Rd.

The 305-seat **Caldwell Theatre Company** (561-241-7432 or 1-877-245-7432; www.caldwelltheatre.com), 7901 N Federal Hwy., is the setting for professional theater musicals and Broadway and off-Broadway shows, and it is one of Florida's four state theaters.

Talented students from around the world, along with artist faculty, present orchestral performances throughout the year at **Lynn University Conservatory of Music** (561-237-9000; www .lynn.edu/music), 3601 N Military Trail.

Delray Beach

The historic **Delray High School** (circa 1925) at Old School Square (see *Historic Sites*) is the home to **Crest Theatre** (561-243-7922; www.old school.org), 51 N Swinton Ave. The 323-seat theater presents a variety of professional productions, such as Broadway, cabaret, music, and dance, throughout the year. Special guest artists are often featured in the six restored classrooms and two art studios. Performances are on Fri.–Sun. evenings and Sat. and Sun. matinees ($40–45).

The 238-seat **Delray Beach Playhouse** (561-272-1281; www.delray beachplayhouse.com), 950 NW Ninth St., overlooking scenic Lake Ida, is one of the nation's oldest community theaters, presenting theatrical and musical productions for nearly 50 years.

MIZNER PARK

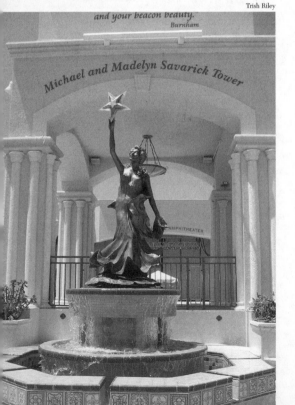

Trish Riley

✳ Selective Shopping

Boca Raton

Stroll through the palms at trendy **Mizner Park** (561-362-0606; www .miznerpark.org), 433 Plaza Real, where you'll be surrounded by boutiques, restaurants, a movie theater, art galleries, and lots of schmoozing. On the north end, the **Amphitheater** has special musical events, and in the central park, art festivals and vintage automobile events are often scheduled.

Boutique shops and trendy restaurants are set in old-world elegance at **Royal Palm Place** (561-362-8340; www.royal palmplace.com), 101 Plaza Real South.

Anchored by such biggies as Neiman Marcus, Macy's, Bloomingdales, Saks Fifth Avenue, and even Sears, the **Town Center at Boca Raton** (561-368-6000; www.towncenteratboca raton.com), 6000 Glades Rd., also has your basic mall stores in between and then some. Check out the new Nordstrom wing for specialty shops such as Coach, Cole Haan, Williams-Sonoma, Kate Spade, and Crane & Co., which has an extensive stationery selection for those who still write by hand.

Delray Beach

Stroll down quaint brick sidewalks in the charming **Atlantic Avenue District** (561-278-0424), where you'll find traditional downtown shopping, gourmet restaurants, a cozy bistro, and more than 150 different boutiques, art galleries, and antiques shops along Atlantic Avenue and Swinton Avenue.

"You're in good hands" at **Hands' Stationers** (561-276-4194), 325 E Atlantic Ave., where this family-owned office supply store has served downtown Delray shoppers for 75 years with its stock-in-trade being a wide variety of art supplies—including inks, canvases, paint, papers, and drafting tables—as well as local books and memorabilia, children's books, and fun ephemera. Closed Sun.

Serious readers will love the **Levenger Outlet** (561-347-3707 or 1-888-592-7461; www.levenger.com), 6000 Glades Rd., at the Town Center, where fine reading accessories are sold, including pens, briefcases, lamps, leather goods, reading tools, and furniture.

Go shopping at **Mercer Wenzel** (561-278-2885), 401 E Atlantic Ave., established in 1930. It's perhaps the very last old-fashioned two-story department store left in Florida, and the current owner—who bought the place in 1957—still works in the men's department. Selling sensible resort wear for men and women, children's clothing, and home decor in a setting where Sinatra croons; yes, you can find old-fashioned handkerchiefs, robes, and slippers here, too. Open 9 AM–5 PM Mon.–Sat.

A popular stop for mystery authors on book tours **Murder on the Beach** (561-279-7790; www.murderonthebeach.com), 273 Pineapple Grove Way, has hundreds of your favorite authors in stock, with a special emphasis on Florida authors and who-dun-its set in Florida. Open daily.

In the Pineapple Grove historic district, you'll find great shopping at the **Ocean City Lumber Company** (561-276-2323). This one-time lumber yard is now an entertainment district. Browse through the trendy boutiques, art galleries, and restaurants in the former lumberyard and areas between NE Second Avenue and Pineapple Grove Way.

GREEN MARKETS
Boca Raton
Every Saturday from November to May, fresh fruits and vegetables, along with fresh cut flowers and arts and

Downtown Delray
GETTING COZY AT MURDER ON THE BEACH

crafts, can be found at the **Boca Raton Greenmarket** (561-368-6875), Royal Palm Plaza south parking lot (intersection of South Mizner Blvd. and Federal Hwy.). The nonprofit market also features a continental breakfast and live music 10 AM–noon.

Delray Beach
Delray Beach Greenmarket in the Park (561-276-8640), in downtown Delray Beach, 20 North Swinton Ave., is the place to go for fresh produce each Saturday October through April.

✸ Special Events
Last Saturday of the month: Take a 30- to 60-minute **Nature Walk** through sand dunes and gardens at the Sandoway House Nature Center (561-274-7263; www.sandowayhouse.com), 142 S Ocean Blvd., Delray Beach, while discovering the beautiful flora and fauna of Florida. The $4 fee also includes admission to the nature center (see *Nature Centers*).

January: The first-class **Annual Downtown Delray Festival of the Arts** (561-278-3755), on Atlantic Ave., Delray Beach, offers works of art for everyone's taste and budget, from $50 to more than $20,000. Free parking and no admission.

When the sun goes down in January and the temperature begins to dip into the 60s, Floridians call that a cold night, so there's no better way to warm up than with the sizzling **Art & Jazz on the Avenue** (561-279-1380, ext. 17; www.downtowndelraybeach.com), Delray Beach. Restaurants, art galleries, and shops along Atlantic Avenue and Pineapple Grove Way open their door in the evening from 6 to 10 on selected Thursday nights October through June. Call for dates. Free.

February: For more than 20 years, the **Annual Outdoor Juried Art Festival** (561-392-2500) at the Boca Raton Museum of Art (561-392-2500; www.bocamuseum.org), 501 Plaza Real, Mizner Park, Boca Raton, has been showcasing works of art from more than 250 artists from around the world. (See *Museums.*)

You'll discover flora, fauna, and fun at the annual **Everglades Day Festival** (561-734-8303), Loxahatchee National Wildlife Refuge at 10216 Lee Road, Boynton Beach. Educational activities and live animal presentations are featured. Free.

March: The **Hatsume Fair** at the Morikami Museum (561-495-0233; www.morikami.org), 4000 Morikami Park Rd., Delray Beach, celebrates the first bud of spring. The festival features three entertainment stages and has demonstrations ranging from martial arts to bonsai care. Artisans and food vendors are also present at the Morikami's largest event. (See *Museums.*) Admission fee.

Start the year with the **Oshogatsu-Japanese New Year Celebration** at the Morikami Museum (561-495-0233; www.morikami.org), 4000 Morikami Park Rd., Delray Beach. The annual event features a sado tea ceremony, hands-on calligraphy and New Year's card making, and games. (See *Museums.*)

The two-day **Annual Boca Bacchanal—A Celebration of Wine** (561-395-6766) is presented by the Boca Raton Historical Society, Boca Raton. The festival, a benefit for local children's charities, features a gala auction. Admission ranges from $85–100 per person. Usually held at the Centre for the Arts in Mizner Park (501 Plaza Real).

Pack your breath mints and head to the **Annual Garlic Fest** (561-279-7511; www.dbgarlicfest.com), Old School Square Grounds, in downtown Delray Beach.

March–April: Learn about the galaxy at the Sandoway House Nature Center (561-274-7263; www.sandowayhouse.com), 142 S Ocean Blvd., Delray Beach, through telescopes and lectures at the monthly **Astronomy Night,** usually held on Wednesday. The $3 fee also includes admission to the nature center (see *Nature Centers*).

April: ✐ The annual **Kidsfest** (561-368-6875) is one day of continuous entertainment and activities held at the Children's Museum, 498 Crawford Blvd., Boca Raton (see *Museums*). Admission $5.

✐ Hands-on activities take center stage at the **Morikami Museum's Children's Day Celebration** (561-495-0233; www.morikami.org), 4000 Morikami Park Rd., where you'll learn the fine art of Japanese toy making, origami, and fish painting or make a giant carp streamer. Several stages fea-

ture Japanese and American performances. $5 for all ages. (See *Museums.*)

August: **Bon Festival,** inspired by
Obon, a three-day holiday honoring
ancestors, is celebrated at the Morikami Museum (561-495-0233; www
.morikami.org), 4000 Morikami Park
Rd., Delray Beach. Highlights include
taiko drumming and traditional Japanese folk dancing, followed by an
evening ceremony where lanterns are
lit and placed on the Morikami Pond
to guide the ancestors' souls home.
The evening culminates with a fire-
works display. Adults $10, children $5,
under 3 free. (See *Museums.*)

October: Don't miss the annual **Delray Beach Orchid Society Show &
Sale** (561-404-2000; www.aos.org) held
at the Old School Square, 51 Swinton
Ave., Delray Beach, where you'll see
the best of elegant and colorful
orchids, along with a variety of supplies
and classes on "how to" care for them.
(See *Historic Sites.*)

October–April: Free **outdoor movies**
are shown on one Friday night each
month at the Old School Square
Entertainment Pavilion (561-243-
7922), Delray Beach. If you don't have
your own lawn chair, you can rent one.
From 6 PM on.

October–June: Downtown Delray
Beach sizzles with **Art & Jazz on the
Avenue** (561-279-1380, ext. 17; www
.downtowndelraybeach.com). Restau-
rants, art galleries, and shops along
Atlantic Avenue and Pineapple Grove
Way open their doors on select
evenings from 6 to 10 on selected
Thursdays. Call for dates.

November: The **Southern Handcraft
Holiday Show & Sale** showcases
beautiful decorations, ornaments, and
more to decorate your home with
Southern flair. Located at the Old
School Square, 51 Swinton Ave. (see
Historic Sites), Delray Beach. The
annual three-day event is Thursday
through Saturday.

December: The **Annual Boca Raton
Holiday Boat Parade** (561-845-9010;
www.bocaratonboatparade.org) lights
up the holiday night as colorful boats
sail up the Intracoastal Waterway from
Boca Raton toward Delray Beach.

The family-friendly, nonalcoholic **First
Night** New Year's Eve Celebration
(561-279-1380; www.downtowndelray
beach.com) is held each year all
through the downtown Delray Beach
area.

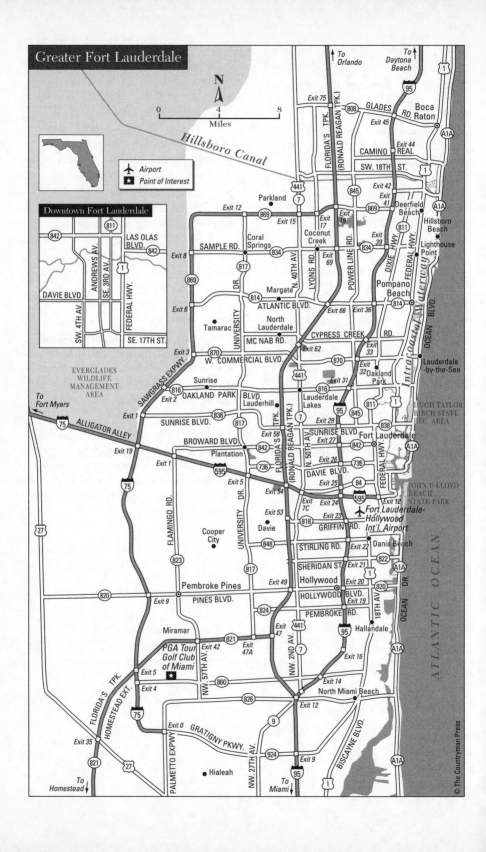

Greater Fort Lauderdale

N

0   4   8
Miles

✈   Airport
★   Point of Interest

Downtown Fort Lauderdale

842
811
842
LAS OLAS BLVD.
Exit 8
1
ANDREWS AV.
SE. 3RD AV.
DAVIE BLVD.
FEDERAL HWY.
SW. 4TH AV.
SE. 17TH ST.

Hillsboro Canal

To Orlando
To Daytona Beach
95
1
Exit 75
808 GLADES RD. Boca Raton
Exit 45
A1A
CAMINO REAL
Exit 44
SW. 18TH ST.
1
441
7
845
Exit 42
869
Exit 41 Deerfield Beach
A1A
Parkland
Exit 12
869
Exit 15
Exit 17
Exit 19
Coconut Creek
Hillsboro Beach
811
Lighthouse Point
Coral Springs
834
N. 40TH AV.
LYONS RD.
POWER LINE RD.
Exit 39
834
SAMPLE RD.
817
Exit 69
DIXIE HWY.
FEDERAL HWY.
Margate
814
ATLANTIC BLVD.
Exit 66
Exit 36
814
Pompano Beach
BLVD.
OCEAN BLVD.
Intracoastal Waterway
Tamarac
North Lauderdale
MC NAB RD.
CYPRESS CREEK
RD.
Exit 62
Exit 33
Lauderdale-by-the-Sea
870
W. COMMERCIAL BLVD.
441
870
Oakland Park
Exit 32
EVERGLADES WILDLIFE MANAGEMENT AREA
Exit 3
SAWGRASS EXPWY.
Sunrise
816
Exit 2
OAKLAND PARK
816
HUGH TAYLOR BIRCH STATE REC. AREA
To Fort Myers
Exit 1
838
BLVD.
Lauderhill
Lauderdale Lakes
811
1
SUNRISE BLVD.
817
7
95
845
838
75
ALLIGATOR ALLEY
BROWARD BLVD.
Exit 58
FLORIDA'S TPK. (RONALD REAGAN TPK.)
SUNRISE BLVD.
Exit 27
Fort Lauderdale
842
A1A
Exit 19
Plantation
842
N. 50TH AV.
Exit 26
FEDERAL HWY.
595
736
DAVIE BLVD.
736
JOHN U. LLOYD BEACH STATE PARK
27
Exit 1
Exit 5
Exit 54
Exit 25
84
75
Exit 53
Exit 7C
Exit 24
595
Exit 12
Cooper City
Davie
818
Exit 23
Fort Lauderdale-Hollywood Int'l. Airport
848
GRIFFIN RD.
Exit 22
Dania Beach
823
817
STIRLING RD.
822
A1A
SHERIDAN ST.
Exit 21
1
Pembroke Pines
Exit 49
Hollywood
Exit 20
820
OCEAN DR.
820
PINES BLVD.
HOLLYWOOD BLVD.
Exit 19
824
18TH AV.
PEMBROKE RD.
Miramar
Exit 47
441
95
Hallandale
A1A
PGA Tour Golf Club of Miami
821
Exit 42
Exit 47A
7
Exit 16
NW. 57TH AV.
NW. 2ND AV.
Exit 5
860
Exit 4
Exit 14
826
North Miami Beach
FLORIDA'S TPK.
HOMESTEAD EXT.
Exit 0
GRATIGNY PKWY.
Exit 12
9
Hialeah
PALMETTO EXPWY.
NW. 27TH AV.
924
Exit 9
75
Exit 35
821
27
To Homestead
To Miami
95
1
A1A
BISCAYNE BLVD.
ATLANTIC OCEAN

© The Countryman Press

SUNNY HOMETOWN:
GREATER FORT LAUDERDALE

T oday, Broward County, sandwiched between the upper crust of Palm Beach and spicy Miami, is white-bread land, where grandmas live and people pretend to lead normal lives, basking in the glory of the perpetual sunshine and days much too beautiful to spend lingering long at the desk. Like all of the Gold Coast, the area is relatively newly populated, thanks to its development following Flagler's railway at the beginning of the 20th century.

In the late 1800s South Florida was virtually an untapped frontier, with only a few dozen Seminole families inhabiting the region. **Dania** (now Dania Beach) is the oldest incorporated city (circa 1904). **Pompano,** at the northern end of the county, became the second town to incorporate in 1908. Henry Flagler's railroad reached **Fort Lauderdale** in 1896. Once a small pioneer village of 250 residents, the city became the central hub of the county. Incorporated in 1915, the county was named for governor Napoleon Bonaparte Broward. It includes popular beach-side towns such as Deerfield Beach, Hollywood, **Lauderdale-by-the-Sea,** and **Wilton Manors.** The western reaches of the county weren't developed for another 50 years, when the Army Corps of Engineers drained the Everglades. Sunrise and Davie being the first to push west, and developers continued westward to build on former swampland, creating family-oriented communities such as Coral Springs and Weston (see *Inland: Western Broward County*).

Known as America's Venice thanks to the extensive canal system and rivers criss-crossing the city, Fort Lauderdale was launched to fame by Marilyn Monroe and *Where the Boys Are,* the happy little film that spawned the spring break frenzy. It was fun while it lasted, but the spring break shenanigans were eventually squelched due to excessive debauchery and replaced with wholesome fun for the whole family.

In addition to a wealth of museums and attractive walking areas, such as River-walk along the New River and Las Olas Boulevard, Fort Lauderdale's legendary beaches are indeed beautiful. Broward County's beaches have been recognized with the Blue Wave award, a voluntary program that ensures that beaches are well maintained and regularly tested for dangerous conditions, including rip tides and pollutants, problems that can pose dangers for swimmers.

With nearly 10 million visitors a year and a projected residential growth of 46 percent over the next 20 years, Broward County officials are actively working to meet the demands of increased population and a strong tourism industry. The Broward County Office of Urban Planning projects population growth of almost 1 million in the next 25 years, with all land used by 2015. Planners continue to grapple with infrastructure ramifications, urging development of "smart" cities and urban redevelopment, the protection of beaches and older neighborhoods, and the creation of growth-management strategies and transportation solutions. Such forward thinking will help protect the paradise of south Florida for future generations.

GUIDANCE Contact the **Greater Fort Lauderdale Convention and Visitors Bureau** (954-765-4466 or 1-800-22SUNNY; www.sunny.org), 100 E Broward Blvd., Ste. 200, Fort Lauderdale 33301, for more information on the area.

For information about Hollywood contact the **Hollywood Office of Tourism** (867-672-2468; www.visithollywood.org), 330 N Federal Hwy., Hollywood 33019.

GETTING THERE *By air:* **Fort Lauderdale–Hollywood International Airport** (1-866-435-9355; www.broward.org/airport) has easy access to I-95, US 595, I-75, and FL 1, as well as Port Everglades.

By car: **I-95** runs north and south and is a good route to take for the areas in the east section of the county, however it is a high-traffic road. Some drivers prefer to pay a few dollars to use the less-traveled **Florida Turnpike,** which runs north and south more toward the center of the county. I-595 is the major artery carrying traffic between the eastern and western regions of the county. The Sawgrass Expressway is a segment of the Turnpike that runs around the northwestern edge of the county, delivering drivers from the Florida Turnpike to Coral Springs and Weston then southward to Miami and the Keys, also crossing I-595 at the west where it turns into I-75 for those bound to Naples.

By rail: **AMTRAK** (1-800-872-7245; www.amtrak.com) provides regularly scheduled service to Fort Lauderdale. Beware—I have sat at the station for hours awaiting delayed trains.

There are **Tri-Rail Stations** (1-800-TRI-RAIL; www.tri-rail.com) throughout the county, mostly paralleling I-95, listed here north to south:

Deerfield Beach station (1300 W. Hillsboro Blvd., Deerfield Beach 33442)

Pompano Beach station (3491 N.W. Eighth Ave., Pompano Beach 33064)

Cypress Creek station (6151 N. Andrews Way, Fort Lauderdale 33309)

Fort Lauderdale station (200 S.W. 21st Terrace, Fort Lauderdale 33312)

Fort Lauderdale/Hollywood International Airport at Dania Beach (500 Gulf Stream Way, Dania Beach 33004)

Sheridan Street station (2900 Sheridan St., Fort Lauderdale 33070)

Hollywood station (3001 Hollywood Blvd., Hollywood 33021)

By bus: **Greyhound Line** (954-764-6551, 1-800-231-2222; www.greyhound .com),515 N.E. Third St., Fort Lauderdale 33301

GETTING AROUND *By car:* Some savvy residents use the acronym COSBY to help remember the layout of the area and to determine where you are at any given time along I-95: When traveling from north to south, "C," for Commercial Boulevard, will bring you to the northern sections of Fort Lauderdale, such as Pompano Beach to the east and Coral Springs to the west; "O," Oakland Boulevard, and "S," Sunrise Boulevard, will bring you all the way from the Fort Lauderdale beaches to western Broward cities such as Sunrise and Plantation; and "B," Broward Boulevard, will bring you to the heart of Fort Lauderdale and the Arts and Science District. Finally, use "Y" as a marker for I-595. The city of Hollywood can be reached off I-95 south of the airport from Griffin, Stirling, or Sheridan. Scenic SR A1A runs along the beaches.

By bus: **Broward County Transit** (954-357-8400; www.broward.org/bct) provides bus service throughout the county.

By streetcar: The complimentary **Downtown A&E Trolley Line** operates throughout Fort Lauderdale's Riverwalk Arts & Entertainment District on Friday 5–midnight and Saturday noon–midnight. The route travels from the Arts & Entertainment Garage (opposite the Broward Center for the Performing Arts) through Old Fort Lauderdale Village, Las Olas Boulevard, the Museum of Art, and Stranahan House, with stops along the way.

Holly Trolley (954-980-9777; www.visithollywood.org) operates from Hollywood hotels to its historic downtown and dining, shopping, and beach areas. Regular fare $1 round-trip. Children under 12 ride free. Call or check Web site for schedule; stops every 30 minutes.

By water taxi: A great way to see luxurious homes along the Intracoastal Waterway is on the **Water Taxi** (954-467-6677; www.watertaxi.com). The route runs from Oakland Park Boulevard to the Riverwalk Arts & Entertainment District. You can also use the water taxi to visit many restaurants, hotels, and attractions located along the waterways of the city. Adults $5 one way, children and seniors $2.50; all-day fare $7. Multiday tickets available at reduced prices. The Water Taxi also offers day trips on Tuesday and Saturday to Miami's South Beach Art Deco District for only $18.

Call **Bradley Executive Limousine** (954-370-0505; www.fla-limo.com); **Dolphin Limousine Service** (954-989-5466; www.dolphin-limo.com); or **The Tri-County Airport Express** (954-561-8888; www.floridalimo.com) to reserve shuttle service to the airport.

PARKING Fort Lauderdale city parking garages are located at the Arts & Science District, 101 SW Fifth Ave.; Bridgeside Place, 3020 NE 32nd Ave. (near Oakland Park Blvd.); City Park, 150 SE Second St.; and City Hall. Rates differ from coin by the hour to flat rates per entry. Some garages have attendants and some have meters. See www.fortlauderdale.gov for more information.

You'll find metered parking throughout Fort Lauderdale, Hollywood, and the beach areas.

PUBLIC RESTROOMS The beach areas and most city parks have rest rooms available to the public at no cost.

VALET Most restaurants and luxury hotels in the beach area offer valet services. Some restaurants and hotels have only mandatory valet parking. Inquire when making reservations.

MEDICAL EMERGENCIES Several hospitals are located throughout Broward County. Many belong to the Broward Health network (www.browardhealth.org).

Broward General Medical Center (954-355-4400; www.browardhealth.org), 1600 S. Andrews Ave., Fort Lauderdale 33316.

Memorial Regional Hospital South (954-966-4500) 3600 Washington St., Hollywood 33021.

Imperial Point Medical Center (954-776-8500) 6401 N Federal Hwy., Fort Lauderdale 33308.

Memorial Regional Hospital (954-987-2000), 3501 Johnson St., Hollywood 33021.

North Broward Medical Center (954-941-8300), 201 E Sample Rd., Deerfield Beach 33064.

Plantation General Hospital (954-587-5010) 401 NW 42nd Ave., Plantation 33317.

Westside Regional Medical Center (954-473-6600), 8201 W Broward Blvd., Plantation 33324.

OCEANSIDE: EASTERN BROWARD COUNTY

The flow of beachside communities on the eastern side of the county are the cities most likely to be of interest to travelers and provide a wealth of hotels, restaurants, and attractions to enjoy from Deerfield Beach to Hollywood.

✳ To See

ART GALLERIES

Fort Lauderdale

Third Avenue Art District (954-763-8982; www.thirdavenueartdistrict.com),505 NE Third Ave., offers tours of artist's studios by appointment. An annual Artwalk is held the first Saturday of February each year. **Broward Art Guild** (954-305-1854; www.browardartguild.org), 1350 E. Sunrise Blvd. (Located at ArtServe), provides 14 exhibitions per year and encourages local artists to participate. Free.

Hollywood

The Art & Culture Center of Hollywood (954-921-3274; www.artandculture center.org), 1650 Harrison St., was founded in 1975 to promote contemporary and innovative artists. Housed in a 1924 Spanish mansion in the heart of downtown Hollywood, it has become the center of this city's art district and offers theater performances, gallery exhibitions, and classes for children and adults. 10 AM–5 PM Mon.–Sat., 12 PM–4 PM Sun. Adults $7; students, seniors, and children 4–13 $4.

Owner Robyn Crosfield's gorgeous award-winning mosaics are just one of the reasons to stop at **Mosaica** (954-923-7006; www.emosaica.com), 2020 Hollywood Blvd. I love art glass and found the starfish and showy bowls intriguing. Select from large objets d'art such as Robyn's mirrors and mosaic-trimmed furniture to small gifts such as the metal art lizards and enameled boxes. Open daily.

Deerfield Beach
Deerfield Beach Historical Society (954-429-0378), 380 E Hillsboro Blvd., oversees several sites from Deerfield Beach's early days in the 1920s that are now on the National Register of Historic Places. They include the 1920 Old Deerfield School, renovated by the city and open for tours; the 1920 Butler House, now a museum and office for the historical society; the 1926 Deerfield School, today the Deerfield Beach Elementary School; and the 1926 Seaboard Coast Line Railway Station, now serving as the area's Tri-Rail station. The historical society also manages the 1930 Kester Cottage. Visit and tour the Butler House Museum (fee), built in 1923 by James and Alice Butler, 9 AM–4 PM Mon.–Fri., 10 AM–2 PM the first and third Sat. of the month.

Pompano Beach
Hillsboro Lighthouse (954-942-2102; www.hillsborolighthouse.org); The Sands Marina, 125 N Riverside. In operation since 1907, the Hillsboro Lighthouse continues to protect ships from running aground along the shoreline near the Hillsboro Inlet. Maintained by the Coast Guard, the lighthouse has occasional tours conducted by the Hillsboro Lighthouse Preservation Society. Charter bus tours leave from the Pompano Beach city parking lot. Fee includes one-year membership in the preservation society.

Fort Lauderdale
In the heart of Fort Lauderdale sits the **Bonnet House Museum & Gardens** (954-563-5393; www.bonnethouse.org), 900 N Birch Rd., named after the yellow water lily that once grew in the property's marshland. Once home to Frederic Clay and Evelyn Fortune Bartlett, both avid art collectors, the plantation-style home now houses a historical museum and art gallery. Tours are available, with the last tour starting at 2:30. Open year-round 10 AM–4 PM Wed.–Sat., noon–4 PM Sun. As you tour the grounds, you'll walk under mangrove trees and through fruit groves of avocado, mango, and guava, while Brazilian squirrel monkeys watch you with great interest. Admission to the grounds: $10; admission to the grounds and plantation home: adults $20, seniors 60+ $18, students 6–12 $16, children under six free. Call ahead for tour schedules, as the plantation home may be closed for wedding parties.

King Cromartie House (954-463-4431), 229 SW Second Ave. Built in 1907, the girlhood home of Frank Stranahan's wife, Ivy Cromartie, has been preserved to offer a glimpse of pioneer life. The home is reminiscent of a grandparent's bungalow, furnished with period antique furniture and decorated with lace doilies and china dolls. (*Also see Stranahan House below*) Open 10 AM–4 PM Tues.–Sun. Fee.

Old Dillard Museum (754-322-8828), 1009 NW 4 St. Built in 1924, Fort Lauderdale's first school for African Americans is now a museum that displays local African American culture and artifacts. Open 11 AM–4 PM Mon.–Fri. Free; donations welcome.

Old Fort Lauderdale Village and Museum, 1905 New River Inn, 237 SW Second Ave. Originally an inn for Fort Lauderdale's turn-of-the-20th-century visitors, the renovated building makes a great museum. Located in the Old Fort Lauderdale area, the village is composed of a cluster of historical buildings at the site where Flagler's railway crossed the New River. Open 10 AM–5 PM Tue.–Fri., noon–5 PM Sat.–Sun. Fee: adults $8, children 6–16 $3, children under 6 free.

The turn-of-the-20th-century (circa 1913) Florida Vernacular–style **Stranahan House** (954-524-4736; www.stranahanhouse.org), 335 SE Sixth Ave. (corner of Las Olas Blvd.), Fort Lauderdale, is the oldest structure in Broward County. Ohioan Frank Stranahan was Fort Lauderdale's first postmaster. He married Ivy Julia Cromartie, the area's first teacher, and soon their house was the center of social events (*see King Cromartie House above*). It remained their personal residence until her death in 1971. Furnished with antiques and memorabilia from their life, the house is open 1 PM–3 PM every day. Adults $12, children under 12 $7. (*See also The Elbo Room in Eating Out, Cap's Place in Dining and Riverside Hotel in Lodging*)

MUSEUMS

Fort Lauderdale

The **Fort Lauderdale Antique Car Museum** (954-779-7300; www.antiquecar museum.org), 1527 SW First Ave. (Packard Ave.), is dedicated to the preservation and history of the Packard Motor Co. The extensive collection includes 22 Packard automobiles dating from 1909 to 1940, such as the 1922 Packard Model 1-16 Sport Phaeton and the 1929 Packard Model 645 Dual Cowl Phaeton previously owned by the Schmidt family of Schmidt Brewing Company. The museum also contains the FDR gallery and library dedicated to the late Franklin D. Roosevelt, and many related automobile memorabilia, including hood ornaments and vintage tools. Open 10 AM–4 PM Mon.–Fri.; 12 PM–3 PM Sat. Donation.

Host to national and international aquatic competitions, the **International Swimming Hall of Fame Museum & Aquatic Complex** (954-462-6536; www.ishof .org), One Hall of Fame Dr., features a 10,000-square-foot museum full of Olympic memorabilia from more than 100 nations. Adults $8, students $4, seniors $6, children under 12 free. Open 9 AM–5 PM daily.

In 1986 the **Museum of Art** (954-525-5500; www.moafl.org), One E Las Olas Blvd., opened its 65,000-square-foot building designed by renowned American architect Edward Larabee Barnes, after growing from a small storefront space on Las Olas Boulevard (which is now Johnny V's; see *Dining Out*) from 1958. Today it has an additional 10,000 square feet and draws crowds from around the world for its permanent art collections and large-scale exhibitions such as Princess Diana, St. Peter and the Vatican, and King Tut. In 2009 and 2010, the museum will show a Norman Rockwell exhibit, photographs of Haitian refugees, and much more. The permanent collection features more than 6,200 various artworks from American impressionist William Glackens, Picasso ceramics, contemporary Cuban art, and CoBrA, one of the country's largest collections of works by the Northern European artists (Copenhagen, Brussels, and Amsterdam). Adults $10, seniors and students $7, children $3. Ticket prices vary for special exhibits. Open 9 AM–5 PM daily.

One of the area's best-kept secrets, the 256-seat **Norma & William Horvitz Auditorium,** at the Museum of Art, is home to the **Inside Out Theatre Company** (954-385-3060; www.insideouttheatre.org), which offers diverse and intelligent productions such as *Whose Life Is It, Anyway?* and *A Year with Frog & Toad,* based on the children's book. (See *Performing Arts.*)

Plan to spend an entire day at the **Museum of Discovery & Science** and the five-story **Blockbuster 3D IMAX Theater** (954-467-6637; www.mods.org), 401 SW Second St. The 52-foot-high Great Gravity Clock greets you as you enter the atrium, and then you can explore living plants and animals at Florida's Ecoscapes and try several interactive adventures in Gizmo City. The Discovery Center is specifically geared toward little ones younger than six. Theater: Open 10 AM–5 PM Mon.–Sat. and noon–6 PM Sun., with extended hours for the IMAX theater on the weekend. Tickets can be purchased separately for the museum or IMAX theater. Museum ticket: adults $9, seniors $8, children 2–12 $7. IMAX and museum ticket: adults $15, seniors $14, children 2–12 $12, children under 2 free.

Dania

Fun for fishers awaits at the **International Game Fish Association (IGFA) Fishing Hall of Fame & Museum** (954-922-4212; www.igfa.org), 300 Gulf Stream Way, with an art gallery, fish gallery, tackle gallery, historical displays, and exciting interactive experiences, including simulated fishing. My brother, an avid angler, took the deep-sea fishing challenge and landed a big virtual marlin! Open 10 AM–6 PM Mon.–Fri., 12 PM–6 PM Sun. Adults $8, children 3–16 and seniors 62+ $5. Parking is free and within walking distance to Outdoor World Bass Pro Shops (see *Selective Shopping*), where you can pick up rods and reels.

Hollywood

See native wildlife, such as alligators and the Florida panther, up close at the **Seminole Okalee Indian Village & Museum** (954-797-5466; www.seminole tribe.com), 5716 Seminole Way. Education shows include alligator wrestling and also on display is an excellent collection of Seminole cultural and historical arti-facts. Open 9 AM–5 PM Tues.–Sat., 10 AM–5 PM Sun. Adults $10, seniors and chil-dren 4–12 $8, children under 4 free.

WILDLIFE VIEWING Thousands upon thousands of live butterflies surround you at **Butterfly World** (954-977-4400; www.butterflyworld.com), 3600 W Sample Rd., Coconut Creek, an 8,000-square-foot conservatory. The beautiful 10-acre tropical gardens are also home to hummingbirds, lorikeets, and an insectarium. Walk among waterfalls, orchids, and peaceful ponds while you learn about these graceful winged creatures. Open 9 AM–5 PM Mon.–Sat., 11 AM–5 PM Sun. Adults $25, children 3–11 $20, children under 2 free.

✳ To Do

BICYCLING Take a bike tour of Fort Lauderdale (954-588-9565) along the beach, through historical neighborhoods, and through trendy Las Olas Boulevard. Tours depart from the **Tour Hut,** 101 S SR A1A (1 block south of Las Olas Blvd.). Small groups ride for about two hours. $30; includes bike rental.

BOAT TOURS

Fort Lauderdale

Sail along Millionaire's Row and the Venice of America on **Carrie B. Harbor Tours** (954-768-9920; www.carriebcruises.com), 440 North New River Drive East. The one-and-a-half-hour, fully narrated tours go out at 11 AM, 1 PM, and 3 PM. Adults $18, children $10. Check the Web site for coupons.

For more than 60 years, the **Jungle Queen Riverboat** (954-462-5596; www .junglequeen.com), 801 Seabreeze Blvd. (SR A1A), has cruised along Fort Lauderdale's Intracoastal Waterway for sight-seeing and dinner cruises. Choose from two narrated tours: the three-hour sight-seeing cruise (adults $17, children $13) or the all-you-can-eat barbecue and shrimp dinner cruise (adults $40, children $22).

The Sea Experience (954-394-8732; www.seaxp.com), Bahia Mar Beach Resort, 801 Seabreeze Blvd., offers glass-bottom boat tours for those who want to stay dry. Adults $28, children $15. Snorkeling and scuba diving is also available (see *Snorkeling*).

Tropical Sailing Catamaran Charters (954-579-8181; www.tropicalsailing.com), 801 Seabreeze Blvd., offers full-moon, stargazing, sight-seeing, wine-tasting, and sunset cruises on the *Spirit of Lauderdale* catamaran. Three trips daily; rates start at $29.

CARRIAGE TOUR Whether you want a quick tour, or if romance is in the air, a great way to see Las Olas is in a **Royal Horse Drawn Carriage** (954-971-9820; www.royalcarriagesfl.com). Percheron or Clydesdale horses carry you though Las Olas and the Arts District and along the Fort Lauderdale beach. Rides depart Wed.–Sun. from SE Eighth Ave. and E Las Olas Blvd.

ECOTOUR A full day of ecoadventure awaits at **Everglades Day Safari** (239-472-1559 or 1-800-472-3069; www.ecosafari.com), Fort Lauderdale, where you'll be taken on a boat ride through mangroves, a nature walk deep into a cypress swamp, a wildlife drive through the backcountry, and an airboat ride through the Everglades "River of Grass" with Miccosukee natives. Safaris depart Fort Lauderdale at 7:45 AM and return about 5:30 PM. Adults $135, children under 12 $99. Lunch is included.

FAMILY ACTIVITIES Drive go-carts and bumper cars at **Boomers** (954-921-2416; www.boomersparks.com), 1700 NW First St., Dania. They also have mini golf, arcade games, laser tag, and batting cages. Open 12 PM–11 PM Mon.–Thurs., noon–2 AM Fri., 10 AM–2 AM Sat., 11 AM–11 PM Sun. Admission $24 and up.

GAMING

Dania
Dania Jai Alai (954-920-1511 or 954-426-4330; www.dania-jai-alai.com), 301 E Dania Beach Blvd., Dania. Originating in the Basque region of Spain, the sport found its way into many cultures and is common in Latin America. A wicker basket is attached to a player's arm, who then uses it to hurl a rubber ball against a three-walled court. The game is much faster than racquetball, with balls reaching speeds of 150 miles per hour. Bets can be placed on players.

Hollywood
Seminole Hard Rock Hotel & Casino (954-327-7625; www.seminolehardrock hollywood.com), One Seminole Way, just off US 441. I call this place the "Seminole's Revenge," for the money they rake in from those desperate to win. Compared to Vegas, the gaming area is much more open and the noise level is higher, but you'll still find the throngs playing slots (no quarters, however—it's all done with bills and tickets) or gathering at the poker tables. Open 24 hours, 7 days a

week, and you can never tell exactly what time it is inside. The complex has a separate high-stakes bingo hall as well, several restaurants and night clubs, and a hotel.

GHOST TOUR **Fort Lauderdale Ghost Tour** (954-290-9328; www.fortlauder daleghosttour.com). The 60- to 90-minute walking tour meets at SE Sixth Avenue and E Las Olas Boulevard and takes you along Las Olas Boulevard and the historical New River. The tour covers a lot of area, so wear comfortable shoes. Adults $15, children 5–10 $10, children under 5 free. Reservations required. No credit cards.

PADDLING

Fort Lauderdale

Paddle past unique architecture, historical sites, and unique wildlife with **Full Moon Kayak Co.** (954-328-5231; www.fullmoonkayak.com). The fully guided and narrated tours operate in both urban and natural settings.

Hollywood

Rent kayaks or canoes at **Anne Kolb Nature Center** (see *Nature Centers*) and explore on your own through tidal wetlands, mangrove forests, and out onto the lake.

SNORKELING If you can't get to the Keys for snorkeling, hop on the **Sea Experience** (954-394-8732; www.seaxp.com), Bahia Mar Resort, 801 Seabreeze Blvd., Fort Lauderdale, for a snorkeling tour. Adults $35, children $21, including all gear. Glass-bottom boat tours are also available (see *Boat Tours*). You can also snorkel right off the beaches in Fort Lauderdale and Dania if you're willing to swim a bit offshore.

SURFING Hang 10 at **Deerfield Beach** (see *Beaches*), where surfing is allowed in select locations. The folks over at **Island Water Sports Surf Superstore** (see *Selective Shopping*) offer free surf lessons every Saturday morning at the Deerfield Beach Pier.

WALKING TOURS The arts and culture center of Broward County is in the **Riverwalk Arts & Entertainment District** (954-468-2540), between SW Seventh Ave. and SW Second Ave., Fort Lauderdale, where you can stroll along the river from the Broward Center for the Performing Arts to the shops on Las Olas Boulevard. The **Riverwalk/Espanade Park** (954-561-7362; www.goriverwalk .com), 1350 W Broward Blvd., Fort Lauderdale, is in the heart of the upbeat and thriving area.

✳ Green Space

BEACHES Wherever you are in Broward County, you can almost always head east and find a beach, though most do not allow dogs (see Canine Beach below). Here are a few of the standouts:

Deerfield Beach

The **City of Deerfield Beach** (www.deerfield-beach.com) has one of the prettiest, family-friendly beaches in the county. The award-winning "Blue Wave" beach

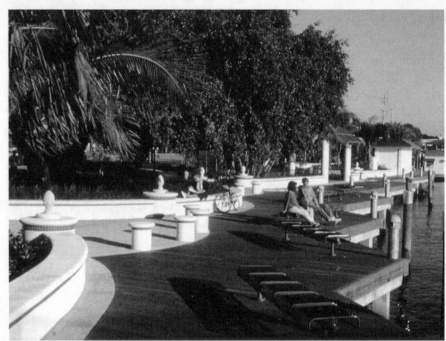

courtesy Greater Fort Lauderdale Convention and Visitors Bureau

RIVERWALK, FT. LAUDERDALE

earned this distinction for their clean water and beach conditions, safety, and their conservative efforts. The 1-mile stretch of beach has nine lifeguard towers with lifeguards present every day from 9 to 5. Take your short or long board, as surfing is permitted on the north side of the pier and south of tower #9. Check the Web site for beach conditions and surf cam.

Lauderdale-by-the-Sea
A quaint little village sits on the beach, a pier for fishers and waves for surfers all combine to make this a popular vacation destination for families looking for quiet time together on the shore.

Fort Lauderdale
Fort Lauderdale's main beach area along SR A1A was once the hot spot for spring break. When the Tonga swimsuit was banned in the 1980s in an attempt to quiet the area, the spring breakers went elsewhere. The beach now beckons a more open-minded audience geared toward an alternative lifestyle. Note the very cool, wavy neon wall that runs along the edge of SR A1A. On the other side of the street, numerous beachfront shops, restaurants, and nightclubs look out on one of the prettiest beaches in Fort Lauderdale.

🐾 **Canine Beach** (954-828-7275; www.ci.ftlaud.fl.us/cityparks/canine_beach), Sunrise Boulevard at SR A1A, from the center line of Sunrise Boulevard at A1A north to Lifeguard Stand # 5 (100-yard section of beach). This is the only area beach that allows dogs, and only Fri.–Sun., from 3 PM–7 PM in winter and 5 PM–9 PM in summer. Pet owners must purchase a weekend permit from the park ranger on duty, $7.

Dania Beach

⚓ Sea turtles nest along the shore at **John U. Lloyd Beach State Park** (954-923-2833; www.floridastateparks.org/lloydbeach/default.cfm), 6503 N Ocean Dr., and when the hatchlings emerge each fall, there can be up to 10,000 of them headed for the surf! Located just south of Port Everglades, the park is a crucial natural habitat on a shoreline crowded with development, and it's one of the most pleasant places to enjoy a commercial-free beach studded with trees instead of condos and shops. Enjoy the beaches, walk the nature trail, or bring a kayak and ply the mangrove-lined channels. Dogs are allowed in the park but not on the beach. Open 8 AM–sunset daily. Fee.

Hollywood

Hollywood Beach is lined with a "broadwalk," shops, small restaurants, and vintage hotels. It's a popular area for biking, and for families and travelers who'd rather not contend with the high-priced glam that characterizes South Beach in Miami.

NATURE CENTERS

Coconut Creek

& ⚓ An oasis in this densely populated area, **Fern Forest Nature Center** (954-970-0150), 201 Lyons Rd. S, has more than 2 miles of nature trails to wander, including the Cypress Creek boardwalk, which follows the rocky edge of now-dry Cypress Creek, a sad comment on the canalization of the county's natural waterways. More than 34 species of ferns grow throughout this verdant park. Stop at the nature center first for an overview of the habitats before hitting the trails. Open 8 AM–6 PM daily. Free.

Dania

& ⚓ Broward County's first nature center, **Secret Woods Nature Center** (954-791-1030), 2701 W FL 84, is hidden in a tangled jungle of mangroves along the New River. The center features interpretive displays and an active beehive; visitors come to enjoy the extensive boardwalk through the mangrove forest, where you can always spot ibises along the waterway. Open 8 AM–6 PM daily. Free.

Hollywood

At West Lake Park, **Anne Kolb Nature Center** (954-926-2410), 1200 Sheridan St., sits above the south side of an extensive mangrove-lined lagoon, West Lake. Two interpretive trails radiate from the center, which features interpretive displays, rotating art exhibits, and a tall observation tower accessed by elevator. The park features extensive paved biking trails, ecotour operators from a dock next to the nature center, and kayak rentals for you to explore this ecosystem on your own. Open 9 AM–5 PM daily. Fee.

PARKS

Coconut Creek

Tradewinds Park (954-968-3880), 3600 Sample Rd., is so packed with activities that you can spend a full day there. Sample Road breaks the park into two sections, North and South. Beyond the traditional pursuits of walking and biking, ball fields and picnicking, there are some very different things to do. At North Tradewinds Park, kids and rail fans will get a blast from the one-eighth life-sized live steam engines running out of Godwin Station, pulling train cars that you can sit on and ride. See the **Tradewinds & Atlantic Railroad** (www.livesteamers.org) schedule for operating times and dates. The 600-plus-acre park also has **Tradewinds Stables** (954-968-3875), offering guided trail rides ($23) and a farm with barnyard animals. **Batting cages** are also available ($15 for 30 minutes). In South Tradewinds Park, visit **Butterfly World** (see *Wildlife Viewing*), said to be the largest butterfly conservatory in the world. You can also rent canoes and kayaks to ply the chain of lakes, bring your Frisbee to tackle the disc golf course, or slip back along the trails at the southernmost end of the park to find a boardwalk through a primeval pond apple swamp.

Deerfield Beach

Deerfield Island Park (954-360-1320), 1720 Deerfield Island Park Rd., provides an opportunity to "get away from it all" on an island in the Intracoastal Waterway, with 1.3 miles of trails and boardwalks to explore. This day-use park can be accessed only by boat. Free shuttle boats leave at prescheduled times; call ahead for schedule.

Fort Lauderdale Beach

✍ Right across the street from the beach, **Hugh Taylor Birch State Park** (954-564-4521; www.floridastateparks.org/hughtaylorbirch/default.cfm), 3109 E Sunrise Blvd., is the former estate of Chicago attorney Hugh Taylor Birch and protects a coastal hammock in this urban area. Built in 1940, Birch's home, TerraMar, displays both Mediterranean and art deco styles and serves as the park's visitors center (open 10 AM–4 PM daily). The quiet park is nestled between the beach and the downtown area, providing a serene escape from the hustle and bustle of city life. The park also has two nature trails, canoe rentals for plying the waters of a coastal dune lake, and plenty of picnic spots. You can walk over to the beach or picnic along the Intracoastal Waterway. This is one of the best places for in-line skating, with a road that passes under a peaceful canopy of trees and then along the water. Open 8 AM–sunset daily. $4 per vehicle.

Hollywood

Broward County Parks and Recreation (954-357-8100; www.broward.org/parks) lists several natural areas throughout the county. One of my favorites is 1,500-acre **West Lake Park** (954-926-2410; www.broward.org/parks), 750 Sheridan St., which offers hiking, biking, and paddling opportunities. Canoeists and kayakers can rent or bring their own, and then paddle through mangrove trails and out onto wide-open lakes. Don't miss the nature exhibit in the main building, where you'll learn about tidal marshes and local wildlife. The **Anne Kolb Nature Center** (see *Nature Centers*) also has a fishing pier and five-story observation tower. Fee.

Oakland Park

✍ Despite the road noise from nearby I-95, **Easterlin Park** (954-938-0610), 1000 NW 38th St., is a pretty little place with camping along a pond and a "designated urban wilderness" where a nature trail winds through the tropical forest and ancient cypresses rise from the edge of a swamp. Playgrounds, picnic areas, and fishing round out the experience. Call for camping reservations. Open daily. Fee on weekends and holidays.

✳ Lodging

COTTAGES

Pompano Beach 33062

Cottages By The Ocean (954-956-8999; www.4rentbythebeach.com), 3309 SE Third St., offers six 1940s Key West–style studio cottages only 2 blocks from the beach and is a member of Superior Small Lodging. The cottages were renovated only a few years ago and include king-sized beds, a barbecue area, and cable television. Nonsmoking; small dogs welcome. Rates $500–1,100 weekly; $1,500–3,500 monthly.

HOTELS, MOTELS, AND RESORTS

Pompano Beach 33062

Sands Harbor Resort and Marina (954-942-9100; www.sandsharbor.com), 125 N Riverside Dr. In business for more than 50 years, Sands Harbor was one of the first businesses to settle Pompano Beach, building a yacht basin to serve visitors and residents from Palm Beach to Miami. On the Intracoastal Waterway near the Hillsboro Inlet, the Sands is convenient to local yacht brokers, dive shops, glass-bottom boat rentals, and snorkel tours. A favorite of fishers and boaters, the resort hosts two annual fishing tournaments, the Pompano Beach Fishing Rodeo in May and the Pompano Beach Saltwater Slam in June. Accommodations in the tall, balconied waterfront building range from hotel rooms to penthouse apartments. $169 and up.

Lauderdale-by-the-Sea 33308

☙ **Courtyard Villas on the Ocean** (954-776-1164; www.courtyardvilla .com), 4312 El Mar Dr.This quaint, private inn offers oceanfront rentals at reasonable rates. $125 and up.

☙ **High Noon Resort** (954-776-1121 or 1-800-382-1265), 4424 El Mar Dr.

A fabulous old beachfront hotel with rooms and suites that are perfect for those seeking a peaceful beach getaway. Advance planners may wish to inquire about renting the rare beach house on the property—it's a great place for a beachfront wedding! $130 and up; $315 and up for the 2 bedroom beach house.

Fort Lauderdale 33304

The Atlantic (954-567-8020; www.the atlantichotelfortlauderdale.com), 601 N Fort Lauderdale Beach Blvd. Newly opened in 2004, the Atlantic is a premier luxury offering on Fort Lauderdale's beach. With sleek styling and spacious rooms decorated with colorful accents and complementary earth tones and black marble baths, the hotel offers the latest amenities, including poolside cabanas and a spa. $269 and up.

☙ **Avalon Waterfront Inns, Beach Resort Waterfront Inn** (954-564-4341 or 1-800-543-2006; www.water frontinns.com), 521 Fort Lauderdale Beach Blvd. (SR A1A). This family-owned enterprise is holding strong against the wave of corporate invasion of Fort Lauderdale Beach. The hotel has earned several awards for their attentiveness to customer service and personal approach to business, all of which add up to better experiences for guests. Rather than raze vintage 1950s inns, the approach is to bring them into the future as boutique hotels. The Beach Resort has 59 fully renovated and redecorated rooms with all the modern amenities, such as Internet access, massage services, and conference facilities (for an intimate group of 12). Across the street from the beach (no hotels mar the beachfront on this stretch of A1A), the hotel also offers a pool. $159 and up.

✦ **Bahia Mar Beach Resort & Yachting Center** (954-627-6357 or 1-

888-802-2442; www.bahiamarhotel
.com), 801 Seabreeze Blvd. Access is
everything—and this hotel has access
to the marina, so if you've brought
your boat or plan to spend some serious time fishing, boating, or diving,
then this could be the best place for
you. $169 and up.

Courtyard Fort Lauderdale Beach
(954-524-8733; www.marriott.com),
440 Seabreeze Blvd. It's hard to beat
the ocean views at this hotel in the
heart of Fort Lauderdale's "Strip,"
where vacationers sun on the beach by
day and hike from restaurant to pub by
night. If that's what you're here for,
this (and a few others up and down the
street) is the place. $259.

◆ **Gallery One Doubletree Guest
Suites** (954-565-3800; www.doubletree
galleria.com), 2670 E Sunrise Blvd.
This lovely hotel, on the Intracoastal
Waterway, is within walking distance of
the beach and the Galleria Shopping
Mall. The rooms are nice, clean, and
well cared for. $219 and up.

◆ **Embassy Suites** (954-527-2700;
www.embassysuitesftl.com), 1100 SE
17th St. Off the beaten path (i.e., the
beach), this hotel is convenient to the
Broward County Convention Center
and the Intracoastal Waterway. Its nice
yet comfortable atmosphere and interi-
or courtyard and hallways make it a
good choice for group events. $259
and up.

▼ **The Flamingo** (954-561-4658;
www.theflamingoresort.com), 2727
Terramar St., Fort Lauderdale 33304,
a luxury gay hotel, is in the heart of the
gay district only a few blocks from the
beach. British West Indies decor
includes such details as four-poster
beds and crisp clean white-on-white
linens. Many of the spacious rooms
and suites open through French doors
directly into the courtyard, where
you'll find fountains, gardens, and a

heated swimming pool. Other amenities include continental breakfast and
full concierge service. Rooms and
suites $150–370.

◆ **Hyatt Regency Pier Sixty-Six**
(954-525-6666; www.pier66.com), 2301
SE 17th St. Causeway. One of Fort
Lauderdale's most enduring landmarks
on the Intracoastal Waterway, the
Hyatt maintains the aura of glamour
and sophistication the rooftop restaurant has always brought to the hotel.
Elegant, well-cared-for rooms. $249
and up.

Hidden from the hustle and bustle of
the main roadways, **Lago Mar Hotel
Resort and Club** (954-523-6511 or 1-
800-LAGOMAR; www.lagomar.com),
1700 S Ocean Ln., Fort Lauderdale
33316, is located directly on one of the
best beaches in the area. Spacious
rooms and luxury suites are decorated
in tropical splendor. Beds are oh so
soft, from the pillow-top mattresses to
the sumptuous duvet covers. Amenities
include an Olympic-sized pool, a
9,000-square-foot lagoon-style pool set
in a tropical paradise, a 500-foot beach
with private beach cabanas, an on-site
full-service spa, a fitness center, beachfront volleyball, tennis courts, a children's play area, a giant outdoor
chessboard, shuffleboard, putting
course, private oceanfront balconies,
and other services found at major
resorts. Guest rooms, executive suites,
and a penthouse with beachfront views
$150–755 depending on season. Valet
parking is available if you need it, but
self-parking is close at hand.

◆ **Marriott's Harbor Beach Resort**
(954-525-4000 or 1-800-222-6543;
www.marriottharborbeach.com), 3030
N Holiday Dr. A longtime Fort Lauderdale hotel, this one has a corner on
the beach—literally. It's located at the
end of the public beach, with a wide
section it calls its own, providing

plenty of fun in the sun for guests. The hotel is large and popular with meeting planners, and its spa is highly regarded. $349.

✦ **Pelican Grand Beach Resort** (954-568-9431; www.pelicanbeach .com), 2000 N Atlantic Ocean Blvd. Family owned since 1989, the Pelican recently underwent a massive renovation project to create an all-new resort. Freshly redecorated to recall the charm of old Florida, rooms feature French-paneled doors, wrought-iron beds, and colorful, plush linens and upholstery. Most have balconies with ocean views and include coffeepots and Internet access. With a rare beachfront location, the resort also features two pools and a tube ride for the kids. $302 and up includes complimentary breakfast for two.

Shhh, **Pillars at New River Sound** (954-467-9639; www.pillarshotel.com), 111 N Birch Rd., Fort Lauderdale 33304, is a secret! This low-key luxury boutique hotel has 23 rooms and suites located in a tropical paradise right on the Intracoastal Waterway. The fully restored 1938 property was previously a private residence. Tastefully appointed rooms feature 14-foot ceilings with British Colonial and island plantation themes. The cozy library features hundreds of books and videos and even a baby grand piano. There is a heated freshwater pool and a waterfront courtyard with a lush tropical garden, and the beach is nearby. Queen- or king-sized beds in superior rooms and suites $300–700.

▼ "1" Located in Victoria Park, **Pineapple Point Guest House & Resort** (954-527-0094 or 1-888-844-7295; www.pineapplepoint.com), 315 NE 16th Terrace, Fort Lauderdale 33304, is within walking distance to the trendy Las Olas district and nearby Wilton Manors. The 1930s guest house

is comprised of seven Old Florida buildings housing 27 luxury rooms and suites within a tropical garden setting. The resort caters to gay men only, and clothing is optional around the heated pool. Several types of accommodations are available: double and king-sized beds in rooms, bungalows, suites, cottages, one- to four-bedroom villas ($199–679), and a three-story villa with four bedrooms and an elevator ($750–900 depending on season). Suites offer separate living rooms and dining areas along with full kitchens. Amenities include high-speed wireless Internet, refrigerators, cable TV, and VCRs, and there is a swimming pool, a lap pool, and two whirlpools.

Old-world charm and elegance will captivate you at **Riverside Hotel** (954-467-0671 or 1-800-325-3280; www.riversidehotel.com), 620 E Las Olas Blvd., Fort Lauderdale 33304. Located in the vibrant Las Olas Boulevard district, the city's oldest hotel (circa 1936) was a favorite of the Du Pont family and later, former President Ronald Reagan and other well-known celebrities. Guest rooms and suites ($125–295) are spread between the original six-story landmark building and a 12-story tower, which caters to executives. Modern amenities include a swimming pool, cable television, data ports, and refrigerators. Over in the Executive Tower you'll find two-room suites ($600) with oversized Jacuzzi tubs.

▼ Plush towels, designer linens, and spa amenities are just a few details that are offered at **The Royal Palms Resort** (954-564-6444 or 1-800-237-7256; www.royalpalms.com), 2901 Terramar St., Fort Lauderdale 33304. The clothing-optional resort caters exclusively to gay men. Amenities include a tropical heated pool, Wi-Fi, cable TV, and refrigerators. Queen- or king-sized beds in pool or garden rooms or suites $189–340.

🦐 🐚 **Sheraton Yankee Clipper** (1-866-716-8106; www.starwoodhotels .com/sheraton/property/overview/index .html?propertyID=664) 321 N. Atlantic Blvd., Fort Lauderdale 33304. The Yankee Clipper has helped define the Fort Lauderdale beach since I was a kid (a long time). Maintaining its popularity as well as its property, the hotel offers distinctive accommodations for business travelers, with easy access to the convention center, airport, and port, and vacationers enjoy the proximity to the beach, shopping, and the marina. $188 and up.

Dania Beach
⊷ **Sheraton Fort Lauderdale Airport** (954-920-3500 or 1-866-716-8106; www.starwoodhotels/sheraton), 1825 Griffin Rd. Convenient to the airport and just a few miles from the beach, the Sheraton is also right next door to the fascinating DCOTA (Design Center of the Americas), where the latest and most unusual items for home and business are displayed in hundreds of designer showrooms. It's a clean, friendly hotel with meeting space and restaurants. $176 and up.

⊷ **Hilton Fort Lauderdale Airport** (954-920-3300; www.hilton.com), 1870 Griffin Rd. At the Hilton there are finely appointed rooms for business travelers, as well as a few amenities the family might enjoy, including a pool, Web TV, and Nintendo games. Convenient to the airport, DCOTA, and the Dania antiques district. $161 and up.

Hollywood
The Westin Diplomat Resort and Spa (954-602-6000 or 1-888-627-9057; www.westin.com/diplomat), 3555 S Ocean Dr. The largest hotel in the

county, with 1,000 rooms, this is a bit of an anomaly on Hollywood's beach. The flashy high-rise came into being with lots of promises to bring revenue and glamour to the city. Some headaches were included, however, such as a problem with beach erosion that makes the towering building look as if it could tumble into the surf at any moment (don't worry, it probably won't). But the end result is an undeniably beautiful hotel, with rooms fit for royalty. $419 and up.

✳ Where to Eat
DINING OUT
Lighthouse Point
Cap's Place (954-941-0418; www .capsplace.com), 2765 NE 28th Ct. A National Historic Site, Cap's Place is a small seafood restaurant afloat in the Intracoastal Waterway, accessible only by boat. (The restaurant provides a motor launch.) Cap's has been serving dinner to the famous, infamous, and the rest of us since the 1920s, when a few enterprising souls tied a few shacks to a barge and floated them from Miami to this small island, creating a casino and rum-running drop point during Prohibition. Party animals such as Al Capone and Meyer Lansky have passed time at the joint, as have Franklin Roosevelt, Winston Churchill, Vanderbilts and Rockefellers, George Harrison, and Mariah Carey. The award-winning dinners of fresh seafood, island chicken, filet mignon, and hearts of palm salad aren't quite as exciting as the boat ride and historic ambience. Reservations recommended. Open daily at 5:30 Jan.–Apr.; closed Mon. May–Dec. $23 and up.

Pompano Beach
Joe's Riverside Grill (954-941-2499; www.joesriversidegrille.com), 125 N Riverside Dr. This award-winning,

four-star restaurant has specialized in deliciously prepared fresh local seafood for 10 years as of 2008, with stone crabs a house favorite, but aged beef also highlights the menu. Try the blackened tuna steak, rum peppercorn–marinated tuna, or jerked grouper for some of the best seafood around. Whatever you choose, you're sure to enjoy the waterfront location on the Intracoastal Waterway. $16 and up.

Romantico (954-946-9100; www.romanticoristorante.com), 1903 E Atlantic Blvd. Romantico serves a small but exquisite Italian menu that includes memorable pasta dishes, salmon with lemon sauce, and seafood and lobster specials. Live music, open daily. $23 and up.

Lauderdale-by-the-Sea

The beachfront **Aruba Beach Cafe** (954-776-0001; www.arubabeachcafe.com), right on the beach at Commercial Blvd. and FL A1A, offers Caribbean and West Indian favorites. Lunch, dinner, and a Sunday breakfast buffet are served.

The trendy art deco–inspired **Blue Moon Fish Co.** (954-267-9888; www.bluemoonfishco.com), 4405 W Tradewinds Ave., is located directly on the Intracoastal Waterway and is known for its Sunday gospel brunch. Lunch and dinner served daily.

Fort Lauderdale

Hard to find, but worth the search is **By Word of Mouth** (954-564-3663; www.bywordofmouthfoods.com), 3200 NE 12th Ave. The restaurant and caterer built its reputation completely by word of mouth more than two decades ago and continues to be one of the best gastronomic delights, always rating high on reviewers' "best of" lists. Start off your meal with portobello mushrooms with lump crabmeat ($14)

or escargots with Pernod crème in pastry shell ($13), and then select an entrée such as shrimp with sweet curry basil ($16), roasted vegetable lasagna with béchamel sauce ($14), or pan-seared grouper with spinach Chardonnay reduction ($17). Finish with one of their specialty cakes, such as Chocolate Orgasm, or our favorite, Carrot Praline ($8). Menu and bakery selections change daily, but if you call a few days in advance, they may make one of their 50 gourmet desserts specifically for your visit. They will also make full-sized cakes for you to take home. (We bring home the Carrot Praline cake too often to mention.) Lunch is served Mon.–Fri. starting at 11 AM; dinner is served Wed.–Sat. starting at 5 PM. (This restaurant's primary business is catering.)

Cafe Martorano (954-561-2554; www.cafemartorano.com), 3343 E Oakland Blvd., at the corner of FL A1A, is a fantastic restaurant, but please leave the kids at home. This *Sopranos*-type restaurant feels like you might be in Little Italy instead of a few steps from Fort Lauderdale Beach. During dinner, gangster movies play overhead on flat screens, while disco lights and '80s music keeps things lively. Be forewarned that your waiter will explain the menu in descriptive detail, but without the benefit of pricing (if you have to ask, then you shouldn't be here—for those who have to ask, most entrées are $25–65). Our family loves this place for the meatball appetizers (two enormous meatballs with a small salad for $14 are just how our in-laws make them back home). Fresh, authentic ingredients are imported from places such as Tuscany, Salerno, Calabria, Sicily, and Modena. If you want a unique dining experience with a very good chance of seeing celebrities (such as James Gandolfini, Liza Minelli, and Dan Marino), then this is the place. Reservations are not accepted, so expect lines on the weekends and in-season of at least an hour. Open 5 PM daily.

The 1920s **Casablanca Cafe** (954-764-3500; www.casablancacafeonline .com), 3049 Alhambra St. on Fort Lauderdale Beach, offers a fabulous ocean view in an historic Moroccan-style villa. Menu items from tropical to North African are served nightly (about $20–30). You often find waiters, and sometimes guests, singing along at the downstairs piano bar in the casual atmosphere. Cozy corners can be found upstairs, with the outside deck offering a view of the beach. Valet parking recommended, as street parking is hard to find. And they don't take reservations, so get there early. Open daily until 1 AM; dinner served until 11 PM.

Charley's Crab (954-561-4800; www .muer.com), 3000 NE 32nd Ave., is a must for locals and tourists alike. The restaurant overlooks the Intracoastal, so you'll often see a nice-sized yacht moored at the dock. Eat inside with modern elegance or on the outside terrace. Lunch and dinner are served daily.

Creolina's (954-524-2003), 209 SW Second St. Chef and owner Mark Sulzinski keeps his Culinary Institute of America diploma posted in the ladies' room, and while I don't know what that's about, his training shines through without the document. He crafts a mean gumbo, serves it up with rice topped with green onions, and calls it an appetizer—add a salad (served with a delicious ginger house dressing) and it's the perfect meal. Heartier appetites may prefer the crawfish étouffée, all washed down with a couple of bottles of Blackened Voodoo, a rich, dark Dixie beer. $14 and up.

A longtime favorite is the **15th Street Fisheries** (954-763-2777; www.15 streetfisheries.com), 1900 SE 15th St., a casual seafood restaurant overlooking the Intracoastal. They serve more than 12 fresh fish items for lunch and dinner daily. $19 and up.

French Quarter (954-463-8000), 215 SE Eighth Ave. Let yourself be pampered at this delightful French eatery. Just a block off the beaten path, this is one to find and enjoy for its attention to detail and for its refusal to rush you through a pleasant dining experience. Enter the restaurant and enjoy the cozy, gardenlike atmosphere of lush plants, old brick arches, and sunlit ceilings. The menu, which includes French and continental cuisine with a Cajun–New Orleans twist, brings you oysters Rockefeller, crab cakes, Brie, or pâté to start; French onion soup, gumbo, or vichyssoise; and entrées of quail, beef Wellington, or medallions of veal *au citron*. This place is warm, friendly, dark, and delicious. $14 and up.

Greek Islands Taverna (954-568-0008), 3300 N Ocean Blvd. While the delicious Greek fare served at this busy spot is popular, the Taverna's not the place for heady romance: it's your table is ready, ma'am; eat; and out. Start with *saganaki* (fried cheese)—don't skip the salad—and consider an entrée of roast leg of lamb or charbroiled swordfish. Save room for the baklava. Rich! $14 and up.

Hi-Life Café (954-563-1395; www .hilifecafe.com), Plaza 3000, 3000 N Federal Hwy. This cozy, comfortable café and bar, owned by Chuck Smith, has earned a Zagat's rating as a Top 40 Favorite. Hi-Life boasts a rich wine list with a number of "great value" selections for the modest budget, paired with delicious yet moderately priced entrée selections. Chef Carlos Fernandez creates unique dishes with a French foundation that are inspired by whimsy and tropical flavors. Reservations are recommended. Closed Mon. $17 and up.

Local celebrity chef Johnny Vinczencz recently opened his own restaurant, **Johnny V** (954-761-7920; www.johnny vlasolas.com), 625 E Las Olas Blvd., after working as a sous chef for Dennis Max, a pioneer in South Florida cuisine in the 1980s and '90s, and then as executive chef for Astor Place in Miami Beach and De La Tierra in Delray Beach (see *South Palm Beach County*). Gourmets take note: Johnny V creates such appetizers as Jamaican jerk seared fresh tuna; Callaloo Stew; Bammy, aka coconut yucca cakes ($13); roasted garlic clams sautéed with Jamon Serrano red chile corn broth; and JV BBQ "Stix" ($14). Entrées may include fresh corn crusted yellowtail snapper, lemon Boniato mash, roasted corn sauce, and smoked pepper relish ($27); red chile venison chop, venison sausage, a trio of baby baked potatoes, wilted spinach, and blackberry demiglaze ($32); or the famous wild mushroom pancake "short stack" with roasted portobello, balsamic syrup, and sun-dried tomato butter ($11). An extensive selection of more than 40 cheeses is available paired with intricate salads and fresh fruits. Desserts are equally impressive. Open for lunch and dinner. Reservations recommended.

A Broward institution, **Lester's Diner** (954-525-5641), 250 FL 84, is open 24/7, offers an extensive menu, and serves breakfast all day. Another location is out west in Sunrise (see *Inland: Western Broward County*).

A longtime favorite of tourists and locals alike, the **Mai-Kai Polynesian Restaurant and Dinner Show** (954-563-3272; www.maikai.com), 3599 N Federal Hwy., brings the South Seas to life within their Polynesian garden restaurant. Hostesses dressed in sarongs serve exotic tropical drinks, and the Polynesian floor show (adults $11, children under 12 free) makes for a fun evening with family or friends. Dinner served nightly. Expect valet parking as street parking is limited.

River House (954-525-7661; www .ftlauderdaleriverhouse.com), 301 SW Third Ave. Located in a historic home on Fort Lauderdale's New River in Old Town, River House's outdoor patio provides a scenic and pleasant dining destination, and the indoor dining and bar are equally charming. The food matches the atmosphere, with fresh flavors spiking traditional favorites such as horseradish-crusted salmon and anise-ginger calamari served in generous portions. Happy hour (all days except Sat.; complimentary sushi); Sun. brunch, reservations recommended. Closed Mon. $19 and up.

You can crack your own crabs at the casual, waterfront **Rustic Inn Crabhouse** (954-584-1637; www.rusticinn .com), 4331 Ravenswood Rd. The steamed garlic blue crabs are served on newspaper-covered tables. Lunch and dinner served daily.

Sage (954-565-2299; www.sagecafe .net), 2378 N Federal Hwy. Delicious country French cuisine is served in a sophisticated yet comfortable atmosphere. Meals begin with an olive tapenade that's irresistible, but don't spoil your appetite—the real fun is yet to come. Try the mustard-crusted *poulet* (chicken) or a crêpe for dinner or dessert. Nice selection of wines, reservations recommended. $14 and up.

Shula's on the Beach (954-355-4000; www.donshula.com), 321 N Atlantic Blvd. (SR A1A). Come here for the lovely setting, lovely view, and the classic menu of aged beef and fresh seafood, presented by chef Chris Gilmore and former Dolphins coach Don Shula, whose successful restaurants now span the nation. While the aged Angus beef is the star here, the house salad—crumbled blue cheese and sugared-walnut vinaigrette over a wedge of iceberg lettuce—is also unforgettable. $19 and up.

✧ **Sublime World Vegetarian Cuisine** (954-539-9000; www.sublimeveg .com), 1431 N Federal Hwy. Animal-rights activist and dishy bikini babe Pamela Anderson came to town to herald the opening of this upscale vegetarian palace in 2003, and the restaurant seems to have warranted the attention. With its cool stone interior and waterfall wall, Sublime's atmosphere helps diners feel as good as the guilt-free fare. Like many Sublime dishes, the sundried tomato carpaccio and arugula with black olive tapenade and garlic chips is unique as well as delicious. The raw avocado and organic beet soup is also lovely. Who could miss meat with entrées such as eggplant Parmesan, veggie lasagna, and grilled portobello with Swiss chard, rutabaga, mango, and ginger? $14 and up.

Sushi Rock (954-462-5541) 1515 E Las Olas Blvd. The epitome of cool hides behind this unassuming though colorful facade. Dark, fun, and chic, the restaurant has a small sushi bar, as well as tables. This little bar not far from the sea has a big-city feeling and some of the best Japanese cuisine around. $9 and up.

Casual dockside dining along the New River is at **Shirttail Charlie's** (954-463-3474; www.shirttailcharlies.com), 400 SW Third Ave. Pull up your boat and dig into local fresh seafood, alligator, and conch. The waterfront restaurant offers a free after-dinner river cruise, or you can take the boat to and from a performance at the Broward

Center for the Performing Arts (see *Performing Arts*). Lunch and dinner served daily.

Once a spring break favorite, **Shooter's Waterfront Cafe** (954-566-2855; www.shooterscafe.com), 3033 NE 32nd Ave., still attracts a lively crowd. Cigarette boats and luxury yachts line the dock along the Intracoastal Waterway. You can eat in or out, or just hang out at the bar. Open daily until late.

Hollywood

Revitalized downtown Hollywood has an amazing array of international restaurants. For the best Spanish food, there's **La Barraca Tapa Bar & Cafe** (954-925-0050), 115 S 20th Ave.; for Irish food and entertainment, there's **O'Hara's Jazz Cafe & Swing Street Bistro** (954-925-2555), 1903 Hollywood Blvd.; Romanian food is served at **Transylvania** (954-929-0777), 113 S 20th Ave.; and you'll find good Mediterranean cuisine at **Zaraka Restaurant & Lounge** (954-966-6669), 715 S 21st Ave.

EATING OUT

Dania Beach

✧ Celebrating 50 years of goodness in 2006, **Jaxson's** old-fashioned ice cream parlor (954-923-4445; www.jaxsonsice cream.com), 128 S Federal Hwy., is a must for any tourist or local. Ice cream and toppings are prepared daily right on the premises. The huge sundaes ($8–11) are almost impossible to finish, but we keep trying. Other cool creations are the old-fashioned banana split ($10), colossal parfaits ($9), and, for parties of four or more, there's the Kitchen Sink ($10 per person). This amazing sundae is served in an actual kitchen sink and is a creation that you make with the guidance of Jaxson's own professional soda jerks. For a truly special event, get a dozen of your close friends together and order the Punch

Bowl Sundae ($90). Oh, and Jaxson's also serves excellent salads ($9), burgers ($8), sandwiches ($7–9), wraps ($8), and junior meals ($6). Just make sure to save room for the ice cream!

Fort Lauderdale

Anthony's Coal-Fired Pizza (954-462-5555; www.anthonyscoalfiredpizza.com), 2203 S Federal Hwy. (There are several other Anthony's Coal-Fired restaurant locations in South Florida.) Regulars flock to the various Anthony's eateries for the thin pizzas with the signature almost-burned tastiness. Baked in 800-degree ovens, the pizzas are the featured items at these popular neighborhood-style restaurants. The well-done pizzas pair nicely with a heaping bowl of Anthony's fresh green Italian salad. Or go for an arugula salad served atop the pizza. Apart from an array of pizza options, the menu is relatively simple. Other items include focaccia sandwiches, side dishes of broccoli rabe and sausage, and cheesecake for dessert. $17 and up.

Chef's Palette Café and Grille (954-760-7957), 1650 SE 17th St. Feeling like a guinea pig? Have no fear. Chef's Palette is the laboratory restaurant of the culinary division of the Art Institute of Fort Lauderdale. Students prepare and present meals, serving the public gourmet cuisine for a song. Reservations recommended. Closed Sun. and Mon. $12 and up.

Croissan' Time (954-565-8555), Sunrise Square, 1201 N Federal Hwy. After driving by this place for months, I finally got a tip that this little pastry shop served up some of the finest French pastry around. The tip proved true. Open for more than 20 years, the shop turns out baguettes, croissant, and breads throughout the day, as well as a wide variety of fine pastries. Eat in the shop or grab a prepared dish of pâté, beef burgundy, or any number of gourmet meals to eat at home. $7 and up.

Downtowner Saloon (954-463-9800), 408 S Andrews Ave. This casual restaurant and bar, on the waterfront under the New River Bridge and tucked behind the county jail, offers sandwiches, seafood, and steak. $9 and up.

Since 1938, **The Elbo Room** (954-463-4615; www.elboroom.com), 241 S Fort Lauderdale Beach Blvd., Fort Lauderdale, has been the area's number-one watering hole. World War II sailors came here in the 1940s, and then spring breakers dominated the scene during the later part of the century when the movie *Where the Boys Are,* with Connie Frances and George Hamilton, made Fort Lauderdale Beach spring break central. Today people 21 and older stop by for a drink and to check out tiny bikinis and a bit of history.

The Floridian (954-463-4041), 1410 E Las Olas Blvd. This friendly, bustling place on trendy Las Olas is a great place to catch a late-night snack or early-early breakfast. Open 24/7. $7 and up.

✎ **Pizza Fusion** (954-358-5353; www.pizzafusion.com), 1013 N Federal Hwy. (Franchises in several other Florida towns and across the country.) Pizza Fusion is a totally unique Green Restaurant—they even invited me to have a book party to announce my latest book, *The Complete Idiot's Guide to Green Living* (Alpha Books 2007)! The food and the business philosophy at these relaxed and informal restaurants revolve around an earth-friendly attitude. The buildings are furnished with recycled and reused tables, floors are environmentally friendly, ovens vent heat for reuse either as heat or for water, delivery vehicles are hybrid cars, ingredients include organic vegetables. Along with oval pizzas, the fare

AUTHOR TRISH RILEY SIGNING BOOKS AT PIZZA FUSION, FT. LAUDERDALE

includes sandwiches, breadsticks with olive tapenade, wraps and salads— some with an exotic flair. The Pacific Rim salad features organic greens, fresh mandarin oranges, red cabbage, cucumbers, snow peas, baby corn, and water chestnuts. The Greek pizza includes kalamata olives, feta cheese, artichoke hearts and fresh basil. For those with precise dining preferences, plenty of items on the menu are labeled as vegan, gluten-free, or organic. $14 and up.

At **Stork's Las Olas** (954-522-4670; www.storkscafe.com), 1109 E Las Olas Blvd., Jim Stork offers 13 different varieties of coffee beans, breakfast pastries, garden salads and sandwiches, mousses, and cakes, tortes, and pies— by the slice, or take home a whole one. All bakery items are made fresh daily, from scratch, using top-notch ingredients.

Tom Jenkins Bar-B-Q (954-522-5046; www.tomjenkinsbbq.com), 1236 S Federal Hwy. Jenkins's own downhome hot and spicy barbecue sauce comes slathered on chicken, ribs, beef, or pork straight off the fiery, constantly rotating rotisserie just off the small, picnic table–filled dining area. Collard greens, hush puppies, and sweet potato pie round out the meal. Take-out is available, or buy the sauce by the bottle and (try to) make your own. Closed Sun. and Mon. $7 and up.

Hollywood

Universe Café (954-920-3774; www .universecafe.net), 1925 Hollywood Blvd., offers salads ($6 and up) and sandwiches, crab cakes, and more. Open daily for breakfast and lunch with live music on the weekends.

Wilton Manors

▼ "I" Fresh gourmet coffee, cappuccinos, iced lattes, macchiato, chai tea, fruit smoothies, and an assortment of desserts can be found at **Java Boys** (954-564-8828), 2230 Wilton Dr. Not for everyone, the mostly male hangout bears the rainbow flag and has buff nude photos on the walls. Bring your laptop to make use of their Wi-Fi hookup.

✳ Entertainment

Fine or casual dining, shopping, art galleries, and all sorts of entertainment from dancing to movies can be found along the **Las Olas Riverfront** (954-522-6556; www.riverfrontfl.com), 300 SW First Ave., Fort Lauderdale. The Sunday Jazz Brunch is held the first Sunday each month. A parking garage is on SW First Avenue, meters and valet parking available as well.

DINNER SHOW Mai-Kai Polynesian Restaurant and Dinner Show (see *Dining Out*), Fort Lauderdale, authentically re-creates a Polynesian village, complete with tiki torches, thatch roof, and wooden plank entrance.

PERFORMING ARTS

Fort Lauderdale

See a show at the **Broward Center for the Performing Arts** (954-462-0222; www.browardcenter.org), 201 SW Fifth Ave. Overlooking the New River and Riverwalk Arts District, the state-of-the-art complex showcases Broadway productions and the **Florida Grand Opera** (1-800-741-1010; www.fgo.org).

All the productions at the **Fort Lauderdale Children's Theatre** (954-763-6882; www.flct.org), 640 N Andrews Ave., are performed by children ranging in age from 6 to 18, and the technicians and backstage crew are also younger than 18. Come see what these talented youngsters can do at shows such as *Aladdin's Lamp* and *Les Miserables School Edition.* Drama classes and camps are also available. Adults $18, children under 12 $15.

Socially relevant and thought-provoking theater is presented at the **Inside Out Theatre Company** at the **Museum of Art Fort Lauderdale** (see *Museums*). Tickets $30, with discounts for students and museum members.

Hollywood

The Art & Culture Center of Hollywood (see *Art Galleries*), in the heart of downtown Hollywood, has professional dance and theatrical performances, gallery exhibitions, and classes for children and adults. The Center hosts the annual Ocean Dance, free performances on Hollywood Beach at Johnson Street in December. The Art & Culture Center also manages the programs at **The Hollywood Central Performing Arts Center** (954-921-3274; www.artandculturecenter.org), 1770 Monroe St., where dance performances are presented. Adults $25, seniors $23, members and students $20.

✳ Selective Shopping

ANTIQUES AND COLLECTIBLES

Fort Lauderdale

Great vintage, antique, and consignment furniture and accessories can be found at **Beachcomber Consignments** (954-630-0911), 3042 N Federal Hwy.; **Decades Design Group** (954-564-0454), N Federal Hwy.; and **June Sharp Antiques and New Trends** (954-565-8165), 3000 N Federal Hwy.

Flagler Antiques (954-463-0994; www.flaglerantiques.com), 720 N Flagler Dr., specializes in art nouveau and art deco French antiques.

For the best in midcentury and atomic modern, check out **Space Modern** (954-564-6100; www.space-modern.com), 2335 NE 26th St., or **Art Modern** (954-567-9502), 2673 N Federal Hwy. (which has a second location in Wilton Manors).

Victoria's Attic (954-463-6774), Gateway Plaza, 1928 E Sunrise Blvd. Proprietor David Fernan has an eclectic collection of consignment furniture from Victorian to midcentury modern, and he'll try to find whatever you're looking for if it's not already among the goods packed wall to wall in his shop. A narrow path winds through the showroom so you can see it all, but his overflow has found another home, Victoria's Attic is in the Gateway Plaza, which has several interesting shops, restaurants, and an offbeat movie theater. Open 12 PM–6 PM Sun.–Thurs., 12 PM–10 PM Fri.–Sat.

Wilton Manors

You'll find lots of fun and funky items at **50's, 60's, 70's Living** (954-767-8000; www.50s60s70sliving.com), 2207 Wilton Dr.; **Modern Rage** (954-328-6834), 2205 N Dixie Hwy.; and **Nostagia Modern** (954-537-5533), 2097 Wilton Dr.

For those looking for country decor, make sure to stop into nearby **Shabby Cottage Chic** (954-564-2740), 2415 N Dixie Hwy.

BOUTIQUES AND SPECIALTY SHOPS

Oakland Park

🐾 If your dog is really your child, take him over to **Central Bark Doggy Day Care and Boutique** (954-568-DOGS; www.centralbarkusa.com), 3699 N Dixie Hwy., where your canine is treated like one of the family. For only $23 you can drop off your pooch for an entire day, so you can enjoy local attractions or do some shopping. For an extra fee the Doggie Salon will have your best friend groomed and gorgeous upon your return. This haven for dogs also offers doggie birthday parties! Make sure to check out their extensive boutique shop. Updated shots and behavior assessment required. The advance application can be downloaded from the Internet.

Fort Lauderdale

🐾 Open since 1999, **The Bone Appetite Bakery** (954-565-3343), 3045 N Federal Hwy., offers healthy treats for both dogs and cats. Bring your pets along so they can pick out their own treats, or have a gift basket made up to bring home. Pet-related gifts are also available.

Groovy and funky things can be found at **Jezebel** (954-761-7881), 1980 E Sunrise Blvd., which also offers excellent vintage clothing.

Along **Las Olas Boulevard** (www.lasolasboulevard.com) you'll want to stop by several shops. In 1917 the charming area was just a dirt road that brought visitors to the famous Fort Lauderdale Beach. Now it is lined with quaint boutiques, art galleries, bistros, and cafés. At **Bijou and Color** (954-600-7349), 701-B E Las Olas Blvd.,

you can select one of their signature pieces of jewelry crafted from natural gemstones found all over the world, or design one yourself with the assistance of their talented in-house design team. **Needlepoint Originals** (954-463-1955; www.needlepoint-originals.com), 702 E Las Olas Blvd., features hand-painted needlepoint canvases designed by the very talented Joan Bancel, along with adaptations inspired by the works of modern masters.

Sometimes you find the unexpected in unusual places—that's the fun in exploring. Such a place is at **Outrageous Framing** (954-537-9320; www.outrageousframing.com), 3020 N Federal Hwy. The small gallery is one of the best in the area for quality custom picture framing, including museum-quality work. While framing is their forte, this shop is also an excellent place for unique gifts and accessories. Check out the showcase with exquisite handmade purses and hair accessories fashioned by local artisans.

Styline (954-523-3375; www.stylinefurniture.com), 116 SE 6 Ave., just south of Broward Blvd., offers an eclectic and unique selection of European furnishings. Call for hours or appointment.

Whole Foods Market (954-565-5655), 2000 N Federal Hwy., is the place to go for all your natural grocery needs. The full hot and cold salad bar, juice bar, and café make this a great place for lunch or a quick and easy dinner. Two other stores are located inland: 810 University Dr., Coral Springs (954-753-8000), and 7720 Peters Rd., Plantation (954-236-0600).

Hollywood

Intricate masks, musical instruments, and large pieces of hand-carved furniture from the Far East take center stage at **Chantik Imports** (954-920-6009), 1911 Hollywood Blvd.

Spend a day in downtown Hollywood browsing the many shops in the **Downtown Hollywood Art and Design District** (www.downtown hollywood.com), encompassing the blocks from 20th Avenue to Young Circle on Hollywood Boulevard and Harrison Street, where the streets are packed with boutiques, galleries, bistros, and sideway cafés.

Hollywood Mama (954-929-8886), 2037 Tyler St., offers a great deal of hip and happening inventory. From trendy T-shirts to elegant evening dresses, you'll be sure to find a unique and glamorous wardrobe to celebrate the diva in you.

With art directly imported from Africa, **Indaba Gallery** (954-920-2029; www .indaba.com), 2029 Harrison St., offers a unique selection of stone and wood sculptures, handwoven baskets and beadwork, and beautiful batiks. Open daily.

Step into the mystic at **The Jeweled Castle** (954-920-2424; www.the jeweledcastle.com), 1920 Hollywood Blvd., an otherworldly realm of crystals, gargoyles, Egyptian art, New Age books and music, and an on-site tarot reader. Open daily.

☙ If your little one is a pint-sized canine, then head over to **Teacups Puppies & Boutique** (954-985-8848), 8991 Taft St., which specializes in canine couture and luxury items for your teeny-weenie pooch. Here you'll find designer dog carriers, bows and collars studded with Swarovski crystals, and sumptuous dog beds.

Trader John's Book & Record Exchange (954-922-2466), 1907 Hollywood Blvd., a densely packed bookstore selling used titles covering every subject you can think of; antiquarian books sold as well. Open daily 10 AM–10 PM.

MALLS AND OUTLETS The **Festival Marketplace** (954-979-4555; www .festivalfleamarket.com), 2900 W Sample Rd., Pompano, is a welcome retreat from the South Florida heat. The indoor, air-conditioned flea market is home to more than 600 vendors that feature new merchandise at reduced prices. Open daily. Valet parking available.

The Galleria at Fort Lauderdale (954-564-1036), 2414 E Sunrise Blvd. Home to the finest department chains, the Galleria is a shopping destination for those seeking pricey gifts from trusted names. Shops include Saks Fifth Avenue, Neiman Marcus, Burdines-Macy's, and Dillard's. Open 10 AM– 9 PM Mon.–Sat., noon–6 PM Sun.

FARMER'S MARKETS For more than 70 years, **Mack's Groves** (1-800-327-3525; www.macksgroves.com), 1180 N Federal Hwy., Pompano Beach, has been a local favorite for Florida-grown naval oranges, pink seedless grapefruit, tangerines, honey bells, and even beefsteak tomatoes. In 1954 Ed and Frankie Vrana purchased the roadside business, and rather than change the name, they decided to keep Mack's Groves in honor of Mr. Mack, who had already operated the successful business for 20 years. And you don't mess with success! Now run by the fourth generation of Vranas, the business still offers fresh Indian River fruits and gift baskets with fruit, nuts, jams, and candy. Shipping is available within the United States and to most areas of Europe.

Hollywood

↬ **Organics by Josh** (Harrison St. at the Broadwalk), This fabulous organic market, on an outdoor terrace facing the beach, offers a wide range of fresh organic fruits and vegetables gathered from local and global sources. Open 10 AM–6 PM Sun.

Dania

Outdoors enthusiasts should head to **Outdoor World Bass Pro Shops** (954-929-7710; www.basspro.com), 200 Gulf Stream Way, where they'll find fishing, boating, and camping supplies in a 160,000-square-foot showroom. Make sure to check out the International Game Fish Association (IGFA) Fishing Hall of Fame & Museum next door (see *Museums*).

Deerfield Beach

Surf's up at **Island Water Sports Surf Superstore** (954-427-4929 or 1-800-873-0375; www.islandwatersports .com), 1985 NE Second St., where you can get all you need in surf or skate products. Free surf lessons are given every Saturday morning at the Deerfield Beach Pier. All equipment is provided; just bring your towel. Call the store to sign up. Open 9 AM–8 PM Mon.–Sat. and 9 AM–6 PM Sun. Check out the surf on the Web cam or call the Surf Report line at 954-421-4102.

Fort Lauderdale

Head to **Peter Glenn** (www.peter glenn.com) for fine sporting attire, wakeboards, kayaks, and camping gear. But don't be surprised to see lots of ski wear and mountaineering equipment: South Florida has one of the largest ski clubs in the nation. Since 1958 the Vermont-based store has offered excellence in outdoor wear and equipment. There are two Fort Lauderdale locations: 2901 W Oakland Park Blvd. (954-484-3606) and 1771 E Sunrise Blvd. (954-467-7872).

✳ Special Events

Weekly Events: **Pompano Beach Green Market Time,** Flagler Ave. and NE First St. Local vendors offer fresh fruits, vegetables, plants, and more. Proceeds benefit the Pompano

Beach Historical Society. Open 8 AM–2 PM Sat. Oct.–May.

Josh's Organic Market (see *Selective Shopping*), 10 AM–5 PM Sun., Hollywood Beach.

Monthly Events:
SunTrust Sunday Jazz Brunch (954-828-5985; www.fortlauderdale.gov), downtown Fort Lauderdale and the Riverwalk. Held the first Sunday of every month from 11 AM to 2 PM, this is a nice opportunity for a peaceful and pleasant stroll along the waterfront, with three or four jazz bands set up along the way, in the gazebo, in the amphitheater, and on the green. In between the stages are booths offering signature dishes and drinks from several area restaurants, although some prefer to bring a picnic and blanket or chairs to enjoy the easygoing festivities. Free admission; fee for food booths.

Second and Fourth Friday of the month: **Broadwalk Friday Fest** (954-924-2980), Hollywood Beach. Listen to live jazz along Hollywood's signature 2.5-mile "Broadwalk" from 7 AM to 10 PM. Free.

Annual Events:
January: The **Country Chili Cookoff** (954-764-7642), held at C. B. Smith Park, Pembroke Pines, features country music with celebrity singers along with a competitive chili cook-off.

Florida Renaissance Festival Quiet Waters Park (954-776-1642; www .ren-fest.com), 401 Powerline Rd. Each year the Florida Renaissance Festival comes to Broward County for five consecutive weekends of medieval history come to life. Ladies and lords, fairies, magicians, jesters, and jousters gather in full medieval regalia to play out the past for the entertainment of thousands of fascinated fans. Join a game of human chess, dine on food fit for a king, and learn the ropes of master falconers in the birds of prey exhibit. Twelve stages provide continuous entertainment. You can also learn how to make period crafts and buy the handiwork of artisans.

The **Deerfield Beach Festival of the Arts** (954-480-4433), NE Second St. and Pioneer Park, Deerfield Beach, has been going strong for nearly three decades and features more than 100 juried artists.

One of the top art festivals in the nation, the **Las Olas Art Fair** (954-472-3755), Fort Lauderdale, features the best in art, music, and food.

February: The best jazz acts in the country converge at the **Annual Riverwalk Blues & Music Festival** (954-523-1004), Riverwalk Park, downtown Fort Lauderdale.

More than 300 tribes celebrate Native American culture at the **Annual Seminole Tribal Fair** (954-797-5551), One Seminole Way, Hollywood, at the Seminole Hard Rock Hotel & Casino. The cultural event has been running for more than 35 years.

All ye lords and ladies head over to the **Florida Renaissance Festival** (954-776-1642; www.ren-fest.com) for jousting knights, fanciful fairies, and maids spreading merriment. Located at Quiet Waters Park, Deerfield Beach, for six weekends from February to mid-March.

March: **Las Olas Art Fair II** (954-472-3755), Fort Lauderdale. A second dose of the January show, where you'll find national and local artists, such as the wildlife color photography of South Florida native Mark J. Thomas (www.blueiceberg.com).

April: ▼ The **Florida Gay Rodeo Association's (FGRA) Sunshine Stampede Rodeo** (954-680-3555; www.fgra.org/stampede/), Bergeron Rodeo Grounds, 4271 Davie Rd.,

Davie. The Florida Gay Rodeo Association has hosted the first ever IGRA-sanctioned rodeo in Florida since 2005.

Air and Sea Show (www.national salute.com), an estimated 4 million people crowd onto Fort Lauderdale's beaches to watch this two-day military air show. Free.

April Pompano Beach Seafood Festival (954-570-7785; www.pompano beachseafoodfestival.com), Atlantic Blvd. and SR A1A. Relax beachside for a few hours or a few days to the sounds of classic rock (performed by national vintage bands and cover shows, including local retro-rockers the Low Tides). Also enjoy games, crafts, and more seafood than you can imagine from several area restaurants. This is a nice spring festival—don't forget your beach gear and chairs.

Ocean Fest Dive & Adventure Sports Expo (954-839-8516; www .oceanfest.com), Lauderdale-by-the-Sea. This festival offers scuba and snorkel instruction, more than 200 dive-related exhibits, an underwater treasure hunt, an underwater music festival, shore diving, and prizes.

May: Continuous live Cajun zydeco music, creole food, and lots of crawfish can be found at the **Cajun Zydeco Festival** (954-771-7117; www.cajun -fest.com), Quiet Waters Park, 401 S Powerline Rd., Deerfield Beach.

The annual **Fort Lauderdale International Boat Show** (954-764-7642) is always a busy event. The largest boat show in the world covers six sites around Fort Lauderdale, with more than 1,600 vessels and 60 super yachts.

June: **Mango Festival** (954-421-0069; www.deerfield-beach.com), Westside Park, Deerfield Beach. This fun festival celebrates the beautiful ripe mango and the multicultural population that enjoys the delicious fruit throughout the tropics. With more than 100 vendors, visitors can enjoy mango jellies and shakes while listening to rhythm and blues, gospel, hip-hop, and poetry and perusing arts and crafts. The weekend festival kicks off with a Saturday-morning parade.

National Week of the Ocean Festival (954-462-5573; www.national-week -of-the-ocean.org), not just a single event, National Week of the Ocean is a banner under which many ocean-related activities are joined to help raise awareness of the seas. During this week a school fair is held to showcase student projects, community beach and waterway cleanups are held, and special events are held at area attractions and retailers, including a marine fair at the IGFA Hall of Fame Museum (www.igfa.org; 300 Gulf Stream Way, Dania Beach 33004). Price varies by event.

Oceanwatch Reef Sweep and Beach Cleanup (954-467-1366; www .oceanwatch.org). Hundreds of divers and beach walkers pitch in to clean up Broward and Palm Beach County beaches and reefs. The total take since 1989 is more than 24 tons of trash. Call for the beach and dive location where you can join the fun. Free.

September: **Hollywood Beach Clam Bake** (954-924-2980; www.hollywood beachclambake.com), Hollywood Broadwalk. This all-American celebration, which takes place in August and September, includes sand castle displays and a contest as well as a treasure hunt on the Broadwalk. Free admission.

October: **Fort Lauderdale International Film Festival (FLIFF)** (954-760-9898; www.fliff.com), Cinema Paradiso, 503 SE Sixth St. Film screenings of more than 100 movies are shown at FLIFF's home, Cinema Paradiso, and in theaters from Boca Raton to Miami.

November: Pompano Park Racing in Pompano Beach is home to the annual **Broward County Fair** (954-922-2224; www.browardcountyfair.com), where you'll find lots of midway rides and exhibits.

Hollywood Jazz Festival (954-424-4440 or 1-877-877-7677; www.south floridajazz.org), Hollywood Central Performing Arts Center, 1770 Monroe St. This weekend festival features national jazz performers. The South Florida JAZZ is dedicated to promoting the American art of jazz by providing educational programs, opportunities for local musicians to share their talents, and a venue for national performers.

December: You have to see the **Fort Lauderdale Winterfest Boat Parade** (954-767-0686; www.winter festparade.com) at least once in your lifetime. The quality event is often televised, but seeing it in person is a unique and unforgettable experience. The boat parade travels from the Port Everglades to Lake Santa Barbara, and many hotels offer packages so you can view the show from your room.

Ocean Dance (954-921-3274; www .artandculturecenter.org/oceandance) is performed free of charge on Hollywood Beach the last few days of the month.

The western reaches of Broward County remained virtually untouched until the 1950s and '60s, with **Sunrise** and **Davie** as the first to be incorporated. **Plantation** was originally developed with 1-acre "long lots" where produce and fruit trees could be grown to support the rapidly expanding beachside areas. Then, several family-oriented communities, such as **Coral Springs** and **Weston,** stretched the edge of the Everglades west as developers created "planned neighborhoods." The expansion continued through the 1990s, when environmental efforts halted any further expansion into the Everglades.

✳ To See

ART GALLERY The Coral Springs Center for the Arts (954-344-5999; www .coralspringscenterforthearts.com), 2855 Coral Springs Dr., Coral Springs, is a performing-arts facility and a museum of fine art. Private meeting rooms and catering are available.

AUTOMOBILES Local car clubs converge at a local shopping mall parking lot for one of the largest collection of vintage hot rods and late-model suped-up cars and tricked-out rides each Friday night at the **Tower Shops** on University Drive, Davie, just south of US 595.

HOCKEY The Florida Panthers take to the ice at the **BankAtlantic Center** (954-835-8000; www.bankatlanticcenter.com), 2555 Panther Pkwy., Sunrise, which is also a main venue for concerts and family shows.

MUSEUMS

Davie

🐾 The hands-on **Young at Art Children's Museum** (954-424-0085; www.young atartmuseum.org), 11584 West State Rd. 84, provides a variety of activities to expand your child's mind and release some of that expressive energy. At Global Village you'll dig for artifacts, visit an African village, and learn about origami. In EarthWorks you'll climb aboard a giant recycling truck and learn about resource management. Kenny's Closet takes you through the psychedelic world of international artist Kenny Scharf, where works of art are lit by black lights and your child can create her own pop art masterpiece. A special gallery, Playspace for Toddlers, allows the little ones to explore movement and hands-on activities specific to their age level. Open year-round 10 AM–5 PM Mon.–Sat., noon–5 PM Sun. Closed Thanksgiving, Christmas, and New Year's Day. Adults and children $8, children under two free.

Plantation

🐾 The hands-on, interactive **My Jewish Discovery Place Children's Museum** (954-792-6700; www.sorefjcc.org), 6501 W Sunrise Blvd., is full of Jewish culture and history. You'll discover how to cook a festive holiday meal in Home for the Holidays; blast off in Discovery Station, complete with NASA jumpsuits; dress up as a doctor or ambulance driver at Hadassah Hospital; and write your wishes and prayers on the stone replica of Jerusalem's Western Wall. Open 12 PM–4 PM Tues.–Thurs. Admission $5.

RODEO Since 1986 the **Five Star Davie Rodeo** (954-384-7075; www.fivestar rodeo.com), Davie Arena, Davie, has featured championship barrel racing, bronco riding, team roping, steer wrestling, and bull riding.

STARGAZING Learn about the sky at **Buehler Planetarium and Observatory** (954-201-6681; www.iloveplanets.com), Broward Community College, Central Campus, 3501 SW Davie Rd., Davie. The state-of-the-art planetarium provides interesting shows about legends of Native Americans, New World explorers, galaxies, Egyptian lore, and even a solar experience through a magic rocket. The observatory houses 20 telescopes for celestial viewing, including the 16-inch LX200 telescope. Call for schedule. Fee.

✳ To Do

ECOTOURS For a quick ecotrip, the **Everglades Holiday Park** (954-434-8111 or 1-800-226-2244; www.evergladesholidaypark.com), 21940 Griffin Rd., Fort Lauderdale, offers one-hour guided tours on airboats, or rent a fishing boat and explore a bit of the Everglades on your own. Adults $20, kids $10; includes one-hour airboat ride followed by a 15-minute alligator show. Fishing guides and gear are also available. A Florida fishing license (required) can be bought on-site. Check the Web site for coupons.

Sawgrass Recreation Park (954-389-0202 or 1-800-424-7262; www.everglades tours.com), US 27 (2 miles north of I-75), Fort Lauderdale, features an 18th-century Native American village, alligator wrestling, birds of prey, and airboat rides. Open daily, with guided airboat tours 9 AM–5 PM. Adults $20, children $10.

FAMILY ACTIVITIES ✐ "Kids can do what they wanna do" at **Wannado City** (954-838-7100 or 1-888-926-6236; www.wannadocity.com), Sawgrass Mills Mall, 12801 W Sunrise Blvd., Sunrise. The indoor theme park takes children's museums and supersizes them with America's first indoor role-playing venue, which allows kids to participate in tons of different careers. Open daily. Adults $7, children $30, children under two free.

SKATE AND BIKE PARKS ✐ The 333.3-meter concrete track at the **Brian Piccolo Velodrome** (954-437-2626; www.broward.org/parks), 9501 Sheridan St., Cooper City, has a maximum banking of 28 degrees. It is open for public use for $3–4, depending on time of day. Bikes are available for rent for an additional fee. The free criterium course adjacent to the velodrome is used by cyclists and in-line speed skaters.

TRAIL RIDING The Bar-B-Ranch (954-424-1060; www.bar-b-ranch.com), 1300 Peaceful Ridge Rd., Davie, is Broward County's oldest and largest public riding stable. Equestrians of all ages and experience levels can ride ponies or horses on scenic trails. Lessons are also available. Open 9 AM–5 PM daily.

WATER PARK Splash around at **Paradise Cove** (954-357-8115), C. B. Smith Park, 900 N Flamingo Rd., Pembroke Pines, where you'll find two interactive water playgrounds, water slides, and a tube ride. Open daily 9:30 AM–5:20 PM May–Labor Day; weekends only Apr., Sept., and Oct. Admission $8.50.

BOTANICAL GARDENS The 60-acre **Flamingo Gardens & Wray Botanical Collection** (954-473-2955; www.flamingogardens.org), 3750 S Flamingo Rd., Fort Lauderdale, is a unique not-for-profit wildlife sanctuary. Take a tour through a citrus grove and a 200-year-old hammock, check out the bird of prey center and free flight aviary, and see alligators and pink flamingos. Open 9:30 AM–5 PM daily; closed Mon. during the hot summer months. Adults $17, children 4–11 $11, children under 4 free. Discounts available for seniors, students, AAA members, and armed service personnel.

DOG PARKS

Coral Springs
❀ Coral Springs was recently listed as one of the top 10 cities for dogs. **Dr. Paul's Pet Care Center Dog Park** (954-752-1879; www.toppetcare.com), 2915 Sportsplex, is a spacious 2-acre dog park that allows enough room for all breeds to run, play, and socialize unleashed. Agility equipment, a wading pool, and a track that wraps around the perimeter of the park offer even more opportunities for exercise. Sit on a bench and observe your pooch from under a canopy of trees or at one of the shaded picnic tables. A separate play area for small dogs and puppies ensures a safe area where the little ones won't get run over by the larger breeds. The nonprofit organization holds the annual Dog Day Run & Kids Dog Show along with a Gala Auction each March (see *Special Events*).

Plantation
❀ **Happy Tails Dog Park** (954-452-2510), 6600 SW 16th St. at Seminole Park, is the place for the annual **Doggie-Palooza Dog Expo** (see *Special Events*). Dog-related events, vendors, and demonstrations by Police K-9s. Dogs of all sizes are welcome to mix and mingle, but they must have current inoculations.

Sunrise
❀ **Markham Park** (see *Parks* below) provides a special section for canine pals to play in water pools and other toys while their people rest on nearby benches.

NATURE CENTER Go bird-watching and look for wildlife as you walk along boardwalks at **Fern Forest Nature Center** (954-970-0150), 201 Lyons Rd. S, Coconut Creek. Broward County Parks and Recreation (954-357-8100; www.broward.org/parks) offers several natural and family recreational areas throughout the county.

PARKS

Davie
& ✐ At **Tree Tops Park** (954-370-3750), 3900 SW 100th Ave., off Nob Hill Rd., you can rent a canoe and paddle the ponds, fish in the ponds and wetlands, have a picnic, or take the kids to the playground and Safety Town. It's a great site for wildlife watching, with several miles of paved and unpaved paths winding through beautiful live oak hammocks, along open flatwoods ponds, and out into adjoining Pine Island Ridge Natural Area, an archaeological site where the Miccosukee had a large village prior to the Second Seminole War. Open 8 AM–sunset daily. Fee on weekends and holidays.

Plantation

✍ A former University of Florida agricultural experimentation farm, **Plantation Heritage Park** (954-791-1025), 1100 S Fig Tree Ln., offers picnicking under the trees, fishing in its ponds, a large playground, and the Anne Kolb Memorial Trail, a 0.25-mile loop through representative native plant communities. Open 8 AM–7:30 PM daily. Fee on weekends and holidays.

Sunrise

✍ 🐾 Covering more than 650 acres along the edge of the Everglades, **Markham Park** (954-389-2000), 16001 W SR 84, offers a variety of pursuits, including a mountain bike trail, model airplane field, biking and jogging path, swimming pool complex with misters, target range, picnic shelters, rental canoes to ply the lakes, and nature and equestrian trails. The park also has an 86-site campground for RVs and tents, and a 3-acre **dog park** for your favorite canine. Open daily; hours vary by season. Free.

PRESERVES

Coral Springs

& ✍ A wonderland of oversize ferns surrounds you on the 0.5-mile boardwalk through **Tall Cypress Natural Area** (954-357-8100), Turtle Run Blvd., north of Sample Rd. Birders, bring binoculars to watch for downy woodpeckers.

Parkland

& ✍ The 20-acre **Doris Davis Foreman Wilderness Area** (954-357-8100), Parkside Dr., south of Loxahatchee Rd., has a beautiful 0.5-mile nature trail through a tropical forest and cypress swamp, with a long boardwalk as a major feature. Open 8 AM–6 PM daily. Free.

Tamarac

& ✍ 🐾 Tiny **Woodmont Natural Area** (954-357-8100), NW 80th Ave., 0.2 mile north of McNab Rd., is a 22-acre patch of pine flatwoods, the last undeveloped land in Tamarac, with a 0.4-mile walking trail great for birding. Open 8 AM–6 PM daily. Free.

WILD PLACES Visible from the Sawgrass Expressway and I-75 North, the **Everglades Conservation Area** consists of natural sawgrass marshes broken into three impoundment areas that provide water for the people of Broward and Miami-Dade Counties. Public access is off ramps along the Sawgrass Expressway and through the Francis S. Taylor WMA, with boat launches off I-75, and public use is primarily for fishing along canal banks or from small craft.

✳ Lodging

HOTELS, MOTELS, AND RESORTS

Plantation 33322

🐾 **Plantation Holiday Inn Express Hotel & Suites** (954-472-5600), 1701 N University Dr., is ideally situated for the business traveler, but it makes for a great central location for vacation travelers as well. Deluxe accommodations or suites have complimentary Wi-Fi hookups, on-site guest laundry, and a fitness center—those are just a few of the perks. A complimentary shuttle service is provided to local attractions and shopping areas. This hotel is especially friendly to pets, with complimentary pet treats, a welcome letter from the General Manager's dog or cat, and information on local pet-friendly restaurants, specialty shops, dog parks, and boarding. Litter boxes, pet pads, and walking services can also be arranged. And when the maid comes to turn down your bed, a small treat will be left for your pet as well. Rooms $109–189; suites about $40 more.

Weston
➷ **Courtyard Fort Lauderdale Weston** (954-343-2225; www.marriott .com/hotels/travel/fllwc-courtyard-fort-lauderdale-weston/), 2000 N Commerce Pkwy. If business or family connections deem your Fort Lauderdale stay should be in the far western suburb city of Weston, Courtyard promises to take good care of you in this green hotel. $189 and up.

✳ Where to Eat
EATING OUT

Coral Springs
🐾 Well-behaved dogs are welcome outside at **Gold Coast Grill** (954-255-3474; www.goldcoastseafoodgrill.com), 2752 N University Dr., in The Walk. Seafood is their specialty, with dishes such as almond-crusted mahimahi ($20), Dijon tomato horseradish crusted salmon ($20), and orange-honey glazed Chilean sea bass ($24). For landlubbers there's the 8-ounce center cut filet ($20), mustard crumb stuffed chicken ($19), and Missouri smoked baby back ribs ($19). Lunch is served Mon.–Fri.; dinner nightly.

Since 1986, **Larry's Ice Cream Parlor** (954-752-0497), 749 University Dr., has been the local favorite of middle school kids and their parents. We moved to South Florida in 1987, and it took no time at all for my kids to find it, often caught sneaking across the street to spend their allowance. Lunch sandwiches are available, but let's face it—we are all going there for the ice cream. Even though larger stores have been built up around it, the family-friendly shop is still the same after all these years. Shakes, malts, sundaes, and such are under $6. Open daily until 6 PM.

Lauderhill
Rosey Baby Crawfish & Cajun House (954-749-5627; www.rosey baby.com), 4587 N University Dr. This little strip-mall pub offers unusual fare—crawfish fresh from New Orleans—and music to match. Locals love it, and it's a nice suburban relief from the glitzy, touristy places. Late-night live music and food. $11 and up.

Plantation
The Grapevine (954-475-1357; www .grapevinegourmet.com), Plantation Community Plaza, 256 S. University Dr., Plantation 33324. This family-owned gourmet shop is a food lover's paradise. With deliciously prepared items for lunch or dinner or to take home for later, the Grapevine also offers fine wines to accompany the meal, as well as the rare ingredients that make the dishes so special. $$.

PLANTATION, VIGNETTO'S RESTAURANT
Trish Riley

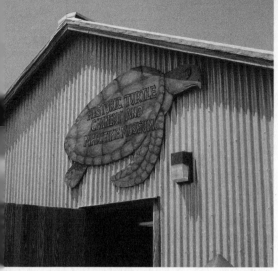

TURTLE KRAWLS MUSEUM, KEY WEST

Vignetto's Italian Grill (954-915-0806), 1633 S University Dr. A friendly Italian eatery tucked into the corner of one of South Florida's ubiquitous strip malls, this unassuming restaurant serves reliably delicious lunch and dinner in overflowing dishes. I'm fond of the egglant rollatini, spaghettini marinara, and huge house salad. Excellent choice anytime. $12 and up.

Sunrise

Lester's Diner (954-525-5641), 1399 NW 136th Ave., is your best bet for a great meal near the Sawgrass Mills Mall. Open 24/7, they offer an extensive menu at reasonable prices that will make everyone happy, with breakfast served all day. A huge selection of pies, cakes, and pastries are baked on the premises daily and are displayed in a case just as you walk in the door. Yum! There is another location east toward the airport (see *Oceanside: Eastern Broward County*).

Poppy's Pizza South (954-474-0671), 8373 W Sunrise Blvd., is known more for their take-out pizza than anything else. For 25 years, the family-owned business has offered patrons great pizza ($6–15) and Italian dinners ($6–15). Open daily for lunch and dinner.

You won't find a better sandwich shop anywhere in Sunrise than **Sharpie's Hoagies** (954-845-0999), 13101 W Sunrise Blvd., in the Sawgrass Commons Shopping Plaza. Sandwiches and salad platters are made fast to your specifications in this sports-themed eatery. Locals line up during the lunch hour, yet they still manage to get everyone back to work on time. Sandwiches are served hot or cold for $5–9. Open daily for lunch until early dinner.

Udipi (954-748-5660) 2100 N University Dr. South Indian vegetarian cuisine served on the buffet for a rich yet inexpensive lunch topped with mango lassie to drink. Very popular authentic restaurant, always filled with appreciative India natives. Daily lunch buffet and dinner 5:30-10 PM. $7 and up.

Davie

Chinatown (954-473-8770; www.chinatown-davie.com), 8934 SR 84. Chinese and Japanese specials, including a fresh sushi bar, are offered at this delicious neighborhood restaurant, located in a deceiving strip mall. I love the sashimi; the Yummy Roll (a wild concoction of crab, shrimp, masago, and avocado with crunchy tempura flakes); the avocado salad, with an unusual blend of seasonings and sauce; the Kamikaze salad, with seafood and cucumber in a spicy mustard sauce; the fresh, clear soups; and the fried banana dessert. Owner Sue Chan works around the clock (with an occasional catnap in the back) to serve and satisfy her customers. $10 and up.

Weston

The Cheese Course (954-384-8183; www.thecheesecourse.com), 1679 Market St. A delightful selection of cheese plates and sandwiches. Open 10 AM–8 PM Sun.–Thurs., 10 AM–11 PM Fri.–Sat. $10 and up.

Pei Wei (954-398-7330; www.peiwei
.com), 4517 Weston Rd. The best fast
food on the market—Asian treats
quick and cheap. $10 and up.

✳ Entertainment
FINE ARTS
Coral Springs
The **Coral Springs Center for the
Arts** (954-344-5999; www.coralsprings
centerforthearts.com), 855 Coral
Springs Dr., features several national
touring theatrical and musical performances for the western county's residents, along with an excellent fine arts
museum.

Plantation
Dedicated to contemporary and original works, the **Mosaic Theatre** (954-
577-8243; www.mosaictheatre.com),
12200 W Broward Blvd., is a welcome
addition to the western county's cultural experience. Professional shows
Thurs.–Sat. evenings, with matinees on
the weekends. Adults $35, seniors $29,
students $15.

✳ Selective Shopping
ANTIQUES AND COLLECTIBLES
Davie
J.C.'s Collectibles (954-648-5611),
6870 Stirling Rd. (enter from inside
the Birdcage Bar & Restaurant) and
6761 W Sunrise Blvd., Bay 2, Plantation, offers antique car and racing collectibles.

BOUTIQUES AND SPECIALTY
SHOPS
Coral Springs
Accent on Country (954-755-3939),
11530 W Sample Rd., a cute country-
themed store, has a huge display of
Dept 56 villages. The ever-changing
displays and lovely ladies have kept me
coming back for nearly two decades. If

you can't find it here, you don't need
it. Watch for guest appearances of collectibles artisans, such as Jim Shore.

A Nose for Clothes (954-753-0202;
www.anoseforclothes.com), 28080 University Dr., sets the trend with the
newest, latest, and greatest fashion
finds. The owner travels the world
(and the New York garment district)
looking for unique contemporary
designer fashions that are fun, chic,
and wearable for women of all ages.
Boutique wear is in both the original
designer look as well as the less-expen-
sive version. You'll find items here that
you won't find anywhere else.

If you long for turquoise, terracotta,
and the other earthy colors of the
Southwest and Mexico, then head into
Southwest Sensations (954-341-
8111; www.southwestsensations.com),
7467 W Sample Rd. This piece of
heaven stands out with an extensive
array of pottery, accessories, and furniture. Owner Ben Fritti or any of his
staff will be happy to assist you while
you browse through the well-laid-out
studio.

Plantation
🐾 Take Fluffy or Spot to **Three Dog
Bakery** (954-424-3223), 236 S University Dr. (across from the Broward
Mall), for the world's best all-natural
dog treats. The large pastry case displays more than 100 fresh baked treats.
The shop also has a neat collection of
doggie boutique wear. Leashed dogs
are welcome. Open daily.

For a quick bite, organic produce,
gourmet cheeses, natural groceries,
or vitamins, **Whole Foods Market**
(954-236-0600), 7720 Peters Rd., is
the place to go, with other locations
in Coral Springs (954-753-8000),
810 University Dr., and Fort Lauderdale (954-565-5655), 2000 N Federal
Hwy.

THE BAREFOOT MAILMAN

By the mid-1800s, before there were roads or railways, people began to make their way south, settling up and down the coast of South Florida. With mail delivery only as far south as Palm Beach, the U.S. Postal Service soon needed a way to deliver mail to the pioneers along the stretch of coastline between Lake Worth and Biscayne Bay. So in 1885 they enlisted a few young men to carry the mail along the only solid path—the beach. Since it was steaming hot and impossible to travel through the sand with any speed, the mail carriers soon went barefoot and walked along the edge in the surf, and the legendary "Barefoot Mailman" was born. Starting by boat in Palm City (now Palm Beach), mailmen were brought as far as the Boynton Beach Inlet and then ventured forth on foot along the 80 miles of coastline to Miami, which was then known as Lemon City. The entire 136-mile round-trip took six days to complete by trudging along the beach by foot and an additional 56 miles by small boats, which they had secretly stashed along the shores. With only one day to rest, the carrier started his exhausting expedition all over again by Monday morning. As for the wages, carriers were paid $175 every three months. The service came to an end when one of the mailmen was killed en route, probably by an alligator while crossing the Hillsboro Inlet, which he had to swim because someone had used his boat, leaving it on the wrong side of the inlet. A memorial statue of the "Barefoot Mailman," Ed Hamilton, stands at the Hillsboro Lighthouse.

MALLS AND OUTLETS Broward Mall (954-473-8100; www.broward mall.com), 8000 W Broward Blvd. Shop the Gap, Victoria's Secret, Burdines-Macy's, and Sears at this centrally located shopping mall. Open 10 AM–9 PM Mon.–Sat. and 11 AM–6 PM Sun.

The king, queen, and kingdom of shopping is out west at the **Sawgrass Mills Mall** (954-846-2300; www.saw grassmillsmall.com), 12801 W Sunrise Blvd., Sunrise. The mile-long mall has more than 300 name-brand stores, outlets, and restaurants. Open daily.

✳ Special Events

January: **Doggie-Palooza Dog Expo** (954-452-2510), Happy Tails Dog Park, 6600 SW 16th St., at Seminole Park. Dog contests, adoptions, vendors, and working dog demonstrations.

MAGIC CITY:
MIAMI-DADE COUNTY

M iami, land of glitter and glitz, glamour and mystique, is known as the Magic City thanks to its practically instant development at the turn of the 19th century, and Miami's magic continues to evolve. Miami is the foundation of south Florida, where you'll find everything imaginable and more.

The area was populated by Paleoindians 10,000 years ago, and 2000-year-old evidence of a Tequesta settlement was discovered at the Miami Circle (www .miamicirclesite.com) in 1998, when condo builders unearthed a stone circle formation on the shores of the Miami River at Brickell Avenue. Archaeologists carbon dated the stones, determining they were laid in AD 100 by the Tequesta. Construction was halted and the state and county together paid $27 million for the site, and although preservation and plans to create public access haven't been established, the condos continue just beside the circle, casting their shadow as an ironic bit of a pall on history. In 1566 Spaniards arrived in Miami and the Tequesta

MIAMI BAYFRONT

Trish Riley

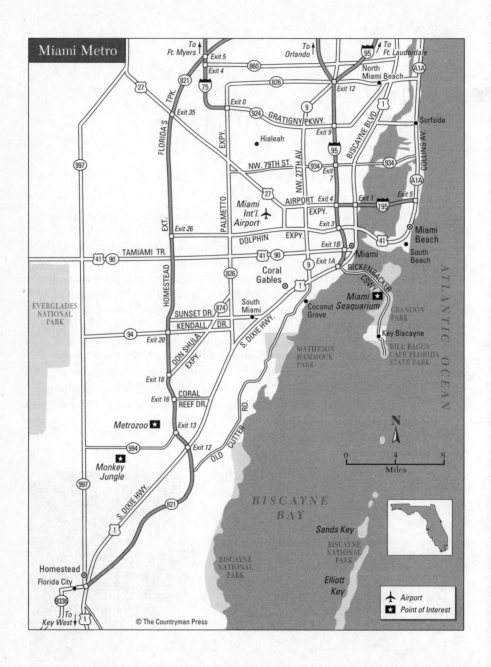

Miami Metro

To Ft. Myers
Exit 5
860
Exit 4
To Orlando
95
To Ft. Lauderdale
A1A

27
821
75
826
North Miami Beach
Exit 12
9
Exit 0
924
GRATIGNY PKWY.
1
Surfside

FLORIDA'S TPK.
Exit 35

Hialeah
Exit 9
95
BISCAYNE BLVD.
COLLINS AV.

NW. 79TH ST.
934
934
A1A

NW. 27TH AV.
Exit 7
A1A
Exit 5

27
AIRPORT
Exit 4
Exit 1
195

Miami Int'l. Airport
EXPY.
Exit 3
Miami Beach

PALMETTO EXPY.
DOLPHIN EXPY.
Exit 1B
South Beach

Exit 26
41 90
Exit 1A

TAMIAMI TR.
41 90
41
Miami

HOMESTEAD EXT.
826
Coral Gables
9
RICKENBACKER CSWY.

EVERGLADES NATIONAL PARK
874
South Miami
1
Miami Seaquarium
CRANDON PARK

SUNSET DR.
Coconut Grove
Key Biscayne

94
KENDALL DR.
Exit 20
S. DIXIE HWY.
MATHESON HAMMOCK PARK
BILL BAGGS CAPE FLORIDA STATE PARK

DON SHULA EXPY.
Exit 18

CORAL REEF DR.
Exit 16

Metrozoo
Exit 13
N

994
Exit 12
OLD CUTTER RD.
0   4   8
Miles

Monkey Jungle

997
S. DIXIE HWY.
821
BISCAYNE BAY
Sands Key
BISCAYNE NATIONAL PARK

1
BISCAYNE NATIONAL PARK
Elliott Key

Homestead
Florida City
9336
To Key West
1
© The Countryman Press

✈ Airport
★ Point of Interest

ATLANTIC OCEAN

were soon decimated by European diseases and conflict. By the 1800s, the first permanent settlers arrived, attracted to the region by government offers of 160 free acres to those who would homestead. Miami was incorporated by American settlers in 1896, thanks to pioneers Mary Brickell and Julia Tuttle—Miami is said to be the only city in the nation settled by women. These women invited Henry Flagler to consider bringing his railway to their town after a freeze rendered his resort mecca of Palm Beach too cold for fun. They drove their point home with a gift of fresh citrus blossoms, untainted by the recent freeze that had devastated crops in central Florida and Palm Beach. The train soon was under way, although some early Miami settlers, including Commodore Ralph Munroe of Cocoanut Grove (as it was spelled at the time), were not so excited to see the signs of progress. Munroe understandably preferred to keep his paradise to himself, but progress came to town just the same, and more quickly than Munroe could stop it. Flagler's train arrived on April 13, 1896.

Progress continued and the city flourished until it was wiped out by the Great Miami Hurricane in 1926, just preceding the Great Depression that cast a plague across the nation. During the depression, Jewish settlers developed Miami Beach, creating the signature buildings now preserved as the Art Deco District of South Beach. Along with the rest of the country, Miami slowly recovered and development began to surge again after World War II, when servicemen who'd been stationed on our sunny shores returned to the city in retirement. The invention of air-conditioning helped make south Florida a more attractive destination for new residents.

Soon, land became scarce, and regional governments worked with the Army Corps of Engineers to drain the swampy Everglades with an elaborate 1,400-mile canal system to open up more land for development and agriculture. The area south of Miami continues to produce a large proportion of the nation's winter produce and a unique selection of tropical fruits today, but the population exploded for decades. However the destruction of half of the Everglades threatens the health of the remaining natural land, the Florida Bay, and the freshwater supply for south Florida. A massive state and federal project to protect what's left of the Everglades and the water supply was begun under President Bill Clinton and Florida Governor Lawton Chiles, and Congress appropriated $7.8 billion for the project in 2000 (after Chiles's death in 1998), but progress has been slow and projected costs continue to rise. In 2008, Florida Governor Charlie Crist arranged for the state to buy some sugarcane farmland that contributes pollution to the Everglades, but the impact of that plan has yet to be seen.

Following World War II, Miami gave birth to the cruise ship industry, with more than a dozen gargantuan vessels lined up along "Cruise Ship Row" off downtown Miami. Its home port of call is "Cruise Capital of the World." Since the 1960s, thousands of Cuban immigrants have come to this area to escape Castro's Cuba. The Art Deco Historic District, between Ocean and Alton Roads, was listed in 1979 on the National Register of Historic Places.

Today Miami is known as the Gateway to the Americas because it serves as an entry point for cargo and immigrants from Cuba, and Central and South America. The Latin influence is more than noticeable in Miami—the population is now more than half Hispanic, with more than 125 languages spoken in homes across Miami-Dade County. This is the land of opportunity, and countless thousands of people have risked their lives and disrupted their families for the chance to come here and achieve the American Dream.

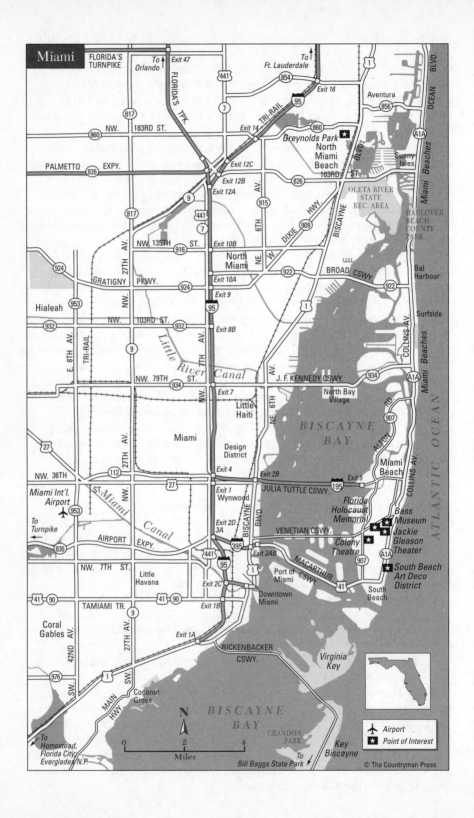

Miami

FLORIDA'S TURNPIKE

To Orlando

Exit 47

To Ft. Lauderdale

FLORIDA'S TPK.

441

854

Exit 16

95

856

Aventura

817

NW. 183RD ST.

7

TRI-RAIL

Exit 14

860

A1A

860

Exit 12C

Greynolds Park

North Miami Beach

Sunny Isles

Miami Beaches

PALMETTO EXPY.

826

9

Exit 12B

Exit 12A

826

163RD. ST.

OLETA RIVER STATE REC. AREA

817

441

7

915

6TH

DIXIE

HWY.

909

BISCAYNE

BLVD.

HAULOVER BEACH COUNTY PARK

924

27TH

NW. 135TH

916

ST.

Exit 10B

North Miami

NE.

W.

922

BROAD CSWY.

Bal Harbour

GRATIGNY PKWY.

924

Exit 10A

Exit 9

922

COLLINS AV.

Surfside

Hialeah

953

NW. 103RD ST.

932

95

Exit 8B

1

Miami Beaches

932

E. 8TH AV.

TRI-RAIL

9

Little River Canal

NW. 7TH

ST.

AV.

J. F. KENNEDY CSWY.

934

A1A

NW. 79TH

934

Exit 7

Little Haiti

North Bay Village

RD.

907

ATLANTIC OCEAN

27

27TH

AV.

Miami

Design District

BISCAYNE BAY

ALTON

NW. 36TH

112

27

Exit 4

Exit 2B

Exit 5

Miami Beach

COLLINS AV.

Miami Int'l. Airport

953

Exit 1

Wynwood

195

JULIA TUTTLE CSWY.

Florida Holocaust Memorial

Bass Museum

To Turnpike

ST. Miami Canal

Exit 2D 3A

BISCAYNE

BLVD.

VENETIAN CSWY.

Jackie Gleason Theater

836

AIRPORT EXPY.

395

441

95

Colony Theatre

907

A1A

NW. 7TH ST.

Little Havana

1

Exit 2AB

MACARTHUR CSWY.

South Beach Art Deco District

41

90

Exit 2C

Port of Miami

South Beach

41

90

TAMIAMI TR.

41

90

Exit 1B

Downtown Miami

Coral Gables

42ND AV.

27TH AV.

9

Exit 1A

RICKENBACKER CSWY.

Virginia Key

976

1

SW.

MAIN HWY.

Coconut Grove

BISCAYNE BAY

CRANDON PARK

Key Biscayne

N

To Homestead, Florida City Everglades N.P.

0   2   4

Miles

To Bill Baggs State Park

✈ Airport

★ Point of Interest

© The Countryman Press

This amazing diversity brings many riches to the city. Visitors can sample a huge variety of authentic cuisines, as well as culinary offerings from nationally acclaimed, cutting-edge chefs, many of whom either started here or found their way to this international hot spot. Foodies will love visiting the Homestead farm-land during the December–June growing season for fresh strawberries, tomatoes, and the wide variety of tropical fruits.

Shopping opportunities are exceptional here, too, thanks to the fact that our port welcomes goods from worldwide trade markets. Look to South Beach and Lincoln Road for the offbeat, to Bayside for international gifts, to Coral Gables for sophisticated goods, and to Coconut Grove for quirky fun.

In 2007, Miami hosted 12 million visitors, a record-setting year with an impact of $17 billion on the local economy, and figures for the first half of 2008 indicate that the trend continues. Travelers are kings and queens in this town. While the traveling life can often be a little tedious, you can bet that you won't find the same old shops and the same old restaurants in Miami—there's nothing humdrum here. Miami has some of the best-known names in retail and cuisine, and the most wonderful corners of this beautiful town can't be found anywhere else in the universe.

GUIDANCE The **Greater Miami Convention and Visitors Bureau** (305-539-3000 or 1-800-933-8448; www.miamiandbeaches.com) is the main connection for tourist information. Call for a vacation guide—they often have special discount offers for hotels and attractions.

GETTING THERE *By air:* **Miami International Airport** (305-876-7000; www.miami-airport.com) is centrally located in the county of SR 836 between the Florida Turnpike and I-95. **Fort Lauderdale–Hollywood International Airport** (1-866-435-9355; www.broward.org/airport) is also within easy access at I-95 just east of I-595.

MIAMI INTERNATIONAL AIRPORT

Courtesy Greater Miami Convention and Visitors Bureau

By bus: **Greyhound** (1-800-231-2222; www.greyhound.com). Several locations will take you to the main areas of Miami-Dade County: **Miami North** (305-688-7277), 16000 NW 7th Ave.; **Miami Central** (305-871-1810), 4111 NW 27th St.; **Miami Downtown** (305-374-6160), 1012 NW 1st Ave.; and for the south end of the county, **Miami Cutler Ridge** (305-296-9072), 10801 Caribbean Blvd., at the American Service Station.

By rail: **AMTRAK** (1-800-872-7245; www.amtrak.com) provides regularly scheduled service to Miami. The **Miami Station** (305-835-1221) is at 8303 NW 37th Ave.

GETTING AROUND *By bus:* **Metrobus,** Miami-Dade Transit, Customer Services (305-770-3131; www.miamidade.gov/transit). With 90 routes from Miami Beach and Key Biscayne to West Miami–Dade, as far north as Diplomat Mall in Broward County, and as far south as Homestead, Florida City, and the Middle Keys, you can easily get to your destination. Bus 57 goes to Miami International Airport and also connects with the Tri-Rail Station. You can pick up printed Metrobus route maps and schedules at the airport's information center in Concourse E. Bus 34, the Busway Flyer, will bring you south to Florida City and Homestead. You can also transfer from several routes to the Metrorail and Metromover (see *By rail,* below).

By trolley: ✑ The ecosensitive hybrid-electric **Coral Gables Trolley** (305-460-5070; www.citybeautiful.net) takes you throughout the Gables, sometimes with entertainment such as vintage-style barbershop quartets and workers dressed in period costumes. The trolley has routes along Miracle Mile and Ponce de Leon Boulevard from Douglas Road to SW 8th Street running every 15 minutes. The free service also has stops at the Venetian Pool and the Biltmore Hotel.

By rail: **Tri-Rail** (1-800-874-7245; www.tri-rail.com) is a convenient way to travel from Miami to West Palm Beach. Tickets are not sold on the train. You must purchase a ticket at the station on the day of use. The train runs in six sections, and tickets are purchased according to the number of sections. A ticket from West Palm Beach to Miami costs around $5.50. On weekends and holidays, the full fare for the entire system is a flat rate of $4. The Tri-Rail ticket allows you to transfer to Metrorail for a $.50 transfer fee. The electric-powered **Metrorail** covers 22 miles of the city on an elevated track, from Kendall to Medley. Full fare: $2. The **Metromover,** an elevated people mover covering nearly 4.5 miles of the Miami business district, including Brickell Avenue, is free to ride. Metrorail, Metrobus, and Metromover are part of Miami-Dade Transit, Customer Services (305-770-3131; www .miamidade.gov/transit).

PARKING Make sure to have some change on hand, as most districts have metered parking. Some parking areas have maximums, so check the meter for restrictions. Solar-powered Pay and Display (P&D) machines require payment at a central location, usually within four cars. These meters take not only coins and dollar bills but also VISA and MasterCard. Private and government parking lots and garages are conveniently located around town. Fees range from $1 to $1.25 per hour to flat rates of $4–15.

VALET You'll be hard-pressed to find a restaurant, hotel, or shopping district that doesn't offer valet services; sometimes you'll have no choice, as some establishments don't allow self-parking. You'll find most of the area's valet parking managed by private companies. All reputable establishments will have one that carries a liability policy. In most situations, however, you won't be able to add the valet parking fee to your hotel or dining bill. In South Florida it is customary to tip when you drop off your car, *and* when you pick it up. Most valets are happy with $1–2, but if you are driving a luxury vehicle or fancy sports car and want them to keep a close eye on it, expect to tip them $5–10. Inquire about valet policies when making reservations.

MEDICAL EMERGENCIES You'll find the best of the medical profession at several medical centers around the Miami metro area. For general emergencies, head to **University of Miami Hospital** (305-325-5511; www.umiamihospital.com), 1400 NW 12th Ave., or to **Jackson Memorial Hospital** (305-585-1111; www.jhsmiami.org), 1611 NW 12th Ave. **Bascom Palmer Eye Institute** (305-326-6000 or 1-800-329-7000; www.bascompalmer.org), 900 NW 17th St., is known the world over for the best care in ocular diseases and surgery. At the north end of Miami, seek out **North Shore Medical Center** (305-835-6000; www.northshore medical.com), 1100 NW 95th St., Miami, or **Jackson North Medical Center** (305-651-1100), 160 NW 170th St., N Miami Beach, for general emergencies. **Mount Sinai Medical Center** (305-674-2121; www.msmc.com), 4300 Alton Rd., specializes in cardiovascular and cancer services. In South Miami–Dade you'll find **South Miami Hospital** (786-662-4000; www.baptisthealth.net), 6200 SW 73rd St., just one of many hospitals in the Baptist Health network. The medical center located the farthest south is **Homestead Hospital** (786-243-8000; www.baptist health.net), 975 Baptist Way (SW 312th St. and SW 147th Ave.), and is the only emergency center for 18 miles in all directions of the city. For diver emergencies, **The Hyperbaric Problem Wound Center** is at **Mercy Hospital** (305-854-0300; 24/7 hotline 1-800-NOBENDS or 911 if emergency; www.hyperbarics.com), 3663 S Miami Ave.

NORTH MIAMI AND MIAMI BEACH

North Miami Beach is primarily residential, including Bal Harbour, Surfside, and Sunny Isles. In the late 1800s, settlers were granted 160 acres by the government. In 1890, Capt. William H. Fulford homesteaded the section of North Miami Beach, selling the entire plot, and then some, in 1917, to Ohio newspaper owner Lefe Allen and Joshua Flaynold. The wide-open streets are a testament to Mr. Allen's plan for a perfect city. In 1927, North Miami Beach was incorporated as the City of Fulford, after the original homesteader. The name was changed to its current moniker in 1931. Locals call the area north of 41st Street "Condo Canyon." From the 1950s through the '70s, unrestricted zoning codes led to this stretch of tall cubical-like structures.

Aventura is an upscale residential and shopping community on the northeast tip of Miami, a land of high-rises, high-style stores, and high prices. North Miami is a nice place to get away from the glitz of the Gold Coast for a few hours and spend an evening as a local. The strip of Northeast 123rd Street (exit I-95 at 125th Street and head east; it curves into 123rd) is mellow and a little easier on the pocketbook than most shorefront activities. On Friday nights special events are frequently offered at both the Museum of Contemporary Art (MOCA) and the Luna Star Café.

Passing from mainland Miami over to the beachfront is definitely a move from one world to another. If you should happen to cross on the Broad Causeway, 125th Street, you'll pass through yet another world on your way: the Bay Harbor Islands. The village of Bay Harbor is a quaint and cozy community that was conceived and built by visionary Shepard Broad on a pair of mangrove-covered sandbars. Incorporated in 1947, the self-contained community manages to keep its 1950s atmosphere in spite of slightly rising apartment buildings on its eastern shorelines, a concession to the increased expenses of running a tiny city. In the shadow of the most coveted destination in the world, the Bay Harbor Islands comprise less than 1 square mile and have 5,100 residents, many of whom grew up here and are now raising their own families in the same neighborhood. Mr. Broad served as mayor for 26 years and lived in the community until his death at age 95 in 2001. Primarily residential, the area has a few fine restaurants lining the causeway before it arrives in Bay Harbor on Miami Beach at 96th Street.

Bal Harbour (Haulover Inlet to 96th Street) is perhaps the ritziest of the Miami Beach communities, calling itself the Gold Coast (although the rest of the state considers the moniker Gold Coast to encompass the entire tri-county area of Palm Beach to Miami). The area is home to the most exclusive department stores—Neiman Marcus and Saks Fifth Avenue—and features fashion boutiques of the best names in the industry, such as Louis Vuitton, Chanel, Giorgio Armani, Prada, and Pratesi, while Cartier, Bulgari, and Tiffany's polish the look at Bal Harbour Shops.

Haulover Beach to the north of Bal Harbour is known as the city's official nude beach (though many bathers go topless at Miami Beach, too), and Haulover also has a popular gay beach area.

The coast is lined with condominium high-rises, home to those who love to shop and dine at only the best. Naturally, there is a nice collection of delicious restaurants, most within walking distance of the condominiums, which is convenient for the retirees who call the area home. Sunny Isles (from Aventura to Haulover Inlet) has been renovated in recent years as father-and-son team Michael and Gil Dezer single-handedly (well, with the help of Donald Trump) razed the vintage Rat Pack hotels (we lament the loss, though we'll admit they were looking rather old and shabby) and replaced them with tall, shiny, view-obstructing condo hotels such as the Trump Sonesta Beach Resort.

Surfside (96th Street to 87th Terrace) is a small beachside city with a bit more modesty, though it's still incorporated as part of the Gold Coast. The community is well known for its clean, peaceful beach and community center, which is open to the public for a fee. North Bay Village boasts a few trendy restaurants and a nice community feel, though I did encounter a skirmish between local kids after a late dinner one night. The kids had no interest in me, fortunately.

✳ To See

HISTORIC PLACES

The oldest building in the Western Hemisphere, the **Ancient Spanish Monastery** (305-945-1461; www.spanishmonastery.com), 16711 West Dixie Hwy., North Miami Beach, was built in Segovia, Spain, in 1141. Brought to America by William Randolph Hearst, the monastery was reassembled in 1952 on its current site. Private weddings here are common, so call before you go. Open 9 AM–5 PM

Mon.–Sat., 1:30 PM–5 PM Sun. Adults $5, seniors 55+ $2.50, students $3, children under 12 $2.

You'll find a two-sided marker at **Haulover Beach,** originally known as Lighthouse Dock. Legend has it that a man named Baker "hauled over" fishing boats from the bay to the ocean around 1810. The dock was built in 1926, by Capt. Henry Jones, with the first dock permit from the War Department. International sport-fishermen docked here in the early 1900s, using charter boats to fish the waters for such big game as marlin and sailfish. The dock was replaced in 1952 by the marina.

✳ To Do

GOLF

Aventura

Two renovated, 18-hole courses designed by Robert Trent Jones Sr. are located at **Turnberry Isle Resort & Club** (305-932-6200; golf concierge, 786-279-6580; www.fairmont.com/turnberryisle), 19999 W Country Club Dr. The tropically landscaped par 70 **Miller Course** plays around Lake Boros, while the watery par 71 **South Course** tests your driving skills. More than 40,000 balls are retrieved from the 64-foot waterfall each year at the last hole, the famous "Island Green." The golf course is open to guests of the resort or club members.

Haulover Golf Course (305-940-6719; www.miamidade.gov/parks/Parks/haulover_golf_course.asp), 10800 Collins Ave., Haulover Golf Course offers a quick game of golf at an unbeatable price, right on Biscayne Bay. Try the nine-hole, par-3 course. Open 7:30 AM–7 PM daily. $10 and up.

✳ Green Space

BEACH You'll always see kites fluttering over **Haulover Park Beach** (305-947-3525 or 305-944-3040; www.miamidade.gov/parks), 10800 Collins Ave., Miami Beach, a 1.5-mile stretch of coconut palm–lined beach just north of Bal Harbour. With lifeguards and concession stands handy, it's one of the more popular public beaches in the region, especially for surfers. A large portion at the north end of the beach is officially "clothing optional." Gawkers and improper behavior are not tolerated; once on the beach, you'll want to check in at the information flag to receive a flyer on beach etiquette, rules, and a brief orientation. While everyone gets along quite nicely, there are distinct sections for gays and straights. On the Intracoastal side, the beach has a full-service marina and restaurant, a nine-hole golf course, and a kite shop. Open sunrise–sunset. Fee.

PARKS A mecca for mountain bikers, **Oleta River State Park** (305-919-1844; www.floridastateparks.org/oletariver/default.cfm), 3400 NE 163rd St., North Miami, offers more than 10 miles of challenging mountain bike trails—amazing for such an urban area! There are shorter trails for novices, including a paved trail. The park spans from the mangrove forests of the Oleta River to the Atlantic Ocean, enabling visitors to enjoy the beach or kayak through a maze of mangroves. On-site outfitter **Blue Moon Outdoor Center** rents kayaks, canoes, and bikes. Open 8 AM–sunset. Fee.

Featuring a natural limestone arch that was the original "Gateway to Miami" and a bridge on the Military Trail of the 1800s, **Arch Creek Park** (305-944-6111), 1855 NE 135th St., protects a sliver of tropical hammock that is a known archaeological site, a village of the Tequesta between 500 B.C. and A.D. 1300. Nature trails wind through the lush landscape, scant steps from Biscayne Boulevard. The arch itself collapsed in the 1980s but has been reestablished in place with a little human help. A small museum on-site explains the historical and archaeological significance of this small but important park. Open 9 AM–5 PM. Free.

The site of a turn-of-the-20th-century rock quarry, **Greynolds Park** (305-945-3425), 17530 W Dixie Hwy., protects 249 acres nestled along the Oleta River, including the mangrove-lined riverbanks and old quarries filled with water and surrounded by tropical hardwood hammocks. The tower, built of leftover stone, is a prominent manufactured feature. The park offers a popular municipal golf course, canoe and paddleboat rentals, hundreds of picnic tables, and two nature trails. The Lakeside Nature Trail circles the old quarries, while the Oleta River Nature Trail is a boardwalk through a dense mangrove forest. Open sunrise–sunset. Fee on weekends.

✳ Lodging

HOTELS AND RESORTS Each of the suites at the **Lilypad Suite Hotel** (305-866-9266; www.lilypadhotelmiami .com), 9400 Collins Ave., offers a full kitchen, nice-sized bathroom, and tasteful decor; standard rooms have two double beds and a writing desk. Suites $85 and up.

The luxurious rooms and suites at the European-style **Sea View Hotel** (305-866-4441 or 1-800-447-1010; www .seaview-hotel.com), 9909 Collins Ave., Bal Harbour, will treat you to the finest in service and luxurious accommodations. Although it's located on the beach, you'll also want to lounge around the heated swimming pools. The poolside cabanas are reminiscent of a time gone by. Well worth the extra price, the Key West–style cabanas have refrigerators, a walk-in closet, bathroom with showers, and their own private patio. On rainy days, you'll be glad you're only a block from the elite Bal Harbour Shops (see *Eating Out* and *Selective Shopping*). Rooms feature rich furnishings, and all have refrigerators. For those with allergies, hypoaller-genic bedding can be requested. $153–500.

Trump Sonesta Beach Resort (305-692-5600; www.sonesta.com/sunnyisles) 18001 Collins Ave., Sunny Isles Beach. This all-new complex has 390 rooms, some with hot tubs on the balconies, all exquisitely appointed and spacious. The beachfront pool complex has waterfalls, a spa, air-conditioned cabanas, water sports, a fitness center, and kids' activities. Salon; restaurants. $199–700.

One of the last small family motels along the strip, the **Best Western Ocean-front Resort** (305-864-2232; www.bwoceanfront.com), 9365 Collins Ave., Surfside, sits oceanfront with balconies overlooking the swimming pool, tropical atrium, or the sea. Although some of the rooms do show their age (the challenge of seaside accommodations), most are recently renovated and include mini kitchens with fridge, microwave, coffeemaker, and toaster. Junior and one-bedroom suites ($179 and up) include an oceanfront continental breakfast with tropical fruit and juice.

✳ Where to Eat

DINING OUT

Aventura

Allen Susser is a friendly celebrity chef in an industry where ego is dominant; Chef Allen is a leader in charitable work, devoting great personal involvement to the homeless and elderly. **Chef Allen's** (305-935-2900; www .chefallens.com), 19088 NE 29th Ave., offers a comfortable atmosphere, and his warm personality has infected his staff. You'll enjoy creatively prepared entrées such as pistachio-crusted black grouper with fricassee of rock shrimp, mango, leeks, and coconut rum ($26), yellow fin tuna with macadamia nut basmati rice and pinot noir pan sauce ($26), or the double cut Berkshire pork chop with baked chili, sweet potato wedges, and mango chutney ($22). The double Valhrona chocolate souffle ($18) is a delicious treat for dessert, served with warm chocolate ganache and chantilly cream. Bring your camera; each menu item is a unique piece of art, and you'll want to remember the experience. Open for dinner nightly starting at 6 PM.

Bal Harbour

While shopping at the elite Bal Harbour Shops, you'll want to take lunch at **Carpaccio** (305-867-7777; www .carpacciobalharbour.com). At this elegant indoor, and casual outdoor, restaurant, power lunchers reign. You'll find a variety of fresh salads, pastas, and of course thinly sliced carpaccio. A great place for people-watching and celebrity spotting; but keep your camera at home, as cameras aren't allowed anywhere in the mall. Open for lunch 11:30 AM–4:30 PM, dinner 4:30 PM–11 PM. Entrées $8–19. Valet parking at the mall is $12.

Bay Harbor Islands

Caffe Da Vinci (305-861-8166; www .caffedavinci.com), 1009 Kane Concourse/96th St. With the best-seller *The Da Vinci Code* propped on the host's desk and reproductions of the *Mona Lisa* and other Leonardo Da Vinci masterpieces gracing the walls, this multi-award-winning restaurant makes no bones about its heritage: executive chef Ricardo Tognozzi's culinary skill was honed in his hometown south of Rome. A long list of regular celebrity customers as well as locals and tourists enjoy the fabulous fresh homemade pasta and sauces along with inventive salads, including Insalata del Maestro, a salad of baby greens, fennel, Granny Smith apples, and Gorgonzola cheese with a honey-mustard vinaigrette; Ravioli Stolichnaya, cheese ravioli in a pink vodka sauce; and Agnolotti al Filetto, ricotta- and spinach-stuffed ravioli with fresh tomato and basil sauce. The house specialty is seaweed *spaghetini* (a flourless and eggless pasta with just 3 carbohydrates and 10 calories) tossed with a tomato-basil sauce and topped with baby shrimp and shiitake mushrooms. When I visited, my server was unusually accommodating, offering to split entrées for my friend and I when we couldn't decide. Entrées $10 and up.

The London Tavern and Islands Café (305-868-4141), Bay Harbor Inn, 9660 E. Bay Harbor Dr. The rich wooden bar and dark, ornately carved furnishings of a London tavern were imported from an old English hotel, lending a warm, familiar atmosphere to this tiny, eight-table pub. The bar has a Cheers sort of neighborhood feeling. Billie Holiday wails from the stereo, and white-coated students busy themselves delivering trays of fruit and fresh herb garnishes to the bar and the Islands Café. The Bay Harbor Inn is owned and operated by the famed culinary arts school Johnson and Wales

University, which guarantees that dining here will be a provocative experience. New American cuisine is served inside, or enjoy a poolside appetizer and cocktail. The inn offers live jazz on weekends and a famous Sunday brunch that features salads, bagels and lox, blintzes, and seafood and chicken entrées with vegetable sides. The Thursday-night seafood menu includes smoked salmon, shrimp and scallop scampi, bacon-wrapped scallops with guava barbecue sauce, black jack tenderloin, and raspberry sorbet or chocolate decadence cake. You can't go wrong. Breakfast daily; dinner served Tues.–Thur. (no lunch) with live entertainment, Sun. brunch. $10 and up.

Sushi Republic (305-867-8036), 9583 Harding Ave., has all the sushi favorites, including rolls, special rolls, and sashimi ($3–11) and combo dinners ($12–19). Open daily for lunch and dinner; hours vary.

Timo (305-936-1008; www.timo restaurant.com), 17624 Collins Ave. Try northern Italian fare courtesy of chef Tim Andriola, formerly executive chef at Mark's South Beach, named

Gourmet's number-one Miami favorite during his reign. Enjoy pizzas from the wood-burning oven, fresh pastas, or full entrées of seafood, veal, or chicken complemented with Parmesan and polenta. Entrées $10 and up.

EATING OUT
Bal Harbour
On the second floor of the Bal Harbour Shops, you'll enjoy imported teas and French pastries at **Lea's Tea Room & Bistro** (305-868-0901). The European-style café serves a delightful selection of baked goods and ice creams. At lunch you can order salads and sandwiches. Open 9:30 AM– 8:30 PM. Breakfast dishes $6–8; lunch and dinner $7–14. Valet parking $12.

✳ Entertainment

ART GALLERY
North Miami
With more than 400 works in its permanent collection, the **Museum of Contemporary Art (MOCA)** (305-893-6211; www.mocanomi.org), 770 NE 125th St., N Miami, displays cut-

MUSEUM OF CONTEMPORARY ART, NORTH MIAMI

Courtesy Greater Miami Convention and Vistior's Bureau

ting-edge contemporary pieces in a wide variety of media. You'll see pieces from abstract impressionist Louise Nevelson, photographic images from Zoe Leonard, and works relating to music by visual artist Christian Marclay. Open 1 PM–9 PM Wed., 11–5 Tues., Thurs., Fri., Sat.; noon–5 PM Sun.; and 7 AM–10 PM the last Fri. evening of every month with jazz performances. Adults $5, seniors and students with ID $3. Free for MOCA members, North Miami residents, and children under 12.

✳ Selective Shopping

Bal Harbour Shops (www.balharbour shops.com) is the shopping center of the rich and famous. While $600 shoes and $2,000 blouses are available, you can also find nice bargains and excellent sales. Hey, the rich like to save money, too. Built in 1965 by owner-developer Stanley Whitman on an old World War II army barracks, the alfresco mall creates a relaxing environment. Take your cue from the turtles in the lush tropical koi pond—slow down and relax; this is a mall of grace and calm. Start your day at **Lea's Tea Room & Bistro** (see *Eating Out*) for a cup of tea and French baked goods; spend the day exploring the shops; and then grab lunch or dinner at **Carpaccio** (see *Dining Out*). The mall is anchored by Neiman Marcus (305-865-6161; www.neimanmarcus.com), and you'll find many "firsts" here. **Giuseppe Zanotti** (305-868-0133; www.giuseppe-zanotti-design.com) offers a unique collection of bejeweled shoes and purses. The fine craftsman dictates that every woman own at least one pair. You'll want to stop in at the **House of Harry Winston** (786-206-6657; www.harrywinston.com) just to see the unique jewels. The connoisseur of gems, Winston created an entirely new way to cut stones, and their brilliance is evidence of his mastery. Winston's most famous piece, the Hope Diamond, resides at the Smithsonian Institution. While the ladies shop, men will enjoy **The Art of Shaving** (305-865-0408; www.theartofshaving.com), where they can get the Royal Shave or an aromatherapy treatment. Part old-fashioned barbershop and part day spa, the shop features shaves the old-fashioned way. Starting with a hot face towel and facial massage to open and cleanse the pores, the barber then applies warm shaving cream with a badger brush, and with an authentic straight razor skillfully shaves your whiskers, not once, but twice—first down, then up. Afterward a mask is applied to rejuvenate the skin. The finishing touch is a splash of rosewater and lavender oil. You'll feel like a new man. My son begs for this treatment each birthday. You can purchase their line here as well. The Straight Razor Shave is $35, the Royal Shave $55. So that superstars can shop like normal people, Bal Harbour Shops have a strict paparazzi policy—no cameras. If caught using a camera, you may be escorted out of the mall; so leave yours in your car or purse. Open 10 AM–9 PM Mon.–Sat.; mall stores 12 PM–6 PM Sun. Parking $12.

Surfside's business district offers interesting shops to explore. **Absolut Flowers** (305-866-5288), 9481 Harding Ave., is jam-packed with trendy home decor and tall glass vases. Reminding me of the marketplace in Goa, West Indies, **Lace Star Designer Fabrics** (305-868-5550; www.lace star.com), 9593 Harding Ave., has a stunning display of beaded fabrics and boasts the "most variety of one-of-a-kind beaded French lace in the world."

THE GABLES, THE GROVE, AND DOWNTOWN MIAMI

Coral Gables, home to the University of Miami and formerly the National Hurricane Center, the city is called the City Beautiful for its 1920s Mediterranean-style architecture of native coral rock and limestone nestled under towering oak, banyan, and royal poinciana trees. Developer George Merrick carefully planned and laid out the city in keeping with the trend of the times to create palatial living for America's elite. With the historic Biltmore Hotel as its centerpiece, the area is still known for its affluent citizens, who create a rich cultural oasis of theaters and fine boutiques.

Coconut Grove is the site of one of Miami's earliest settlements, and this bayside community's roads and sites are named after the pioneers who first settled here, such as the Ingraham Highway, named for Flagler Railway scout James Ingraham. Some of the grand homes of the early 20th century still grace the shoreline, from Vizcaya to the Barnacle to the Deering Estate. Affectionately called "the Grove," the city served as an early Bahamian immigrant community, and in the 1960s it became quite popular with musicians and hipsters. Anyone who was there then will regale listeners with tales of intimate musical gatherings with David Crosby, Joni Mitchell, Fred Neil, and Jimmy Buffett. But the popularity of the community seemed to bring its downfall, as so often happens. In an effort to capitalize on the crowds, developers quickly swooped into the community with early versions of festival marketplaces—palaces of retail and restaurant trade designed to woo the music-loving public and to capture their dollars.

As it turned out, there wasn't a lot of money to be made from the hipsters of the 1960s, and the retail behemoths continue to pose a challenge for the community. But in the process the charming sense of a village atmosphere was lost and has never been fully recovered.

Nonetheless, the Grove maintains a hint of grooviness, and the streets of Coconut Grove still offer a plethora of kinky shops and sidewalk cafés of the sort that the hip-

MIAMI SKYLINE AND MARINA

Courtesy Greater Miami Convention and Visitors Bureau

pies of yesteryear might have found interesting—including head shops and lingerie and sex toy shops. Designer boutiques also line the streets, and mainstream shopping can be found at the Mayfair and Coco Walk. The Grove may not be the same as wistful natives recall, but it's still a comfortable, casual place to enjoy an evening.

Downtown Miami is home to the American Airlines Arena, where you can see the Miami Heat along with several featured concerts. With a stunning skyline, the city is remarkably resilient to the up and down turns of weather and the economy. Today, many new condominium towers sit empty, awaiting the resurgence of buyers who will likely find bargains in paradise for a few years to come. The multicultural community offers a colorful array of building styles and dining options. Neighborhoods within the city include Brickell Avenue, Miami's Wall Street; MiMO, Miami Modern, the area of north Biscayne Boulevard with trendy antiques shops and dining; Little Havana, where Cuban and Latin Americans often begin their stay in the United States gently enveloped within their own culture; the Design District, where trendy interiors, cuisine and nightlife abound; and the newly developing Wynwood, a growing arts community.

✳ To See

ARCHAEOLOGICAL SITES While clearing a site for new development in 1998, workers uncovered the ancient **Miami Circle,** 401 Brickell Ave. Archaeologists and the people of Miami went to great lengths, which included heated debate, to preserve this site, believed to be a Tequesta site dating back 1,800 to 2,000 years. Consisting of 24 holes cut into limestone bedrock, the Circle has been speculated to be a central ceremonial site or possibly a celestial calendar. Located at the mouth of the Miami River, the 38-foot-wide circle is not currently accessible to the public, though it can be viewed through chain-link fences. Many artifacts found at the site, such as shell tools, stone axe-heads, and human teeth, are on display at the **Historical Museum of Southern Florida** (305-375-1492; www.hmsf.org), 101 W Flagler St., Miami (see *Museums*), where you'll also see a scaled-down replica of the Miami Circle. The Historical Museum of Southern Florida has been designated to manage the site and plans to develop tours beginning in 2009.

ART GALLERY The **MOCA at Goldman Warehouse** (305-573-5441; www .mocanomi.org), 404 NW 26th St., is a satellite branch of the Museum of Contemporary Art, with exhibits from the MOCA collection along with works by emerging artists. Open 12 PM–5 PM Wed.–Sat., noon–5 PM Sun. Admission by donation.

ATTRACTIONS **Jungle Island** (305-400-7000; www.jungleisland.com), 111 Parrot Jungle Trail, Miami, is located on Watson Island, just off the MacArthur Causeway. Formerly known as Parrot Jungle, it was previously located farther south, where Pinecrest Gardens now stands (see *South Miami–Dade: Food and Wine Country*). You'll find the same colorful macaws (there are thousands of them), but the park has other creatures as well. Marvel at Crocosauras, a 2,000-pound, 20-feet long, 35 year-old saltwater crocodile; Hercules, the Liger (part lion, part tiger); and Peanut and Pumpkin, twin female orangutans. Guests will enjoy the spectacular animal shows in the Parrot Bowl and Winged Wonder, or a relaxing walk through the beautiful tropical landscape. Open daily 10 AM–6 PM. Adults $29.95, children 3–10 $23.95, under 2 free. Senior, military, and student courtesy discounts are a few dollars less. Parking $7 per vehicle.

Coconut Grove

The oldest home in Miami-Dade County, in its original location, is situated on the shore of Biscayne Bay at the **Barnacle Historic State Park** (305-442-6866; www.floridastateparks.org/TheBarnacle/), 3485 Main Hwy. Built in the 1800s as the home of a prominent Coconut Grove pioneer, Ralph Middleton Munroe, it is surrounded by a hardwood hammock, the last of its kind in the area. In the home you'll see unique architecture, sweeping verandas, and furnishings of the era. Open 9 AM–5 PM Fri.–Mon., with Yoga by the Sea 6–7:30 PM Wed. Guided tours are offered at 10 AM, 11:30 AM, 1 PM, and 2:30 PM. $1 for ages six and up, under six free.

An incredible display of grandeur and one of the more beautiful pieces of architecture in South Florida is the **Vizcaya Museum and Gardens** (305-250-9133; www.vizcayamuseum.org), 3251 S Miami Ave. It was built as a winter home (1916–1925) during the Gilded Age for James Deering, vice president of International Harvester and brother to Charles Deering (see Deering Estate in *South Miami–Dade: Food and Wine Country*). The home features 34 rooms, decorated with art and furnishings from the 15th to the 19th centuries, where several important documents have been signed, such as the first Free Trade Agreement between the United States and a South American country (Chile). Outside, exotic orchids can be seen in the David A. Klein Orchidarium, and fountains grace 10 tropically landscaped gardens. Open 9:30 AM–4:30 PM daily. Adults $15, Miami-Dade residents $10, children 6–12 $6, under 6 free.

Coral Gables

Coral Gables Merrick House (305-460-5361; www.coralgables.com), 907 Coral Way (circa 1899–1907), is the boyhood home of George E. Merrick, founder of Coral Gables. The home features the Merrick family's art, furniture, and memorabilia of the 1920s. Guided tours are presented Wednesday and Sunday at 1 PM, 2 PM, and 3 PM. Adults $5, seniors and students $3, children 6–12 $1, under 6 free.

Miami

Built in 1825 and rebuilt in 1846, the **Cape Florida Lighthouse** at Bill Baggs Cape Florida State Park (www.floridastateparks.org/capeflorida/; see *Beaches*) is the oldest standing structure in Miami-Dade County. Park staff and volunteers offer free guided tours of the lighthouse at 10 AM and 1 PM Thurs.–Mon., self tours 9 AM–5 PM; show up a half hour before departure to reserve a space. It's a spiral climb of 109 steps to the top, with a bird's-eye view of downtown Miami and Biscayne Bay as your reward. The Light Keeper's Quarters are included on the tour.

Completed in 1925, the 255-foot **Freedom Tower** (305-375-1492), 600 Biscayne Blvd., was built as a memorial to Cuban immigrants and is often referred to as Miami's "Ellis Island." A striking centerpiece in downtown

VIZCAYA

Sandra Friend

Miami, the federal government used the building to process Cuban refugees until the late 1980s. Now owned by Miami Dade College, the Mediterranean Revival building houses a museum, with displays on the boat lifts of Cuban refugees and the history of Cuba, a library, a meeting hall, and the Cuban American National Foundation.

MUSEUMS

Miami

At the **Historical Museum of Southern Florida** (305-375-1492; www .hmsf.org), 101 W Flagler St., you'll see artifacts from the Miami Circle (see *Archaeological Sites*) while learning about South Florida history dating back 10,000 years. Walk down into a small-scale replica of the Miami Circle, about 12 feet in diameter, and see some of the artifacts found at the site. Marvel at the workmanship on the *Miami Centennial Quilt*, which has

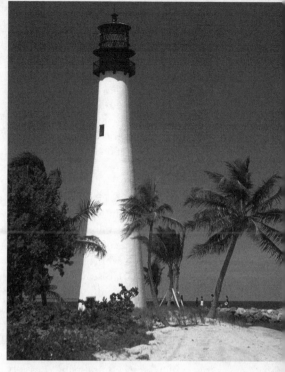

CAPE FLORIDA LIGHTHOUSE

blocks representing the Barefoot Mailman (see *South Palm Beach County*), the Biltmore (see *Lodging*), and Julia Tuttle's Orange Blossoms, which were sent to Henry Flagler (see *Central Palm Beach County*) to inform him that Miami was a great paradise to which he should consider extending his railroad. Exhibits, such as the History of Miami Beach, change throughout the year. Tours available in English and Spanish by appointment. Call for prices. Open 10 AM–5 PM Mon.–Sat., 10 AM–9 PM Thurs., 12 PM–5 PM Sun. Adults $8, children 6–12 $5, under 6 free.

✐ Kids will have fun in 14 galleries at the **Miami Children's Museum** (305-373-5437; www.miamichildrensmuseum.org), 980 MacArthur Causeway. The museum offers many interactive exhibits. At the Castle of Dreams, climb through a two-story castle and see sands from around the world; learn how to be a vet at Pet Central; or become a camera operator at Television Studio. Open 10 AM–6 PM daily. Adults and children $12, babies under 12 months are free. Parking is $1 per hour.

The **Miami Science Museum** (305-646-4200; www.miamisci.org), 3280 S Miami Ave., is not your ordinary science museum. At the **Falcon Batchelor Bird of Prey Center** (305-646-4244), you'll see rare birds of prey, from the tiny burrowing owl to the majestic bald eagle. Throughout the museum experience live science demonstrations, interactive exhibits, and theater shows. At the planetarium you can view the galaxy on the 65-foot-diameter domed projection screen, or take in a laser show to the sounds of Pink Floyd, Nine Inch Nails, and the Grateful Dead on the first Friday of every month. Make sure to browse through the excellent museum store before leaving. Open 10 AM–6 PM daily; last ticket sold at 5:30.

Adults $18, seniors 62+ and students with ID $16, children 3–12 $13, under 3 free.

The **Miami Art Museum** (305-375-3000; www.miamiartmuseum.org), 101 W Flagler St., presents international art of the 20th and 21st centuries. The permanent collection, Miami Currents: Linking Community and Collection, showcases Miami artists. You'll also view several U.S. and international artists' works, such as Nairobi-born Wangechi Mutu's piece, *You tried so hard to make us away,* created of ink, acrylic, glitter, fur, contact paper, and collage, or George Segal's painted plaster sculpture, *Abraham's Farewell to Ishmael.* Open 10 AM–5 PM Tues.–Fri., noon–5 PM Sat. and Sun. Adults $8, seniors $4, children under 12 and students free. Entrance to the museum is free on the second Saturday of each month and every Sunday.

SPORTING EVENTS Florida loves its sports teams. In Miami, the **Miami Dolphins** football team (www.miamidolphins.com) and the **Florida Marlins** baseball team (www.marlins.mlb.com) both play at Dolphin Stadium (305-623-6100; www.proplayerstadium.com), 2269 NW 199th St. The **Miami Heat** basketball team (www.nba.com/heat) plays at the American Airlines Arena (786-777-1000; www.aaarena.com), 601 Biscayne Blvd. And you'll find the **Florida Panthers** hockey team (www.floridapanthers.com) up in Broward County at the BankAtlantic Center (954-835-7000; www.bankatlanticcenter.com), One Panther Pkwy., Sunrise.

TOURS ✤ **Dragonfly Expeditions** (305-774-9019 or 1-888-992-6337; www.dragonflyexpeditions.com), 1825 Ponce de Leon Blvd., Coral Gables, believes in true "green" travel, immersing travelers in unique destinations, with minimal impact on the environment. Their tours incorporate flora and fauna, along with history and culture. You'll enjoy Miami Magic City Bus and Walking Tour, which explores the area's colorful heritage. On the Ghosts and Gravestones tour you'll uncover the mystery of the Miami Circle (see *Archaeological Sites*) with an expert archaeologist, and then visit the Miami Cemetery to learn about Miami's pioneers and settlers. On the Havana Nights tour you'll be transported to another world, where you'll enjoy a dinner on Little Havana's lively main street, Calle Ocho, then watch the art of cigar rolling and later learn Latin dances at a Cuban nightclub. The Everglades Backwater tour explores the areas of the Everglades most tourists can't reach—wade in swamps with field biologists. The Middle Keys Discovery Paddle explores the keys—sailing, snorkeling, hiking. Tour prices depend on group size and some include meals. $30–100.

✳ To Do

FAMILY ACTIVITIES ✑ Have a blast at the **Crandon Park Family Amusement Center** (305-361-5421), Key Biscayne, at Crandon Park (see *Beaches*), which includes a 1949 carousel, an old-fashioned outdoor roller rink, a dolphin-shaped splash fountain, and a beachside playground as well as a Tropical Jungle Hayride. Open 10 AM–7 PM $2 fees for carousel and hayride.

GOLF

Coral Gables
Play on an 18-hole, par 17 course with the grandeur of the **Biltmore Hotel** (305-460-5366; www.biltmorehotel.com), 1210 Anastasia Ave., as a backdrop. The hotel

and golf course were built in 1925 by architect Donald Ross. Also run by the Biltmore is the inexpensive and easy to play 9-hole **Granada Golf Course** (305-460-5367), 2001 Granada Blvd. Three dogleg fairways provide a good challenge for both novice and experienced golfers, and the small course has no water hazards.

Doral

The famed **Doral Golf Resort and Spa** (305-592-2000, 305-592-2030, or 1-800-71-DORAL; www.doralresort.com), 4400 NW 87th Ave., offers 90 holes on the Blue, Great White, Silver, Gold, and Red Courses. Opening in the 1960s, the courses have been host to many of golf's greatest champions. You'll enjoy driving where legends played on the Blue Monster with its famous fountain at the 18th hole, or the palm tree–lined Great White Course, redesigned by Greg Norman in 2000, with coquina sand and 222 Scottish-style bunkers.

Key Biscayne

The 18-hole par 72 championship **Crandon Park Golf Course** (305-361-9129; www.miamidade.gov/parks/parks/crandon_golf.asp), 6700 Crandon Blvd., is a nature lover's delight. Mangroves and lush tropical foliage surround you at the secluded setting overlooking Biscayne Bay. At the last hole you'll find water on both sides of the fairway.

HIKING At Crandon Park, **Bear Cut Nature Preserve** (see *Nature Centers*), Key Biscayne, provides a place to stretch your legs. The 1.3-mile Osprey Beach Trail is a broad path along the coastal dunes with beach crossovers. It ends at a paved path; follow that to walk a boardwalk through the mangrove forest to an overlook of a 6,000-year-old fossil reef on Biscayne Bay. Near the nature center are two loop trails to introduce you to the tropical hardwood hammock: the Bear Cut Nature Trail and the Tequesta Hammock Trail, each 0.3 mile. Open 8 AM to sunset daily.

SWIMMING Spend a day in paradise: Nestled in the heart of Coral Gables is a unique swimming hole, the **Venetian Pool** (305-460-5357; www.venetianpool .com), 2701 DeSoto Blvd. You'll enjoy swimming in and out of caves carved out of coral rock, and under stone bridges and waterfalls. The cool water comes from natural springs beneath the pool. Then lie on the sandy beach, or lounge on the lawn. Surrounded by a lush tropical landscape and exquisite architecture, the historic landmark is designed to resemble a Venetian-style lagoon. Open all year, with reduced hours in winter. Apr.–Oct. open seven days: adults $10, children 3–12 $6.75. Nov.–Mar. open Tues.–Sun., closed Mon.: adults $6.75, children 3–12 $5.50. No babies or toddlers; children must be 38 inches tall and show proof that they are 3 years old.

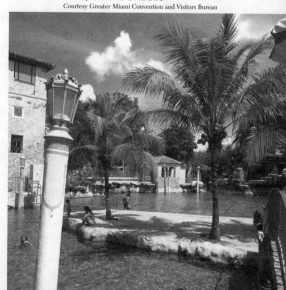

VENETIAN POOL, CORAL GABLES
Courtesy Greater Miami Convention and Visitors Bureau

✳ Green Space

BEACHES

Key Biscayne

The sparkling waters of Biscayne Bay invite at **Bill Baggs Cape Florida State Park** (305-361-5811; www.floridastateparks.org/capeflorida/), 1200 S Crandon Blvd., which is rated as one of the Top 10 beaches in the United States. Bask in the sun in the shadow of the historic **Cape Florida Lighthouse** (see *Historic Sites*); rent bicycles or surreys to enjoy the bayside bicycle path with its view of Stiltsville, a collection of old fishing shacks in the shallows offshore; walk the 1.5-mile nature trail through coastal habitats; or rent sea kayaks at the marina to ply the bay waters. The embers were still smoldering from a fire at the Lighthouse Café the day I arrived, but the park promises to have this popular restaurant up and running by late 2006. Open 9–8:30 daily. $5 per car.

With 2 miles of beach to choose from, **Crandon Park** (305-361-5421), 4000 Crandon Blvd., is a popular choice for sun worshipers. Opened in 1947, the park spans from Biscayne Bay to the Atlantic Ocean, and an offshore sandbar protects the famed white-sand beach, making it an ideal swimming and shelling spot. Lifeguards are always on duty, and coconut palms and sea grapes frame the view. In addition to the beach, the park offers solitude at **Bear Cut Nature Preserve** (see *Nature Centers*) or laughs at the **Crandon Park Family Amusement Center** (see *Family Activities*). **Crandon Park Golf Course,** an 18-hole championship golf course, is also on the grounds. Open 9 AM–5 PM daily. Fee.

BOTANICAL GARDENS

Coconut Grove

Listed on the National Register of Historic Places, the 8-acre **Kampong** (305-442-7169; www.ntbg.org/gardens/kampong.html), 4013 Douglas Rd., is part of the National Tropical Botanical Garden. Noted plant expert David Fairchild selected plants from around the world that he thought would add aesthetic value to the nation, bringing them here to cultivate. You'll walk through a wide variety of colorful flowering and tropical fruit trees. Open 9 AM–2 PM Mon.–Fri. Guided tours available.

Coral Gables

The expansive **Fairchild Tropical Botanic Garden** (305-667-1651; www.fairchildgarden.org), 10901 Old Cutler Rd., established in 1938, is a peaceful tropical paradise. Walk through the 83-acre botanical garden, where you'll enjoy seven regions, including Windows to the Tropics, a 16,428-square-foot conservatory featuring rare orchids, aroids, bromeliads, and fruit trees; the McLamore Arboretum, which displays more than 740 species of tropical flowering trees on 8 acres; and the world-renowned Montgomery Palmetum, with an impressive selection of palms from all parts of the globe. The newest section, the William F. Whitman Tropical Fruit Pavilion, features a 38-foot-high pavilion where you can view exotic tropical fruit species from areas such as Borneo and the Amazon. The Keys Coastal Habitat, a local favorite, attracts migratory birds and Florida fauna with plants native to South Florida and the Florida Keys. Narrated open-air tram tours, and guided walking tours. Gift shop sells a nice selection of tropical gardening books. Open 9:30 AM–4:30 PM every day except Christmas. Adults $20, seniors 65+ $15, children 6–17 $10, children 5 and under and Fairchild members free.

NATURE CENTER ♿ Offering art exhibits, interactive displays, aquariums, and a beautiful little gift shop, the **Marjory Stoneman Douglas Biscayne Nature Center** is the gateway to **Bear Cut Nature Preserve** (305-361-5421), 6767 Crandon Blvd., Key Biscayne. This little-known preserve lies at the far northern end of the **Crandon Park** (see *Beaches*) parking lots. Protecting 280 acres of natural habitats on Biscayne Bay, the preserve has several nature trails that introduce you to tropical forest, coastal dunes, and the mangrove forest, as well as a paved pathway for bicycles and wheelchairs. Not to be missed is the boardwalk to the fossil reef overlook on Biscayne Bay. Open 9 AM–5 PM daily. Fee.

PARKS Natural pine flatwoods and a spot of rare pine rocklands habitat are the focal points of the 65-acre **A. D. Barnes Park** (305-666-5883), 3401 SW 72nd Ave., where paved trails radiate from the **Sense of Wonder Nature Center** (9 AM–6 PM Mon.–Fri., 10 AM–6 PM Sat. and Sun.) into the surrounding tropical hardwood hammock and pines. When the nature center is closed, use the **Leisure Center** entrance, which has some interesting outdoor art. Open sunrise–sunset. Free.

✳ Lodging
HOTELS, MOTELS, AND RESORTS

Coconut Grove 33133
At **Grove Isle Hotel & Spa** (305-858-8300 or 1-800-884-7683; www.grove isle.com), Four Grove Isle Dr., you'll be greeted with exotic jungle murals and towering gold columns topped with green palm fronds in the main lobby. After check-in, curl up on one of the hammocks overlooking the bay, play life-sized chess with 3-foot pieces on the pool deck, and on cool nights cozy up at the outdoor fire pit. You'll find luxury accommodations ($279–529) in a variety of choices. The five Grand Luxury Bayfront Suites are situated on the corners of the hotel, providing the best water views. They include such plush amenities as a flat-screen plasma TV and a four-poster king bed. For romance, the spacious Bay Suite Studios feature an elevated bedroom with king canopy beds and butterfly netting. Elegant Colonial decor is found in the Luxury Bayfront Rooms, with either king- or two queen-sized beds. And overlooking the marina, you'll watch sailboats glide by from one of the Luxury Bay Suites with king- and queen-sized beds.

Coral Gables 33134
ⓣ Old-world elegance greets you at the **Biltmore Hotel** (305-445-1926 or 1-800-915-1926; www.biltmorehotel .com), 1200 Anastasia Ave. Built in 1926, the grand hotel has seen its fair share of presidents, royalty, and celebrities, so you'd expect it to be expensive. However, it's very affordable during the summer months. Stepping back in time, you'll find white-glove service greeting you upon your arrival and throughout your stay. The European ambiance is evident, from the gargoyles on the staircases to the tiny finches in the grand-lobby birdcage. Once in your room you'll be treated to feather beds, Egyptian-cotton duvet covers, and signature robes and slippers. You won't miss your high-tech toys—high-speed Internet, cable TV, digital on-demand movies, and Sony PlayStation are in each room ($279–589). The hotel features the lush tropical landscaping of Canary palms, bougainvillea, and hibiscus; romantic balconies; complimentary carriage

rides throughout Coral Gables, an on-site spa, a championship golf course (see *Golf*), fine dining (see *Dining Out*), and the largest pool in the continental United States. The 700,000-gallon pool once hosted water ballets and water polo. For that special night, the 1,830-square-foot two-story Everglades "Al Capone" Suite features hand-painted ceiling scenes of the Everglades, a private elevator, and a baby grand piano ($4,800–5,500 per night).

Hotel St. Michel (305-444-1666 or 1-800-848-HOTEL; www.hotelstmichel .com), 162 Alcazar Ave., is very European. Built in 1926, the charming inn has 27 rooms ($175–325), all with different personalities. Weary travelers will appreciate the attentive service, which starts at check-in and continues throughout your stay. Fresh fruit, rich imported chocolates, and an assortment of fine toiletries, including a mending kit, provide nice touches to the rooms. Rooms are decorated in elegant antiques, buttery walls, and—true to European style—the windows open so you can enjoy the balmy night air. Each morning you'll enjoy continental breakfast featuring croissants, fresh-squeezed orange juice, and coffee or a variety of European teas. The hotel is conveniently located only a block from the famed Miracle Mile shopping district (see *Selective Shopping*).

Miami 33131

↬ **Four Seasons Hotel Miami** (305-358-3535; www.fourseasons.com), 1435 Brickell Ave., is one of the most sleek and sophisticated hotels in town. Elegance is the standard here, from the amenities and rooms to the spa and signature restaurant, Acqua, serving Latin American ceviche and Italian specialties. $425–440.

↬ **Intercontinental Hotel** (305-577-1000; www.ichotelsgroup.com), 100 Chopin Plaza. Featuring two restaurants, an outdoor pool, and a fitness center, the Intercontinental Hotel serves Miami's business crowd and elite visitors who prefer a little distance from the celebrity scene, but not too much. It's right downtown on Biscayne Bay, adjacent to Bayside Marketplace. $329–729.

❝❞ 🐾 Guests with pets will enjoy the **Mandarin Oriental** (305-913-8288; www .mandarinoriental.com/miami), 500 Brickell Key Dr., where they can walk their dogs on the beautiful South Lawn and private beach overlooking Biscayne Bay. The Mandarin provides privacy and exclusivity to celebrities and sophisticated travelers who desire— and can afford—the best in accommodations. The hotel's sparkling guest list includes the King and Queen of Spain, Mick Jagger, Whitney Houston, Jada Pinkett, and Will Smith. In the Asian themes of the hotel's corporate foundation, bamboo and orchids, sliding rice-paper doors, cool marble, and linens all combine to create an air of privilege and perfection. The hotel is also home to one of the nation's top spas, where guests and visitors may luxuriate in a variety of massage and relaxation techniques from around the world, including Thailand, India, China, Europe, and Bali. Yoga, Pilates, Tai Chi, and meditation classes are conducted regularly. A popular and unique service called "Time Rituals" allows guests to simply book spa space and professionals by the hour for custom-designed service packages. Your pet will be provided with a plush pet bed, food bowls, and a fun treat. Rates are $233–1,283. The luxurious Biscayne Suite goes for $2,283 during low season, $3,566 during high season.

Miami River Inn (305-325-0045 or 1-800-468-3589; www.miamiriverinn .com), 118 SW South River Dr., claims to be Miami's only Bed and Breakfast hotel. The Miami River Inn, a collection of four historic buildings circa 1906–10, is Miami's longest continually run rooming house/hotel, where rooms once rented for $14 a night. The fully restored inn is unique in an environment of big money and fast-talking politicians. Furnished with antiques, the inn's quaint rooms are in buildings surrounding a peaceful pool and garden area, a lush retreat set against a rather harsh urban backdrop. $99–199.

Hyatt Regency Miami (305-358-1234; http://miamiregency.hyatt.com), 400 SE Second Ave. Overlooking Biscayne Bay and the Miami Circle (which is now obscured by a protective covering of soil but marked by indicators), the Sheraton Biscayne Bay offers convenience to downtown as well as the pleasure of water views. With cool, colorful Miami styling, the hotel's amenities include a lobby bar, pool, patio garden, and fitness center. $189–349.

✳ Where to Eat

DINING OUT

Downtown Miami
Azul (305-913-8288), Mandarin Oriental Hotel, 500 Brickell Key Dr. With the most distinguished rating of any restaurant in Miami—the AAA five-diamond award—Azul is a force to be enjoyed. With an open-air kitchen and cool champagne bar, the restaurant is guaranteed to soothe and relax diners with its peaceful, feng shui–inspired decor, which includes a waterfall wall and a raindroplike curtain of dripping water lining the kitchen. Make time. Closed Sun. Entrées $40 and up.

Gloria and Emilio Estefan Jr.'s **Bongos Cuban Café** (786-777-2100; www.bongoscubancafe.com), 601 Biscayne Blvd., features Cuban cuisine in a tropical art deco–style café where you can gaze at the cruise ships, at the Port

of Miami, Biscayne Bay, and the Downtown Miami skyline. The lively restaurant is a great place to go before or after a game or concert at the American Airlines Arena. You'll find Cuban menu items such as *ropa vieja* and *bistec la Milanesa*. Kids have their own menu with *bistec de Palomilla* (a Cuban-style grilled steak), and *chicharrones de pollo* (lightly floured boneless chicken nuggets). Open for lunch 11:30 AM–5 PM Fri.–Sun., dinner 5 PM–11 PM Wed.–Sun.

The power lunch is king at **The Capital Grille** (305-374-4500; www.thecapitalgrille.com), 444 Brickell Ave. Located next to the Miami Convention Center, it is known for its dry-aged steaks and outstanding wine list. You'll find dry-aged steak au poivre with Courvoisier cream sauce and the Grille's signature veal chop to be some of the juiciest. Your toughest executive decision will be selecting from the more than 5,000 bottles of wine on the wall. When celebrating landing the big deal, you'll want to order a wine from the Captain's List, which features rare wines and champagnes.

DOWNTOWN MIAMI
Courtesy Greater Miami Convention and Visitors Bureau

Gordon Biersch Brewery Restaurant (786-425-1130; www.gordon biersch.com), 1201 Brickell Ave., is a chain steakhouse that offers fresh-brewed beer and a hearty menu of beef and seafood in fresh-flavored modern incarnations, located in Miami's financial district. You'll pass tiny protected 100-year-old homes, which are contrasted against the steel and glass skyscrapers of the money keepers. Bankers and financiers naturally frequent this locale. Entrées $15 and up.

Grass (305-573-3355; www.grass lounge.com), 28 N.E. 40th St. One of the hottest tickets outside of South Beach, Grass is a walled enclave in the Design District. Entry is by reservation only, and it must be made well in advance. Diners may linger only two hours to make way for the next seating. The dining room is an outdoor terrace with low tables, banquettes, and a bar covered by a large tiki hut. More tables rest under the stars. But in spite of the exclusive velvet-rope routine, the atmosphere inside the kingdom is as comfortable and casual as the decor, which includes pots of grass decorating the tables under the grass hut. Chef Pedro Duarte favors delicate flavors with Asian and Latin distinctions. I loved the golden gazpacho, Mérida mixed ceviche (there were several to choose from), and Morayaki chicken with teriyaki and raspberries. Entrées $20 and up.

Karu & Y (305-403-7850; www.karu-y .com), 71 NW 14th St., is the place where art and culinary cuisine meet. Sit back and enjoy the striking architecture and artistic pieces on the wall and on your plate. The menu features flavors of *Alta Cocina* ("Cuisine of the Americas"). Open for dinner 7 AM–11 PM; stay late in the "Y" Ultra Lounge and garden.

Michael's Genuine Food and Drink (305-573-5550), 130 NE 40th St. The Design District is hot, and Michael's is one of the hottest new spots in the district. Michael Schwartz, whom diners might know from his first South Beach restaurant, Nemo, has created a welcoming spot that is both a friendly neighborhood bar and a restaurant that wins national raves. Schwartz plays with his food in the best sense, matching up everyday ingredients to create the sublime, as he does, for example, in his crispy beef cheek with celeriac puree, celery salad, and chocolate reduction, or in his crispy sweet and spicy pork belly with kimchi, crushed peanuts, and pea shoots. Entrées $16 and up.

Prime Blue Grille (305-358-5900; www.primebluegrille.com), 315 S Biscayne Blvd. Great steak, great seafood served in a chic space with expansive views of Biscayne Bay. Prime Blue Grille serves hormone-free, aged beef and plenty of local seafood. Chef Tindaro Losurdo designed the menu to take advantage of seasonal specialties and the abundance of local seafood. Featured steaks are all corn-fed and hormone free. Entrées $15 and up.

Provence Grill (305-373-1940), 1001 S. Miami Ave. This is my favorite place to go for dinner before attending musical events at nearby Tobacco Road. The authentic French cuisine is delicious, and the patio dining is pleasant. Try the palate-pleasing homemade pâté with vegetable sides and poached salmon in white wine sauce. Entrées $15 and up.

Set in the richness of deep mahogany walls, the award-winning **Morton's the Steakhouse** (305-400-9990; www.mortons.com), 1200 Brickell Ave., features the best in steaks and wines. Whether you select Oskar or filet Diane, end with Morton's legendary hot chocolate cake. You'll want to dress up a bit at this restaurant and, depending on beverage choices, expect dinner for two to be about $170. Open for lunch and dinner.

Coconut Grove

🐾 With tiny monkeys hanging off chandeliers, you'll know you're in for a unique treat at the bohemian-style **Baleen,** located in the Grove Isle Club and Resort (305-857-5007; www.groveisle.com), Four Grove Isle Dr. You'll find plump oversized crab cakes and Asian bouillabaisse. Breakfast 7 AM–10:30 AM, lunch 11 AM–2:30 PM, dinner 6:30 PM–10 PM, staying open until 11 PM on Fri. and Sat. nights. Dinner entrées $28–48.

Jaguar Ceviche Spoon Bar and Latam Grille (304-444-0216; www.jaguarspot.com) 3067 Grand Ave. Enjoy a sampler of ceviches with Latin flavors including mango, jalapeno, and avocado while enjoying passersby at this sidewalk café on the main drag in Coconut Grove. Lunch and dinner specials starting at $11.

Monty's Stone Crab Raw Bar (305-856-3992; www.montysstonecrab.com), 2550 S Bayshore Dr., offers live calypso and reggae music playing. You'll feel like you're on a Caribbean island as you dine on fresh, no-nonsense seafood while looking out over Biscayne Bay. Start with their famous she-crab soup, loaded with crab, for only $6. Then savor such dishes as mango barbecue salmon ($24), island-style red snapper ($24), or Florida bouillabaisse ($25). Entrées $15–39; crab and lobster dishes at market price. Open 11:30 PM–1 AM daily, sometimes later on the weekends.

Go up, up on the rooftop and you'll be rewarded with a stunning view while dining at **Panorama Restaurant** (305-447-8256; www.sonesta.com/coconutgrove), 2889 McFarlane Rd.

The contemporary restaurant is on the eighth floor of the Sonesta Hotel. Panorama serves Peruvian, Nuevo-Andean, and contemporary American food. And you'll keep your waistline intact, as they feature a complete South Beach Diet menu. Open daily for breakfast, lunch, and dinner. Entrées $18–27.

Coral Gables 33134

While visiting the **Biltmore Hotel** (305-445-1926; www.biltmorehotel.com), 1200 Anastasia Ave., you'll want to experience their world-class cuisine. Featuring the finest in French food and wine, the chic **Palme d'Or** is a favorite of both locals and celebrity guests. Entrées include duck confit, pan-seared wild striped bass, and seared baby lamb chop ($39–93). Open for dinner only. At **Fontana,** you'll dine in the open courtyard on Mediterranean and Italian fare. Entrées $22–39. Open for breakfast, lunch, and dinner. Poolside at **Cascade Poolside Bar & Grill,** you'll find light Caribbean specialties such as chilled Andalusian gazpacho and Don Quixote salad. Entrées $7–15. Open for lunch and dinner.

DELECTABLE CEVICHE SAMPLER AT JAGUAR IN COCONUT GROVE

Trish Riley

Canton Chinese Restaurant (305-448-3736; www.cantonrestaurants.com), 2614 Ponce de Leon Blvd., has been a local favorite for more than 25 years. Maybe it's the huge portions, or honey chicken and canton steak served family-style, or simply the friendliness of the staff that keeps everyone coming back year after year. Open for lunch and dinner. This place is busy, so reservations are a good idea.

Now in Doral you'll experience Hispanic cuisine at its finest at the lively **Chispa** (305-591-7166; www.chispa restaurant.com), 11500 NW 41st St. Sample such signature dishes as roasted sweet peppers and goat cheese ($7), salmon ($23) or shrimp ceviche ($10), roasted mahi *relleno* ($21), and shrimp and *lechon asado* risotto with *sofrito* sauce ($27). Open for breakfast, lunch, and dinner.

Christy's Restaurant (305-446-1400; www.christysrestaurant.com), 3101 Ponce de Leon Blvd., is famous for midwestern beef, such as the 16- to 18-ounce prime rib of beef ($38), and fresh Florida seafood, such as the fresh filet of snapper amandine ($29). Save room for the impressive baked Alaska for two ($11). Reservations required. Open for lunch 11:30 AM–4 PM Mon.–Fri., dinner 4 PM–10 PM Sun.–Thurs. and 4 PM–11 PM Fri. and Sat.

Jake's Bar and Grill (305-662-8632; www.jakesbar.net), 6901 Red Rd., offers excellent New American fare. Start with a selection of tapas ($10) or pan-roasted jumbo lump crab cake with smokehouse almond tartar ($12), then move on to *churrasco* grilled skirt steak with chimichurri, tostones, and beans and rice ($21). Open for dinner.

Another culinary celebrity, Chef Douglas Rodriguez, brings his Latin influence to a traditional steakhouse. At **Ola Steak** (305-461-4442; www.ola steak.com), 320 San Lorenzo Ave., Ste. 1320, in the Village of Merrick Park, you'll feast on 100 percent certified organic Uruguayan wet-aged beef and Black Angus dry-aged beef.

Dine outside overlooking Matheson Hammock at **The Red Fish Grill** (305-668-8788; www.redfishgrill.net), 9610 Old Cutler Rd. Start with a nice ceviche of the day, and then spice things up with a *churrasco* steak with Argentinean chimichurri, red peppers, and Spanish rice ($29). Entrées $19–38. Open for dinner only.

EATING OUT

Downtown Miami

Big Fish (305-373-1770), 55 SW Miami Ave. This funky, comfortable, mostly seafood restaurant puts you right on the edge of the Miami River, with an interesting and unique view of the city. The blend of crisp white linens on a decades-old dock seems a bit incongruous, but the elegance is a charming feature, as is the outdoor bar wrapped around a huge banyan tree. Entrées $10 and up.

Bijan's on the River (305-381-7778), 64 SE Fourth St. Here you can get seafood specialties at business-lunch prices, but the really cool thing about this place is the fact that it's located in Fort Dallas Park in a historic building that was part of the estate of Miami pioneer Julia Tuttle, who lived on the river in the early 1930s. Entrées $10 and up.

Charcuterie (305-576-7877), 3612 NE Second Ave. This small, simple French café tucked under an overpass on the south side of the Design District is much loved by locals in the know. The delicate yet rich French specialties include wild salmon baked *en papillote* (in a pastry-crust pillow), escargots, scallops *en croute* (also baked in a pastry crust), and tricolored fish tartare. Save room for the crème brûlée. Limited hours; closed Sun. Entrées $10 and up.

Garcia's Seafood Grille and Fish Market (305-375-0765), 398 NW North River Dr. A family concern for more than 30 years on this working riverfront, the restaurant has its own fishing enterprise, which guarantees the freshest possible catch—ask your server what's fresh. The snapper in champagne sauce was memorable. Entrées $10 and up.

Joe's Seafood Market and Restaurant (305-381-9329), 400 NW North River Dr. Joe's serves seafood in a casual atmosphere that's popular with the working crowd near the river. It's just a few blocks west of downtown on the Miami River. Entrées $10 and up.

Los Tres Amigos (305-324-1400), 1025 NW 20 St. A bit off the beaten path and out of the way of most tourist attractions, this little hole-in-the-wall Mexican restaurant is not fancy, but it's truly an authentic treasure—bring your Spanish dictionary. It's located just north of the Ryder Trauma Center and Jackson Memorial Hospital at the University of Miami School of Medicine. You'll feel more like you've come to the home of good friends when welcomed by the genuine, friendly hospitality that Mexicans call their own. My husband and I wheeled our patient, son Bud, into the restaurant to help lift his spirits when we visited him at the hospital. The staff helped us cheer him up and sold us a cool Mexican T-shirt for him to pull over his hospital PJs. Entrées $7 and up.

One Ninety Restaurant (305-576-9779) 190 NE 46th St. Chef/owner Alan Hughes presents a tasting menu in a comfortable, urban atmosphere that fits nicely in this old Miami community of Bueno Vista, near Morningside, which was once grand and is now up and coming again. Nestled in a vin-tage storefront, the concrete floors and dingy windows belie the bohemian, eclectic flair within. After hours One Ninety becomes a hipsters' club that showcases live performances, DJs, and dancing. Spanish tapas, South American ceviche, and French and Asian flavors all are represented in the edgy offerings. Sun. brunch (with surprisingly traditional dishes). Closed Mon. Entrées $10 and up.

Tobacco Road (305-374-1198), 626 S Miami Ave. Known as the oldest bar in town, Tobacco Road was built on the site of a Native American trading post on the Miami River and has hosted such luminaries as Billie Holiday and Cab Calloway. Today it serves up the best local music on weekends along with steak and lobster specials and a mean Greek salad. It's great for after work or after the clubs have closed. $10 and up.

UVA (305-754-9022; www.uva-69.com), 6900 Biscayne Blvd., offers delectable Latin-inspired cuisine in the MiMO district of Miami. I enjoyed a Caribbean avocado and mango crab salad, and my terrier was treated to grilled chicken breast, cut in tiny bites and served with a side bowl of water. Friendly service and comfortable atmosphere. Entrées $10 and up.

Wine 69 (305-759-0122; wine69miami.com), 6909 Biscayne Blvd., is a favorite among my friends who live in the area for its ambiance and for the friendliness of owner Ben Neji, who serves up a variety of wines with cheeses, olives, nuts, fruit, and all the best menu items to complement the wines. Entrées $12.95 and up.

Coconut Grove
Mix and mingle with local residents at the **Greenstreet Outdoor Lounge & Restaurant** (305-444-0244; www .greenstreetcafe.net), 3468 Main Hwy. The popular spot with red velvet sofas

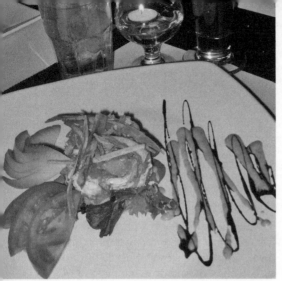

CARIBBEAN AVOCADO AND MANGO CRAB SALAD AT UVA IN MIAMI'S MiMO (MIAMI MODERN) DISTRICT

on the sidewalk offers something for everyone, from tabbouleh salad ($8), jalapeño poppers ($8), or fried calamari ($8.50) as appetizers to pesto ravioli ($16), a margarita pizza ($12), or orange duck ($19) for an entrée. You'll want to be early in line for Sunday breakfast, to get one of their famous muffins. Open for breakfast, lunch, and dinner daily 7:30 AM–10:45 PM, and till 11:45 PM on Fri. and Sat.

The Nicaraguan steakhouse, **Los Ranchos Steak & Seafood Cantina** (305-461-8222; www.losranchossteakhouse .com), 3015 Grand Ave., is known for its *churrasco* ($17–20) served with *gallo pinto* (spiced rice and beans). You'll also want to try their *tres leches* ("Three Milks") dessert. Entrées $11–20. Open for lunch and dinner noon–10 PM Sun., 11:30 AM–10 PM Mon.–Fri., noon–11 PM Sat.

Scotty's Landing (305-854-2626; www.sailmiami.com/scottys.htm), 3381 Pan American Dr., next to the Grove Key Marina and Miami City Hall. At this charming local favorite, enjoy live local music (I especially like Valerie Wisecracker and the 18 Wheelers) and

fresh seafood on the outdoor patio overlooking the water. It's nothing fancy, but it's a great place for a sunny afternoon lunch or dinner. Entrées $10 and up.

Little Havana

Casa Juancho (305-642-2452; www .casajuancho.com), 2436 SW Eighth St. Serrano hams hang from the wood ceiling, against a backdrop of brick walls and a terra-cotta tile floor, creating an inviting, warm den of luscious smells and jovial patter. A piano player works a corner of the bar, busy red-and-green-vested waiters full of information float all around, and there's a long dessert table filled with everything from cakes and pies to pastries. Seasoned every few months during the 18-month drying process, the hams are the restaurant's signature offering. Sliced to paper thinness, the meat is a tasty combination of salt and seasonings. Casa Juancho is also famous for its paella, a mixture of rice, vegetables, sausage, chicken, and fish. Live Latin and Flamenco music nightly. $12 and up.

Hy-Vong (305-446-3674), 3458 SW Eighth St. As incongruous as it seems, this authentic Vietnamese restaurant sits right on Callé Ocho, the main drag of Little Havana. Passersby might never guess that in this tiny hole-in-the-wall storefront is the best Vietnamese in town, and thanks to its lack of fluff and puff, it's extremely reasonably priced. The place has its own little history, even if it's not about Cuban boat lifts. Owner Kathy Manning, a math teacher, took in a Vietnamese refugee sponsored by her church in 1975, and five years later the pair created the restaurant together. It's a complete success. Chef Tung Nguyen still cooks in the back, and Kathy is hostess and server. There are only a dozen tables, and they don't take reservations, so there's pretty much always a waiting line outside. But the home-made kim chi (an appetizer of fermented cabbage), lettuce rolls, roast duck with black currant sauce and avocado, grouper in mango sauce, and watercress and ripe tomato salad are always worth the effort. There's an eclectic imported beer list, too. Closed Mon. $12 and up.

Versaille's (305-445-7614), 3555 SW Eighth St. A neighborhood fixture for 30 years, Versaille's, with its white Formica tables and green vinyl and chrome dinettes contrasted against regal wooden columns and chandeliers dangling from the ceiling, is a favorite stop for visiting presidents and politicos. It's well known for its ardent discussions among earnest cigar lovers. Forsake your diet for a day when you choose to dine here—Cuban food is not known for its slimming qualities. The delicious, comfort-style fare is rich with starches and buttery sauces. Each dish, served by white-shirted waiters with black bowties, includes a pile of rice, either white, yellow, or the dark, smoky-flavored *moros*, with black beans. Don't forget to sample the sangria. The thick dessert confections are voluptuous treats offered with warm smiles and *cafecito Cubano*. $10 and up.

✳ Selective Shopping
BOOKSTORES
Coral Gables
You'll always find something new at the independent **Books & Books** (305-442-4408; www.booksandbooks .com), 265 Aragon Ave. Inspiring readers and writers with its architectural beauty, the 9,000-square-foot Mediterranean-style building (circa 1927) is on the Coral Gables Register of Historic Places. Note the original tile floors, fireplace, beamed ceilings, and floor-to-ceiling dark-wood shelves. The

locally owned bookstore also has locations in Miami Beach and Bal Harbour (see *South Beach and Miami Oceanside*). And at the Levenger Outlet in Delray Beach (see *South Palm Beach County*), you'll find book accessories and reading tools. Open 9 AM–11 PM every day.

Enjoy browsing rare and antique books at the quaint **Fifteenth Street Books** (305-442-2344; www.fifteenthstreet books.com), 296 Aragon Ave. The bookstore has a nice collection of Cuban and rare 15th-century books, and a comfy reading room. It also houses Gladioli's, an antiques and art gallery with furnishings, jewelry, and miscellaneous collectibles. Open 11 AM–10 PM.

FARMER'S MARKET The **Coconut Grove Farmers Market** (305-794-1464), 3300 Grand Ave. and Margaret St., is open 10 AM–5 PM Saturdays, year-round. It's run by Glaser Organic Farm, specializing in vegan and natural food. You'll find everything from tropical produce to exotic plants here.

SHOPS
Coral Gables
Anchored by Neiman Marcus and Nordstrom, the exclusive shopping destination **Merrick Park** (305-529-0200; www.villageofmerrickpark.com), 358 San Lorenzo Ave., is known for firsts. Designers such as **CH Carolina Herrera** (305-448-3333; www.carolina herrera.com), **Donald J Pliner** (305-774-5880; www.donaldjpliner.com), and **Jimmy Choo** (305-443-6124; www.jimmychoo.com) are among the first boutiques to grace South Florida at Merrick Park. Trendy moms will also want to bring the kids to **Janie & Jack** (305-447-0810; www.janieand jack.com), and **Pottery Barn Kids** (305-446-6511; www.potterybarn

kids.com). Not your average mall; the upscale village atmosphere features tropical foliage, elegant fountains, and unique architecture. You'll also have a wide selection of fine eateries from which to choose. Shops are open 10 AM–9 PM Mon.–Sat., 12 PM–6 PM Sun.

Downtown Miami

You'll be in the heart of downtown Miami, but you'll feel like you are at a Caribbean market at **Bayside Marketplace** (305-577-3344; www.bayside marketplace.com), 401 Biscayne Blvd. Located near the American Airlines Arena, the lively open-air mall features calypso and reggae music in the central entertainment area.

Little Havana to Go (305-857-9720), 1442 SW Eighth St. Find all manner of colorful Cuban-style souvenirs, including the popular cotton shirts, *guayaberas;* colorful hammocks; replicas of toy soldiers; chessmen; and other artifacts from Cuba's pre-Castro days. Open 11 AM–6 PM Mon.–Sat. and 11 AM–5 PM Sun. Open late on "Cultural Fridays," last Fri. of the month 11 AM–11 PM.

Old Cuba, the Collection (305-643-6269), 1561 SW Eighth St. The store features books of Cuban history and others with beautiful pictures of the off-limits island, as well as Cuban music, artwork, clothing, and trinkets. These souvenirs of the past are available for a single purpose—to keep Cuban culture alive and thriving for those who don't know, and for those who can't forget. Owner Jackie Perez keeps the memories alive for her parents, and for those like her, who were raised in the United States. Open 10 AM–6 PM Mon.–Sat.

Stoneage Antiques (305-633-5114; www.stoneage-antiques.com), 3236 N.W. South River Dr. This mishmash of stuff spilling across the grounds looks like a junkyard shack, but the warehouse full of 30 years' worth of collected treasures stacked floor to ceiling is sure to deliver something of interest to everyone. Whether you're in the market for vintage fishing gear, a Native American–style dugout canoe, signs from Florida landmarks long gone, maps, headlights, lanterns, wringer washers, or coils of ships' rope, you'll find it here. Run by father-and-son team Gary and Ryan Stone, the store specializes in nautical antiques. Providing film props is a substantial chunk of their business. Open 9 AM–4:45 PM Mon.–Sat.

✳ Entertainment

MUSIC

Coral Gables

You'll find several world-class jazz and classical artists performing at **Coral Gables Congregational Church** (305-448-7421), 3010 De Soto Blvd., Coral Gables. The beautiful church (circa 1923–1925), built in the Mediterranean Revival style of that era and across from the beautiful Biltmore Hotel, features a bell tower and grand Baroque entranceway—a favorite of brides. The church presents several renowned artists and musical programs, such as their Summer Concert Series, throughout the year.

Plymouth Congregational Church (305-444-6521; www.plymouthmiami .com), 3400 Devon Rd., Coral Gables, offers musical performances and author speaking engagements—I saw Susan Sontag there. Built in 1897, the church is a fine architectural treasure.

Miami

For more than six decades the **Florida Grand Opera** (1-800-741-1010; www.fgo.org), 1300 Biscayne Blvd., has been thrilling audiences throughout South Florida with performances of favorites such as *The Barber of Seville, Madama Butterfly,* and *Carmen.*

Olympia Theater at Gusman Center for the Performing Arts (305-374-2444; www.gusmancenter.org), 174 E. Flagler Ave. The beautifully restored Olympia Theater lends insight into the glamour enjoyed in Miami during the city's early heydays. Opened in 1926 as a silent-movie house, the theater must have been extremely popular, as it was the first air-conditioned building in the South. Rescued from demolition and renovated to its original splendor by Miami philanthropist Maurice Gusman in 1975, the theater's exquisite architecture and design are stunning. The stage has hosted Elvis Presley and Luciano Pavarotti and continues to be the most sophisticated venue in town for traveling entertainers. It's home to Miami's Maximum Dance Company and the Miami International Film Festival. Tickets $10 and up.

THEATER

Downtown Miami
The new **Adrienne Arsht Center for the Performing Arts** (305-9494-6722; www.miamiperformingartscenter.org),

13000 Biscayne Blvd., has opened near Biscayne Bay to offer world class musical and Broadway shows.

Coral Gables
The 600-seat **Actors' Playhouse at The Miracle Theatre** (305-444-9293; www.actorsplayhouse.org), 280 Miracle Mile, presents professional award-winning theatrical productions for all ages. The balcony of the main stage has been transformed into the 300-seat Children's Theatre. In the intimate 100-seat black box, you'll experience innovative new work and cutting-edge experimental theater. In 2009, expect performances such as *Les Miserables* and the world premiere of *Havana Bourgeoisie* by Florida playright Carlos Lacamara. Mainstage performances: Wed.–Sat. evenings, and Sun. matinee. $48 Fri. and Sat.; $40 all other times. At the Children's Theatre, all seats are $15.

GableStage at the Biltmore (305-445-1119; www.gablestage.org), 1200 Anastasia Ave., presents innovative and thought-provoking productions, including premieres of award-winning plays in South Florida. Performances Thurs.,

PLYMOUTH CONGREGATIONAL CHURCH, CORAL GABLES

Trish Riley

Fri., and Sat. at 8 PM; Sun. at 2 PM and 7 PM. Tickets: $43 Sat., $37 all other times.

Miami Design District

Contemporary performances are presented at the **Miami Light Project** (305-576-4350; www.miamilightproject .com), 3000 Biscayne Blvd., where you'll see cutting-edge productions along with performances by the world-renowned Mad Cat Theatre Company.

✳ Special Events

January: The annual **International Chocolate Festival,** held by Fairchild Gardens (305-667-1651; www.fairchildgarden.org), 10901 Old Cutler Rd., is for the true chocolate addict. Watch cooking demonstrations, buy chocolate orchids and cacao trees, attend lectures, explore Fairchild's gardens and—of course—taste some of the greatest chocolate ever made! Admission is $20 for adults, free for

ORCHIDS IN THE CONSERVATORY AT FAIRCHILD GARDENS

Sandra Friend

children under five. Held in the last week of Jan.

February: The annual **Coconut Grove Art Festival** (www.coconut groveartsfest.com), McFarlane Rd., South Bayshore Dr., and Pan American Dr., is the number one arts festival in the nation. More than 300 artisans are selected by jury, with only the best showcasing their arts and crafts. Usually held over the President's Day holiday weekend, 9 AM–6 PM Fri.–Mon. Admission $7 per day or $17 for all three days.

Early June: The annual weeklong **Goombay Festival** (305-448-9501), 3802 Oak Ave., Coconut Grove, celebrates the Grove's heritage. First settled by Bahamian immigrants in the 1890s, today the Grove transforms Grand Avenue into Nassau's Bay Street. You'll see bright and colorful Junkanoo costumes, eat Bahamian foods, and shop a wide variety of crafts while listening to the lively Caribbean beat. The festival has become the largest black heritage festival in the United States.

July: Taste something different at the **International Mango Festival** (305-667-1651; www.fairchildgarden.org), Fairchild Tropical Botanic Garden, 10901 Old Cutler Rd., Coral Gables, where you can learn more about how to cook with this tropical fruit. Enjoy the Mango Brunch and Mango Auction, while kids enjoy special activities.

October: The **Miami Carnival** (305-653-1877; www.miamicarnival.net), Bicentennial Park, 1075 Biscayne Blvd., has been an annual event since 1984. Miami sizzles with traditional celebrations of the West Indies. Come for the Main Parade and Jr. Kiddies Parade to see the colorful costumes (NE 36th St. and NE Second Ave.), and then stay for the food and live music, which goes on until 11 PM.

MIRACLE MILE SHOPS IN CORAL GABLES

My favorite shopping area is the **Miracle Mile** (305-569-0311; www.shopcoralgables.com) in Coral Gables. Its spacious streets, great eateries, and friendly people are worthwhile reasons to take a drive away from the beach and explore inland. Service seems to be tops at every shop. **M & M's Maternity** (305-448-7386), 357 Miracle Mile, provides a personal dresser to greet you and help you select just one piece or an entire wardrobe. There's no pressure, though; you can browse on your own if you like. The staff want you to feel comfortable and are willing to wait on you hand and foot—a nice treat when you're tired and puffy. And the prices are low ($8–30 for tops; $12–60 for bottoms), too. While the shopping district of Miracle Mile is flush with bridal boutiques, you'll also find specialty shops such as **The Dog Bar** (305-441-8979; www.dogbar.com), 259 Miracle Mile, where you can dress up your dog or cat in the finest apparel, then spoil your pet further with a unique toy or healthy treat. Open 11 AM–7 PM Mon.–Wed., 11 AM–9 PM Thurs. and Fri., 10 AM–7 PM Sat., 12 PM–5 PM Sun. Also on Jefferson behind Lincoln Rd. in South Beach (see *South Beach*). To get that cool Miami look, head to **Guayaberas Etc.** (305-441-9891; www.guayaberashirt.com), 270 Miracle Mile, for chic tropical wear. Open 10–7 Mon.–Sat. And along with **Graziano's Restaurant** shop (305-460-0001; www.grazianosgroup.com), 394 Giralda Ave., you'll also find more than 40 places to eat. When your feet get tired, hop on the free **Coral Gables Trolley** for a view of the city (see *Getting Around*).

SOUTH BEACH

Trendy South Miami Beach has been a mecca for the "beautiful people" for decades. All along Ocean Drive you'll find celebrities, party-goers, models, and moguls, but South Beach (SoBe) is very family friendly as well. Rich with art and architecture, the Art Deco Historic District is between Ocean Drive and Alton Road. Here pink, turquoise, and yellow boutique hotels and neon eateries dominate the skyline. All along Collins Avenue and Lincoln Road you'll find high-fashion shops and eateries. Partygoers will want to take an afternoon siesta. While most clubs open at 10 PM, they typically don't get moving until after midnight. Even if you aren't into club hopping, you'll want to experience at least one club, as this area is like no other in the United States. For those who remember the TV show *Miami Vice*, Española Way is where most of the outside shots were filmed.

✳ To See

ART GALLERY Located in the Art Deco Historic District, **The Wolfsonian-FIU** (305-531-1001; www.wolfsonian.org), 1001 Washington Ave., South Beach, displays fine arts produced between 1885 and 1945. You'll see European and American exhibits, such as a poster from the World's Fair and many from the age of machinery. My favorite piece, in the Celtic Revival style, is by acclaimed Irish illustrator and stained-glass artist Harry Clarke. The stained-glass window panel was commissioned in 1926 for the International Labor Building, League of Nations, Geneva, but it was never installed. The 71.5-by-40-inch window features, in exquisite detail, 12 vignettes of Irish poets' and writers' works, such as *The Weaver's Grave* by Seumas O'Kelly. Open 12 PM–6 PM Sat.–Tues., 12 PM–9 PM Thurs. and Fri. Closed Wed. Adults $7; seniors, students, and children 6–12 $5; under 6 free.

HISTORIC PLACES

South Beach

The marker on Española Way indicates the **Art Deco Historic District,** a 1-square-mile area in South Beach. With its Spanish and nautical influence, this popular district includes some of the finest architectural examples of the Bohemian period. Note the cobalt blue neon on the 1939 Breakwater Hotel, the window eyebrows on the 1954 Shelbourne, and the porthole windows and smokestacklike neon tower of the 1938 Essex House Hotel. Art deco buildings were initially painted white, off-white, or beige with a contrasting color on just the trim. It was not until the 1980s that vibrant colors covered the main sections of the buildings, when Leonard Horowitz of the Miami Design Preservation League (MDPL) designed the color schemes for more than 150 buildings. The late 1930s and early '40s brought the "streamline" period, with the sleek nautical design of luxury cruise ships. You'll see this design incorporated into many boutique hotels. The mid-1950s brought larger buildings with a minimalist midcentury modern style of architecture that signaled the end of the art deco period.

Walking along Ocean Drive, you'll find yourself standing in front of the **Versace Mansion.** The home is only a few feet from the sidewalk, providing an excellent view of its architecture. **Casa Casuarina,** at 1116 Ocean Dr., was built in 1930. It was modeled after the Alcazar de Colon in Santo Domingo (built by Christopher Columbus's son circa 1510), reputed to be the oldest home in the Western Hemisphere. In 1992, famed fashion designer Gianni Versace purchased the home as a beach house. Designer of the 1980s series *Miami Vice* look—a pastel T-shirt and white jacket often seen on Don Johnson's "Sonny Crockett"—Versace was influential in creating the new South Miami Beach scene. Soon after his arrival it became the "place to be seen," and many posh eateries and boutiques popped up along Ocean Drive, making SoBe a destination for the rich and famous. Madonna, Sly Stallone, and Elton John were frequent guests at the mansion. Unfortunately the life of the much-loved Versace was cut short in 1997 when he was murdered at the steps of the home. Casa Casuarina has since been sold to a private owner. The home is now a members-only club and can be rented out for functions if you have the dough—rentals start at $10,000 and are creatively catered by **Barton G** (see *Dining Out*).

MEMORIAL & **The Holocaust Memorial** (305-538-1663; www.holocaustmmb .org), 1933–1945 Meridian Ave., Miami Beach. Emotional and moving, hundreds of bronze sculptures of tormented men, women, and children cling to a giant arm tattooed with a number from Auschwitz, the arm reaching to the sky in search of hope and life. The central sculpture is accessed from a tunnel where haunting voices of Israeli children sing songs of the Holocaust over an audio speaker. The granite Memorial Wall details the chilling period during which more than 6 million Jews were murdered. The memorial is outdoors and free to all. Open 9 AM–9 PM daily.

MUSEUMS

The **Bass Museum of Art** (305-673-7530; www.bassmuseum.org), 2121 Park Ave., located in the heart of the historic Art Deco Historic District, offers a fine display of European paintings and exhibitions of contemporary art. The 1930 art deco building houses five galleries, a café, and an extensive gift shop. On the grand ramp is a monumental tapestry, an altar piece by Botticelli and Ghirlandaio. Open 10 AM–5 PM Tues.–Sat., 11 AM–5 PM Sun. Free docent tours every Sat. at 2. Adults $8, seniors and students $6, children under 6 free. The second Thursday of each month is free from 6 AM to 9 PM.

The **Jewish Museum of Florida** (305-672-5044; www.jewishmuseum .com), 301 Washington Ave., is housed in a 1936 synagogue. The art deco building features 80 stained-glass win-

Courtesy Greater Miami Convention and Visitors Bureau
HOLOCAUST MEMORIAL, MIAMI BEACH

dows, a marble bimah, and a copper dome. The museum displays traveling exhibits reflecting Florida Jewish history from 1763. Open 10 AM–5 PM ues.–Sun. Adults $6, seniors 65+ and students $5, children under 6 free. On Saturday the public enjoys free admission.

✳ To Do

WALKING TOURS A trip to South Florida wouldn't be complete without a tour of the nation's largest **20th-Century National Register Historic District** (see *Historic Places*). Starting at the Miami Design Preservation League (MDPL) Art Deco Welcome Center, you'll be guided past some of the 800 historical buildings created in the 1920s and '30s. The 90-minute tour of the **Art Deco Historic District** (305-672-2014; www.mdpl.org), 1001 Ocean Dr., Miami Beach, features three dominant architectural styles: art deco, Mediterranean Revival, and MiMo (Miami Modernism). Tours begin at 10:30 AM Wed., Fri., Sat., and Sun., and at 6:30 PM Thurs. Adults $20, seniors and students $15, children under 12 free.

If you want to view the area on your own the Art Deco Welcome Center offers **self-guided audio tours** of the Art Deco Historic District in English, Spanish, Portuguese, German, or French. Offered 10 AM–4 PM daily. Adults $20, seniors and children $15.

✳ Green Space

BEACH South Beach is the scene for glamorous babes and beefcake guys. It's fair game to lose your shirt and wear that racy thong—if you dare. The beautiful shoreline is a sight to behold.

BOTANICAL GARDEN Miami Beach Botanical Garden (305-673-7256; www.mbgarden.org), 2000 Convention Center Dr. Nestled between the busy streets of Miami Beach lies a green oasis that's a perfect spot for a quick break from the day. A half hour spent strolling the small, shady patch of growth or contemplating life from a bench overlooking a pond filled with water lilies in the Japanese garden can restore your enthusiasm. A bamboo garden and stone pagoda complete the peaceful ambiance. A circular fountain lined with dark red miniature roses graces the entryway, and the garden's boardroom and the glass-roofed conservatory flank a terrace with tall

Trish Riley

BABES OF SOUTH BEACH, MIAMI BEACH

hedges. A tall palm frond stretches through the second-story ceiling of the glass shelter, which protects the garden's collection of more than 300 hundred orchids. The gardens are cool and colorful, with native butterfly catchers and fragrant subtropicals forming a hedge against the city streets, but the roar of traffic can still be heard over the cackling green parrots roosting in the trees. A gift shop sells gardening implements and accessories, artwork, and unusual books. Special art and music events are frequently held here; call for details. Open 9 AM–5 PM Tues.–Sun. Free.

GOLF Miami Beach Golf Club (305-532-3350; www.miamibeachgolfclub.com), 2301 Alton Rd. Totally renovated from its earliest days in 1923, this course has been patronized by Miami Beach pioneers and served as a training ground for soldiers during World War II. It continues to be a beautiful course in a great location. Open daily 6:30 AM–8 PM. Price includes cart and range balls.

✳ Lodging

HOTELS, MOTELS, AND RESORTS The Alexander Hotel (305-865-6500; www.alexanderhotel .com) 5225 Collins Ave. This oceanfront hotel is an impressive renovation on Miami Beach's Millionaire Row between Bal Harbour and South Beach. Its Caribbean decor of deep, rich woods and colorful fabrics lends elegance to the popular hotel. Features include conference facilities, a spa, oceanfront pools and dock, and the premier restaurant for beef, Shula's Steakhouse. One- and two-bedroom suites. $150 and up.

☙ The Angler's Boutique Resort (305-534-9600; www.theanglersresort .com), 660 Washington Ave. This new all-suite boutique hotel offers a wide array of unusual amenities, such as private rooftop terraces and gardens with outdoor showers. The fully renovated historic property two blocks off Miami Beach is said to have been a favorite vacation destination for Ernest Hemingway. Bring a pen; perhaps you'll find inspiration here. Pet-friendly. $250 and up.

Avalon Hotel (305-538-0133 or 1-800-933-3306; www.avalonhotel.com), 700

Ocean Dr. Decorated with Danish-style furnishings and plush linens, the 104 rooms at the Avalon also have data ports and refrigerators. Complimentary breakfast buffet. $175 and up.

The Blue Moon (305-673-2262; www.bluemoonhotel.com), 944 Collins Ave. Renovated from a pair of art deco and Mediterranean hotels, this 75-room vintage property boasts smallish but stylish rooms featuring all the amenities. There's also a sensuous lounge, a nice respite from the SoBe swirl. $150 and up.

Clevelander Hotel (305-531-3485 or 1-800-815-6829; www.clevelander .com), 1020 Ocean Dr. This is a hot spot for the hip. Ear plugs and dark window shades are among the amenities offered at the Clevelander, which is party central on South Beach. Currently undergoing renovations, guests may be rerouted to the Clevelander's sister hotel, the Essex, during some phases of the project. The rooms are small, simple, bright, and cool, but what else do you need? Even if you're not staying here, chances are you'll enjoy a few drinks at one of the five bars, such as the alluring poolside bar that opens onto Ocean Drive at 10th—where "the buzz" starts, they say. $90 and up.

Comfort Inn and Suites South Beach (305-531-3406), 1238 Collins Ave. This beautifully renovated 1929 boutique hotel features 28 rooms and suites with crisp damask linens and cool lines. Retro terrazzo lobby and bar, conference room, continental breakfast, and multilingual staff. A fitness center is close by. $90 and up.

Crescent Suites: Miami Beach Hotel (305-531-5197 or 1-800-634-3119; www.crescentsuites.com), 1420 Ocean Dr. This all-suites boutique property is clean and super convenient, with rooms with kitchenettes and separate bedrooms—a plus for families. The decor is SoBe chic. $150 and up.

The Delano (305-672-2000 or 1-800-555-5001; www.delano-hotel.com), 1685 Collins Ave. Created by Ian Schrager of Studio 54 fame in New York, this is not your average hotel. Oozing cool, sleek chic, it's simple and breezy, with polished wood floors and gauzy curtains suspended from high ceilings. At the legendary pool, designed by Philippe Starck, the water actually flows over the edges. Surrounded by private bungalows and dining cabanas, the pool actually makes the beach in the background seem a lesser destination. Rooms are white on white and, like the rest, sleek yet bare. This is a place for the haves: the rich and famous are at home here. $150 and up.

Eden Roc Renaissance Resort and Spa (786-276-0526; www.edenroc resort.com), 4525 Collins Ave. Designed by famed architect Morris Lapidus in 1956, the Eden Roc has been updated to refresh yet preserve Lapidus's unique and luxurious styling, which includes beautiful natural materials such as black marble and

MIAMI BEACH
Courtesy Greater Miami Convention and Visitors Bureau

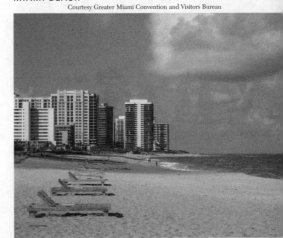

mahogany. The broad lobby welcomes guests with a vast view of the ocean. I attended a wine tasting at the Eden Roc with my friend Kathleen one afternoon only to get drenched as we ran from the car to the hotel. We found our way to the famous Spa of Eden, where we were welcomed with hair dryers and towels. The atmosphere is so glamorous that we kept imagining stars such as Elizabeth Taylor, Ann Margret, and Frank Sinatra visiting the hotel in the past. More recent guests include gorgeous George Clooney and the beautiful Whitney Houston. $150 and up.

Fontainebleau Miami Beach (305-538-2000; www.fontainebleau.com), 4441 Collins Ave. One of Miami Beach's older and memorable properties, the Morris Lapidus–designed Fontainebleau has just completed a major renovation, but it retains its charm and glamour while jet-setting into the future with the latest in room styling and amenities. The large complex includes pools, the beach, and fitness and business accoutrements to meet the needs of everyone in the family. $150 and up.

The Hotel (305-531-2222 or 1-877-843-4683; www.thehotelofsouthbeach .com), 801 Collins Ave. Even though it's a block off Ocean Drive, you can still catch a view of the ocean from the rooftop pool of this exclusive Todd Oldham–designed boutique hotel. J. Lo and Lenny Kravitz are said to have stayed here before buying their own Miami Beach digs. The Hotel features a full gym, a lounge bar, and the nationally famous Wish restaurant. The whimsical rooms are decorated in earthy hues with tie-dyed accents. $150 and up.

Hotel Impala (305-673-2021 or 1-800-646-7252; www.hotelimpalamiami beach.com), 1228 Collins Ave. Mick Jagger, Julia Roberts, Sean "P. Diddy" Combs, and Danny Glover are among the luminaries who have availed themselves of this Mediterranean-style treat, which has just 17 carefully appointed rooms and an award-winning restaurant, Spiga. $90 and up.

The Loews Miami Beach Hotel (305-604-1601; www.loewshotels.com), 1601 Collins Ave. Tall, imposing, and relatively new compared to the historic properties around it, the Loews has its own cachet. From its beautiful grand entrance to its sculpted beachfront pool, this hotel was created with your pleasure in mind. Fitness club, kids' camp, data ports, and six restaurants and lounges. $250 and up.

The Marlin (305-604-5063 or 1-800-OUTPOST; www.marlinhotel.com), 1200 Collins Ave. Created by music-industry honcho and hotelier Chris Blackwell, the Marlin caters to the music crowd. If you like the hip-hop and techno that prevail on the beach today, you'll love the sleek, sci-fi stainless look and pulsing activity that never ends at this locale. It's home to South Beach Studios, where rock 'n' roll reigns. $150 and up.

The National Hotel (305-532-2311 or 1-800-327-8370; www.nationalhotel .com), 1677 Collins Ave. If you like to swim laps, you'll love the challenge of the 205-foot-long pool at this hotel. Built in 1939 at the start of the Beach's art deco days, the National continues to serve as an icon of sustainability in a fast-paced environment. Fully renovated in 1996, the family-owned hotel is one of the largest in the historic district, with 150 rooms and a trilevel penthouse, conference facilities, restaurant, pool lounge, and martini bar. It's a favorite among those who like historic tradition as well as upscale amenities in a chic setting. City view and oceanfront rooms. $250 and up.

The Palms (305-534-0505 or 1-800-550-0505; www.thepalmshotel.com), 3025 Collins Ave. A large, business-oriented hotel located just north of the nightlife, the Palms has the beach, a pool, and elegant dining in addition to conference and meeting facilities. The rooms are sleek and spare, decorated for function as well as form. $90 and up.

The Raleigh (305-534-6300 or 1-800-432-4317; www.raleighhotel.com), 1775 Collins Ave. With its beautiful, elegantly outlined pool made famous by Esther Williams's water ballet, the Raleigh has retained its original art deco charm and historic beauty throughout the decades, and it continues to generate rave reviews from *Condé Nast Traveler* and *Travel + Leisure*. Decorated in a casual island style, the rooms are cool and charming. In addition to the restaurant, bar, lounge, and pool, the hotel features a ballroom and conference facilities. The 104 rooms and penthouse feature Egyptian cotton, 400-thread-count sheets as well as gourmet mini bars. $150 and up.

The Ritz-Carlton, South Beach (786-276-4000; www.ritzcarlton.com), 1 Lincoln Rd. How about your own beachside bed? Cabanas at the Ritz-Carlton are curtained plush beds perfect for daytime sunbathing, massage, and private evenings *à deux* (or *trois?*). Renovated from the 1953 DiLido Hotel and designed by legendary architect Morris Lapidus, this Ritz is definitely ritzy. Diners may enjoy fine cuisine outdoors on the beach at the DiLido Beach Club or "restyled American" cuisine—comfort food with a twist—at Americana. Just about all other cuisines, including Asian, Mediterranean, African Euro, and Caribbean, are offered at the hotel's other restaurants and lounges. The

Parisian spa exemplifies the elegance of this hotel, unmatched on South Beach. There are 376 rooms, including an exclusive VIP club level and penthouse. $250 and up.

Royal Palm Resort Hotel (786-837-6164; www.royalpalmmiamibeach-px.trvlclick.com), 1545 Collins Ave. This traditional high-rise, with art deco touches and 1950s–'60s MiMO (Miami Modern) flair, has modern amenities. It's a short walk to the SoBe nightlife and celebrity-studded beach. Restaurant, pool, lounge. $250 and up.

The Shore Club (305-695-3100 or 1-877-640-9500; www.shoreclub.com), 1901 Collins Ave. Another exclusive property created by Ian Schrager, the Shore Club has Asian- and Moroccan-inspired gardens, a sleek rooftop pool and spa, a penthouse, and shops. Its sultry Red Room lounge features glowing red walls and a polished red floor, and the world-renowned SkyBar is a late-night destination of the hip and famous. $250 and up.

The Tides Hotel (305-604-5070; www.thetideshotel.com), 1220 Ocean Dr. Renovated from an enduring landmark into a destination hotel considered to be one of the most beautiful on Ocean Drive, the Tides's wide-stair entry sets a dramatic stage for the most exciting events. Built in 1936, this property has seen its share of celebrities, including Lauren Hutton, Katie Couric, Ben Affleck, and J.Lo. (My parents, who are celebs in my book, honeymooned here in 1946.) Today, instead of its original 115 rooms, the hotel has 46 rooms and suites, each coolly appointed with crisp cottons, polished wood, CD players with CDs, and a telescope to keep a close eye on what's arguably the most famous beach in the country. $250 and up.

The Tudor Hotel (305-534-2934 or 1-800-843-2934; www.tudorsouth

beach.com), 1111 Collins Ave. This basic hotel in the heart of South Beach is not as chic as some, but it's not as expensive, either. The rooms have tile floors and dark decor, and the penthouse suites have nice rooftop terraces. $90 and up.

Waldorf Towers Hotel (305-531-7684; www.waldorftowers.com), 860 Ocean Dr. This small, cool hotel in the heart of the SoBe action has a terrace restaurant from which diners can keep an eye on passersby—the thing to do on Ocean Drive. Famous guests have included Ivana Trump and Florida governor Jeb Bush. In-house restaurant Primetime offers breakfast, brunch, and dinner. Rooms have city or ocean view. $90 and up.

Essex House Hotel and Suites (305-534-2700; www.essexhotel.com), 1001 Collins Ave. Built in 1938, it features art deco lines from luxury cruise ships—in the lobby as well as the 61 rooms and 19 spacious suites, where beige and russet linens accent rich mahogany furnishings. The bathrooms will make any diva squeal with delight. They're so enormous, you can spread out when getting ready for a night of clubbing. They also have several mirrors, including a lighted makeup mirror. After a night on the town, you'll be glad the spacious Jacuzzi is large enough so that your entire party can sit around it soaking their feet. Between beach time and clubbing, enjoy sitting in the tropical courtyard with cascading bougainvilleas and a burbling fountain, or lounging in the lobby where you'll be sure to meet new people. Service is excellent and the concierge will be more than happy to make dinner reservations for you or put you on your favorite nightclub's list (see *Nightclubs*). You'll find phenomenal deals in low season with rates from $89 to 139. High-season rates run $179–249.

Hotel Astor (305-531-8081 or 1-800-270-4981; www.hotelastor.com), 956 Washington Ave. You'll know you are in for a new experience as you approach the breathtaking cut coral stone façade of this 1936 art deco hotel. In the lobby, the original Vitrolite wall panels surround stark white modern furniture, and a dramatic staircase leads you down to the Metro Kitchen and Bar. Outside you can relax in the garden by the vertical water sculpture. The quaint boutique hotel offers 40 rooms and suites ($170–420) decorated in crisp whites, soft taupes, chocolates, and brushed chrome. Impressively clean for a boutique hotel in South Beach; the housekeeping attendants are restricted to a minimal number of rooms to ensure every attention to detail. The 1,100-square-foot Astor Suite books for upward of $1,000.

✳ Where to Eat

DINING OUT Barton G, The Restaurant (305-672-8881; www.bartong.com), 1427 West Ave. This restaurant takes all the stuffiness out of fine dining with fun drinks, yummy entrées, and wildly creative desserts. Start with their signature drink, the Sabrinatini, made with Absolut Mandarin, Watermelon Pucker & Champagne, with a tiny chocolate monkey that hangs on the edge of the glass ($12). For an appetizer ($8–21) try the trio of crab tacos with cilantro, red pepper kimchee, and yellow pepper ginger, or Lobster Pop-Tarts (lobster and Gruyère in a flaky crust), with a trio of sauces. You'll enjoy such entrées as the Bar-G-Cola salmon with Coca-Cola sauce, sunflower seed crusted grouper with saffron mash, or the pear and walnut brioche crusted lamb chops ($16–64). Save room for dessert ($13–34). The Big Top Cotton Candy will have everyone sharing, and the

Cup Cake Picnic with, vanilla and chocolate cupcakes, ice cream and do-it-yourself sprinkles and icing will send you over the edge. Reservations are recommended, and dining is inside or in the garden.

Carnevale (305-672-3333; www.carnevalerestaurant.com), 907 Lincoln Rd. The fresh Venetian fare served here is getting attention from the locals. Quattro Formaggi (four cheese) pizza could be just the thing for a casual night at the pedestrian mall, or step inside the small, unassuming dining room for Pagila and Fieno shrimp Absolut (wine and green spinach spaghetti in a vodka pink sauce), scampi, or veal Marsala. Happy hour. $12 and up.

Creek 28 (305-672-7825; www.creek 28.com), 2727 Indian Creek Dr. Chef Kira Volz led my guest and I on a tour of her organic gardens, stopping to pull Surinam cherries from hedge bushes— a colorful landscape plant with berries as yet undiscovered, apparently—and mused about creating a sauce with the smoky-flavored delicacy. The taste was exquisite and I'm hoping she comes through . . . Volz is an experimenter who enjoys the musky and hot flavors of the Mediterranean and Middle East to create exotic dishes sure to please the palate. Dine in the torchlit outdoor garden if you can. Entrées $15 and up.

Doraku (305-695-8383; www.sushi doraku.com), 1104 Lincoln Rd. Japanese-trained executive chef Hiro Terada serves two styles of Japanese cuisine: Kansai, a traditional style, and Tokyo, a contemporary style. Appetizers ($6–14) include the Maine lobster sushi roll. Sushi and sashimi ($2–6 a piece) have unique delicacies such as sea urchin and octopus. The extensive selection of sake is imported from various regions of Japan, along with their signature fruit sake infused with pineapple, cher-ry, and mango. Lunch noon–3:30 PM Mon.–Fri.; dinner 5 PM–midnight Mon.–Thurs., 5 PM–1 AM Fri., 3 PM–1 AM Sat., 3 PM–11:30 PM Sun. A fabulous Happy Hour is held Monday through Friday from 5 to 8, with a complimentary buffet on Friday.

Escopazzo (305-674-9450; www.escopazzo.com), 1311 Washington Ave. Husband-and-wife team Giancarla and Pino Bodoni use all organic fresh and imported ingredients to create exceptional Italian fare from their homeland. Flavors such as pumpkin and amaretto enhance ravioli; homemade pastas blend with truffles, cream, and cheese. Famous diners include Patti LaBelle, Cameron Diaz, Harrison Ford, Michelle Pfeiffer, David Geffen, and the late Gianni Versace. Closed Mon. $12 and up.

The glamorous **Forge Restaurant** (305-538-8533; www.theforge.com), 432 41 St., has been a Miami Beach landmark for decades. The award-winning American steakhouse offers white-tie service in an antique setting and features more than 300,000 wines in their eight-room wine cellar. Choose -between lamb osso buco with seafood saffron risotto, Forge Duck with black currant sauce, or the veal chop with sun-dried tomatoes, encrusted with fresh mozzarella. Broiled steaks feature four complimentary house sauces: Classic Java, Forge A.1., Four Mustard Horse-radish Lime, and Béarnaise. Select dessert early, as the made-to-order Belgium chocolate or Grand Marnier citrus soufflé take 30 minutes to prepare. The Forge Blacksmith Pie has been a classic for more than two decades. Open 6:30–midnight Mon.–Thurs.; 6:30 PM–3 AM Fri. and Sat., 6:30–midnight Sun. Expect prices $51 and higher.

At the moderately priced **Grillfish** (305-538-9908; www.grillfish.com),

1444 Collins Ave., you'll first take note of the floor-to-ceiling erotic mural behind the large stone bar. Ornate columns, massive mirrors, and candlelight continue the ambiance of sensuality. Chalkboard menus, situated around the room, feature such freshly caught fish as mahimahi ($18), whole yellowtail snapper ($20), and wahoo ($17). Each fish dish is served with a choice of sweet onion or creamy garlic tomato sauce and is accompanied by pasta or salad. The menu also offers a selection of meats, such as filet mignon with horseradish cream ($24) and veal Marsala ($17). Save room for one of their desserts, such as black Russian banana split ($6) or mango Key lime pie ($7). Open daily, 5:30 till late.

For fresh crab, **Joe's Stone Crab Restaurant** (305-673-0365; www .joesstonecrab.com), 11 Washington Ave., can't be beat. Growing from a little lunch counter to the present-day homage to the crab, the restaurant founded by Joe Weiss in 1913 is as much of Miami Beach's history as Flagler's Railroad (see *Palm Beach County*). The restaurant operates on a seasonal schedule, dependent on the crabs (typically Oct. 15–May 15). You can't make reservations, so you'll want to get there early, or expect to wait. Entrées $7–49, with market prices dictating. Open for lunch 11:30 AM–2 PM Tues.–Sat., dinner 5 PM–10 PM Mon.–Thurs., 5 PM–11 PM Fri. and Sat., 4 PM–10 PM Sun.

Maison d'Azur (305-534-9600), 660 Washington Ave. Reflecting Paris and St. Tropez in both atmosphere and menu, this new yet highly acclaimed restaurant features fresh seafood and caviar, delivered to your room at the brand new Angler's Resort, poolside, and in the indoor and outdoor dining rooms. $12 and up.

Metro Kitchen + Bar at the Hotel Astor (305-531-8081; www.hotelastor .com), 956 Washington Ave. Dark woods, crisp linens, stainless, and stone—all bathed in bright light—set the stage for no-nonsense yet whimsical and creative cuisine. A fusion of French, Italian, and Asian cuisines reflects the Caribbean and Latin cultures of south Florida, resulting in dishes such as jerked mahimahi, guava and mascarpone spring rolls, and foie gras with lychees. A quiet respite from the SoBe hustle, the Metro lounge serves its signature martinis nightly and at its hot Tuesday-night parties. $12 and up.

Talula (305-672-0778; www.talulaon line.com), 210 23rd St. One of Miami Beach's most acclaimed new restaurants, Talula is the brainchild of a couple of award-winning chefs, Frank Randazzo and his wife, Andrea Curto-Randazzo, who have both achieved great national fame. Together they've created an intimate atmosphere with warm woods, brick, and copper, as well as a garden terrace for those who enjoy south Florida's temperate clime. Billed as New American cuisine, the menu offers many worldly variations on the theme, such as conch ceviche and Australian lamb. Barbecue quail gets rave reviews as a starter, and comfort foods such as acorn squash and collard greens provide homestyle flavors. Closed Mon. $12 and up.

Tantra (305-672-4765; www.tantra restaurant.com), 1445 Pennsylvania Ave. Sensuous and suggestive, Tantra's decor is designed to be aphrodisiac. Fragrance wafts from hookah pipes scattered about, and the low lights, grass floors, pillows, and reclining lounges beckon. Moroccan cuisine with rich flavors and spicy aromas melts the last of the holdouts. It's extremely pricey, but if you have someone hot to dine with, the ambiance is worth it. Open late. $26 and up.

Wish (305-531-2222; www.wish restaurant.com), The Hotel, 801 Collins Ave. Wish is one of the best restaurants in the world according to *Condé Nast Traveler*. It's chef, Marco Ferraro, presents amazing fare. Try the signature salad of endive, radish, and cashews in a ginger-lime dressing, Hamachi sashimi, or lobster ravioli. Sip perfect margaritas and strawberry daiquiris on the lushly planted outdoor patio as you wait for the sun to fall and the nightlife to begin on one of the most famous party strips in the world. Or, if you're a guest of the hotel, take it to the rooftop pool for a view of the surf or a rubdown under the sun before siesta. $12 and up.

EATING OUT A classic **kosher** deli, **Roasters 'n' Toasters** (305-531-7691; roastersntoasters.com), 525 41st St., is a busy breakfast nosh, with bagels and lox, pickled green tomatoes, and eggs several ways. 6 AM to 3:30 PM every day.

The neon sign beckons you to **Jerry's Famous Deli** (305-532-8030; www .jerrysfamousdeli.com), 1450 Collins Ave. The lively deli, where you'll often spot a host of celebrities, is open 24 hours every day. Hefty portions and friendly service dominate with such varied entrées as white spaghetti ($11), corned beef and cabbage ($15), fajita plate ($14), and chicken breast schnitzel ($17). You'll find more than 600 traditional deli favorites, along with enormous sandwiches, salads, and pizzas. Plan to stop by often for dessert, as their bakery features such delights as walnut cake for only $4.

Also open 24 hours (see **Jerry's,** above) is the **News Café** (305-538-6397; www.newscafe.com), 800 Ocean Dr. A great place to celebrity-watch, the café is a central meeting point for top models. Start your day with breakfast. For only $7 you can order the

Continental Special with assorted pastries, hot coffee, and juice. For heartier appetites they have Benedicts, omelets, quiche, French toast, and pancakes ($6–11). Later in the day, you'll enjoy entrées such as seafood paella ($23); the vegetarian favorite, portobello mushroom with spinach and tomato over rice ($9); and a variety of pasta, pizza, and Mediterranean dishes.

Nexxt (305-532-6643), 700 Lincoln Rd. Enjoy soups and salads, eggs, steaks with Mediterranean influences, and gorgeous pastries indoors, fast-café style, or outside under umbrellas on the mall (fans keep diners cool while they remain immersed in the scene). Sun. brunch. $10 and up.

✳ Selective Shopping

ANTIQUES AND COLLECTIBLES At **Antique Collectible Market** (305-673-4991; www.antiquecollectible market.com), you'll find 80 or more dealers lined up in the open-air mall on Lincoln Road. The market is open only on Sunday from 8 to 5. Located just a couple of blocks from the Lincoln Road Farmers Market held the same day (see *Farmer's Markets*).

BOOKSTORES Staving off the major bookstores, the independent **Books & Books** (1-888-626-6576; www.books andbooks.com) at Miami Beach (305-532-3222), 927 Lincoln Rd., and Bal Harbour (305-864-4241), 9700 Collins Ave., is the main bookstore to head to for a wide selection of reading and fun. It's not unusual to see a best-selling author browsing the isles or signing books. The large magazine collection and newsstands contain publications and papers from around the world. The locally owned bookstore also has locations in Coral Gables (see *The Gables, the Grove, and Downtown Miami*), and at Levenger Outlet in

Delray Beach (see *South Palm Beach County*), where you'll find book accessories and reading tools. Open 10 AM–11 PM Sun.–Thurs., 10 AM–midnight Fri. and Sat.

SHOPPING The **1950s-style mall** on Lincoln Rd. at 16th St. (305-531-3442) is a perfect place to shop, dine, or just have fun with the family, even the dog. Closed to traffic, the pedestrian-only mall covers 8 city blocks. When looking for a night-out ensemble, seek out **Chroma** (305-695-8808), tucked in an alcove at 920 Lincoln Rd. A favorite of mine is **White House/Black Market** (305-672-8006; www.whiteandblack .com), 1106 Lincoln Rd. No big-name brands here; the shop features private labels made in a timeless style. And the reasonably priced quality clothes and accessories can be worn day or night. Don't forget your pet. **The Dog Bar** (305-532-5654; www.dogbar.com), 1684 Jefferson Ave., has duds, toys, and treats for both dogs and cats in the SoBe style. Open daily; most shops open by 11 AM. City parking for Lincoln Road Mall is available between Lincoln Rd. and 17th St.

Epicure (305-672-1861; www.epicure -market.com), 1656 Alton Rd. This market of the stars serves the needs of the most discriminating residents and visitors to the beach. Here you'll find all manner of fresh seafood, meats, breads, produce, deli items, flowers, fine wines, and a coffee bar—the best of everything. It's a small shop with friendly service. Open 10 AM–8 PM Mon.–Sat., 10 AM–7 PM Sun.

FARMER'S MARKETS The special event company, **The Market Company** (305-775-2166; www.themarket company.org), runs a cool version of the farmer's and festival markets. Locals know that the **Lincoln Road Farmers Market,** 600 Block of Lin-

coln Rd. (between Lenox Ave. and Washington Ave.), is the freshest market around. Featuring local fruits, vegetables, fresh cut flowers, baked breads, and jams and honey. Open year-round on Sun.: 9 AM–7 PM Apr.–Oct.; 9–6 Nov.–Mar. **Española Way Weekend Festival** features multicultural gifts, clothing, and jewelry in the South Beach Historic Spanish Village. You'll find the market on 428 Española Way (between 14th St. and 15th St., and Drexel Ave. and Washington Ave.), 10 AM–6 PM Sat., 11 AM–9 PM Sun.; and **FestivArt,** Fri. and Sat. 7 AM–midnight. The **Market Company store** is at 428 Española Way.

✴ Entertainment

DANCING We are so lucky to have **The Miami City Ballet** (1-877-929-7010; www.miamicityballet.org), 2200 Liberty Ave., and luckier to have artistic director Edward Villella leading it. With an operating budget of more than 10 million, the company of 50 dancers is one of the largest ballet corps in the United States. The founder of the company, Villella, in 1997 received the prestigious National Medal of Arts from President Clinton and was also named a Kennedy Center Honoree. Marrying the classical techniques of choreographer George Balanchine with his own style, Villella brings a fresh approach to dance. His four-act ballet, *The Neighborhood Ballroom,* premiered in 2003. The company's repertoire includes 82 ballets, with masterworks from George Balanchine, Twyla Tharp, and Paul Taylor, along with original works from Villella and other gifted choreographers. Call for show times, location, and pricing.

NIGHTCLUBS

Miami Beach/South Beach
South Beach nightlife is the hottest

late-night scene in south Florida for the over-21 crowd. The club parties don't begin until after dinner, and many clubs offer happy hours from 10 or 11 PM until midnight, when the fun gets started and lasts until the clubs close at 5 AM. Clubs open and close like swinging doors in South Beach. The hottest clubs continually reinvent themselves. Often just the street address is enough to direct you to the newest hip and happening club. No matter what, there is always a club for everyone, but if celebrity-watching is high on your list of priorities, look for the velvet ropes and long lines that signal exclusivity and expect to pay cover charges of $20 and way up from there.

Cameo (305-532-2667), 1445 Washington Ave. The high-tech DJ and dance scene is for those who are here to be discovered or do some discovering of their own. This is the ultimate nightclub, with unrelenting beat, pulsing lights and music, and piles of bodies on the dance floor, on the catwalk, in the curtained cubbyholes, and in the upstairs VIP room.

Jazid (305-673-9372) 1342 Washington Ave. There's jazz downstairs and a new room upstairs decorated in stainless steel, cool blue, and sci-fi chic that features electronica and techno pop, blues, and rock.

Mansion (305-532-1525; www.the opiumgroup.com), 1235 Washington Ave. Mansion is making a good showing as a major club on the scene, thanks to owners Eric and Francis Milon, whose track record was proven by forerunners Opium Garden, next door, and the exclusive private club Privé. It hardly seems fair that a pair of pretty French boys (Eric is a former model for Giorgio Armani and *GQ*) should have all the luck, but their Midas touch, partnered with music scene insider Roman Jones, son of gui-

tarist Mick Jones of Foreigner, is the last word. Mansion is in a huge old building that served as a casino in the 1930s. On Friday hip-hop rules, with Euro dance next door at Opium, and on Saturday the scene switches clubs, with Euro at Mansion and hip-hop at Opium, to keep the crowds flowing between them. Open until dawn.

Nikki Beach Club (305-538-1231), 1 Ocean Dr. Everyone knows Nikki Beach, perhaps because it's always been here, or maybe because it's the only place to go for those awake during the daylight hours. SoBe insiders hang here for what they call "nightlife during the daytime" on Sunday. Go ahead, lie on the sand while sipping piña coladas. The night scene here is hot, too.

Opium Garden (305-531-5535; www .theopiumgroup.com), 136 Collins Ave. Another Milon brothers and Roman Jones project, Opium Garden has withstood the fickle phasic nature of South Beach chic—it's been here since 2000 and is still going strong. The Thai-inspired outdoor courtyard rocks all night long. If the famous SoBe nightlife is what you're here for, this is the place.

Pearl (305-673-1575), 1 Ocean Dr. Upstairs from the Nikki Beach Club, Pearl dominates the traditional beach-party scene with its SoBe art deco–*Jetsons* look and glowing ambience. Sean Penn, Sting, and Naomi Campbell have been seen sidling up to the bar here. DJ party on Thursday nights.

SkyBar Miami Beach (305-695-3100), 1901 Collins Ave. SkyBar is the pool/beach bar of the legendary Ian Schrager's Shore Club—a place for late-night relaxing, dancing, drinking, and rendezvousing in private cabanas and cubbies scattered about the grounds. Come sip and sizzle with the best of them. Thursday and Saturday are the big nights here.

THEATER Opening in 1934 as a movie house for Paramount Pictures, the **Colony Theatre** (305-674-1040), 1040 Lincoln Rd., is a fine example of the art deco style and is listed on the National Register of Historic Places. Redesigned with new acoustics, but retaining the historical architecture, the theater is host to a variety of performing arts such as dance, concerts, comedy, and film festivals.

Under the direction of Jude Parry "the mistress of pantomime," the **Gold Coast Theatre Co.** (305-538-5500; www.britishpanto.org) specializes in mime and physical theater with strolling characters, improvised fun, and at times audience participation. The company often plays to homeless shelters and at safe houses for victims of domestic abuse. Public performances are often held at the Colony Theatre on Lincoln Road (see above). Call for locations and current schedule.

✳ Special Events

January: **Miami Beach Art Deco Weekend Festival** (305-672-2014; www.mdpl.org), along Ocean Dr., between 5th St. and 15th St. You'll love the big bands and artistic antiques as you step back to the art deco period (circa 1925–1945). Presented by the Miami Design Preservation League.

February: The **Miami International Boat Show and Strictly Sail** (www.miamiboatshow.com) takes over the Miami Beach Convention Center and many marinas around the city. More than 2,300 marine manufacturers showcase vessels of your dreams, along with accessories such as nautical clothing, teak deck chairs, and the all-important sunglasses.

March: **Callé Ocho Festival / Carnaval Miami** (305-644-8888; www.carnavalmiami.com), etween 4th Ave. and 27th Ave., on SW Eighth St. The annual Callé Ocho Festival, a Latin cultural celebration that draws an estimated million partyers, is billed as the premier Hispanic event in the United States. The pinnacle event of Carnaval Miami, it's a street festival that features huge pans of paella, a Spanish dish of rice, seafood, and sausage; music, dominoes, and fun. Free admission; food and events fee.

July: **International Mango Festival** (305-667-1651; www.ftg.org), Fairchild Tropical Garden, 10901 Old Cutler Rd., Coral Gables 33156. Celebrate the luscious pink, purple, green, and gold fruit of subtropical Florida with aficionados of the sweet and tangy fruit. Try mango punch, mango pastries, mango pie, and mango brunch. Sample the many varieties of the fruit, buy bags full, buy mango trees and learn to care for them, and learn how to prepare the fruit. This is one of south Florida's most popular festivals. 9:30 AM–4:30 PM Sat. and Sun. Fee.

August: **Miami Spice Restaurant Month** (305-539-3000; www.miamirestaurantmonth.com). Restaurants throughout Miami and Miami Beach offer prix fixe menu specials throughout the month of August.

October: Experience the excitement and colors of a 2000-year-old traditional sporting event. Sponsored by the United Chinese Association of Florida, the **South Florida Dragon Boat Festival** (305-345-8489; www.miamidragonboat.com) is held at **Haulover Park and Marina** (see *Beaches*). More than two-dozen slim canoelike boats are decorated with brilliant colors and a hand-painted dragon's head. Teams of up to 20 rowers each race against each other, many for local

NAVIGATING NIGHTCLUBS

You don't have to be a millionaire, celebrity, or a 20-something size 2 to gain entrance to the famous clubs of South Beach. The trendy dance-club atmosphere of SoBe is like no other. Even if you never go to clubs, plan to experience at least one. A simple black outfit is all you need. Or take time to shop **Lincoln Road** (see *Selective Shopping*) to get the latest "in" outfit. Next, arrive early—around 10–11 PM. Even then, expect to wait. Clubs don't typically get hopping until well after midnight, and waits of an hour are not uncommon. Just be patient; everyone eventually gets in. The clubs also like to show a lengthy line to create an atmosphere of "this must be the place to be tonight," and a full club is much more entertaining. Getting in is easier if you cluster in small groups. Groups of men should break up or attach themselves to a group of women. I don't know why, but men will stand in line forever if they are grouped together. When approaching the doorman, don't say anything—just smile. If you have bought a table or know your name is on The List, then give your name and wait patiently. And don't bother to grease doormen's palms. They'll think even $50 is cheap, and you won't get in any faster. If you plan on frequenting the same club for several nights, however, you might slip them a $20 or more *after* they move you past the velvet rope, just on the off chance that they might remember you each night. Be forewarned: Tipping may not get you in any faster. The easiest way to ensure entrance is to put your name on a list, which can be done in a number of ways. The first is to have your hotel concierge call and put your name on The List. Although this is a free service, $10 is a nice gesture to give the concierge when the reservation is made. The second, and more expensive, way to gain entrance is to buy a table. You'll have to cough up several hundreds of dollars to reserve one, but a reserved table includes a bottle or bottles of your choice of liquor ($225 per bottle and up). All mixers are provided, and you'll be assured table service. If you haven't reserved a table, don't even think of sitting down unless invited. Unlike the days of "get there early to get the best seat," all tables are available by reservation only. Even if you don't reserve a table, plan to spend a bundle. Admission to clubs varies but typically runs around $20. Once inside you'll spend about $7 for beer and wine, and $12 and up for mixed drinks, so a table reservation may be the best bargain for a group. If you haven't been clubbing in a long time, or ever, you may want to book a club tour. The tour host can gain immediate entrance to numerous clubs, and the tour often includes some drinks. Call the **Greater Miami Convention and Visitors Bureau** (see *Guidance*) for a selection of approved club-tour operators. Most clubs are open 10 PM–5 AM.

charities. You'll enjoy a weekend of fun with martial arts demonstrations, an egg roll eating contest, a kid's kite contest, and authentic Asian food booths.

November: **Miami Book Fair International** (305-237-3258; www.miami bookfair.com) 300 NE Second Ave., downtown Miami, Miami-Dade College, Wolfson Campus. This premier celebration of books features titles and authors from South America and the islands, as well as the U.S. mainland. A week of events leads up to a festival weekend of high-profile lectures and demonstrations, including a children's arena and colorful book sale stalls. Free admission and lectures, but bring a little cash for snacks, drinks, and book bargains.

NASCAR Finals Ford Championship Weekend (1-866-409-RACE; www.homesteadmiamispeedway.com), One Speedway Blvd., Homestead. Finale of the national NASCAR series held around the country. A huge draw for fans, who fill hotels throughout Homestead, South Miami, and the upper Keys, as well as the infield and multiple camping lots on-site.

December: **Art Basel Miami Beach** (305-674-1292; www.artbasel.com/ miami_beach), Miami Beach Convention Center, 1901 Convention Center Dr., Miami Beach. This huge art party, a gallery hop that stretches from South Beach to the Design District, brings a bit of Switzerland to Miami. Fee.

Art Miami (305-573-1388 or 1-866-727-7953; www.art-miami.com), art show in the **Wynwood Art District,** 2242 NW 2nd Ave., Miami. Parties and perspectives mark this four-day festival, which has formed the foundation of an arts reputation that is fast becoming Miami's own. Artists from around the world display their wares at edgy new galleries. Fee.

SOUTH MIAMI–DADE: FOOD AND WINE COUNTRY

At the tip of Miami-Dade County lies an area teaming with tropical agriculture. It was first opened to settlers in 1898, and for decades the only access to the county was via the Homesteaders Trail. It wasn't until Henry Flagler's railroad accessed this remote county, bordered by the Atlantic Ocean to the east and the Everglades to the west, that the area began to develop. Severe hurricanes have hit here twice—in 1926, and again in 1992 when Hurricane Andrew struck. True to the pioneer spirit, however, residents have consciously rebuilt and restored many historic buildings, including the Mediterranean Revival buildings in the quaint business district on Krome Avenue. Expansion has been rapid in Miami-Dade County, one of the last areas in South Florida still open for development. The Homestead Miami Speedway is the really big event here, but it's just one of many attractions in this tropical location. Florida City, considered the gateway to the Everglades and offering many ecofriendly activities, has seen an increase in tourism. Once thought of as a place to pass through on the way to the Keys, the southern cities of Miami-Dade County have blossomed into an area rich with gourmet delights while preserving their agricultural heritage—nearly half of the country's winter vegetables in the United States are grown here. U-pick and roadside fruit and vegetable stands are abundant. You'll find avocados, guava, mangos, mamey, and papaya picked fresh from the fields. And because this region is so close to the harvest, it has seen a growth in tasty eateries and innovative wines such as Lychee and Carambola.

✳ To See

ARCHAEOLOGICAL SITES At the **Deering Estate at Cutler Ridge** (see *Historic Sites*) join a walking tour (included in admission) for a glimpse into prehistory, meandering through the tropical forest, through the site of the 1800s village of Cutler, and across a stone bridge, and culminating in a walk to a Tequesta burial mound from the 1600s.

ART GALLERIES The not-for-profit artist community at **ArtSouth** (305-247-9406; www.artsouthhomestead.org), 240 N Krome Ave., Homestead, is spread over 3.5 acres. You'll find the studios of 35 fine artists on the campus. In the two-story Fine Arts Building, you'll feel strong emotions when viewing the works of Joe Parker, and an organic connection with Carol Jaime's soulful woodcarvings. You'll also experience the human condition with the rich tropical flora of Vanessa Bryson's oil, watercolor, and pastel paintings. The new Fine Crafts & Sculpture Building features pottery, ceramics, and works in metal. Over at the historic Sanctuary, various performing arts are presented throughout the year. An Open House, with all studios open and live entertainment, is held each month on the second Saturday.

The garden paths will draw you in to several quaint shops and galleries in **Cauley Square Historic Village** (305-258-3543; www.cauleysquareshops.com), 22400 Old Dixie Hwy. (US 1), Miami. Open 10 AM–5 PM Tues.–Sat., 12 PM–5 PM Sun.

ATTRACTIONS Romance knows no limits at **Coral Castle** (305-248-6345 or 1-800-366-0264; www.coralcastle.com), 28655 S Dixie Hwy., Homestead. From 1923 to 1951, Latvian immigrant Edward Leedskalnin built a stunning architectural structure to recapture the unrequited love of Agnes Scuffs. After the young lady canceled the wedding just one day before the event, the 26-year-old jilted groom began a lifelong quest to win her back. Working alone, Leedskalnin carved more than 1,100 tons of coral rock by hand, placing each section on 10 acres, all without the use of machinery. Originally called Rock Gate Park, Coral Castle features the Heart Table, Moon Garden, Polaris Telescope, and even the AC-Generator. To protect his privacy, he surrounded the castle with 8-foot walls that are 3 feet thick with a functional stone gate. Thirty-minute audio tours provide details of the castle in four languages, explaining the many interesting facts of Ed Leedskalnin's life ("Sweet Sixteen" by Billy Joel was written about Leedskalnin's lost love). The young runaway bride eventually married someone else. Ed's remains are buried in Miami Memorial Park Cemetery. Open 9 AM–8 PM Mon.–Thurs., 9 AM–9 PM Fri.–Sun. Adults $9.75, seniors 62+ $6.50, children 7–12 $5, under 7 free.

AVIATION A wide selection of classic and military aircraft is on display at the Wings Over Miami Museum (305-233-5197; www.wingsovermiami.com), Kendall-Tamiami Executive Airport, 114710 SW 128th St., Miami. Aircraft is displayed in the hangar, outside, and at times in the air. Open 10 AM–5 PM Thurs.–Sun. Adults $10, seniors $7, children $6.

Cutler Ridge

Step into South Florida's past at **The Deering Estate at Cutler Ridge** (305-235-1668; www.deeringestate.org), 16701 SW 72 Ave., where pioneer families settled the village of Cutler, one of the first in the region, and the Richmond family built a grand home in 1896 overlooking Biscayne Bay. In 1900, they opened the Richmond Cottage, the first hotel between Coconut Grove and Key West. These two buildings are among the last examples of early Frame Vernacular architecture in South Florida. Purchased by industrialist Charles Deering in 1913, the estate expanded with additional buildings, including his grand Mediterranean Revival "Stone House" and a boat basin, where today manatees frolic. Now a county park, the estate encompasses nearly 450 acres, a large portion of it left as natural tropical forest and accessible on guided tours only, where you'll see the remains of the original village and a burial mound from the 1600s. Adults $10, children $5; includes guided tour of the Stone House and the trails at set times throughout the day. Open 10 AM–5 PM daily, except Christmas and Thanksgiving.

Redland

In the **Redland Historic Agricultural District** north of Homestead, the cultivation of tropical fruits, flowers, and palm trees is big business, with nearly 300 ornamental growers, vegetable farms, bonsai, and water lily nurseries. According to some of its residents, Redland is Brigadoon, a fabled land that no one else can see. Only one home is allowed on every 5 acres, and the dark, rich soil is perfect for tropical flora grown nowhere else in the United States.

Several **historic coral rock houses** built by the region's early pioneers can be seen in the vicinity of the original Orchid Jungle, SW 157th Ave., at Newton Rd., Homestead, now **Hattie Bauer Hammock Park.** At 15730 SW 272nd St., **"Windwood"** is a beautiful example of a coral rock home; the **Cooper Residence,** 14201 SW 248th St., built in 1933, has wrought-iron gates; the home and carriage house are mortared coral rock. The **Redland Farm Life School** on SW 162nd Ave. is the region's original schoolhouse.

MUSEUMS

Florida City/Homestead

The 1904 Frame Vernacular **Florida Pioneer Museum** (305-567-0262; www.pioneerfloridamuseum.org), 826 N Krome Ave., Florida City, was built as a residence for an agent of the Florida East Coast Railroad. The 1.5-story home, listed on the National Register of Historic Places, features turn-of-the-20th-century memorabilia. Tues.–Sat. 10 AM–5 PM. Adults $5, seniors $4, and children five and under free.

♟ At the **Historic Homestead Townhall Museum** (305-242-4463), 41 N Krome Ave., Homestead, you'll discover artifacts and memorabilia of the area, including more than 400 historical pictures. Open 11 AM–5 PM Tues.–Sat. Free.

NATIVE AMERICAN PLACES Originally members of the Creek Nation, the Miccosukee natives have adapted to several changes in their history. From the struggle with early settlers to the draining of their land during the Land Boom, they have kept with their traditions while adapting to the modern world. At the

Miccosukee Indian Village (305-223-8380; www.miccosukee.com), Mile Marker 70, US 41, Tamiami Trail, you'll be guided on a tour that explores their history, culture, and lifestyle. **Miccosukee Resort & Gaming** (305-242-6464 or 1-877-242-6464; www.miccosukee.com), 500 SW 177th Ave., Miami, offers exciting hours of video pull-tab machines, Lighting Lotto, and 58 poker tables. Many locals head to High Stakes Bingo, where you can win thousands of dollars. Village open 9 AM–5 PM daily. Gaming open 24 hours.

ORCHID GROWERS This county is one of the largest orchid-growing regions, the Redland, and you can visit a number of local nurseries. Stop in and inhale the sweet fragrance at **Soroa Orchids** (305-247-2566; www.soroa.com), 25750 SW 177th Ave., or venture a few streets back to fabled **R.F. Orchids** (305-245-4570; www.rforchids.com), 28100 SW 182nd Ave. In its third generation of growers, this family operation is the most-awarded grower in the United States, and the owner is a top speaker on the subject of orchids. We were greeted with cherry limeade and encountered a profusion of colors and aromas of the finest orchids, as written about in *The Orchid Thief.* I know little about orchids, but the array of varieties was simply dazzling; this is a must-stop for orchid collectors. Open 9 AM–5 PM Tues.–Sun.

Baldan Orchids (305-232-8694), 20075 SW 180th Ave., are open 9:30 AM–5 PM Sat. and Sun., and feature blooming-size *Phalaenopsis.* **Redland Orchids** (305-246-2473), 26620 SW 203rd Ave., specialize in *Cattleas, Oncidiums,* and *Encyclias* and are open 8–4 Mon.–Fri. You'll find a wide variety of orchids and tropical exotics at **Impact Orchids & Exotics** (305-257-5771), 14400 SW 248th St. The folks at **Whimsy Orchids** (305-242-1333), 18755 SW 248th St., are open 8:30 AM–4 PM Tues.–Sat., with *Equitant oncidiums (Tolumnia)* as their specialty. Call for appointment. Pick up an *Orchid Guide to South Florida* at the Tropical Everglades Visitor Center, for a wider listing of these growers.

RAILROADIANA Ride the rails at **The Gold Coast Railroad Museum** (305-253-0063; www.gcrm.org), 12450 SW 152nd St. (Miami Metrozoo Entrance), Miami. The museum features the history of trains, along with real—yes, you can ride them—trains. Starting in 1956, Richmond Naval Air Station, a former World War II airship base, was transformed into a living museum with more than 3 miles of tracks and an assortment of working historic trains. Inside the enormous airship hangar, you'll explore the armor-plated Ferdinand Magellan, which served Presidents Roosevelt, Truman, and Eisenhower; the Silver Crescent, a California Zephyr with visa-dome observation deck; a 1922 steam locomotive, a Seaboard wooden caboose, and many more trains. Sit in the passenger coach and enjoy a 20-minute ride on a diesel-electric standard-gauge train, or ride up front with the engineer in the cab. Kids will love the Edwin Link Children's Railroad, which runs on 2-foot track. The beautifully landscaped tracks over in the Floyd McEachern Model Train Exhibit provide inspiration to collect your own railroadiana. Open 11 AM–4 PM Tues.–Sun. Adults $6, children under 12 $4. Train rides available on weekends for an additional $2.25–11.

WILDLIFE VIEWING You'll spot a variety of wildlife all along any of the roads in this region. In particular, head out on Palm Drive and along US 192 at dusk or dawn; you'll be sure to spot ibis, egrets, and the occasional opossum. Head south on US 192 to reach **Everglades Outpost and Everglades Alligator Farm** (see *Wildlife Rehabilitation & Zoological Parks*).

WINERY ❦ A garden paradise awaits you at **Schnebly Redland's Winery** (305-242-1224 or 1-888-717-WINE; www.schneblywinery.com), 30205 SW 217th Ave., Homestead, where from the visitors center you can sit and taste wine as twin waterfalls drop 18 feet into a cool tropical pond. Denisse and Peter Schnebly began as tropical packers. Realizing that the slightly blemished fruit not suited for the marketplace could be turned into unique wines, they sought out a vintner, Doug Knapp, and over several years developed distinguished wines made from such tropical fruits as carambola, passion fruit, guava, mangos, and Asian lychees. The Schneblys' entrepreneurial spirit has created a mecca for a new agricultural business in southern Miami-Dade County. Agri-tours, wine festivals, and walks through the orchards are just part of the new Food and Wine Country. While the wines aren't likely to compete with French champagne or Sonoma merlot, if you like the spark and vitality of these delectable fruits, you're sure to find these wines an interesting diversion for your palette. Try the Carambola, made from star fruit, which is reminiscent of Pinot Grigio. The Mango, resembling a White Zinfandel, might work with pasta. For a wine that's good with just about everything, try the unique taste of Rose Guava. Lychee is light and crisp, while the Passion Fruit complements dessert. Wines are reasonably priced at $14–20 per bottle. The wine-tasting room is open 10 AM–5 PM Mon.–Fri., 10 AM–6 PM Sat., 12–5 Sun.

ZOOLOGICAL PARKS & WILDLIFE REHAB

Homestead

✐ You'll see thousands of gators at **Everglades Alligator Farm** (305-247-2628; www.everglades.com), 40351 SW 192nd Ave. At this real working alligator farm, hundreds of tiny alligators live in "grow out" pens, while the larger reptiles lounge along a vast tropical lake. Make sure to check out the Sebastopol geese. These snowy-white fowl have unique curled feathers, preventing flight. The clean grounds have a rustic feel, providing you with a natural experience. The farm is home to a wide assortment of nonreleasable wildlife and carries the best collection of animal educational books around. Airboat rides take you along the "river of grass," where you'll see an abundance of wildlife, including gators, in their natural habit. Admission includes the airboat ride. Open 9 AM–6 PM daily except Christmas. Adults $17, children 4–11 $10, under 4 free.

❦ The **Everglades Outpost** (305-247-8000; www.evergladesoutpost.org), 35601 SW 192nd Ave., is primarily a rehabilitation and release facility of wild and exotic animals. The sanctuary provides a safe and nurturing atmosphere for nonreleasable wildlife and exotic species, such as those confiscated by authorities. Founders Bob Freer and Barbara Tansey welcome you to the facility to view the various animals and to learn more about these injured or abused creatures and their plight. Among some of the "guests" you might encounter are Florida panthers; albino and orange tigers; a grizzly bear and a cinnamon black bear; mandrill, macaque, and capuchin monkeys; fallow deer; a pair of sloths; a lesser anteater; and wolves, including Tasha, a female timber wolf, and Yukon, the alpha male artic wolf. One-day membership: adults $7, children under 12 $5; annual membership: $50; family membership (up to five people): $100. Closed Mon. and Wed. Their adopt-an-animal program allows you to sponsor an animal for a year.

Miami

⌀ One of the best zoos in the nation, **Miami Metrozoo** (305-251-0400; www .miamimetrozoo.com), 12400 SW 152nd St., features more than 1,300 animals and is cageless. After passing through the entrance, you'll soon come upon the Bengal tigers, including a rare white Bengal in the Pride of Asia habitat. You can sit for hours watching these majestic beasts as they play in and out of their swimming pool, with Asian ruins as the backdrop. Another favorite are the Cape hunting dogs with their beautiful tan, white, and black markings. You'll often see them frolicking with pups. You'll smell the eucalyptus as you get near the peaceful koala exhibit, where the first koala on the East Coast was born. Throughout, animals are grouped according to geographic territories that cover most areas of the world. The park is huge, so expect a lot of walking. Tired feet will be happy to take the free monorail, which runs throughout the property, hop on a guided tram tour, or rent one of the covered bicycle carriages. Open daily 9:30 AM–5:30 PM; ticket booth closes at 4. Adults 13+ $16, children 3–12 $12, under 3 free. Bicycle carriages are rented out for two-hour periods. The smaller carriage carries three adults and two children ($22); the larger carriage carries six adults and two children ($32). The new Wild Earth Jeep Simulator, which will take you on virtual African safari, is $5.

Since 1935, **Monkey Jungle** (305-235-1611; www.monkeyjungle.com), 14805 SW 216th St., has been the place where "the humans are caged and the monkeys run free." Experience mammals close to our hearts and genetic makeup while enjoying the 30-acre tropical rain forest. You'll see monkeys swinging freely overhead or playing in the swimming pool. Presentations on primates are offered throughout the day to enrich your adventure. Home to more than 400 primates, representing 30 species, the Monkey Jungle is a protected habit for endangered primates, and one of a few in the nation. Gibbons, guenons, spider monkeys, colobus, and the tiny endangered Golden Lion Tamarin are just some of the primates you'll encounter. The park also houses more than 5,000 specimens of fossil deposits. Open 9:30 PM–5 PM daily. Adults $29, seniors 65+ $28, children 3–9 $24.

Village of Pinecrest

⌀ The lovely oasis at **Pinecrest Gardens** (305-669-6942; www.pinecrestgardens .com), 11000 SW 57th Ave., also has a **Petting Zone** (see *Botanical Gardens*). Open 8–sunset daily. The Petting Zone is open periodically throughout the day, in short sessions, at 10 AM, 12 PM, 2 PM, and 4 PM. Free for everyone.

✴ To Do

FAMILY ACTIVITIES ⌀ Rev your engines on two high-quality go-cart tracks at **Speed Demons of Florida City** (305-246-0086; www.speeddemonskarting.com), 453 N Krome Ave., Florida City. Whether you're young or old, experienced or novice, the European-designed carts are sure to satisfy your need for speed. The challenging 0.25-mile main track is a favorite of seasoned drivers, ages 15 and up. The rooftop junior track is for younger or less experienced racers; adult carts are available on the junior track for those who wish to race with their kids. PRO Track and Game Room open 3 PM–10 PM Mon.–Fri., 11 AM–10 PM Sat., 11 AM–9 PM Sun.

Rookie track opens a few hours later and closes earlier. Member and nonmember admission fees. PRO (15 years and up): single race $17–20, five races $75. ROOKIE (8–14 years): single race $12–15, five races $50.

HIKING **Everglades National Park** (305-242-7700; www.nps.gov/ever/index .htm), 40001 SR 9336. Most of the region's hiking is concentrated in the vast wilds of Everglades National Park. Travel west on Palm Drive to 192nd Avenue (the Robert Is Here roadside market is on the corner), go south, and then follow signs to the park entrance. The Everglades are unique. This park was created in 1947 thanks to Marjory Stoneman Douglas, who created awareness of the "River of Grass," and to former president Harry S. Truman, who designated its national park status. Activity is limited to quiet pastimes and explorations. Peaceful visitors who don't disturb or frighten the wildlife are likely to see alligators and, during the migratory seasons, rare birds. Other creatures who call the 'Glades home, such as Florida panthers, bobcats, dolphins, and manatees, tend to remain scarce to humans. Environmental concerns remain important: the Everglades are considered to be endangered today because of encroaching development and agriculture and diminishing water supply and quality. Open 24/7. Fee.

Enter the park from the north, off US 41, at **Shark Valley** (see *Wild Places*), the Bobcat Boardwalk is an enjoyable 0.5-mile stroll through a tropical hammock and out through the sawgrass prairie. The 1-mile rugged **Otter Cave Hammock Trail** follows a rough limestone trail through a dense tropical hammock and is prone to flooding.

Along the Main Park Road in Everglades National Park, numerous short trails, most a half mile long or less, enable you to explore specific habitats. All trailheads are signposted and most have parking areas. The popular **Anhinga** and **Gumbo Limbo Trails** at Royal Palm Hammock provide excellent wildlife-watching and take only an hour or so of gentle meandering to complete. The **Pinelands Trail** is a 0.5-mile paved trail through a rare pine rocklands area. **Pay-hay-okee** showcases the vast sawgrass prairie with its cypress domes. **Mahogany Hammock** is a loop through a dense tropical hammock. **West Lake** has a boardwalk loop through the mangrove forest out to the lake. **Eco Pond,** at Flamingo, is a gentle stroll around a roosting area for herons and roseate spoonbills.

Hikers willing to pack on a few miles should head for the **Snake Bight Trail,** which leads 1.6 miles straight out to an overlook on Florida Bay; the **Rowdy Bend Trail,** a 2.6-mile narrow track through fields of salt hay and buttonwoods; the **Bear Lake Trail,** a 3.2-mile round-trip through dense mangroves to the shores of Bear Lake; and the **Christian Point Trail,** a 3.6-mile round-trip that takes you through the mangrove forest close to Florida Bay. At the back of the campground in Flamingo, the **Bayshore Loop** leads you 2 miles along Florida Bay and through the remains of the old village of Flamingo.

MOTOR SPORTS **Homestead Miami Speedway** (305-230-7223; www.home steadmiamispeedway.com), One Speedway Blvd., Homestead, is where you'll find the championship finals of NASCAR, Indy, Grand Am, and stock cars racing up to 190 mph on 20-degree turns. The track is also a venue for motorcycle races.

PADDLING The granddaddy of long paddling trips in Florida is the 99-mile **Wilderness Waterway,** stretching from Flamingo to Everglades City. Snaking through the Ten Thousand Islands, a maze of mangrove islands where the freshwater sheet flow of the Everglades and Big Cypress meet Florida Bay, the Wilderness Waterway is a true challenge for paddlers. Nautical charts show marked campsites on islands, and on chickee platforms built where there is no dry land. The route takes nine days to paddle, and solid logistical planning for safety and enjoyment of the trip. A backcountry permit is required from Everglades National Park to use the campsites. Check in at either the Flamingo or Gulf Coast Visitor Centers (www.nps.gov/ever/index .htm) prior to your departure.

If you're bringing your canoe or kayak to Everglades National Park, you'll find many launch points along the southern portion of the Main Park Road. Canoe trails near Flamingo include the 5.2-mile **Nine Mile Pond Loop;** the 2-mile **Noble Hammock Trail;** the 11-mile **Hells Bay Trail,** winding through a maze of mangroves; the **Bear Lake Canal Trail,** which you can follow for up to 22 miles round-trip; the 6.8-mile **Mud Lake Loop;** and up to 15.4 miles round-trip on the **West Lake Trail,** through heavy alligator and crocodile habitat. Check in at any of the park's visitor centers for information and maps for these trails.

SCENIC DRIVES At Everglades National Park, the 38-mile **Main Park Road** provides an interesting South Florida scenic drive, starting at the park entrance gate near the Ernest Coe Visitor Center and ending at Flamingo Visitor Center, the jumping-off point for excursions into Florida Bay.

SKYDIVING Take your bravery to new heights at **Skydive Miami** (305-759-3483; www.skydivemiami.com), 28730 SW 217th Ave., at Homestead General Airport, Homestead. How high can you go? Tandem jumps start at 8,000 feet, but you'll want to experi-

Trish Riley

HOMESTEAD SPEEDWAY

THE TEN THOUSAND ISLANDS

Naples Marco Island Everglades CVB

ence the jump from 13,500 feet to enjoy a full one minute of free fall. Open six days a week, closed Tuesday. Basic Tandem (8,000 feet) $199, Deluxe Tandem (10,000 feet) $229, Extreme Tandem (13,500 feet) $249. To prove your daring, make sure to get a video, photo package, or DVD: $69 each, or all three for $99.

SNORKELING Biscayne National Park (305-230-7275; www.nps.gov/bisc), 9700 SW 328th St. Explore this national underwater park's coral reefs and mangrove shorelines. It's popular for boating, sailing, fishing, snorkeling, diving, and camping, or take the glass-bottom boat cruise over the coral reefs and a shipwreck or artificial reef. The three-hour park-tour boat trips depart at 10 daily for the living coral reefs or the nearby Elliott or Boca Chita Keys, depending on the weather. Four-hour snorkel/Scuba trips depart at 1:30. The visitors center is open 9 AM–5 PM daily; the park is open 7:30 AM–5:30 PM daily. Free admission.

Take a short drive to **Keys Diver Snorkel Tours** (305-451-1177; keysdiver.com), 99696 Overseas Hwy., Key Largo, for some of the finest snorkeling in the region. Tour departs at 9 AM, $28. (See also *Upper and Middle Keys*.)

TOURS Dragonfly Expeditions (see Miami Tours) offers the Everglades Experience, where you'll meander through an ancient cypress dome. Make sure to sign up early for the exceptional Photography Expedition with award-winning "Wild Florida" photographer Jeff Ripple. $30–100.

You'll enjoy canoeing, wet walks in a cypress dome, stargazing, and sight-seeing at **Everglades Hostel Guided Tours** (305-248-1122; www.evergladeshostel.com), 20 SW 2nd Ave., Florida City. On each tour a wilderness expert will guide you through a variety of habitats. Full-day tour runs $80 for registered guests, $100 for walk-ins. Half-day tours also available.

Experience the diversity of the Redland Historic Agricultural District on the **Redland Tropical Gardens Tours** (305-247-2016; www.theredland.org), 22540 SW 177th Ave., Redland, which showcase the growers of this unique region. Tours run 9 AM–1 PM. Half day tours $25, full day tours $60.

Rob's Redland Riot Tour (305-443-7973; www.redlandriot.com) is by far the best way to see the rural farming and historic areas of southern Miami-Dade County. Rob's informative tours provide interesting information, visit historical sites, and stop at several tropical roadside stands. You'll visit such places as Cauley Square, Redland Fruit and Spice Park, R.F. Orchids, Schnebly Redland's Winery, Robert Is Here, Florida Pioneer Museum, Redland Hotel, Historic Homestead, and a number of designated Historic Homes. Prices vary. You can also walk or drive the tour yourself: a free self-guided map is on the Web site.

& Explore the "river of grass" on **Shark Valley Tram Tours** (305-221-8455; www.sharkvalleytramtours.com), Shark Valley Visitor Center, Everglades National Park. The two-hour tram ride follows a 14-mile paved loop (shared with bicyclists) through the open sawgrass prairie to a large observation tower, where you disembark and spend 15 minutes or so enjoying the view; you can see for miles. Your guide points out wildlife and indigenous flora along the way and explains how the Everglades formed and are nourished by a steady flow of water. Tours run 9 AM–4 PM daily, Dec.–Apr. (reservations a must), and 9:30 AM–3 PM, May–Nov. Adults $16, children $10. Mosquito head nets and full insect protection recommended on summer tours.

✴ Green Space

BEACH One of the region's little-known secrets is **Homestead Bayfront Park** (305-230-3033; www.miamidade.gov), 9698 SW 328th St., Homestead. A great family beach, the saltwater lagoon fluctuates with the tide. A playground, picnic areas, barbecue grills, and a sandy beach are surrounded by beautiful palm trees. Open sunrise–sunset. Admission $4 per vehicle.

BOTANICAL GARDENS

Village of Pinecrest

✍ Once the location of Parrot Jungle, **Pinecrest Gardens** (305-669-6942; www .pinecrestgardens.com), 11000 SW 57th Ave., has continued nurturing the decades-old natural areas. The original Parrot Jungle opened in 1936 and is now in Miami (see Jungle Island, *The Gables, the Grove, and Downtown Miami*). In 2002, the Village of Pinecrest purchased the 22-acre site and created an oasis for all to enjoy. Walk under towering banyan trees with a flock of albino peacocks; stroll through the botanical garden searching for rare plants; sit and gaze at the graceful waterfowl at Swan Lake; or just enjoy the tropical landscape and natural streams. Kids 3–12 can get wet and silly at Splash 'N Play and will also enjoy the petting zoo, butterfly exhibit, and playground. Open 8 AM–sunset daily. Splash 'N Play and the Butterfly Exhibit are open from 9 AM to one hour before park closing. The Petting Zone is open in four short sessions throughout the day, so as not to tire the animals. Free for everyone.

Redland

&. From its humble beginnings—cultivars donated by local growers—**Redland Fruit and Spice Park** (305-247-5727; www.fruitandspicepark.org), 24801 SW 187th Ave., has blossomed into a showcase of tropical fruits, flowers, and spices grown commercially in this region. As you walk the pathways through themed gardens, it's okay to sample fruits that have fallen to the ground—just avoid them in the poisonous plants area. A network of trails fans out throughout the park to enable you to explore at your own pace, or you can join a guided tour on a tram that stops at points of interest. Browse the gift shop on your way out for cookbooks, scholarly books on fruit, and fruit products. Open 10 AM–5 PM. Admission $7 adults, $1.50 for children.

THE TRAM AT SHARK VALLEY

Sandra Friend

PARKS

Cutler Ridge

✍ At **Bill Sadowski Park & Nature Center** (305-255-4767; www.miami dade.gov/parks), 17555 SW 79th Ave., walk the Old Cutler Ridge Nature Trail to immerse in an ancient hardwood hammock, a primeval forest of Old Florida surrounded by today's suburbia. The park also features a nature center with live animals, native tree arboretum, butterfly garden, playground, canoe launch, and picnic area. A public observatory is open Saturday nights 8–10 PM. Free.

Kendall

♬ Just a few blocks from Florida's Turnpike, **Kendall Indian Hammocks Park** (305-596-9324; www.miamidade.gov/parks), 11345 SW 79th St., protects a stand of natural forest known as the Snapper Creek Glade. Trails meander through the tropical hammock, and a picnic area and playground adjoin. Free.

Redland

♬ At **Castellow Hammock Park** (305-242-7688; www.miamidade.gov/parks), 22301 SW 162nd Ave., explore a remnant of the original habitat of the Redland, a tropical jungle with a rocky limestone floor and deep solution holes. The nature center has a great overview of the region, as well as a butterfly garden popular with photographers. Behind it, you'll find an 0.5-mile nature trail, well worth a visit to understand just how radically the land in South Florida has been changed. Open sunrise–sunset. Free.

WILD PLACES Biscayne National Park (305-250-PARK; www.nps.gov/bisc/), 9700 SW 328th St., Homestead. One of Florida's offshore parks, Biscayne protects the mangrove coastline of South Dade, living coral reefs, and islands that managed to escape development. Recreational opportunities include snorkeling and scuba diving, canoeing and kayaking, and hiking and camping on the islands of the park, but access to the park is only by boat. For an overview of the park's habitats and resources, stop at the Dante Fascell Visitor Center, exit 6 off Florida's Turnpike (follow the signs). Open 9 AM–5 PM daily. A park concessionaire (305-230-1100) provides snorkeling, scuba diving, and glass-bottom boat tours of the reefs; call for reservations and cost.

✳ Lodging

BED & BREAKFAST

Redland 33170

Fruit trees from every continent create an oasis in the farming district at the **Grove Inn Country Guesthouse** (305-247-6572; www.groveinn.com), 22540 SW 177th Ave., a delightful getaway. The 14 rooms are named for tropical fruits, and you can walk around the garden and sample their namesakes in-season. It has the feel of an updated 1940s motel with shabby chic decor; each cozy room includes a kitchenette with a mini fridge and a microwave. Paul Mulhern and Craig Bulger coaxed this phoenix from the ashes of a rundown motel, and the transformation is simply amazing. Add your name to the autograph tree, and then relax in the pool, or the hot tub, or under the arbor as the Christmas lights and candles flicker. A gourmet breakfast is served from 8 to 10 in the main dining room. Call for rates.

CAMPGROUNDS

Everglades National Park

Everglades National Park (1-800-365-CAMP) has two major campgrounds along the Main Park Road south of Homestead, at Long Pine Key (nearest the park entrance) and Flamingo (at the very end of the road). Reservations required Dec.–Apr.; otherwise, sites are first-come, first-served. (See also *Everglades National Park.*)

Homestead 33034

You'll enjoy luxury when you hook up at **Gold Coaster** (305-248-5462 or 1-800-828-6992; www.goldcoasterrv .com), 34850 SW 187th Ave. In the heart of Food and Wine Country, the mobile home park offers a heated swimming pool and spa, a playscape, and laundry facilities. The high level of customer service is what keeps families coming back, so make your reservations early. Day ($50), week ($295), month ($850), and season ($2,700). Pets welcome.

Miami 33177

The first-class **Larry and Penny Thompson Campground** (305-232-1049; www.miamidade.gov/parks/), 12451 SW 184th St., is located next to the Miami Metrozoo. Dedicated to the memory of Larry Thompson, a popular columnist with the *Miami Herald,* the campground was once part of the Richland Naval Station. A true destination location; you'll enjoy the natural setting with its 270 acres of nature, bridal, and hiking paths, including a 20-station fitness course. The campground has 240 sites for RVs and tent camping, and a choice of places to cool off. The large clear blue freshwater lake has it own white-sand beach, and three mammoth waterslides carved into a rock mountain empty into a heated pool. RV rates ($30 daily; $170 weekly; $500 monthly) include full hookup, water, and sewer. Tent sites are $15 nightly.

HOSTEL Ever wonder about staying at a hostel? Often thought of as inexpensive lodging for college kids, independent travelers of all ages are staying at these unique accommodations, many with resort-type features, for a fraction of the price. Most have a central entertainment area with community kitchen where you can cook your own meals. And you'll be required to pick up after yourself, which may include being assigned a small chore, such as sweeping. Plan to bring your own bedding, although they will often supply this if requested in advance.

Florida City 33034

ⁱ¹ The **Everglades Hostel** (305-248-1122 or 1-800-372-3874; www.ever gladeshostel.com), 20 SW Second Ave., is a great place to see if hostelling is for you. The clean, friendly hostel is in the heart of Florida City, where you can hop a bus and head to the Keys or Miami. The hostel also offers several types of tours into the Everglades, where you can wet walk in a cypress dome. They also rent canoes and bicycles so you can explore the area on your own. The hostel will nurture your mind and spirit, offering such amenities as a meditation gazebo, a whimsical tropical garden, and a glow-in -the-dark life-sized chessboard. Guests often gather around the fully equipped kitchen to chat, lounge in the "living room" while watching the large-screen cable TV, or surf the Net with free Web and wireless access. You'll also stay connected with free long-distance phone calls (within the United States). Office hours are 9–9, but once you check in you can come and go as you please. Camping in the garden with your own tent $18, dorm beds $25, private rooms $75. Discounts for Hostelling International (HI) members. Bring your own sheets or pay $2 for linen rental. Pets are welcome with prior management approval.

HOTEL Redland Hotel (305-246-1904, 1-800-595-1904; www.redland hotel.com) 5 S Flagler Ave. Built in 1904, this building, which has suffered fires and poverty and nearly met the wrecking ball, was discovered and saved by Katy and Rex Oleson with the help of friends Nancy and Jerry Gust in 1997. Today the restored hotel has 22 rooms, a vintage bar, and an expansive veranda. $75 and up.

✳ Where to Eat
DINING OUT
Homestead/Florida City

✐ At first glance you would think that the **Mutineer Restaurant** (305-245-3377; www.mutineer.biz), 11 SE First Ave., Florida City, was just another tourist trap. You'd be wrong. While tourists do flock here, they come for good reason. For lunch, serious seafood lovers should head straight to the all-you-can-eat seafood buffet ($10). Salads, sandwiches, and burgers are priced from $5 to 11. This little gem really shines at night with appetizers such as she-crab soup—creamy lobster bisque served in a bread bowl ($5.25). For landlubbers there's prime rib ($17–20). Make sure to save room for the Key lime pie and chocolate truffle mousse cake ($5). Decorated in a nautical theme, the chocolate walls and old-world drapes complement the cheery yellow polo shirts worn by the waitstaff. Patrons can take their turn at the piano in the lobby, and you'll want to take the kids over to their petting zoo just for fun. Open 11 AM–9:30 PM daily, and a bit later on the weekends in-season.

Prepare to be enchanted at the **White Lion Café** (305-248-1076; www.white lioncafe.com), 146 NW 7th St., Homestead. This delightful restaurant features excellent food in a historic home, with comfortable surroundings that spill out into the lush garden patio. Dine in or out, or just come for dessert. The extensive bakery selection will be a hazard to your diet, but the goodies are worth it. Lunch 11–3 Mon.–Sat. Dinner from 5 PM "until the fat lady sings," Tues.–Sat. Lunch entrées $7–9, dinner entrées $9–22. The open-air bar features live blues, jazz, and swing on Friday and Saturday nights.

EATING OUT
Homestead/Florida City

It's worth traveling off US 1 to find **Alabama Jack's** (305-248-8741; www.alabamajacks.com), 1500 Card Sound Rd., Key Largo. Located 13 miles southeast from Homestead, just before the toll, this eatery is a "must" for those heading to the Keys. The inexpensive pub food ($7–13) includes the *best* conch fritters in the region ($7). Country-western bands play on the weekends. Overlooking the canal, you'll enjoy watching huge mangrove snappers begging for treats. You'll feel like you are in the middle of nowhere, and you are, and it's worth it. Of course once you are there, you won't want to leave. Open 11 AM–7 PM daily.

The historic **Capri Restaurant** (305-247-1542; www.dinecapri.com), 935 N Krome Ave., Florida City, has been open since 1958. While you'll find a great selection of Italian dishes, such as chicken, veal, and seafood pasta ($12–22), or their certified Black Angus beef ($22–43), you'll also want to try one of their famous World Martinis, such as the Mango ($7), or a tropical drink, such as the West Indies Yellow Bird ($7). Open for lunch and dinner Mon.–Sat.

Head to the **Captain's House** (305-247-9456), 404 SW First Ave., Florida City, for their lump crab cakes ($11), grouper sandwich ($9), or famous lobster Reuben ($14). Entrées ($9–18), such as whiskey peppercorn snapper, come with a choice of two sides. The kid's Minnow's Menu ($5) covers even the pickiest appetite. All seafood is fresh from the Keys.

For eat-in or take-out Italian fare, call **Romano's Pizza** (305-246-7788), 110 N Homestead Blvd. (US 1), Homestead. Twelve- to 18-inch pizzas ($6–16) and traditional entrées such as manicotti, lasagna, and chicken parmigiana ($5–7). Open 10–9 Mon.–Sat; delivery available 11 AM–2 PM and 5–9 PM.

❦ If you're looking for real Mexican food, then look no further than **Rosita's Mexican Restaurant** (305-246-3114), 199 W Palm Dr., Florida City. The modest restaurant has developed a broad reputation for it delicious, authentic Mexican food, such as huevos rancheros ($4) for breakfast and *mole rojo de pollo* (red mole—a spicy chocolate sauce—with chicken, $8) for dinner. Green enchiladas with chicken, cheese, or beef include beans, rice, and salad ($5). Shrimp rancheros ($8). Desserts only $2. Open 8:30 AM–9 PM daily.

Redland

Try the "secret recipe" campfire stew at **Redland Rib House** (305-246-8866), 24856 SW 177th Ave., a favorite around these parts for their St. Louis–style barbecued ribs, fresh-ground char-grilled burgers, black beans and corn, and homemade pies. Half a slab of ribs $10; a whole slab of baby backs $16.

✳ Entertainment

Most of the nightly entertainment is on the weekends at local restaurants. You'll find relaxing blues and jazz in the garden at **White Lion Café** (305-248-1076; www.whitelioncafe.com), 146 NW 7th St., Homestead. **Main Street Café** (305-245-7575), 128 N Krome Ave., Homestead, livens things up with folk, country, blues, and classic rock on Saturday and Sunday nights, and open-mike night every Thursday. Open 8 AM–midnight.

✳ Selective Shopping

ANTIQUES, BOUTIQUES, AND SHOPS

Homestead

For 8 blocks along Krome Avenue in Homestead, you'll find an array of quaint antiques shops, art galleries, and restaurants. Or enjoy the wide selection of antiques and collectibles at **Jacobsen's** (305-247-4745; www.jacobsensantiques.com), 144 N Krome Ave., with 12 different dealers under one roof. The recently renovated **Historic Downtown** features turn-of-the-20th-century buildings, including the 1917 Town Hall.

Miami

A true hidden find, many of the pioneer buildings in **Cauley Square Historic Village** (305-258-3543; www.cauleysquareshops.com), 22400 Old Dixie Hwy. (US 1), date to 1903, when millionaire farmer William Cauley shipped tomatoes on Henry Flagler's railroad (see *Palm Beach*). On the 10-acre site sit several pioneer homes and warehouses converted into quaint shops, an artisans' village, and a tearoom. You'll enjoy walking the lush tropical grounds as you explore more than a dozen reasonably priced shops; many sell to the boutiques on South Beach. On weekends, live music is featured in the gardens. The Village is open 10 AM–5 PM Tues.–Sat., noon–5 PM Sun.

OUTLETS Shoppers looking for brand-name bargains will want to head to **Prime Outlets at Florida City** (305-248-4727; www.primeoutlets.com), 250 E Palm Dr., Florida City. Open 10 AM–9 PM Mon.–Sat.; 11 AM–6 PM Sun.

PRODUCE STANDS, FARMER'S MARKETS, FISH MARKETS, AND U-PICK

Homestead/Florida City/Redland
Everyone gathers at the **Farmers' Market** (305-242-0008), 330 N Krome Ave., Florida City, for locally grown tropical fruits and fresh vegetables. Open 10 AM–3 PM Sat.

Gardner's Market (305-255-2468; www.gardnersmarkets.com) 8287 SW 124th St., Pinecrest. Great food and wine since 1912. This most delightful market has the finest of foods, wines, cheeses, fresh-baked breads and pastries, fresh meats and seafoods, and all the eclectic ingredients a discriminating cook could desire. Farmer's market on Sunday morning during the local growing season (Nov.–Apr.). Open 8 AM–8 PM Mon.–Sat. and 8 AM–6 PM Sun.

Knauss Berry Farm (305-247-0668), 15980 SW 248th St., Homestead. A visit to this better-than-average farm stand always anchors my visits to the Redland. The German Baptists who farm the Homestead fields during the fall and winter months produce delicious herbs, greens, tomatoes, strawberries, and flowers. As an added bonus, fresh-baked pies and breads are always available and in demand at this popular spot, as are the fruit milk shakes that have made the place famous. Open 8 AM–5 PM Mon.–Sat. from Thanksgiving through Easter.

Robert Is Here (305-246-1592; www.robertishere.com), 19900 SW 144th St., Florida City. At the age of seven, Robert started his roadside fruit stand with a small table, a few fruits, and a sign that simply said, "Robert Is Here," and has grown this "lemonade stand" into a modern-day success story. You'll find more than 20 different varieties of locally grown tropical produce with strange names such as anon (a sugar apple), atemova, canestel (egg fruit), mamey, monstera, and even "ugly fruit." The stand also has a huge selection of commonly known fruits and vegetables such as Florida oranges, grapefruit, and sweet onions. In addition to all the fresh fruit and vegetables, you'll find a large selection of honey, jams, marinades, and dressings such as Florida Orange Poppyseed, Key Lime Honey Mustard, Key Lime Caesar Peppercorn, and Creamy Vidalia Onion Cucumber. Unless he is in the fields, you'll probably find Robert behind one of the counters. Out back you'll enjoy the quirky zoo, an eclectic collection of rescued and abandoned animals, including emus, parrots, donkeys, and iguanas. At the observation hive you can view live bees making honey. The Southern Most Purple Martin House is as nice as any beachfront condo. Don't leave without one of Robert's famous Key lime milk shakes; you can also get them in a variety of flavors. Open daily.

Laura Oswald used to sell fresh produce by the side of the road for 13 years, and then opened **The Tomato Lady's Hodgepodge** (305-251-1348), 20286 Old Cutler Rd., as a permanent location. Here, she offers bee pollen, fresh herbs, dried spices, and local fresh veggies.

Tropical Fruit Growers of South Florida (305-401-1502; www.florida-agriculture.com/tropical), 18710 SW 288th St., Homestead, a coalition of 100 South Florida growers, began in 1988. In this boutique industry, each grower harvests from farms under 100 acres, some as small as 3 acres. You'll handpick tropical favorites such as lychee, carambola, longan, mamey sapote, guava, mango, banana, and green papaya and many other specialty fruits.

✳ Special Events

Second Saturday of every month: Walk through the studios of 35 fine artists while enjoying live entertainment at **ArtSouth** (305-247-9406; www.art southhomestead.org), 240 N Krome Ave., Homestead. The artists' community is set on 3.5 acres in the heart of Homestead.

Last Sunday of every month: Divas are darling at the Hats & High Heels Party at **Cauley Square Historic Village** (305-258-3543; www.cauleysquare shops.com), 22400 Old Dixie Hwy. (US 1), Miami. The fun red-carpet-style event features prizes for "Best Hat" and "Best High Heels."

January: **Redland Natural Arts Festival** (305-247-5727; www.miamidade .gov/parks), Fruit and Spice Park, 24801 SW 187th Ave., Homestead. The Redland is the rich farmland that is a south Florida heritage—for decades, this was the land that fed the nation during the cold winter months. Celebrate the plants, arts, crafts, and music of the growers who settled this land a century ago and whose families still work to feed the world. Fee.

First weekend in March: **Asian Culture Festival,** Fruit and Spice Park, Redland. Enjoy the sensory delights— music, dance, visual arts, food, plants, and more—of Asia during this celebration of cultures. Admission $6; children under 12 free.

April: The Fairchild Tropical Gardens, Miami (305-667-1651), features the International Orchid Festival, the International Chocolate Festival and the International Mango Festival on the beautiful park grounds.

Enjoy old-time fun with music, food, arts and crafts, and entertainment such as juggling and puppetry at the **Redland Natural Arts Festival** (305-247-5727; www.fruitandspicepark.org), Fruit and Spice Park, 24801 SW 187th Ave., Homestead.

Summer: 🐾 In summer the Miami Metrozoo holds their annual **Big Cat-Nap Campout** (305-251-0400; www .miamimetrozoo.com), 12400 SW 152nd St., Miami. The special event allows children six and older to spend a night at the zoo. They'll learn about the animals through behind-the-scenes tours. Campers gather around a campfire, complete with s'mores, and wake to the sounds of lions and tigers. The event also includes complimentary zoo admission the next day, continental breakfast, and a commemorative T-shirt. Held 6 PM–8:30 AM. For members and nonmembers: adults $45–57, children $40–47, family of four $160–198.

October: One of Florida's wildest Halloween parties is **Metroboo** at the Metrozoo (305-251-0400; www.miami metrozoo.com), 12400 SW 152nd St., Miami. A unique trick or treat for kids 12 and under, with costume contests, music, trick or treating, and fun prizes. Held 11 AM–4 PM. Adults 13+ $12, seniors $11, children 3–12 $7, under 3 free.

December: **Arts & Craft Show** at **Cauley Square Historic Village** (305-258-3543; www.cauleysquare shops.com), 22400 Old Dixie Hwy. (US 1), Miami, features more than 50 vendors in a village filled with nostalgia and merriment.

EVERGLADES NATIONAL PARK

"There are no other Everglades in the world." So began *River of Grass,* the 1947 classic by Marjory Stoneman Douglas. Dedicated on December 6, 1947, by President Harry S. Truman, **Everglades National Park** (305-242-7700), 40001 FL 9936, Homestead, was the culmination of decades' worth of effort to preserve and protect the uniqueness of South Florida, with visionaries like Ernest Coe, David Fairchild, John Pennekamp, and Ms. Douglas leading the charge. Within the 2,358 square miles of Everglades National Park, the park boundaries protect the largest sawgrass prairie in North America, the largest mangrove forest in the Western Hemisphere, and dozens of intriguing and rare habitats like tree islands and pine rocklands. Landscapes are majestic here, sweeping panoramas of marsh and cypress.

What many visitors don't realize, however, is that the Everglades extend far beyond the protected boundaries of Everglades National Park, that the "river of grass" was once fed directly by Lake Okeechobee, and flowed both south and east toward the sea. Land reclamation efforts in the early 1900s uncovered rich black muck beneath the Everglades, kicking off an agricultural boom around the lake as the swamp was drained. When the population exploded along Florida's east coast, more Everglades were drained to provide land: first for farms, and more recently for subdivisions and shopping malls pushing ever farther west, consuming about half of what was once the Everglades, ancient swampland now disguised with ornamental plantings and sod. Despite the vastness of Everglades National Park, its boundaries cannot prevent the life-sustaining sheet flow of water into the park from carrying harmful agricultural and residential runoff generated by surrounding regions through the Everglades and into Florida Bay. The boundaries cannot prevent the wind from spreading the seeds of invasive exotic shrubs and trees, nor can they prevent thoughtless people from releasing tropical pets into the wild, creatures like pythons and iguanas and parrots that thrive without natural predators and compete with indigenous wildlife for resources.

Everglades National Park provides a place to contemplate a wilderness dependent on water, where the wildest of Florida's creatures still roam. Despite the issues that threaten its future, it is still a place of grandeur, where thunderheads form above vast prairies, and panthers slink through tree islands. To learn more, explore!

An important note about visiting Everglades National Park: Mosquitoes are an ever-present force, even in winter. They are at their peak in midsummer (tent campers, beware) and wane in January; but they never, ever leave. Carry mosquito head nets, bring your favorite repellent (if you don't want to use synthetic chemicals, scientists say that natural essential lemon-eucalyptus oil is just as effective), and use full-body coverage (long-sleeved shirt, long pants) when hiking, especially after a rainfall.

If you plan to wander off-trail, consult a park ranger before doing so, for safety's sake. Everglades National Park has unique natural hazards to consider, including jagged deep holes in the limestone karst, extremely poisonous plants, and plenty of wildlife. A ranger can help guide you away from any known trouble spots.

EVERGLADES VISITORS CENTERS

Shark Valley Visitor Center (305-221-8776), Tamiami Trail, open 8:30 AM–5 PM daily, has two-hour narrated tram rides (see *Tours*) along a 14-mile paved loop through the "river of grass," with a stop at an observation tower. Visitors are also welcome to bike or hike the loop, but there is no shade. Off-trail "slough slogs" get you up close and personal (adults 13+ $15, children 12 and under $7). To reach Shark Valley, follow US 41 (Tamiami Trail) west from Miami. The park's entrance is within the Miccosukee Reservation. The main portion of the park is reached via US 1 or Krome Avenue in Florida City to FL 9993. Unless you visit the park with a local tour operator, a car is essential for getting around.

At the beginning of the Main Park Road to Flamingo, the **Ernest Coe Visitor Center** (305-242-7700) is the snazziest of the visitors centers in the park, with detailed exhibits on ecosystems, history, and the flora and fauna of this vast preserve, as well as a large-screen movie theater to introduce you to the world's only Everglades. Purchase tickets here for guided activities, which include the two-and-half-hour Everglades Wet Walk (adult $15, children $7), which takes you out into the rugged "river of grass," and the Three-in-One Bike Hike ($20, bike included; $15 if you bring your own bike and helmet) through pine rocklands and sawgrass prairies on a system of rugged old limestone roads. Freebie interpretive walks are also still offered on a regular basis on the Anhinga Trail and at Mahogany Hammock.

The **Royal Palm Visitor Center**, 4 miles west of the main entrance station, is a relict of Royal Palm State Park (circa 1916) and the starting point for two of the park's most popular walks, the Anhinga Trail and the Gumbo Limbo Trail. Open 8 AM–4:15 PM daily. Free ranger-guided walks include the Anhinga Amble at 10:30 AM and the 'Glades Glimpse at 1:30 PM.

The **Flamingo Visitor Center,** at the end of Main Park Rd., offers exhibits, information, and backcountry permits. Staff are on hand 9–5 daily, late Nov.–May 1. The Flamingo complex includes the visitors center, marina, and the Flamingo Campground. The classic National Park lodge and cabins have been demolished after destruction caused by hurricanes Katrina and Wilma.

The Conch Republic: The Florida Keys

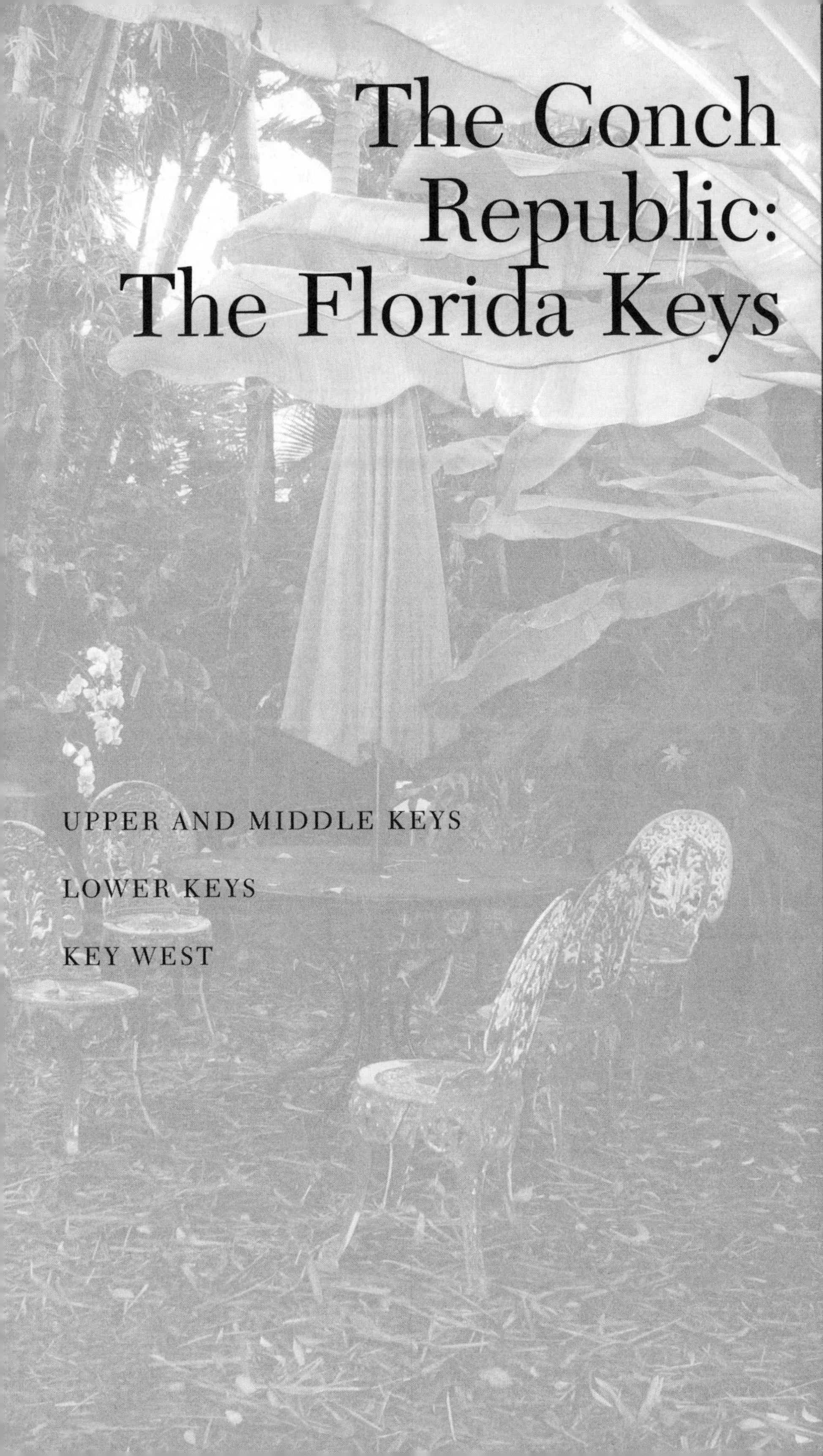

5

UPPER AND MIDDLE KEYS

LOWER KEYS

KEY WEST

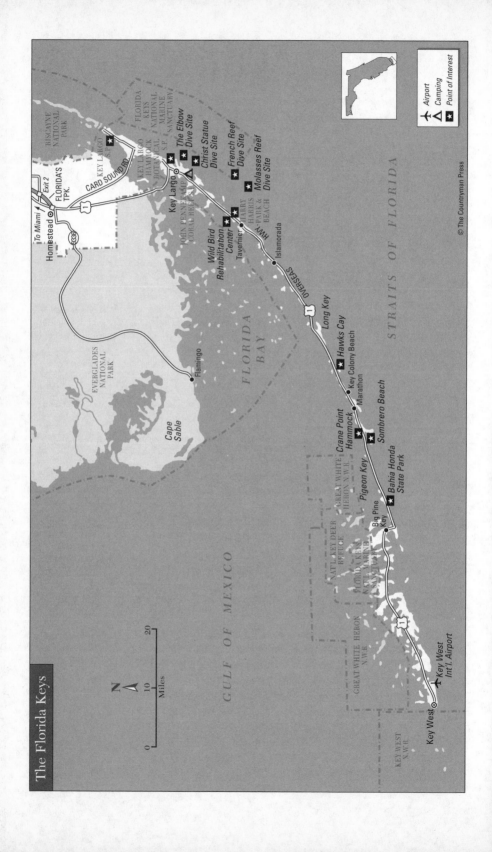

The Florida Keys

N

0 10 20
Miles

Airport
Camping
Point of Interest

BISCAYNE NATIONAL PARK

FLORIDA KEYS NATIONAL MARINE SANCTUARY

To Miami
Exit 2
FLORIDA'S TPK.
Homestead
336

KEY LARGO

CARD SOUND RD.

Key Largo

KEY LARGO HAMMOCK BOTANICAL S.P.

The Elbow Dive Site

Christ Statue Dive Site

French Reef Dive Site

Molasses Reef Dive Site

JOHN PENNEKAMP CORAL REEF S.P.

Wild Bird Rehabilitation Center

Tavernier

HARRY HARRIS PARK & BEACH

Islamorada

OVERSEAS

STRAITS OF FLORIDA

EVERGLADES NATIONAL PARK

Flamingo

Cape Sable

FLORIDA BAY

Long Key

Hawks Cay

Key Colony Beach

Marathon

GREAT WHITE HERON N.W.R.

Crane Point Hammock

Sombrero Beach

Pigeon Key

Bahia Honda State Park

NAT'L KEY DEER REFUGE

FLORIDA KEYS NAT'L MARINE SANCTUARY

Big Pine Key

GULF OF MEXICO

GREAT WHITE HERON N.W.R.

KEY WEST N.W.R.

Key West

Key West Int'l. Airport

© The Countryman Press

THE CONCH REPUBLIC:
THE FLORIDA KEYS

A string of pearls set in an emerald sea, the **Florida Keys** are connected by an amazing engineering feat—43 bridges that enable the Overseas Highway to island-hop more than 110 miles to reach one of Florida's oldest cities, Key West. With lush tropical foliage, expansive views of both shallow Florida Bay and the calm Atlantic waters, and the largest living coral reef in the United States, this is a special place, mostly disconnected from the rest of Florida and absolutely disconnected from the most of the world. Life is on "island time," people are friendly, and the atmosphere is casual virtually everywhere you go. It's no wonder authors have flocked to the Keys over the years, from luminaries such as Ernest Hemingway, Truman Capote, and Tennessee Williams to modern-day best-sellers such as Carl Hiaasen and James W. Hall. Artists, too—you'll find them here in profusion, with their roadside galleries, and musicians making a living working the endless supply of bars and restaurants up and down US 1. It's a different world, one that invites you to slow down and savor the sun, the breeze, and the coconut trees—the mellow world of the Keys.

Ponce de Leon is credited as the first explorer to encounter the Florida Keys, although when he found them on May 15, 1513, they were populated with native tribes of Calusa and Tequesta. Since the islands were difficult to access, most activity for the following 300 years reflected the life of the sea. Pirates occasionally inhabited the islands and often crashed into the coral reefs lining the shores. A flourishing wrecking industry was established to collect pirates' treasure and the bounties of cargo ships caught between the Caribbean islands and Europe and South America. Key West became the wealthiest city in the nation in the late 1800s and early 1900s, and it quickly developed into a more bustling city than any other in slow-growing south Florida. Pioneers from Palm Beach to Miami and Fort Myers visited Key West for supplies and to connect with the distant worlds of Washington, D.C., New York City, and Europe. Meanwhile, sponging, cigar making, and farming industries emerged in the Keys.

Henry Flagler is credited with opening up the Florida Keys to wealthy vacationers as well as the general public thanks to his "railroad that went to sea." The project took 20,000 men seven years and cost $50 million. During construction, 250 lives were lost and there were three hurricanes. The sponge trade died when blight killed the sea creatures, and the farmers were put out of business when

Flagler's railway made it possible to feed America's northern cities more cheaply with produce from Cuba. Alas, the train was laid to rest at sea by the Labor Day hurricane of 1935, which wiped out the railroad bridge along with most of Islamorada. The combination of the Depression era and the loss of revenue from Flagler's railway tumbled the fortunes of the Keys. Franklin Delano Roosevelt helped to reemploy local residents by commissioning the building of the Overseas Highway, which helped reestablish the Keys tourism industry and revived the local economy.

Today tourism is the leading industry in the Keys, where visitors can revel in the laid-back atmosphere and enjoy the perpetual sunshine and crystal blue sea with the nation's only living coral reef. Residents strive to protect the natural resources that make the Florida Keys the premier place in the nation for sport fishing, scuba diving and snorkeling, boating, and relaxing. The tiny chain of islands represents a fragile and unique ecosystem that provides habitat to many species of wildlife, marine life, and botanicals, all of which create the Keys paradise visitors and residents enjoy. More than 2,800 square nautical miles of water surrounding the island chain are designated as the Florida National Marine Sanctuary, where sea life, plants, and coral reefs are protected from destruction and pollution. The National Wildlife Refuges of the Florida Keys protect 416,000 acres of land and sea, as well as the many plants and animals that depend on these unique habitats.

A downside to the incredible draw of this luscious paradise is that the tourism industry has become such a commercial behemoth that it's pushing out local residents, who can no longer afford to live here because of sky-high real estate values and low labor wages. With an exodus of residents who once served diners and cleaned hotel rooms, there is a dearth of workers. Larger companies truck staff in from Homestead and Miami by bus each day, but it's sad that business has displaced the locals from their homes.

The Overseas Highway is currently under construction in an effort to improve safety and evacuation traffic flows on the 18-mile stretch of road connecting the Keys to the mainland. The $147.8 million dollar project includes adding a 7,500-foot-high bridge to carry some of the traffic and separating north and southbound lanes with a concrete barrier. Traffic continues to traverse the roadway during the construction project, which is slated for completion in 2009, but at press time, summer 2009, work is still underway.

UPPER AND MIDDLE KEYS

Many words have been written to praise the tropical beauty and splendor of the crystal-clear water around the coral reefs of **Key Largo.** For landlubbers, the island has one distinction that truly sets it apart—I know of nowhere else where you'll encounter a Crocodile Crossing road sign. The saline lakes of upper Key Largo are home to the last significant colony of American crocodiles in the world, protected by Crocodile Lakes National Wildlife Refuge. Key Largo is also the first dense outpost of truly tropical flora as you drive south, with protected thickets of some of the largest Caribbean trees on earth. It is the home of the most accessible coral reefs in the United States, where the first ever underwater preserve was established, and as such, is a mecca for divers and snorkelers alike. At 27 miles long, Key Largo is the largest of the Keys and includes the town of **Tavernier** at the Largo Sound end of the island. The first community on Key Largo was established at Rock Harbor in 1870. Key Largo, at the beginning of the long chain of islands, is a transitional sort of place. It has a strong sense of island charm, where boating and fishing are mainstays of activity, and its convenience to the mainland draws a big weekend tourist crowd. Yet since it is closest to the mainland, its atmosphere is still very traditional, very businesslike. There is a great deal of commerce and business here, and many residents commute to the mainland to work. Some might say Key Largo is the best of both worlds.

Islamorada is where you first feel like you're driving in the tropics, where placid aquamarine waters stretch off to the horizon on both sides of the road as you drive the causeways connecting the islands. Called "the purple islands" (*morada*) by the Spanish explorers who sailed these seas, the islands sport lush foliage hiding a variety of small waterfront mom-and-pop motels and artist studios. Settlement began in 1907 with a subdivision called the "Townsite of Isla-morada," and when the Overseas Railroad touched the islands, it adopted that name for the railroad station. The four major islands include Plantation Key, Windley Key, Upper Matecumbe, and Lower Matecumbe.

The largest of the island chains, **Marathon,** saw its first modern-day settlers in the 1830s, when Bahamian immigrants started a subsistence farming village on Vaca Key, near a source of freshwater; visit the remnants of Adderly Village at Crane Point Hammock. It wasn't until Henry Flagler's ambitious project hit this jumping-off point that the place fairly bustled with inhabitants, gathered here to engineer an amazing feat—crossing 7 miles of open ocean with a railway trestle. The marathon of work necessary to complete the railroad on Flagler's timetable

423

gave the 13-island chain its name. Once completed, the piers of the Seven Mile Bridge created eddies that attracted tarpon, which in turn attracted anglers to the water's bounty, making Marathon another favored destination for sportsmen. The island is home to the only airport in the Keys outside of Key West.

GUIDANCE The Florida Keys & Key West Tourism Council (305-296-1552 or 1-800-FLA-KEYS; www.fla-keys.com), 1201 White St., Ste. 102, Key West 33040, is your source for trip planning, and they have a number of excellent booklets and brochures to make it a breeze. Ask for information on a specific island or on a specific theme, such as diving, and they'll be happy to help. At 10600 Overseas Hwy., the **Key Largo Visitor Center** (1-800-822-1088; www.keylargo.org) is open 9–6 daily. The **Islamorada Chamber of Commerce** (305-664-4503; www.islamoradachamber.com), 83244 Overseas Hwy., has brochures and information on fishing the area. The **Greater Marathon Visitor Center** (305-743-5417 or 1-800-262-7284; www.floridakeysmarathon.com), 12222 Overseas Hwy., is just before Vaca Cut.

GETTING THERE *By car:* The Overseas Highway, **US 1,** is the only way to drive the Keys.

By air: To reach the Upper Keys, use **Miami International Airport** (see The Gables, the Grove, and Downtown Miami section. For the Middle Keys, a commuter flight to **Marathon Airport** (305-289-6060), 9400 Overseas Hwy., Ste. 200, is in order.

By bus: **Greyhound** (305-871-1810; www.greyhound.com) stops all along the islands; call for specific pickup locations and rates.

GETTING AROUND *By car:* **US 1** connects the islands; destinations along the road are designated by mile markers, with directions generally expressed according to "MM." When you get to MM0, you'll know you've reached the southernmost point of the United States in Key West. Enjoy the trip!

By bus: Since **Greyhound** links the islands, it's possible to use the bus to island-hop.

By taxi: If you fly into Marathon Airport, you can get where you're going with **Action Taxi** (305-743-6800) or **Sunset Taxi & Transportation** (305-289-7422).

MEDICAL EMERGENCIES One of the most serious medical emergencies a diver can experience is the bends, and with all the diving going on in the Keys, the **Key Largo Recompression Chamber** (911 if emergency, 1-800-NO-BENDS for information) can be a lifesaver for those in need. General emergencies should head to **Fisherman's Hospital** (305-743-5533; www.fishermanshospital.com), 3301 Overseas Hwy., MM 48.7, Marathon, where there is a 24-hour emergency room, or **Mariner's Hospital** (305-434-3000), at 91500 Overseas Hwy.

* To See
ART GALLERIES

Islamorada
More than 400 artists from around the country are represented in the fine work found at **Gallery Morada** (305-664-3650), 81611 Overseas Hwy.—Particularly

beautiful are the citrus-colored, wheel-thrown "bowl sculptures" of Marge Mar-guiles, part of the vast array of "practical art" in the gallery. Open 10–6 daily.

The Rain Barrel Artist Village (305-852-3084), 86700 Overseas Hwy., MM 86, is a haven for artists, each with their own gallery space and working studios where you can look over their latest projects. Among them are the **Lawler Gallery** (305-853-7011), the studio of longtime artist Dan Lawler, who paints a variety of sub-jects in a cartoon style, and the **Jefferson Clay Creations** (305-852-6911), with whimsical, free-form porcelain sculptures that reflect the plant and animal life in the Keys.

You'll find Stacie Krupa's bold, large paintings at **Stacie Krupa Studio Gallery** of Art (305-942-0614; www.staciekrupa.com), 82935 Overseas Hwy., MM 83.

Inside a historic Conch home, the **Wellington House Gallery** (305-664-8913), 81599 Overseas Hwy., showcases the handmade furnishings, acrylics and watercol-ors, sculptures, and tapestries of local artists.

Key Largo

At **The Gallery at Kona Kai** (305-852-7200; www.g-k-k.com), on the grounds of Kona Kai Resort (see *Lodging*), MM 97.8, view interpretations of South Florida as seen through the eyes of the finest artists—the pointillist ocean scenes of John Halver, the massive canvases of Stacy Krupa, Franco Passalauga's dreams of fish. It's also the only gallery in the Keys that represents Clyde Butcher's fine-art pho-tography.

Marathon

The **Bougainvillea House** (305-743-0808; www.bougainvilleahousegallery.com), 12420 Overseas Hwy., is the local artist's collective, featuring 26 Keys artists. Some of the works you'll see here include Georgina Hosek's glazed mosaics of sea life, fish rubbings by Jeannie Johnson, and Allison Schaeffler-Murphy's fascinating jew-elry and glass art. Stop in for Art on the Porch exhibits the second Saturday of each month. Closed Mon.

HISTORIC SITES

Islamorada

Swaying palm trees carved into tall slabs of coral rock are the centerpiece of the **Hurricane Monument** on Upper Matecumbe Key, a beautiful but solemn reminder of the hundreds who perished when a tidal wave engulfed the islands of Islamorada during the 1935 Labor Day hurricane. You'll find the monument oceanside in a small park at MM 81.6. The **Pioneer Cemetery,** MM 82, is on the grounds of Cheeca Lodge in Islamorada; the angel statue here is one of the few objects that survived the hurricane. **Windley Key Fossil Reef Geological State Park** (see *Parks*) at MM 85.5 showcases historic quarry equipment used in Henry Flagler's day to slice coral rock from several quarries now encompassed by the park.

Key Largo

If you're a film buff, you might enjoy the **Caribbean Club** (305-451-9970), MM 104 bayside; it's the only place in the Keys where scenes from the movie *Key Largo* were filmed in 1947, and the walls of the bar (yes, it's still a bar) are covered with memorabilia.

Marathon

Accessed from a visitors center at the southern tip of Marathon, **Pigeon Key** (see *Railroadiana*) was a work camp for workers on the Overseas Railroad, with historic homes, barracks, and outbuildings dating from the early 1900s. At **Crane Point Hammock** (see *Museums*), the **Adderly House** is hidden in the tropical forest along the hiking trails. On the National Register of Historic Places, it's the oldest remaining building on the island and was built of tabby in Bahamian style and completed in 1906. George Adderly's home became the focal point of a small African American settlement called Adderly Town, which persisted on Vaca Key through the completion of the railroad.

Islamorada

At **Theatre of the Sea** (305-664-2431; www.theatreofthesea.com), 84721 Overseas Hwy., brick paths meander beneath a bower of tropical plantings, past gibbons and parrots and deep saltwater pools lined with coral rock where loggerhead turtles and parrot fish glide. It's changed very little and grown more lush and interesting since Kenny McKenny opened these 17 acres as a tropical roadside attraction in 1946, created from old rock quarries left behind from the Overseas Railroad. The same family still owns and operates the park, nature trails lead out to a beach and into the mangrove forest to introduce you to native habitats. Open 9:30 AM– 4 PM daily. Adults $29.95, ages 3–10 $18.95. Reservations are essential for special programs, including several offshore cruises offered by the park.

MUSEUMS

Islamorada

Telling the story of the quest to explore beneath the sea, the **Florida Keys History of Diving Museum** (305-664-9737; www.divingmuseum.com), MM 83, showcases artifacts from the long history of diving in the Keys. Founders Joe and Sally Bauer have been collecting historic diving artifacts for more than 30 years and claim the world's largest collection of this unique niche. The museum opened in 2006 but already has a history of diving and treasure hunting in South Florida. Donations appreciated.

Marathon

✍ Carved out of a dense tropical hammock, **Crane Point Hammock Museums & Nature Center** (305-743-9100; www.cranepoint.net), 5550 Overseas Hwy., has something for everyone. Administered by the nonprofit Florida Keys Land Trust, this 63-acre preserve includes the last intact thatch palm hammock in the Keys. There are two museums on-site. In the Museum of Natural History of the Florida Keys, walk through a replica reef, see a 600-year-old dugout canoe, and learn the gamut of Keys history, from its indigenous peoples through wreckers and "Flagler's Folly." In the Children's Museum, the kids will love the engaging outdoor exhibits that put them on the deck of a pirate ship or in a Native American village or railroad station, with touch tanks and an iguana house, too. But the beauty of this park is how it immerses you in the outdoors. Mulched trails lead through a lush primordial forest of ferns, where orchids hang high overhead; a boardwalk crosses a solution hole lined with mangroves. Butterflies flutter in a butterfly garden under the buttonwoods. Walk the trails to discover the **Adderly House** (see *Historic Sites*), the **Marathon Wild Bird Center** (see Wildlife *Rehab*), and a boardwalk out to

Florida Bay. Open 9 AM–5 PM Mon.–Sat. and noon–5 Sun. Adults $11, seniors $9, students 6 and up $7, children under 6 free.

RAILROADIANA After running his Florida East Coast Railroad the length of the Atlantic Coast in Florida in the early 1900s, Henry Flagler proposed the "Key West Extension," bridging 153 miles of open seas to reach the port at Key West. The newspapers derided it as "Flagler's Folly," yet Flagler had the deep pockets to make it happen. Thousands of workers swarmed into the Keys to blast coral rock, build support piers, and lay girders to make Flagler's dream come true, despite a 1910 hurricane that displaced part of the railroad in the Lower Keys. On January 22, 1912, Flagler stepped out of his private railcar to the cheers of half the population of Key West, officially inaugurating the **Overseas Railroad.** It was a hit with tourists, bringing eager sportsmen to previously undiscovered islands, and it encouraged commerce to and from the port of Key West. Then tragedy struck. In 1935 the Labor Day hurricane bore down on the Middle Keys. A 17-foot tidal wave struck the islands, toppling a train with more than 500 World War I veterans who worked for the railroad into the sea. Miles of track and bridges were demolished. It was the end of the line for "Flagler's Folly," and much of the right-of-way was soon turned over to the transportation department to build the Overseas Highway, which began construction in the late 1930s. A large memorial on Matecumbe Key is dedicated to those who died in the storm. Remnants of **railroad trestles** (now used as fishing piers) and a **caboose** parked in Islamorada across from Matecumbe Station are some of the relics left behind.

Pigeon Key Historical Railroad Site (305-743-5999; www.pigeonkey.net), MM 48 on Knight's Key, oceanside before the Seven Mile Bridge, kicks right off with a bit of railroad history—the visitors center where you pick up the tram is "Old 64," a **Flagler railroad Pullman car** owned by George Kyle. A nonprofit organization, these folks run tours 10–4 daily (adults $11, ages 5–13 $8.50). Visit the **Pigeon Key Museum** for detailed background on the building of the Overseas Railroad and the original Seven Mile Bridge, which our tour guide asserted is better built than the one used by cars today; it's survived nine hurricanes. Several historic buildings, such as the Bridge Tender's House and the Paint Foreman's House, also tell the railroad's story. After the railroad's demise, the island became a stopping-off point for motorists crossing the Seven Mile Bridge and later passed into private hands before being acquired to tell its history. Open 9:30 AM–4 PM daily; tours leave on the hour 10 AM–3 PM.

WILDLIFE REHAB
Key Largo
At the **Florida Keys Wild Bird Center** (305-852-4486; www.fkwbc.org), MM 93.6 bayside, wander a boardwalk through enclosures with wild hawks, osprey, roseate spoonbills, and other birds that could not be released after rehabilitation. The nonprofit center rescues and rehabilitates injured birds in the Upper Keys. Donations appreciated.

Marathon
✄ On the grounds of Crane Point Hammock, the **Marathon Wild Bird Center** (305-743-8382; www.marathonwildbirdcenter.org) cares for injured and orphaned

birds, particularly raptors, with the intent of rehabilitation to release them back into the wild. See ospreys, owls, and hawks in their flight cages, and pelicans that were injured by improperly discarded monofilament fishing line.

A nonprofit rescue mission for sea turtles, **The Turtle Hospital** (305-743-2552; www.turtlehospital.org) is the only state-certified veterinary hospital in the world that cares just for sea turtles. Working with donated medical equipment, experienced veterinarians stabilize, care for, and rehabilitate ill and injured sea turtles. Guided tours (adults $15, ages 4–12 $7.50) last 45 minutes and are offered daily at 10, 1, and 4. Reservations are required; tours subject to cancellation due to turtle emergencies and/or weather.

✳ To Do

BICYCLING The **Florida Keys Overseas Heritage Trail** (see *Greenways*) provides miles of paved bike trail for you to roam, including the entire length of Key Largo and several long stretches in and around Islamorada.

BIRDING Along the **waysides of the Overseas Highway** and at any of the *Green Space* stops listed, you'll have the opportunity to view ibises, herons, and other wading birds. **Curry Hammock State Park,** MM 56.2 (see *Beaches*) boasts some of the best seasonal birding in the Keys—it's on the flyover route for most migrating raptors and has a tall observation tower for you to bring your binoculars and watch. The Florida Keys Birding and Wildlife Festival is held in September through October annually at Curry Hammock State Park (305-289-2690; www .keysbirdingfest.org).

BOATING The folks are friendly at **Robbie's Marina** (305-664-9814 and 1-877-664-8498; www.robbies.com), MM 75.5, Little Matecumbe Key, and you have lots of options for getting out on the water. Rent a boat, from a 15-foot skiff to a 26-foot Rendezvous, hop a boat out to the offshore state parks, arrange a snorkeling trip on a captained boat (see *Ecotours*), charter for offshore game fishing, head out fishing on the flats, or check in at adjacent **Florida Keys Kayak & Sail** (305-664-4878) for backcountry tours ($39 and up) and kayak or sailboat rentals. But the really big deal here is that you can feed the tarpon. The schools of huge fish that hover under the docks and wait for the nearly constant handouts have made Robbie's famous. The fun began in 1986 when marina owners Robbie and his wife, Mona, found an injured tarpon under their dock. The fish needed stitches for a slash in his jaw, and the couple nursed him back to health for six months before releasing him. Dubbed Scarface, the fish came back to visit and brought his fish pals along, and soon the feeding tradition was established.

DIVING

Key Largo
With the only living reef in the United States, the Florida Keys are a mecca for divers eager to enjoy the colorful underwater gardens of coral and to explore the many offshore wrecks. **Key Largo** is diver central, with dedicated dive resorts that cater to folks in wetsuits, dive shops, and charters to get you out on the reefs, which start 6 miles offshore. Sadly, and a great loss for science, the reefs are said to be diminished by 90 to 95 percent today, mostly from pollution and global warming.

Be careful not to touch the living coral when you swim, snorkel or dive, because just touching the fragile sea life can damage and kill the precious little that's left.

A favorite for snorkelers, **Keys Diver Snorkel Tours** (305-451-1177 or 1-888-289-2402; www.keysdiver.com), 99696 Overseas Hwy., makes a point of avoiding the crowds and provides top-notch gear for your experience out on the reef. Their small groups, safety-conscious practices, and responsible ecosnorkeling make them especially good for families and those a bit timid in the water. **Amy Slate's Amoray Dive Resort** (305-451-3595 or 1-800-426-6729; www.amoray.com), MM 104, US 1 bayside, 104250 Overseas Hwy., is the place for divers and wannabes. Since 1978 Amy Slate has offered cozy shelter, instruction, and boat trips for those anxious to enjoy the beautiful coral reefs, shipwrecks, stingrays, sharks, sea life, and dolphins. Single rooms and waterfront apartments are available, $99–$329. Since 1962, **Ocean Divers North** (305-451-1113; www.oceandivers.com), 105800 Overseas Hwy., has served visiting divers with a large stock of rental Scuba Pro equipment, PADI instruction, regulator repair service, and daily diving and snorkeling trips departing at 8 AM and 1 PM. **Silent World Dive Center** (304-451-3252 or 1-800-966-DIVE; www.SilentWorldKeyLargo.com), MM 103.2 bayside, offers instruction and leads 14-passenger trips out to the reefs in Pennekamp and the Key Largo National Marine Sanctuary. At the Bonefish Bay Motel and Cottages, **Abyss Dive Center** (305-743-2126 or 1-800-457-0134; www.abyssdive .com), MM 53.5, offers instruction, rentals, and a dive boat to get you out on the reef. See *Dive Resorts* for other stay-and-play options. If you're an experienced diver and want a truly unique vacation, book **Jules Undersea Lodge** (305-451-2353; www.jul.com), 51 Shoreland Dr. at MM 103.5; it's the world's first undersea hotel, boasting a two-bedroom, air-conditioned suite 30 feet below water in Emerald Lagoon, and yes, they offer room service.

Marathon

The Florida Keys National Marine Sanctuary Shipwreck Trail (www.florida keys.noaa.gov) commemorates five centuries of ships wrecked on the reefs surrounding the keys. Visit their Web site or pick up a brochure at a visitors center to pinpoint where the wrecks are located.

Beginners dive at **Sombrero Reef,** a coral garden where parrot fish and stingrays play, while advanced divers head out to the Thunderbolt, a sunken research vessel that is home to barracuda, moray eels, and at least one goliath grouper dubbed "Bubba."

ECOTOURS

Key Largo
The **Key Largo Princess glass bottom boat** (305-451-4655 or 1-877-648-8129; keylargoprincess.com) leaves the Holiday Inn docks (MM 100) at 10, 1 and 4, offering trips to Molasses Reef and others at Pennekamp as well. Adults $30 and children $15.

Islamorada
Robbie's Marina has ecotours—two hour trips through seagrass beds and protected shallow bays; mangroves and hammock islands; not predetermined but based on group interest. (305-664-9814 or 1-877-664-8498; www.robbies.com), MM 75.5, Little Matecumbe Key.

FISHING There are few better places than the Keys to spend your days fishing. There are hundreds of places along US 1 where you can pull off and cast a line. The waters of Florida Bay are shallow and clear for flats fishing, and on the ocean side, the outer edge of the reef drops off into an abyss where some of the best "big game" fish are found, including wahoo, sailfish, dolphin, kingfish, and marlin. Flats fishing is especially popular because of the ease with which you can catch the "Big Three"—tarpon, bonefish, and permit. Tarpon fishing is best April through June, and permit and bonefish most common from spring through fall. You'll find charter boats and fishing guides at every marina, because fishing is the lifestyle of the Keys. Keys charter captains recommend using friendly fishing hooks that don't injure the fish when sportfishing. Consider using these hooks to protect the sport for years to come. Check at **Robbie's Marina** (see *Boating*) or **Suzanne Fishing Charters** (305-664-9202; www.suzannefishingcharters.com), Whale Harbor Marina, Islamorada, to book a deep-sea trip; at **World Wide Sportsman** (see *Selective Shopping*) for deep-sea fishing; and **Florida Keys Anglers** (305-712-0258; www.floridakeysanglers.com) for sight fishing the flats.

HIKING Most people don't associate hiking with the Keys, but there are great little walks that introduce you to the tropical habitats. You'll find two pleasant short nature trails at **John Pennekamp Coral Reef State Park,** a network of five short trails at **Windley Key Geological State Park,** and one of the best hikes in the Keys at **Long Key State Park. Curry Hammock State Park** has a new bayside loop trail, and **Crane Point Hammock** (see *Museums*) offers several miles of hiking trails in a dense tropical hammock. But the wildest place of all to hike is on Key Largo. Check in at Pennekamp's ranger station for a backcountry permit to go beyond the nature trail and wander the forest roads of **Key Largo Hammocks Botanical State Park,** which encompasses nearly 3,000 acres of tropical forest adjacent to Crocodile Lakes National Wildlife Refuge.

HOUSEBOATING Imagine drifting through the crystal-clear shallows of Florida Bay . . . on a houseboat! Rent a fully equipped houseboat that sleeps up to six and includes access to a private island for your docking and tropical pleasure (305-879-1101; www.rentmyhouseboats.com) from $2800 per week.

LOBSTERING August 6 through March 31 marks the annual **Florida lobster season,** when you're welcome to scuba or snorkel for your own dinner (Beware: I heard the lobster scream when I caught one!). Limits are 6 per day or 24 per boat, and specific areas, such as the waters of John Pennekamp Coral Reef State Park and Everglades National Park, are excluded. For the full list of rules and regulations, contact the **Florida Marine Patrol** (1-800-342-5367 or 1-800-ASK-FISH) or the **National Marine Fisheries Service** (813-570-5305 or 305-743-2437).

PADDLING Sea kayaking is the best way to explore the thousands of mangrove-lined passageways on Florida Bay, and you'll find plenty of outfitters ready to set you up on a paddling trip. At MM 104 on Key Largo, **Florida Bay Outfitters** (305-451-3018; www.kayakfloridakeys.com) offers instruction and rentals ($40 and up), with guided tours starting at $50; **Marathon Kayak** (305-743-0561; www.marathonkayak.com), 7849 Overseas Hwy., has rentals and guided tours available. At Duck Key, **Hawk's Cay** (305-743-7000 or 1-888-313-5749; www.hawkscay

.com), 61 Hawk's Cay Blvd., offers ecokayak adventures for $35–40, or you can rent your own kayak for $20–30 per hour.

SAILING You'll experience the wind in your hair and the spray of the sea at **Colgate's Offshore Sailing School** (www.offshore-sailing.com) at **Hawk's Cay Resort** (see *Lodging*). Founded in 1964 by Olympic and America's Cup sailor Steve Colgate, the school offers a variety of courses to fit your schedule. The two-hour clinic gives you a chance to experience the thrill of sailing. The 3- to 6-day Learn to Sail courses on Colgate 26 sailboats combine classroom and offshore sailing, while leaving you enough time each day to enjoy the resort. You'll sail on 46-foot Hunters down to Key West on the Live Aboard Cruising course, while tacking, jibbing, reefing, learning about wind direction, what to do in weather conditions, and reading nautical maps. Or totally immerse yourself on the 10-day Fast Track to Cruising course, which includes both the Learn to Sail and Live Aboard Cruising courses, along with boat mechanics and how to plan your own sea adventure.

SCENIC DRIVE You don't have much of a choice—US 1 is the only highway linking the Keys, and it's one of the most scenic drives in Florida, often offering simultaneous views of the Atlantic Ocean and Florida Bay, especially through Islamorada south to Marathon. The Overseas Highway was recently named an "All American Road," the top designation for a scenic highway in the nation. Relax and enjoy.

SPA THERAPY The **Calm Waters Spa** at Hawk's Cay (305-289-4810; www.hawkscay.com), 61 Hawk's Cay Blvd., nourishes your body after a long day in the sun. The yoga-inspired Thai Massage ($130–160) loosens tense muscles through a variety of stretches and relaxation techniques. Their signature Keys Style Margarita Salt Loofa treatment ($90) exfoliates you, starting with the tropical rain room, then continues with the Margarita Salt massage, followed by botanical tequila gel and their lime body lotion. Teens will love the Jazzy Island Manicure ($25) and Jazzy Island Pedicure ($30).

Avanyu Spa at Cheeca Lodge (305-517-4485), MM 82, US 1 oceanside, 81801 Oceanside Hwy., Islamorada, lets you relax your back and brain at this full-service spa open to the public. Enjoy an Avanyu Swedish massage or several different variations, with or without the fragrance of essential oils, or invigorate your circulation with a salt scrub, mud wrap, or hydrotherapy. There are facials, sun-damage treatments, and special services for kids and teens, too.

Island Body & Sol Spa At The Moorings (www.islandbodyandsol.com), MM 81.6, oceanside, 123 Beach Rd., Islamorada, provides peaceful ambiance in a warm, dark, and quiet spa with all types of body treats available, from Japanese facial massage to aromatherapy with warmed oils or Native American treaments with hot stones. The perfect enhancement to your beach vacation. Open daily by appointment.

WATER SPORTS

Key Largo
There's lots to do at **Caribbean Watersports** (305-852-4707; www.caribbean watersports.com), 97000 Overseas Hwy., MM 97 at the Westin Beach Resort, where you can grab a Hobie Cat or a sailboard, or sign up for a sailing lesson or

snorkeling trip. Lounge at their sandy beach, and kick back and enjoy the sunset. At **Key Largo Parasail** (305-747-0032; www.keylargoparasail.com), MM 104, rise a thousand feet into the air on the sea breeze . . . if you dare!

✳ Green Space

BEACHES One little secret about the Upper and Middle Keys: Beaches are few and far between. The islands are mangrove lined, so when you find a stretch of natural beach, it's truly a delight. **John Pennekamp Coral Reef State Park** (see *Parks*) offers two small beaches, but you might prefer swimming off the sandy beach at **Harry Harris County Park,** MM 92, Tavernier, or at **Founder's Park,** MM 86, in Islamorada. **Anne's Beach,** MM 73.5 between Islamorada and Marathon, has a boardwalk through the mangroves and fishing areas as well as two small sandy beaches. On Marathon, check out **Sombrero Public Beach,** 2 miles south of MM 50 at the end of Sombrero Beach Road, where there's a playground, picnic tables, and restrooms, and **Curry Hammock State Park** (305-289-2690), 56200 Overseas Hwy., which offers picnic tables, a brand-new campground, and a short nature trail.

GREENWAYS Making use of the remaining bridges and right-of-way of the Overseas Railroad, the **Florida Keys Overseas Heritage Trail** (305-853-3571; www .dep.state.fl.us/gwt/state/keystrail/default.htm), Three La Croix Court, Key Largo, is a paved path paralleling the Overseas Highway to enable bikers and pedestrians a safe way to travel through the Keys. The trail currently stretches 60 miles with plans to eventually extend it the full 106 miles between Key Largo and Key West.

PARKS

Key Largo
The first undersea park in America, **John Pennekamp Coral Reef State Park** (305-451-1202), MM 103, offers landlubbers some fun as well. Start off at the visitors center to see the saltwater aquariums, including a 30,000-gallon tank, that orient you to the sea life found in this 70-nautical-square-mile park, and then explore the park's two nature trails. The Wild Tamarind Trail is a short loop through the dense tropical hardwood hammock—look closely at tree limbs to spot colorful tree snails. On the Mangrove Trail, walk a boardwalk through tunnels formed by the mangroves, with an observation deck over the meandering saline creeks. Keep alert for giant iguanas—nonnative, but nevertheless roaming the berm along the park road. There are two beaches for swimming and an underwater snorkeling trail. All this without getting on a boat! If you plan to visit the reef (and you should), the park concession (see *Ecotours*) offers diving, snorkeling, and glass-bottom boat trips. Fee.

Long Key
With its fine selection of oceanfront campsites, **Long Key State Park** (305-664-4815), 67400 Overseas Hwy., MM 67.5, has always been a favorite for tent campers, and you will enjoy exploring the mangrove-lined lagoons by kayak. But I love this park most for its hiking trail. **The Golden Orb Trail** loops only a little more than a mile, but it's one of the most fascinating hikes in the Keys, passing through five different plant communities, including the desertlike coastal berm, where salt-tolerant plants grow on layers of coral.

Offshore from Little Matecumbe Key, **Lignumvitae Key Botanical State Park** (305-664-2540) protects a rarity in these parts—a virgin tropical hardwood forest. A small part of the island was cleared for William J. Matheson, a wealthy Miami chemist, to build a caretaker's home in 1919; the stone structure is now the visitors center. Visitors must walk with a ranger to explore the botanical wonders, which include a gnarled lignum vitae tree more than 2,000 years old. Tours start at the dock and are given twice daily, Thursday through Monday; bring insect repellent and, if it isn't the dead of winter, a mosquito head net! Fee. Check at Robbie's Marina (see *Boating*) for daily tour boat times, which may vary.

✐ At **Windley Key Fossil Reef Geological State Park** (305-664-2540), MM 85.5, Henry Flagler's workmen quarried Key Largo limestone—a fossilized coral— to use in building structures along the Overseas Railroad. The quarry continued in active operation through the 1960s, producing decorative stone for building facades. Stop at the visitors center (open 8 AM–5 PM Thurs.–Mon.) to orient yourself to the history of this site, and then wander the trails to enjoy the shady tropical hammocks and to examine the incredible detail of fossils in the coral walls. There is a small picnic area on-site. Fee.

WILD PLACES In the Keys, it doesn't get wilder than out on and *in* the water. The **Florida Keys National Marine Sanctuary** (305-743-2437; www.floridakeys .noaa.gov) encompasses 2,800 nautical square miles along the entire island chain. Both Florida Bay and the flats behind the Atlantic-side reefs have hundreds of small, uninhabited islands buttressed by mangroves and accessible only by boat. The sanctuary includes the waters of the Key Largo National Marine Sanctuary and John Pennekamp Coral Reef State Park.

Key Largo Hammock Botanical State Park (305-451-1202), CR 905 just north of US 1, offers a wild walk through the "land of little giants," the largest collection of the smallest National Champion trees in the United States, growing in the densest and largest tropical hammock in the country. Backcountry permits are available to allow you to roam more than 2,000 acres of tropical forest on forest roads. Avoid the temptation to go off-road unless you know your poisonous trees well. Fee. Adjacent **Crocodile Lakes National Wildlife Refuge** (305-451-4223; www.fws .gov/southeast/crocodilelake), covering nearly 7,000 acres, is not open to the public for good reason—it has the highest population of endangered American crocodiles on earth, and they need to be left undisturbed.

✳ Lodging

CAMPGROUNDS

Key Largo 33037
🐾 Shaded campsites are the norm at **Florida Keys RV Resort** (305-451-6090), 106003 Overseas Hwy., a resort with full hookups ($35 and up), a pool and spa, and a 2-acre fishing lake.

✐ **Key Largo Kampground and Marina** (305-451-1431 or 1-800-526-7688; www.keylargokampground.com),

101551 Overseas Hwy., has a handful of waterfront sites on the Atlantic Ocean, a boat ramp, and dockage. Two beaches and a pool make this a great family destination; full hookup and tent sites available, starting at $33.

Marathon 33050
Relax at **Jolly Roger Travel Park** (305-289-0404 or 1-800-995-1525;

www.jrtp.com) along Florida Bay, where campsites are $45.

COTTAGES

Marathon 33050

On its own private island, **Conch Key Cottages** (305-289-1377 or 1-800-330-1577; www.conchkeycottages.com), MM 62.3, is a quiet retreat once known as Walker's Island, where some of the cottages date from the 1920s and have wonderful "old Conch" interiors with varnished wooden walls and ceilings. A path winds through the well-manicured grounds with tropical gardens to each of the cottages, which are painted in pastels and named after seashells. There are no phones to puncture the bliss of your stay, but use of a kayak comes with every unit. Rates run $398 for one bedroom. Enjoy the pool tucked under the sea grapes, or swim at their own private beach.

DIVE RESORTS

Key Largo 33037

Amy Slate's Amoray Dive Resort (305-451-3595 or 1-800-4-AMORAY; www.amoray.com), 104250 Overseas Hwy., is a dedicated dive resort with dive-stay packages, instruction, and underwater weddings; rates start at $99. Specializing in small, personalized diving expeditions, **Kelly's on the Bay** (305-451-1622 or 1-800-226-0415), 104220 Overseas Hwy., is a small family-owned resort with 32 bayside units ($70–175).

HOTELS, MOTELS, AND RESORTS

Key Largo 33037

Step between the carved wooden palms into another world at **Kona Kai Resort & Gallery** (305-852-7200 or 1-800-365-STAY; www.konakairesort .com), 97802 Overseas Hwy., where

Joe and Ronnie Harris wrought magic on a 1940s seaside motel to transform it into one of the most intimate and relaxing resorts in the Keys, centered around a classy fine-art gallery. Tastefully decorated with art, the tropical gardens boast nearly 40 types of rare palms, a tropical fruit garden, and more than 400 species of orchids in Ronnie's orchid house—if you love tropical flora like I do, ask for a map. Each room is named for a tropical fruit: our one-bedroom Key Lime Suite ($339–419) included an incredible host of amenities, including a full kitchen with new appliances, glass-block accent walls, remote controls for the CD player and fans, island music and books, and original artwork decorating the rooms. Televisions are included, but no phones. The regular guest rooms ($244–369) are very spacious and include a mini fridge; there are one- and two-bedroom suites as well ($608–789). After watching the sunset from the dock on Florida Bay, we enjoyed a soak in the Jacuzzi and a swim in the pool. Guests have use of kayaks and paddleboats, too. Pampered? You bet. I can't wait to return.

Largo Lodge Motel (352-451-0424 or 1-800-468-4378; www.largolodge .com), 101740 Overseas Hwy. Hidden in a palm hammock, this intimate resort caters to adults only, with rooms and cottages on the bay starting at $95.

Several years ago I stayed at the **Marriott Key Largo Bay Beach Resort** (305-453-0000 or 1-866-849-3733; www.marriottkeylargo.com), 103800 Overseas Hwy., and was delighted by the size of my room ($199 and up) and its view of Florida Bay. Down at the lushly landscaped pool area, I grabbed a margarita at the tiki bar and relaxed with my favorite novel—the perfect end to a busy day of research. It's a large complex, with restaurants, meeting facilities, and a full-service spa, but still small enough to wander around in your sandals without feeling out of place.

I've always found **Popp's Motel** (305-852-5201; www.popps.com), 95500 Overseas Hwy., a visually appealing destination. Owned by the same family since 1951, it offers 10 affordable "home away from home" cottages ($99–119) with kitchens, a boat ramp, and a private sand beach on Florida Bay.

Long Key 33001
Nestled in a coconut grove along Florida Bay, the intimate **Lime Tree Bay Resort** (305-664-4740 or 1-800-723-4519; www.limetreebayresort.com), has a waterfront pool, great snorkeling offshore, and an appealing selection of 33 motel rooms ($89 and up) and one- and two-bedroom suites ($205 and up), many with stunning views. With a family in tow, I'd go for the Zane Grey, a two-bedroom unit with island decor, a writing desk, wooden blinds, and wraparound windows with an awesome view of Florida Bay.

Duck Key 33050
◢ **Hawk's Cay Resort** (305-743-7000 or 1-888-443-6393; www.hawkscay .com), 61 Hawk's Cay Blvd., encompasses 60 acres on a tropical island, just east of MM 61. You can choose from 161 guest rooms and suites in the main hotel or stay in one of their two-bedroom villas with living room and fully furnished kitchen. The Marina Villa is all on one floor, while the two-story Conch Villa has an optional tropical spa on your own private deck. For those needing more space or privacy, the Sanctuary Villa, at 1,750 square feet, comes with its very own private pool. All are tropically decorated and have a private porch or deck where you can watch the sun rise over the

Atlantic Ocean or set on the Gulf. Once you've settled in, there's a lot to do. At the **Indies Club,** kids can splash around and "slide the plank" at the **Pirate's Ship** pool, complete with water cannons. The **Treehouse** features S-curve and rocket slides, monkey bars, a tire swing, and a climbing wall. Fun kids' activities also include the **Hermit Crab Derby** for the little ones and **Island Scavenger Hunt** for teens. Preteens and teens will love hanging out at **The Cove** (fee), where they can dance, sing karaoke, or play air hockey and Xbox. Couples will want to snuggle on the **Sunset Champagne Cruise** ($35), and anglers will want to charter a boat and head to the backcountry flats ($325–675) or near the Gulf Stream for offshore or reef fishing ($550–1,300). Other water activities run the gamut from Jet Skiing ($59 and up an hour), wakeboarding ($89 and up per lesson), snorkeling ($35), and ecokayaking tours ($35–45) to **Colgate's Offshore Sailing School** (see *Sailing*), where professional U.S. sailing–certified instructors, under the direction of Olympic and America's Cup sailor Steve Colgate, teach you on Colgate 26 sailboats and 46-foot Hunters. Clinics run from two hours to 10 days. The **Calm Waters Spa** (see *Spa Therapy*) takes you further into nirvana with their Pineapple Coconut Sugar Glow Body Treatment ($65) or their Tropical Breeze Escape Massage ($80–125). The Tropical Teaser ($216) pairs the two and adds a Mini-Botanical Facial for a full two hours of relaxation and rejuvenation.

Islamorada 33036
Chesapeake Resort (305-664-4662 or 1-800-338-3395; www.chesapeake -resort.com), 83409 Overseas Hwy., offers something for everyone: a place to relax with a view of the Atlantic framed by coconut palms, your choice

of standard motel rooms or deluxe accommodations in spacious ocean-front rooms ($195 and up), and an oceanside pool and spa adjoining the sunning beach.

A gigantic retro sign on US 1 beckons you into **The Islander Resort** (305-664-2031 or 1-800-753-6002; www .islanderfloridakeys.com), P.O. Box 766, MM 82.1, but there's nothing retro about this updated oceanfront resort. Every spacious room has high ceilings and a tiled floor; is decorated in shades of blue and white; and is sparkling clean, even the full kitchen. Walkways lead to the oceanfront, where you can enjoy two zero-entry pools or nearly a quarter mile of Atlantic Ocean beach. Your choices include studio lanai ($149–235), one-bedroom ($205–385), and two-bed-room ($305–505) units.

On Florida Bay, the tropical **Kon-Tiki Resort** (305-664-4702; www.kontiki -resort.com), 81200 Overseas Hwy., is a collection of 1960s-era villas with updated furnishings in spacious rooms; most have two bedrooms, full living room, dining area, and kitchen, and a screened porch ($127 and up, with dis-counts for weekly and monthly stays). Dockage is available for boats up to 25 feet long, but personal watercraft are not permitted.

🦐 ♿ 🐾 "Think pink!" at the **Sands of Islamorada** (305-664-2791 or 1-888-741-4518; www.sandsofislamorada .com), 80051 Overseas Hwy., a charm-ing little old-fashioned beach resort under the same ownership for 20 years. Dressed in bold tropical colors, the airy rooms and efficiencies ($165 and up) feature tile floors, high ceil-ings, full-sized refrigerator, coffeemak-er, and microwave. Relax in the pool or hot tub and listen to resident parrots Tela, Dolly, and Scootie squawk and squabble, or enjoy their beachfront on

the Atlantic Ocean, where the water is crystal clear for snorkeling. A boat ramp and dockage are available for your craft.

Cheeca Lodge & Spa (305-664-4651 or 1-800-327-2888; www.cheeca.com), MM 82, US 1 oceanside, 81801 Oceanside Hwy., Islamorada, is a self-contained, nationally acclaimed resort and makes the perfect getaway for those who require privacy yet desire the utmost in service and amenities. Cheeca, established as an inn in 1946, offers 27 acres of ultramanicured fun for celebrities such as former president George H. W. Bush, for whom the lodge's grandest suite is named. The resort was recently renovated, with all suites reflecting a West Indies decor including mahogany furniture and marble bathrooms. Some units are available for sale as condo-hotel suites. In addition, a new private club with oceanfront dining room and outdoor lounge has opened. Private beach, fish-ing boats, and an Ernest Heming-way–inspired clubhouse are still planned for owners and members to enjoy, along with other member-exclu-sive privileges such as preferred pric-ing on amenities. With a palm-lined beach, sunset cruises perfect for wed-dings, and long, lighted dock, Cheeca easily lives up to its trademark "bare-foot elegance." $150 and up.

The Moorings Village and Spa (305-664-4708; www.mooringsvillage andspa.com), MM 81.6, oceanside, 123 Beach Rd., is a charming collection of modern Keys-style cottages clustered under palms and coconut trees on a private beach. Enjoy the spa, kayaking, and sailing at this exclusive and peace-ful enclave. From $250 per night to $9,000 per week. Worth it.

Holiday Isle Beach Resorts and Marina (305-664-2321 or 1-800-327-7070; www.holidayisle.com), MM 84,

US 1 oceanside, 84001 Overseas Hwy., Islamorada, is legendary for its tiki bar, which serves tropical rum runners and piña coladas all day and night to the hundreds who've chosen to stay here or in the near vicinity (there is a complex of hotels, shops, and restaurants clustered here). The atmosphere is big and busy, loud and fun—it's a place where anglers, boaters, tourists, and kids coexist in a crowd of ticky-tacky fun. Stay at Harbor Lights, 0.5 mile from the tiki bar ($75 and up for a single), or on the ocean at Holiday Isle ($250 and up for the presidential suite).

Marathon 33050

Hidden in a thickly canopied jungle of banana palms and other tropical plants on Marathon, **Banana Bay Resort & Marina** (305-743-3500 or 1-866-689-4217; www.bananabay.com) is a retreat in itself. Enjoy clean, spacious guest rooms ($95–225) with continental breakfast served next to the oversized pool with adjoining whirlpool. The resort offers watersports rentals and fishing charters in addition to a heated freshwater pool, swim-up tiki bar, and private beach.

Coral Lagoon Resort (305-289-1323;

Trish Riley

WATERFRONT VIEWS AT CORAL LAGOON RESORT

www.corallagoonresort.com), MM 53.5, 123999 Overseas Hwy., is a newly built collection of lovely two- and three-bedroom townhouses featuring full amenities from waterfront porches to laundry machines and a boat dock and storage marina. Rent as low as $199 per night or buy one for $500,000–1.2 million.

✐ Settle into a cute cottage at **Crystal Bay Resort** (305-289-8089 or 1-888-289-8089; www.crystalbayresort.com), 4900 Overseas Hwy., a 1950s resort with updated interiors. The suites are large and open and make great use of the natural light. It's a perfect place to bring the family, with an on-site miniature golf course (go ahead, knock that ball into the gator's mouth!), a shaded playground, and a pool next to the bay as well as a marina and dock for your boat. Cottages start at $85, efficiencies at $110, and suites at $140.

Retro rooms and a tiled pool make the charming **Flamingo Inn** (305-289-1478 or 1-800-439-1478; www.the flamingoinn.com), 59299 Overseas Hwy., a fun place to stay; it has curb appeal, a boat ramp, and basic accommodations for reasonable prices ($50–159).

HOLIDAY ISLE, ISLAMORADA

James Steele

Captain Pip's Marina and Hideaway (305-743-4403 or 1-800-707-2844; www.captainpips.com), MM 47.5, US 1 bayside, 1410 Overseas Hwy., Marathon. It pays to stay at a fishing marina: Captain Pip's offers the use of an 18- or 21-foot boat during your stay, which is a big savings on boat rental. Crafted of rustic whitewashed Dade County pine and shaded with colorful blue awnings, the rooms have refrigerators, microwaves, and toasters, while suites have gulf-front views and full kitchens. There are also efficiencies, apartments, and suites, some available by the week only. The lowest rates are from September to December. $75 and up.

Rainbow Bend Fishing Resort (305-289-1505 or 1-800-929-1505; www.rainbowbend.com), MM 58, US 1 oceanside, 57784 Overseas Hwy., Grassy Key, Marathon, offers a variety of room options, from a standard hotel room to two-bedroom oceanfront suites and several in between. In business for three decades, Rainbow Bend maintains its authentic Keys charm with rooms that are clean and neat though not fancy. Fees include half-day use of a small motorboat, free kayaks and sailboats, and free breakfast daily. As an added bonus, Rainbow Bend is home to the award-winning Hideaway Café, open for breakfast and dinner. Pets under 40 pounds permitted for an extra fee; children three and older and additional adults in the room are extra. $75 and up.

Seabird Key (305-669-0044; www.seabirdkey.com), Marathon, offers your own private 10-acre island for your Keys getaway. There's room for eight in this privately owned home, with two double bedrooms and baths plus a loft for kids with four bunk beds and another bath. There are also two outdoor showers and a white-sand beach. This ultimate ecoresort relies on solar power (with backup generators) for electricity. Built from river-dredged cypress, the tropical cottage is raised high off the ground to capture ocean breezes, and floor-to-ceiling louvered window shades help keep the air flowing through the home, so no air-conditioning is needed. Most other conveniences of modern life are available, though, including a telephone, microwave oven, and even a coffee-bean grinder, and music is piped all the way to the beach. Rainwater is collected in a cistern, and laundry wastewater is recycled for irrigating the lush tropical gardens. Yard wastes and seaweed are recycled as compost, and table scraps are fed to fish and wildlife or composted. You'll have your own 19-foot boat (which would otherwise cost a bundle for the week) and Sunfish sailboat, as well as snorkeling, swimming, and fishing gear. A library of books, CDs, and videotapes is on hand, or make your own music at the piano. The island is a five-minute boat ride from Marathon and an hour's drive from Key West. Summer specials are sometimes available. About $7,000 per week.

TOWNHOME PORCH AT CORAL LAGOON RESORT

Trish Riley

Trish Riley

BANANAS IN THE LUSH GARDENS OF
SEABIRD KEY

✳ Where to Eat

DINING OUT

Key Largo

The Fish House (305-451-4665), MM
102.4, US 1 oceanside, is an excellent
choice for lunch or dinner as you pass
through the upper keys. A local institution, the restaurant delivers fresh
seafood in authentic conch-style dishes. Clam chowder, lobster bisque,
fresh catch grilled, blackened, or fried
with coleslaw and cold beer will sate
your yearning for the delicious seafood
famous in the Keys. Lunch and dinner
daily.

A fish camp in the 1930s, **Ballyhoo's
Historical Seafood Grille** (305-852-
0822), MM 97.8 in the median, is now
a popular seafood grill with the catch
of the day ($14 and up) served a dozen
different ways and all-you-can-eat
stone crab for $38. They also have
daily specials for you landlubbers—try
out the Cajun sausage with red beans
and rice or open-faced roast beef and

mashed potatoes. Your salad comes
accompanied with a unique bread
I can best describe as a hot pretzel
loaf, and the sweet tea (served in
Mason jars) is perfect.

Watch sunset turn the waters of Florida Bay from blue to gold from your
table at the **Bayside Grille** (305-451-
3380; www.keylargo-baysidegrill.com),
MM 99.5 bayside, a classy restaurant
with a view as romantic as they get.
Dine on fresh yellowtail, grouper, dolphin, and jumbo shrimp; leave room
for the luscious Florida orange cake.
Open for lunch and dinner daily.

Duck Key

Hawk's Cay Resort (305-743-7000 or
1-888-443-6393; www.hawkscay.com),
61 Hawk's Cay Blvd. Three of the
many restaurants on the property
include **Terrace,** where you'll enjoy
a lavish gourmet breakfast buffet with
super huge muffins and made-to-order
omelets; **Tom's Harbor House,** at
the marina, for steaks and seafood;
and **Alma,** for romantic fusion of Latin
and Floridian cuisine in elegant
surroundings.

ENTERING THE HOTEL AT
BANANA BAY RESORT

Sandra Friend

Grassy Key

Whole roasted duck à la Hideaway ($28) is the specialty at **The Hideaway** (305-289-1554; www.hideaway cafe.com), MM 57.5, US 1 South. Hosts Robert and Jackie serve excellent gourmet fare, such as chateaubriand ($32) and seafood puttanesca, which has shrimp, scallops, and shellfish in a spicy red sauce ($2). Residents say that the Hideaway Café, a five-star restaurant with patio dining overlooking the ocean, is the place to go. The award-winning restaurant has tables dressed with white linen tablecloths and fresh roses, and waiters in shirts and ties—a rarity in the Keys. Numerous recommendations for the rack of lamb proved true, and the fresh Keys pink shrimp were delicious. Reservations required. It's tucked away at Rainbow Bend Resort, and you may want to call ahead for directions as the restaurant is tricky to find (hence "The Hideaway"). Open daily from 4:30 PM.

Islamorada

Morada Bay Beach Café (305-664-0604; www.moradabay-restaurant .com), MM 81.6, US 1 bayside, 81600 Overseas Hwy., is known for its bayside beach café, sunset dining, and full-moon parties, Morada Bay serves sophisticated breakfast, lunch, and dinner fare on its beachfront porch, in the Moroccan- and Tibetan-furnished dining room, or upstairs in the more formal Pierre's restaurant. Relax with a cigar and cognac in the Green Flash Lounge after a continental dinner. Reasonable prices for fine waterfront dining.

Out on the docks behind **World Wide Sportsman** (see *Selective Shopping*), **Islamorada Fish Company** (305-664-9271; www.islamoradafishco.com), 81532 Overseas Hwy., has the perfect setting for savoring seafood. Entrées ($14–27) cater to seafood lovers, featuring tuna steak wasabi, dolphin chardonnay, and stuffed Florida lobster.

With all this fresh fish around, **Kaiyo** (305-664-5556; www.kaiyokeys.com), 81701 Old Overseas Hwy., makes the most of it with an upscale sushi bar with hardwood floors, beautiful mosaics, and a Zen garden out front. Relax in this fine bistro setting and enjoy Asian cuisine with Florida flair— Key lime lobster roll using fresh Florida lobster, pan-seared conch cake, and more. Open noon–10 PM Mon.–Sat., closed Sun.

Marathon

For a classy dinner out, visit **Annette's Lobster & Steak House** (305-743-5516; www.annetteslobster.com), 3660 Overseas Hwy., where dinner entrées ($14 and up) include dozens of exquisite selections, such as roast duckling, macadamia grouper, and rack of lamb. Reservations recommended.

The **Key Colony Inn** (305-743-0100), US 1, is a classic—one that locals frequent and tourists return to. The extensive menu includes a bowl of salad presented tableside. A great dining spot for families. Open daily for lunch 11 AM–2 PM and dinner 5 PM– 10 PM. Reservations suggested.

EATING OUT

Key Largo

Giant biscuits! Great grits! You'll find them at **Harriette's Restaurant** (305-852-8689), 95710 Overseas Hwy., where Harriette Mattson and her trusty kitchen staff whip up a breakfast that'll keep you going until dinner. The menu includes a conch fritter burger, crab cakes Benedict, apple and peach crêpes, and breakfast burritos (real big ones); breakfast will run you $3–8. Open 6–2 daily; closed major holidays.

Copper Kettle Restaurant at the Tavernier Hotel (305-852-4131 or

1-800-515-4131; www.tavernierhotel
.com), MM 91, US 1 oceanside, 91865
Overseas Hwy., Tavernier, offers breakfast, lunch, and dinner served inside in
a cottage atmosphere or out in the tropical courtyard. Conch chowder, seafood
specials, liver and onions, and award-
winning Key lime pie are just a few of
the menu offerings. Moderate prices.

Islamorada
**Lorelei Restaurant and Cabana
Bar** (305-664-4656; www.loreleiflorida
keys.com), MM 82, US 1 bayside, 96
Madeira Rd., is marked by a giant
mermaid sign, which is like a siren
beckoning you in to sample the basic
but hearty seafood fare at this longtime
Keys institution. Dine overlooking the
water or outdoors on the waterfront.
Live music nightly, reasonable prices.

Hungry Tarpon Diner (305-664-
0535), in front of Robbie's Marina,
MM 77.5, is small and unpretentious.
It dates from the 1940s and serves real
Florida cuisine, such as Grits and
Grunts (two eggs, biscuits, grits or
hash browns, and fried fish) for breakfast and fresh-as-it-gets hogfish, yellowfin tuna, and Florida lobster for
dinner.

Boasting "the best breakfast in the
islands," **Mangrove Mike's Café**
(305-664-8022), MM 82.2 at the Sunset Inn, sports a 1950s motif and
serves up winners such as wraps,
omelets, and hotcakes ($5–7) 6–2 daily.

If the sweet aroma of the smoker
outside doesn't make you take a beeline to **Time Out Barbecue** (305-664-
8911), MM 81.5 on the Old Overseas
Hwy., I hope this will—there's not a
barbecue restaurant I can recommend
more highly south of Lake Okeechobee. But I'm partial to Kansas City
style, where the pulled pork is slow
cooked in barbecue sauce and it comes
out so succulent you don't need to add

another drop of sauce. Daily lunch
specials such as "Your Mama's" pot
roast or fried catfish and hush puppies
run $6, and their fish is fresh every
day—"when it's gone, it's gone." 11
AM–10 PM.

Marathon
After a long day on the water, grab a
drink and a sandwich and watch the
sun go down at local favorite **Bur-
dine's Waterfront ChikiTiki** (305-
743-5317; www.burdineswaterfront
.com), 1200 Ocean St., where you'll
find huge chili burgers and fried Key
lime pie. At MM 47.5 at the end of
15th St.

An open-air restaurant along US 1, the
Cracked Conch Café (305-743-2233;
www.conchcafe.com), 4999 Overseas
Hwy., serves conch in several unique
preparations, including conch-stuffed
chicken. Pronounced "konk," it's the
soul food of the Keys, pulled from a
shellfish found offshore, and it's also
the proud nickname of the natives.
Nightly specials include tropical dolphin and grouper Oscar, with entrées
$12–23.

Locally caught seafood is abundant at
the oldest fish market and restaurant
in Marathon. **Fish Tales Market &
Eatery** (305-743-9196; www.florida
lobster.com), MM 54 oceanside at
117th St. across from Vaca Cut Bridge,
offers selections at the raw bar, salads
($7), sandwiches, or platters ($4–10),
and draft beer by the glass or pitcher.
The full-service fish house offers not
only local seafood but also hand-cut
aged choice and prime steaks, and
homemade bratwurst. Open 11
AM–6:30 PM Mon.–Sat.

You'll find the best prices for seafood
straight off the boat at **Keys Fisheries
Market & Marina** (305-743-4353;
www.keysfisheries.com), MM 49 bayside, on the water. Groups of up to six

can join a commercial lobster or stone crab boat crew for a taste of a working day at sea, learning about the industry and the history of the Keys from your captain, a professional commercial fisherman. At day's end, the bounty of the day can be prepared for your dockside dinner at the Keys Fisheries restaurant. The restaurant offers all varieties of fresh local fish—grilled, blackened, or fried—along with crab cakes, crab Alfredo, and Key lime pie. The Famous Lobster Reuben is a huge sandwich of chunks of lobster bathed in Thousand Island sauce, smothered with Swiss and sauerkraut and slapped between two massive slices of Texas toast. Huge and tasty. Place your order at the counter, along with the name of your favorite criminal or celebrity (so when the servers call out "Jesse James" or "Marilyn Monroe," you'll know when they're looking for you), and then dine at picnic tables while birds and tarpon volley for handouts. The market also offers fresh fish to go or will ship it far and wide. Try their crab rangoon ($5) or gator nuggets ($6).

Since 1954, the breezy **7 Mile Grill** (305-743-4481), 1240 Overseas Hwy., has been a great breakfast stop before you head south to the Lower Keys. Choose from nine different omelets (including fresh veggie), the 7 Mile muffin, eggs Benedict, blueberry hotcakes, or just plan old eggs and grits ($3–7). Open for lunch and dinner, too.

Sombrero Marina and Dockside Lounge (305-743-0000), MM 50, US 1 oceanside, 35 Sombrero Blvd., Marathon, is a local favorite. At Sombrero's boaters can stop by to grill their catch and do their laundry, pick up supplies at the liquor store, relax with friends at the Tiki Dock, or dine at the Dockside Lounge, a local hot spot with live music nightly and Sunday local open-jam sessions. Warning from a local: don't let shabby neighborhood deter you—it's safe and fun. Casual fare includes pizza, wings, burgers, and local seafood. $10 and up.

🐾 Oceanside breakfast, lunch, and dinner can be enjoyed at **Cabana Breezes** (305-743-4849), MM 53.5, Key Colony Beach. $10 and up.

COFFEE SHOP

Marathon

A giant coffee cup urges you to pull in to **Leigh Ann's Coffee House** (305-743-2001; www.leighannscoffeehouse.com), 7537 Overseas Hwy., at MM 50, where your favorite cup of Joe is an accompaniment to delectable fresh made salads and pastries such as Sharon's Key lime éclairs along with daily lunch specials, such as stuffed peppers.

✳ Selective Shopping

Key Largo

Stop in the **Book Nook** (305-451-1468), 103400 Overseas Hwy., where owner Joel keeps an outstanding stock of Florida guidebooks and local nonfiction on the front table. There's a full shelf of Florida mystery writers to choose from, as well as a nice selection

OCEANSIDE BEACH VIEW FROM CABANA BREEZES AT KEY COLONY BEACH

Trish Riley

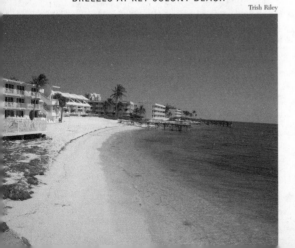

of literary nonfiction, some genre paperbacks, and books on maritime history.

The **Florida Keys Gift Company** (305-453-9229; www.keysmermaid .com), 102421 Overseas Hwy., has vibrantly painted fish from Jeannine Bean, beautiful gyotaku (Japanese fish prints) by artist Al Weinbaum, decorative art glass, hand-colored photos, and inspirational art, including greeting cards with clever sayings like "Adventure without risk is Disneyland."

Great gifts await at **Largo Cargo** (305-451-4242; www.largocargo.com), 103101 Overseas Hwy., where the works of local artists include some very funky pottery, mermaids and palm trees, and seashore scenes—all that you expect in the tropics. Largo Cargo also sells tourist fare: kites, T-shirts, and gifts.

Shell World (305-451-9797; www .shellworldflkeys.com), 97600 Overseas Hwy., has a vast selection of tropical gifts, seashells, and coral. It's also the first large gift shop you see after leaving the mainland, and the massive coral strewn about outside will catch your attention. Their stock includes furniture and art imported from Indonesia, the usual T-shirts, and children's books and games.

Tavernier
The Shell Man (305-852-8149; www .theshellman.com), 92439 Overseas Hwy., has toys, a giant rooster, monkey-faced coconuts, and lots of shells and coral within a sprawling complex that includes a Christmas room. Buy fish fresh at **Key Largo Fisheries** (305-451-3782; www.keylargofisheries .com), 1313 Ocean Bay Dr., Key Largo, where amberjack, snapper, swordfish, and mahimahi come in daily, and lobster and stone crab in-season. They'll ship it via FedEx anywhere!

With a spacious bistro feel, **Cover to Cover Books** (305-853-2464), 91272 Overseas Hwy., offers java with your James W. Hall. Books are displayed as if they were pieces of fine art—an author could not feel prouder to be included on these shelves. Open daily, until 9 PM Mon.–Sat. and 10 PM on Fri.

Islamorada
You can't miss **Treasure Village** (305-852-2458), MM 86.7, with the giant lobster out front. It's a mini mall of shops and galleries surrounding a shaded courtyard, where tropical birds twitter and squawk. Among the many selections are **Spirit Dance** (see *Art Galleries*); **Island Body and Sol,** with aromatic soaps and bath salts; and **Bluewater Potters.**

In the front of **Hooked on Books** (305-517-2602; www.hookedonbooks floridakeys.com), 82681 Overseas Hwy., you'll find plenty to read on maritime topics and the Florida Keys; an entire bookcase is devoted to Florida authors (hooray!). There's a mix of new and used books, many Ballantine and Penguin literary titles, and an entire room devoted just to children's literature.

At **The Banyan Tree** (305-664-3433; www.banyantreegarden.com), 81997 Overseas Hwy., garden paths meander under the shade of gumbo limbo, sea grapes, and a large banyan tree, which also shades the shop full of antiques and home decor (look for Tiffany glass here), outdoor furniture, and plants and flowers.

Ernest Hemingway's boat *Pilar* rests on the sales floor of **World Wide Sportsman** (305-664-3398 or 1-800-327-2880; www.basspro.com), 81576 Overseas Hwy., which is only one of many reasons to stop in and see one of the largest nautical outfitters in South Florida. This two-story department store of the outdoors focuses on fishing, befitting its location, with an excellent selection of technical wear, guidebooks, and tackle. Relax in the Zane Grey lounge, or ask about booking a deepwater charter trip; a full-service marina and waterfront restaurant are out back.

Marathon

It's not often a person gets cast as a character in a novel, but Charlie Wood, the owner of **Marathon Discount Books** (305-289-2066), 2219 Overseas Hwy., and his store managed that distinction in one of Tim Dorsey's madcap tomes. Great selection of new fiction, books of regional interest, and especially—bless you—Florida authors. It's no surprise, since Charlie credits John D. MacDonald for luring him to the Keys. Browse rare books and used books, as well as new books. Open daily.

Get your tropical gifts at **Marooned in Marathon** (305-743-3809), 7849 Overseas Hwy., a place with silly toys, whimsical playful sculptures, painted handbags in bold colors, and big papier-mâché blossoms. Other gift shops on the island: **Shipwrecked by Design** (305-743-3808) at Quay Village, MM 54, has nautical gifts, glass and metal art, lots of tropical Christmas ornaments, and treasure maps; and **Jules LaVerne's Overseas Adventure** (305-743-2277) at Quay Village is full of unusual objects such as beaded balls, Buddha icons, and plastic flamingos.

✳ Special Events

January: **Art Under the Oaks** (305-664-5241), a free annual festival at San Pedro Catholic Church, MM 89.5, US 1 bayside, Islamorada.

Islamorada Waterfront Home Tour (305-664-4503; www.islamorada chamber.com) is your chance to view the lifestyles of the rich and fortunate. $25 and up.

February: ♦ **Florida Keys Chili Cookoff** (305-451-1302; www.keylargo rotary.org), second Sat., Key Largo. Sanctioned by the International Chili Society, it's a cookoff where everyone is welcome. Live bands and a petting zoo for the kids. Held at Rowell's Marina, MM 104.5 bayside.

Pigeon Key Art Festival (305-743-5999), second weekend. For more than a decade, artists have gathered here on historic Pigeon Key under the Old Seven Mile Bridge to showcase the fine arts. Live bands, kid's corner, and free T-shirt drawings.

March: Marathon Garden Club presents the **Annual Marathon House & Garden Tour** (305-743-4971), first Sat., 10 AM–4 PM, and has done so for three decades.

The Easter Bunny goes diving to host an **Underwater Easter Egg Hunt** (305-338-3395; www.floridakeysbest .com/florida_keys/kids_in_special _situations.htm), last Sat., Key Largo, benefiting a local children's charity. Prizes and a diver in a bunny suit.

Enjoy the bounty of the surrounding seas at the **Original Marathon Seafood Festival** (305-743-5417; www.floridakeysmarathon.com), an annual celebration since 1982.

April: **Seven Mile Bridge Run** (305-743-8513), third Sat. More than 1,500 runners run across the longest segmented bridge in the world in this annual footrace, during which the Overseas Highway is closed to traffic. The first run, in 1982, was held to commemorate rebuilding the bridges.

May: **Island Festival Featuring the Taste of Islamorada** (305-664-4503; www.islamoradachamber.com), second weekend, Plantation Key. Enjoy music, art, and lots of food; presented by the Islamorada Chamber of Commerce.

July: **Key Largo Celebration of the Sea** (305-451-4747; www.celebration ofthesea.com), last Sat. Concerts, films, scuba gear displays, and more.

October: Celebrate Indian Key's history at the **Indian Key Festival** (305-664-4087), first weekend, Indian Key, with living history and reenactments.

November: **Annual Island Jubilee** (www.keylargo.org), first weekend, Harry Harris Park, Tavernier. Now more than 20 years old, this festival includes an arts and crafts show, barbecue, and a cardboard-boat regatta.

At **Indian Key Historic State Park** (305-664-2540; www.floridastateparks .org/indiankey/), offshore between Tea Table and Lower Matecumbe in Islamorada, walk the streets of the original county seat of Dade County. Known to

One of the favorite pastimes for nondivers visiting Key Largo is to grab a narrated tour on a glass-bottom boat over the reefs. At **John Pennekamp Coral Reef State Park** (see *Parks*), the official tour operator (305-451-6300; www.pennekamppark.com) runs three glass-bottom boat tours daily ($24 adults, $17 ages 12 and under) plus snorkeling ($30 adults, $25 ages 12 and under; plus equipment rental) and scuba tours ($60, plus equipment rental). As I'm not a diver, I opted to see the reef via the *Spirit of Pennekamp.* Forty years ago, they did this with a rowboat and a bucket. Today, it's a sleek modified catamaran (one of only five in the world) that can put on some speed as it snakes through the narrow mangrove-lined passages out to the open water of Largo Sound. It's a 6.5-mile trip across the open ocean to Molasses Reef, so if your stomach is weak, take advantage of the Dramamine the staff offers you *before* you get on the boat. Once out at the reef, the captain drifts across the incredible walls of coral, a living garden of constant movement. Sea plumes wave like ferns in a breeze, and colorful rainbows form as a school of parrot fish flashes past. Our narrator, Matt, filled us in on all sorts of details about the reef, including the fact that coral spawns on the August full moon, spewing exploding volcanoes of luminous eggs and sperm. You could spend hours staring at the color and form of the tropical reef beneath you, and the trip is over too soon. Yes, the glass windows do tint the view—for true color, you'd need to dive or snorkel—but most visitors opt for this experience because of their lack of expertise with open water and a fear of sharks and barracuda, which are curious about divers, but rarely a problem. On a previous snorkeling trip to the reef, once my snorkel partner had climbed back into the boat, I found myself alone and surrounded by a school of barracudas, all sneering at me with their vicious-looking teeth. I laughed out loud just to let them know I admired them and was happy to see them . . . they lost interest in me and swam away. But when I spotted a big, swishing forked tail on the ocean floor, I decided that swimming with sharks was more than I could deal with and gave up my solo snorkeling.

Spanish explorers in 1527 as the passage at the "Wells of Matecumbe," this coral rock island stands sentinel at a 2-mile passage between the reefs to Florida Bay that the earliest sailing ships could navigate. Yet more than 300 ships wrecked within sight of the island within one year. A small wrecker's settlement established by renegade wrecker Jacob Houseman evolved into a trader's stop, where John James Audubon rested during his 1832 visit to the Keys. Houseman succeeded in having the settlement named the county seat in 1836 when Dade County was carved out of Mosquito County. In 1838 noted botanist Henry Perrine moved his family here and began to experiment with cultivating various tropical plants, particularly agave—which runs rampant on the island today. As the Second Seminole War dragged on, residents of the settlement feared an attack because of their well-stocked storehouses. It happened on August 7, 1840. When the Native Americans attacked, Houseman and his wife escaped; other residents hid in the post office and under tables. Perrine's first thought was for his family. Since their house sat above the water, he let them through a trapdoor to the turtle kraal below, and then turned to defend the exit by trying to reason with the Native Americans. Perrine was killed and the house set on fire. Fourteen-year-old Henry Jr. saved the rest of the family by sailing them to nearby Tea Table Key.

As you explore the island, note the foundations of the three-story warehouses, one with a "flushing commode" in the corner—the tide cleans out the hewn stone privy. The ruins of a cistern and post office are still here, as is Jacob Houseman's grave. A park ranger gives tours at 9 AM and 1 PM Thursday through Monday; you must arrange your own transportation to the island. Use your own watercraft or check in at **Robbie's Marina** (see *Boating*) for the official state park ferry, which also serves **Lignumvitae Key Botanical State Park** (see *Parks*) on the opposite side of the channel.

■ LOWER KEYS

T he essence of the Lower Keys begins across the Seven Mile Bridge where the land widens and the Overseas Highway immediately takes a turn toward the west. For 30 or so miles you will be in the backcounty, where, among pine forests and secluded mangrove islands, a wealth of eco-opportunities exists. Your first clue that life as you know it is slowing down is on **Bahia Honda Key** at MM 37, where the Bahia Honda State Park (see *Beaches*) provides a wealth of natural activities on and off land. **Big Pine Key** is the central hub of shopping and activities, and where you'll find the **National Key Deer Refuge** (see *Wild Places*). Spanish documents from 1627 show Big Pine Key's earliest name as Cayos de Cuchiaga, a Native American name cited by Hernando D'Escalante Fontaneda, a Spanish explorer who was shipwrecked in the mid-1500s and lived with the Calusa tribe for nearly two decades before his rescue in 1566. In 1678, it was found on Spanish charts as Cayo Pinero, or Pine Island—*pinar* means "grove of pines," and *pino* is "pine tree," of which there were many on the island. The British charts identified it in 1772 as New Castle Island, and in 1774 charts were again referencing "Pine Island" (Pinara Kays). The name Big Pine Island was specifically referenced in Ferdinand H. Gerdes's 1849 journals, which he wrote while doing reconnaissance of the Florida reef.

Continuing on, you'll drive several miles through residential keys such as Big, Middle, and Little Torch Keys; Summerland Key; Cudjoe Key; **Sugarloaf Key;** and Big Coppitt Key, where you can stop at the occasional roadside restaurant for a quick bite. While in the Lower Keys, you'll enjoy kayak tours where you may see a pod of dolphins or a nurse shark in the shallow waters. Discover skates, horseshoe crabs, colorful fish, and the occasional barracuda just a few feet off the sandy shores. Key deer are plentiful, and to protect them there is a speed restriction. The best time to see the dog-sized Key deer, a subspecies of the Virginia white-tailed deer, is at dawn or dusk in the National Key Deer Refuge or on one of the quiet roads on No Name Key. Please don't feed this protected species—it's illegal; tame deer learn to come to the roadsides, where they get struck by cars.

Leaving the Lower Keys, tourist life returns as you cross over the Boca Chica Bridge and into Key West.

GUIDANCE The official contact for visitors to the Keys is **The Florida Keys & Key West Tourism Council** (305-296-1552 or 1-800-FLA-KEYS; www.fla-keys .com), 1201 White St., Ste. 102, Key West 33040, where you will find information on all the Keys. The **Lower Keys Chamber of Commerce Visitor Center** (305-872-2411 or 1-800-872-3722; www.lowerkeyschamber.com), MM 31, 31020 Overseas Hwy., Big Pine Key 33043, offers great information specific to Big Pine Key.

GETTING THERE *By car:* Once you enter the Keys, one road links the islands—the Overseas Highway, **US 1.**

By air: To reach the Lower Keys, use **Miami International Airport** (see the *The Gables, the Grove, and Downtown Miami* section); **Marathon Airport** (305-289-6060), 9400 Overseas Hwy., Ste. 200; or **Key West International Airport** (305-296-5439; www.keywestinternationalairport.com).

By bus: **Greyhound** (305-296-9072, 305-871-1810, or 1-800-231-2222; www.greyhound.com) stops all along the islands; call for specific pickup locations and rates.

By rail: **AMTRAK** (1-800-USARAIL; www.amtrak.com) takes you as far south as Fort Lauderdale. There, you can transfer to the Keys Shuttle.

By shuttle: Call 24 hours ahead for the **Florida Keys Shuttle** (305-289-9997 or 1-888-765-9997; www.floridakeysshuttle.com), which offers door-to-door service from Miami International Airport to numerous points in the Keys.

GETTING AROUND *By car:* **US 1** connects the islands; destinations along the road are designated by mile markers, shown as"MM." Marathon, MM 63–MM 47, is about a 2 hour drive to Key West.

By bus: Since **Greyhound** (see *Getting There*) links the islands, it's possible to use the bus to island-hop.

By taxi: If you fly into Marathon Airport, you can get where you're going with **Action Taxi** (305-743-6800) or **Sunset Taxi & Transportation** (305-289-7422). If you fly into Key West, take **Friendly Cab Co.** (305-292-0000).

PARKING Parking is readily available in the Lower Keys without charge.

MEDICAL EMERGENCIES General emergencies should head to **Fisherman's Hospital** (305-743-5533; www.fishermanshospital.com), 3301 Overseas Hwy., MM 48.7, Marathon, or **Lower Keys Medical Center** (305-294-5531; www.lkmc .com), 5900 College Rd., Key West. The **Key Largo Recompression Chamber** (911 if emergency, 1-800-NO-BENDS for information) is the closest resource for divers experiencing the life-threatening "bends."

✳ To See

ART GALLERY Several talented local artists are shown at **Artists in Paradise Gallery** (305-872-1828; www.artistsinparadise.com), Big Pine Shopping Center, 221 Key Deer Blvd., Big Pine Key.

ECOTOUR Take a five-hour island-hopping tour on glass-bottom boats with **Island Excursions** (305-872-9863 or 1-800-654-9560; www.strikezonecharter .com), 29675 Overseas Hwy., MM 29.5, Big Pine Key. Journey into the backcountry along tidal flats and mangroves to seek out the elusive Key deer while dolphins swim nearby. The glass-bottom boats allow you to see starfish, sponges, tropical fish, and sea turtles up close. You will also have the chance to snorkel and do some light fishing while you learn about the history of the islands and its first inhabitants along with the local flora and fauna. The tour ($49) also includes the world-famous fish fry.

HISTORIC SITES The **Old Bahia Honda Bridge,** MM 37, in Bahia Honda State Park (see *Beaches*), was once part of Henry Flagler's Overseas Railroad and is listed on the National Register of Historic Places. During the Great Labor Day Hurricane, September 2, 1935, a 17-foot wall of water washed over the bridge, destroying the railroad. The bridge offers an excellent panoramic view of the area and an eerie reminder of what a hurricane's storm surge can do.

Surviving several hurricanes, the **Perky Bat Tower** on Sugarloaf Key has become somewhat of a legend. In 1929, Richter C. Perky built the tower to reduce the island's mosquito population so that he could build a resort complex. Located bay-side down a side road directly off MM 17, the odd structure was supposed to be a welcoming home for bats, but the nocturnal creatures had other ideas, and they never took residence in the tower. Today it stands as a tribute to Mr. Perky's good intentions.

WILDLIFE VIEWING **Blue Hole**, a freshwater sinkhole on Key Deer Blvd., Big Pine Key, is an old quarry from the Flagler railroad days. In the heart of **National Key Deer Refuge** (see *Wild Places*), it offers excellent viewing opportunities for Key deer, alligators, iguanas, turtles, and freshwater fish. The natural area contains an interpretive display, observation deck, and nature trails.

✳ To Do

BICYCLING Bicyclists will enjoy nearly a dozen miles of roads that run off MM 30, Wilder Road, and Key Deer Boulevard on Big Pine Key. Don't forget to cross over and explore No Name Key, where nearly all residents are independently powered by solar energy.

DIVING What better place to dive than in the Keys? From only a few feet off-shore to ships sunk at depths of 110 feet, the Lower Keys are alive with underwater adventure. Dive boats can take you 5 miles offshore to **Looe Key Reef** (see *Coral Reefs*), where you can snorkel with colorful fish and coral, or 3 miles offshore down to the *Adolphus Busch*. The 210-foot-long ship is a great place for experienced divers, where they can swim through large holes cut in the sides of the ship, through the wheel-house, and out the smokestacks. There are lots of tropical fish in the artificial reef, and lucky divers may even spot the gargantuan Jewfish, which weighs about 400 pounds. Sitting upright at 100 feet in crystal-clear water, the freighter's towers are only 40 feet down.

SEA TURTLE
Courtesy Greater Miami Convention and Visitors Bureau

Without a doubt, **Strike Zone Charters** (305-872-9863 or 1-800-654-9560; www .strikezonecharter.com), 29675 Overseas Hwy., MM 29.5, Big Pine Key, is the best when snorkeling or diving Looe Key Reef and the Lower Keys. Gayle and Mary, and their adorable chihuahuas, keep things safe on their 40- and 45-foot custom-built glass-bottom catamarans. On board you'll find things super clean and ship-shape. Tuck your belongings in dry storage and relax under the 350-foot canopy or grab some sun while motoring out to the dive site. So that you can explore with confidence, your guides will carefully go over instructions for a safe dive, and then the geography and ecology of the reef. At Looe Key Reef, you'll see a variety of colorful tropical fish, such as the bright orange clownfish and royal blue tang swimming among staghorn, elkhorn, piliar, and star corals to depths from just inches to up to 30 feet. Over at the HMS *Looe* wreck, those staying on board may even spot the smokestack through the boat's glass bottom. To ensure anyone can get in and out of the water with ease, they are even equipped to handle those with special needs. A freshwater shower is also available to rinse off the salt water after diving—or it can be used by those staying on board, who might want to cool off. Glass bottom $25; snorkel $30; scuba dive reef $40; scuba dive wreck $50.

FISHING Strike Zone Charters (see *Diving*) offers deep-sea and flats fishing in the warm blue waters of the Atlantic Ocean or in the sandy flats near and around the Keys. You'll fish for sailfish, tuna, snapper, and marlin on the deep-sea excursion and tarpon, bonefish, and shark on the flats charter. Deep-sea fishing: full day $595, half day $450; flats fishing: full day $425, half day $325.

PADDLING The best backcountry guided tours are by Bill Keogh's **Big Pine Kayak** (305-872-7474 or 1-877-595-2925; www.keyskayaktours.com), Big Pine Key, where you'll kayak or canoe through mangrove tunnels teeming with wildlife. Or rent your own boat and explore the mangroves and peaceful waterways on your own. You'll want to pick up Bill's book, the *Florida Keys Paddling Guide* by Countryman Press, to learn all about the wildlife and ecosystems that you'll encounter. Two locations are at **the Old Wooden Bridge Fishing Camp** and **Parmer's Resort** (see *Lodging*).

✳ Green Space

BEACH Boasting one of the most popular beaches in the Keys, **Bahia Honda State Park** (305-872-2353; www.floridastateparks.org/bahiahonda), 36850 Overseas Hwy., also offers a full slate of recreational opportunities besides lolling in the sun. Walk the Silver Palm Nature Trail through the last significant silver palm hammock in the United States; rent a kayak and wind through the mangrove mazes and paddle offshore; camp or rent a cabin at one of the campgrounds; explore a portion of Henry Flagler's Overseas Railroad.

CORAL REEF Five miles off Big Pine Key, oceanside, is the beautiful coral formation **Looe Key Reef.** Under the protection of the Florida Keys National Marine Sanctuary, the refuge is named after the HMS *Looe,* a British ship that foundered on the coral in 1744 while towing a captured French ship. The reef is about 200 yards by 800 yards and formed in the shape of a U with several "fingers," so you can snorkel the high points or scuba in between. This is an amazing reef that you can spend an entire weekend exploring. Brightly colored tropical fish swim with you and graze on the coral canyons below. You'll come face-to-face with yellowtail and sergeant majors while schools of angelfish swim nearby. Look closely to see moray eels hiding in more than 50 species of corals, such as staghorn, brain, and fire corals, some more than 7,000 years old. Listen carefully to hear parrot fish munching and crunching and shrimp crackling. This reef is large, and as such expect to see several barracuda and the occasional shark—none of which seemed interested in me when I was floating about, but it can be a bit unsettling. At times the water can be rough, so check the surf report if this bothers you. Experts recommend munching on ginger before taking to the seas to ease nausea. For those not quite ready for such a large reef or the wide-open ocean, the reefs off Key Largo are smaller (see *Upper and Middle Keys*).

WILD PLACES Since the 1930s, the little-known **Great White Heron National Wildlife Refuge** (305-872-2239; www.fws.gov/southeast/greatwhiteheron), managed by National Key Deer Refuge, has protected the Lower Keys's "backcountry," including more than 186,000 acres of marine waters across hundreds of unpopulated mangrove islands between Marathon and Key West. The islands are important nesting and roosting places for more than 250 species of birds. Access to the region is only by boat. Open dawn–dusk. Free.

North America's smallest deer roam in herds through the **National Key Deer Refuge** (305-872-2239; www.fws.gov/nationalkeydeer), 28950 Watson Blvd., MM 30, where 800 or so of the 2- to 3-foot-tall deer range across 8,500 acres of mangrove forests, tropical hardwood hammocks, and pine rocklands across the Lower Keys. On Big Pine Key, stop in at the visitors center in the Winn-Dixie shopping center off Key Deer Boulevard for an orientation before heading out to look for deer. **Blue Hole** (see *Wildlife Viewing*), off Key Deer Blvd., is a good place to see deer at dusk and dawn coming to a rare freshwater water source. Farther up the road are two nature trails that wind through deer habitat. Open dawn–dusk. Free.

✴ Lodging

CAMPGROUNDS

Bahia Honda Key 33043
Bahia Honda State Park (305-872-2353; www.floridastateparks.org/bahiahonda; reservations: 1-800-326-3521 or www.reserveamerica.com), 36850 Overseas Hwy., MM 37, has oceanfront tent camping and smaller RVs sites, typically 30–40 feet long, with a beautiful beach and nature trail. The remnants of Henry Flagler's railroad offers excellent panoramic views. Rental boats, kayaks, bicycles, snorkeling, and fishing gear are available. Eighty sites ($32 per night) come with water, some with electricity. Duplex cabins ($137 per night) sleep six. No

KEY DEER

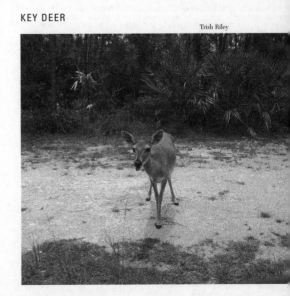

Trish Riley

weekly or monthly rates. Maximum stay is limited to 14 days.

Ohio Key 33043

The 75-acre private island is simply paradise at **Sunshine Key RV Resort & Marina** (305-872-2217 or 1-800-852-0348; www.RVontheGO.com), 38801 Overseas Hwy., MM 39, located just off Big Pine Key. The largest RV resort in the Keys, it boasts 400 RV sites and a 172-slip marina, and it has full amenities such as a heated pool, tennis, volleyball, laundry, marina café, dive shop, boat rentals, and more. Monthly rates range from $1,030–9,225. Check the Internet for specials.

Big Pine Key 33043

One of the best campgrounds for kids is at **Big Pine Key Fishing Lodge** (305-872-2351), MM 33, where you'll find a heated pool, shuffleboard, horseshoes, playground, and a game room. A boat ramp, dock, and marina area are also on-site, and you can charter a boat for saltwater fishing, or paddle the backcountry with Bill Keogh's Big Pine Kayak (see *Paddling*). Tent sites and full RV hookups. Call for rates.

Sugarloaf Key 33044

Whether you want to tent camp, bring your own RV, or stay in one of their Airstream RVs, **Sugarloaf Key Resort KOA** (305-745-3549 or 1-800-562-7731; www.koa.com), 251 CR 939, MM 20, offers a chance to relax and unwind in tropical paradise. Only 20 minutes from Key West, it provides all the necessary amenities, including private beach, swimming pool, hot tub, sauna, and waterfront pub. Call for rates.

FISH CAMP

Big Pine Key 33043

The **Old Wooden Bridge Fish Camp** (305-872-2241; www.old woodenbridge.com), 1791 Bogie Dr., dates from the 1950s, when only six cottages provided fishing opportunities to wintering visitors. Located off the beaten path, the original building (circa 1943) still stands as the camp store at the base of No Name Key Bridge. Today you can camp out in 14 guest cottages along the shoreline of the Bogie Channel. The one- and two-bedroom cottages have been fully renovated to include modern luxuries such as a stove, refrigerator, microwave, cable television, and, of course, air-conditioning. The full bait and tackle store is also stocked with snacks and beverages, so you don't have to drive into town for supplies. Bill Keogh's Big Pine Kayak (see *Paddling*) departs to the backcountry from here. Rates: $95–230 per night; $980–1,354 per week.

HOTELS, MOTELS, AND RESORTS ⌖ **Deer Run Bed & Breakfast** (305-872-2015; www.deer runfloridabb.com), MM 33 oceanside, P.O. Box 431, Long Beach Dr., Big Pine Key, offers a vegetarian, all-organic B&B, and was the fifth accommodations business in the Florida Keys to meet the state's Green Lodging standards. The owners make an effort to conserve water and electricity, compost biodegradable material, use native plants for landscaping—all business practices that are beneficial for our environment. Sit on the beach in back of the house while Key deer graze the lawn of this bed & breakfast. Comfortable and quiet, peaceful and pleasant, rooms offer oceanfront or garden views. Bike or canoe; relax in the ocean, in the hot tub, or in a beachfront hammock; or fish and barbecue your catch for dinner. No children or pets; three-night minimum on holidays. $75 and up.

Little Torch Key 33042

To get to **Little Palm Island Resort & Spa** (305-515-4004 or 1-800-343-8567; www.littlepalmisland.com), 28500 Overseas Hwy., MM 28.5 oceanside, you must first check in at the guest welcome station on Little Torch Key, where they immediately offer registered guests and diners with reservations fresh fruit and ice cold water, or you can order a PT 109, Gumby Slumber, or Jamaica Me Krazy drink while waiting for the ferry. You'll then board the historic *Truman* yacht for a short ride over to paradise. Leave your electronics behind, as this resort doesn't allow them, not even a cell phone, although there is a quaint phone booth if you have to reach the mainland. Once there, you'll be captivated by the peace and quiet as you walk under shady palms on your way to your own private, waterfront, thatched-roofed bungalow. There's lots to do on the 5-acre private island: play life-sized chess under balmy palm trees; take a walk through the Zen garden and up to the full-service SpaTerre for a Javanese Lulur Royal Treatment ($250) or Tropical Essence Massage ($140–180); slip into the freshwater lagoon-style pool shaded under a canopy of palms; take to the water on one of the Windsurfers, day sailers, or kayaks; grab a chaise and stretch out along the beach; or swim out to the floating tiki hut. The poolside bar has a wide selection of top-line liquors, beer, and wines. At sunset enjoy a gourmet dinner pretty much anywhere you choose or in their elegant Colonial dining room. Listen to live music each night on the west side of the island, then gaze at the crystal-clear night sky before retiring to your own private bungalow or grand suite. Twenty-eight Bungalow suites ($700–1,500 per night) come with king-sized bed, living room, whirlpool bath, indoor and outdoor showers, and a private veranda. The two Island Grand Suites ($1,000–2,500 per night), also have his-and-hers bathrooms and an outdoor hot tub. Both Bungalow and Island Grand Suites require a two-night minimum stay. All money is handled over at Little Torch Key, so there's no need carry your wallet. Tipping is handled that way, too, with 10 percent added for staff, and an 18 percent gratuity for food or beverages. An optional two- or three-meal menu plan is available for an additional cost. Little Palm Island is a special treat for romantics or those who need some peace and quiet and extreme pampering.

Tucked away on 5 tropical acres, **Parmer's Resort** (305-872-2157; www.parmersplace.com), 565 Barry Ave., MM 28.5, offers quiet waterfront accommodations. The air-conditioned rooms, some with vaulted ceilings, come with cable TV and a private porch. Efficiencies have complete kitchens and come with one, two, or three bedrooms. Take a dip in the heated pool surrounded by lush tropical landscaping, and then walk down the garden paths to discover more than 70 exotic birds in their aviary. Ice chests and pets are forbidden in the rooms, and you'll be subjected to a hefty fee if you break the rules. Rooms $99–1144; efficiencies $129–194. Complimentary continental breakfast buffet is included.

Looe Key Reef Resort and Dive Center (305-872-2215 or 1-800-942-5397), MM 27.5, US 1 oceanside, 27340 Overseas Hwy., Ramrod Key, is recently renovated with the rooms in basic motel style for those with diving in mind. Back doors open onto the dock, and the pool is used for diver certification classes. Snacks and tropical refreshments can be had at the cash-only tiki bar and at Julio's Grill.

Prices vary from single to six-person suites; some may require a minimum three-night stay. $75 and up.

Sugarloaf Key 33044

At MM 17 you'll find **Sugarloaf Lodge** (305-745-3211 or 1-800-553-6097; www.sugarloaflodge.net), 17001 Overseas Hwy. bayside, a welcome retreat. All rooms are waterfront at the fully equipped resort, complete with full restaurant, Pirate's lounge, and tiki bar. You'll find lots to do here, from tennis, mini golf, and shuffleboard to swimming in the heated pool or snorkeling in the crystal-clear ocean. Anglers will find all the necessary bait and tackle to land the big one. Pet friendly. Rooms $115–165; efficiencies $110–150.

✳ Where to Eat

DINING OUT

Little Torch Key

You don't have to stay overnight at **Little Palm Island Resort & Spa** (305-872-2524 or 1-800-3-GET-LOST; www.littlepalmisland.com), 28500 Overseas Hwy., MM 28.5 oceanside, to enjoy their culinary delights, but you must have a reservation, and you won't be allowed to explore the island without an escort. Check in at the guest welcome station on Little Torch Key, and then you'll motor over on the historic *Truman* yacht. Breakfast, lunch, dinner, and exquisite Sunday brunch are held indoors in the elegant dining room or outdoors on the terrace or even the sandy beach. For breakfast try the lobster hash with red onions, green peppers, bacon, potatoes, eggs any style, and chive hollandaise ($19); cinnamon French toast with blueberry or strawberry compote ($15); or buttermilk pancakes ($15). Brunch includes a host of items that change according to season. Wash it all down

with a mimosa ($12) or Bloody Mary ($9). Lunch brings light fare such as the jumbo lump crab cake appetizer with frisée lettuce and saffron aioli ($22); shrimp wrap sandwich with tomatoes, spinach, shaved red onion, avocado, and chipolte-cilantro aioli ($17); and the mustard-crusted grouper entrée with tarragon-infused potatoes, baby carrots, snap peas, and tomato butter ($23). For those sunset dinners, try the seared scallop and duck foie gras appetizer with curried lentils and banana and orange ginger glaze ($24), and then the exquisite glazed mahimahi with marinated tofu entrée, served with edamame, baby bok choy, scallions, and lemon soy ($43). Worth the price to be romanced in paradise.

EATING OUT

Big Pine Key

My hiker buddies tell me the **Cracked Egg Cafe** (305-872-7030), 30739 Overseas Hwy., MM 31, is the best breakfast around and a welcome treat after logging long miles along the Overseas Highway.

Worth the drive off the beaten path, the **No Name Pub** (305-872-9115; www.nonamepub.com), N Watson Blvd., off MM 30 bayside, is a very cool place with lots of stories. The oldest pub in Big Pine Key, it was built in 1931 originally as a general store. It was rumored to have once been a brothel, and you have to see the way it's decorated to believe it. Sample the Royal Pub pizza ($17–22), spicy Caribbean wings ($9), and a bowl of the famous Pub chili ($3).—With more than 60 types of beer to wash it all down, it's a great place to sneak away just for the fun of it. Open daily.

Rob's Island Grill (305-872-3022), 31251 Ave. A, is a really nice family sports bar with eight satellite connections, so no one needs to miss their hometown game. Rob has had a restaurant on the key since 1985, but this newly built one is only a few years old. Tucked back on a side street, bayside, watch for it or you'll almost miss it when coming from the north as you enter Big Pine Key. The restaurant offers a selection of sandwiches, salads, steaks, and seafood and will even cook your own catch. Vegetarians will also find this to their liking.

Cudjoe Key

A favorite of locals, the **Square Grouper Bar & Grill** (305-745-8880), MM 22.5, is for those special occasions and those wanting a long wine list and excellent gourmet-type Caribbean and Floridian fare.

Little Torch Key

The waterfront **Parrotdise Bar & Grille** (305-872-9989; www.parrot disewaterfront.com), 183 Barry Ave., MM 28.5 bayside, offers fun and food for everyone. Kids will love the shark pool and tropical fish pond, while adults will enjoy the live music from acoustic guitar soloists to jazz festivals (see *Special Events*). For lunch you'll want to try their lobster Reuben in Parrotdise ($15) and for dinner their Parrotdise guava shrimp, sautéed with a Key lime, guava, ginger, and cilantro sauce ($23). After your meal, take a walk on the dock and try to spot the many sea creatures that inhabit the shoreline, such as barracuda, crab, and even the occasional octopus. Then curl up in one of their beach hammocks or go back for some Key lime pie or chocolate pot de crème ($5). Open daily for lunch and dinner, with happy hour 3–7.

Ramrod Key

If you are looking for a party place, then head over to **Boondocks Grille & Draft House & Miniature Golf** (305-872-0020; www.boondocks.us .com), MM 27.5 bayside, which features lively music, drinks, a raw bar, and light fare.

Sugarloaf Key

Not to be missed, **Mangrove Mamas** (305-745-3030; www.mangrovemamas restaurant.com), MM 20 bayside, is the place to stop for one of the best meals in the Keys. Locals come to this tiny restaurant for their light and airy conch fritters ($8), tempura fish (market price), and Black Angus steaks ($25). Lunch favorites are the teriyaki chicken sandwich ($9) or the grouper sandwich (market price), which can be grilled, fried, blackened, or broiled. The intimate garden surroundings are a welcome retreat after days on the open ocean. Open daily, lunch and dinner.

COFFEE SHOP If you find yourself jonesing for a cup of java, then pull over at MM 15 to **Baby's Coffee** (305-744-9866 or 1-800-523-2326; www .babyscoffee.com), 3178 US 1 oceanside, Saddlebunch Key. The roadside café is housed in a 1920s building, and the story goes that the occupants had christened it "Baby's Place" after their youngest son. When New Yorkers Gary Tepinsky and Olga Manosalvas selected the site for their coffee shop, they adopted the name, and Baby's Coffee was born. Taking great care in creating the perfect cup o' joe, fresh beans are carefully selected and roasted to perfection in small batches to ensure consistency and are available in bags or through their mail-order business. A nice selection of fresh baked goods and logo items can also be found. Make sure to take particular note of the fine art on display. The talented Olga expresses herself through a mix of her Ecuadorian heritage and experiences from New York City and living in the Keys. Baby's Coffee is open every day except Christmas, and the coffee can also be found served at restaurants and inns throughout the Keys and Miami.

✳ Special Events

Contact the **Lower Keys Chamber** (305-872-2411 or 1-800-872-3722; www.lowerkeyschamber.com) to learn more about the following events.

March–April: Held at Parrotdise Bar & Grille in Little Torch Key (see *Eating Out*), the Lower Keys Jazz & Art Festival includes a juried art show and smooth jazz.

June: Anglers compete for $4,000 in cash and prizes at the **Big Pine & Lower Keys Dolphin Tournament** (305-872-2411; www.lowerkeys chamber.com), Big Pine Key.

July: Everything happens below the surface at the unique **Underwater Music Festival** (305-872-2411; www .lowerkeyschamber.com) in the Florida Keys National Marine Sanctuary. The annual event broadcasts music for divers and snorkelers at Looe Key to promote reef preservation.

KEY WEST

The Calusa people were the earliest inhabitants of Key West, but the island remained undiscovered until 1521, when Juan Ponce de León arrived, establishing a fishing and salvage village. Visited mainly by Spanish explorers, the island was first deeded to Cuba and called Cayo Hueso, meaning "Bone Island," and in 1815 the governor of Cuba transferred the island to the United States. Because Key West was so remote, townies refused to recognize any nation and became a bit unruly. So, John Simonton, a large landowner, lobbied the U.S. government for a new naval base, hoping its presence would provide some order to the town. In 1823 Commodore David Porter of the U.S. Navy took charge and ran any rowdy residents out of town.

Today, Key West is home to a wealth of exemplary cuisine and charming guest houses with luxuriously appointed rooms. Duval Street is lined with pubs busy from early in the day to late into the night. The creative community welcomes gay and lesbian members, and many businesses and activities cater to gays, such as WomenFest and Fantasy Fest, celebrations held in September and October. Drag shows provide exceptional entertainment for all persuasions, and an easygoing atmosphere ensures fun for all. Key West ascribes to a philosophy dubbed One Human Family, a public declaration adopted on October 17, 2000, that all people everywhere are entitled to equal rights, respect, and dignity and lives free from violence, prejudice, and harassment.

BOAT LAUNCH AND MARINA, KEY WEST
Courtesy Sunset Key Resort

Key West is one of the most unusual cities in the country and one of the most visited, although a high proportion of visitors spend a very limited time in town—just long enough to hike from one end of legendary Duval Street to the other, buy a T-shirt, and have a beer at Sloppy Joe's before jumping back aboard their cruise ship.

This cruise-ship tourism was denounced by former mayor Shirley

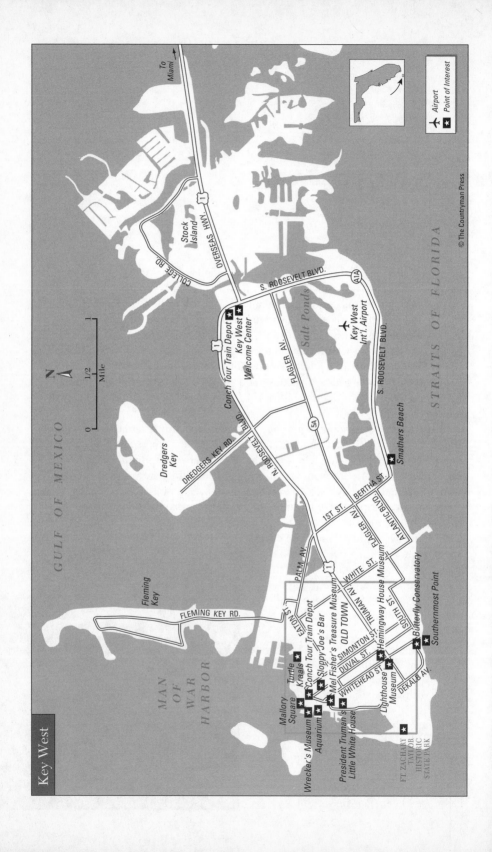

Key West

Trish Riley

LOTUS BLOSSOM IN HEMINGWAY'S
GARDEN, KEY WEST

Freeman as a costly exploitation of the island, and indeed, the ambient spirit that has drawn artists and writers here since before the days when Hemingway made Key West his home in the 1930s does seem to be dwindling at the expense of a hustle to survive. The intense proliferation of hotels, guest houses, and restaurants catering to a well-heeled crowd with pockets full of money is driving real estate prices through the roof, displacing local residents to other islands. Paradise runs the risk of losing its artistic cultural backbone, giving way to carbon-copied galleries, chain restaurants, and hotels. Although Key West has a long history of attracting artistic types and those of non-traditional sexual persuasion, I was surprised to note on a recent visit a high proportion of middle-aged middle Americans; a decidedly different crowd than I'd ever seen here before. It's as if those who chose more conventional lifestyles enjoy the chance to visit a paradise where anything goes—a place where you can sample, if only for a few days, the decadence you turned away from when opting for a more mundane life.

I encourage you to take the time to find and enjoy the flavors of Key West that can't be found anywhere else in the world. Spend time musing, writing, painting, and nourishing your own artistic soul while visiting, enjoying, and at the same time replenishing the spirit that makes the place special. Come drink a toast to Ernest Hemingway with thousands of white-bearded men during Hemingway Days in July, or don (or should I say remove?) your Mardi Gras garb for the wildest Halloween masquerade you've ever seen during Fantasy Fest in October.

Perhaps you've heard of the Conch Republic, noticed the blue and yellow flags flying, or spotted the unique passports available in gift shops. All of these are inspired by the week of independence declared in 1982, creating an independent island nation for a few days. It all started when the U.S. Border Patrol set up a roadblock on US 1 as it exited the Keys in Florida City, searching all cars as they left the islands on a Sunday afternoon. The federal agency said the goal of the roadblock was to apprehend illegal aliens entering the country, yet in four days only 4 illegals were found, while 3,000 were recorded coming into Miami Beach. The car searches also turned up about 3 pounds of pot, which turned out to be another of the Border Patrol's objectives.

POOCHIE'S WILD RIDE, KEY WEST

Trish Riley

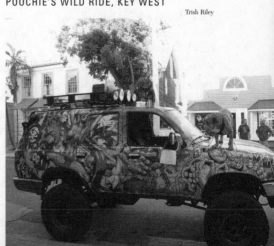

But the fiasco had a greater impact on the Keys. A traffic jam 19 miles long greeted those returning from Keys vacations and discouraged potential visitors. The negative effect on the Keys biggest industry, tourism, was significant. When U.S. citizens were stopped and asked for proof of citizenship before being allowed to pass onto the mainland, Key West officials became angry. Then the mayor decided to take action: since the Keys were being treated like a foreign country, the islands would secede from the nation. A mock ceremony was held at Mallory Square, drawing international attention to the border fiasco.

Called a creative approach to a serious problem, the publicity stunt worked, and the roadblock was removed after five days. The event is commemorated each year in April at the ten-day Conch Republic Independence Celebration. Its motto: "We seceded where others failed."

All over Key West you'll hear residents referred to as "Conchs" (pronounced "Konks"). The label began with early Bahamian immigrants and was adopted by all residents during the 20th century. Today a "Salt Water Conch" is a person born on the island; a "Fresh Water Conch" is born elsewhere but has been on the island so long they are considered a native.

GUIDANCE The official contact for visitors to the Keys is **The Florida Keys & Key West** (305-296-1552 or 1-800-FLA-KEYS; www.fla-keys.com), 1201 White St., Ste. 102, Key West 33040, where you will find information on all the Keys. The **Key West Chamber of Commerce** (305-294-2587; www.keywestchamber .org), 402 Wall St., is another resource once you get to Key West.

GETTING THERE *By car:* Once you enter the Keys, one road links the islands— the Overseas Highway, **US 1.**

By air: To reach the Lower Keys, use **Miami International Airport** (see The Gables, the Grove, and Downtown Miami section); **Marathon Airport** (305-289-6060), 9400 Overseas Hwy., Ste. 200; or **Key West International Airport** (305-296-5439; www.keywestinternationalairport.com).

By bus: **Greyhound** (305-296-9072, 305-871-1810, or 1-800-231-2222; www.grey hound.com) stops all along the islands. Call for specific pickup locations and rates.

By shuttle: Call 24 hours ahead for the **Florida Keys Shuttle** (305-289-9997 or 1-888-765-9997; www.floridakeysshuttle.com), which offers door-to-door service from Miami International Airport to numerous points in the Keys.

GETTING AROUND *By foot:* The best mode of transportation in Key West is by foot. Everything is close by and parking is limited, so stretch your legs and work off all that Key lime pie.

By two wheels: Rent a bicycle or motorized scooter to ease your weary feet, especially on hot days. Vendors are located on almost every corner, and many lodgings provide these for free or for a nominal fee. Pick up a free copy of *Sharon Wells' Walking and Biking Guide to Historic Key West* at many shops, restaurants, and hotels around town for maps and information about local sights.

By car: **US 1** connects the islands; destinations along the road are designated by mile markers, shown as "MM." The hub of Key West's Old Town historic district is found around Duval, Eaton, Simonton, Green, Caroline, and Front Streets.

By bus: Since **Greyhound** links the islands, it's possible to use the bus to island-hop. Once in Key West, the **City Bus for Key West and Stock Island** (305-292-8165; www.keywestcity.com) and **City of Key West Transit** (305-292-8160) take you around the island. A **shuttle service to Key West's Old Town/ Historic District** (305-293-6426) has stops along the entire route.

By taxi: You can get anywhere you're going with **Friendly Cab Co.** (305-292-0000).

PARKING Metered parking is free all over town for guests with handicapped tags.

Park and Ride Garages are at the corner of Caroline and Grinnell Sts. Get reduced rates with a validated shuttle ticket ($1 per hour with a $10 maximum). The open lot at Mallory Square ($3 per hour) has no maximum, so it can add up if you leave your car overnight. The lot at the Schooner Wharf ($2 per hour) on William Street is another option if you're heading out on one of the sailing tours.

MEDICAL EMERGENCIES For general emergencies head to **Lower Keys Medical Center** (305-294-5531; www.lkmc.com), 5900 Junior College Rd., Key West. The **Key Largo Recompression Chamber** (911 if emergency, 1-800-NO-BENDS for information) is the closest resource for divers experiencing the life-threatening "bends."

✳ To See

AQUARIUM ♿ 🐾 The **Key West Aquarium** (305-296-2051; www.keywest aquarium.com), One Whitehead St. at Mallory Square, provides an opportunity to see "goliath grouper," a docile native species that lives under piers and around the reefs. The aquarium opened in 1934 as the city's first tourist attraction. It's a must-see for its classic interior, including the *vero fresco* murals originally painted by Alfred Crimi in 1934 and retouched by local artists Gualberto Alfaro and David Laughlin in 1998. Historic photos of the aquarium and docks are suspended around the central room, which is ringed with tanks of native sea creatures, such as brilliant purple and yellow cheek wrasse, chalk bass, and sergeant major. Staff members feed the stingrays and sea turtles and show off sharks that you're allowed to touch. The touch tank up-front contains conchs, horseshoe crabs, and starfish. A pool rimmed with red mangroves shimmers with tarpon, rainbow parrot fish (who eat coral and excrete the beach sand you see in the Keys), bonnet head sharks, barracuda, and other common denizens of the deep. Open daily 10 AM–6 PM. Adults $11, ages 9–12 $5.

ART GALLERIES A bevy of art galleries can be found on Duval Street, but you will also want to seek out other galleries sporadically located around town, such as **The Lemonade Stand Art Studio** (305-295-6873; www.lemonadestandart studio.com), 227 Petronia St. in Bahama Village; the **Harrison Gallery** (305-294-0609; www.harrisongallery.com), 825 White St., which represents sculptor Helen Harrison along with other talented artists; the **Haitian Art Co.** (305-296-8932;), 600 Frances St., which has been exhibiting a diverse collection of Haitian art since 1977; and **Mary O'Shea's Glass Garden** (305-293-8822; www.keywestglass.com), 613 Eaton St., the largest glass studio in the Florida Keys. Glass Reunions

(305294-1720; www.glassreunions.com), 825 Duval St., is a contemporary gallery with a stunning collection of work by more than 200 glass artists from around the country.

Back on Duval Street you'll find **Alan S. Maltz Gallery** (305-294-0005; www.alan maltz.com), 1210 Duval St., which showcases the fine-art photography of this renowned artist; and you won't want to miss the infamous **Wyland Gallery** (305-292-4998; www.wyland.com), 719 and 102 Duval St., featuring the works of marine-life artist Wyland, along with other environmental artists. Wyland has painted more than 25,000 works since 1971, and his art is cherished by collectors in 30 countries around the world. Globally famous for his colorful large-scale Whaling Walls (see *Murals*), he has worked diligently to educate the world on environmental issues. You'll want to explore the "Wyland Kids, Save Our Blue Planet" section of his Web site, where you can view illustrations of marine animals with your little ones. And kids of all ages will fall in love with his new children's book, *Spouty and Friends*.

BUTTERFLY CONSERVATORY Known for his Wings of Imagination gallery on Duval Street, artist Sam Trophia dreamed of a Victorian flower garden that evoked the sensory magic of stepping into an animated scene from a classic Disney movie. After many years of hard work with partner George Fernandez, the dream is now alive as the **Key West Butterfly Conservatory** (305-296-2988 or 1-800-839-4647; www.keywestbutterfly.com), 1316 Duval St., a half-acre tropical forest under glass where clouds of butterflies drift past as you stand mesmerized. Music adds a touch of magic as you watch blue morphos, giant swallowtails, and heliconias settle down and feast on slices of fruit. Tiny colorful birds—honeycreepers, speckled tanagers, and paradise tanagers—flit about in search of fruit. In the **Wings of Imagination Gift Shop** (www.wingsofimagination.com), one room is devoted to the art of butterflies, where Trophia's creations include mounted butterflies that swirl like luminescent galaxies (see *Selective Shopping*). Open daily 9 AM–5 PM. Adults $10, senior citizens and military $8.50, ages 4–12 $7.50.

HISTORIC SITES Relive the building of the Key West extension of the Florida East Coast Railway at **Flagler Station** (305-295-3562), 901 Caroline St. While naysayers shook their heads, Henry Flagler started construction in 1905 on the first overseas railroad. Spanning 130 miles from the Florida mainland to Key West, "Flagler's Folly" was successfully completed seven years later, allowing the 84-year-old Flagler just long enough to see the first train arrive in Key West. Flagler fell down a flight of stairs at his home in Palm Beach, passing away May 20, 1913 (see **Whitehall** in *Central Palm Beach County*). Open daily 9 AM–5 PM. Fee.

At **Fort Zachary Taylor Historic State Park** (305-295-00376713; www.florida stateparks.org/forttaylor), end of Southard St. on Truman Annex, explore one of the United States's largest fortresses, built to protect the shipping lanes passing Key West. Construction of this massive masonry structure began in 1850. During the Civil War, Federal soldiers occupied the fort, forcing Key West into Union hands. By the time construction was completed in 1866, the fort included a desalination plant and a row of latrines flushed out by the tides. During the Spanish-American War, the top levels of Fort Taylor were cut down to install modern weaponry; only in recent times has it been discovered that in doing so, the soldiers encased the largest known cache of Civil War–era cannons in concrete. As you tour the fort, notice the gothic styling within the various chambers. Fee.

East Martello Fort and Museum (305-296-39131; www.kwahs.com), 3501 S Roosevelt Blvd., was built in 1862 for protection during the Civil War, but the East Martello battery was never used for battle because of obsolete construction methods, although it has been used to house and train soldiers. Today it serves as a suitable repository for historical artifacts, including those from Native American times, from shipwrecking, from the Keys' wealthy days as a U.S. port of entry, from sponging and fishing, and more, through the past few decades of island history. Open 9:30–4:30 daily (except Christmas). Small fee.Take a few moments to wander through the **Key West Cemetery,** where all the graves are aboveground, and many have inscriptions such as I TOLD YOU I WAS SICK engraved on headstones. The 1847 historic cemetery is located in Old Town, bounded by Passover Lane and Frances, Olivia, Angela, and Margaret Streets, with the main entry gates open at the corner of Margaret and Angela. Several tours take you through or past the cemetery, or you can self-tour during the daylight hours.

Open since 1997, the **Key West Historical Sculpture Garden** is located in front of the Waterfront Playhouse (see *Entertainment*) near Mallory Square. The garden displays 36 bronze busts of men and women who were instrumental in the development and evolution of Key West. Plans to add an additional 36 busts are slated for the coming years. *The Wreckers*, by Miami sculptor James Mastin, rises 25 feet at the entrance to the garden and depicts the lives of these early pioneers.

The Sunset Celebration at **Mallory Square** is known the world over. Beginning in the 1800s as a raucous port for pirates, the harbor was next a place for antipirate demonstrations, and then the location from where American forces convened for the Civil War, the Spanish-American War, and World Wars I and II. In the 1960s, hippies took to the docks to watch the sunset, and a carnival atmosphere began. By the 1980s, the town felt they needed to regulate the somewhat lawless partying, so in 1984 Key West Cultural Preservation Society, Inc. was formed to manage the nightly event. Today you can join in the nightly festivities where residents and tourists alike gather to watch the sun set to the west. Preceding sunset, the square comes alive with a unique collection of performing artists, including fire eaters, jugglers, and magicians, while arts and crafts created by local artisans are sold. The square is named for Key West resident Stephen Russell Mallory (1812–73), who held a variety of governmental positions in Key West in the 1800s. Having particular knowledge about naval affairs, he was the Confederate secretary of the navy during the Civil War and one of President Jefferson Davis's most valuable cabinet members.

Mile Marker Zero (0) is located at the corner of Whitehead and South Streets, designating the beginning of US 1. The highway stretches 2,390 miles from here along the U.S. eastern seaboard to Fort Kent, Maine. The marker provides a popular photo spot, as does the **Southernmost Point.** The site is marked by a huge red, yellow, green, and white buoy (circa 1983). Standing 12 feet tall with a reach of 7 feet wide, the buoy received a face-lift in 2005 only to be hammered later that year with Hurricane Wilma. Still standing, it marks the southernmost point in the continental United States that is accessible to the general public, and it is a mere 90 miles from Havana, Cuba. The true southernmost point, on dry land anyway, is within the U.S. Naval Base boundary, just a bit west of the buoy. The actual southernmost point in the United States is on tiny Ballast Key, a federally protected wildlife preserve with no public access. It is located a few miles southwest between Key West and the Marquesas Keys. While you can't step on the southernmost island, you can fly over it on a tour (see *Airplane Tours*).

At 322 Duval St., the **Oldest House** in South Florida is now the **Wrecker's Museum** (see *Museums*). Built in 1829 as a residence for Capt. Francis Watlington and his family, this six-room house with courtyard and outbuildings remained a residence until 1973 and is on the National Register of Historic Places.

The stained-glass windows at **St. Paul's Episcopal Church,** 401 Duval St., are a glorious sight to behold; so much so that Lloyd's of London insures them. You'll want to be sure to visit this spectacular church (circa 1838), but you may not be alone when you do. It's said that the ghost of John Fleming, who donated the land the church rests on, wanders the grounds. When not on his ghostly rounds, Mr. Fleming's earthly remains reside in the churchyard.

MURALS The **Coral Reef** wall at the Historic Seaport wraps around much of the building housing Waterfront Market and Reef Relief on William Street. The mural, which showcases an impressive view of the Florida Keys's coral reef ecosystem, is one of **Wyland's Whaling Wall** projects (see *Art Galleries*). He was joined by artist **Guy Harvey,** best known for his painting of sport fish. Make sure to stop in at Reef Relief's Environmental Center & Gift Store.

You'll need to check in at the office at Glynn Archer Elementary School, 1302 White St., before viewing the mural painted by artist **William Hoffman.** The mural depicts the early years of Key West with Spanish explorers and the construction of the Overseas Railroad.

MUSEUMS At the **Audubon House & Tropical Gardens** (305-294-2116; www.audubonhouse.com), 205 Whitehead St., you'll experience the artistic works

MURAL OF THE EARLY KEYS, LOWER KEYS

Trish Riley

of John James Audubon. You'll see 28 first-edition pieces created by the world-famous ornithologist, along with an audio tour of the 1840s home, furnished with period pieces from the 1800s and built with architectural elements identified with wreckers and salvagers of the time. Enjoy a peaceful walk through the 1-acre tropical garden to calm your mind or enliven your spirits. Don't forget to browse through the gallery and gift shop for inspired and imaginative items. Open daily 9:30 AM–5 PM. Adults $10, students $6.50, children $5.

Trish Riley

POOLSIDE DECOR IN THE COURTYARD AT CASA ANTIGUA, KEY WEST

Casa Antigua, 314 Simonton St., is a little-known hideaway where Hemingway whiled away a few weeks waiting for his new Ford motor car to be delivered in 1928 . . . and wrote *A Farewell to Arms* in the meantime. Tours of the tropical courtyard are $2, or free with a $10 purchase in the adjoining Pelican Poop gift shop. Open 10 AM–6 PM daily.

The Curry Mansion Museum (305-294-5349 or 1-800-253-3466; www.curry mansion.com), 511 Caroline St., built in 1899 by William Curry, a Bahamian immigrant who worked the shores of Key West as a salvager, is listed on the National Register of Historic Places. Curry started construction of the 25-room mansion in 1855, incorporating many design elements common to wreckers. Take particular note of the widow's walk and Tiffany glass door entry. Make your way up the stairs to the attic, where you'll find an array of antique toys and garments from the era. Throughout the mansion, each room is staged in Victorian elegance. You can rest your head at the Curry **Mansion Inn** (see *Lodging*), which offers guest rooms and suites. Open 10 AM–5 PM daily. Fee.

Eco-Discovery Center (305-809-4750; www.floridakeys.noaa.gov), 35 East Quay Rd., provides opportunities to learn about the Keys ecosystem with virtual dives, videos, displays, and gift shop. Open 9 AM–4 PM Tues.–Sat. except Thanksgiving and Christmas.

The Spanish colonial–style **Ernest Hemingway Home and Museum** (305-294-1136; www.hemingwayhome.com), 907 Whitehead St., is a National Historic Landmark. Built in 1851 by salvage wrecker Asa Tift, the home displays items collected by Hemingway during his world travels. A calm and creative environment, this is where Hemingway wrote most of his greatest novels and where you'll find more than 60 descendants of his famous polydactyl cats, who lounge throughout the elegant garden and stately home. Open daily 9 AM–5 PM for tours. Adults $12, children $6, under six free.

At the **Heritage House Museum & Robert Frost Cottage** (305-296-3573; www.heritagehousemuseum.org), 410 Caroline St., you'll view a grand Caribbean colonial house (circa 1830s) with a variety of rare antiques and maritime memorabilia. The **Robert Frost Cottage,** located at the rear of the home, is often used for poetry conferences and can be viewed only from the outside during the tour.

Open 10 AM–4 PM Mon.–Sat., with tours every half hour. The $15 admission also includes admission to the Oldest House and the Audubon House.

Key West Shipwreck Historeum (305-292-8990; www.shipwreckhistoreum .com), One Whitehead St. Your costumed guide, master wrecker Asa Tift, takes you on an engaging tour of the 1800s, when shipwreck salvaging was the means to untold wealth, albeit a perilous livelihood. Learn about the world of wreckers as he spins a tale of the 1856 sinking and recovery of the *Isaac Allerton,* the richest shipwreck in Key West history. See artifacts from this rich and colorful historical period, when wrecking was Key West's main occupation. Open daily 9 AM–5 PM. Adults $11, ages 4–12 $4.50, under 4 free.

Florida's only presidential museum is—the **Little White House** (305-294-9911; www.trumanlittlewhitehouse.com), 111 Front St., at the Truman Naval Station. Walk through rooms filled with history to see where President Harry S. Truman spent 175 days at Quarters A while you listen to stories of historical meetings, elegant soirees, and how he kept the Secret Service on their toes. Modern moguls and CEOs should take note of the tiny desk where Truman signed important documents. Open daily 9 AM–5 PM. Adults $15, senior $13, ages 5–12 $5, under 5 free.

At the **Mel Fisher Maritime Heritage Museum** (305-294-2633; www.melfisher .org), 200 Greene St., you'll see an outstanding collection of shipwreck salvage. Donated in large part (more than $20 million in treasure and historical artifacts) by the man who "saw the ocean paved with coin," founder Mel Fisher established an incredible exhibit. You'll see such items as the "poison cup" gold chalice, an emerald-studded gold cross, gold and silver bars, thousands of silver coins, and other treasures from the 1622 shipwreck of the Spanish galleon *Nuestra Señora de Atocha.* Check out the second floor, where you'll learn more about pirates and life at sea. The Trade Goods museum store features authentic Spanish "cob" coins made into jewelry pieces, and replicas of doubloons and ancient weaponry. Free.

Inside the **Oldest House Wrecker's Museum** (305-294-9501; www.oirf.org/ museums/oldesthouse.htm), 322 Duval St., enjoy a tour of the Watlington house (see *Historic Sites*), built in 1829. Each room is decked out with period paintings, furnishings, and extensive exhibits that evoke the age of the wrecker, an old and storied career in the Conch Republic. In the back of the home, the office of Capt. Francis Watlington (circa 1870) features a "landlubber's tilt," with the windows and boards at a slant. Step out into the shaded courtyard and explore the outbuildings, the kitchen, and a former carriage house with exhibits on the wreckers of the Keys. Artifacts include a book from 1836, fragments of a china doll tea set, and a giant turnbuckle for the iron struts supporting the 1853 Sand Key lighthouse. Open 10 AM–2 PM daily for self-guided tours. Fee.

The bizarre and unnatural can be found at **Ripley's Believe It or Not** (305-293-9939; www.ripleyskeywest.com), 108 Duval St., where more than 500 exhibits in 13 themed galleries include everything from a prehistoric mastodon skeleton to a shrunken torso reputed to have belonged to Ernest Hemingway. Open daily 9:30 AM–11 PM. Adults $15, ages 5–12 $12, under 5 free.

By far one of the most famous homes in Key West is the 1896 **Southernmost House Grand Hotel & Museum** (305-296-3141; www.southernmosthouse.com), 1400 Duval St. Tours take you through the former home of Judge J. Vining Harris, where you'll see 43 original U.S. Presidential signatures, along with other documents dating from 1486. The tour provides you with the rich history of the home and the politics of the time. When Truman snuck out of the Little White House, this is where the Secret Service would find him. The home is also a bed & breakfast (see *Lodging*). Open for tours 10–6 daily. Adults $8, children under 12 free.

At the **Turtle Kraals Museum** (305-294-0209), 200 Margaret St., you'll learn about the turtle rehabilitation program of this former turtle canning facility. Open daily 11:15 AM–4:15 PM. Donation.

RAILROADIANA At the **Flagler Station Overseas Railroad Historeum** (305-295-3562; www.flaglerstation.net), 901 Caroline St., in the historic Key West Seaport, take a journey into the past through the movie *The Day the Train Arrived,* commemorating Flagler's disembarkation on the first train to Key West on January 22, 1912. Walk through a Florida East Coast railroad car with photographs and artifacts, and listen to storytellers describe one of the most awesome engineering feats of the last century. Fee.

WILDLIFE REHABILITATION The **Reef World Educational Facility and Environmental Center**, a nonprofit organization dedicated to protecting coral reefs (305-294-3100; www.reefrelief.org), 201 William St., at the historic seaport, offers free activities about reefs, turtles, dolphins, and sharks, and what you can do to help protect living coral reef ecosystems. At their gift shop there is a great variety of educational materials and books for young and old on this fragile marine environment, and there is also a selection of ecorelevant clothes, gifts, and posters. This is an interesting place to visit and an important stop where the family can learn about the need to protect the fragile environment of the Keys. Free.

Housed in a corner of the Sonny McCoy Indigenous Park (see *Parks*), **Wildlife Rescue of the Keys** (305-294-1441; www.floridakeyswildliferescue.org/fkwr), 1388 Ave. B, cares for sick and injured wildlife in the Lower Keys, particularly shorebirds, with an emphasis on rehabilitation and release. Dedicated volunteers have rescued crocodiles and assisted with whale strandings. Wander through the enclosures to visit with permanent residents such as pelicans, seagulls, and osprey that cannot be returned to the wild. Open 9 AM–5 PM daily. Donation.

✳ To Do

AIRPLANE TOURS Let the wind blow through your hair as you and one other person share the adventure of a lifetime on **Key West Biplane Rides** (305-294-8687; www.keywestairtours.com), 3469 S Roosevelt Blvd., located at the Key West Airport. You'll fly in a 1941 open cockpit WACO UPF-7 biplane as you soar only 500 feet off the ground and over the water. Different tours show you the sites of Key West and nearby islands. For a quick tour take the 18-minute Island Shipwreck Tour ($140) to see the Old

SOUTHERNMOST HOUSE
Courtesy Southernmost House

Town District and shipwrecks in the Fleming Key Channel. You'll spot sharks and stingrays swimming below in the 30-minute Coral Reef/Boca Grande Key Tour ($295), which covers 34 nautical miles over Key West and nearby uninhabited islands. The 50- to 55-minute Hour Tour ($325) takes in all the sites from Hemingway's famous Stilt House to Cotrell Key to look at the coral. All prices are per plane for two people. Call for reservations.

BIRDING Visit the **Key West Tropical Forest & Botanical Garden** (see *Botanical Gardens*) during the month of September for "Migration Mania," as migratory birds stop en masse at freshwater Desbiens Pond to drink deeply before setting off to Central and South America. Our feathered friends also flock to the freshwater pond near the White Street Pier at **Sonny McCoy Indigenous Park** (see *Parks*). **Dry Tortugas National Park** (305-242-7700; www.nps.gov/drto/), P.O. Box 6208, Key West, offers some of the most spectacular birding opportunities in the U.S. Visitors can camp on the virtually unoccupied islands or just visit for the day. Travel there by ferry, seaplane, or private boat ($40 and up). Park admission fee.

CRUISING You'll find golf cart–type electric cars for rent at **Key West Cruisers** (305-294-4724 500 Truman Ave. (at the intersection of Truman and Duval). These two- and four-seaters range from $60 to 80, starting from two hours to three or more days.

ECOTOURS Kayak Eco-Tours (305-294-8087; www.blue-planet-kayak.com) will take you paddling through a wildlife refuge or under the full moon. Guided tours are two and a half hours long ($50). Private tours are also available. Or you can rent a single or tandem kayak for a full day ($40–50) or a half day ($30–40) and explore on your own.

Lazy Dog Island Outfitters & Adventure Company (305-295-9898; www .mosquitocoast.net), 5114 Overseas Hwy., located at the Hurricane Hole Marina at MM 4.2. Lazy Dog takes you on sea kayaks through the backcountry on wildlife and snorkel tours. Rate is $60 per person and includes snacks, bottled water, and mask and snorkel sets. Lazy Dog also offers two-hour kayak tours with your dog ($35).

GHOST TOURS You'll have a spooktacular time with **The Ghosts & Legends of Key West** (305-294-1713 or 1-866-622-4467; www.keywestghosts.com), where you'll learn about the ghouls that inhabit Victorian mansions and secret voodoo rituals. Ninety-minute tours are at 7 PM and 9 PM nightly, starting at the Porter Mansion at the corner of Duval and Caroline Streets. Ages 8 and up $18.

You'll be led by lantern through the dark and narrow streets of historic Old Town for about 90 minutes with **Ghost Tours of Key West** (305-294-9255; www .hauntedtours.com), 423 Fleming St., where you'll learn about the legends of pirates, wreckers, and former Key West inhabitants. The nightly 0.5-mile tour begins in the lobby of the Crowne Plaza La Concha Hotel at 430 Duval Street and covers such sites as **St. Paul's Episcopal Church and cemetery** (see *Historic Sites*) and **Captain Tony's Saloon** (see *Eating Out*). Founded in 1996 by the author of *Ghosts of Key West,* David L. Sloan, this nightly haunt has been featured on numerous television shows, including the History and Discovery channels. Two tours leave at 8 and 9 PM. Adults $15, ages 4–12 $10, under 4 free.

HOCKEY Families skate free at the **Southernmost Hockey Club** (www.keywest hockey.com) on Friday night. Bring your own inline skates to the corner of Bertha St. and Atlantic Blvd. Call the YMCA of Key West at 305-296-YMCA for more information.

SAILING TOURS The 80-foot *Schooner Liberty* and 125-foot *Schooner Liberty Clipper* set sail morning, afternoon, and sunset for two hours on the **Liberty Fleet of Tall Ships** (305-292-0332; www.libertyfleet.com), 245 Front St. You'll enjoy the festive Caribbean barbecue during the season on the *Schooner Liberty Clipper*. Ships depart from Schooner Wharf at the historic seaport. Morning and afternoon sails: adults $40, children 12 and under $20; drinks available for purchase. Sunset sails: adults $65, children $40; includes complimentary drinks. Two-and-a-half-hour-long Caribbean barbecue dinner cruise: adults $85, children $55.

On **Sunny Days Catamarans** (305-292-6100 or 1-800-236-7937; www.sunny dayskeywest.com), at the foot of Elizabeth and Greene Sts., you can choose from a variety of catamaran tours, from snorkeling tours ($35–45) to a full-day excursion to **Dry Tortugas National Park** (see *Parks*) on their *Fast Cat* ($135) (reduced prices for children and seniors). Rates include a continental breakfast, buffet lunch, soft drinks, water, snorkeling gear, and a guided tour of the fort.

The 130-foot **Western Union** (305-292-1766; www.keyweststargazer.com), 202 William St., at Schooner Wharf, is the last tall ship constructed in Key West and is the last sailing cable ship found anywhere. The *Western Union,* launched in 1939, spent the next 35 years laying cable off the shores of the Keys before being used in the Mariel Boatlift and in a program for troubled teens. Now back home, it is heralded as the "Flagship of Key West." On two-hour, fully narrated afternoon and sunset tours, you'll enjoy sailing on one of the few authentic coasting schooners still in sailing condition. Step aboard the varnished mahogany decks, and relax as the ship moves gently out through the shipping lanes while soft music plays. On their 90-minute Stargazer Cruise, you'll discover the mystery of the night sky as astronomer Joe Universe provides you a bit of history and folklore, then uses a green laser beam to show you the stars and constellations overhead. Use your binoculars for a closer inspection of the band of animals that makes up the zodiac. Now owned by Historic Tours of America, the *Western Union* is on the National Register of Historic Places. Sunset and stargazing sails $55 with reduced prices for children.

TRAIN & TROLLEY TOURS Get your ticket for **The Conch Tour Train** (305-294-5161; www.conchtourtrain.com), 201 Front St. in Mallory Square, and then board from Mallory Square or from Flagler Station, 901 Caroline St. Narrated tours depart every half hour and are 90 minutes long. This tour is one way to learn about Key West before you explore on your own. Adults $29, ages 4–12 $14. **Old Town Trolley Tours** (305-296-6688 or 1-800-868-7482; www.historictours.com) is operated by the same company, but this one gives you the option of hopping on and off at 12 locations around town to spend a few minutes or hours at each location. Adults $26, ages 4–12 $13. Those with longer legs may be more comfortable on the trolley.

▼ The **Gay & Lesbian Trolley Tour** (305-294-4603; www.gaykeywestfl.com), 513 Truman Ave., operated by Key West Business Guild and Historic Tours of America, bears the rainbow flag during the 70-minute tour each Sat at 11 AM. You'll learn about the influence the gay and lesbian culture has had on the politics and economy of Key West, along with historical sites of specific interest to gay travelers. Call for departure location. Rates are $20 per person.

WALKING TOURS Duval, the main street of historic Old Town, stretches for 1 mile from the Atlantic Ocean (on the quiet side) to the Gulf of Mexico (on the spirited side), ending at Mallory Square (see *Historic Sites*). You'll find many art galleries, boutiques, restaurants, pubs, and lively music along this well-populated boulevard. Those attempting the "Duval Crawl" (one drink in every bar on Duval St.) should have a designated driver, or at least someone who can carry you home.

Historian and artist Sharon Wells arrived in Key West in 1976 and has been charting the territory ever since. She provides personalized walking or bike tours through her company Island City Strolls and is also author of *Sharon Wells' Walking and Biking Guide to Historic Key West*, available free at locations all around town for those who prefer to make their own way. Either way, if you've taken a liking to Keys architecture or are interested in the old cemetery, literary sites, grand homes and gardens, or gay highlights of Key West, Wells will help you find them. Wells's paintings and photographs of Key West and beyond are displayed at her gallery, KW Light Gallery, at 534 Fleming Street. **Island City Strolls** (305-294-8380; www.seekeywest.com), 534 Fleming St., Key West. **Go GPS Tours** (305-293-8891; www.gogpstours.com), 218 Whitehead St., provide GPS devices with audiovisual tour guides in four languages for your independent explorations.

✳ Green Space

BEACHES Fort Zachary Taylor (see *Historic Sites*), is a popular destination for watching the sunset and the cruise ships sailing past. Enjoy snorkeling or sunbathing on the coral rock sand; amenities include picnic tables, a bathhouse, and a light refreshment stand. Fee. On the Atlantic, **Smathers Beach,** on S Roosevelt Blvd., has shallow water great for the kids, and water sports including parasailing, Jet Skiing, and windsurfing. Free. At the White Street Pier, **Higgs Beach** is a popular family destination for its picnic tables and grills under the coconut palms. 🐾 **Gable Beach,** at Vernon St. and Waddell Ave., is the one dog-friendly beach on the island. And for those who let it all hang out, **Atlantic Shores Resort,** 510 South St., features a private nude beach.

BOTANICAL GARDENS ⅊ In 1936 the Works Progress Administration created a 55-acre botanical garden on Stock Island. But during World War II, pieces of the garden were sacrificed for an army hospital and other public works until the forest was whittled down to 8 acres and eventually abandoned. Thankfully, a group of dedicated volunteers has brought this botanical wonder back to life as the **Key West Tropical Forest & Botanical Garden** (305-296-1504; www.keywest botanicalgarden.org), 5210 College Rd., MM 4.25. Start your tour at the visitors center, which has a film about the biodiversity of the Keys, and pick up a map to walk any of the three self-guided tours through what is one of the top 25 biological hot spots of the world. Duke University students documented the flora of the forest, which includes a dwarf lignum vitae tree, the National Champion Cuban lignumvitae tree, *thrinax* palms more than a century old, and the oldest wild cinnamon tree in the Keys. Endangered white-crowned pigeons nest in the canopy, and thousands of migratory birds drop in for fresh water from Desbiens Pond, where the endangered mud-striped turtle lives. "The pond is like a turnpike stop on the flyway," said Carol Ann Sharkey, president of the nonprofit. At least 30 endangered species live in this last remnant of truly tropical forest on Key West. Plans are to finish removing invasive plants from the existing 8 acres and restore a new 8-acre tract (the former site of the army hospital) back to a formal botanical garden, and establish a medicinal plants research center on the site. The forest and gardens are open 10–5, closed Wednesday and during September. Donation.

For a relaxing break from Duval Street, seek out **Nancy Forrester's Secret Garden** (305-294-0015; www.nfsgarden.com), One Free School Ln. (off the 500 block of Simonton St.). This private paradise features lush tropical landscaping with orchids and an art gallery hides deep in the forest. Nancy Forrester, owner and curator of this last acre of undeveloped land in Key West, works hard to protect the status of her land. Enjoy a walk through the wild jungle paths and chat with resident parrots for a precious reminder of the importance of preserving nature and learning to live harmoniously with our environment. She also offers her property as an artists' retreat, and sometimes she rents out the small Bahamian cottage in the garden—it's lovely, with a porch and kitchenette. Open 10 AM–5 PM daily. Fee.

PARKS Seventy miles off the coast of Key West sits the **Dry Tortugas National Park** (www.nps.gov/drto). It's clear the Florida Keys have been providing happy days for anglers and tourists for more than a century, and the population and plethora of commercial enterprises are the evidence. If you're wondering what the Keys looked like in days past, consider a tour of the Dry Tortugas National Park, seven islands about 70 miles west of Key West. Named after its abundance of sea turtles (*tortugas* is Spanish for "turtles"), the area is a great location for snorkeling and birding, but it is best known for the largest fort in coastal America, Florida's own Alcatraz, **Fort Jefferson**, which served insufficiently as both fort and prison before being abandoned and consigned to the park service. Several tour boats and seaplanes offer transportation to the area with tours of the fort. Park entrance fee; primitive camping is available on Garden Key for a nightly fee. Call the campground at 305-242-7700.

Protecting 5.5 acres of natural Key West, **Sonny McCoy Indigenous Park** (305-293-6418), 1801 White St., encompasses the largest freshwater pond on the island and is home to **Wildlife Rescue of the Keys** (see *Wildlife Rehabilitation*). This is a hot spot for birders, as you can see warblers in migration and various raptors, including swallow-tailed kites. A boardwalk leads to natural surface trails that take you through a forest of silver buttonwoods and thatch palms and a grove of gumbo limbo to an observation deck on the pond. There is a shaded picnic pavilion and restrooms. Open 7 AM–5 PM Mon.–Fri.; tours by arrangement. Free.

PRESERVES Key West Nature Preserve (305-809-3700), Atlantic Blvd. Meander the trail through this strip of natural coastal hammock, where sea grapes crowd the edge of a mangrove swamp and giant land crabs dig holes in the footpath. A boardwalk leads through a bower of nickerbean to an observation deck with a view of the pier and the wrack line on the beach. Open sunrise–sunset daily; no swimming. Free.

✳ Lodging

The zip code for all Key West accommodations is 33040. Key West offers a wide range of accommodations, from single rooms to hotel suites, homes, and cottages, but the majority of lodgings are in restored Victorian and cracker houses scattered throughout Old Town, and they're loaded with charm and amenities. Pets are particularly welcome in Key West, and many lodgings and restaurants welcome them.

BED & BREAKFASTS, GUEST HOUSES, HOMES, AND COTTAGES
Ambrosia House (305-296-9838 or 1-800-535-9838; www.ambrosiakeywest.com), 615, 618, and 622 Fleming St., is smartly decorated in cool, island styles. Ambrosia House and Ambrosia Too offer suites, town houses, and a cottage clustered around tropical pools set in tropical gardens. It's close to Old Town, yet just far enough away to be nicely secluded in its own lush ambiance. Pet friendly. And complimentary breakfast. $179–639.

AMBROSIA HOUSE, KEY WEST

Trish Riley

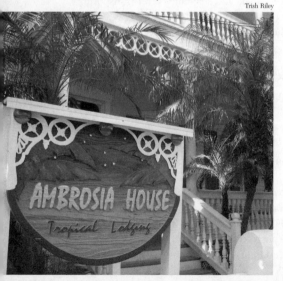

Artist House Key West (305-296-3977 or 1-800-582-7882; www.artisthousekeywest.com), 534 Eaton St. Stepping into the Artist House, said to be one of the most authentically restored Victorian guest houses in Old Town, is like stepping back in time. And some say that not everyone has left the premises from days gone by—is the turret room haunted? $115–265.

Authors of Key West Guesthouse (305-294-7381 or 1-800-898-6909; www.authorskeywest.com), 725 White St. This private compound of conch-style cottages, suites, and rooms is reminiscent of the many writers who have made Key West home. Bring pen and notebook and settle into the quiet atmosphere and peaceful gardens to craft your masterpiece, or just enjoy a few nights in style. Rooms and cottages; no pets. $100–155.

Avalon Bed and Breakfast (305-294-8233 or 1-800-848-1317; www.avalonbnb.com), 317 Duval St. Once a Cuban club at the quiet end of Duval Street, this bed & breakfast offers clean, quiet rooms with cool wood floors and net-canopied beds for guests seeking privacy and perhaps a little romance. Built in 1895, the Avalon is listed on the National Register of Historic Places. Pets welcome. $89–329.

Center Court Inn and Cottages (305-296-9292 or 1-800-797-8787; www.centercourtkw.com) 915 Center St. A collection of several historic properties scattered through Old Town; each has been renovated to sleek perfection. Most include gardens, hot tubs, pools, and kitchens, and many are pet friendly. Rooms and cottages; breakfast included with some accommodations. $178–8,000.

The Curry Mansion House (305-294-6777 or 1-800-633-7439; www.curryhousekeywest.com), 806 Fleming St. Romantic rooms are clustered around the pool of this restored historic Victorian mansion and offer a relaxing vacation reminiscent of a nearly forgotten era. European breakfasts, pool, hot tub, and daily cocktail parties enhance the romance. If you should happen to hear a sad-sounding trombone blaring into the night—that would be the ghost of Miss Petunia, who whiled the hours waiting for her captain to come home from sea by playing her instrument from the Curry House widow's walk. Rumor has it she was felled by a stray cannon blast, but everyone wonders, was it the miserable horn that cost her her life? Very reasonable rates in Key West terms. $109–259.

Curl up in a romantic atmosphere at the **Curry Mansion Inn** (305-294-5349 or 1-800-253-3466; www.curry mansion.com), 511 Caroline St. The elegant 22-room mansion, built in 1899 by Florida's first millionaire family, is open daily for historical tours (see *Museums*), which are free to guests. Rooms and suites are decorated with wicker or antiques from the period, such as graceful canopy beds, and have private baths, wet bars, air-conditioning, ceiling fans, and cable television. You'll enjoy the close proximity to Duval Street for shopping and dining, or relax any time of day at the swimming pool and hot tub, open 24 hours. Accommodations include a full deluxe breakfast and daily open bar. Rooms and suites range from $195 to 365.

↪ **Cypress House and Guest Studios** (305-294-6969 or 1-800-525-2488; www.cypresshousekw.com), 601 Caroline St. A wide variety of room options is available among two homes and a cottage nestled amid the lush flora that characterizes Old Town Key West. Whether you're looking for luxury or are on a tight budget, you'll find garden and courtyard rooms, a suite with

kitchenette and a front porch, master suite with beautiful tiled bath and jacuzzi and hand-painted ceiling mural over the four-poster bed. A rich complimentary breakfast buffet features fresh home-baked breads, fruit, cereal, juices, and more each morning, and a poolside happy hour provides appetizers and a full bar for guests to get a head start on their Key West nights of delight. $165–450.

Duval House Key West (305-294-1666 or 1-800-223-8825; www.duval housekeywest.com), 815 Duval St. Put yourself on the edge of the middle of the action. Duval Street, lined with all the shops and pubs of Key West, is the strip to stroll when twilight fades and the lights take over the night. If you like to be in the thick of things, yet shielded by a white picket fence with a pool in a hidden garden for respite from the excitement of the city, this is the place for you. Small rooms to two-bedroom suites in this collection of 7 Victorian houses with balconies and a gazebo. $125–350.

↪ **The Eden House** (305-296-6868 or 1-800-533-KEYS; www.edenhouse .com), 1015 Fleming St., is nestled on a side street within a short walk to all the activities on Duval. Built in 1924, the art deco–style inn is Key West's oldest hotel and has been lovingly cared for by owner Mike Eden since 1975. The attention to detail is everywhere, from the warm greeting and cool beverage you'll receive on your arrival to the lush tropical gardens, boardwalks, and hammocks found throughout the property. The fun and funky guest house feels like a beach house at times, and at others a quaint country inn. One thing is for sure— their knowledgeable staff knows the best places to eat and play on the island. But you'll want to spend some time right here on-site. Sun lovers will want to bask by the heated pool and Jacuzzi, or up on the elevated sundeck, while those with delicate skin will want to curl up under a canopy of palms in one of the property's eight hammocks, while listening only to the sounds of a waterfall. Enjoy a glass of wine or a chilled drink at the complimentary happy hour from 4 to 5. The comfortable rooms are very clean and efficient, with French doors leading out onto your own porch, some with swing. As this is a guest house, not a bed & breakfast, you'll have to venture out for breakfast; however, an on-site restaurant, Café Med, offers convenient dinners with Mediterranean flavor. Coffee and tea are available in the lobby at all times. Rates range from those for rooms with shared bath ($95–175) to the deluxe conch house with full kitchen ($260–440) and every imaginable configuration in between, with prices going up incrementally with enhancements such as private bath, TV, refrigerator, kitchenette, porch, Jacuzzi, and extra bedroom. Free parking available on-site.

Settle into romance at **The Frances Street Bottle Inn** (305-294-8530 or 1-800-294-8530; www.bottleinn.com), 535 Frances St., where colorful antique bottles adorn the windows and walls of this 1879 home. Innkeepers Mary Beth, Dennis, and Marketa create a comfortable atmosphere with bright pastels and wicker, bookshelves lined with books in the common areas, a quiet garden with a hot tub, and a wraparound veranda on both floors under the poinciana and palms. Over the years, the inn has worn many cloaks—from a private home to a general store, a Presbyterian church, and the starring role in the Fox TV series *Key West* in the 1990s. Each of the seven units ($125–295) has private baths and televisions; there is a phone and data port hookup in the lobby,

where breakfast is served from 8 to 10. I especially appreciate their Green policy, which includes recycling, low-flow toilets, and third-day bed linen changes on your longer stays.

↠ **Gardens Hotel** (305-294-2661 or 1-800-526-2664; www.gardenshotel .com), 526 Angela St. Possibly the most luxurious Old Town guest house in Key West, the Gardens Hotel has rated inclusion in *Condé Nast Traveler*'s list of the world's best places to stay for several years and was rated a readers choice by Trip Advisor in 2006. Gardens was the first hotel in Key West to GoGreen, and general manager Cindy DeRocher says it's one of the best things they've done for hotel management, cost control, and guest satisfaction. "Not only is it good to be a good steward of the environment, it just makes sense," says DeRocher. "Luxury isn't a waste; luxury is the tranquility our guests get to experience here. It's all about service and that's what we do best." For more than 30 years the Gardens Hotel was a private mansion with a carefully cultivated botanical garden, and in the 1990s the property was purchased and renovated into a hotel. Kate Miane, owner of Ambrosia and Ambrosia Too, bought the property for an unprecedented multimillion-dollar price tag, and neighbors waited with bated breath to see whether Ms. Miane could be as successful with this expansive and beautiful property as she has been with Ambrosia. She did not disappoint. Confidence was inspired by her first order of business—refreshing the gardens and bringing back the butterflies. Fresh, elegant, modern rooms and suites. $195–710.

The Grand Key West (305-294-0590 or 1-888-947-2630; www.thegrandguest house.com), 1116 Grinnell St., has been called one of the best deals in

Key West. The Grand offers clean, simple rooms with refrigerators in a nontouristy residential neighborhood. Five blocks from Duval Street in historic Old Town, the Grand had been a private home and rooming house before its current incarnation as a small hotel. Continental breakfast. $98–268.

Heron House (305-294-9227 or 1-800-294-1644; www.heronhouse.com), 512 Simonton St., is lush, charming, and exclusive. Heron House has a private, sheltered atmosphere, as if complicit in sharing your secrets. Once inside its stone privacy wall, guests can gather around the pool or retreat on a private sundeck. A four-crown, four-diamond inn, Heron House is just a block off Duval Street. Rooms and suites available. $120–289.

Hog's Breath Guesthouse (305-296-4222; www.hogsbreath.com/guesthouse .htm), 310 Elizabeth St. In need of a full house for a large group? The Hog's Breath Guesthouse is often used to provide housing for entertainers at the popular nightclub. The 150-year old, two-story house has three bedrooms plus two-bedroom lofts and is fully furnished with washer and dryer, kitchen, private garden, and pool. It's located near the waterfront and Mallory Square, just a few blocks from Duval Street. Three-night minimum, call for current rates.

↬ **La Mer Hotel & Dewey House** (305-296-6577 or 1-800-354-4455; www.lamerhotel.com), 506 South St. One of the few beachfront historic properties in Key West, La Mer and Dewey House, built as a turn-of-the-20th-century guest house and private home, have been meticulously renovated by Southernmost Resorts. Both include continental breakfast and afternoon tea served on the oceanfront veranda and a morning paper. The

Southernmost Hotel collection has been recognized by the state as the largest independently owned Green Lodging in the Florida Keys. $298–418.

▼ **LaTeDa Hotel and Bar** (305-296-6706 or 1-877-528-3320; www.lateda .com), 1125 Duval St. The sultry and sophisticated nightclub here has a 30-year tradition of fame and is said to have the best drag show in town. The decor of the standard, deluxe, and luxury rooms includes traditional home-style furnishing and sleek wood floors, tile, mahogany furnishings, French doors that open onto the garden, Roman tubs (in the luxury rooms), data ports, and refrigerators. $100–375.

Marquesa Hotel (305-292-1919 or 1-800-869-4631; www.marquesa.com), 600 Fleming St. This complex of conch houses in Old Town has been transformed into award-winning luxurious rooms and suites with the finest amenities, from elegant marble baths to plush bathrobes. Lush gardens surround two refreshing pools, and a notable restaurant serves dinner on the premises if walking a block to Duval has lost its appeal. $345–520.

Old Customs House Inn (305-294-8507; www.oldcustomshouse.com), 124 Duval St. This historic home is set off

HERON HOUSE

Trish Riley

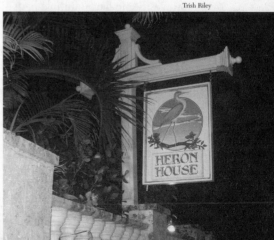

from the street through a gate right on Duval, yet it's private and charming thanks to gardens and trees that shade the porches and balconies. White wicker offsets the white picket fencing around the balconies, and rooms gleam with hardwood floors, tile accents, and Dade County pine furnishings. Studios and suites feature kitchenettes. Pets welcome, but call first. $90 and up.

✧ **Old Town Manor** (305-292-2170 or 1-800-294-2170; www.oldtown manor.com), 511 Eaton St. A blend of Victorian restoration and modern comfort, the Main House, built in 1886, and the William Skelton House, built in 1832, offer plush beds in fresh, sunny rooms, many with verandas overlooking lush historic gardens. Old Town Manor, formerly Eaton Lodge, was among the first lodgings to GoGreen in Key West.The private tropical garden offers a restful escape from the heart of Duval Street, just a block away. Old Town Manor offers some of the most affordable options for overnight travelers. Rooms and the two-bedroom Suite William are available. Pets welcome. $115–335.

Old Town Suites (305-296-5169 or 1-800-413-1978; www.oldtownsuites .com), two cottages, one on Petronia and the other on Center Street, with suites or rent the whole place. Some rooms have kitchens; others have coffeemakers, refrigerators, and microwaves; some have multiple beds for families, jacuzzi, or pool. $129–258.

✧ 🐾 ▼ **Pearl's Rainbow** (305-292-1450; www.pearlsrainbow.com); 525 United St., is a resort exclusively for women with a range of rooms, two pools, and jacuzzis. Pearl's Patio offers a lesbian happy hour daily. Pet friendly. Rooms $89–379.

Simonton Court Historic Inns and Cottages (305-294-6386 or 1-800-944-2687; www.simontoncourt.com), 320

Simonton St. A wide range of accommodations make up Simonton Court, from sleeping rooms in a manor or mansion to quaint cottages and elegant town houses, the largest with four bedrooms. Attention to details, decor, ambience, and atmosphere shows through such touches as tropical gardens, white linens, and natural wood floors. Hot tubs, pools, continental breakfast included. $150–400.

Suite Dreams (305-292-4713 or 1-800-730-2483; www.oldtownsuites .com), 1001 Von Phister St. Part of the luxury accommodations offered by Old Town Suites, which also owns Olivia by Duval, Suite Dreams is a gated home far removed from the hustle of Duval Street, in a suburban setting several blocks away from the tourist crowds. There's a small pool and fishpond on the shared patio and a private pool and gourmet kitchen for the three-bedroom Super Suite. The beach is just a few blocks away. $100–500.

HOSTEL ⁰**I**⁰ Seasoned hostelers will find comfort at the **Key West Youth Hostel** (305-296-5719 or 1-800-468-5516; www.keywesthostel.com), Seashell Motel, 718 South St. Strict rules make this a no-party place. Only 2 blocks from the beach, in Old Town, the hostel is never closed and offers 92 beds, free wireless Internet, kitchen facilities, and a courtyard. Rates $28 per night for hostel members; $31 for nonmembers. Bikes are available for rent.

HOTELS, MOTELS, AND RESORTS Banana Bay Resort Key West (305-296-6925; www.bananabay .com), 2319 N. Roosevelt Blvd. Set apart from the action at Sloppy Joe's, but close enough to walk or bike into town, this resort caters to adults, with romantic rooms, a tropical pool, and fitness and business centers. A beachside gazebo is standing by for weddings, snorkel guides and wild dolphin charters are available, and if you bring your own boat (less than 25 feet), you can dock here for a daily fee. Fully equipped rooms; no kids under 16 or pets allowed. $90 and up.

↪ **Casa Marina Resort and Beach Club** (305-296-3535 or 1-800-626-0777; www.casamarinakeywest.com), 1500 Reynolds St. Originally built by Henry Morrison Flagler for the tourists his train brought to town, this hotel now offers 311 rooms on the oceanfront, with a wide amount of beachfront set aside for guests' use. Rooms are carefully maintained to ensure that guests can enjoy privilege and service. $359 and up.

↪ **Crowne Plaza La Concha** (305-296-2991 or 1-800-745-2191; www .laconchakeywest.com), 430 Duval St. Built in 1925 during Key West's heyday as the wealthiest city in the nation, La Concha is the tallest building on the island, with seven stories. The rooftop offers a popular public lookout over Duval Street at the Top of La Concha Bar, especially great for sunset viewing. With all the extra amenities you'd expect from Crowne Plaza resorts, rooms are standard issue with fine appointments, data ports, and room service at the push of a button. La Concha provides for those whose trust relies on familiar service. Pet friendly. $248–429.

Stay in style on an 1830s estate at the **Key Lime Inn** (305-294-5229 or 1-800-549-4430; www.keylimeinn.com), 725 Truman Ave., vintage motor-court cottages arranged around a central treed courtyard and swimming pool, with a grand 1854 Bahamian British colonial–style home of Walter C. Mahoney. The units include the fully renovated and comfortable cottages, built in 1939 by a former circus per-

Trish Riley

SUNSET VIEW OF KEY WEST FROM THE ROOF AT CROWNE PLAZA HOTEL

former, and a handful of units in the historic home; Rooms 10 and 12 have access to the upper-story porch. There are 37 one-bedroom units and king rooms with a porch or patio and a country bed. Rates run $109 and up in the off-season, $189–309 during the high season, with surcharges for special events.

↪ **Southernmost Hotel** (305-296-6577 or 1-800-354-4455; www .southernmostresorts.com), 1319 Duval St., is indeed the southernmost hotel in the United States. Built in the 1950s, the hotel has been through major renovations to keep up with the fast-growing tourist industry on the island, so guests get a blended feeling of 1950s motel with 21st-century style. Some people prefer the group atmosphere, reliability, and service that's professional, yet maintains the guests' privacy and anonymity. The Southernmost Hotel provides a fine alternative to the many similarly priced guest houses, and it's across the street from the beach. This hotel is part of the Southernmost Hotel Collection, a group of properties that make up the largest Green lodging in Key West and includes an oceanfront extension opened in December 2008. $89 and up.

The Southernmost House Grand Hotel and Museum (305-296-3141 or 1-866-764-6633; www.southernmost house.com), 1400 Duval St. Built in 1896, the Southernmost House is a stunning piece of Victorian architecture on the beach, saved from disintegration by a 1996 restoration costing $3 million. The house has hosted five presidents of the United States and has many museum pieces that reflect that history. Today guests can stay at the hotel, tour the museum, or spend the day enjoying the beachfront pool and bar. An all-day pass (fee) includes museum tour, use of the pool, beach, and a drink. Tours are held daily. Rooms are decorated in period antiques and offer oceanfront or garden views. $225–545.

Sunset Key Guest Cottages (305-292-5300 or 1-888-477-7786; www .sunsetkeyisland.com/resortmain.htm), 245 Front St. Relieve yourself of the congested pubs, restaurants, and shops clustered along Duval Street by staying a boat ride away. Ocean Properties Ltd. of Delray Beach bought what was once known as Tank Island and built a modern island-style village for your private retreat. Now called Sunset Key and franchised by Westin Hotels, the island offers clusters of cottages, all freshly appointed to ensure your comfort, even including a shopping service to stock your cottage with your favorite foods. Some are beachfront, others have views, and some look upon the pool instead, giving parents a nice chance to remain close while their children play. Tennis and basketball courts are on the grounds, in addition to a spa, and there are water sports and other activities. Guests may utilize the launch day and night to partake of city pleasures and then return to quiet island life. Guests may also request the services of a private chef to cook in their cottage, or the Latitudes Beach Café provides oceanside Caribbean dining for guests as well as visitors. If you like Sunset Key so much you don't want to leave, you don't have to. Single-family residences are available for sale. Sunset Key has been rated as the second best place to stay in the United States and Canada by *Travel + Leisure*. Minimum stays may apply. $595–2,295.

SUNSET KEY RESORT

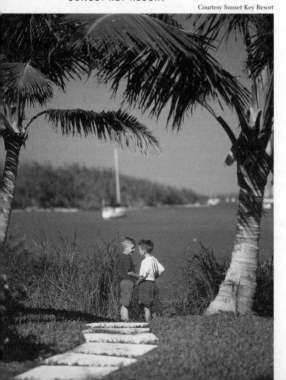

Courtesy Sunset Key Resort

✳ Where to Eat

Key West is a great place to eat. Excellent fresh seafood abounds and chefs make a point to treat it right. Many hotels and guest houses offer complimentary breakfasts to start your day, delectable lunches and appetizers tide you through the afternoon; but save your appetite and your pocketbook for an investment in a rich dinner—you'll find plenty to satisfy your palate.

SUNSET KEY RESORT

Courtesy Sunset Key Resort

DINING OUT ▼ Alice's at LaTeDa

(305-296-5733; www.aliceskeywest
.com), 1125 Duval St. Called New
World Fusion Confusion by *Bon
Appétit,* Alice Weingarten's cuisine has
won a long list of awards. Alice creates
an always beautiful blend of Mediterranean, tropical, and traditional flavors
and styles for breakfast, lunch, and
dinner. Try a seviche martini with gazpacho sidecar for a pair of flavors that
are hard to choose between, or a pure
passion salad with mango, goat cheese,
almonds, and berries over fresh baby
greens and topped with passion-fruit
vinaigrette. Desserts are not to be
bypassed, and don't forget the after-
dinner show in the Crystal Room—it's
the hottest drag show in the city.
Entrées $15 and up.

Azur Restaurant (305-292-2987;
www.azurkeywest.com), 425 Grinnell
St. Serving breakfast, brunch, lunch,
and dinner in the dining room or on
the patio, all dishes promise a Mediterranean flair for culinary delight. From
the charred octopus salad served with
red peppers and lemon zest to grilled
flatbread pizza or seared breast of
duck served with wild mushrooms and
artichokes, meals here seem to live up
to the promise. Entrées $12 and up.

Blue Heaven (305-296-8666; www
.blueheavenkw.com), 305 Petronia St.
Blue Heaven is mostly outdoors, with
chickens running underfoot and a
hanging rope swing to entertain diners
awaiting their brunch, lunch, or dinner.
A rooftop dining area gets a breeze
from surrounding trees, while those
below benefit from shade provided by
sails spread from the tree limbs.
Caribbean flavors spice up the fare,
reflecting perhaps this restaurant's
location in Bahama Village. Its popularity came like wildfire, netting
national acclaim from all angles, but
the fame hasn't changed the atmosphere or spawned a chain. You can still
enjoy a refreshing drink while watching the kids chase chickens and swing
in the trees. Entrées $12 and up.

Café Marquesa (305-292-1919 or 1-
800-869-4631; www.marquesa.com),
600 Fleming St. Chef Susan Ferry has
made a name for herself and Café
Marquesa that permeates the city like

DELICACIES FROM ALICE'S, KEY WEST

Courtesy Alice's, Key West

the fine sauces she creates to accompany the creative dishes she concocts. The small restaurant exudes its charm even when closed and empty, beckoning passersby to come in and enjoy such treats as heirloom eggplant, corn, and tomato salad with Brie or goat cheese, walnut-crusted rack of lamb, and Key lime napoleon with fruits and berries. Open for dinner only–reservations recommended. Entrées $21 and up.

Crabby Dick's (305-294-7229; www.crabbydickskeywest.com), 712 Duval St. You can while away the afternoon here downing inexpensive draughts and nibbling cheap chicken wings, enjoying the breeze on the outdoor patio or the cool bar. Entrées $13.50 and up.

Kelly's Caribbean Bar and Grill (305-293-8484; www.kellyskeywest.com), 301 Whitehead St. After rocketing to celebrity fame in *Top Gun,* actress Kelly McGillis came back to her hometown of Key West and opened a top-flight restaurant, where in the early days she could often be found serving as hostess. With a local writers' library and its own brewery, Kelly's provides a relaxing atmosphere for those seeking a higher plane. Impressive gourmet fare includes seafood dishes with Caribbean flair, such as sesame seared tuna and yellowtail snapper served with tropical fruit, or keep it simple with chicken fettuccine or prime rib. Entrées start at $15.95.

La Trattoria (305-296-1075; www.latrattoria.us), 524 Duval St., is considered by many to be Key West's best restaurant, with a basketful of People's Choice Awards. La Trattoria seduces diners with a sophisticated atmosphere and then fattens them with stunningly delicious treats. And it's not your standard issue Italian: here you'll find superb blends of garlic, olive oil, tomato, and basil with ravioli, tortellini, penne, and gnocchi. After dinner be sure to make your way to the back of the restaurant, where you'll be delighted to find a hidden little jazz bar, Virgilio's, famous for its chocolate martinis. Entrées $13 and up.

Louie's Backyard (305-294-1016; www.louiesbackyard.com), 700 Waddell Ave. The elegant indoor dining room looks out at the ocean, or dine outside, which is a bit more casual. It's even more relaxed at the on-site Afterdeck Bar, where well-behaved, leashed dogs are welcome. Sandwiched between Dog Beach and an apartment once rented by Jimmy Buffett, this mansion, built at the turn of the 20th century by a wealthy wrecker, now offers inspired cuisine. Try the cracked conch roll with horseradish aioli or grilled scallops with spicy mango ketchup—you won't soon forget it. Entrées $18 and up.

☙ Food and art meet at **Mangoes** (352-292-4606; www.mangoeskeywest.com), 700 Duval St., an upscale restaurant featuring floral art from Piero Aversa, sculptures by John Martini, and plaster art from Sergio deVecchi. Infused with music, light, and the aromas from the kitchen, this is a delightful place for a meal. Executive Chef Paul Orchard oversees creations such as passion yellowtail snapper, which came dusted with toasted coconut and drizzled with a sour spicy mango passionfruit sauce. The white conch chowder was luscious and creamy, and the tomato bisque tart had a hint of cheese. Choose from a tempting selection of desserts, including a crème brûlée, delicate and silky with a lingering cappuccino taste, a perfect accompaniment to that after-dinner coffee. Perfection doesn't come cheap—expect to drop $75 for a meal for two. Pets welcome.

Pisces "A Seafood Place" presented by Café Des Artistes (305-294-7100; www.pisceskeywest.com), 1007 Simonton St. Same owner, same chef—different name. Café Des Artistes began in 1982 and underwent renovation in 2002. Much of the architecture of the original building (circa 1892) was restored, setting the stage for an incredible meal. Owner Timothy Ryan thought that with a fresh new look, the restaurant needed a new name, and Pisces was chosen to reflect the "fruits from the sea" concept. Buttery walls accented with plum drapes surround tables set with crisp white linens placed with half wall dividers, so intimate conversations can be held in private. Walls are decorated with original signed Andy Warhol prints, from owner Timothy Ryan's personal collection, framed within architectural arches. You'll especially enjoy the portraits of Marilyn Monroe and Mick Jagger, along with the famous *Campbell's Tomato Soup* and *Cow 1971.* Chef Andrew Berman creates magic with seafood, and his famous Lobster Tango Mango—shelled Maine lobster flambéed in cognac with shrimp in saffron butter, mango, and basil is a winner. You'll also want to try the Aphrodite Pisces, lobster, shrimp, and sea scallops baked in puff pastry with lemon tarragon butter; Yellowtail Snapper Atocha, with lemon brown butter, avocadoes, mint, and peas; and house favorite Raspberry Duck. Save room for the flambéed Rhum Baba, with white chocolate mousse, fresh berries, and mango sauce ($9) or chocolate fondant, an upside-down chocolate soufflé with pistachio and warm Valrhona chocolate sauce ($9). A glass of late harvest dessert wine ($9–15) is a great way to finish it all off. Appetizers $8–24; entrées $27–44. Reservations strongly recommended.

EATING OUT Savor a glass of cabernet while Dino croons at **Abbondanza** (305-292-1199), 1208 Simonton St., a comfortable Italian restaurant that offers all the classic dishes—including spaghetti *Calabrese,* with peppers, onions, and spicy sausage, and linguine *pescatore,* with shrimp, scallops, clams, and mussels. Entrées $9–18.

At **Alonzo's Oyster Bar** (305-294-5880; www.alonzosoysterbar.com), 700 Front St., oysters are the thing—brought in fresh and prepared fresh. Try the Dixie Oyster Spinach Salad, with fried oysters, bacon, hard-boiled egg, and mango touched with passionfruit vinaigrette atop a bed of baby spinach, or oysters prepared with spinach Parmesan, andouille, or Key lime garlic. The oysters come from around the country; daily raw selections are listed on the chalkboard. Entrées $14–19.

Since 1851, **Captain Tony's Saloon** (305-294-1838; www.capttonys saloon.com), 428 Greene St., has been the favorite watering hole of thirsty souls, from wreckers to writers. In the early 1900s it was a cigar factory, bordello, and favorite speakeasy. From 1928 to 1939, Ernest Hemingway met his friends here faithfully every afternoon at 3:30 for a scotch and soda while he was working on such books as *Death in the Afternoon* and *To Have and Have Not.* Hemingway's bar stool is still on view. The 1970s brought Jimmy Buffett and the Coral Reefer Band to the pub for impromptu sessions, and today you'll find a variety of talent, with music and a bit of mayhem nightly.

For the best Cuban *con leche,* head over to **The Five Brothers Grocery** (305-296-5205), 930 Southard St., at the corner of Grinnell. This tiny corner grocery store goes through 24 pounds of authentic Cuban coffee a day and is a great place for Cuban sandwiches.

You come to the **Green Parrot** (1-800-901-9552; www.greenparrot.com), corner of Whitehead and Southard Sts., to drink, not eat. With lots of ice-cold beer and tropical concoctions, you won't go thirsty. This legendary landmark, the last bar on US 1, pumps out great music all the time, and the must-see, one-of-a-kind watering hole has been serving great drinks, darts, and pool since 1890. The bar bills itself as "a sunny place for shady people," but don't be hesitant to scope it out—it really isn't as scary as it looks. Can't wait to see it? There's a live Web cam on their Web site. For those who want to poke their heads in just to say they were there, there's a great gift shop on-site for souvenirs.

Hog's Breath Saloon (305-292-2032; www.hogsbreath.com), 400 Front St. How about a Hog's Breath T-shirt, hat, or beer cup? This Keys club has become a famous brand. It's a fine place for a semi-outdoor evening drink and a little admirable live music. (It's the home of the Key West Songwriters Festival each May; www.keywestsong writersfestival.com.) Enjoy fine wings and fish dip—spiced up with Hog's Breath own hot sauce—burgers, or fish of all kinds. Remember, Hog's Breath is better than no breath at all! Entrées $12 and up.

Jimmy Buffett's Margaritaville Café (305-292-1435; www.margarita ville.com), 500 Duval St., is a must-stop for the infamous Cheeseburger in Paradise ($9), served just like the song says, or the broiled yellowtail snapper sandwich ($10). Wash it all down with one of seven fresh fruit margaritas ($6), such as passion fruit or banana, or order up the original Margaritaville Gold Margarita ($6).

At **Sloppy Joe's** (305-294-5717; www .sloppyjoes.com), 201 Duval St., their namesake sandwich is big, drippy, and sweet, and the chili comes tomato-thick with a bit of a kick. The sliced potato salad is something right out of my childhood. But most folks don't come here for the food; they're here for the legendary drink, from margaritas and Rum Runners to a one-and-a-half-ounce pour on your favorite liquor. Touting themselves as Hemingway's favorite bar, they've been here since 1937.

Turtle Kraals Bar and Restaurant (305-294-2640; www.turtlekraals.com), 1 Lands End Village. It's hard to eat here without reflecting on the fact that this was once a turtle cannery, but just remind yourself that those days are over now. Order a salad, gazpacho, or spinach and artichoke dip if it makes you feel better. Enjoy the open-air view of the waterfront and seaport, and relish the historic charm that emanates from the walls. Or go ahead and indulge in the Cuban- and Southwest-flavored seafood that's famous here, like lobster chile rellenos or mojo grilled shrimp. Wash it down with a bottle of Key West Sunset Ale, and relax in the salty breeze. Entrées $10 and up.

ICE CREAM PARLORS If you love ice cream, you must not miss **Flamingo Crossing** (305-296-6124), 1105 Duval St., where their homemade gelato flavors range into the tropical, including soursop, guava, papaya, mango, and passion fruit. Their Rum Runner sorbet is like a water ice, satisfying and light; the coconut gelato is a thick sweet cream bursting with flavor. Also available are Floridian favorites: Cuban coffee and, of course, Key lime.

At the **Key West Ice Cream Factory** (305-295-3011; www.keywesticecream factory.com), 201 William St., enjoy homemade ice cream flavors packed with fresh tropical fruit, premium tropical smoothies, and their original-recipe Key lime pie ice cream.

✳ Entertainment

THEATER Professional theater, live comedy, drama, music, and cabaret shows are presented November through July at the **Red Barn Theatre** (305-296-9911 or 1-866-870-9911; www.redbarntheatre.com), 319 Duval St. Main-stage shows run Tues.–Sat. at 8 PM. Advanced tickets $25, opening night $29; senior citizens, military, and students receive a 10 percent discount.

At the **Tennessee Williams Theatre** (305-296-1520; www.twstages.com), 5901 College Rd., you'll enjoy great theatrical performances along with art exhibitions, festivals, fund-raisers, and community events. Indoors, the 480-seat theater has added 250 seats in their new Grand Foyer, allowing for intimate recitals and poetry readings. The Grand Foyer can also be converted to bistro seating for cabaret shows. Outdoors overlooking the water, performances can accommodate 2,500 guests.

You'll find Florida's oldest continuously running theater over at Mallory Square. **The Waterfront Playhouse** (305-294-5015; www.waterfrontplayhouse.com), 310 Wall St., has been presenting live theater since 1940, with an array of productions. You may see such musical productions as *Little Shop of Horrors,* dramas such as *A Streetcar Named Desire,* and innovative works such as *Naked Boys Singing.* Tickets $30–35.

✳ Selective Shopping

When traveling in and out of Key West, make sure to pull over at MM 15 to **Baby's Coffee** (305-744-9866 or 1-800-523-2326; www.babys coffee.com), 3178 US 1 (oceanside), Saddlebunch Key, for a great cup of coffee and bakery snacks. (See *Eating Out* in *Lower Keys.*)

The best Key lime pie is found at **Blond Giraffe** (www.blondgiraffe .com), where owners Roberto and Tania Madeira serve a variety of edible Key lime delights, such as the incredible Key lime pie wrapped in chocolate served on a stick. You'll also find a nice selection of bath products, such as their Key Lime Goat Soap. Three locations: 629 Duval St. (305-293-6998); 1209 Truman Ave. (305-295-6776); and their factory store at 107 Simonton St. (305-296-9174). Watch the pies being made!

You'll find an elegant and sophisticated, but not stuffy, boutique at **Blue** (305-292-5172; www.blueislandstore .com), 718 Caroline St. It has a great mix of casual and dressy wear, and I was able to find the neatest, super-soft T-shirts, along with some elegant cocktail outfits. The shop specializes in smart, wearable women's clothing, shoes, purses, and hats. Open daily.

Playful and satirical chicken-related gifts line the shelves at **The Chicken Store** (305-394-3542; www.theChicken Store.com), 1227 Duval St., which is home to the Rooster Rescue Team. For a donation, you can slip into a cottage filled with rescued gypsy chickens, part of Key West's long legacy of foraging fowl. Open 10 AM–5 PM daily.

Cigar aficionados will want to check out **Conch Republic Cigar Factory** (1-800-317-2167; www.conch-cigars .com), 512 Greene Stand **Key West Havana Cigar Company** (305-296-2680; www.keywestcigar.com), 1121 Duval St.

An otherworldly gift shop awaits you at **Ghost Tours of Key West** (305-294-9255; www.hauntedtours.com), 423

Duval St., located at the Crowne Plaza La Concha Hotel. (See *To Do* for more information about the ghost tours.)

At the **Helio Gallery Store** (305-294-7901; www.heliographics.com), 814 Fleming St., you'll find great designs inspired by nature, such as botanical prints, pillows, table runners, totes, and textiles decorated with large banana leaves, coconut palms, butterflies, and more. Open 10 AM–6 PM daily.

From doorstops and footstools to pillows and purses, you'll find great stitchery over at **Julie Pischke Needlepoint Designs** (305-296-6091; www.islandneedlepoint.com), 527 Fleming St., where owner and designer Julie Pischke features her award-winning tropical needlepoint designs. Open Tues.–Sat.

Mary O'Shea's Glass Garden (305-293-8822; www.keywestglass.com), 613

Eaton St. Visit Mary for a friendly chat and to view her glass creations of jewelry, dishes, artwork, and more. Open 10 AM–5 PM Mon.–Sat.

Don't leave Key West without something from **Key West Handprint Fabrics** (305-294-9535 or 1-800-866-0333; www.keywestfashions.com), 201 Simonton St., where you'll find colorful, original hand-print fabrics by local Key West artists. Ladies can select from dresses, skirts, capris, shorts, and assorted jewelry, and men will go wild for their tropical parrot shirts. Girls will want an outfit from their "Mommy & Me" collection. For those who love to sew, fabrics by the yard are $16–26, with quilting squares also available to commemorate your trip.

Since 1976, the **Key West Kite Company** (305-296-2535; www.keywestkites.com), 408 Green St., has made the skies more colorful with their large selection of kites, windsocks, banners, flags, and more. You find an array of single lines, deltas, and parafoils, along with radical frameless stunt kites for kite surfing.

Enjoy unique, tropical wines at **The Key West Winery** (305-292-1717; www.thekeywestwinery.com), 103 Simonton St. The Key Limen wine tastes like a margarita, while the Category 5 white sangria honors hurricanes with a blend of their Key Limen, pineapple, mango, watermelon, and passion fruit wines. You'll also find edible Key lime treats and wine accessories. Open daily, with free wine tastings.

Everyone on land and sea seems to be wearing **Kinos Sandals** (305-294-5044; www.kinosandalfactory.com), 107 Fitzpatrick St. Walk into the small factory shop and you'll see busy shoemakers assembling these comfortable and durable flip-flops. It all began in 1966 with Cuban refugees Roberto "Kino"

COCKS RULE IN KEY WEST

Trish Riley

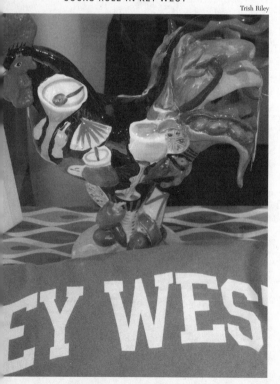

and Margarita Lopez. Roberto had a shoe factory back in Cuba, and he longed to continue his business, but first he needed to save for it. After years as a handyman, he finally had enough to open his factory, and it has been a local favorite ever since. These affordable sandals never seem to wear out. I've had my "Chain" ($11) sandal for three years, and they still look like the day I bought them, despite traipsing through South Florida storms. The "Lili" is the most common style seen on the docks, and it comes in a half dozen colors and in both women's ($11) and men's ($13) sizes. They also have one style for kids ($8). You'll need to check back often, as not all styles and sizes are on hand all the time.

Nellie & Joe's Key Lime Juice (1-800-LIME-PIE; www.keylimejuice .com) is the maker of the original Key West Lime Juice. Beginning 30 years ago in their kitchen, Nellie & Joe's can now be ordered through the Internet or picked up at a variety of stores throughout the United States. You'll find a great selection of their products at **Kermit's Key West Key Lime Shoppe** (305-296-0806; www.key limeshop.com), 200A Elizabeth St., where you can also enjoy a hot cup of coffee and a fresh slice of Key lime pie outside in the beautiful garden. Make sure to stop by during the holidays, as Kermit festively decorates the outside of the store into an award-winning gingerbread house. Kermit is also known for his support of local organizations in the area, such as the Monroe Association for Retarded Citizens, Inc (www .marchouse .org). He pays his staff a fair wage, so they donate 90 percent of all tips received toward this worthwhile organization. **Whitehead Street Pottery** (305-294-5067; www.whitehead streetpottery.com), 322 Julia St., specializes in stoneware, porcelain, and

Trish Riley

TEDDI ADMIRES MARY O'SHEA'S GLASS GARDEN IN KEY WEST

raku-fired containers. Open 10 AM–5 PM; closed Tues.

✳ Special Events

For information on the following events, contact the **Key West Chamber of Commerce** (305-294-2587; www.keywestchamber.org) and check out www.fla-keys.com for additional contact numbers.

January: Big-name sailing skippers compete for five days in North America's largest midwinter yachting races at the **Acura Key West Regatta** (www .premiere-racing.com).

Now more than 20 years old, the **Key West Literary Seminar** (1-888-293-9291; www.KeyWestLiterarySeminar .org), held midmonth, brings in authors from around the world who hold workshops and readings for the likes of you and me, aspiring novelists and fans alike. This two-week festival celebrates the island's long-standing love affair with literature, from the plays of Tennessee Williams to the short stories of John Hershey—and, of course, the Hemingway classics.

You'll see exquisite homes on the **Old Island Days House and Garden Tour** (www.oirf.org), also offered in February and March.

February: Over at Fort Zachary Taylor Historic State Park (www.floridastate parks.org/forttaylor), the **Annual Civil War Heritage Festival** (305-295-3033) re-creates the Civil War with a mock land and sea battle.

More than 100 artisans showcase their talents at the **Annual Old Island Days Art Festival,** held in the historic Old Town district along Whitehead Street from Greene to Caroline Streets.

You'll get a chance to tour ginger-bread-style Victorians and contemporary homes on the **Old Island Days House and Garden Tour** (also offered Jan. and Mar.).

March: You won't want to miss the **Annual Conch Shell Blowing Contest** (www.oirf.org/events), an island tradition. Contestants compete in an attempt to make music on the fluted conch shells.

Check out extraordinary architecture and gardens at the **Old Island Days House and Garden Tour** (also offered Jan. and Feb.).

April: Attend the poetry-writing workshop to hone up on your lyrical skills at the **Annual Robert Frost Poetry Festival** (www.robertfrostpoetry festival.com), held at the Heritage House Museum (see *Museums*).

For more than two decades, the **Conch Republic Independence Celebration** (www.conchrepublic .com) has been held to commemorate the Conch Republic, which was founded in 1982 after response to the U.S. Border Patrol road-blocking traffic in and out of the Keys. Events include parades, drag races, and, of course, lots of partying.

The **Taste of Key West** presents the area's best culinary delights for the annual benefit held at the Truman Waterfront.

May: Offshore captains will want to seek the $15,000 prize at the **Annual Dolphin Masters Invitational.**

Musical sounds are heard at the **Key West Songwriters Festival** (www .kwswf.com), where you can see some of America's best songwriters performing in intimate surroundings.

June: Ladies get a chance to catch the big one at the **Annual Conch Republic Ladies' Dolphin Tournament,** with prizes totaling $7,500.

From Jose Marti to conga lines, Hispanic customs and cultures are brought to life at the **Annual Cuban American Heritage Festival** (www .cubanfest.com).

Celebrating the island's most loved and hated fowl, **Chickenfest,** held mid-month, is four days of fun that includes arts and crafts, food, the Poultry in Motion parade, and lots of crazy events, such as the Shake Your Feathers chicken show, Chicken Soup for the Conch Soul, Chicken Scratch Nine-Hole Miniature Golf Tournament, and the Fowl Follies.

The **Key West Gator Club Dolphin Derby** (www.keywest.gatorclub.com) chases down the colorful fish while raising money for college scholarships.

The annual **Pridefest** (www.pridefest keywest.com) celebrates the gay community in Key West with parades and events throughout the city.

July: The **Del Brown Permit Tournament** celebrates the angling pioneer who fly-fished more than 500 of these hard-fighting fish. The most challenging fish in fly-fishing, fishers can be found in grass and sandy flats, searching for their favorite food—crabs.

Anglers fish in the tropical shallows at the Flats Slam Event of the Key West Fishing Tournament Series.

You'll think you're seeing double at the **Hemingway Days Festival** (www .fla-keys.com/hemingwaymedia), where "Papa" seemingly is spotted throughout town at this annual event celebrating the author and his lifestyle. Bearded men compete at the lookalike contest over at Sloppy Joe's Bar on Duval Street. The festival also includes the **Drambuie Key West Marlin Tournament,** the top event for the mightiest of the offshore species, with $250,000 in prize money.

With a focus on preservation, the annual **Reef Awareness Week** offers a variety of ecotours and environmental education. Call Reef Relief at 305-294-3100 or log on to www.reefrelief .org to learn more about the delicate coral reefs just offshore.

September: ▼ The women take over the city at **WomenFest** (www.women fest.com), a lesbian-oriented event, which presents a variety of art, music, comedy, parties, and fun in the sun.

October: The one, the only, not-to-be-missed event is **Fantasy Fest** (www .fantasyfest.net), where for 10 days the town is packed with costumed participants in the mother of all costume competitions. Features a lavish, and R-rated, parade.

The two-day **Goombay Festival** (www.goombay-keywest.org) pours into the streets of Key West's historic Bahama Village with island-style food, fun, and frolic in Caribbean traditions.

November: "Go fast" powerboats race in the **Key West Offshore World Championships.** The annual event is described as the Indianapolis 500 of powerboat racing.

December: The Bahama Conch Community Land Trust presents the **Annual Key West Island Kwanzaa** festival the week between Christmas and New Year's. Events include African-themed ceremonies, rituals, and feasts.

POLYDACTYL VERSUS POULTRY

Which came first in Key West, the chickens or the cats? According to historians, the cats arrived in the 1500s, escaping from anchored Spanish explorer ships, and later bred with a six-toed polydactyl (many-fingered) cat given to Ernest Hemingway by a visiting ship's captain, possibly from Boston, where the largest population of polydactyl cats can be found. The ubiquitous roaming chickens came later, in the 1800s, when early pioneers brought them down through the Keys for a food source. Now protected, both run amok through the streets of Key West and are controlled to a certain extent through cat adoption clinics, spay/neuter programs, and "chicken lifts" that relocate some of the island's more than 2,000 fowl to farms in central Florida. You'll find more than 50 descendants of the famous writer's cats lovingly cared for at **Hemingway's house** (see *Museums*), while feral cats are equally adored and never have to venture too far for a free meal. Chicken lovers should make sure to stop at the **Chicken Store** on Duval Street (see *Selective Shopping*) and take part in the annual **Chickenfest,** a clucking good celebration held each June (see *Special Events*).

THE A TO Z ON TIPPING

To tip or not to tip? And how much? South Florida is one area where it seems everyone is looking for a handout, from tip jars to valets. Some hotels even have a "resort fee" added. You'll feel your vacation dollars stretched thin if you haven't planned ahead for this inescapable add-on. In defense of the service workers, they hold some of the most underpaid and underappreciated careers. Worse yet, they are taxed on "estimated" tips, whether they receive them or not. Something to think about the next time you are wondering whether you should leave a tip or not. At restaurants, make sure to always read the bottom of your check before tipping. The general rule is any party of more than six should expect the gratuity to be automatically added in. Due in part to the large number of European tourists who are not accustomed to tipping, you'll find many restaurants and bars in the beach areas automatically add in the gratuity. Some hotels, resorts, and even bed & breakfasts, mainly along the southeast coast and into the Keys, have begun adding a daily resort fee that covers all the housekeeping and recreation services. Before you book your reservation, always ask about this fee, as it may add as much as $40 a day to your bill. If you do not intend to use any of the recreational equipment, you may be able to get all or part of this fee waived. At most spas, the tip is usually included on full-service treatments—ask when you book your appointment. A guide to reasonable tipping rates:

AIRPORT SHUTTLE VANS/BUSES
$2 per person to or from hotel.

BARTENDERS AND COCKTAIL SERVERS
15–20 percent

Some bars, especially the trendier areas, have already added the gratuity to the bill, so check carefully before paying.

If you have drinks before dinner, try to settle up before going to your table. Some restaurants require the waiter to tip the bartender and cocktail servers a percentage of their tips. This is often done to keep things moving smoothly and so that the customer has to handle money only once. First ask the bartender if you can settle up. If not, it's okay to ask if she will get a cut from the waiter; e.g., "Does the waiter take care of you?" If they don't, then by all means, tip her—and gener-ously. She'll tell your waiter that you're a good tipper, and you'll almost always be assured great service. And if your bartender has been exceptionally cordial, then it's still nice to leave her a few dollars.

BED & BREAKFASTS

Many bed & breakfasts have a no-tipping policy, so ask before you arrive or upon check-in. I always like to leave something anyway, as it's often a local teenager, col-lege kid, or single mom who cleans the rooms, and they can always use a few extra bucks. Some bed & breakfasts pool and split tips between the maids, cooks, and pool attendants. For those places, tip a little more than you would at a hotel, or about $5 per person per day.

BELLMEN/BELLHOPS

$1–2 per bag upon delivery to your room (arrival and departure). Many of the bet-ter hotels will show you to your room, open your door, and detail the amenities of your room or suite. It's nice to add a few dollars if they do this. If you need to hold your luggage before or after check-in, then consider tipping $1 per bag when they put your bags in storage and again when they retrieve them.

BUFFETS AND CAFETERIAS

First look to see if the tip was included. Tipping is not usually expected in self-serve eateries, but some are adding it to the bill. If you have a server who brings you things, clears dishes, or keeps your drinks refilled, then tip 10–15 percent. If he just refills drinks, then $1–2 is sufficient.

BUSBOYS

Busboys are taken care of by the waitstaff, but if they did something extra, like cleaning up that mess your darling child made, then give them $1–2.

CASINO STAFF

Like food servers, casino workers make most of their income from tips. While it is not necessary to tip when you are losing, it *is* customary to tip a percentage of your winnings. For craps, blackjack, poker, and roulette dealers, tip a $5 chip or more per session or 10 percent of your winnings. For slot machine attendants, tip a $1–2 chip when they repair your machine. And cocktail servers should get at least a $1 chip per drink. Remember, at casinos, drinks are usually free or very cheap.

COMPLIMENTARY BREAKFASTS

If it is self-serve, then tip nothing. But if you sit down and are waited on, then tip $1–2 per person or estimate the price of the breakfast and tip 15–20 percent of that total.

CONCIERGES

A good concierge can score you hard-to-get theater tickets, restaurant reservations, or put your name at the top of the hottest nightclub list, so make sure to tip her $5–10 for each service, or you can give her an envelope covering all your services at the end of your trip. Ask at the front desk which is preferred, as your favorite concierge may have the day off when you check out. If you have been conversing with a concierge before you arrive, then it is also nice to bring her a token gift from your hometown, such as candies, jams, or soaps, along with the gratuity, of course.

DOORMEN

Hailing a cab, $1–2. Hauling your bags in or out of your car, 50 cents to $1 a bag. Sometimes doormen do double duty as bellmen, so tip $1–2 per bag if they carry your bags all the way to the room. Tip the same as a concierge if they are helpful with directions or recommendations. No tip is necessary if they just open the door.

GOLF CADDIES

$15–25 on top of the fee for the caddy.

GUIDES

Some companies have a no-tipping policy. Check when you book the trip. Other operators derive most of their income from gratuities. In most instances, you'll always be safe with 10–15 percent of the cost of the activity. For one-hour tours, such as on airboats and at historical sites, they'll be delighted with $1–2 per person. For three-hour tours, such as ecotours, horseback riding, and day cruises, tip $5–10 per person. For lengthier tours, such as half- or full-day kayaking and fishing charters, tip 15 percent of the cost of the excursion.

LIMO/TOWN CAR SERVICE

10–15 percent (arrival or departure), 20 percent if you have the driver at your beck and call for a block of time.

MAID SERVICE/HOUSEKEEPING

$5 *per person* per day, with a little extra on the day you check out. Tip more if you're traveling with kids and/or pets or if you and your golf buddies have tracked half of the green into the room. You'll want to leave your tip daily because there may be a different maid each day. And make sure it is obvious that the money is for them; you'll often find an envelope on the dresser for this purpose. Personally, I like to leave it in the bathroom on the tray where they put the soap and shampoo. That always seems to ensure that they replenish it. Anytime you ask a maid or someone from housekeeping to come to your room, such as to deliver a hair dryer or for turndown service, always tip $1–2 per item.

MAITRE D'S

Nothing is expected, unless they reserve you a special table or squeeze you onto the "reservation-only" list. Then give $5–10, or more.

MASSAGE THERAPISTS

10–15 percent if they come to your home or hotel room. Ask in advance if this is automatically included in the price. (See also *Spa treatments*.)

MUSICIANS

$2–3 for special requests. If the mariachi band is walking around, tipping is optional. For pianists tip $1–5 at the end of your meal or their performance, whichever is first.

NIGHTCLUB SERVERS

It is not necessary to grease the palms of the bouncer at the door. (See *Navigating Nightclubs* in *South Beach* , *The Gables, the Grove, and Downtown Miami*.) I've heard of people tipping $50 and up, and that still didn't get them in any faster, so don't bother. Once inside, tip bartenders and cocktail servers 15–20 percent. Don't tip on the cover charge if one is included in your bill.

Porters/skycaps (airport baggage handlers) $1–2 per bag.

RESORT/RECREATION FEES

Resort fees can run the gamut from $5 to $40 a day per room. It is important to ask when you book your reservation so as not to be surprised. This fee may cover anything from free use of beach cabanas, snorkel equipment, paddleboats, kayaks, sailboards, sailboats, tennis courts, a round of golf, or simply the use of their swimming pool. For those who plan to vacation entirely at the resort, it may be a bargain.

RESTROOM ATTENDANTS

A dying breed, these silent sentries are usually found at the trendiest nightclubs and restaurants. And you'll be especially grateful at the nightclubs as the night wears on. Attendants pay for the bevy of hairspray, perfume, tissues, and assorted touch-up makeup, so if you use any of it, please leave them $1 per visit.

ROOM SERVICE

Most hotels add the gratuity. If nothing is added, then tack on 15 percent to the total charge.

SPA TREATMENTS

15–20 percent for a full-service treatment. Most spas add this in automatically. If none is included, then tip at the end of the service and make sure to leave $2–5 for locker room and lounge attendants.

SWIMMING POOL/BEACH ATTENDANTS

If you want them to hold the same deck chair or cabana every day, then tip $2–3 per chair and $5–10 per cabana beginning the first day. It is not necessary to tip the keeper of the towels, unless he passes you a fresh one as you get out of the pool; then $1–2 is a nice gesture.

TAKE-OUT

If one of the waitstaff takes your order and packages the food, then tip $1–2 or up to 10 percent. No tip is necessary for drive-up.

TAXIS

15 percent of total fare (add more if the driver helps you with your bags).

TIP JARS

It seems tip jars are popping up everywhere: coffee shops, gas stations, and even fast-food restaurants. Do you leave something or not? It's just inappropriate for any food service establishment that doesn't actually bring you food and replenish your drinks to ask for a gratuity. The flip side is that these workers are generally paid only minimum wage, so if you're feeling generous, drop your change in the bucket.

VALETS

You'll find valet parking your car hard to avoid. South Florida is "valet central," especially in the beach areas, and many places have mandatory valet. Expect to pay $7–15 for parking and to tip $1–5 when you pick up your vehicle. The recent trend is also to tip when dropping off. Note that the valets are often separate concessionaires and not employees of the restaurant or hotel, so liability may be limited.

WAITSTAFF (FULL-SERVICE RESTAURANT)

Waitstaff in Florida are paid only a few dollars an hour and are taxed on all of their sales, so they expect 15–20 percent of the bill. Make sure to figure tips before coupons and discounts are applied. And always check your bill to see if the gratuity was automatically added.

WINE STEWARDS

10–15 percent of wine bill, but only if you used their services.

INDEX